Handbook
of
Thanatology

2nd edition

The essential body of knowledge for
the study of death, dying, and bereavement

David K. Meagher and David E. Balk, Editors

Association for Death Education and Counseling®
The Thanatology Association®

www.adec.org

Published 2013
by Routledge
711 Third Avenue, New York, NY 10017

Simultaneously published in the UK
by Routledge
27 Church Road, Hove, East Sussex BN3 2FA

Routledge is an imprint of the Taylor & Francis Group, an informa business

Library of Congress Cataloging-in-Publication Data
Handbook of thanatology : the essential body of knowledge for the study of death, dying, and
bereavement / David K. Meagher and David E. Balk, editors. — 2nd edition.
    pages cm
  Summary: "*The Handbook of Thanatology* is the most authoritative volume in the field, providing
a single source of up-to-date scholarship, research, and practice implications. The handbook is the
recommended resource for preparation for the prestigious certificate in thanatology (CT) and fellow in
thanatology (FT) credentials, which are administered and granted by ADEC."—Provided by publisher.
  Includes bibliographical references and index.
  ISBN 978-0-415-63055-9 (pbk.) — ISBN 978-0-203-76730-6 (ebook) 1. Thanatology—Handbooks,
manuals, etc. 2. Death—Handbooks, manuals, etc. I. Meagher, David K. II. Balk, David E., 1943-
  HQ1073.H363 2013
  306.9—dc23
                        2013002945

ISBN: 978-0-415-63055-9 (pbk)
ISBN: 978-0-203-76730-6 (ebk)

Handbook of Thanatology
The essential body of knowledge for
the study of death, dying, and bereavement

Introduction to the Handbook of Thanatology
The Essential Body of Knowledge for the Study of Death, Dying, and Bereavement
1st Edition

Thanatology—the study of death and dying—at its core centers on the whole person. Holistic knowledge and holistic practice intertwine in our interdisciplinary efforts. If ever there was an arena requiring that the research-practice gap be bridged, surely it occurs where thanatologists engage with persons dealing with human mortality. Mastering the complex, multidisciplinary arena that is thanatology is a task, however, beyond human capability.

As in all arenas of scholarship and practice, thanatology too has become more vast than any one individual can be expected reasonably to master. The Association for Death Education and Counseling (ADEC)—*The Thanatology Association*—sought to develop a comprehensive resource covering the fundamental and foundational knowledge in thanatology, while acknowledging that no one person can ever know all there is to know in this complex field. As one of the oldest interdisciplinary professional organizations in the field of dying, death, and bereavement, ADEC is dedicated to promoting excellence and recognizing diversity in death education, care of the dying, grief counseling, and research in thanatology. Based on quality research and theory, the association provides information, support, and resources to its international, multicultural, multidisciplinary membership, and through it, to the public. The *Handbook of Thanatology* is just one of these essential resources.

To find out more about the structure of the handbook and how it came to be, see Certifications in Thanatology on page ix. This is not the be-all and end-all of thanatology resources; ADEC expects to release a revised edition of the *Handbook of Thanatology: The Essential Body of Knowledge for the Study of Death, Dying, and Bereavement* in years to come, as our vast field continues to grow.

> David E. Balk
> Editor-in-Chief, *Handbook of Thanatology*
> Professor, Brooklyn College of the City University of New York
> February 8, 2007

Introduction to the
Handbook of Thanatology:
The Essential Body of Knowledge for the
Study of Death, Dying, and Bereavement
2nd Edition

The Body of Knowledge (BOK) Matrix on page xii – xiii of this edition reflects how the basic knowledge of the field of death education, counseling, and research has evolved since the first edition of the *Handbook of Thanatology*. The goal of this edition is to provide substantive content to reflect this evolution and serve as a major resource for those preparing to engage or already professionally engaged in the field.

As in the first edition, the contributors for this edition come from a variety of professional fields: counseling, education, administration, and research. They address a number of topics, many of which include recent controversies; thus, the reader will receive a variety of perspectives from differing viewpoints. Significant changes have occurred within the legal, medical, and ethical arenas with regard to the treatment of the terminally ill and the rights of individuals to actively participate in the decisions around their care and the care of their loved ones. Research has revealed more information about how we humans deal with our own death and the death of our loved ones. Medical advances have resulted in changes in the way we treat the dying. In addition, with the improvements made in organ transplant technology, our ability to prevent death in others has enhanced. Our knowledge of the psychological and emotional responses to traumatic death has also increased our ability to provide immediate and long-term support to affected individuals.

The 21st century may be considered the digital age. To address the impact the Internet has had on death education, grief counseling, and research and in addition to a discussion of this topic in two revised chapters (*Historical and Contemporary Perspectives on Death Education* and *Resources and Research in Thanatology*), we have added a new chapter (*Thanatology in the Digital Age*) to focus solely on this issue.

This edition goes beyond the borders of the United States and Canada. A new international perspective is included with the additions of chapters dealing with issues and programs from Ireland and Israel.

The Editors:

David K. Meagher
Professor Emeritus
Brooklyn College, CUNY
October 1, 2012

David E. Balk
Professor
Brooklyn College, CUNY

Certifications in Thanatology: How the *Handbook of Thanatology* Can Assist

The Association for Death Education and Counseling (ADEC) envisions a world in which dying, death, and bereavement are recognized as fundamental and significant aspects of the human experience. The association, ever committed to being on the forefront of thanatology (the study of death and dying), provides a home for professionals from diverse backgrounds to advance the body of knowledge and promote practical applications of research and theory. In addition, ADEC offers a two-level certification program for thanatology professionals. This program protects the public by creating a standard for thanatology practice while helping professionals develop and demonstrate their mastery of knowledge of thanatology and thanatology-related issues.

ADEC offers Certification in Thanatology (CT) and Fellow in Thanatology (FT), the details of which can be found at http://www.adec.org. *Certification in Thanatology* is a foundation certification that enhances the professional designation established by the academic discipline of each certificate holder. It recognizes the specific educational background in dying, death, and bereavement. Thus, a counselor/therapist or educator is defined by his/her education and work experience. The certification will note the special educational training in the field. The *Fellow in Thanatology* certification is an advanced professional certification for thanatology professionals. It recognizes practitioners and educators in the discipline of death, dying, and bereavement who have met specified knowledge requirements measured through a standardized testing process, and who demonstrate advanced levels of competency in teaching, research, and/or clinical practice through a professional portfolio. Recipients of ADEC certification are required to undergo the recertification process every 3 years.

This *Handbook of Thanatology* emerged as ADEC members serving on the Credentialing Council, the Body of Knowledge Committee, and the Test Committee reflected on efforts to put into operation a reliable and valid exam measuring knowledge considered foundational to thanatology. The structure of this handbook comes directly from the inspired efforts of the Body of Knowledge Committee, chaired by Carol Wogrin, in a 2005 two-day winter meeting during which six categories considered fundamental to thanatology were identified. They are:

Category Definitions

Dying: the physical, behavioral, cognitive, and emotional experience of living with life threatening/life limiting illness, caring for the terminally ill, the dying process, and the experience of death

End-of-Life Decision Making: the medical, legal, ethical and interpersonal choices, decisions and behaviors of individuals, families and professionals as life nears its end, that are often associated with a terminal illness

Loss, Grief and Mourning: the physical, behavioral, cognitive, and emotional experience of and reactions to loss, the grief process, as well as rituals and practices surrounding grief

Assessment and Intervention: information gathered, decisions made, and actions taken by professional caregivers to determine and/or provide for the needs of persons who are dying, their loved ones, and bereaved individuals

Traumatic Death: a death that occurs in a manner that is unanticipated, shocking, or violent; may be inflicted, self-inflicted or unintentional

Death Education: formal and informal methods for acquiring and disseminating knowledge about dying, death, and bereavement

Indicator Descriptors

Cultural/Socialization concerns the effect of diverse cultural and social influences on the experience of death and loss.

Religious/Spiritual addresses the relationship that religious and spiritual belief systems have on the reaction to and coping with dying and bereavement.

Professional Issues deal with the factors that affect professionals' training, abilities and responsibilities in providing care to persons who are dying or bereaved.

Historical Perspective views the historical context, developments, and theoretical paradigms that influenced the death experience and in the development of the field of thanatology.

Contemporary Perspective provides the theoretical perspective, factual context and other factors which have influenced the current perspectives on the death experience and the field of thanatology.

Life Span considers the developmental perspectives on death and dying from the prenatal period to old age.

Institutional/Societal relate to the social organizations and institutions beyond the individual and family that affect the experience of dying, death, and bereavement.

Family and Individual addresses the social, cognitive, physical, interpersonal, and emotional encounters, theories and interpretations of dying, death, and bereavement from the standpoint of one's position within the group of people sharing a relational bond, commitment and who define themselves as family.

Resources and Research involves materials, organizations and groups of individuals who study and facilitate the acquisition of knowledge. Moreover, resources involve the ideas and materials based upon the findings of empirical research and theoretical synthesis that add to the knowledge base of thanatology.

Ethical/Legal pertains to the aspects of dying, death or bereavement that concerns the principles of justice, fairness, and the determination of ethically appropriate options. Legal issues refer to the articulated laws of a society that pertain to thanatology.

The six categories and ten indicators form the Body of Knowledge (BOK) Matrix reproduced on the next two pages. The BOK Matrix is copyrighted by the Association for Death Education and Counseling. The examples in the various cells of the BOK Matrix are illustrative of topics considered probable when categories and indicators intersect. For instance, in the cell with the category Traumatic Death and the indicator Religion and Spirituality, you will see the illustrative examples of "meaning reconstruction" and "rituals." The topics in the BOK Matrix presented below are not considered exhaustive.

As early as July 2003 the Test Committee floated a proposal that ADEC commission its own book on the material considered foundational knowledge in thanatology. After much discussion the current structure for the book got strong endorsement: to write separate chapters using a category-by-indicators focus. Thus, there would be a chapter on culture, socialization, and dying; one on religion, spirituality, and dying; and so forth through all the categories and indicators within the BOK Matrix. After some reflection, the editors decided two indicators (professional issues, resources and research) deserved more treatment that would cut across BOK categories (in contrast to the other chapters that focus on a BOK category by a specific indicator).

What you have in your hands is the product of those efforts. For those interested in thanatology certification, this book is a must-read and will continue to be a valuable resource for your practice.

Body of Knowledge (BOK) Matrix

				Indicators						
Categories	Cultural/ Socialization	Religious/ Spiritual	Professional Issues	Historical Perspectives	Contemporary Perspectives	Life Span	Institutional/ Societal	Family and Individual	Resources and Research	Ethical/ Legal
Dying	perspectives on dying, health care interactions, family roles	facing death, rituals, meaning, suffering, impact on treatment decisions, afterlife, legacies	self care, boundaries, compassion fatigue, burnout, attitudes toward dying	hospice, causes and patterns of death in Western societies, influential theories	global causes and patterns of death and lifestyle choices, gender issues, impact of technology, influential theories, death attitudes, role of complementary/alternative therapies	normative developmental tasks, developmental concepts of death, special populations	hospice, palliative care, impact of politics, interacting with the health care system, special populations	gender roles, communication, cultural impact on family roles, family history, coping strategies	current significant research findings, organizations and journals, media and internet	allocation of resources, ethical principles, legislation/ medical practice
End-of-Life Decision Making	advance care planning, ethnic issues, values and attitudes, gender	advance care planning, values and attitudes, beliefs and doctrines, suffering, sanctity of life, quality of life	communication, understanding patient's rights	landmark legal cases, attitudes toward final disposition, evolution of advance care planning	options and choices, impact of medical technology, impact of media and Internet	impact of age on decision making, determining competency to make decisions	advance care planning, health care legislation, public/mass media and political impact on decision-making	advance care planning, treatment decisions, communication, family systems	media and Internet, professional organizations, current significant research findings	principles of medical ethics, advance directives, landmark cases, legal planning, decision making processes
Loss, Grief, and Mourning	factors affecting experience of and expression of grief, impact on mourning practices	meaning making, impact on mourning practices	burnout, compassion fatigue, awareness of personal loss history, coping strategies, self assessment, self care, boundaries, clinical competency	influential theories, post-death activities	influential theories and models, post-death practices, media and Internet, intervention strategies	impact of developmental stage on loss experience, specific types of loss and impact on grief and mourning	media and Internet, school/ workplace grief, public deaths, political systems	family life cycle, communication, impact of illness trajectory, grief styles, normative grief responses, impact of type of loss	empirical research on current theories, research on effectiveness of intervention	ethics and working with the bereaved, legal aspects of death

© Association for Death Education and Counseling® *The Thanatology Association*®

Assessment and Intervention	advance care planning, cultural competence, communication, meaning of death	components of spiritual assessment, interventions, facilitating integration of meaning and value of one's life	appropriate components of assessments, communication, professional liability and limitations, determining appropriate interventions in concert with evidence and client characteristics, professional responsibilities	changes in determination of death, intervention theories prior to 1990	current assessment models, current therapeutic strategies, controversy about efficacy of interventions, complicated grief, gender considerations, pathologizing of grief	developmental considerations	impact of death system, impact of societal infrastructure, contributions of grief support services	family systems theory, gender issues, assessment of risk factors for complicated/prolonged grief, determining appropriateness of specific interventions	evidence of effectiveness of assessment and intervention, community programs	determination of death, informed consent, ethical principles, legal parameters around death, professional responsibilities
Traumatic Death	cause of death, meaning making, advance care planning, ethnic issues, values and attitudes, gender	meaning making, rituals, impact of religion	appropriate training, professional response, commemorative activities, vicarious traumatization	previous major traumatic occurances	recent/anticipated future traumatic occurrences, impact of communication systems, organ and tissue donation, current approaches	death patterns, issues specific to each developmental phase	meaning making, role of the media and Internet, infrastructure, types of traumatic deaths, impact on specific populations	impact on experience of grief, types of traumatic deaths, coping strategies, individual differences, vicarious traumatization, social support	major national organizations, current significant research findings	criminal justice system, impact on larger society, ethical intervention issues
Death Education	different death systems, diverse views about death	diversity of religious beliefs, diversity of meaning making, diversity of spirituality	evaluation of knowledge, criteria for an effective educator, methods, training specific to parameters of practice, media and Internet	attitudes towards death, history of thanatology as a discipline, historical eras	advance care planning, influence of media and the Internet, social concerns, components of death education	teaching across the life cycle, issues specific to each developmental phase, impact of life transitions	influence of media and Internet, varied educational settings, impact of larger systems, military	formal, informal	types of resources, understanding the research, importance of evidence-based practice, certification, professional organizations	impact of legal system on death, understanding a professional code of ethics, applying principles of ethics

List of Contributors

David E. Balk is a professor in the Department of Health and Nutrition Sciences at Brooklyn College where he directs graduate studies in thanatology. He wrote *Helping the Bereaved College Student*, which Springer Publishing Co. published in 2011. He was editor-in-chief of the first edition of ADEC's 2007 publication *Handbook of Thanatology: The Essential Body of Knowledge for the Study of Death, Dying, and Bereavement*.

Melissa M. Bell, PhD, LSW, is a professor of social work at Chatham University, Pittsburgh, PA, where she also coordinates the social work field placement program. After completing a post-MSW fellowship in clinical services at Yale University, she received her doctorate in social work and doctorate certificate in women's studies from the University of Pittsburgh. Prior to her academic career, she was a psychiatric social worker at a large psychiatric hospital and in private practice. She has presented at the ADEC/International Conference on Grief and Bereavement in Contemporary Society.

Corinne Cavuoti graduated with a master's degree in community health with a concentration in thanatology from Brooklyn College in Brooklyn, NY. Her thesis was titled "Do elderly nursing home residents experience disenfranchised grief?" She previously worked as a patient facilitator, counseling patients experiencing loss at a women's clinic in New York City. She is currently facilitating bereavement groups and developing an online support program for adolescents dealing with loss and bereavement.

Stephen R. Connor, PhD, is an international palliative care consultant and senior fellow to the London-based Worldwide Palliative Care Alliance (WPCA), an alliance of national and regional hospice and palliative care organizations globally. Connor has worked continuously in the hospice/palliative care movement since 1976, as the CEO of four U.S. hospice programs and as vice president of the U.S. National Hospice and Palliative Care Organization, 1998-2008. In addition to being a hospice and association executive, Connor is a researcher and psychotherapist, licensed as a clinical psychologist in two U.S. states. Connor is focused on palliative care development internationally with WPCA and as a consultant to the Open Society Foundation's International Palliative Care Initiative in New York. He also serves as research director for Capital Caring in the Washington, DC, area. He has published more than 75 peer-reviewed journal articles, reviews, and book chapters on issues related to palliative care for patients and their families and is the author of *Hospice: Practice, Pitfalls, and Promise (1998)* and *Hospice and Palliative Care: The Essential Guide* (2009).

Alicia Skinner Cook, PhD, is a licensed psychologist and professor emeritus in the Department of Human Development and Family Studies at Colorado State University. Cook's scholarly work has focused on families and grief and the ethics of conducting bereavement research. She has published more than 45 articles and four books and has been a visiting scholar at the Hastings Center for Biomedical Ethics. She has developed and taught courses on death, dying, and grief at both the undergraduate and graduate level and written a book for grief counselors, *Helping the Bereaved: Therapeutic Interventions for Children, Adolescents, and Adults* (coauthored with Daniel Dworkin).

Charles A. Corr, PhD, is a member of the Association for Death Education and Counseling, the International Work Group on Death, Dying, and Bereavement (Chairperson, 1989-1993), the board of directors, The Hospice Institute of the Florida Suncoast, and the Executive Committee of the National Donor Family Council. Corr is also co-editor of a quarterly e-newsletter sponsored by the CHiPPS (Children's Project on Palliative/Hospice Services) project of the National Hospice and Palliative Care Organization; professor emeritus, Southern Illinois University, Edwardsville; and an adjunct faculty member at King's University College of the University of Western Ontario.

Donna M. Corr, RN, MS, took early retirement as professor of nursing, St. Louis Community College at Forest Park. With her husband Charles, the Corrs' publications include 40 books and booklets, along with more than 100 articles and chapters in professional journals in the field of death, dying, and bereavement. Their most recent book is the seventh edition of *Death & Dying, Life & Living* (Belmont, CA: Wadsworth, 2013).

Gerry R. Cox, PhD, is a professor emeritus of sociology at University of Wisconsin-La Crosse. He is the director of the Center for Death Education and Bioethics. His teaching focused upon theory/theory construction, deviance and criminology, death and dying, social psychology, and minority peoples. He has been publishing materials since 1973 in sociology and teaching-oriented professional journals. He is a member of the International Work Group on Dying, Death, and Bereavement, the Midwest Sociological Society, the American Sociological Association, the International Sociological Association, Phi Kappa Phi, the Great Plains Sociological Society, and the Association for Death Education and Counseling. He serves on the board of directors of the National Prison Hospice Association.

David A. Crenshaw, PhD, is clinical director of the Children's Home of Poughkeepsie in New York. He is a board certified clinical psychologist, a fellow of the American Psychological Association, a fellow in the Division of Child and Adolescent Psychology of APA, and a faculty associate of Johns Hopkins University. Crenshaw is past president of the New York Association for Play Therapy.

Illene Noppe Cupit, PhD, a graduate of Temple University, is professor of human development at the University of Wisconsin-Green Bay. She developed the Dying, Death and Loss course on her campus more than twenty years ago. Cupit's research focuses on college student bereavement, adolescent grief, death education, and developmental issues. Cupit recently co-edited a book with Carla Sofka and Kathy Gilbert entitled, *Dying, Death and Grief in an Online Universe* (Springer Publishers, 2012). She also founded Camp Lloyd, a day camp for grieving children. She is the president of the Association for Death Education and Counseling for 2012-2013.

Lynne Ann DeSpelder, MA, an author, counselor, and a professor of psychology at Cabrillo College in Aptos, CA, holds a Fellow in Thanatology (FT) from the Association for Death Education and Counseling. She conducts trainings and speaks about death, dying, and bereavement both nationally and internationally, recently in Italy, England, and Japan. DeSpelder is on the international editorial board of the journal *Mortality.* Together with Albert Lee Strickland, she is coauthor of *The Last Dance: Encountering Death and Dying,* a college textbook first published in 1983 and currently in its ninth edition, and co-editor of *The Path Ahead: Readings in Death and Dying.* They were recipients of the ADEC Death Education Award in 2003 for contributions to the field. DeSpelder and Strickland are members of the International Work Group on Death, Dying, and Bereavement (IWG) and are life members of ADEC.

Kenneth J. Doka, PhD, is a professor of gerontology at the graduate school of The College of New Rochelle and senior consultant to the Hospice Foundation of America. A prolific author, Doka has written or edited 30 books and more than 100 articles and book chapters. Doka is editor of both *Omega: The Journal of Death and Dying and Journeys: A Newsletter to Help in Bereavement.* Doka was elected president of the Association for Death Education and Counseling in 1993. In 1995, he was elected to the board of directors of the International Work Group on Dying, Death, and Bereavement and served as chair from 1997-1999. The Association for Death Education and Counseling presented him with an Award for Outstanding Contributions in the Field of Death Education in 1998. He is a licensed mental health counselor and ordained Lutheran clergyman.

Dolores M. Dooley, PhD, retired after 30 years, from the Philosophy Department at the National University of Ireland in Cork in 2005. During her tenure there she developed the required ethics course for medical students and, in the 1990s and thereafter, she collaborated in the development of ethics courses for the School of Nursing and Midwifery. She now lives in Dublin and lectures part time on health care ethics and law at the Royal College of Surgeons in Ireland. Her publications include *Ethics of New Reproductive Technologies (2003) and Nursing Ethics: Irish Cases and Concerns* (2nd ed., 2012). She contributed ethics modules for *End of Life Care: Ethics and Law* (2011), an educational resource funded by the Irish Hospice Foundation aiming to improve the culture of care and organization of dying, death, and bereavement in Irish hospitals.

Kathleen R. Gilbert is the executive associate dean of the School of Public Health and professor of Applied Health Science at Indiana University-Bloomington. She received her doctorate from Purdue University and is an ADEC Fellow in Thanatology (FT). She is a former president of ADEC. She is a member and former member of the board of the International Work Group on Death, Dying, and Bereavement. She has published and presented on her research interests: loss and grieving in the context of family, loss and meaning making, stress and resilience in the family, cross-national research, and the Internet as a tool for death education. She has taught an online course on grief in a family context, as well as other courses on interpretive qualitative research, families, stress and resilience in the family, theory, and family life education.

Richard B. Gilbert, **PhD, DMin, CT,** has been an active member of the Association for Death Education and Counseling since the early 1980s. He has served in many posts, including the board, certification chair, co-chair of the conference in Albuquerque, and a frequent presenter. He was awarded the ADEC Distinguished Service Award at the Miami conference (2011). He retired from hospital chaplaincy and related ministries in 2007. He continues speaking, teaching, and writing. A new edition of his book, *Heartpeace* (Centering) was just released, and, in press with Baywood, *Living and Loss: The Interplay of Intimacy, Sexuality and Grief*, co-edited with Brad DeFord. Two other books are in the formative stage.

Madeline Jacobs, **MPA,** teaches health and medical dilemmas at the graduate program in thanatology at Brooklyn College, City University of New York. She has extensive experience developing and evaluating programs in palliative, community, and transitional care for seniors and other at-risk populations living in the community.

John R. Jordan, PhD, is a licensed psychologist in private practice in Pawtucket, RI, where he has specialized in work with survivors of suicide and other traumatic losses for more than 30 years. He is the clinical consultant for Grief Support Services of the Samaritans in Boston, MA, and the professional advisor to the Survivor Council of the American Foundation for Suicide Prevention (AFSP). For over 25 years, Jordan has provided training nationally and internationally for professional caregivers and has helped to lead many healing workshops for suicide survivors. Jordan has published more than 35 clinical and research articles, chapters, and full books in the areas of bereavement after suicide, support group models, the integration of research and practice in thanatology, and loss in family and larger social systems. He is the co-author of three books: *After Suicide Loss: Coping with Your Grief; Grief After Suicide: Coping with the Consequences and Caring for the Survivors* (Routledge, 2011), and the recently published *Devastating Losses: How Parents Cope With the Death of a Child to Suicide or Drugs* (Springer, 2012).

Jeffrey Kauffman is a psychotherapist in private practice in suburban Philadelphia. He is the author of *Helping Persons With Mental Retardation Mourn and the editor of Awareness of Mortality, Loss of the Assumptive World* and *The Shame of Death, Grief and Trauma,* as well as numerous articles on grief and traumatic loss. His interest in the problem of shame has become a central concern and has led to his writing the following articles: "The Primacy of Shame, Making Sense of Being Human" and "(Exposure) In The Eyes Of The Other, On The Primacy Of Shame and the Nature Of God." He has taught at Bryn Mawr College, Widener University, and online for King's University College of the University of Western Ontario. He is a Fellow in Thanatology and has been a member of the Association for Death Education and Counseling since 1986.

Dennis Klass, PhD, is a professor emeritus living on Cape Cod. He earned a doctorate from University of Chicago where began his work in thanatology as an assistant in Elisabeth Kübler-Ross' famous seminar. He is on the editorial boards of *Death Studies* and *Omega, Journal of Death and Dying.* Klass was the professional advisor to the St. Louis Chapter of Bereaved Parents for more than twenty years. In that role he did a long-term ethnographic study of parental bereavement. Over the last two decades Klass has turned his research toward the cross-cultural study of grief. He is the author of *The Spiritual Lives of Bereaved Parents* (Brunner/Mazel, 1999) and *Parental Grief: Resolution and Solace* (Springer, 1988). He is the coauthor of *Dead but not Lost: Grief Narratives in Religious Traditions* (AltaMira, 2005) and co-editor of *Continuing Bonds: New Understandings of Grief* (Taylor Francis, 1996). He has written more than 50 articles or book chapters.

Karolina Krysinska, PhD, is a research psychologist working at the KU Leuven - University of Leuven in Belgium. Her research interests include risk and protective factors in suicide, suicide prevention, thanatology, psychology of trauma, and psychology of religion. She is an author and co-author of book chapters and peer-reviewed articles on different aspects of suicide, trauma, and Bereavement.

Marcia Lattanzi-Licht is a psychotherapist and educator and co-founder of HospiceCare, Boulder, CO (1976). Lattanzi-Licht's numerous publications include *The Hospice Choice* and *Coping with Public Tragedy.* An internationally known educator, she was awarded an honorary doctorate in recognition of her body of work (University of Colorado, 2005), the 1984 Winston Churchill Traveling Fellowship, the 2002 ADEC Educator Award, and NHPCO's 1995 Heart of Hospice. She received the Boulder County District Attorney's highest award in 1988, the Distinguished Service Award, for her work with victims of crime.

David Lester, PhD, has doctorates from Brandeis University (in psychology) and Cambridge University (in social and political science) and is distinguished professor of psychology at the Richard Stockton College of New Jersey. He has written extensively on suicide, murder, life-after-death, and the fear of death.

Ruth Malkinson, PhD, is director of training at the International Center for the Study of Loss, Bereavement and Human Resilience at the University of Haifa. She is the director of the Israeli Center of REBT (Rational Emotive Behavior Therapy). Malkinson is internationally recognized for her expertise in cognitive grief therapy, family therapy, and social work. She has published numerous articles and chapters in these areas. Her book *Cognitive Grief Therapy: Constructing a Rational Meaning to Life Following Loss* was published in 2007 by Norton. With her colleagues S.S. Rubin and E. Witztum, she wrote *Working with the Bereaved: Multiple Lenses on Loss and Mourning.* In addition to numerous articles and chapters, they published *Loss and Bereavement in Israel* in 1993 and *Traumatic and Nontraumatic Loss and Bereavement: Clinical Theory and Practice* in 2000.

Jennifer L. Matheson, PhD, LMFT, is an associate professor in the Department of Human Development and Family Studies at Colorado State University. She has both a master's and doctoral degree in marriage, and family therapy (MFT) from Virginia Tech and a master's in sociology from George Mason University. Matheson is the director of the Center for Family and Couple Therapy at CSU and an award-winning teacher in the MFT master's program. Her current research centers around substance abuse treatment on college campuses where she has received funding through the National Institutes of Drug Abuse (NIDA). Clinically, she is a licensed MFT, an AAMFT Clinical Fellow, and an AAMFT Approved Supervisor. Her clinical expertise revolves around grief and loss, adolescent and family substance abuse treatment, and family play therapy.

David K. Meagher, **EdD, CT,** professor emeritus, Brooklyn College-CUNY, is the founder of its Thanatology Graduate Studies Program at Brooklyn College. He has served on the advisory boards of two hospice programs and ElderPlans' Widowed Support Service in New York. A recipient of ADEC's 2004 Death Educator Award, David is a past president of ADEC. He has also served as consultant to the Office of the Medical Examiner of Suffolk County, NY, the Floating Hospital of NY, the NFDA, and the NYC Department of Education. He is the author of *Zach and His Dog: A Story of Bonding, Love, and Loss for Children and Adults to Share Together.* Meagher was an associate editor of the first edition of the *Handbook of Thanatology* and is the coeditor of the second edition.

Robyn L. Mowery is a licensed marriage and family therapist. She has established a program of research in medical family therapy focused on family decision making regarding end-of-life and palliative care.

Colleen I. Murray is director of the Interdisciplinary Social Psychology doctorate program and professor of Sociology at the University of Nevada, Reno. She received her doctorate from The Ohio State University and is an ADEC Fellow in Thanatology. She serves as chair of the Grief Focus Group of the National Council on Family Relations. Her research involves the intersection of justice and health, including the application of theory to loss; grief of adolescents and families; the coexistence of post-traumatic stress and post-traumatic growth in bereaved parents' narratives and in the music of Hurricane Katrina; and cross-cultural media accounts, attributions, and social construction of mass tragedies involving youth. She has more than 70 contributions to publications such as *Family Relations, Journal of Applied Social Psychology,* and *Journal of Social and Personal Relationships.* Murray teaches courses in research methods, families, adolescence, health, theories, and loss.

Blair Sumner Mynatt, MS, NCC, is a doctoral candidate in counselor education at the University of Tennessee. While a student, she obtained graduate certificates in qualitative research in educational settings; evaluation, statistics, and measurement; and gerontology. As part of her gerontology certificate, she completed over 600 clinical hours in the hospice and assisted-living settings. Her clinical experience includes grief work with adults and children (and their families) with intellectual disabilities and autism. She also has extensive experience working with children with grief issues in the school setting. Blair completed a LEND/UCEED traineeship with the University of Tennessee College of Medicine Boling Center for Developmental Disabilities. Blair is an active conference presenter and received numerous leadership awards while a student. She served as the student representative on the American Counseling Association Governing Council and was selected as a Chi Sigma Iota International Honor Society Leadership Intern.

Robert A. Neimeyer, PhD, is professor in the Department of Psychology, University of Memphis, where he also maintains an active clinical practice. Since completing his doctoral training at the University of Nebraska in 1982, he has published 25 books, including *Techniques of Grief Therapy: Creative Practices for Counseling the Bereaved and Grief and Bereavement in Contemporary Society: Bridging Research and Practice* (both with Routledge), and serves as editor of the journal *Death Studies*. The author of nearly 400 articles and book chapters, he is currently working to advance a more adequate theory of grieving as a meaning-making process, both in his published work and through his frequent professional workshops for national and international audiences. Neimeyer served as a member of the American Psychological Association's Task Force on End-of-Life Issues and chair of the International Work Group for Death, Dying, and Bereavement. In recognition of his scholarly contributions, he has been granted the Eminent Faculty Award by the University of Memphis, made a fellow of the Clinical Psychology Division of the American Psychological Association, and given the Research Recognition and Clinical Practice Awards by the Association for Death Education and Counseling.

Kevin Ann Oltjenbruns, PhD, was a long-time faculty member (31 years) in the Department of Human Development and Family Studies at Colorado State University where she served as vice provost for undergraduate studies for 3 years prior to her retirement in June 2005. She served in many other administrative roles at the university, including serving as the associate dean in the College of Applied Human Sciences. Currently, she is serving as a codirector of the Osher Lifelong Learning Institute through the Division of Continuing Education at Colorado State University. Oltjenbruns's research and teaching focus was in the area of grief and loss. She co-authored a textbook entitled *Dying and Grieving: Lifespan and Family Perspectives* and also wrote numerous articles and chapters, focusing primarily on various issues related to developmental stages and grief. In addition to many other community volunteer activities over the years, Oltjenbruns has been involved with Hospice of Larimer County (in Northern Colorado) and is a frequent guest speaker on topics related to grief. Oltjenbruns served as the editor of ADEC's *The Forum* newsletter for 3 years and was honored as ADEC's Death Educator of the Year in 2006.

Robin Paletti earned a master's in special education from the City University of New York at Queens College. She teaches high school in New York City with a special focus on crisis intervention and bereavement.

Jackson P. Rainer, PhD, ABPP, is a board certified psychologist licensed to practice in Georgia and North Carolina. He is currently the department head of Psychology and Counseling at Valdosta State University, Valdosta, GA. Rainer is known and respected in the professional community, having taught, researched, and supervised in the areas of counseling and psychotherapy, ethics, death and dying, bereavement, and crisis intervention. He is on the editorial board of seven psychotherapy journals and has written extensively on the topics of crisis intervention and systemic response to grief. He is a consultant to the American Academy of Bereavement and the CMI Education Institute.

Lillian M. Range, PhD, is professor of counseling and behavioral science, Our Lady of Holy Cross College, and professor emerita, The University of Southern Mississippi. Her research interests are suicide prevention and health promotion. Fellow, American Psychological Association, and past president, Southeastern Psychological Association, she is associate editor of *Death Studies*. Publications include *Sex Roles*, *Nursing Ethics*, *Health Promotion Practice*, *Violence and Victims*, *Journal of Psychopathology and Behavioral Assessment*.

Paul C. Rosenblatt, PhD, is Morse-Alumni Distinguished Teaching Professor of Family Social Science emeritus at the University of Minnesota. He is author of *Parent Grief: Narratives of Loss and Relationship* (Routledge), *Help Your Marriage Survive the Death of a Child* (Temple University Press), and *African-American Grief* (co-authored with Beverly R. Wallace, published by Routledge). His current projects include an analysis of the concept of complicated grief in crosscultural perspective, an essay (with Elizabeth Wieling) on the links of grieving and trauma in the context of poor urban families in Brazil, an article on grief therapy in crosscultural perspective, and an article on how grief interventions in the western world might be different if they were based on premises of death and grief drawn from other cultures.

Ester Shapiro, PhD, (aka Ester Rebeca Shapiro Rok) is associate professor of psychology, University of Massachusetts and research associate, Gaston Institute for Latino Research and Public Policy. A Cuban Jewish Eastern European immigrant, she is committed to helping all families make the most of their opportunities for improving life chances even when facing adversity, death, and loss. Her teaching, research, and practice apply cultural and ecosystemic approaches to understanding and facilitating positive outcomes during family life cycle transitions by reducing stressors and mobilizing resources linking individual, family, and social/community change. She wrote *Grief as a Family Process: A Developmental Approach to Clinical Practice* (Guilford, 1994), is completing *Promoting Grief and Growth: Family and Cultural Contexts in Bereavement Care,* and was coordinating editor of *Nuestros Cuerpos Nuestras Vidas* (Seven Stories 2000), the Spanish transcultural adaptation of *Our Bodies, Ourselves.* She has published and presented extensively on a sociocultural model of family development, family and culture in bereavement care, participatory research promoting health and educational equity, and designing and evaluating interventions that build resilience among urban, diverse children, adolescents, adults, and families.

Simon Shimshon Rubin, PhD, is chair of the clinical psychology program and professor of psychology at the University of Haifa in Israel. He is founder and director of the International Center for the Study of Loss, Bereavement and Human Resilience at the University of Haifa. Previously, he directed the postgraduate program in psychotherapy there. Rubin has lectured and published extensively nationally and internationally on matters related to bereavement, ethics, and psychotherapy. His work addresses the applied, clinical, research, and theoretical aspects of these fields. His most recent book, *Working with the Bereaved: Multiple Lenses on Loss and Mourning,* was written with R. Malkinson and E. Witztum and was published in 2012 by Routledge. Previously, they published *Loss and Bereavement in Israel* in 1993 and *Traumatic and Nontraumatic Loss and Bereavement: Clinical Theory and Practice* in 2000.

Anne M. Smith, MA, received her master's in community health, thanatology from Brooklyn College, CUNY. She has been working in the field of hospice and bereavement for the past 15 years. In addition to her work as a bereavement counselor at an inpatient hospice, she is currently facilitating bereavement groups at a local hospital and teaching a thanatology course at Ramapo College of New Jersey. She also works with her husband, a veterinarian, to support and educate clients regarding end-of-life issues for pets and pet bereavement.

Carla J. Sofka, PhD, MSW, is an associate professor of social work at Siena College in Loudonville, NY. Drawing upon her clinical experience in medical, psychiatric, and hospice settings, she teaches courses on social work practice. In addition to teaching the research methods course, she also teaches elective courses on death and dying and death in popular culture. Sofka recently co-edited *Dying, Death, and Grief in an Online Universe,* a book describing how thanatechnology serves as a resource for death education and grief counseling. Additional research has focused on how museums serve as healing spaces for coping with tragedy and thanatology-related themes in young adult literature. Sofka served as president of the Association for Death Education and Counseling from 2010 to 2011. She has written the News and Notes column in *Death Studies* and has served as an associate editor for this journal since 1994.

Robert G. Stevenson is currently an associate professor in the Counseling Program of the School of Social and Behavioral Sciences at Mercy College, NY. He has published more than 60 journal articles and book chapters and edited/authored several books. Two of his most recent publications are *Perspectives on Violence and Violent Death* and *What Will We Do? Preparing a School Community to Cope With Crises.* His degrees include a bachelor's (College of the Holy Cross), master's (Montclair State University), and both

MAT and EdD (Fairleigh Dickinson University). He developed the first independent course on death education at the high school level and taught it for 25 years. He is a member of the International Work Group on Death, Dying and Bereavement and the Association for Death Education and Counseling. He has served ADEC on its board of directors, as chairman of the Education Institute and on the board of certification review. He received the 1997 Wendel Williams Outstanding Educator Award and the 1993 ADEC National Death Educator Award for his contributions to those fields. For service during the New York Guard activation in Manhattan after September 11, 2001, he was awarded the New York State Defense of Liberty medal. He co-founded a community grief support center (Jamie Schuman Center) in Hillsdale, NJ. After retiring from secondary school teaching, he worked as a counselor in Paterson, NJ in a program he helped to develop for parolees reentering society from state prisons and with adolescents in recovery from addiction.

Albert Lee Strickland, CT, is a writer and musician. He is a past editor of ADEC's *The Forum* newsletter, received ADEC's Service Award in 1989, and was elected to two terms on ADEC's Leadership Recruitment and Development Committee. His musical presentations centering on themes of loss and death in American blues and gospel music include performances in Australia, Germany, Hong Kong, Canada, Italy, and the United States. Together with Lynne Ann DeSpelder, he is coauthor of *The Last Dance: Encountering Death and Dying,* a college textbook first published in 1983 and currently in its ninth edition, and co-editor of *The Path Ahead: Readings in Death and Dying.* They were recipients of the ADEC Death Education Award in 2003 for contributions to the field. DeSpelder and Strickland are members of the International Work Group on Death, Dying, and Bereavement (IWG) and both are life members of ADEC.

Gordon Thornton, PhD, FT, is an emeritus professor of psychology at Indiana University of Pennsylvania where he has taught a course in the psychology of death and dying since 1975. He is a certified as a Fellow in Thanatology (FT) from the Association for Death Education and Counseling (ADEC). He is a former president of ADEC and chair of the Credentialing Council. He has given presentations on a variety of topics in the area of dying, death, and bereavement and has contributed articles to *Death Studies* and *The Forum.*

Mary Alice Varga is an assistant professor in the Department of Educational Technology and Foundations at the University of West Georgia in Carrollton, GA. She is also a doctoral candidate in educational psychology and counseling at the University of Tennessee in Knoxville, TN, where she served as a graduate research assistant for the Grief Outreach Initiative in the College of Education, Health, and Human Sciences. She is also an active member of the Association for Death Education and Counseling. Her research interests include grief among college students and grieving in online communities.

Andrea C. Walker, PhD, is a specialist in family studies and has focused her research on death and dying in various cultural and religious contexts and across the life span. Specifically, she has studied bereavement, grieving, and spirituality/religiosity in the

Muscogee Creek tribe and with undergraduate college students. Her doctorate is in human development and family studies, and she holds a license as an alcohol and drug counselor in the state of Oklahoma. She is part of the psychology faculty at Oral Roberts University in Tulsa, OK.

James L. Werth, Jr., PhD, is a professor of psychology and director of the Doctor of Psychology (Psy.D.) Program in Counseling Psychology at Radford University. His published work is primarily focused on end-of-life issues, ethics, suicide, and HIV disease. His recent books are *Duty to Protect* (2008, American Psychological Association) and *Counseling Clients Near the End of Life* (2012, Springer). He is the 2013 President of the Clinical Emergencies and Crises Section of the Division of Clinical Psychology of the American Psychological Association where his initiatives focus on rural suicide prevention, foundational training on duty-to-protect issues, and incorporating education on clinical emergencies and crises into doctoral psychology programs.

Eliezer Witztum, MD, is professor in the Division of Psychiatry, Faculty of Health Sciences, at Ben-Gurion University of the Negev in Israel. Witztum is chairman of the School of Psychotherapy at the Faculty of Health Sciences there. He serves as director of Psychotherapy Supervision at the Mental Health Center, Beer Sheva, and as senior consultant psychiatrist at the Community Mental Health Center of Ezrat Nashim Hospital in Jerusalem. He has written more than 200 scientific publications and 15 books including *Social, Cultural and Clinical Aspects of the Ethiopian Immigrants in Israel* published in 2012. Along with his colleagues S.S. Rubin and R. Malkinson, he wrote *Working with the Bereaved: Multiple Lenses on Loss and Mourning*. In addition to numerous articles and chapters, they published *Loss and Bereavement in Israel* in 1993 and *Traumatic and Nontraumatic Loss and Bereavement: Clinical Theory and Practice* in 2000.

Carol Wogrin, PsyD, RN, FT, is the director of the National Center for Death Education, Mount Ida College, and a Fulbright Scholar at Women's University in Africa, Harare, Zimbabwe. She is a licensed psychologist and registered nurse with a background in acute care, home care, and hospice. She has been working with individuals and families coping with illness and bereavement for over 30 years. An author and educator, she serves on the board of directors of the International Work Group on Death, Dying and Bereavement, and formerly served on ADEC's board of directors. She is an associate editor for the first edition of the *Handbook of Thanatology*, and in 2010 was given ADEC's Death Educator Award. She lectures internationally on the care of the dying, the bereaved and the professionals who care for them.

Mary Lou Zanich, PhD, emeritus professor of psychology, was chair of the Psychology Department at Indiana University of Pennsylvania and interim dean of the College of Natural Sciences and Mathematics. She was a member of the board of directors and also staff support facilitator for the local hospice. She co-instructed "Death in the Human Experience," published in *The Forum,* and presented at ADEC conferences.

Dying

Introduction to Part 1,
Chapters 1 – 6

Chapters 1 through 6 focus on dying. The Body of Knowledge defined this major category of thanatology knowledge in this way: **the physical, psychosocial, and spiritual experience of facing death, living with terminal illness, the dying process, and caring for the terminally ill.**

The six chapters of Part 1 focus on dying in terms of these indicators: culture and socialization, religion and spirituality, historical and contemporary perspectives, life span issues, the family and larger systems, and ethical and legal issues. Five chapters were revised from the chapters that appeared in the first edition, and in the case of chapter 6, the contributor wrote a wholly new chapter.

Chapter 1

Culture, Socialization, and Dying

Charles A. Corr and Donna M. Corr

This chapter examines some cultural and social aspects related to persons who are dying or closely approaching death, as well as the care they are offered. The challenge we face is that there are myriad cultural and social variables that may affect dying in any historical and social situation because historical circumstances differ across time and in different communities. Accordingly, societal death systems change in their responses to specific challenges. More importantly, because dying is not the whole of anyone's life, it is critical to keep in mind that *dying persons are living human beings*. Dying is a special situation in living; it cannot properly or fully be understood without taking account of the entirety of a person's life, both individually and within the social systems in which that person is living.

Cultural Factors That Affect Dying

Every human being is born into and raised within a context in which cultural, social, religious, and ethnic factors influence his or her life. As such, these variables, which we subsume here under the broad heading of "cultural factors," affect each individual's views of and interactions with dying and death. This cultural influence is true whether the individual accepts or rejects the acculturation that he or she receives, since even in rejection those cultural factors provide a benchmark against which the individual defines and conducts his or her life.

One way to understand the various factors addressed in this section is to think of culture as "a unified set of values, ideas, beliefs, and standards of behavior shared by a group of people; it is the way a person accepts, orders, interprets, and understands experiences throughout the life course" (Thomas, 2001, p. 40). Clearly, in the United States and in most other countries, there are many, often quite diverse, cultural groups. Coming to know something about those cultural groups helps to improve appreciation of ourselves, other people, and our society as a whole.

For example, if we think for a moment about what we know concerning religious differences in beliefs, attitudes, and practices, we can easily recognize differences between various Christian denominations, between orthodox and reform Jews, and between Sunni and Shia Islamic groups. At the same time, it is all too easy to develop stereotypes around religious and cultural differences. For example, we may perceive members of one religious or cultural group as highly expressive and demonstrative in ways they face loss, while others may be viewed as much more reserved and even stoic. This observation may be true as a generalization about the group, but is it also true of every member of that group? In other words, are we settling for superficial stereotypes in what we think about cultural groups and their diverse members?

So our task is to be equally sensitive both to differences between cultural groups and to diversity within those groups. For this reason, it is notoriously difficult to speak in a general way about how cultural factors influence human beings and what results they produce. What is needed is an effort to enter into specific cultural groups and see how they address issues related to dying, an effort something like the one undertaken by the editors of a five-volume series about *Death and Bereavement Around the World* (Morgan, Laungani, & Palmer, 2002-2009). Our project in this chapter will inevitably be on a much more limited scale.

In this chapter, we focus on selected examples of ways in which cultural factors bear on experiences of dying. Among many possible examples, these include:

- Communication within family or cultural groups and between those groups and outsiders
- Decision making within some family and cultural groups
- Issues about who should be primarily responsible for care of a dying person
- Distrust by members of cultural groups with regard to the larger social system, its health care institutions, and some health care providers

Concerning *communication*, Thomas (2001, p. 42) has written that, "Communication about end-of-life issues is the key to understanding and making rational decisions." Accordingly, there have been numerous reports that maintaining control over communication is an important issue for many Asian Americans and some members of other cultural groups (e.g., Doka & Tucci, 2009; Tanner, 1995; Tong & Spicer, 1994). For example, members of such communities may be quite restrained in communicating to health care providers what they are experiencing when they are in distress and dying. Also, some family members may place a high priority on not telling dying persons that they are dying. Health care providers who do not share such values or who lack cultural sensitivity may become frustrated when they are caring for a dying person from such a cultural group.

Closely related to attitudes associated with communication are those related to *decision making*. Because patriarchal and hierarchical structures are prevalent in some cultural groups, in such groups it is often the oldest male or at least an older member of the family who is expected to make decisions about the care of dying family members (Blackhall, Murphy, Frank, Michel, & Azen, 1995; Braun, Pietsch, & Blanchette, 2000).

To outsiders, this practice may appear to deny or at least infringe upon the autonomy of the ill person.

Another significant issue in which cultural factors play an important role has to do with *who should care for a dying person*. In contemporary American society, the provision of such care is often primarily assigned to outsiders—to staff and volunteers in hospitals, long-term care facilities, and hospice programs. Studies of certain Hispanic cultural groups (e.g., Cox & Monk, 1993; Delgado & Tennstedt, 1997; Gelfand, Balcazar, Parzuchowski, & Lenox, 2001), however, have noted that this role is primarily and insistently held within the family and there most often assigned to female members.

Distrust has many causes and is often quite deep-seated. For example, among African Americans some have traced it back to the general implications of slavery and particularly to the Tuskegee study conducted by the United States Public Health Service. Begun in 1932, the study initially offered the only known treatments at the time to poor African-American sharecroppers in Alabama with syphilis. Tragically, participants were eventually allowed to go untreated until they died in order to study the natural progress of the disease. This research design occurred even after penicillin became available in the mid-1940s and was shown to be effective in treating syphilis. The study was not halted until it was exposed in the press in 1972 (Jones, 1992; Washington, 2006). More recent reports have addressed ongoing racial injustice in health care (e.g., Freeman & Payne, 2000; Geiger, 2002). As a result, many African Americans believe the health care they receive is less adequate than that offered to Caucasian Americans (Tschann, Kaufmann, & Micco, 2003; Waters, 2001).

These issues affecting dying persons and care of the dying are intertwined with ways in which individuals and members of groups in our society view the importance of family, the role of religion, and the importance of being present at a death. They also influence other matters, such as whether or not persons are willing to making advance plans for end-of-life treatment, to consider opportunities for organ donation, or to take part in physician-assisted suicide.

Death Anxiety and Concerns That Affect Dying

Much attention in recent years has been given to the concept of death anxiety and its measurement (e.g., Neimeyer, 1994; Neimeyer, Wittkowski, & Moser, 2004). For example, many reports suggest that women report higher death anxiety than men in our society, while older adults appear to report less death anxiety than some younger persons. It has also been argued that death anxiety is a complex concept, one that varies with both demographic and personality factors, as well as with life accomplishments and past or future regrets (Tomer & Eliason, 1996).

Further, death-related attitudes may reflect very different concerns and responses such as those focused on:

- *My own dying*: Will it involve a long, difficult, painful, or undignified dying process, especially in an alien institution under the care of strangers who might not respect my personal needs or wishes—if so, I might wish that my dying would occur without any form of distress or prior knowledge, and in my sleep, or perhaps I might take deliberate action to prepare an advance directive or to seek out opportunities for physician-assisted suicide (sometimes called "death with dignity" or "aid in dying;" Corr, 2012), thereby hoping to avoid unacceptable ways of experiencing my dying; by contrast, concerns about my own dying might lead me to wish to avoid a sudden, unanticipated death, allowing time to address "unfinished business," bid farewell to loved ones (Byock, 2004), and "get ready to meet my Maker."

- *My own death*: Will it release me from hardships and suffering, or will it involve losing the life and everything it involves that has been and still is so important to me?
- *What will happen to me after my death*: Am I anxious about the unknown and fearful of judgment or punishment after death, or am I anticipating a heavenly reward, a passage to a better life, or a reunion with someone who had died earlier?
- *The bereavement of someone I love*: Am I mainly concerned about the burdens that my illness and dying are placing upon those whom I love and/or am I worried about what will happen to them after I am gone?

Dying in Our Social System: Once Upon a Time

In times past in the United States of America and in many other developed countries around the world, what Glaser and Strauss (1968) identified as *dying trajectories* were relatively brief and largely predictable experiences. Mainly caused by communicable diseases, dying typically involved clear and recognizable symptoms such as fever, diarrhea, nausea, vomiting, or muscle ache. Family members, friends, and those professionals who might have been available would have been able to recognize that individuals displaying these symptoms were seriously ill. On the basis of past experiences with similar patterns of disease, it could often be predicted whether or not an individual afflicted in these ways would recover or would die and possibly also when the outcome would be known.

Care given to such individuals would largely have been supportive in nature, offered in the hope that the body would heal itself and concerned not to interfere in that process. This care would likely have focused on providing a place to rest, shelter from the elements, a cool cloth to wipe a feverish brow, and nourishing food ("chicken soup"). Various forms of spiritual intercession would often have accompanied it. Many fortunate individuals would have been cared for at home and by family members. Hospitals likely would not have been available. Even when they were, they often took the form of charitable institutions (almshouses) with large, crowded wards that were typically dark, stuffy, unpleasant, and even life threatening since they threw together many different types of people with very different disabilities and often contagious conditions.

As Western culture became more urbanized, hospitals began to change. During the latter half of the 19th century, a biomedical model emerged that viewed disease as involving specific entities and predictable causes. Therapy became intended to "fix" malfunctioning parts of the human body. Specialization in carrying out therapeutic tasks became the norm. A division of labor came to characterize both health care providers and health care institutions. In particular, hospitals—now often called "medical centers" or "health centers"—came to focus on acute care in which scientific medicine sought to cure disease. A paradoxical result of this new focus on hospital-based, acute care is that within the very institutions in which nearly half of all Americans now die death often began to be perceived as involving a kind of failure.

Following passage of the Social Security Act of 1935, which added federal funding to the personal resources of individuals and their relatives, health insurance, and retirement packages, long-term care facilities began to be developed. These long-term care facilities (often called "nursing homes") filled the need for chronic care as families had often become small, nuclear groupings in which individuals frequently lived at a distance from their kin instead of extended clusters living nearby in the same community. Chronic care became especially important as average life expectancy increased, individuals were no longer able to work or had decided to retire from work well before their deaths, and many required assistance in caring for themselves and in performing activities of daily living as they lived out the last years of their lives.

Many long-term care facilities in our society provide excellent services, but some have been hesitant when requirements for chronic care evolved into needs for end-of-life care. Some coped by transferring residents to acute care hospitals shortly before their deaths, while others tried to make do or to develop their capacities to care for dying persons. However that may be, approximately 22 percent of all Americans currently die in long-term care facilities.

Recent Efforts to Change Social Systems and Improve Care for the Dying

During the early decades of the second half of the 20th century, new perspectives were advanced concerning the situation of those who were coping with dying, the nature of pain when one is dying, and appropriate therapeutic regimes for such persons. Above all, these new perspectives questioned how the social organization of programs serving those who are coping with dying affected the care provided and they stressed the value of holistic, person-centered care and interdisciplinary teamwork. That led to the development of the hospice movement, heightened interest in palliative care, and efforts to apply hospice principles in hospitals, long-term care facilities, and other settings.

Unfortunately, there is evidence that these efforts have not benefited all who are dying in our society, especially those in the best of our acute care institutions. For example, the research project called SUPPORT (Study to Understand Prognoses and Preferences for Outcomes and Risks of Treatments; SUPPORT Principal Investigators, 1995) examined end-of-life preferences, decision making, and interventions in a total of 9,105 adults hospitalized with one or more of nine life-threatening diagnoses in five teaching hospitals in the United States. The 2-year first phase of the study observed 4,301 patients and documented substantial shortcomings in communication, overuse of aggressive cure-oriented treatment at the very end of life, and undue pain preceding death. The 2-year second phase of the study compared the situations of 4,804 patients randomly assigned to intervention and control groups with each other and with baseline data from Phase 1. Physicians with the intervention group received improved, computer-based, prognostic information on their patients' status. In addition, a specially trained nurse was assigned to the intervention group in each hospital to carry out multiple contacts with patients, families, physicians, and hospital staff in order to elicit preferences, improve understanding of outcomes, encourage better attention to pain control, facilitate advance care planning, and enhance patient-physician communication.

The SUPPORT study used multiple criteria to evaluate outcomes, such as the timing of written do not resuscitate (DNR) orders, patient and physician agreement (based on their first interview) whether to withhold resuscitation, the number of days before death spent in an intensive care unit either receiving mechanical ventilation or comatose, the frequency and severity of pain, and the use of hospital resources. Results were discouraging. Phase 2 intervention "failed to improve care or patient outcomes" (p. 1591) and led to the conclusion that "we are left with a troubling situation. The picture we describe of the care of seriously ill or dying persons is not attractive" (p. 1597).

We are left to hope that the hospice movement—consisting of an estimated 5,000 programs that cared for 1.58 million dying persons in 2011 (almost 42% of all Americans who died that year), nearly 67% of whom were able to die in a place they called home (NHPCO, 2012)—and the related palliative care movement will eventually have a more favorable influence on care of the dying in hospitals and long-term care facilities.

Some Concluding Thoughts

Dying persons have always been members of the human community and responsibilities for their care have always been with us. In the preface to her celebrated book, *On Death and Dying* (1969), Elisabeth Kübler-Ross reminded readers that we should pay attention to dying persons and to all who are coping with dying for three reasons (Corr, 2011):

1. They are *still alive* and often have "unfinished business" they want and need to address.
2. We need to *listen actively* to them in order to identify with them their tasks and needs so that we can be effective providers of care.
3. They have *much to teach us* about our shared humanity and the final stages of life with all its anxieties, fears, and hopes.

To say this message in another way, we pay attention to dying persons because they are living human beings, because we want to improve our society for all its members, and because we want to have better systems in place to care for ourselves and for our loved ones when we face our own dying and death at the end of life.

Chapter 2

Religion, Spirituality, and Dying

Marcia Lattanzi-Licht

There are times in all of our lives when we are forced to reach deep into ourselves to feel the truth of our real nature. For each of us there comes a moment when we can no longer live our lives by accident. Life throws us into questions that some of us refuse to ask until we are confronted by death or some tragedy in our lives (Wayne Muller, 1997).

Religion and spirituality are complex, overlapping concepts, each with different significance for individuals. The focus for persons facing death typically includes addressing spiritual needs, both religious and nonreligious. Religious needs center around one's relationship with God, and others, and possibly for preparing oneself for the afterlife. Generally, religious concern center on a specific faith congregation or community and are attached to an agreed-upon set of doctrines. (Lattanzi-Licht, Mahoney, Miller, 1998). Religion for some people is the most important factor that keeps them going (Koenig, 1998). Religion may also contribute to spiritual pain or suffering as well as spiritual healing.

The Consensus Conference (Puchalski, et al., 2009) defined spirituality as involving the ways individuals search for and express meaning and also the ways they experience connectedness. Connections to the moment, to self, to others, to the sacred, and to nature are all seen as part of spirituality.

For seriously ill persons, spirituality is often a bridge between feelings of hopelessness and a renewed sense of hope and meaning (Frankl, 1959). Spiritual needs are not limited to religion and are often a thread that runs through physical, emotional/psychological, and social needs and concerns. Persons facing the end of life acknowledge a greater spiritual perspective and orientation than nonterminally ill or healthy persons (Reed, 1987).

Facing Death

Recognizing that dying is more than a bio-psychosocial event, there have been human spiritual "tasks" identified for coping with dying. The work of these tasks centers on identifying, developing, or reaffirming sources of spiritual energy that can encourage faith and hope (Corr, 1992; Saunders, 1967). Those who care for people facing the end of life recognize and attend to a broad range of related spiritual needs:

- re-examining beliefs
- reconciling life choices
- exploring one's lifetime contribution
- examining loving relationships
- exploring beliefs about an afterlife
- discovering meaning.

Spiritual needs typically involve personal reflection and examination. Some people do the exploration in a solitary way, offering possibilities for understanding and healing that may never be communicated directly with another. Others find the reflection and feedback of another person helpful and an aid in discovery. Active listening and being present promote the opportunity for persons who are seriously ill and dying to explore spiritual concerns. Weisman (1972) identified open communication and warm personal relationships as two of the important conditions that define an "appropriate death." In the unknown realm of sorrow and grief, caring human closeness is essential and can offer considerable spiritual strength (Lattanzi-Licht, Mahoney & Miller, 1998).

In 1997, a Gallup Poll commissioned by the Nathan Cummings and Fetzer Foundations examined spiritual concerns at the end of life (Gallup, 1997). The telephone interviews of 1,200 adults explored how people find comfort in their dying days, and things that worry people when they think about their own death. They also explored how people plan for disability or death, including considering physician-assisted suicide as a possibility. Survey findings highlighted the importance of human contact as a source of both spiritual and emotional support at the time of death. Respondents reported looking to family (81%) and close friends (61%) to offer this support. Only 36% of people believed clergy could provide effective spiritual support and comfort.

The Gallup study (1997) showed 24 different matters that might cause concern for respondents as they consider their own deaths. Medical situations of suffering great pain or living in a vegetative state are at the forefront of worry for all age groups. Specific spiritual concerns move to the forefront for younger adults and include worries about not being forgiven by God (72% of 18-24 year olds) and fear about death cutting them off from God or a higher power (63%). One explanation might be that younger people are still developing their personal spirituality and may feel less certain about facing ultimate questions.

In the realm of relationships and connections, the Gallup survey (1997) found that those who responded equally feared "not being forgiven by God" (56%) and "not reconciling with others" (56%). Respondents also expressed significant concern about dying when feeling removed or cut off from God or a "Higher Power" (51%).

Faith has the potential to strengthen and comfort us in difficult times of our lives.

Recent studies report on the personal importance of religion and its significant role in the adjustment to illness. Religious coping (for instance, prayer, meditation, religious study) can offer a sense of comfort, control, personal growth, and meaning when facing life-threatening illness. In a recent multicenter study, 88% of patients with advanced cancer reported religion and spirituality to be personally important in adjusting to their illness (Balboni et al., 2007).

Williams (2006) suggests a spectrum of spirituality at the end of life that includes spiritual work (forgiveness, self-exploration, search for balance), spiritual despair (alienation, loss of self, dissonance), and spiritual well-being (connection, self-actualization, consonance). Spiritual well-being offers a measure of protection against end-of-life despair and depression in persons facing death (McClain, Rosenfeld, & Breitbart, 2003).

A recent investigation into spiritual caregiving and spiritual assessments led analysts to propose a model defining spirituality that distinguishes between the dimensions of spiritual well-being (e.g., peace), spiritual cognitive behavioral context (spiritual beliefs, spiritual activities, and spiritual relationships), and spiritual coping, highlighting the relationships between the dimensions. (Gijsberts et al., 2011).

Both religion and spirituality offer the possibility to transcend personal concerns and focus on a belief that is sustaining, including the belief in a caring or knowing presence. In general, religious involvement and spirituality are associated with better health outcomes.

Meaning

While there is an ongoing interest in distinguishing religious and spiritual concerns, there is also an evolving understanding of the significance of "spirituality." In general, spiritual experiences can be seen as important opportunities for learning, growth, and meaning. Theologian John Shea (2000) presents the term *spiritualities* as the beliefs, stories, and practices that respond to a basic, shared human need to find an integrated meaning. These beliefs, stories, and practices are generated from social actions and interactions and may or may not be linked to religious beliefs, practices, or communities.

Meaning can refer to a spiritual sense of purpose in life, which centers around the capacity of an individual to feel the worth of his or her individual life. Most major psychological and spiritual theorists, including Frankl, link meaning to one's contribution to the world through work, and to one's important loving relationships. Meaning can also refer to the attempt to understand and shape the personal response to a loss of physical capacity or function, or physical pain, or to the death of a loved one.

The question of meaning can be perplexing and insoluble. Meaning relates to a search for coherence or personal significance (Yalom, 1980). The challenging process of discovering and creating meaning can help an individual grow spiritually. Frankl (1959) offers three avenues for discovering meaning: creating a work or doing a deed, experiencing something or encountering someone, and, the attitude we take toward unavoidable suffering.

Exploring and attending to spiritual meaning is an essential focus for persons facing death. A growing body of research indicates that a sense of meaning in life is associated with improved psychological well-being, satisfaction with life, and overall quality of life (Winkelman et al., 2011; Maxotti et al., 2011; Fry, 2000; Fryback & Reinert, 1999; Cohen, et al., 1996; Rizzo, 1990). Spiritual individuals also tend to be more hopeful and to experience more meaning or purpose in life (Mahoney & Graci, 1999).

Treatment Decisions

Religious beliefs can be a significant influence upon ethics and upon decision making at the end of life. A person's beliefs and values can profoundly affect how a person copes with illness, as well as the treatment of illness.

In health care, the most common end-of-life dilemmas that require hard choices can be influenced significantly by religious beliefs. These decisions center on attempting resuscitation, utilizing artificial nutrition and hydration, hospitalizing, and shifting from treatment goals to comfort goals (Dunn, 2001). Recent studies find positive religious coping in people with advanced cancer is associated with receipt of intensive life-prolonging medical care at the end of life (Phelps et al., 2009). Areas that pose religious conflicts include utilizing ventilators, antibiotic treatment, and pain control. Media coverage of the Terry Schiavo case and worries over health care "death panels" highlight the differences in religious beliefs and values among members of our larger society as well as family members (see Beutler, 2011).

In a clear representation of choice and personal comfort, nearly 70% of people interviewed in the Gallup study wanted to die at "home" (1997). This decision, along with others about continuing futile treatment, are often not discussed with people, or are only offered in the final stage of an illness. By not giving people full information, their perceptions of time and opportunities can be distorted. The time people believe they have to spend meaningfully can be greatly diminished.

In recent studies, the vast majority of people (86-88%) feel it is important for health care professionals to address spiritual concerns (Winkelman et al., 2007; Balboni et al., 2007). Sadly, the Balboni (2007) report also showed that 72% of the people reported that their spiritual needs were supported minimally or not at all by the medical system.

The religious beliefs of physicians can be another influence upon decision making (Seale, 2010). Health care professionals have a sacred trust to offer seriously ill persons truthful information, balanced with realistic hope. A person's religious beliefs, or hope for a miracle, should not be a barrier to referral to hospice or to offering timely and excellent end-of-life care (Sulmasy, 2010). Many people continue to hope for a miracle long after they know that the illness is rapidly progressing and treatment options are without reasonable promise. In a spiritual framework, the focus becomes healing in a symbolic, relational context, not from a physical standpoint.

Suffering

Suffering can be defined as an actual or perceived threat to the integrity or continued existence of the whole person (Cassell, 1982). Facing the end of life brings inevitable suffering, on physical, emotional, social, spiritual, and existential dimensions. Dame

Cicely Saunders (1967), founder of the modern day hospice movement, described the realm of suffering by persons who are dying as "total pain," involving the interaction of physical, social, psychological, and spiritual pain.

Beliefs can be enabling mechanisms for survival. They create a framework for us to live inside, where comfort and meaning can be found. Cultural and religious beliefs influence personal ones in ways we may not recognize—and may complicate—coping or increase suffering. For example, Puritan beliefs center around a God that punishes people with illness based upon their actions or omissions. Questions of punishment, guilt, and "deserving" illness or suffering all create distress. Old Testament images of a god of retribution (Kushner, 1988) can create increasing feelings of isolation and abandonment. Protestant beliefs in predestination could engender a sense of powerlessness in some people. Even New Age beliefs can create a sense of failure or wrong living (what goes around comes around). And beliefs in Karma leave one wondering about past lives and past transgressions.

Frankl (1959) learned in his experience at Auschwitz that suffering itself is not destructive; suffering without meaning has the potential to destroy a person. It is possible to address physical suffering for a person facing the end of life. The possibility of continued emotional-spiritual suffering was a significant death-related concern for 51% of people in the Gallup study (1997). The intrinsic challenge of emotional or spiritual suffering is to engage in the discovery of personal meaning. Existential suffering and deep personal anguish at the end of life are some of the most distressing conditions that occur in persons who are dying. The ways to address and respond to such suffering are not well-understood (Boston et al., 2011).

Quality of life, including an emphasis on addressing spiritual needs, has been a main focus for hospice and palliative care. By addressing the spiritual dimensions of personhood through care practices and research, it is possible to decrease suffering and enhance the quality of time remaining for individuals facing death (Chochinov & Cann, 2005).

Rituals

Rituals are both religious and spiritual. They may follow prescribed religious formats and they are markers to communicate meaning and guide responses to change and loss (Irion, 1999). In a multicultural society, persons may express their spiritual nature in a variety of philosophical and religious beliefs and practices. These practices and rituals may differ greatly depending upon religion, race, sex, class, ethnic heritage, and experience (International Work Group, 1999).

Some people may express a longing for religious rituals or spiritual support at the end of life. Individuals can carry out specific practices (prayer, meditation, dietary practices, religious service attendance, etc.) as part of their religious or spiritual life. In settings where persons who are facing death are cared for, spiritual assessments look at ways to address the conditions or events that limit the ability to practice religious or spiritual rituals (e.g., weakness, immobility, hospitalization, depression).

Rituals are ways to address the great mystery of death and the profound questions it raises. Rituals related to dying are essential and offer three important elements of comfort to participants: They bring people together, they acknowledge a significant experience/event, and they create opportunities for support or comfort. Religious rituals that recognize the profound human experience of death focus on the process of grief, including separation, transition, and incorporation (van Gennep, 1960).

The use of ritual, expressive arts, and narrative are ways to create connection and foster meaning. Art-based or verbal methods for eliciting individual and family narratives can build relationships among the person who is ill, family members, and practitioners (Romanoff & Thompson, 2006). These relationships can be therapeutic and potentially transformative for all involved.

In some religious traditions sacraments mark significant passages or times in life. In the Catholic church, the sacraments that are involved with the end of life include the Sacrament of the Sick, Reconciliation, and the Eucharist. Each of these sacraments blesses the person who is ill in unique ways. The Sacrament of the Sick, or Anointing of the Sick, contains healing elements of restoring or renewing the person's relationship with their religious community. It contains a penitential rite of forgiveness, can relieve suffering, and offers consolation and hope. The blessing and laying on of hands also symbolically reduces isolation and asks for guidance for the journey ahead (Picchi, 2011). John O'Donahue (2004), renowned Catholic theologian and writer, spoke of the sacred nature of the deathbed, and of the sacramental importance of *tending the spirit* of the person who is dying.

Religious and faith communities can contribute to spiritual comfort or healing in many ways, but particularly through rituals. Rituals offer recognition of the finality of a life, as well as a connection with transcendence, of the life to come. As rituals mark a turning point between an old reality and the new, they serve to help mourners find comfort and strength for the journey ahead.

Afterlife

Religious or spiritual ideas about immortality range from Christian beliefs about resurrection to the cycles of rebirth in Eastern faiths like Buddhism and Hinduism. Some who martyr themselves performing terrorist acts are assured by religious/political leaders that their sacrifice will earn them a place in heaven. Some religious practitioners sacrifice animals to gain protection from death. All of these beliefs imply freedom from one's biological finiteness, of living at a higher level of existence.

Beliefs in an afterlife can hold great comfort for persons facing death, as well as for their family members. Most religious beliefs in an afterlife are predicated upon decent behavior in the present human existence. Notions of reward or punishment permeate conceptions of the afterlife. Some traditions believe that it is impossible to know whether life continues, but encourage ethical behavior as the key to any potential continuation of life.

Numerous authors describe a "spiritual world" and afterlife experiences (McEneaney, 2010; Weiss, 1988). The notion of an "unbroken connection" has some validity in the context of the relationship transformation involved in developing continuing bonds. It seems less important to examine whether these experiences are "real" than it is to understand that for a number of people who are dying, and their loved ones who survive them, they offer spiritual comfort and hope.

Legacy and Symbolic Immortality

In concert with the growing emphasis on spirituality and religion at the end of life, there is emerging interest in legacy, and the power it has as a tool for clarifying the dimensions of the life that has been lived, and of discovering the aspects of the self that is left for others (Fink, 2011; Hunter, 2007-2008). Legacy work involves communicating meaning and valued connections, two important dimensions of transcendence and spirituality (Puchalski et al., 2009). By its very nature, legacy work affirms the value and meaning of a person's life,

There are many approaches and tools for legacy work with someone who is facing the end of life. (Hunter 2007-2008; Fink, 2011). The essential task of legacy work is meaning making, and specific approaches like reminiscence therapy, life review therapy, dignity therapy, ethical wills all create opportunities for discovering threads of coherence in one's life narrative.

Robert Jay Lifton (1979) shaped a comprehensive theory based upon the human need to symbolize continuity between death and life. Lifton defined a sense of "symbolic immortality," and believed that life is threatened when death is not transcended. The first of Lifton's five modes of immortality is "biological immortality," or the sense of living through and in one's children. Lifton also describes, as many great religions have maintained, a "theological immortality" that typically involves a form of personal afterlife and a type of reunion with the divine or release to existence on a higher plane. The third mode of immortality is achieved through "works," or creating an enduring human impact, the sense that one's contribution will not die. "Natural immorality" diminishes the pain of death as a person's body returns to the earth where it is absorbed and utilized for new life or survival by nature itself. And, finally, "experiential transcendence" involves a psychic state so intense that in it, time and death cease to exist, a continuous present. Adults can grow in their sense of symbolic immortality and purpose in life, and it acts to help them cope with the fear of death (Drolet, 1990).

Symbolic immortality, with its links to history and biology, can be seen as a way of trying to overcome the finality of death through contribution. Lifton made an important point about nuclear danger threatening cultural symbols of immortality while propagating haunting images of annihilation. The possibilities that all means for transcendence will be destroyed creates fear that some believe has led to the growth of cults and religious fundamentalism, and to contemporary drug "epidemics."

In his writing on symbolic immortality, Lifton refers to Otto Rank who stressed humanity's need for reassurance about the eternal survival of the self. Rank (1958) held that humans manipulate the natural environment and create culture to sustain spiritual identity.

Conclusion

Religion and spirituality are important considerations for persons facing death, and for their family members. Understanding the influence of a person's religious and/or spiritual beliefs, practices and experiences can enhance comfort and care at the end of life.

Dying can be seen as a spiritual journey. Images of supporting people at the end of life often include journeying with them, following their lead. In addition to providing physical and emotional care and comfort, those who care for persons facing death join with them in exploring their beliefs and deepest life experiences, and sharing their questions about the mystery that mortality presents.

Another image that applies to people facing the end of life is that of a spiritual search. The search for meaning, connection, or hope does not involve an end or completion point, but rather is a continuing, sometimes transcendent process, a process that engages one's spirit.

Chapter 3

Historical and Contemporary Perspectives on Dying

Kenneth J. Doka

Early Efforts

While many people associate the historical roots of the study of dying with Kübler-Ross' epochal book *On Death and Dying* (1969), in fact, the roots of the field are earlier. In this section, I will explore some of the early and contemporary contributions to the study of the dying process. This chapter begins with a brief history of some of the early formative work, reviews the development of the concept of anticipatory grief, describes more contemporary efforts to develop task models of dying, and discusses theorists who have viewed dying as a developmental and transformative experience. This chapter in no way presents a comprehensive review of all the work that exists on the field. Rather, it represents the author's perspective of influential work that has contributed to the care of the dying. Persons who wish a more all-inclusive view may wish to consult varied social histories of the field (Pine, 1977; 1986; Corr, Doka, and Kastenbaum, 1999).

Perhaps one of the earliest efforts to understand some of the psychosocial processes of dying was Lindemann's (1944) study of grief reactions that introduced the concept of *anticipatory grief*—a topic that will be explored later in this section. Feifel's *The Meaning of Death* (1959) was one of the first publications and early efforts in the field. Though the book had a broad focus, some of the articles did address the dying process. In that same year, Cicely Saunders, who founded St. Christopher's Hospice, published a series of articles focusing on nursing and the dying (Saunders, 1959). In 1962, Weisman and Hackett published a study on dying patients and the predilection to death.

Glaser and Strauss also published, in that era, two books that would contribute some enduring concepts to the study of the dying process. In *Awareness of Dying* (1965), Glaser and Strauss studied what dying people knew or suspected about their impending deaths. It is important to remember that in that period, general practice was not to discuss death with individuals who were dying. Nonetheless, Glaser and Strauss documented that dying individuals experienced four different awareness contexts. In *closed awareness*, the dying person had no inking of his or her impending death. As Glaser and Strauss noted, this context was unstable and unlikely to last long as dying individuals began to respond to both external and internal cues. In *suspected awareness*, dying individuals expected their impending death—often trying to test their suspicions with medical staff or family. A third context—*mutual pretense*—was the most common. Here patients and family were aware of the impending death, but to protect the other each person pretended that the patient would recover. A last context—*open awareness*—occurred when both patients and family were aware of and could discuss the possibility of death. Glaser and Strauss' (1965) work played a significant role in questioning the veil of silence that had surrounded the dying process.

Their second work, *Time for Dying* (Glaser and Strauss, 1968), focused on the temporal organization of death within the hospital. They noted that most deaths followed certain expected trajectories. "Badly timed" deaths, where the death did not follow an expected trajectory, often created great difficulty for staff.

Sudnow's *Passing On: The Social Organization of Dying* (1967) was an ethnographic account of dying in two hospitals. While Sudnow's work was wide-reaching and touched on numerous themes, one of his most enduring contributions was the introduction of the concept of *social death*. Social death referred to his observed phenomenon that family and staff often treated many comatose patients, though technically living, as if they were dead.

Hospice: A Way to Care for the Dying

In this early period, Saunders founded St. Christopher's Hospice, often credited as the first hospice, in the London area. Saunders emphasized that dying was not simply a biomedical or physical event but also had psychosocial, familial, and spiritual implications. Care of the dying needed to be holistic and centered on the ill person and his or her family as the unit of care. St. Christopher's tried to create a homelike atmosphere that sought a holistic, family-centered way to allow dying persons to live life as fully as possible, free from debilitating pain and incapacitating symptoms. Both the hospice philosophy and the growth of hospice did much to improve the treatment of dying persons and to encourage the study of the dying process

The hospice movement's remarkable history is well-noted in other sources (see for example, Stoddard, 1978). It is, perhaps, one of the most successful grassroots movements in the last quarter of the 20th century. The holistic philosophy of hospice has permeated much of medicine now—at least in terms of a recognition that a patient's quality of life means meeting not only physical needs but psychological, social, and spiritual needs as well. Moreover, the success of hospice has led others to seriously question how well the medical system generally meets the needs of those who are dying as a result of multiple serious chronic illnesses (Myers & Lynn, 2001).

St. Christopher's became a beacon both of research and practice generating seeds that would grow throughout the world. Literally many of the pioneers who would influence the development of hospice and palliative care visited or trained there.

In the United States the success of St. Christopher's resulted in the development of Hospice Inc. outside of New Haven, CT, in 1974. Branford also had a small home care unit. But it was William Lamers, a founder of a hospice in Marin County, CA, that viewed home care as both the heart and future of hospice. To Lamers, the idea of a homelike environment could best be offered within the patient's actual home. Lamers offered a model that freed interested individuals from fundraising for new facilities. This home care model of hospice quickly spread throughout the United States sponsored by a range of groups from churches and interfaith groups to junior leagues. Hospice then took a very different cast in the United States compared to England in that, in the United States, hospices primarily offered home care and heavily stressed psychosocial care and the use of volunteers (Connor, 1998).

Not everyone learned the same lesson at St. Christopher's. St. Christopher's impressed Balfour Mount, a Canadian physician. However, Mount was convinced that the lessons of St. Christopher's need not necessarily lead to a new form of care but could be applied even in the high-technology environment on the modern hospital. When he returned to the Royal Victoria Hospital in Montreal, Canada he pioneered the development of a hospital-based palliative care model.

To Saunders and Kastenbaum (1999), the growth of hospice was a reaction to a number of trends. First, technology-driven medicine focused on cure, seemingly abandoning those who were no longer responsive to treatment. Second, hospice resonated with two other themes of the era—consumerism and return to nature. Both trends converged on the idea that individuals could create alternative, more natural organizations, where persons could take control of their lives—and their deaths.

The hospice movement, both directly and indirectly, also accelerated interest in complementary and alternative therapies. Complementary therapies may be defined as those treatments, such as imagery or diet, that are employed *in addition to* conventional medical approaches, while alternative approaches are those that are used *instead of* conventional medical treatment (Doka, 2009). The holistic nature of hospice care has led to a range of additional treatment modalities including bodywork, acupuncture, and expressive therapies to provide palliation (Kalauokalani, 2006). The same consumerist orientation that supported hospice also fueled interests in alternative approaches.

Kübler-Ross and *On Death and Dying*

Few of these efforts, at least in the very beginning, captured as much public attention as did the publication of Kübler-Ross' *On Death and Dying*. The book appeared at the right moment. Kübler-Ross was a charismatic woman who spoke of a "natural death" at a time when there was an increased aversion to technological and personal care (Klass & Hutton, 1985). Her message found a ready audience.

Kübler-Ross posited that dying persons went through a series of five (now famous) stages—denial, anger, bargaining, depression, and acceptance. Through her case vignettes, she made a powerful plea for the humanistic care of the dying patient. In an excellent evaluation of Kübler-Ross' contributions, Corr (1993) suggests that this call for humanistic care and her affirming message to talk to dying persons, along with the heuristic value of the work, are the enduring legacies of the book.

The stages, though still popular in lay literature, are far more problematic. Evaluations of her theory of stages (see, for example, Doka, 1993) note many problems. Some are methodological in nature. Kübler-Ross never really documented her material. It is unclear how her data were collected or how many patients experienced what reactions. Nor has research supported the concept of stages (e.g., Schulz & Aderman, 1974). There are other problems as well. While Kübler-Ross insisted that the stage theory was not to be understood literally or linearly, the book clearly offers an impression of linear stages. As such, individual differences and the diverse ways that persons cope are often ignored. In addition, it is unclear whether the stages represent a description of how persons cope with dying or a prescriptive approach that stresses that dying individuals ought to be assisted to move through the five stages and eventually embrace acceptance.

Weisman's (1972) work on denial suggests another difficulty—denial and acceptance are far more complicated than Kübler-Ross perceived. In his work, Weisman described orders of denial emphasizing that patients might deny symptoms, diagnosis, or impending death. Weisman notes that denial is not always negative. It allows patients to participate in therapy and sustain hope. Weisman introduces a very significant concept of *middle knowledge*—meaning that patients drift in and out of denial; sometimes affirming, other times denying the closeness of death. To Weisman the important question was not "Does the patient accept or deny death?" but rather "When, with whom, and under what circumstances does the patient discuss the possibility of death?"

In summary then, the 1960s and 1970s were a formative time for the study of dying. In this period many of the classic works and key concepts were developed. It also was a period when hospice continued to develop and begin to expand.

The Evolution of the Concept *Anticipatory Grief*

In the closing section of his study on acute grief, Lindemann (1944) noted that grief reactions could be in anticipation of loss. Fulton and associates (Fulton & Fulton, 1971; Fulton & Gottesman, 1980) attempted to develop this concept. Fulton's concern was that the term was easily misused. Fulton wrote at a time when many clinicians attempted to "encourage" family members to experience anticipatory grief under the assumption that the acknowledgement and processing of the grief prior to the loss would mitigate grief experienced after the death. He later described this approach as a "hydrostatic" perspective of grief—indicating a zero-sum notion of grief, that is, that there is just so much grief or tears that can be expended. Therefore whatever is experienced earlier on in the illness will not need to be encountered later (Fulton, 1987). Moreover, foreknowledge or forewarning of death does not seem necessarily to imply that anticipatory grief occurs. It is little wonder that research found little evidence that the anticipation of loss positively influenced later grief outcomes (see Rando, 2000, for an extensive review). Fulton has since reevaluated the concept, stating "I have serious reservations regarding the heuristic value—either theoretical or practical—of the concepts 'anticipatory grief' and 'anticipatory mourning'" (Fulton, 2003, p. 348).

Rando (2000a), though, has offered an extensive revision of the concept. Rando acknowledges that the term *anticipatory grief* is a misnomer. Yet, she still finds it useful. Rando redefines *anticipatory grief* referring to the phenomena as *anticipatory mourning*. This is a critical distinction. Anticipatory grief refers to a reaction while anticipatory mourning is a far more inclusive concept referring not only to reactions experienced but also the intrapsychic processes that one uses to adapt to and cope with life-limiting illness. Rando also redefines the concept as referring not only to the grief generated by the possibility of future loss but primarily as a reaction to the losses currently experienced in the course of the illness. The patient is not the only person to incur these losses. Family members and even professional caregivers may experience these losses as the patient continues to decline. Rando's reformulation then frees the concept from much of the earlier misconceptions that proved problematic.

Task and Phase Models of Coping With Life-Threatening Illness and Dying

Worden's publication of *Grief Counseling and Grief Therapy* (1982) represented a paradigm shift in the way we understand mourning—one that would contribute to the study of dying as well. While prior models offered a more linear stage or phase theory to explain the mourning process, Worden conceptualized mourning as a series of four tasks. As Corr (1992) noted, the use of tasks offered certain advantages. Implicit in the concept of tasks was an inherent assumption of individuality and autonomy not often seen in stage models. Bereaved individuals might find it easier to cope with some tasks than with others. They would complete tasks in their own unique ways. And grieving persons would complete these tasks on their own timetable or even choose not to address certain tasks. Also unlike stage theories, there was no assumption of linearity. Moreover a task model had clear clinical implications. A grief counselor could assist clients in understanding what tasks they were struggling with and facilitate these grieving clients as they sought to work on these difficult tasks.

Both Corr (1992) and Doka (1993, 1995) applied the concept of tasks to the dying process. To Corr, coping with dying involved four major tasks that correspond to the dimensions of human life—physical, psychological, social, and spiritual. The physical task was to satisfy bodily needs and to minimize physical distress in ways that are consistent with other values. Corr defined the psychological task as to maximize psychological security, autonomy, and richness. The social task was to sustain and enhance those interpersonal attachments that are significant to the person concerned and to sustain selected interactions with social groups within society or with society itself. Corr's spiritual task was to address issues of meaningfulness, connectedness, and transcendence and, in doing so, to foster hope.

Building on the work of both Pattison (1978) and Weisman (1980), Doka (1993, 1995) suggested that a life-threatening illness can be understood as a series of phases, noting that not all phases would appear in any given illness. The *prediagnostic phase* concerns itself with the process of health seeking. It refers to the time prior to the diagnosis. One of the most common, but not the only context, would be the time between when an individual notices a symptom and seeks medical assistance. The *acute phase* refers to the crisis period surrounding the diagnosis of life-threatening illness. The *chronic phase* refers to that period when the individual struggles with the disease and treatment. Many individuals may recover from the illness. However, Doka reminds that in the *recovery phase*, individuals do not simply go back to the life experienced before illness. They still have to adapt to the aftereffects, residues, and fears and anxieties aroused by the illness. The *terminal phase* revolves around adapting to the inevitability of impending death as treatment becomes palliative.

At each phase, individuals have to adapt to a series of tasks. These tasks derive from four general or global tasks—to respond to the physical facts of disease, to take steps to cope with the reality of the disease, to preserve self-concept and relationships with others in the face of the disease, and to deal with affective and existential/spiritual issues created or reactivated by the disease.

Though these models seem to have interesting implications for understanding the ways that individuals cope with dying and life-threatening illness, they have not been widely applied. Yet, they still represent a possible direction as we strive to develop new approaches and models of the dying process.

Future Trends

Dying continues to evolve. In recent years the four leading causes of death in the United States and many industrialized countries include cardiovascular diseases, cancer, cerebrovascular diseases, and respiratory diseases. Moreover as the population ages, it is not unusual that many patients will have multiple chronic conditions at end of life. This aspect of aging has made medical management of the dying process more complicated both ethically and medically. Ethically, it raises the question of whether some chronic conditions should be treated when the goal of care has become palliative. Medically it means that multiple conditions are being simultaneously treated, making both treatments complex, and the dying trajectory less predictable. This emerging medical reality has led to an interest in concurrent care—or medical treatment where palliative care is offered concurrently with life-extending treatment.

The Possibilities in Dying

In addition to coping with dying, there has been some work on possibilities for continued growth and development throughout the dying process. Kübler-Ross (1975), in her edited book, *Death: The Final Stage of Growth*, suggested that accepting the finiteness of life allows us to more fully live life—discarding the external roles and petty concerns that are essentially meaningless. Dying persons are our teachers, she asserts, since accepting the limited time left in their lives they can focus on what is truly important and meaningful.

Byock (1997) in his book *Dying Well: The Prospect for Growth at the End-of-Life* suggests that once a dying patient is freed from pain, that person retains the human potential to grow and the possibility to use his or her remaining time to express love, finish significant and meaningful tasks, and reconcile with others.

The key caution is to remember that these are possibilities—possibilities to be embraced by the dying person. They become a danger when others, whether family members or health professionals, see it as their goal to induce the dying person to achieve such possibilities. Shneidman (1992) offers a fitting caution that no one has to die in a state of "psychoanalytical grace."

Conclusion

While the study of grief abounds with exciting ideas and the hospice movement has expanded exponentially, the study of the dying process has been relatively neglected. It can be hoped that the next decade will be one of increased attention to and development of new ways to conceptualize the ways that individuals experience dying and evidence-based interventive strategies to assist dying persons, their families, and their caregivers.

Chapter 4

Life Span Issues and Dying

Mary Alice Varga and Robin Paletti

A central issue in thanatology research involves the physical and psychosocial experiences of dying and implications across the human life span. For individuals facing death, negotiation of the dying process is often fraught with developmental challenges. This chapter aims to provide an exploration of these concerns, including such relevant factors as normative developmental task fulfillment, death attitudes across the life span, and palliative care issues. It should be noted that the varied experiences of dying—and human development itself—are shaped in large part by social, cultural, and historical factors (Morgan & Laungani, 2002; Parkes, Laungani, & Young, 1997); a comprehensive examination of these influences, however, lies beyond the scope of this chapter, which instead offers a distinctly Western perspective, rooted theoretically in Erikson's (1963, 1968) widely recognized ideas concerning human life span development.

The term *life cycle* has been defined as the underlying order of the course of human life (Neugarten & Datan, 1973). The most generally accepted theories of human life span development describe a series of normative transitions through which an individual progresses from infancy through adulthood (Erikson, 1963; Freud, 1917; Jung, 1933/1971). Among the most influential of these, Erikson's (1963) task-oriented model characterizes the human personality as evolved through social experience. During each of the eight distinct stages of development, an individual is presented with a psychosocial conflict and masters challenges and developmental tasks in a normative process. Failure to fulfill these developmental tasks impedes the maturation process. For terminally ill individuals, confrontation with death poses significant barriers to normative task completion, giving rise to a number of urgent developmental concerns. As individuals across the life span strive towards personality fulfillment in the face of death, their experiences provide valuable insight into the dying process, and pave the way for the improved care of the terminally ill.

Infancy and Childhood

The term *childhood* generally refers to the first 10 to 12 years of life, encompassing four basic developmental stages: infancy (birth through approximately 12-18 months), toddlerhood (infancy through approximately 3 years), early childhood (approximately 3 to 6 years), and middle childhood (6 years to puberty) (Erikson, 1963). While childhood deaths are rare, the National Center for Health Statistics (Murphy, Xu, & Kochanek, 2012) reports the largest number occurring during infancy. The overall infant mortality rate in the United States is approximately 614 deaths per 100,000 live births. Statistics, however, reveal discrepancies among racial groups. The mortality rates among Hispanic and Caucasian Americans are 537 and 528, respectively and the rate increases to 1,100 deaths per 100,000 live births for African Americans. For older children, ages 1 to 4 years, the total number of deaths declines to approximately 27 deaths per 100,000 people. The leading causes of these deaths are accidents, followed by congenital malformations, and homicide. Among older children, the death rate decreases to approximately 13 children per 100,000, with the leading cause remaining accidents, followed by cancer (malignant neoplasms).

Developmental Issues

According to Erikson (1963, 1968) each of the four stages in childhood may be characterized in terms of a particular developmental task including trust, autonomy, initiative, and industry. Confrontation with death during any of these stages may hinder the maturation process. The developmental work of infants, for instance, involves the cultivation of trust versus mistrust, thus allowing children to develop a sense of hope, along with a perceived ability to rely on others to fulfill needs. For chronically ill infants, extended hospital stays, constantly changing environments, and painful and confusing medical procedures may interfere with the ability to develop a psychic bond with adults and to develop the trust crucial to development (Doka, 1996).

Later in childhood, an overriding tension emerges between a child's sense of autonomy and external control factors (Erikson, 1963). The primary developmental task at this stage of development involves the establishment of a sense of independence and self-control. Physical limitations for terminal toddlers, caused by illness and parental overprotectiveness, may compromise the ability to develop a sense of self-control and autonomy (Doka, 1996).

Terminal illness during early and middle childhood presents additional challenges. Between the ages of approximately 3 to 6 years, a child must begin to balance personal desires with moral responsibility (Erikson, 1963). Children begin taking initiative exploring new activities, making choices and judgments, and gauging their level of capabilities. In older childhood, children between ages 6 to 12 years become more concerned with productivity and mastering complex skills. Interests and abilities are also discovered, resulting in a sense of industry. These two stages and the resolutions of initiative and industry are critical for the development of self-confidence. For dying children, however, inconsistent discipline, coupled with parents' reluctance to set behavioral limits, may undermine these resolutions (Doka, 1996). In older children, the struggle to meet academic demands while coping with terminal illness may compromise the achievement of mastery and competence and negatively affect self-esteem. Physical limitations, as well as parental safety concerns, may also impede the development of children's industrial capacity.

Childhood Death Attitudes

Children's attitudes towards death are largely influenced by cognitive developmental levels, socialization, religion, and prior experience with death and dying and vary by age and gender (Florian, 1985; Mahon, Goldberg, & Washington, 1999; Silverman, 2000a; Walker and Maiden,1987; Yang & Chen, 2009). In general, research surrounding children's death concepts suggests three distinct developmental stages and includes components of nonfunctionality, irreversibility, and universality (Nagy, 1948). Nonfunctionality addresses the understanding that functions such as breathing and eating characterize something as living, and the functions created at death. Irreversibility focuses on the concept that a human body cannot physically return from death. Universality is the understanding that living things will eventually die. For children under 5 years of age, death may be perceived as reversible, or the result of magical or medical intervention (Speece & Brent, 1992). Among children ages 5 through 9, death is often personified, or perceived as a contingency, and viewed as escapable. Children beyond age 9 are able to recognize that death is universal, irreversible, and that human functioning ceases; however, research also shows children developing mature understandings of death as early as age 6 (Hunter & Smith, 2008; Mahon, et al., 1999; Nagy, 1948). Furthermore, male children are more likely to accept and confront death while female children express more negative emotions and resistance toward death (Yang & Chen, 2009).

As terminally ill children learn about their condition, they often develop heightened levels of anxiety (Corr, 1999). Unsurprisingly, death anxiety among dying children is greater than among their healthier peers (Waechter, 1971). In early childhood, this anxiety arises from a fear of parental separation, while older children more often fear destruction and body mutilation following death (Corr, 1999).

Implications for Care

Consideration of developmental issues is crucial for effective care of terminally ill children. In addition to providing maximum physical relief of symptoms, caregivers may facilitate children's psychosocial development by encouraging active communication throughout the dying process (Adams & Deveau, 1987). Corr (1999) cites music, art, or drama therapy as particularly helpful in this regard. Assigning children appropriate roles in the management of illness and treatment decisions is also critical toward the development of mastery and the maintenance of a healthy self-esteem. Caregivers must allow children to function as active partners in treatment, allowing for the development of a crucial sense of autonomy, while supporting social interaction by facilitating access to peers.

Adolescence

Adolescence is generally understood as the period of life ranging from age 12 to approximately 18 years (Erikson, 1963); however, there is recognition of fluidity about the beginning and end of the adolescent years due to early onset of puberty and extended delays in achieving autonomy; the NCHS (Murphy et al., 2012) cites the number of deaths among younger teens at approximately 13 per 100,000 people, with accidents and cancer the two leading causes. For older adolescents, this rate increases to approximately 68 per 100,000 people, with accidents again the leading cause of death, followed by suicide. Normally a time of burgeoning possibilities, adolescence is a dynamic period in the human life span. When death occurs at this stage, it is accompanied by a number of complex psychosocial considerations.

Developmental Issues

Adolescents are confronted with a host of unique transitional issues in their biological, cognitive, social, and affective development (Noppe & Noppe, 2004). Along with profound physical changes, for instance, teenagers must also negotiate pressing psychosocial concerns surrounding the attainment of independence, peer acceptance, and self-esteem. Erikson (1968) describes the primary task of adolescence as identity formation, citing teenagers' struggle to formulate personal and occupational goals, and to address issues of sexuality and gender. Klopfenstein (1999) conceptualizes this period in terms of three substages: early adolescence, middle adolescence, and late adolescence. Early adolescence (ages 10 to 14 years) involves a predominant shift in attachment from parents to peers. Middle adolescence (ages 15 to 17 years) encompasses the development of individual self-image, experimentation, and the cultivation of abstract reasoning ability. Late adolescence (late teens to 20 years) describes a period of increased self-acceptance, concern for others, and an increasingly future-oriented view of the world.

Confrontation with death in terminally ill patients during adolescence poses challenges to identity formation and frustrates the normative developmental processes in several ways. Physically, changes associated with puberty may be delayed, replaced by unwelcome side effects of treatment, including hair loss, acne, weight fluctuations, or disfigurements (Freyer, 2004). The psychosocial development of terminally ill teenagers is also profoundly affected by the dying process. The crucial struggle for independence and mastery is often exacerbated in various instances. For example, physical and emotional dependence may increase as treatment progresses (Nannis, Susman, & Strope 1978; Freyer, 2004). Peer relations, critical to the development of adolescent identity, may also be hindered by chronic illness. Difficulty participating in social or athletic activities, a lack of sexual outlets, prolonged hospital stays, frequent outpatient visits, or home medication regimens may impede socialization and lend themselves to a sense of isolation among terminally ill teens (Freyer, 2004).

Adolescent Death Attitudes

Research suggests that teenagers' conceptions of death evolve over the course of three stages of adolescence and are intrinsically related to developmental issues (Noppe and Noppe, 1996). Concepts of death among younger teens most often involve parental separation, while individuals in midadolescence tend to focus on death's impact on others. For college-age youth, consideration of one's legacy supersedes concern with personal mortality. Teenagers' burgeoning abstract-thinking skills give rise to more fully developed concepts of death than those found in younger children, and by adolescence, most individuals understand death as universal and irreversible (Foley & Whittam, 1990). Still, the struggle to construct an identity may also impede a logical understanding of death, resulting in increased anxiety among adolescents (Noppe & Noppe, 2004). Death anxiety, in fact, is at its highest levels among teens that possess "less stable ego pictures" at the peak of identity formation (Alexander & Alderstein 1958, p. 175).

Implications for Care

Caring for dying adolescents should address physical and psychosocial concerns. Special consideration should be taken to support unique developmental needs, including the application of treatment models, which emphasize ego identity through acceptance of death (Nannis et al., 1978). In an effort to enhance a sense of autonomy and independence for terminal teenagers, caregivers might also allow for appropriate graduated participation in treatment decisions, although such choices may be complicated by questions surrounding cognitive capacities (Freyer, 2004). Schoeman (1980) also stresses the importance of family privacy, autonomy, and responsibility in end-of-life decision making among terminally ill adolescents.

Adulthood

Adulthood is a life stage that may also be conceptualized in three parts: young adulthood (ages in 20s and 30s), middle adulthood (ages in 40s, 50s, and early 60s), and late adulthood or maturity (ages beyond 65) (Cook & Oltjenbruns, 1998; Erikson, 1963). Death rates among the latter group are the highest, at approximately 6,859 deaths per 100,000 people (Murphy et al., 2007). Among the elderly, heart disease is the primary cause of death, followed by cancer. In midadulthood, the death rate decreases to approximately 629 per 100,000 people, with cancer and heart disease again the two leading causes. Among younger adults, the death rate decreases further, to 103 deaths per 100,000 people, with accidents and cancer as the predominant causes. At each stage of adulthood, confrontation with the dying process demands negotiation of an array of pressing psychosocial issues.

Developmental Issues

The primary developmental tasks of adulthood involve the exercise of responsibility and the expansion of competencies (Cook & Oltjenbruns, 1998). For young adults, love relationships are a principal focus, as individuals strive to achieve intimacy versus a sense of isolation (Erikson, 1963). At this stage of life, adults have established their identity and may commit to close friendships, marriage, career, and parenthood. When terminal illness intrudes upon these developmental tasks, many young adults are fiercely resistant (Pattison, 1977). Intimate relationships may also be threatened by the onset of terminal illness, as partners become alienated by their own fears surrounding the dying process (Cook & Oltjenbruns, 1998). Nevertheless, close relationships often serve to allay fears of isolation and aid the terminally ill in feeling valued as individuals.

As adults age, psychological emphasis shifts to contemplation of achievements and generativity (Butler & Lewis, 1982; Erikson, 1963). Relationships remain important at this stage of life, along with a sense of individual and familial security (Pattison, 1977). Erikson (1968) describes middle adulthood in terms of generativity versus stagnation, as individuals focus increasingly on parenting and the next generation. Death at this stage usually follows considerable introspection and a reevaluation of one's accomplishments (Cook & Oltjenbruns, 1998).

In the elder ages of adulthood, death and dying emerge as more immediate concerns. Among the elderly, dying is often characterized by a process of life review (Butler, 1963), as individuals strive to maintain ego identity in the face of despair (Erikson, 1963). Successful resolution of this stage of development allows for the cultivation of wisdom, feelings of contentment, and a sense of acceptance and fulfillment. Failure to achieve these virtues results in a sense of hopelessness, derived from an individual's disappointment in a life perceived as poorly lived (Erikson, 1982).

Adult Death Attitudes

Death attitudes in adulthood vary and are influenced by a number of factors, including gender, ethnicity, physical and psychological health, religious beliefs, environmental factors, generational differences, experience with death and aging, and life satisfaction (DePaola, Griffin Young, & Neimeyer, 2003; Fortner & Neimeyer, 1999; Walker & Maiden, 1987). In general, studies suggest that death anxiety decreases from midlife to old age. However, Russac, Gatliff, Reece, and Spottswood (2007) found that peaks in death anxiety for women appear during the age range of the mid-20s and then again in the early 50s, which they attribute to female reproductive statuses.

Research also provides specific insight on death anxiety and death attitudes among adults. Among older adults, women report more death anxiety than men (Azaiza, Ron, Shoman, & Gigini, 2010; Besser & Priel, 2007; Circirelli, 2001; DePaola et al., 2003; Suhail & Akram, 2002). Differences in death attitudes among various ethnicities have also been cited. Whereas older Caucasian adults report fears pertaining to the dying process, African Americans report fear of the unknown, consciousness when dead, and the status of the body after death (DePaola et al., 2003). Older adults with less religiosity exhibit greater anxiety about various dimensions of death (Cicirelli, 2002; Suhail & Akram, 2002; Wu, Tang, & Kwok, 2002). Older adults living in institutions show more fear of death when compared to older adults living independently (Azaiza et al., 2010; Fortner & Neimeyer, 1999). Finally, it is also suggested that older adults with increased physical and psychological concerns experience greater death anxiety (Moreno & Moore, 2008; Wu et al., 2002).

Implications for Care

Similar to cases involving children and adolescents, key developmental issues must be addressed in caring for dying adults. As intimacy is a critical concern for individuals in this age group, its expression ought to be encouraged through open communication and, when applicable, marriage therapy. Modified continuation of occupational roles might also be encouraged for young adults with terminal illness to gain a sense of accomplishment and achievement (Cook & Oltjenbruns, 1998). At middle age, treatment choices ought to support generativity processes through the continued realization of social roles and relationships. Allowing individuals a prominent role in postdeath arrangements is often helpful in this regard. Such participation in end-of-life decision making is also an important aspect of treatment for the elderly, for whom autonomy is vital to the maintenance of a positive self-concept (Corr, Nabe & Corr 2003). According to Corr, Nabe, and Corr, caregivers should encourage older adults to conduct life reviews, perhaps using photos as stimuli. Individualized care, either at home or within a personalized institution, is also suggested, in order to help dying adults achieve maximum physical and psychic comfort levels. DePaola et al. (2003) also recommends encouraging the elderly to conduct life reviews to increase ego-integrity and reduce overall death anxiety.

Conclusion

From infancy to adulthood, individuals are faced with various crises throughout their life span that can significantly affect development and normative task fulfillment. Individuals confronting death are often presented with specific physical and psychosocial crises that intensify the developmental process and present complex concerns. Ultimately, the struggle toward normative development and personality fulfillment in the face of death characterizes the dying process across the human life span.

Chapter 5

The Family, Larger Systems, and the Dying Process

Stephen R. Connor

Thirty-five years ago those working in the new field of death, dying, and hospice believed that the need for specialists who cared for the dying would be obsolete in 20 years. Good care for the dying would become part of the larger health care system and separate organizations such as hospice would no longer be needed. While a laudable goal, it is now clear that the need for those who specialize in care of the dying will continue for the foreseeable future.

Improvements have been made in the way our health system provides care for the dying, and in this chapter we will explore the evolving structures and systems that have emerged to deliver care, including: hospice care, palliative care, professional certification and hospice and palliative care as a new medical subspecialty, care of the dying in institutions, care for underserved populations such as prisoners, the disabled, minorities, those with uncertain prognoses or stigmatizing conditions, those in very rural areas, and the mentally ill. In addition, the impact of death and dying on our evolving concept of family or attachment network will be examined including the biomedical–psychosocial–spiritual model, the stress of caregiving, and the current thinking on awareness of dying and the impact of differing trajectories of dying. Hospice care in the United States has been one of the most successful experiments at delivering palliative care to date despite a number of significant limitations.

Hospice Care

The National Hospice and Palliative Care Organization (National Hospice and Palliative Care Organization [NHPCO], 2000, p. ii) definition of hospice states:

> Hospice provides support and care for persons in the last phases of an incurable disease so that they may live as fully and as comfortably as possible. Hospice recognizes that the dying process is a part of the normal process of living and focuses on enhancing the quality of remaining life. Hospice affirms life and neither hastens nor postpones death. Hospice exists in the hope and belief that through

appropriate care, and the promotion of a caring community sensitive to their needs that individuals and their families may be free to attain a degree of satisfaction in preparation for death. Hospice recognizes that human growth and development can be a lifelong process. Hospice seeks to preserve and promote the inherent potential for growth within individuals and families during the last phase of life. Hospice offers palliative care for all individuals and their families without regard to age, gender, nationality, race, creed, sexual orientation, disability, diagnosis, availability of a primary caregiver, or ability to pay.

Hospice programs provide state-of-the-art palliative care and supportive services to individuals at the end of their lives, their family members, and significant others, 24 hours a day, 7 days a week, in both the home and facility-based care settings. Physical, social, spiritual, and emotional care are provided by a clinically directed interdisciplinary team consisting of patients and their families, professionals, and volunteers during the:

1. Last stages of an illness;
2. Dying process; and
3. Bereavement period.

Modern hospice care began with Cicely Saunders' founding of St. Christopher's Hospice outside London in 1967. Today there are more than 16,000 hospice or palliative care services worldwide in 136 countries (Lynch, Connor, & Clark 2012). The first U.S. hospice began serving patients in 1973 (Connor, 2009; Stoddard, 1992). Today there are more than 3,000 U.S. companies that deliver hospice services at more than 5,150 offices serving defined areas. In 2010 an estimated 1.58 million patients and families received services from a hospice provider (NHPCO, 2011). Of those served, approximately 1,029,000 died, 292,759 were carried over into 2011, and 259,000 were discharged for a reason other than death, usually due to improved condition.

In 2010 there were an estimated 2.465 million deaths in the United States from all causes (Centers for Disease Control [CDC], 2012). Therefore, if 1,029,000 people died under hospice care in 2005, then almost 42% of all people who died that year had at least one day of hospice care before they died—a really remarkable feat for palliative care in the United States and a benchmark internationally. The true denominator for the need for hospice or palliative care is unknown, but if we eliminate those who clearly would never access hospice or palliative care including those dying of sudden trauma, non-HIV infectious diseases, sudden heart attack or stroke, and those who become acutely ill and die but who were not dependent prior to their illness, we can eliminate almost one-third of all deaths from the denominator (Connor, 1999). Hospice in the United States is now reaching well over half of those who need care, and this statistic does not include those receiving palliative care outside of hospice.

However, are people getting hospice care for a long enough period prior to death to benefit? In the early days of hospice care in the United States average length of service was about 70 days. For hospice to be maximally effective some (Iwashyna & Christakis,

1998) have suggested that 2-3 months of care are needed. This duration is to allow enough time to prepare and educate caregivers, to assist in getting affairs in order, to prevent anticipated and distressing symptom problems from occurring, and to form a therapeutic relationship with the patient and family.

The length of service for hospice had dropped to a low of 48 days in 2001 and 2002 and has now climbed to a relatively steady average of around 68 days. However a more accurate measure of the typical hospice patient's experience is the median length of service, which was only 19.7 days in 2010, and more troubling, the percent of hospice patients on service 7 days or less was more than 35% (NHPCO, 2012). The number of hospice patients on service over 6 months climbed to 11.8% in 2010.

The length of service for hospice has been influenced by several factors. During the late 1990s hospices received increased government scrutiny focused on patients who were on hospice care for more than 6 months. In addition the Medicare Hospice Benefit prevents patients from receiving hospice care while currently receiving "curative" care. Each hospice provider is allowed to determine which treatments are curative and which are palliative. There is disagreement over the definition of curative with many treatments aimed less at cure than prolongation of survival for usually short periods but at considerable expense. Many patients and families demand continuation of these treatments, thus in some cases delaying hospice referral or admission. Some of the more progressive hospices have increased their average length of service by admitting patients that are still receiving these prolongative treatments. The resulting income has been enough to pay for the added treatment costs.

Hospice payment under Medicare is governed by regulations referred to as Conditions of Participation or COPs (Centers for Medicaid and Medicare Services [CMS], 2006). These rules have been in place since enactment of the Medicare Hospice Benefit (MHB) in 1983 and specify how hospice care must be organized and delivered to qualify for payment. Key provisions of the Conditions of Participation require hospices to:

- admit eligible patients with a terminal illness with a prognosis of 6 months or less who agree not to continue curative treatment and agree to hospice care;
- recertify surviving patients as being terminally ill at specified intervals (90 days, followed by another 90 days, followed by ongoing 60 day recertification periods);
- meet administrative requirements including a governing body, an interdisciplinary team, a plan of care for each patient, a medical record for each patient, a medical director, regular training, quality assurance, use of volunteers, and maintenance of professional management of the program; and
- provide core services by hospice employees including a physician, nurse, counselor, and medical social worker, and provide other noncore services including physical, occupational, and speech therapy, home health aides/homemakers, medical equipment and supplies, medications, and short-term inpatient care for symptom management and respite.

MHB payment is made for each day of hospice care on a per diem basis at one of four rates: routine home care, continuous home care for crisis periods in lieu of hospitalization, general inpatient care for severe symptom management, and inpatient respite care to give up to 5 days break for caregivers.

The COPs underwent revision in 2008, and in the recent health care reform legislation additional changes were made including a new requirement for a face-to-face visit with a hospice physician or nurse practitioner to recertify patients every 60 days after the initial 6 months of hospice care.

Several organizations also provide voluntary accreditation for hospices including the Joint Commission on Accreditation of Healthcare Organizations (JCAHO), Community Health Accreditation Program (CHAP), and the Accreditation Commission for Health Care (ACHC). At present almost 60% of hospices are accredited by one of these bodies (NHPCO, 2012).

Palliative Care

Palliative care is defined as "Patient and family-centered care that optimizes quality of life by anticipating, preventing, and treating suffering. Palliative care throughout the continuum of illness involves addressing physical, intellectual, emotional, social, and spiritual needs and to facilitate patient autonomy, access to information, and choice." (Definition recommended by CMS in the revised Medicare Hospice Conditions of Participation and adopted by the National Quality Forum (NQF), with agreement by NHPCO and the Center to Advance Palliative Care (CAPC).)

The World Health Organization defines palliative care as:

Palliative care is an approach that improves the quality of life of patients and their families facing the problem associated with life-threatening illness, through the prevention and relief of suffering by means of early identification and impeccable assessment and treatment of pain and other problems, physical, psychosocial and spiritual. Palliative care:

- provides relief from pain and other distressing symptoms;
- affirms life and regards dying as a normal process;
- intends neither to hasten or postpone death;
- integrates the psychological and spiritual aspects of patient care;
- offers a support system to help patients live as actively as possible until death;
- offers a support system to help the family cope during the patient's illness and in their own bereavement;
- uses a team approach to address the needs of patients and their families, including bereavement counselling, if indicated;
- will enhance quality of life, and may also positively influence the course of illness;
- is applicable early in the course of illness, in conjunction with other therapies that are intended to prolong life, such as chemotherapy or radiation therapy, and includes those investigations needed to better understand and manage distressing clinical complications. (WHO, 2012).

This definition is much more expansive than that the one used in the United States.

All of hospice care is palliative; however, not all palliative care is provided by hospices. In the last 15 years primarily hospital-based palliative care has grown in the United States. The American Hospital Association and the Center to Advance Palliative Care report that there are now more than 1,635 hospitals in the United States that provide palliative care services (CAPC, 2012). In addition many hospice programs are now adding palliative care programs and services for patients who do not qualify for reimbursement as hospice patients. (see Clinical Practice Guidelines for Quality Palliative Care at http://www.nationalconsensusproject.org/Guidelines_Download.asp)

Professional Certification

In September of 2006 the American Board of Medical Specialties voted to approve hospice and palliative medicine as a new subspecialty. Any currently recognized specialty can add hospice and palliative medicine as a subspecialty. So far 10 cosponsoring boards have agreed, including Internal Medicine, Family Medicine, Surgery, Anesthesiology, Physical Medicine and Rehabilitation (PM&R), Obstetrics/Gynecology, Pediatrics, Neurology/Psychiatry, Radiology, and Emergency Medicine. This important achievement represents years of work mainly led by the American Academy of Hospice and Palliative Medicine and the American Board for Hospice and Palliative Medicine (ABHPM).

The National Board for Certification of Hospice and Palliative Nurses (NBCHPN) continues to certify advanced practice nurses, registered nurses, licensed practical/vocational nurses, and nursing assistants. As of 2012 there were more than 17,000 professionals certified by ABHPM. The NHPCO and the National Association for Social Workers now offer an Advanced Certified Hospice and Palliative Social Worker credential. The Association for Death Education and Counseling (ADEC) Certification program is the only certification program for those practicing generally in the field of death, dying, and bereavement. ADEC offers a two-level certification program for thanatology professionals. ADEC offers Certification in Thanatology and Fellow in Thanatology. Recipients of ADEC certification are required to undergo the recertification process every 3 years.

Care of the Dying in Institutions

The World Health Organization (WHO, 2006) estimates that there are 57 million deaths annually worldwide. In the developed world there is a much higher rate of death in institutions than in the developing world where death continues to come at earlier age and usually at home. Even in transitional countries like Romania home deaths are still over 80% of all deaths. In the United States and generally in Europe hospital death rates are high. In the United States in 2007 36% of all deaths occurred in the hospital and an additional 7% in the hospital outpatient or emergency department. Nursing home deaths were reported at 21.7%, while 25.4% were at personal residences. Interestingly 9.9% were in "all other places." This catch-all category likely includes many people in assisted living, as well as those where the location of death was not specified or in nontraditional locations such as prison, homeless, and in shelters (CDC, 2012).

Care of the dying in institutions continues to be a serious concern. A major study of dying in institutions was conducted by the SUPPORT Investigators (1995) with funding by the Robert Wood Johnson Foundation. The study looked primarily at teaching hospitals and found that overall pain control continued to be poor, patients' wishes for care were routinely ignored, and advance directives were often disregarded. In the first phase of this study only 47% of physicians knew when their patients preferred to avoid CPR, 38% of patients who died spent at least 10 days in an intensive care unit, and for 50% of conscious patients who died in the hospital, family members reported moderate to severe pain at least half the time. The development of hospital-based palliative care has improved this situation in recent years. Along with the recognition of hospice and palliative care as a subspecialization in medicine it is now more common for patients to receive a palliative care consult in the hospital by a hospice physician or nurse practitioner.

More and more people are dying in nursing facilities annually. Average survival for chronically ill patients admitted to nursing homes is estimated to be 18 months (Rothera, Jones, Harwood, Avery, & Waite, 2002). As such they are a natural population for palliative care. Hospice care to patients in nursing facilities has been shown to lead to a number of positive outcomes including: (1) hospice patients had superior pain assessments and hospice patients in daily pain are twice as likely to receive strong pain relievers than are nonhospice residents in daily pain; (2) a 93% increased likelihood that patients in daily pain will have at least some attempt made at managing their pain; (3) lower proportions of hospice patients compared to nonhospice patients had invasive procedures such as physical restraints, IV feeding, or feeding tubes; and (4) less likelihood of return to acute care facilities (Miller, Gozalo, & Mor, 2000).

In 2010 16.7% of hospice patients were admitted in nursing facilities and 18% died in nursing facilities (NHPCO, 2011), a relative decline from previous years, mainly due to increased government scrutiny. From these data we can surmise that only about 1% of hospice patients are transferred from other settings to nursing homes before death. For the remainder the nursing home was essentially the patient's home. For the hospice or palliative care provider, the nursing home staff, along with any other family, becomes the patient's de facto family and a recipient of support from the hospice team.

Care for Underserved Populations

Palliative care has spread slowly for many underserved populations. Hospice care in the United States began mainly in more affluent areas where minority populations were less well-represented. In the UK hospice has been criticized as deluxe dying for the few (Douglas, 1992). Over the last 30 years the proportion of minorities receiving hospice care has increased but is still not believed to be at par with the population (Connor et al., 2008). In 2010 less than 6% of hospice patients were Hispanic/Latino, about 11% were African American, and Caucasians accounted for 77% of admissions (NHPCO, 2011).

The prison population is another disenfranchised population that has had limited access to hospice or palliative care. Since the early 1990s tougher sentencing laws resulting from the Get Tough on Crime campaign and the Three Strikes and You're Out law have increased the number of inmates housed in prisons. The number of inmates housed in federal, state, and private correctional facilities has increased steadily. During 2010, state, federal, and private correctional facilities held 2,266,800 inmates, The number of inmates who died in jails and prisons in 2010 was 4,356. Between 2000 and 2009, suicide (29%) and heart disease (22%) were the leading causes of deaths in jails, accounting for over half (51%) of all deaths in jails. Death by drug or alcohol intoxication (7%) was the third leading single cause of death in jails between 2000 and 2009. No other single cause of death accounted for more than 5% of jail deaths during this period. Among the causes of inmate deaths in jails, AIDS-related deaths had the largest decline, decreasing by more than half (54%) between 2000 and 2009 (Bureau of Justice Statistics, 2011).

Although prisoners are entitled to health care that is commensurate with community standards, most inmates dying in prison do not have access to end-of-life care that meets these standards (Craig & Craig, 1999). Over the past decade efforts have been made to improve hospice and palliative care for inmates (Craig & Craig, 1999; Yampolskaya & Winston, 2003). However, several challenges remain such as reconciling incarceration practices with hospice practices, providing palliative care that complies with correctional goals, providing adequate pain management in an environment lacking of trust between inmate and staff members, and involving family within the confines of visitation restrictions. For resources on serving patients in correctional facilities go to the NHPCO resource page http://www.nhpco.org/i4a/pages/index.cfm?pageid=5371.

Patients with developmental disabilities have also had limited access to hospice and palliative care. Many with developmental disabilities until recent years had lived in specialized inpatient facilities and died at relatively early ages. Today only those with the most profound disabilities are institutionalized, and many are living to older age with the usual accompanying chronic diseases. One percent of the population is developmentally disabled, and most now live independently or in group homes. Professionals working with the developmentally disabled have limited knowledge of palliative care principles, and palliative professionals have limited knowledge of the special challenges of care for the developmentally disabled. Patients with physical disabilities also face added challenges receiving palliative care.

Dying Trajectories

It has been proposed that there are four primary trajectories to dying. They include (1) sudden death; (2) death from predictable decline such as cancer; (3) death from solid organ failure, and; (4) death from old age including frailty and/or dementia (Lunney et al., 2003).

This categorization may oversimplify the variations in the way people die and certainly some of these trajectories will overlap; however, it is a useful way to understand most common pathways to death. Obviously those dying suddenly will not be able to avail themselves of palliative care, except that families may benefit from bereavement support and some who sustain trauma will have a period of need for symptom control prior to their deaths.

Caregiver Issues/Gender Roles/Awareness of Dying

One of the factors that makes hospice and palliative care so successful is a focus on empowerment of caregivers. At the time of admission to a hospice or palliative care service a thorough assessment of family and caregiver history, needs, and capacities is done. A defining characteristic of all palliative care is the idea that the patient and family are the unit of care, not just the patient. By family we mean those who are involved in the emotional life and care of the person dying, regardless of blood or marital ties.

In palliative care families are taught to do almost anything a nursing professional can do, to the extent that the family member has the internal strength or ability to do this work. One of the reasons it is thought that families do better in bereavement after participating in hospice care (Connor & McMaster, 1996; Schulz, et al., 2001; Christakis & Iwashyna, 2003) is due to their effective involvement in caregiving. Postdeath, noncaregivers have been found to show more depression and weight loss.

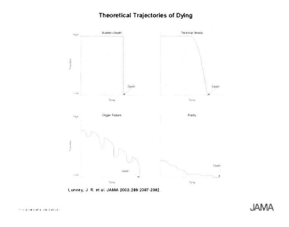

Theoretical Trajectories of Dying

Lunney, J. R. et al. JAMA 2003;289:2387-2392

JAMA

To facilitate their involvement many families will need support. The International Work Group on Death, Dying, and Bereavement has published *Assumptions and Principles for Psychological Care of Dying Persons and Their Families* (Psychological Work Group of the International Work Group on Death, Dying, and Bereavement, 1993), which includes a statement on families' need to be cared for in order to give care.

Caregiving can lead to positive outcomes as well as stressful negative outcomes. What determines positive or negative outcomes in caregiving depends largely on timing, circumstances, and perception of the meaningfulness of the work (Folkman, 1997; Schulz et al., 2001). In general caregiving that is time-limited in some way is easier to cope with, as in the case of hospice care. When caregivers perceive their job of caregiving as personally meaningful there is less stress and when the relationship to the person cared for is not an ambivalent one.

Caregiving in the United States is primarily done by women, who comprise 75% of caregivers. Two-thirds of caregivers are also employed and are between 35 and 64 years old. Numerous resources on caregiving can also be found on the Caring Connection website (http://www.caringinfo.org/i4a/pages/index.cfm?pageid=3279) including information on physical caregiving, comfort care, services available to assist caregivers, and caring for the caregiver.

Awareness of dying remains a difficult issue for dying persons and their caregivers. The term *conspiracy of silence* was used by Glaser & Strauss (1965) to describe the phenomena of physicians and families conspiring to keep information on the seriousness of a patient's condition from them. The underlying premise is that if you tell a patient he or she is dying it will result in the patient becoming depressed, giving up, and dying sooner than he or she might otherwise have if he or she remained in blissful ignorance.

The problem with this premise is that patients usually know how serious their condition is even if not told directly. Instead of being protected from difficult information the patient is left in what Weisman (1972) refers to as a state of lonely apprehension. The more the conspiracy of silence is maintained the worse the situation gets. This example illustrates a circumstance where what one is trying to do to solve the problem actually makes the situation worse as honest communication becomes more difficult to convey over time. Most of what we perceive to be denial on the part of the patient or family is generally in the service of preserving interpersonal relationships. Avoiding discussion of the seriousness of the patient's condition is due to fear that open communication will somehow harm the person or drive people away, when it is the lack of communication that is really creating discomfort.

What is known about the impact of truth telling on a dying person's emotional state is that, after a sometimes strong emotional reaction to the bad news, the patient usually adapts to the situation or chooses to ignore the information. No research has ever shown that telling a patient an accurate prognosis has any negative impact on survival. In fact some research has shown that truth telling can result in positive responses (Connor, 1992). And some research indicates that open family communication about dying can have a positive impact on the health and survival of widowed persons (Christakis & Iwashyna, 2003; Connor & McMaster, 1996).

In fact we now have growing evidence that the delivery of palliative care may lead to improved survival in patients themselves (Connor, Pyenson, Fitch, & Spence, 2007; Temel et al., 2010). We do not know how palliative care is associated with improved survival, and it runs counter to the philosophical notion that we neither hasten nor prolong dying, but we may speculate that palliative patients get better general care management and may avoid some of the perils of aggressive treatment in our health care systems.

Chapter 6

Ethical and Legal Issues Related to Dying and End-of-Life Care

Madeline Jacobs

The American medical system is fraught with ethical dilemmas at every turn: Should children be immunized against infectious diseases? How much risk is acceptable in testing new therapies and treatments? How should scarce health care resources be distributed? What are the right treatment decisions for any given situation? Should embryos be utilized to find new treatments? Should women be given the legal right to terminate pregnancies? When does life start? When does it end?

Is access to health care an issue of justice? Is it a right or something that should be earned? Is rationing health care morally or ethically defensible? How is rationing defined? Many people warn of rationing if we switch to a national health care system, but health care services are already unavailable to tens of millions of Americans based on the ability to pay. Isn't that rationing? Who should be entitled to health care services? Can the country afford to provide ideal benefits based on the answers to these questions?

The last 30 days of a beneficiary's life account for the highest portion of Medicare dollars per member. In fact, one-fourth of the entire Medicare budget is spent in the last year of a patient's life and, of that amount, 40% is spent in the last 30 days. With the cost of health care skyrocketing and limits on access imposed by cost, availability of resources (hospitals, doctors, medications), should there be a discussion on whether it is ethical to spend so much at the end of life, at the expense of dental care, primary care access, and treatment for younger patients?

Who really makes the decisions about acceptable practice, access to resources, or accepted definitions of life and death? There is no single answer, but a continually evolving process, with multiple stakeholders and contexts. Technology, a disjointed funding system, and a heterogeneous population have created a complex, often confusing web of competing interests and information for each situation.

According to the *U.S. History Encyclopedia*, bioethics "addresses the moral and ethical issues arising from clinical practice, medical and biological research, resource allocation, and access to biomedical technology." Modern bioethics has been shaped over the past century by social, political, and technological developments. It provides a theoretical foundation for sifting through the multiple interests and complex issues involved in caring for patients at the end of life and is based on the central concept of patient autonomy. Several core concepts pertinent to bioethics are examined in Table 1.

Table 1

Core Bioethical Concepts

Autonomy: The right to make decisions about one's own life and body without coercion by others. To have the right to act in terms of your own values.

Beneficence: Doing what's best for the patient, helping others

Nonmaleficence: Do no harm

Justice: Treating each patient impartially

Distributive Justice: Assured access to care

Capacity: The degree to which a person is able to understand health care options and make decisions for themselves. A person's capacity is task specific and is determined in context to each situation.

Competence: A legal term. A person is assumed competent to act and decide for unless a judge legally declares otherwise. A judicial declaration of incompetence can be global—when a person can't make any kinds of decisions for himself or herself, or limited to specified decisions, such as financial matters, personal care or medical decisions.

Paternalism: Doctor knows best—any action, decision, rule, or policy made by a physician or other caregiver, or a government, that dictates what is best for the patient without considering his/her own beliefs and value system and does not respect patient autonomy.

Substituted Judgment: When someone else makes decisions for an incapacitated or incompetent patient by making all efforts to determine the preferences of the patient—how the patient would have decided if capable—based on whatever evidence can be found.

Foundations of Modern Bioethics

Modern physicians still take the Hippocratic Oath—a pledge to follow moral standards in their practice. While it has been updated since the days of ancient Greece, the Oath still reflects a deeply held belief in the physician as a healer and critical member of society. Traditionally, good and evil have been defined by religious traditions. Good people follow God's law and evil people don't. Before the late 18th and early 19th Century, all ethics and moral discussions were based in the belief that all good comes from a God or creator.

In the 18th and 19th centuries, philosophers and politicians began to develop social contract theories that were independent of a belief in God. These theories were based in the belief that people need rules to rise above their base natures and live in society. The work of the philosophers Immanuel Kant, Jeremy Bentham, and John Stuart Mill deal with how people can live together in society productively and what ideals and values should help shape behavior and relationships within that society. These philosophers thought about why people should behave morally and how a society should assign benefit to an action.

Immanuel Kant believed that people should behave morally because it is the right thing to do as a duty, not because they feel like doing the right thing. He also was an elitist who believed that most people weren't capable of following moral, ethical rules. The essential ideal for the Utilitarians in late 18th and 19th century England was to provide the greatest benefit—good—for a maximum number of people. The Utilitarians were focused on outcomes and were not interested in intentions. These broad theories often don't apply to complex, nuanced situations. What the rules say—rule utilitarianism—is different from how people act—act utilitarianism. Utilitarianism is a central tenet of public health and triage, the goals of which are to help as many people as possible while deciding how to allocate scarce resources.

Mill's work *On Liberty* in 1859 places bioethics in a political context. Are questions of life and death public or private concerns? Mill's *harm principle* posits that private actions only become public when someone is harmed in the doing. He states "that the only purpose for which power can rightfully be exercised over any member of a civilized community, against his will, is to prevent harm to others. His own good, either physical or moral, is not a sufficient warrant… Over himself, over his own body and mine, the individual is sovereign" (Mills, 1859, p. 62).

This idea of individual as independent from the state or community is a very modern, Western value. It is a fundamental building block in the American principle of patient self-determination. In practice, however, it often clashes with the values of patients and providers who come from cultures and communities that hold more traditional, paternalistic views of individual rights.

In a secular, pluralistic society such as the United States, there is no state-sanctioned religion that provides parameters and definitive judgments to solve ethical dilemmas. Modern bioethicists build on early ethical theorists and develop systematic approaches to morality and ethics to guide practitioners. For example, there is in the medical ethics literature a debate between the views of Tom Beauchamp and James Childress (2001), known as the Georgetown mantra, and a moral system proposed by Gert, Culver, and Clouser (1997). The Georgetown mantra provides four ethical principles—autonomy, nonmaleficence, beneficence, and justice (see Table 1 with core bioethical concepts for definitions). Gert, Culver, and Clouser (1997) propose a moral system based on 10 rules and five ideals:

The Ten Moral Rules:
1. Do not kill.
2. Do not cause pain.
3. Do not disable.
4. Do not deprive of freedom.
5. Do not deprive of pleasure.
6. Do not deceive.
7. Do not cheat.
8. Keep your promise.
9. Obey the law.
10. Do your duty.

The first five always lead directly to harm if violated. The second five, if violated, often lead to harm, but not as directly as the first five.

The Five Moral Ideals:
1. Prevent or reduce (risk of) death.
2. Prevent or reduce (risk of) pain.
3. Prevent or reduce (risk of) disability.
4. Prevent or reduce (risk of) loss of pleasure.
5. Prevent or reduce (risk of) loss of freedom.

Practitioners look to such academic debates for guidance in dealing with real-life situations and conflicts, and judges and legislators look to them when developing legislation and determining legal precedent.

Patient Self-Determination

The American ethic of patient self-determination developed over the course of the 20th century and was shaped largely in the legal arena. Each of these landmark cases further shifted the balance of power in medical decisions from the provider and the community to the patient.

In 1914, a New York State Court of Appeals judge, Benjamin Cordozo (who went on to serve on the Supreme Court of the United States), ruled in *Schloendorff vs. the Society of the New York Hospital* that "Every human being of adult years in sound mind has a right to determine what shall be done with his or her own body; and a surgeon who performs an operation without the patient's consent commits an assault for which he is liable for damages.... This is true except in cases of emergency when the patient is unconscious and when it is necessary to operate before consent can be obtained."

This ruling signaled a significant shift in health care norms. Historically, the relationship between physicians and patients was one of paternalism—father knows best—where the physician is the father figure. Basically, doctors made the decisions for patients, often without consulting the patient or obtaining consent.

While the 1914 Cordoza ruling enhanced the legal standing of patients to control their own health care decisions, it took a long time for informed consent to become a standard of medical practice. In 1961, a study by Oken found that 90% of physicians at Michael Reese Hospital reported that they withheld cancer diagnoses from patients in order to "sustain and bolster patient hope," even though earlier studies had established that patients overwhelmingly preferred to know their diagnoses.

The Oken study was published at a time of great social and political change. America in 1960 was in social upheaval, when the society at large began to reject paternalism and individualism became the norm in all aspects of life. People didn't want to just do what they were told anymore.

A number of movements sprang up with different groups of people—minorities, women, consumers—asserting their right to participate fully in society. The idea of a patient's right to decide the course of treatment was a natural outgrowth of the civil rights and women's rights movements, and the Oken study added fuel to the fire.

When the study was repeated by Novack and colleagues less than 20 years later in 1979, a full 97% of the physicians reported telling cancer patients their diagnoses.

The 1991 Patient Self-Determination Act

In the years following *Schloendorff*, the courts established the parameters of informed consent by considering the rights of patients to information and their role in medical decision making. Some cases were about patients who didn't want to know their diagnoses. In *Cobbs vs. Grant* (Cal 1972), the court ruled that "a medical doctor need not make disclosure of risks when the patient requests that he be not so informed" (Mosk, 1972, p. 12).

Two landmark cases of young women who suffered massive brain damage and were kept alive artificially, Karen Ann Quinlan and Nancy Cruzan, dealt with making end-of-life decisions for incapacitated patients who didn't leave a written record of their preferences. The cases ultimately led to the Patient Self-Determination Act in 1991.

On November 5, 1990, Congress passed the Patient Self-Determination Act (PSDA) as an amendment to the Omnibus Budget Reconciliation Act of 1990 (see chapters on end-of-life decision making). Concurrent to these legal developments, the delivery of medical care became more impersonal and institutionalized. The relationship between physicians and patients was transformed by increasingly sophisticated treatment technologies and medications. The ethical responsibility to treat the suffering and pain caused by these interventions became recognized as a requirement of good care.

Redefining the Goals of Care at the End of Life

It may seem immaterial to study the ideas of the ancient Greeks, Christians, and European philosophers, but they have profound influence on how we continue to define the roles and responsibilities of society, physicians, and patients. Modern technology blurs the definitions of good care—what does it mean to heal, especially at the end of life? The technological imperative seems to point to doing everything possible technically to preserve life, because it's possible. But the suffering caused by such a course of action can be seen as doing harm to the patient, who is in the last stages of life and can never be cured and put whole. What constitutes compassionate, competent care in these situations?

The Intensive Care Unit (ICU) is the hospital location where patients at the end of their lives are brought. According to Joseph Fins, "In the face of end-stage disease, these patients are often over-treated, subjected to poor pain management, and deprived of contact with family as death approaches" (p. 153). Surveys have shown that patients find routine ICU treatments and tests, such as arterial blood gasses, to be extremely painful. Why should patients at the end of their lives be subjected to these tests and procedures which do not contribute to appropriate end-of-life goals of care?

The ICU is a prime example of how death is equated with failure in the culture of a hospital. Illness is attacked as an enemy and seen mostly as a physical problem. Symptoms and system failures are treated by specialists who myopically see only the part or system that they know how to treat, without regard to the whole prognosis or stage in life.

One result of all this patching together is to confuse the patient and families into thinking that the patient is actually getting better or recovering, rather than extending the dying process technologically. Many of the technologies currently used in the course of routine hospital care, such as cardiopulmonary resuscitation, were created to save lives on the battlefield. Instead of stabilizing young soldiers so they could recover and go on to lead productive lives, these technologies are used routinely to bring old and ill bodies back from the dead. In essence, medical technology has created a form of what Nancy Dubler calls "life in death on machines" (p. 260).

The hospital team has managed to bring patients back from the brink of death multiple times, allowing them precious time with their families and renewed hope for more such miraculous escapes. Thus, the family is understandably confused when the medical team tells them that any further treatment would be futile and may do more harm than good. Modern medicine has worked its last miracle and there are no other treatments, medications, surgeries, or interventions to plug the dike of death.

The issue of futility is a tricky one and is compounded by other issues, such as culture, religion, and even politics. For example, minority patients may believe that they are not being offered all that is available and that, based on history, they are being discriminated against. Studies show definitive disparities in access to, and levels of, care for racial and ethnic minorities. In addition, the United States has a shameful history of knowingly using minorities (and servicemen) as subjects in scientific research. The most famous case was the Tuskegee Study in which 399 African American men with syphilis were purposefully left untreated in order to study the long-term effects of the disease. Given this context, why should minority patients trust that hospitals are really providing them with all the best care that they deserve?

In 1995, the results of the Study to Understand Prognoses and Preferences for Outcomes and Risks of Treatments (SUPPORT) were published. The investigators found that less than half of the physicians knew their patients' wishes regarding do not resuscitate (DNR) orders, almost half of the DNR orders were written within 2 days of death; 38% of the patients who died spent 10 days or more in the ICU, and family members reported that conscious patients who died were in severe or moderate pain at least 50% of the time. An intervention aimed at improving physician–patient communication at the end of life failed to improve any of the indicators.

The SUPPORT study revealed that people were suffering terrible deaths in hospitals, in pain and with no power to control the last stage of their lives. In essence, technology has outstripped our ability to effectively treat dying patients and ignores the final stages of decline and disease. Not surprisingly, a right to die movement has sprung up, calling for people's right to avoid such painful and humiliating ends. In his self-written obituary, Derek Humphrey (2005), the founder of the Hemlock Society, wrote that his purpose for writing the *Final Exit* was to educate and advise thousands of dying people to know how to bring about their peaceful ends when dying, trapped in a ruined body, or just plain terminally old, frail, and tired of life.

The SUPPORT study was a wake-up call to the medical profession. In essence, the choice being provided to patients at the end of their lives was to either suffer or commit suicide. This dilemma was unacceptable, and the medical establishment began to look for alternatives and new methods of treatment to improve these choices. An entirely new medical specialty, palliative medicine, has developed specifically to better treat people at the end of life and recognizes the relief of suffering as a central goal of care. Other solutions, such as the expansion of hospice and palliative care units into hospitals, community palliative care, slow medicine, and many new laws and tools for documenting and following patients' wishes continue to be developed, based on a constantly evolving foundation of legal precedent.

End-of-Life Decision Making

Introduction to Part 2, Chapters 7 – 13

Chapters 7 through 13 focus on end-of-life decision making. The Body of Knowledge defined this major category of thanatology in this way: **the aspects of life threatening illness/terminal illness that involve choices and decisions about actions to be taken, for individuals, families, and professional caregivers.**

The seven chapters of Part 2 focus on end-of-life decision making in terms of these indicators: culture and socialization, religion and spirituality, historical and contemporary perspectives, life span issues, the family and larger systems, and ethical and legal issues. Four of the chapters (7, 9, 10, and 11) were revised from chapters found in the first edition, one (chapter 8) was carried over unchanged, and two chapters are wholly new: Chapter 12 on ethical and legal issues, and chapter 13, an Irish perspective on end-of-life decision making.

Chapter 7

Culture, Socialization, and End-of-Life Decision Making

Andrea C. Walker

Culture is multifaceted, multidimensional, and embedded in time and history. Culture involves a series of interactions and adjustments, negotiations and agreements of a person, or group of people, with their environment. Interwoven into culture is a series of expectations, perceptions of "rightness" regarding sources of power, values, social structures, religion, etc. Socialization involves learning the rules, beliefs, and expectations within a particular society, many of which are influenced and/or defined by culture.

Culture has been suggested to encompass an even broader contextual overlay of variables such as spirituality, religiosity, age, gender, sexual orientation, socio-economic status, and health/disability status (Hayslip, Hansson, Starkweather, & Dolan, 2009). The degree of acculturation to the dominant group's values adds further nuances; a Muscogee Creek Indian, for example, may integrate into mainstream culture for employment and social group while a member of his or her family speaks only his or her native tongue. Cultural diversity is highly complex, especially in relationship to end-of-life decisions, and there may be much more variation within than between groups. Kagawa-Singer and Blackhall (2010) recommended "finding a balance between cultural stereotyping and cultural empiricism…by neither disregarding culture nor assuming one is part of a list of stereotypical characteristics" (p. 331).

This chapter thus provides a description of research findings about end-of-life decisions as influenced by individuals' socialization processes within cultural contexts. It provides an overview of five general groups' cultural values related to death, and then presents findings on end-of-life decisions related to those cultural values. This chapter does not deeply explore the values within each culture. Any reference made to a particular group rests on the assumptions that (a) there may be only a few commonalities among the group members and (b) an overlay of individual and situational factors defines the experience. All of those factors cannot be discussed in this venue, but I encourage readers to consider the information presented here with that in mind.

Cultural Values Regarding End-of-Life Decisions in the United States

The impact of Western medical ethical principles on Caucasian Americans' end-of-life decisions cannot be overstated. The principles promote: (a) beneficence, honesty, respect, and all possible benefit to the patient; (b) nonmaleficence, bringing no harm to the patient; (c) justice in matters of health care; and (d) patient autonomy. Such principles have been taken so seriously that they have been legislated into public policy with the Patient Self-Determination Act (Henig, Faul, & Raffin, 2001), which was passed as part of the Omnibus Budget Reconciliation Act of 1990 to increase patient autonomy regarding treatment options, advance directives, and when to discontinue treatment (Young & Jex, 1992). The passing of the Patient Self-Determination Act has brought up ethical issues revolving around withholding and/or withdrawing treatment, as well as more controversial issues of: (a) physician-assisted suicide, obtaining a physician's aid in committing suicide; (b) indirect euthanasia, the physician allowing a patient to die using more passive, less intrusive means, and; (c) direct euthanasia, the physician's purposeful intervention to hasten death (Horacek, as cited by Marrone, 1997). As such, Caucasian Americans typically consider the patient's quality of life and do not always opt for life-prolonging treatments.

Cultural conflicts with the principles around the Patient Self-Determination Act have been explored in literature (Werth, Blevins, Toussaint, and Durham, 2002). A benefit to Caucasian Americans may be perceived differently by other Americans. For instance, "the humane choice" of removing a ventilator from an infant whose brain is severely injured may be a cultural assault to a father from a Saudi culture embedded in Islamic values (Sayeed, Padela, Naim, & Lantos, 2012). Moreover, removal from tube feeding of a terminal, unconscious patient to minimize suffering may be perceived as giving up to some in an African-American culture. As respect for the patient's value system and justice in treatment are likely to be important in all cultures, components of value systems and perceptions of justice may diverge. The idea of fidelity, forthright communication from the physician regarding the patient's diagnosis, prognosis, and treatment options, while important in the dominant culture, may seem cruel and inappropriate to some Chinese Americans (Yeo, 1995). Finally, the value of autonomy may not be seen as self-determination in many cultures, as it is in the United States (Winzelberg, Hanson, & Tulsky, 2005). Furthermore, some have challenged the idea that the Western view of autonomy is always in the best interest of the patient. Hallenbeck, Goldstein, and Mebane (1996) described the ethical principles in the United States as having "sustained and reinforced a pervasive reductionism…and dominance of self-interest in decision making…" (p. 394). Quite simply, members of minority cultural backgrounds may not share dominant U.S. values of independence, self-reliance, and fear of being dependent on others as a result of lingering treatment (Kagawa-Singer & Blackhall, 2010).

Sociohistorical Context and Meaning of Death

Each major cultural group in the United States evolves from unique sociohistorical contexts, enveloped in experiences encompassing country of origin, religious background, immigration to the United States, and position in mainstream society. Psychosocial and demographic variables such as age, socio-economic status, religion, education, perspective of health care, and meaning of death may account for the variation within cultural groups. For instance, in a study of older adults' personal preferences if faced with terminal illnesses and/or physical conditions (Cicirelli, 1997), many older adults were socialized to regard the physician as authority figure and, thus, themselves as having less decision-making authority in their health care. In addition, African-American participants' end-of-life decision preferences remained consistent across circumstances, socio-economic status, and religiosity, suggesting that the unique social history may have helped form a strong sense of survival in the face of trauma unique to the culture (Cicirelli, 1997).

African-Americans as a group tend to have a strong focus on religiosity, often in Protestant Christianity, believing that suffering is redemptive and that God has more authority over life and death than physicians (Kagawa-Singer & Blackhall, 2010). Research has found that African-Americans favor health care that prolongs life at a significantly higher rate than Caucasian (Hopp & Duffy, 2000; McKinley, Garrett, Evans, & Danis, 1996; Shrank, Kutner, Richardson, Mularski, Fischer, & Kagawa-Singer, 2005; Winter & Parker, 2007), and this choice for prolonging life appears to be related to a strong sense of religiosity (Mitchell & Mitchell, 2009). In addition, there may be a legitimate lack of trust by African-Americans in the medical establishment (Bullock, 2006) based on experiences of injustice in health care, disregard for autonomy, and disproportionate involvement in research and experimentation. Several historical events, including but not limited to slavery; medical experimentation; the Tuskegee syphilis experiment, in which treatment was knowingly withheld from patients to track their digression; and lack of federal funding when AIDS spread to the African-American community (Dula, 1994), along with social pressures of economic challenges and unequal rates of incarceration (Crawley et al., 2000), have resulted in some African-Americans questioning whether they should trust the health care system (Amelle, Lawrence, & Gresle, 2005). Research is mixed, however, suggesting diversity within the group. For example, African-Americans have more commonalities than differences with Caucasian in their perspectives of tube feeding elders with dementia (Modi, Velde, & Gessert, 2010), communicating prognosis to those with terminal illnesses, and favoring patient autonomy over family decision making (Blackhall, Murphy, Frank, & Mischel, 1996). Furthermore, older African-Americans and Caucasian were later found to be similar in terms of their death-related fears (Cicirelli, 2000). African-American ambulatory cancer patients, indeed, reported trust in the health care system and feeling that physicians treated them equally well, regardless of race (McKinley et al., 1996).

The term *American Indian* covers over 500 tribes in the United States, each with its own cultural considerations. Much of the current culture within each tribe is influenced by the degree of acculturation and the influence of Christianity (McCabe, 1994). Some sociocultural commonalities may be observed. Many American Indians experience distrust in mainstream health care and educational systems (Walker, 2009), resulting from a history of forced acculturation, relocation, and dishonored agreements with the U.S. government. In some tribes, such as the Muscogee Creek, children attended boarding schools where they were not allowed to use their native language (Thompson, personal communications, 2002), accelerating their evolution away from their native culture. Spirituality is a part of every facet of life, especially for Chippewa (Stately, 2002), though largely ignored throughout history. Many tribes were at one time based on a communal structure, relying on consensus for decision making (Chaudhuri & Chaudhuri, 2001). Navajos have a strong sense of autonomy, though decisions are typically made with input from other tribal members, making the Western ethic of confidentiality seem strange (McCabe, 1994). Finally, American Indians often have a particular disposition toward a balanced perspective of life and a more accepting position toward death; death is an event neither to be feared nor anticipated (Walker& Balk, 2007).

Hispanic Americans are comprised of many diverse groups, including Mexicans, Cubans, Puerto Ricans, and Latin Americans with traditions influenced by both Spain and Africa. Representing a growing population in mainstream United States, there may be a few similarities across groups despite the diversity. Many of these groups openly celebrate Day of the Dead to remember their loved ones, indicating a familiarity and acceptance of death, as well as emphasis on remembering family after death (Soto, personal communications, 2000). Importance of family appears to be common across most groups, and end-of-life decisions may be based on the family rather than the individual wishes; in fact, Hispanics are more likely to prefer family-centered decision making (Kwak & Haley, 2005) though they report a strong value of autonomy, similar to African and Caucasian Americans, when facing death (Volker & Wu, 2011). Religious beliefs, usually Roman Catholic, are often intertwined with the view of death as natural, though caused by sin, and as a path to resurrection (Miller, 2002). Many Mexican Americans thus see life and health as a gift from God, and enduring the suffering of sickness may be a sign of strength (Klessig, 1992).

Asian-Americans represent yet another vastly diverse category of minority cultures in the United States, comprising Chinese, Japanese, Filipino, Vietnamese, Korean, Native Hawaiian, among numerous others. Many immigrated to the United States during several waves over the past 200 years, enduring some U.S. resistance evident in the Chinese Exclusion Act of 1882 and the Oriental Exclusion Act of 1924. Many Asian-Americans, except Filipinos who are dominantly Catholic, originate from Buddhist and Taoist backgrounds (Braun & Nichols, 1996), in which death is not distinct from life, is a conditioned state, and is impermanent (Kawamura, 2002). This Buddhist perspective may influence the decision of several groups, including Chinese, Japanese, Filipino, Asian/Pacific Islander, and others, to enroll in hospice less frequently, and have shorter stays when they do enroll, than Caucasian patients (Ngo-Metzger, Phillips, & McCarthy,

2008). Chinese incorporate the Buddhist value of not causing suffering or burden on others (Bowman & Singer, 2001). Native Hawaiians experienced much loss of life upon their initial contact with the West when European missionaries arrived on their islands a few centuries ago. Influenced by a combination of Christianity and their native religion, Native Hawaiians appear to accept death as a transition to the next life (Braun & Nichols, 1996). Koreans tend to perceive death as return to familial, cultural, and spiritual homes (Kwon, 2006). The value of duty to family or filial piety, respect and care for one's parents and elders in the family, influences end-of-life decisions in Asian groups, particularly the Chinese (Bowman & Singer, 2001; Yeo, 1995) and Asian Indian families (Sharma, Khosla, Tulsky, & Carrese, 2012).

Research About End-of-Life Decisions and Culture

Members of mainstream European American culture are more likely to have knowledge and use of advance directives, withdraw life-sustaining treatments in futile conditions, and support physician-assisted suicide than those of minority cultures. As a whole, minority cultures tend to be less supportive of decisions that result in earlier death.

Advance Care Planning

Advance care planning provides family and health care with a person's treatment preferences prior to incapacitation through the living will, written specification regarding administration of life support due to terminal illness, and durable power of attorney, giving another person legal authority to make one's medical decisions when he/she is unable to do so (Doukas & McCullough, 1991). Caucasian Americans have shown to be the most likely group to have advance directives, with African-Americans and Hispanics significantly less likely (Carr, 2011). African-Americans were more likely to have negative attitudes toward advance directives due to distrust of the system, lack of access to health care, increased spirituality, a survivalist view of suffering and death, influence of social support systems, and other unknown reasons while controlling for socio-economic status (Bullock, 2006; King & Wolf, 1998; Kwak & Haley, 2005; McKinley et al., 1996). Because elderly Chinese rely on their children, they may see little value in advance care planning (Bowman & Singer, 2001). Braun and Nichols (1996) found that few Native Hawaiians had a living will, as property typically goes to the spouse and children, and family carried out the dying person's verbal wishes regarding death and/or funeral. Also, many Japanese participants actually had advance directives, Chinese believed in them but few had them, some Filipinos had them if they had been in the United States long, and Vietnamese participants were typically not familiar with advance directives (Braun & Nichols, 1996).

Life Support/Tube Feeding

Life support involves the use of mechanical devices such as intravenous tube feeding to sustain life when the patient would not otherwise remain alive. Repeatedly throughout literature, research indicates that African-Americans more strongly prefer the use of life support regardless of physical condition than other cultural groups (Amelle et al., 2005; Caralis, Davis, Wright, & Marcial, 1993; King & Wolf, 1998; Kwak & Haley, 2005;

McKinley et al., 1996; True et al., 2005) although some research suggests similar attitudes in African and Caucasian Americans (Modi, Velde, & Gessert, 2010). Hispanics seem to prefer life-prolonging treatment (Caralis et al., 1993), but women reported not wanting a feeding tube (Duffy, Jackson, Schim, Ronis, & Fowler, 2006). To increase longevity, the likelihood of Chinese families to choose life support if the dying person is younger than expected also increases (Yeo, 1995). Elderly Chinese may actually prefer to not engage in life-sustaining treatments in futile conditions, even though their children may feel an obligation to do so (Bowman & Singer, 2001). When compared to Caucasians, non-Jewish participants, Chinese, Filipino, and Korean Americans were much more likely to agree to start, as well as less likely to terminate, life support, and Iranians, whose Muslim beliefs dictate that no one has the right to choose death, usually oppose terminating life support regardless of condition (Klessig, 1992). For Orthodox Jews, life support may be continued in any situation, but for non-Orthodox Jews the dying process should not be prolonged (Klessig, 1992).

Communication About Medical Condition

Many minority cultures in the United States, including Chinese, Japanese, Korean, Ethiopian, Greek, Italian, French, Eastern European, Mexican, Central and South American, and Native American believe that withholding the truth about a terminal medical condition from a person is more compassionate and ethical, and disclosure of information regarding diagnosis, prognosis, and treatment preferences is discouraged (Kagawa-Singer & Blackhall, 2001; Kwak & Haley, 2005). Japanese resident physicians are more likely than U.S. residents to discuss medical information with family before the patient (Gabbay et al., 2005). As full disclosure may be seen as distressing in some Hispanic families (Yeo, 1995), the value of filial piety may also make it difficult for some Chinese Americans to communicate bad news, as this disclosure may cause harm and discouragement to the dying person (Muller & Desmond, 1992; Orona, Koenig, & Davis, 1994; Yeo, 1995). Some studies have indicated that such communication is not discouraged among many African and Caucasian Americans (Kagawa-Singer & Blackhall, 2001), as well as some Hispanics (Caralis et al., 1993). African-Americans request more spiritually oriented information, however, while Caucasian Americans prefer more information about medical options and associated costs (Shrank et al., 2005).

Locus of Decision Making

Whether a culture has a tendency toward individual or family/communal structure heavily influences who makes decisions. Personal autonomy may be less important in many cultures than in the mainstream United States Asian and Hispanic Americans tend to prefer removing the burden of treatment decisions from the patient, while African-American families tend to promote the individual person's wishes (Kwak & Haley; 2005). African-Americans do prefer to include more family, friends, and spiritual leaders in end-of-life discussions, however, while Caucasian Americans are more exclusive (Shrank et al., 2005). Chinese, Hispanic, Korean, Filipino, and Mexican Americans are much more likely than European or African-Americans to believe the family should be the primary decision maker (Kagawa-Singer, 2001; Klessig, 1992; Orona et al., 1994; Yeo, 1995), and Japanese resident physicians are more likely than U.S. residents to fulfill families' choices over individual patients' choices (Gabbay et al., 2005). Some Hispanics are more likely to refer to the physician's recommendation (Caralis et al., 1993). In a case study by Carter and Sandling (1992), an American Indian mother deferred to the tribal elders her decision whether to allow her tragically deformed child to be kept alive by intravenous feeding, demonstrating the cultural tendency to consult group opinion when making individual choice.

Autopsy and Organ Donation

The dominant U.S. culture finds little ethical dilemma with either autopsies or organ donations, but some Asian groups have indicated otherwise. Chinese have divergent opinions of wanting to help others while not wanting to destroy their bodies, seen as gifts from parents; Japanese indicated hesitance to mutilate the body but acceptance, with Buddhist desire to help others, as long as body appeared intact; Filipinos indicated a greater tendency to agree with the longer time spent in the United States; Vietnamese were generally against organ donation because of not wanting to be born into the next life missing an organ (Braun & Nichols, 1996). Those Asian-Americans who do intend to donate organs are motivated more by social responsibility than individual rights (Park, Shin, & Yun, 2009). Hispanic Americans reported willingness to donate or receive an organ from a family member but great hesitation in discussing the donation with the person (Siegel, Alvaro, Hohman, & Maurer, 2011). Mexican Americans tend to prefer not having autopsies or organ donations because of the beliefs that the soul remains with the body for some time after death and that making such plans before death is equitable with giving up on treatment (Perkins, Supik, & Hazda, 1993). African-Americans, on the other hand, tend to concur with the Protestant Christian belief that the soul leaves the body upon death and may be more likely to choose autopsies and to help others through organ donation (Perkins et al., 1993). Additional evidence indicates that willingness to donate organs is much lower in African than Caucasian Americans (Lichtenstein, Alcser, Corning, Bachman, & Doukas, 1997). Distrust in the health care system contributes to negative attitudes, but the relationship varies according to education level, marital status, and other factors (Russell, Robinson, Thompson, Perryman, & Arriola, 2012). American Indians, traditionally desiring to enter the spirit world with an intact body, are reexamining beliefs based on high need due to prevalence of diabetes (Fahrenwald & Stabnow, 2005).

Suicide and Euthanasia

This controversial topic has received diverse opinions, even from members of mainstream U.S. society. In Lichtenstein et al.'s (1997) comparison study of African and Caucasian Americans, both supported legalizing voluntary and physician-assisted suicide, but Caucasian were much more likely than African-Americans to request it themselves (Caralis et al., 1993), possibly due to a stronger religious commitment and cultural condemnation of suicide among African-Americans. Wasserman, Clair, & Ritchey (2005-2006) found that, though African-Americans distrust the health care system, their attitudes toward euthanasia seem to be due to spiritual issues. Mexican Americans also have much less positive attitude toward assisted suicide (Mouton, Espino, Esparza, & Miles, 2000). Native Hawaiians are tolerant of suicide and in favor of passive euthanasia; Chinese tend to believe that suicide is wrong except in cases of rape and prisoners of war, and euthanasia is generally acceptable if it reflects the person's wishes and does not damage filial piety; Japanese are tolerant of suicide and support the family's decision in euthanasia; Filipinos are generally not supportive of suicide or euthanasia; Vietnamese usually believe suicide is wrong and accept euthanasia only if family cannot afford continued health care (Braun & Nichols, 1996). These Asian group differences appeared to reflect education level and length of time in the United States (Braun & Nichols, 1996). Mexican Americans generally report negative attitudes toward physician-assisted suicide, but a recent study found that males preferred legalization over Caucasian Americans (Espino et al., 2010).

Conclusions and Recommendations

In concluding this chapter, a couple of points must be made. First, findings on culture and end-of-life decisions are evolving. Since the first edition of the handbook, studies have been conducted that challenge our understandings; we are finding a more complex interplay of variables that appear to interact with sociohistorical context. Second, we need to take more deliberate steps in our research to explore this evolving understanding. In the past, the empirical knowledge base has largely focused on quantitative and/or crosscultural comparisons. While this approach has informed scholars and practitioners of some general threads, results indicate that decisions also depend on individual factors, such as spirituality/religiosity, available information/education, acculturation, and communication with health care providers. The comparison studies have done just what they were intended to do. Now, a closer picture of individuals' and families' experiences is needed to provide a richer context with which to understand how the values of culture impact choices made at the end of life. End-of-life literature will benefit from increased focus on the specific decisions people face as they are embedded in the nuances of familial relationships, circumstances around the illness or death, and beliefs about death and life. Indeed, recent trends suggest that this type of shift is in the making.

All of us desire to create meaning amidst our end-of-life experiences. The uncertainty embedded in the event itself only adds to the uncertainty already felt in facing a wave of health care decisions. Caregivers of African, Hispanic, and Caucasian Americans felt burdened with end-of-life decisions when they were uncertain of their loved ones' preferences (Braun, Beyth, Ford, & McCullough, (2008). As grief therapists, professional counselors, psychologists, and medical care providers, steps can be taken to help ease the burden for families of dying loved ones. We draw upon Laungani's (1992) model of understanding culture for the following suggestions: (a) determine the locus of decision making in the family, whether patriarchal or matriarchal, individual, or family as a unit;

(b) observe closely the communication styles and patterns within the family, including language used and whether unidirectional or bidirectional; (c) determine the family's locus of control, whether reality is perceived as deterministic or as a set of choices; (d) analyze how reality is perceived and expressed, whether through cognitive or emotional means; (e) understand how the family attributes causation of events, whether through scientific, material explanations, or spiritual forces; and (f) adapt decision-making processes to accommodate diverse perspectives toward end-of-life issues. Doka (2005) recommends that practitioners consider all factors, complicating and facilitating, and realize that the process of providing appropriate care may take time and may not end at the family member's death.

Ultimately, culturally competent research and culturally responsible and effective practice will occur when a theme of sensitivity and respect is incorporated into interactions with each person. Doing so involves a reflexive evaluation of our own culture, socialization process, and values involved in our personal beliefs about end-of-life choices, a critical review of how our own personal biases might affect our interactions with those of other cultures and value systems, and finally, compartmentalization of our belief systems to objectively and compassionately embrace and respect perceptions of truth outside our own.

Chapter 8

End-of-Life Care: Spirituality and Religion

The Reverend Richard B. Gilbert

Introduction

Joyce Hutchinson and Joyce Rupp (1999) have a rich history of capturing the essence of the human experience and the spiritual implications within these experiences. They suggest that the two most vital moments, defining moments, in the human experience are birth and death. How a person approaches dying becomes the bulwark on which rests all that affords meaning and integrity for a person.

Rupp contends, with reference to the practices of her coauthor, that caring for the dying is a privilege and is, indeed, a sacred time for the dying, their loved ones, and also for those who are beckoned to approach the bedside of the dying. She says, "Joyce [Hutchison] visualizes herself as accompanying each dying person to the door that opens to the other side. She walks them home with loving care, quiet joy, tenderness and compassion" (p. 19).

End-of-life care requires us to at least be available to the dying and their loved ones around the issues of meaning, beliefs, rituals, and their longing for peace as they face whatever may be ahead for them. This accessibility means our willingness, with competence, to be available to others around spiritual concerns, wounds, religious issues, unresolved issues, guilt, sin, fears about tomorrow, a lack of certainty surrounding their faith and a sense of estrangement from God (or that which is their empowerment), or their religious connections. It requires us to stand firmly in their presence as guest, nonjudgmentally, while also tracking our own spiritual/religious issues, challenges, and shortcomings.

To assist our discussion we will follow this outline:
- Spirituality and religion: definitions
- Spiritual care: the invitation placed before all providers
- Spiritual assessment tools
- The place for ritual in the care of the dying (including diversity)

- "Managing" diversity within the family (especially points of dispute)
- When our spiritual/religious self feels inadequate or threatened as providers/caregivers
- Making better use of chaplains

Spirituality and Religion: Definitions

Three points are essential here. The first is that everyone has something that he or she expresses and experiences as spiritual. This expression and experience takes on a new priority and intensity when a person is approaching the end of life. In the tension between "lasts" and "firsts" there may be an internal challenge or conflict previously unknown to the dying person and surrounding loved ones. Second, as caregivers (in whatever role) we must be particularly present and nonjudgmental while monitoring and keeping watch over our own spiritual and religious beliefs and practices.

The third point is particularly important. While the murmurings of the dying and of the loved ones may seem almost profane in distancing from things spiritual, these longings and struggles for wholeness at the time of death's approach, paradoxically, serve as the ultimate fulfillment and the ultimate destruction. This longing isn't necessarily about heaven and hell, though it may be for some, but the reality that this is the final test of anyone's beliefs and practices. Even those who have experienced a profound spiritual sense throughout their life journey may feel their faith parched by the draining demands of unfamiliarity on the spiritual walk when dying. Said another way, this person has not faced death before, and this spiritual walk becomes the final stretch or wilderness. Gentle, nonjudgmental, reassuring listening will be the mark for the providers so that the patient can be free to say, believe, or search in any direction yet feel safe enough to risk moving onward to the tomorrow that awaits within the boundaries of his or her faith.

In their training manual for hospice physicians, the American Academy of Hospice and Palliative Medicine (1997) speaks of the search for meaning:

> The search for meaning is often characterized by a process that involves exploring questions of value and worth, letting go of former roles and expectations, and reframing events to support renewed hope and an enlarged sense of efficacy. When traumatic losses threaten or occur, patients and families begin the difficult process of adaptation by trying to make sense of what is happening to them. They search for meaning … (p. 17).

Then will unfold the questions of who, what, when, and why? as we try to configure some pathway that we can follow that will make sense out of all of this. Seldom, of course, is it sensible. It is doable when we are enabled to make the right connections which, after all, is a person's expressed spirituality.

It is during this entanglement between life and death, doubt and belief, that some thread of hope is woven. Terminal illness is not necessarily the absence of hope. People can find a measure of hope, even confidence, as they again bringing together living/dying and their beliefs and practices.

The experience of dying and death is a first-time experience for us, even if we had faced the deaths of many loved ones and friends. The spiritual framework, often felt to be crushed under the strong winds of death, are the same reference points that, upon moving through the worst of death's storm, may be the first familiar ground we recognize.

A death is the interruption of a human relationship—whether through a sudden death in an emergency room; a lingering on through disease, perhaps in a nursing home or hospice; or the stealing away of the breath of life in pregnancy. Painful interruptions, wrong by human standards, are a part of life, the created order. We grieve, we hurt, we lash out at the God we want to blame for all of this (Gilbert, 1995, p. 115).

In addressing the gay, lesbian, bisexual, and transgendered community, a lifestyle so frequently immersed in isolation and abandonment, a strong religious criticism from many, it becomes clear why many in this community could suffer severe spiritual and/ or religious doubts and wounds. Sweasey (1997), in citing spirituality as one coming to know the self, speaks of spirituality in this way, "Having a deeper sense of oneself, addressing the whole of life, and a connection with something bigger" (p. 12).

Religion often serves as the practical or structured (framing) around which we find a measure of community, familiarity, and dependability. (Corr, Nabe, & Corr, 2006) "[Religion is] experience, tradition, and shared attitudes had prepared individuals and the community as a whole to support each other and to contend with the cycles of life and death in their midst" (p. 45).

In his study on spirituality and aging, David Moberg (2001) reminds us that this separation between spirituality and religion has not been an easy separation, should not be seen as a divorce, and is relatively recent in its happening. He suggests that spirituality emerged as an in term, in part, because of a growing suspicion of, and separation from, religion. Spirituality became positive and religion was experienced as negative. Spirituality and religion share the common purpose of enhancing a person's self-worth, beliefs, coping with life, and that which is eternal for them.

Spiritual Care: The Invitation Placed Before all Providers

Spiritual care is to remove our shoes, in a sense of humility and awe, as we tread upon the sacred ground that is defined and trusted by the dying patient. This intimate sharing is always scripted by the dying, and our ability to step into it is by invitation only. We bring our beliefs and practices, and we have myriad spiritual assessment tools.

Sadly, some strong testimony suggests that spiritual care has been an area of some turf warring. Some hospices have not been honestly committed to professional standards for chaplains. Others have good chaplains who are blocked out by nurses and social workers "who determine when the chaplains will visit," as one chaplain shared with me in a personal conversation.

Spiritual care is the work of all of us. If it rests with the patient primarily, and secondarily with the family, it is their right to extend the welcome mat to whom they wish. Obviously the team must build mutual trust and respect that replaces heroism with collaboration. The patient, for many reasons, may feel more comfortable with the doctor or the housekeeper, the nurse or the volunteer. Let it happen as it should happen, even when referrals come too late (to hospice) that the patient often has no opportunity to explore these important ingredients in their recipe for peace and wholeness.

Rachel Stanworth (2004), in remarks preceded by a strong case for chaplains and pastoral care, states, "The point I wish to make is that unless transparency to an ultimate horizon is valued in principle by employers, there is a danger that providers of palliative care will come to regard spiritual issues as a purely subsidiary interest of psychotherapeutic support, an impoverishment this book strongly resists"(p. 237).

Spiritual Assessment Tools

To assess is to value story, things said and unsaid, the collaborative viewpoints of the team, patient and family concerns, blending them together into, at least for palliative care, the medical model that then guides all team members in the care of the patient.

In part because of time constraints (staffing, late referrals, ability of patient to communicate when heavily medicated, no available family or family disruption that eliminates accurate reporting), along with our own comfort levels around spiritual and religious matters, spiritual assessment is frequently compromised. It has become easier to fit the person into the assessment tool, as one chaplain reminded me when visiting a patient in the hospital where I served. "I have no time to visit with you. I must complete the assessment form."

This practice is common and, equally common, is the risk for spiritual neglect and abuse. Once we have put processes first we have crossed a definitive boundary that, unless reclaimed, will confound despair and pain and further distress the person whose death approaches. It is about fitting who we are and what we offer into the story, the personhood, of the patient. To reverse that intention is to cross that boundary.

Several assessment questions are here offered as resources to guide you as the patient chooses to let you in. David Moberg (2001) suggests several approaches.

1. Questions for discussion and mapping the journey:
   - Do you feel that you have become more religious as you have grown older?
   - How would you describe your own spirituality and your own spiritual life?
   - What is your perception of death? Your attitudes toward death?
   - Are you afraid to die? Why or why not? (pp. 80-81)
2. Moberg shares these marking-points that allow patients to identify their spiritual health and need.
   - Assurance of God's continuing love
   - Certainty that life is protected
   - Relief from heightened emotions as of fear, guilt, grief
   - Relief from loneliness
   - A perspective for life that embraces time and eternity
   - Continue spiritual growth
   - A satisfying status in life as a person

- The illusion of continued worth and usefulness (p. 93)

Gilbert (1996) offers these assessment questions that can work well when offered conversationally.

- When you are discouraged or feeling despondent, what keeps you going?
- What are your sources of energy and courage?
- Where have you found strength in past experiences of loss or struggle?
- Where have you have found hope in the past? How do you define hope?
- Who have you looked up to? Who inspires you?
- What does dying mean to you?
- What does suffering mean to you?
- What does "religious community" mean to you?
- What does "religious leader" mean to you?

Another approach is to consider, by observation, assessment, and conversation, the signs or "symptoms" of spiritual wounds or crises. Donna O'Toole (1995) provides these statements as possible markers in the story.

- Feeling lost and empty
- Feeling forsaken, abandoned, criticized, or judged by God
- Questioning why to go on with life
- Extremes of pessimism or optimism
- Feeling or not feeling God (or other significant experiences) in life
- Needing to give or receive forgiveness
- Needing to give or receive punishment
- Feeling spiritually connected to what/who is lost

Gilbert (1995) offers these approaches around feelings expressed, demonstrated or sensed as absent:

- "I feel that I am letting God down..."
- "It's all my fault"
- "God will take care of me [often shield protecting further discussion or deeper examination]"
- "Why did this happen to me? Why now?"
- "My heart aches. Where are the pills?"
- "There is no hope."
- "Does God still love me?"
- "What if God knew this ...?"
- "I don't know how to pray any more."
- "Can you teach me how to pray?"
- "I am going home."
- "Will you pray with me?"
- "I want to see a priest."
- "I thought God promised..."

- "The Lord is my shepherd."
- "Prayed, and prayed, and prayed..."

The Place for Ritual in the Care of the Dying

Ritual is the marker, the stamp of approval that denotes where a person is on the journey, what is happening or has happened, and the spiritual significance of the moment. It can both comfort and clarify and serves as a conduit to a person's faith, spiritual connections, and religious sense. It is the anchor holding the person firmly in a most turbulent of seas.

It is important to bear in mind that, while rituals, especially sacramental ones, have a more universal definition and outcome, are important, they are still the product or choice of the patient and must not be imposed. This topic can be particularly tricky when the family is divided around spiritual and/or religious matters, each producing his or her own agenda. Questions like, What rituals are important to you?, What does a religious leader mean to you?, and that which probes what keeps a person connected to God and religious community, may be your pathways for inquiring about patient wishes.

Any discussion about ritual needs to consider not only the diversity of religious expressions, even within a common group or denomination, but also the diversity of culture. It is imperative that providers keep clear in both thoughts and actions the differences between *diversity* and *different*. Several extensive bibliographies on diversity and other related subjects are available free, by email, from this author.

African-Americans: As one minister noted, "We Blacks are very spiritual and we are very loud about it." African-Americans often speak about "passing" rather than dying. They generally reject organ donations, especially older generations, because they believe you must be whole to meet the Risen Christ. The religious leader often takes on a much larger role as minister, advocate, legal consultant, and ethicist.

Hispanics or Latinos: Do note carefully that we are speaking not only of diversity within families, communities, and nation, but from one country to the next. What works with Mexicans, for example, may not be the approach of people from Argentina. "Death is different in Mexico (Irish et al., 1993, p. 69)." Death can be feared, and emotions and emotional needs run high. They are expressive, use art, religious objects, chants, and prayers. The priest has a strong responsibility, both rooted in power and empowerment. Some providers may note, for the first time, something of the magical use of religion. The line can blur. The rule of thumb is to follow the lead of patient and family.

In addition to the reminder of differences by families and countries, it is also a generational division. First generation Latinos, especially from Mexico, even those who are legal, are so frightened of any authority (and thus place even more authority on the role of the priest) that they will say yes to any statement by a professional, out of fear, often never understanding their right to say no. Diversity, then, is not about translating words, but of helping people understand content (words), options (choices), and rights.

Even those who break away from Roman Catholicism and follow other denominations may still seek the rituals and sacraments that are more traditional. There can be variations from generation to generation, especially when moving from first to second generation. Providers must carefully facilitate both needs. Many Mexicans will need guidance around American funeral practices and also often need assistance when burial in Mexico is preferred.

Jews: There is variation, of course, by traditions: Hasidic, Orthodox, Conservative, Reformed, Reconstructionist. There can be language and cultural additions to the discussion. Some will pick and choose, preferring to see themselves as cultural Jews. Many will require burial within 24 hours, and with specific preparations, including bathing and dressing. This requirement becomes a potential point of difficulty when an autopsy is requested or demanded, and, quite frankly, American society, especially around the logistics for death certificates and other vital statistics, is not a 24-7 operation. A Friday afternoon death might well, simply due to paperwork, be delayed until Monday.

Roman Catholics have much diversity, including cultural. Some national groups will go back to old traditions, including Extreme Unction, refusing the strongest persuasion of the changes since Vatican II. They might seek both anointing (now stressing reconciliation) and last rites. The threefold burial rites of the wake (often with the recitation of the rosary), the funeral mass and the burial are important. Some plans can be frustrated by the shortage of priests or the refusal of some priests or dioceses to facilitate options.

Hinduism, including the sect, *Jainism,* represents the oldest major world religion. It combines many religions and many beliefs. There also can be strong practices around caste and gender. This cultural influence has strong implications for providers. Organ donations generally are not opposed, and burial is within 24 hours, usually by cremation. The switch to crematories, now an American mainstay, is a significant cultural shift. Caskets are always open, and sacred books and food play a significant part.

Buddhism stresses that the person passes through many reincarnations. This passage is imperiled when there are delays at the time of the death, including pronouncing the death, paperwork, organ donation discussion and funeral arrangements. This aspect is well-discussed by Donald Irish and his colleagues (1993).

Muslims and the Islamic faith, have become a contentious issue for many due to world events, politics, and, at times, prejudice, and fear. There is also variation due to country of origin, and frequently issues around gender and authority. Muslims view death as a universal reckoning, when people are called upon to account for their actions. They find their faith expressed in the Five Pillars. The casket is never open, there are readings from *The Qur'an,* prayers are recited, and the deceased is buried (not cremated). Many times the graveside ceremonies are attended only by men.

Native Americans (first-generation Americans) is a complex collection best described as diverse. There are strong tribal customs and differences, generally a profound sense of spirituality, and much that does not fit neatly into the American traditions. There are also generational differences. Oftentimes in communities with large Native American communities, one of the funeral homes is particularly expert in the needs of that community.

In all of these groupings, and there are many more, the key reminder is always that, while being informed about general practices and expectations, let the person tell you.

Managing Diversity Within the Family

While there is no one way to do a burial (albeit while respecting state and community laws), there can be strong expressions around practices that are less acceptable for a particular family or family member. This conflict is often mirrored in issues surrounding religious diversity (Christian vs. non-Christian, religious vs. nonreligious, born again vs. those following a different definition or set of criteria). Some opinions or objections may be rooted in the nature of the relationship to the dying patient as well as in old wounds, bitterness, or feuds. Sometimes there are secrets, others, as Ken Doka (1989) expresses so well, are disenfranchised and have voice that is not heard. Remarriage and blended families, especially when there are adult children who have not accepted the new mom or dad, can be very conflictual. The patient's advance directives, even the fact that the family did not know there were any advance directives, may dictate things in ways unsuitable to the family or parts of the family.

These predicaments often create what feels like a conflictual role for providers. It is important that the *team* plans around these concerns and maintains a common approach. It may be necessary for one member of the team to be directive. While we stress that we follow the wishes of the patient, it is too easy to hide in that caveat and fail both to address the needs of the family (within reason) and how those needs, practices, and memories help or hinder the patient as death approaches.

When Our Spiritual/Religious Beliefs Feel Inadequate or Threatened

Even under the best of circumstances, the constant parade of dying patients brings significant challenges to providers. Various patients will hook you, snag you less in their stuff and more in yours. Sometimes it is the accumulation of deaths. For others it is the circumstances around the dying, the patient's age or gender, and the patient's family can contribute to this entanglement. These stressors are neutral unless they impact on the patient or compromise our ability as providers. For most of us it is missing the opportunity for us to explore our own beliefs and practices.

Sometimes our frustration is an invitation to learn, such as questions or a sense of inadequacy when responding to a person who represents different values, gender, beliefs, or lifestyle.

Just as we need to listen to patients intentionally, as a guest, and nonjudgmentally, so we require that for ourselves. Many of us have trouble acknowledging and actualizing this fact. There must be a component of the team process that provides debriefing and the opportunity not only to review the case, but to review ourselves. Management must know how to discern team needs and when an intervention might be necessary for the group (team) or for an individual. This discernment is also a good use of the chaplain's presence with team members.

Making Better Use of Chaplains

Chaplains have long served in the care of the dying. Even before the modern hospice movement there were various expressions of hospitality and care of the dying, often provided by monks and monastic communities.

Chaplains are specialists, usually with additional training and accountability, to work in a variety of traditional and nontraditional workplaces, including hospice. They need to be included as active members of the team, and it is important that they have full access to patients, families, staff, and charts. Chaplains have the responsibility of both being actively present while also standing at a distance, viewing the wider picture, including the needs of the staff.

Conclusion

Few events in life both depend upon and stress a person's spiritual resources than to be approaching the end of their life. This ending is a time of profound, exaggerated experiences, feelings and needs, all of it at an intensity frequently unknown previously. For some, this new experience is more than their spirituality can bear. For others, things spiritual are the only things that will move them through it.

Exploring the spiritual dimension is crucial for patients, families, and providers when approaching end-of-life care.

Chapter 9

Historical and Contemporary Perspectives on End-of-Life Decision Making

James L. Werth, Jr.

Introduction

This chapter is intended to briefly review several areas that have implications for end-of-life decision making. To the degree possible, I have based the discussion on research and will provide both historical and contemporary perspectives on each area, although the length of time reviewed will vary by topic. I defined end-of-life decision making as choices made by dying individuals, their loved ones, or professional caregivers that take place during a person's dying process and/or have an effect on the manner and timing of death. Examples of end-of-life decisions include whether to create advance directives (i.e., a living will, a durable power of attorney for health care) and, if so, determining the specifics related to them; whether to continue on, withhold, or withdraw life-sustaining treatment; whether to more actively hasten death such as by voluntarily stopping eating and drinking or requesting (or providing, in the case of personal and professional caregivers) assisted suicide or voluntary euthanasia (see also Kleespies, 2004). I will not deal with end-of-life decisions made and enforced by health care providers without the awareness of the dying person or loved ones (e.g., involuntary euthanasia) or over the protestations of the dying person/loved ones (e.g., futility determinations).

Demographics of Death

According to the National Center for Health Statistics (Kochanek, Xu, Murphy, Minino, & Kung, 2011), in 2009 nearly 2.5 million people died in the United States. Over 70% of those who died were 65-plus while less than 2% were under the age of 20. Because the majority of people who die are adults, as well as the fact that decision making for infants and children is complicated by a variety of factors, the focus on this chapter is on end-of-life decision making by and for adults.

In the United States, in 2009, the average person could expect to live to be over age 78 (Kochanek et al., 2011); in 1900 life expectancy was only 47 years (Field, 2009).

There are longevity differences based on sex and race/ethnicity (Kochanek et al., 2011). Women, on average, can expect to live to be 81, while the average life expectancy for men is 76. Thus, women are more likely to be single/widowed near the end of life, and the current cohort of women is more likely to be poor because they did not work to the same extent as today's women (Stillion, 2006). The average life expectancy for Caucasian is 79, while it is 74.5 for African-Americans and 81 for Hispanics. Combining these data, Hispanic women have the longest life expectancy, followed by Caucasian women, Hispanic men, African-American women, Caucasian men, and then African-American men; other groups are harder to track.

In many other countries, life expectancy has also increased, but in some nations there has been little improvement. For example, Stillion (2006; see also World Health Organization [WHO], 2012, Table 1) noted that Japan (83 years in 2009) and Sweden (81 years in 2009) have also seen significant increases in longevity in the last century. Just as in the United States there are gender differences in longevity in most countries reporting mortality statistics, with women living longer (Stillion, 2006; WHO, 2012). On the other hand, life expectancy of someone in many countries in Africa may be 55 or less (WHO, 2012, Table 1).

Although not technically a death demographic, it is noteworthy that as people continue to live longer, the likelihood of some sort of cognitive decline increases, even without considering the people who develop dementia (Park, O'Connell, & Thomson, 2003). Thus, there is the possibility that eventually any person may lose the capacity to make her or his own health care decisions, which has implications for the end-of-life decision making process.

Causes and Patterns of Dying

Just as longevity has changed in the past century, so too have the causes of death, the places where death occurs, and the ways that people die, all of which may impact decisions.

Causes of Death

During the early 1900s, the leading causes of death were diseases and conditions that led to death fairly certainly and rapidly (e.g., pneumonia); however, more recently, the primary causes of death are chronic conditions that often have an uncertain path and timeline (e.g., cancers, heart conditions; see Field, 2009; Leming & Dickinson, 2007; Stillion, 2006).

The patterns of dying differ based on age group, sex, and race/ethnicity. For example, in 2009, for people over 65, heart disease and cancer are clearly the two leading causes of death, while for those aged 15-24, unintentional injuries, homicide, and suicide are the top three (Kochanek et al., 2011). In 2008, Alzheimer's disease, influenza and pneumonia, and suicide were in the top 10 lists for Caucasians but not for African-Americans whereas homicide, septicemia, and HIV disease were in the top 10 for African-Americans but not Caucasians (Heron, 2012).

Internationally, the causes and patterns of death look very different (WHO, 2012, Table 2). For example, the mortality rate for communicable diseases is much lower in the region of the Americas and the European region than the African region. Similarly, the mortality rate associated with chronic respiratory conditions is much higher in the Southeast Asia region and the African region than in the region of the Americas and the European region. The patterns of death underscore Ditto's (2006, footnote 1, p. 136) point that end-of-life decision making in the United States, much of Europe, and other industrialized and technologically advanced countries probably is very different from other parts of the world.

Where Death Occurs

Just as the causes of death have shifted over the last 100 years, the same is true of the places where death occurs, at least in the United States (Field, 2009; Stillion, 2006). Although death used to take place in the home with the person surrounded by loved ones, according to the National Vital Statistics System (n.d.; Table GMWK309), in 2005 over 75% of deaths occurred in institutions where people were likely to be surrounded by health care workers. More specifically, about 45% of people died in hospitals and about 22% died in a nursing home; almost 25% died at home. According to the National Hospice and Palliative Care Organization (NHPCO, 2012), in 2010, nearly 42% of people who died were receiving hospice care, which may take place in a variety of settings including a personal home or an institution (hospice will be discussed more fully below).

How and When People Actually Die

Given the information above—that people who die are primarily older adults who have chronic conditions and are in institutions—it should not be surprising that the dying process and ways in which people die today reflect these changes. Instead of fading away at home as the body shuts down (i.e., "naturally"), the majority of people who die in the United States in modern times do so after a decision has been made to stop or not start treatment (Faber-Langendoen & Lanken, 2000). Thus, although technically people may die of an underlying condition, such as kidney failure, they actually typically die when treatment (e.g., dialysis) is withheld or withdrawn, so the timing and manner of their death is orchestrated or negotiated in some way by a combination of the dying person, loved ones, the health care team, and sometimes the courts. As with the other areas mentioned above, there are differences based on demographics; some of the possible reasons for these differences will be discussed in the next two sections.

Obstacles to Health Care

The issue of health care disparities has received significant attention in the last decade (e.g., Gamble & Stone, 2006; Satcher & Pamies, 2006). Given the history of exclusion of non-Caucasians from hospitals as well as the unethical medical experimentation on racial/ethnic minority individuals in the United States, it is not surprising that there are sociocultural barriers to equal access and care that continue today (Shavers & Shavers,

2006). There are also differences in health-related quality of life based on demographic factors (Lubetkin, Jia, Franks, & Gold, 2005), including treatment based on age (e.g., Schrag et al., 2001) and sex (Wizemann & Pardue, 2001). One of the major obstacles to health care is mistrust of the medical system, based on historical issues such as the Tuskegee syphilis study (Werth, Blevins, Toussaint, & Durham, 2002).

Pain management provides an example of how discrimination has continued into the present, can create obstacles to appropriate care, and therefore can have implications on decision making. A number of studies conducted in various settings and geographic locations have demonstrated that there are significant differences in the provision of pain medication across a variety of settings and for all types of pain (for a review see, Green, Anderson, et al., 2003). For example, a study of patients who presented with musculoskeletal pain demonstrated that race (black vs. Caucasian) and age (older vs. younger) were two factors leading to fewer prescriptions of opioids and pain medication in the emergency room and upon discharge (Heins et al., 2006); similarly, in another study, blacks were less likely to receive opioids than Caucasians (Chen et al., 2005).

This lack of appropriate pain management has extended to chronic and terminal illness situations. Research has demonstrated that in such situations members of ethnic minority groups with cancer-related pain are less likely to receive the recommended amount of pain medication (and may even receive no medication) than European Americans (Werth et al., 2002). A related issue is that even if they receive prescriptions for the proper amount of pain medication, members of ethnic minority groups may not be able to get these prescriptions filled in pharmacies in their own neighborhoods because of insufficient supplies (Green, Ndao-Brumblay, West, & Washington, 2005; Morrison, Wallenstein, Natale, Senzel, & Huang, 2000). These problems with proper access and treatment have been linked to some of the decision-making differences near the end of life attributed to ethnicity.

Diversity Issues in End-of-Life Decision-Making

The literature on the apparent impact of cultural diversity on end-of-life decisions is fairly large and growing. Thus I cannot cover all aspects of diversity and must rely on gross generalizations in the areas I do discuss (Blevins & Papadatou, 2006). I highlight some results related to age, ethnicity, and gender.

The impact of age on end-of-life decision making is difficult to identify because of confounding variables such as cohort effects (Blevins & Papadatou, 2006) and religiosity. This difficulty may explain the inconsistency in the literature regarding the beliefs of older adults about end-of-life decisions such as withholding or withdrawing treatment and having advance directives (i.e., living wills or durable powers of attorney; Werth et al., 2002).

On the other hand, research on the attitudes and actions of various ethnic groups has been fairly consistent (Werth et al., 2002). Given that they may be less likely to receive proper and timely care in the first place, it should not be surprising that members of ethnic minority groups appear to be less likely to make decisions that appear to limit care or potentially hasten death, such as requesting treatment be withheld or withdrawn (either in person, in a living will, or through a proxy). In addition, longevity may be perceived as an intrinsic good, either for the person himself or herself or in order to extend the length of relationships (Mutran, Danis, Bratton, Sudha, & Hanson, 1997; Werth et al., 2002). European Americans are more likely to have positive attitudes toward advance directives, assisted suicide, and euthanasia; to actually complete advance directives; and to request and receive assistance in dying, whether legally in Oregon or in unregulated fashion (Werth et al., 2002).

The literature on gender differences in end-of-life decision making seems to show some possible differences in a few studies on particular types of decisions, but overall the differences appear to cancel each other out (Werth et al., 2002). Yet, Kastenbaum (1995) noted that illness, debility, and death may have a different meaning for men and women, given cultural gender role expectations for women as caregivers of others and for men to be providers for their families. In addition, some research has shown that women are more concerned about having a "dignified death" than men (Bookwala et al., 2001).

Treatment Options

When diagnosed with a life-threatening condition, there are often many possible treatments, depending on the situation (Leming & Dickinson, 2007; Stillion, 2006). Some options may be physical or biological, such as medication, surgery, transplantation, chemotherapy, radiation, and/or complementary therapies; other possibilities include behavioral changes, psychosocial interventions, or spiritual activities. Different groups (e.g., immigrants) may be more or less likely to select a given treatment option based on cultural values, including religious beliefs (Juckett, 2005). For example, some cultures ascribe to a belief that there must be a balance between hot and cold and that imbalances cause disease, so if a person has a hot condition (e.g., a rash) and the physician prescribes a hot treatment (e.g., vitamins), an Asian or Latino person may disregard the advice and may have less confidence in the medical doctor (Juckett, 2005). Some cultures have their own diagnoses and treatments as well (Juckett, 2005). Further, in some groups, depending on the family relationships involved, the patient may not be the treatment decision maker and in fact the family may not want the person told of her or his condition, especially if death may be involved (Werth et al., 2002).

Although many of the treatments for conditions that may lead to death are medical, the National Institutes of Health (NIH, 1997; NIH Technology Assessment Conference Statement, 1995) has acknowledged that psychological interventions are efficacious for some conditions and may be especially beneficial when used in concert with medical treatments. Psychosocial interventions can be useful in dealing with the emotional reactions to the various medical treatments and the side effects of such approaches.

Kleespies (2004) stated that "conventional care" is focused on acute care and cure, especially in hospitals where advanced technology can be used, which works well for many people but not for those who are dying. Thus, another treatment option is palliative care, the goal of which is to alleviate or prevent symptoms and suffering that cause distress without striving for cure (Kleespies, 2004). Palliative care is often considered to be implemented when a person is dying, but actually can be offered in conjunction with other treatments (Stillion, 2006); however, it is true that hospice (see next section) is one particular type of palliative care that is reserved for people near the end of life.

Although some would not call them "treatment" options, withholding/withdrawing treatment, assisted suicide, and euthanasia are options for some people. These possibilities may get discussed in terms of quality vs. quantity of life, with different people having different goals (Rodriguez & Young, 2006). As noted earlier, most people in the United States die after a decision to withhold or withdraw treatment, but there is marked variation across countries (Sprung et al., 2003). Similarly, laws permitting physician-assisted suicide under certain circumstances exist in Oregon and Washington but no other state has passed a law allowing it and euthanasia remains illegal in all states (Kleespies, 2004). The Montana State Supreme Court has stated there are no legal precedents or Montana statutes prohibiting physician-assisted suicide, but the Montana legislature has passed no law regarding physician-assisted suicide (Knickerbocker, 2010). Only a few other countries (e.g., The Netherlands, Belgium, Switzerland) have legalized assisted suicide and/or voluntary active euthanasia while others (e.g., Australia, England) have explicitly rejected efforts to allow either action (see Finlay, Wheatley, & Izdebski, 2005; Materstvedt et al., 2003; and accompanying commentaries).

Holistic Approaches

One treatment option that offers a holistic approach is hospice. Widely considered to offer the gold standard in care near the end of life (Casarett, 2006; Connor, Lycan, & Schumacher, 2006), the modern hospice began in England in 1967 when Cicely Saunders started St. Christopher's (Stillion, 2006). The first modern hospice in the United States was established in New Haven, CT, in the early 1970s (Connor et al., 2006) and placed emphasis on home care as opposed to inpatient services. In 1982, the U.S. Congress added coverage for hospice through Medicare (Stillion, 2006). Today there are over 5,000 hospices in the United States, which served almost 1.6 million people in 2010—over 77% of whom were European American, over 35% had cancer, 56% were women, and nearly 83% were 65-plus years old (NHPCO, 2012).

Hospices utilize a multidisciplinary team of nurses, aides, social workers, chaplains, and volunteers, under the direction of a physician, to provide biopsychosociospiritual care of the dying person and her or his family, often in the person's home (Connor et al., 2006; Kleespies, 2004; Leming & Dickinson, 2007). Hospice personnel excel at treating and alleviating pain and suffering. Once a person has been given a prognosis of six months or less to live, she or he becomes eligible for hospice, although the median length of stay in hospice is only 21 days, with about 35% of people dying within a week of admission (NHPCO, 2012). One potential reason for this short stay is that in order to access hospice care, the person must agree to forgo any more attempts at curative treatment; thus some people (including physicians, patients, and caregivers) can interpret this decision as giving up and therefore resist enrolling in hospice (Casarett, 2006). This phenomenon demonstrates that the way hospice is explained to dying individuals and their loved ones can have a significant effect on the decisions of whether and when to enroll in hospice.

Death Anxiety

The general concept of death anxiety has been the focus of significant empirical attention. However, exploration of the impact of death anxiety on end-of-life decision making is, almost necessarily, a theoretical enterprise. There has been some research on gender and age differences (Kastenbaum, 1995; Leming & Dickinson, 2007) but to truly examine how death anxiety influences decision making, one would need to conduct research involving death anxiety measures with people who are dying or in conjunction with some measures of end-of-life decision making, such as attitudes about or completion of advance directives. A search of the literature did not find any work specifically on this topic.

Landmark Legal Cases

Earlier, the topic of withholding and withdrawing treatment was mentioned. The fact that people in the United States can choose to not start or to stop life-sustaining treatment for themselves or loved ones is the result of a series of legal cases that involved state and federal courts up to and including the U.S. Supreme Court. Three cases that deserve special mention are *In re Quinlan* (1976), *Cruzan v. Director, Missouri Department of Health* (1990), and *Schiavo ex rel. Schindler v. Schiavo* (2005a, 2005b), hereinafter referred to as *Quinlan*, *Cruzan*, and *Schiavo*, respectively (Cerminara, 2009).

In *Quinlan*, a young woman was in a persistent vegetative state and her father wanted to discontinue the use of a ventilator. The woman's physicians along with the hospital and county and state legal officials objected. The New Jersey Supreme Court ruled that there was a constitutional right to privacy under the 14th Amendment along with the New Jersey constitution. They took into account the technological developments that allowed life to be prolonged. Importantly, the *Quinlan* case demonstrated that surrogates could make decisions for people who were unable to express themselves.

Cruzan also involved a young woman in a persistent vegetative state, but she could breathe on her own and was kept alive through the provision of artificial food and fluids, which her parents wanted to stop in order to allow her to die. The issue here was the degree of evidence required to allow the withdrawal of life-sustaining treatment when someone had not named anyone as a proxy in the event of being unable to speak for herself or himself. The U.S. Supreme Court ruled that there is a right to refuse life-sustaining treatment and that a state could set a high standard to demonstrate that a person would want treatment withheld or withdrawn but was not required to do so.

More recently, a protracted battle ensued between the judicial branch and the executive and legislative branches in the case of Theresa Marie Schiavo, who also happened to be in a persistent vegetative state and was receiving artificial nutrition and hydration. Her husband believed she would have wanted the treatment stopped and asked a judge to decide (for more discussion of this case see the entire issue of *Death Studies*, Volume 30, Issue 2: "The implications of the Theresa Schiavo case for end-of-life care and decisions"). The courts ruled that the treatment should be stopped, but the Florida legislature and governor, U.S. Congress, and President George W. Bush tried to intervene. However, the courts' rulings held, and Schiavo died after the tubes were removed.

Conclusion

There have been many developments in the last century that have affected end-of-life decision making. I have mentioned a few, including technological advances and other changes in when, where, and how people die; obstacles to health care and related cultural diversity issues; traditional and holistic treatment options; and court cases that have helped define options for end-of-life decisions.

Chapter 10

Life Span Issues and End-of-Life Decision Making

Andrea C. Walker

Consider the experience of a teenager with acute lymphoma that is unresponsive to any treatment, with a prognosis of death in the next 2 weeks, being approached by her staff nurse about where she would like to spend the rest of her days. On the other hand, imagine a healthy widower of 94 years with several children and numerous grandchildren and great-grandchildren, approached by his physician about end-of-life choices should an accident or unexpected illness occur, robbing him of his capacity to make decisions at that time. Finally, ponder the 40-year-old female diagnosed with Level 3 breast cancer, recommended treatment of biweekly chemotherapy, whose prognosis is unknown. The experiences of these individuals vary dramatically, as likely will their responses to end-of-life choices. A large part of the difference in responses relates to each individual's developmental place in the span of life.

Life span development is multidimensional, with cognitive, social, emotional, spiritual, physical, and behavioral elements; multidirectional, with increasing and decreasing capacities; based on context; subject to environmental and cultural changes; and ranging across the entire life, from infancy to the oldest old in scope. Erikson (1997) provided a noteworthy contribution to the life span perspective by explaining development in terms of psychosocial stages into late adulthood, with each new stage presenting an opportunity to reach higher development if "tasks" are resolved properly. The stage in which an individual is in his or her life largely influences how challenges are perceived and approached. The purpose of this chapter is to look at how life span issues affect the end-of-life decisions we make. We will begin with a literature review of end-of-life decisions at different life stages, move to a discussion about vulnerable populations, and conclude with implications for caregivers.

End-of-Life Decisions Across the Life Span

Because end-of-life choices are usually made by those anticipating death, research typically involves older adults and terminally ill patients. Death occurs at all ages, however, and certain tasks may characterize the experiences at different developmental stages. Corr's (1991) task-based approach to coping with dying provides us with a conceptual framework for considering end-of-life issues that arise throughout the life span. The model identifies (a) physical, (b) psychological, (c) social, and (d) spiritual dimensions of coping, and Corr proposed that each of the tasks inherent in the four dimensions are undertaken within the larger context of development and must be resolved for effective coping to occur. Thus, physical, psychological, social, and spiritual tasks may be embedded within the dying person's experience in varying degrees and with diverse implications across the life span.

Infancy and Young Childhood

The death of an infant or child is considered by most of society to be a nonnormative event and looked upon as a tragedy. Health care thus tends to take on the role of fixing the problem, doing whatever possible to prevent the tragedy from occurring. Mothers reported wanting everything done for their extremely premature infants (Moro, Kavanaugh, Savage, Reyes, Kimura, & Bhat, 2011). In such cases, it is necessary to weigh the consequences of decisions to reach the best possible outcome for the child and parents, who often need assurance that all treatments outside of futility have been tried. With terminally ill children in palliative care, however, the younger the child the more likely treatment will be withdrawn (Tan, Totapally, Torbati, & Wolfsdorf, 2006). Infants who are deemed to have no chance of survival or extremely poor quality of future life in Belgium and Netherlands may be deliberately given medication with the intention of ending life (Wyatt, 2007). As surviving infants and young children seek to develop trust, autonomy, initiative, and industry (Erikson, 1997), dealing with a traumatic illness, the treatment of which sometimes confines the child's activities and interactions, may leave them with unresolved tasks later in life. Should a life-threatening illness or death occur at this stage, much of the decision-making responsibility falls to the parent or guardian.

For children, both healthy and those facing death, more mature death understanding relates to lower death fear (Slaughter & Griffiths, 2007). Discussions about treatment and death, conducted according to the child's developmental level, thus provide more reassurance to the child than silence, and whenever possible the child's wishes about his or her treatment should be fulfilled (McConnell, Frager, & Levetown, 2004). Some argue that children should be given more autonomy to make decisions regarding donation of their own organs (Brierley & Larcher, 2011). In a child facing death, physical and psychological comforts are highly important (Sourkes, 1996), and a feeling of influence on a child's surroundings may provide that comfort to some degree.

As the perceived role of many parents is to protect their children, end-of-life decisions can be exceptionally stressful for them. Berg et al. (2007) describes two mothers' experiences with critically ill young children, one a highly educated mother who lost a premature daughter after intensive struggle for life, the other a working mother who lost a toddler daughter to brain tumor. Both shared their experiences and needs for more engaged, sensitive health care staff. Parents ultimately face serious decisions regarding do not resuscitate orders, artificial feeding, and terminal sedation to relieve symptoms, so information about the prognosis, treatment options, and the child's reaction to treatments must be communicated clearly. Prognosis and treatment, as well as demographic characteristics, have been found to influence end-of-life decisions for young children, highlighting the need for open communication (Tan et al., 2006) and continued discussion between health care, parents, and, as much as possible, to the child.

Adolescence

Adolescence is characterized by pubertal and physical changes, increased emphasis on relationships with peers, increased need for autonomy and self-definition, and the beginning of separation from family (Erikson, 1997). The prefrontal cortex, part of the brain responsible for complex decision making, is still developing and will not be fully mature until the mid-20s. Facing a terminal illness at such a critical life stage, during which the search for independence and identity heightens, the desire for autonomy grows, but the full capacity for complex decision making has not been reached, can be especially challenging. Adolescents may have cognitive ability to think abstractly but regress to earlier concrete thinking and behavior when faced with crisis (Stevens & Dunsmore, 1996). This regression can result in family role alteration during illness, as was the case with a female adolescent dying of cancer (Penson et al., 2002); decision making began with the adolescent and, as her health regressed, transferred to the parent. Still, the health care system recognizes adolescents as having the capacity to participate in treatment choices (Children's Rights Task Force of the Midwest Bioethics Center, 1995) and generally encourages adolescents to participate. Indeed, adolescent cancer survivors reported valuing autonomous decision making, without excluding their parents from the process (Pousset et al., 2009).

Studies have confirmed adolescents' willingness and ability to participate in end-of-life decisions and have compared their choices with those of individuals much later in the life span. Both ill and healthy adolescents have been found to want to participate in decision making (Lyon & Lyon, 2009; Lyon, McCabe, Patel, & D'Angelo, 2004; Pousset et al., 2009). Participants in McAliley, Hudson-Barr, Gunning, and Rowbottom's (2000) study of mostly healthy adolescents were found to be competent enough to understand advance directives, comfortable discussing them, and believe in their importance, though they chose medical and surgical interventions over choices to end life at a higher rate than have adults in past studies. When compared with healthy adolescents, however, adolescent cancer survivors were found to be more accepting toward end-of-life decisions that had a life-shortening effect (Pousset et al., 2009). Collectively, these data suggest that the more experience persons have with death-related issues, the more accepting they are of life-shortening choices. Health care should thus center around the family (Lyon et al., 2009), incorporating the specific health situation, as well as the needs and experiences of the entire family, particularly those of the adolescent patient.

Young and Middle Adulthood

Young and middle adulthood is characterized by establishment of intimate relationships, family growth, and development of generativity (Erikson, 1997). Decisions of whether or not to terminate life-sustaining treatments in young and middle adults may be influenced by hope of recovery through treatment or medical discovery. Young adult college students, as well as some older adults, see withdrawal from treatment in similar terms as suicide and see those patients as less competent (Wellman & Sugarman, 1999). On the other hand, the greater the condition interferes with valued life activities, the more likely it is to lead to a choice to end life (Ditto, Druley, Moore, & Danks, 1996). Having a negative attitude toward death predicted higher likelihood to prolong life in college students. When the prognosis of death is certain, whether a person has dependents and arranged provisional care of those dependents can influence decisions. Moreover, religiosity and spirituality, particularly in middle-aged cardiac arrest patients (Ai, Park, & Shearer, 2009), as well as type of life-sustaining treatment (Mills & Wilmoth, 2002) are important factors in end-of-life decisions. In this complicated stage of life, as the chance of their own terminal illness increases, young and middle-aged adults are also more often faced with the possibility of end-of-life decisions of a terminally ill child or of their elderly or terminally ill parents. End-of-life decision making can touch individuals in this age range with more complexity than in others.

Older Adulthood

The majority of research on advance care planning focuses on elderly adults, who are often nearing retirement and needing to reassess priorities, values and hobbies, to ensure a sense of integrity over their lives (Erikson, 1997). A strong need at this stage involves maintaining social relationships (Ditto et al., 1996). In his book *The Virtues of Aging*, Jimmy Carter (1998) shared his experiences leaving the White House and makes recommendations for life after retirement. Carter discusses a need for information and end-of-life planning, emphasizing the importance of retaining one's lifelong character and personal dignity during dying. Lester (1996) also suggested that end-of-life choices relate to five concepts of an appropriate death, including (a) having a role in one's death, (b) maintaining integrity of the body, (c) consistency with lifestyle, (d) appropriate timing, and (e) different types of death (social, cognitive, biological, etc.) occurring simultaneously. These needs seem to be common for most older adults.

Who Makes Decisions?

In a large sample of 4,500 older adults, who were healthy, Caucasian, Midwestern high school graduates, 80% preferred independent decision making, and this preference was associated with being less avoidant of thoughts of death and valuing quality over length of life (Moorman, 2011). Surprisingly, health status may not be related to whether or not a person makes preparations, but discussions initiated by physicians are influential (Kahana, Dan, Kahana, & Kercher, 2004). In a study of 700 elderly New Yorkers, predictors of completing advance care planning were (a) having established primary care physicians,

(b) personal experience with mechanical ventilation, (c) knowledge about the process of advance care planning, and (d) physicians' willingness to initiate discussions (Morrison & Meier, 2004). Moreover, those who complete advance directives are more likely to receive care at the end of their lives that is consistent with their preferences (Silveira, Kim, & Langa, 2010).

What Choices Are Made?

Researchers are somewhat divided in what predicts end-of-life decision making and/ or advance planning, with social, religious, demographic, and psychological factors being considered. Older adults have been found to not necessarily want aggressive treatment interventions at the end of life but prefer those that will minimize their discomfort (Nahm & Resnick, 2001) and improve life quality (Moorman, 2011), consistent with Ditto et al.'s (1996) finding that belief in one's ability to perform valued life activities predicts older adults' choices to prolong life. Elders with greater religiosity are more likely to extend their lives regardless of their condition, and those with lower religiosity and higher value of quality of life are more likely to hasten death (Cicirelli, MacLean, & Cox, 2000). Older adults consider perceived mental capacity, family burden, and pain to be the most important factors in end-of-life decisions (Mills & Wilmoth, 2002). Cicirelli (1997) suggested that choices may also result from psychosocial and demographic factors. In his study, those who preferred maintaining life regardless of conditions tended to be African-American, of lower socio-economic status (less education and lower occupational status), and with greater subjective religiosity; they placed less value on the quality of life, had less fear of the dying process, and more fear of destruction of the body. Inversely, those who favored ending their lives tended to be Caucasian, of higher socio-economic status, and with lower subjective religiosity; they placed higher value on the quality of life and had more fear of the dying process. A surprising result of the study was that the majority of participants chose to continue living even with lower quality of life, which may indicate a survival instinct and/or socialized inhibitions against self-destruction.

Marital status, age, lack of psychological well-being, and gender have been found to have no influence on end-of-life decisions (Cicirelli, 1997). This conclusion was later challenged by Bookwala et al. (2001) who found that men prefer life-sustaining treatments more than women, and Kahana et al. (2004), who found that unmarried and younger individuals were more likely to have made end-of-life plans. Due to the heterogeneity of views, end-of-life decisions of older adults may not be predictable, and providers need to ask specific questions to consider each person's preferences individually (Vig, Davenport, & Pearlman, 2002).

The Role of Dementia

Older adults are living longer, the population of older adults is growing, and the need for competence of psychologists in areas of dementia and family caregiving is thus increasing (Karel, Gatz, & Smyer, 2012). The existence or potential for dementia in an older adult with a progressive disease such as Alzheimer's underscores the importance of advance planning. Research has indicated that upon admittance to nursing homes, most patients are beyond the cognitive capacity to complete health care proxies, and many families are too emotionally distraught (Lacey, 2006). Families thus face difficult decisions in ensuring quality of life while determining what the relative with dementia wants based on past conversations, highlighting the need for ongoing communication among the patient, family, and health care providers (Hennings, Froggatt, & Keady, 2010). Further, though health care staff and family members of the patient are usually motivated by what is best for the patient, their opinions on end-of-life choices can diverge due to differences in religion and perspective (Rurup et al., 2006). The number of studies measuring dementia and end-of-life decisions has multiplied in recent years; the following overview merely scratches the surface, and further exploration of literature is encouraged.

Irwin (2006) expressed skepticism regarding life-prolonging treatments, particularly tube feeding, based on the bioethical principles. Empirical evidence generally supports Irwin's perspective, indicating that predictors of satisfaction of end-of-life care for nursing home residents with advanced dementia include elimination of tube feeding, as well as specialized treatment for dementia, focus on patient comfort, and improved communication (Engel, Keily, & Mitchell, 2006). After watching a video on care for those with dementia, the majority of older adults preferred comfort care over life-prolonging care (Volandes et al., 2011). Family caregivers reported most often that the wish of their relative, before becoming debilitated with dementia, was to not be kept alive by "extraordinary measures" (Black et al., 2009). On the other hand, some suggest that the use of tube feeding does promote comfort and reduce distress at the end of life, arguing that literature does not provide undisputed data for or against the use of tube feeding (McCarron & McCallion, 2007). Much of the uncertainty, however, associated with end-of-life decisions of an older adult with dementia can be alleviated with completion of advance directives.

Vulnerable Populations

Persons with Disabilities

End-of-life care for individuals with disabilities can take on a particularly complex situation. Disabilities may involve (a) individuals who were born with or developed a disability very early in life, (b) individuals who acquired a disability suddenly due to illness or trauma, and (c) individuals who have suffered from a progressive, chronic disease (Robinson, Phipps, Purtilo, Tsoumas, & Hamel-Nardozzi, 2006). Forbat and Service (2005) applied several case studies of end-of-life decision making to a hierarchy model utilized within the Coordinated Management of Meaning (CMM) approach (Cronen, Pearce, & Changsheng), emphasizing the contextual interaction of history, religion, culture, legal implications, financial status, and proposed patient's perspective to decisions such as tube feeding, do not resuscitate orders, and type or duration of home care.

The highly publicized case of Terri Schiavo (involving a long battle between family, delaying decision about her life and ongoing treatment for 7 years) brought to light the importance of developing policies to help families make good end-of-life decisions for their loved ones who cannot speak for themselves (Ditto, 2009) in the face of highly complex medical situations. Some argue that Terri faced "disability discrimination" as the assumption was made that she wanted to die (Johnson, 2006). Individuals with disabilities are especially vulnerable in end-of-life care, and health care providers must practice self-reflexivity when giving medical advice; their status as highly functional clinicians may bias their perspectives regarding quality of life (Robinson et al., 2006).

Most agree that a sensitive, person-centered approach should be used to help developmentally disabled individuals communicate their end-of-life wishes. Whether these persons should be able to choose assisted death, however, has been a highly controversial topic. Mayo and Gunderson (2002) present a impassioned refute of the suggestion to eliminate the option of physician-assisted suicide for disabled persons, arguing that trying to prevent this option actually represents a return to medical vitalism and a shift away from the value of patient self-determination that currently dominates the medical system. Indeed, rates of physician-assisted dying have shown no evidence of heightened risk for disabled individuals (Battin, van der Heide, Ganzini, van der Wal, & Onwuteaka-Philipsen, 2007). Others discuss a difference between "formerly competent" and "never competent individuals;" they argue that those who have never had full autonomy are not able to suddenly be autonomous, and the surrogate should make the most compassionate decision to preserve the life and dignity of the disabled individual (Cantor, 2005). Research continues to emphasize participation of disabled patients in decisions, however. For instance, adults with Down syndrome have been found to need increased involvement in end-of-life treatment (Watchman, 2005). One parent of a Prader-Willi[1] child indicated that though her child's disease is complex and will require assistance in end-of-life care decisions, she believes the best thing for her child is to remain as autonomous as possible (Hannefield, 2006, personal communications).

Persons With Serious Mental Illness

Persons with serious mental illness have been found to be able to designate treatment preferences, with most participants choosing aggressive treatments against pain and most disagreeing with physician-assisted suicide (Foti, Bartels, Van Citters, Merriman, & Fletcher, 2005). Empirical evidence provides no support for the notion that those with psychiatric illnesses are at higher risk in terms of physician-assisted dying (Battin et al., 2007). As physician-assisted suicide in the United States is currently legal only in Oregon and Washington, the debate is still significant for persons with mental illnesses, so the question regarding individuals with these issues is far from resolved.

---

1 Prader-Willi is "a complex genetic disorder that includes short stature, mental retardation or learning disabilities, incomplete sexual development, characteristic behavior problems, low muscle tone, and an involuntary urge to eat constantly, which, coupled with a reduced need for calories, leads to obesity" (retrieved January 29, 2007, from http://www.thearc.org/faqs/pwsynd.html).

Persons With HIV/AIDS

Although HIV/AIDS affects all age groups, its occurrence in young and middle adults is more frequent. The prognosis can be ambiguous at best, complicating questions regarding end-of-life treatment. Unfortunately, empirical evidence evaluating the proportion of physician-assisted death in people with AIDS suggested that this population is the only one to be at heightened risk (Battin, 2007). Suggestions in literature regarding the importance of communication with health care about end-of-life planning are particularly poignant with people with HIV/AIDS. Women with HIV and HIV patients with children in the household were found to be the most likely to communicate with practitioners about end-of-life issues, and African-Americans, Latinos, intravenous drug users, and less educated individuals were least likely to have had these discussions with physicians (Wenger et al., 2001). For adolescents with HIV, family-centered advanced care planning resulted in less decisional conflict, better communication, and more congruence in adolescent/surrogate preferences for end-of-life care (Lyon et al., 2009). The prognosis of HIV-infected individuals has improved with medical advances, likely influencing the choice for life-sustaining treatments in this population.

Conclusions and Implications for Practitioners

Literature repetitively acknowledges a need for improvement in physical and mental health care practices regarding end-of-life issues. The results of several of the studies referenced in this chapter have validated the importance of communication and the interactive processes among the terminally ill person, the family, and the health care practitioner in advance care planning. Vulnerable populations are at particular risk and must be considered individually, while maximizing the person's dignity and sense of autonomy. Further, implications for care may vary slightly at each general stage across the life span, depending largely on the person's ability to make informed decisions.

For infants and young children, more mature understandings of death led to less fear (Slaughter & Griffiths, 2007). Ongoing communication among child, parents, and health care provider, therefore, is paramount (Tan et al., 2006) so that the needs of everyone in the family system are considered. Awareness of culture and family processes is important, and McConnell et al.'s (2004) cycle of pediatric palliative care decision making includes (a) assessing communication styles, culture, and beliefs; (b) assessing knowledge and perspectives; (c) assessing decision-making capacity; (d) choosing the people and place for discussion; (e) opening discussions and framing decisions; (f) evaluating options and making informed choices; (g) preventing conflict and ensuring continuity; and (h) ongoing reassessment to ensure cultural and familial sensitivity. McConnell recommends following each step in this cycle when working with seriously ill children.

Terminally ill adolescents should be allowed to express their individuality as much as possible, particularly by ensuring their privacy, allowing them to create their own space, and encouraging them to participate in their own end-of-life decisions to the degree with which they are comfortable (McConnell et al., 2004). Adolescents and their families benefit from working with a multidisciplinary health care team. Parents report that stress associated with making end-of-life decisions for their children can be alleviated if they know everything has been tried and there are no other options (Penson et al., 2002). Adolescents have been found to be willing, capable, and interested in discussing end-of-life issues (Lyon & Lyon, 2009; Lyon, McCabe, Patel, & D'Angelo, 2004; McAliley et al., 2000; Pousset et al., 2009)).

Since adults tend to base their end-of-life decisions on quality of life with a given treatment, discussions about advance directives in terms of desired outcomes and valued behavioral functions might be a meaningful approach (Ditto et al., 1996). Caregivers must be self-aware and focused on not allowing their own needs to interfere with the medical system's ethical values of autonomy, beneficience, nonmaleficience, and justice for the patient. Six critical care nurses, who suffered from extreme physical, emotional, and psychological stress from their jobs, were interviewed regarding their role in the end-of-life decision making of their patients (Jezuit, 2000). These nurses routinely experienced conflict between meeting the patients' needs and their own moral beliefs. The nurses upheld ethical principles, as well as trustworthiness and compassion, and consistency in practice through embodiment of a deontological view of ethics, that is, a view stressing moral obligations and duties. Jezuit discussed a Theory of Duty, in which caregivers should act from the obligation of duty, which gives the action inherent moral worth. Using contributions from Kantian philosophy, Jezuit indicated that patients should be treated as "ends in and of themselves and not just as means to an end" (p. 49) and that any decision regarding patient treatment has morality if it can be generalized to other patients in similar situations.

Chapter 11

The Family, Larger Systems, and End-of-Life Decision Making

Blair Sumner Mynatt and Robyn L. Mowery

Introduction

Historically, families were primarily shaped by the experience of death of family members. In the United States, as the advent of end-of-life care increased life expectancy, the beneficent and often paternalistic voice of medicine began to progressively drown out the voices of patients and families whose values suggested that there may be fates worse than death (Field & Cassel, 1997). Over the course of the last few decades, recognition of the interdependence and mutual influence between the patient and the family as a whole progressively disappeared in institutionalized medicine (Nelson & Nelson, 1995). This holistic perspective of the family's role at the end of life has been replaced, to a large extent, with an instrumental view of the family's sole purpose as service to the individual, rather than also bearing in mind the ways in which individuals within a family collectively contribute to the entire family system. The institution of the family has lost its decision-making voice within the institution of medicine (a term used interchangeably with *the health care system*), and is now seen primarily as a substitute voice for a dying individual when the patient is unable to speak for him or herself (Nelson & Nelson, 1995; Winzelberg, Hanson, & Tulsky, 2005).

Relations between the institutions of the family and medicine have been significantly shaped by the institution of law. In an attempt to have the values of family life heard, families turned to the legal system for support. Principally through the process of litigation of several landmark cases (e.g., Quinlan, Bouvia, Kevorkian, & Cruzan) as well as the enactment by Congress in 1990 of the Patient Self-Determination Act (PSDA), there emerged a legal consensus that amplified the voice of individual patients (Meisel, 2005; Werth & Blevins, 2002). The courts declared that end-of-life care decisions should be guided (either directly or through proxy methods) by the dying individual's wishes, and the PSDA required health facilities to inform patients of their right to refuse medical treatment and formulate advance directives (Meisel, 2005). The legal system based its conclusions on an individual's right to privacy and self-determination (i.e., autonomy) without formally recognizing the moral or practical significance of other voices in the decision-making process (Nelson & Nelson, 1995; Winzelberg, Hanson, & Tulsky, 2005). In this way, the legal system effectively reified the medical system's modern tendency to focus on the individual patient without fully recognizing the significance of interrelated and interdependent family relationships.

This individualistic approach to end-of-life decision making, in which families are predominantly reduced to being extensions of the patient's voice at the end of life, has very recently begun to be challenged. Leading biomedical ethics scholars at the Hastings Center suggest that existing consensus thinking on end-of-life care is founded on several profound misconceptions and oversimplifications. Murray and Jennings (2005) assert that the current approach has been excessively rationalistic and individualistic. Hastings Center scholars further claim that problems with end-of-life decision making have been misdiagnosed as flawed practice at the individual patient and physician level when the shortcomings of end-of-life care may be more structural and institutional in nature (Lynn, 2000, 2005; Murray & Jennings, 2005). From this perspective, the excluded voice of the family system may have much more to do with differences between institutional cultures (Turner, 2005) and the contextual features that shape their practices than any intentional devaluing of family life. In short, the values and goals of one institution may make it deaf to the values and goals of another (Nelson & Nelson, 1995).

Using the practice of institutional analysis, Palmer (2000) suggested looking across institutions and asking which institutional processes are most likely to help (or hinder) society's optimal response to end-of-life care. The remainder of the chapter will employ the language of systems theory to explore the interrelated voices of medicine and law in the United States and the practical implications for how institutional factors may unwittingly constrain both the voice of the family and the patient in end-of-life decision making. As detailed reviews of the legal, religious, and spiritual aspects of end-of-life decision-making occur in separate chapters, the emphasis here will be limited to the broader notion of the institution of law and its relationship to the institution of medicine (not to be confused with the National Institutes of Health's Institute of Medicine), while religion and spirituality, through certainly relevant, will not be highlighted.

Systemic Factors Influencing End-of-Life Decision Making

Systems theory posits that the whole is greater than the sum of its parts and, like a mobile in constant motion, each part simultaneously influences and is influenced by other parts (Bowen, 1985). Families are fundamentally more than simply a group of separate individuals, the institution of medicine is more than a compilation of discrete health care professionals or facilities, and the institution of law is more than a collection of attorneys and judges, independent court cases, or acts of legislation. Systems of people (including social institutions) develop idiosyncratic goals, beliefs, values, and ways of expressing themselves. They are governed by implicit and explicit roles, rules and procedures, and have boundaries which may be open or closed, rigid or flexible. Health care providers, family members, and attorneys are all socialized into the larger culture of their respective institutions as well as the particular version of their immediate contexts (e.g., hospital or nursing home, nuclear or extended family, county or state legal system) (Turner, 2005). While all three institutions have overlapping aims, each deploys different mechanisms for achieving its mission, which may not function efficiently across institutional systems.

Institution of Medicine

Broadly considered, the primary end of medicine is the provision of health care, traditionally conceived as the cure of acute illnesses and restoration of functioning (Preston & Kelly, 2006). Foundational to acute care is the idea that clear diagnosis leads to clear treatment protocols (Machado, 2005). As the threat to life increases, so does the reliance on medical specialists and advanced technology for diagnosis and treatment. Roles for health care professionals are often highly specific and organized according to type of disease and the degree and type of intervention needed (i.e.; primary, secondary, and tertiary care). All types of care occur in a specialized setting with its own implicit and explicit rules (e.g., limited visiting hours in intensive care units) and norms (e.g., the expectation that life must be preserved at all costs). Thus, decision making within an acute care context tends to be focused on discrete issues and fragmented solutions. However, this decision making strategy for dealing with acute illness has created problems of its own.

As Joanne Lynn (2006) observed, "[The] great success of modern medicine has been to transform acute causes of death into chronic illnesses" (p. S14). This transformation has occurred precisely because the mechanisms of modern medicine (e.g., advanced technologies and pharmaceuticals) have been so successful in achieving their purposes that living with and dying from chronic conditions have resulted in novel circumstances for which new mechanisms for making complex decisions have yet, or are only beginning, to appear. The role financial reimbursement mechanisms play in shaping end-of-life care within institution medicine cannot be underestimated.

For example, nearly half of all Americans 65 years of age or older will enter a nursing home before they die, and most of these residents will have incurable chronic illnesses (Zerzan, Stearns, & Hanson, 2000). Like acute care hospitals, however, policies governing nursing homes emphasize the goals of rehabilitation and the restoration of functioning (Johnson, 2005). Reimbursement mechanisms such as Medicare, Medicaid, and private insurance companies encourage the reliance on technological interventions to meet rehabilitation goals, thereby limiting options during decision making for terminal care (Morrison, 2005; Zerzan, Stearns, & Hanson, 2000). Furthermore, funding mechanisms do not reimburse health care providers for the time it takes to invest in nurturing relationships with patients even though research reinforces the importance of psychosocial support for health outcomes and quality of life (Morrison, 2005).

In addition to advanced physical care requirements, chronic terminal illness increases the need for caring relationships, which can facilitate and sustain the slow transformation of one's identity and interactions with others over the course of the illness and dying process. From the perspective of institutional analysis (Palmer, 2000), the institution of medicine as it is currently organized is not well-suited for developing these relationships. The institution of the family, however, has the development of individual and family identity and sustained intimate relationships as core to its mission.

Institution of the Family

The provision of health care in the context of the family is a secondary end, a derivative product of a shared identity forged by a moral commitment to the well-being of one another (Nelson & Nelson, 1995). This moral commitment is why death cannot be conceived of and dealt with solely in individual terms, and why dying patients frequently express more concerns about the suffering of their loved ones than their own physical status (Kogan, Blanchette, & Masaki, 2000; Murray & Jennings, 2005).

> [The] family as a whole dies along with one of its members—it will never be the same again. Every aspect of the family's life and functioning is undergoing change, a change imposed against its will. Inevitably, these changes create stress within the family. The way a family has functioned in the past profoundly influences the way it deals with the dying of one of its members (Davies, Reimer, Brown, & Martens, 1995, p. 89).

The role(s) the dying individual played in the family can affect the family decision-making process. For instance, if the patient played the role of peacekeeper or scapegoat within the family, his or her impending departure will likely destabilize relationships between other family members because there is no one now available to help manage or take the blame for conflict. Additionally, Davies et al. (1995) empirically delineated eight dimensions of family functioning, each representing a continuum of functionality, that affect the success or difficulty families face when confronted with the impending death of a loved one: Integrating the past, dealing with feelings, solving problems, utilizing resources, considering others, portraying family identity, fulfilling roles, and tolerating differences. The more strengths families exhibit in each of these dimensions, the smoother the decision making process will be, while the opposite is also generally true. For example, families with rigid or closed boundaries are often suspicious of others, tend to function in isolation, and have trouble collaborating with others during a time of need (Kristjanson & Aoun, 2004). Closed or rigid family systems may have difficulty adjusting to new information or ideas, thereby struggling during the decision making process (Csikai & Chaitin, 2006; see also chapter 19 in this handbook).

The dimension of "considering others" (Davies, et al., 1995) is especially relevant from the perspective of institutional analysis. Being part of a family means being morally required to make decisions on the basis of not simply what is best for oneself, but based on thinking about what is best for all concerned (Hardwig, 1990). Ivan Boszormenyi-Nagy, a founding theorist in family therapy, argues that "relational ethics" is critical to healthy family functioning, and that failure of each family member to give due consideration to the interests of other members is seen as the heart of family dysfunction (Boszormenyi-Nagy, 1987; Boszormenyi-Nagy, Gruebaum, & Ulricj, 1991). Boszormenyi-Nagy claims that family functioning is enhanced when members of the family can trust the family system as a whole, and that this trust will instigate the process of balancing consideration of the well-being of oneself with considerations of the well-being of others (Boszormenyi-Nagy, et al., 1991).

Indeed, clinical observation suggests that when healthy families are given permission to voice their own interests in the decision-making process (i.e., when health professionals give due consideration to the family as moral stakeholders), they have an easier time giving due consideration to the patient's needs and wishes; often yielding growth and development for all (see also Foster & McLellan, 2002). This observation is consistent with Panke and Ferrell (2005) who note that "opportunities for growth for both patient and family are tremendous even while they are coping with countless difficulties and sorrows as the patient's disease progresses" (p. 985).

However, relying on this model of shared decision making based on relational ethics within the family, stands in stark contrast to individually focused biomedical ethics and a legal consensus about end-of-life decision making that is founded on the principle of an individual's right to privacy and autonomy (See chapters 6 and 12 in this handbook). The conflict between these models over decision making occurs because the surrogate or proxy model of end-of-life decision making was initially forged in response to cases of extreme conflict between the institution of medicine and the institution of the family over the best interests of individual patients (Burt, 2005).

Institution of Law

While the institutional goal of medicine is protecting health and the institutional goal of the family is protecting development within a web of intimate relationships, the goal of the institution of law can be understood, at least in part, as protecting citizens' rights. Litigation and adjudication of narrowly defined questions and the legislation of broad socially sanctioned policies are the two primary mechanisms used by the institution of law to protect the rights of citizens.

The goals of the recently enacted Patient Protection and Affordable Care Act (PPACA) (2010) include reducing the number of uninsured Americans and overall costs of health care, improving healthcare outcomes, and simplifying the delivery of health care services. The original version of the PPACA included wording that would have reimbursed physicians for holding advanced care planning discussions with patients (Giovanni, 2012); however, due to misunderstandings regarding the nature of these advanced care planning discussions, this language was removed from the bill. The PPACA largely avoids most issues related to end-of-life care for terminally ill patients, thus neglecting this important issue (Giovanni, 2012).

The courts protected individual rights of patients against paternalistic medicine via landmark cases such as Quinlan, Bouvia, and Cruzan, which explicitly established the legal rights of patients to refuse medical treatments either directly or indirectly by designated health care surrogates. But just as medicine's solution to acute health crises created additional problems, the court's reliance on the language of individual right has created its own set of problems, especially for the family (Hardwig, 1990; Machado, 2005).

The legal consensus about end-of-life decision making assumes the existence of conflict whereby the rights of individuals to make their own decisions must be assiduously protected from either an overzealous health care system or coercive family members (Nelson & Nelson, 1995). Court cases such as Cruzan, Quinlan, and, most recently, Schiavo, highlight the need for such protection in extreme circumstances, but the media attention these cases received tended to obscure the fact that they represent exceptions of family functioning rather than the rule.

> Most families don't use the health care delivery system as a means of mistreating the helpless. Why, then, construct a policy that treats all families as if they did? It might be thought that a default assumption of mistrust is safer, because it does prevent actual abuse and hurts no one where families are loving [or a health care system is appropriately benevolent] rather than abusive. But in point of fact, it does hurt people in loving families: It courts a real danger of breaking down the intricate network of relationships—already strained by serious illness—within which the patient is situated. Routinely and systemically treating people [within families and/or between families and health care providers] as if they were adversaries of mistrust sets up emotional barriers among family members at the precise moment when they need all the comfort intimacy can give them (Nelson & Nelson, 1995, pp. 115-116).

If, therefore, Nelson and Nelson's (1995) and Boszormenyi-Nagy's (Boszormenyi-Nagy, et al., 1991) views of family functioning and relational ethics are correct, a purely individualized approach to ethical decision making at the end of life in the context of family dynamics may itself be a morally questionable activity that increases the risk of harm to the family system (Mowery, 2005). Furthermore, it would suggest that being in intimate relationships with others changes the level of influence on ethical decision making considered to be appropriate, particularly in contrast to nonintimate relationships (Mowery, 2005).

Practical Implications

What have been the results of this individual emphasis during end-of-life decision making? During the last 40 years while the legal consensus was being developed, home hospice care grew from a grassroots movement originating as a patient and family-friendly alternative to end-of-life care in institutional settings, to a federal and state subsidized form of health care. Despite these efforts, only 30% of individuals receive hospice services at the end of their life (Gazelle, 2007). The vast majority of American still die in hospitals without having documented advance directives and with families having limited voice in the process (Field & Cassel, 1997; Merrick, 2005).

Advanced Care Planning and Treatment Decisions

Ninety percent of patients in the Intensive Care Unit are admitted without advance directives (Boyle et al., 2005), and because these conversations are often not held ahead of time, the patients and family members may experience difficulty regarding end-of-life decisions. Advance directives were designed to provide a means for people to retain autonomous control over their future medical care by documenting their treatment preferences in writing and designating someone who would make surrogate decisions on their behalf in the event that they no longer had the capacity to communicate their desires (Burt, 2005). Consistent with the types of carefully circumscribed questions posed in the court cases from which advance directives arose, and a medical system designed to apply curative treatments to clearly diagnosable acute conditions, these documents have tended to focus on narrowly defined treatment options (e.g.; do not resuscitate orders).

Hickman, Hammes, Moss, & Toole (2006) summarized numerous limitations of advance directives, while also reviewing recent alternatives. Newer approaches to advance care planning have emphasized the articulation of values and goals of care such as quality (i.e., freedom from pain and suffering) rather than quantity of life (e.g., Five Wishes) or increasing portability across treatment settings (i.e., Physicians Orders for Life-Sustaining Treatments, (POLST)). All of these approaches to advanced planning emphasize the need to discuss one's wishes with a designated health care surrogate as well as making these wishes known to health care providers to make sure one's autonomy is respected and advance decisions are carried out.

Yet, these improvements still fail to recognize that an autonomy driven approach to end-of-life decision making has not consistently served the interests of patients and families (Winzelburg, Hanson, & Tulsku, 2005). Recent attitudinal research suggests that most patients do not prefer a purely autonomy driven approach to end-of-life decision making (Nolan, Sood, Kub, & Sulmasy, 2005). These researchers found that while patients retain decision making capacity, most prefer to share decision making with physicians and/or loved ones (i.e., give due consideration to the medical expertise of the physician and the interdependent needs of the family), with additional weight given to the input (not necessarily substituted judgment) of loved ones once the patient loses decisional capacity.

> In addition, it is known that even some patients who would opt, should they lose capacity, for having their surrogate perform a substituted judgment may be doing so not to express autonomy but as a means of relieving their surrogates of the burden of making a 'best interests' decision. These considerations suggest that a process far more complex than a desire for autonomous preference satisfaction is at work in end-of life decision making (Nolan, et al;, 2005, p. 349).

Assisted Death

Current consensus that it is the individual patient's right to refuse medical treatment, even if doing so hastens one's death, has led to controversy about whether the morally accepted view to permit "nature to take its own course" (i.e., passive euthanasia) can and/or should be extended to permitting a terminally ill patient to 'direct nature's course' (i.e., active euthanasia or physician-assisted suicide, (PAS)). The question is whether there is a moral distinction between intentionally allowing a disease process to result in death or intentionally causing death though the use of additional means (usually pharmaceuticals) to stop a disease process. Health care providers, bioethicists, and families are divided in response to this question. The federal courts have said this extension of the principle of autonomy in end-of-life decision making is an issue that must be resolved through the legislative process in each state (Emanuel, Fairclough, & Emanuel, 2000). To date, two states (Oregon and Washington) have legalized a process whereby patients can seek prescriptions from physicians for the express purpose of committing suicide (i.e., PAS) (see also chapter 9 in this handbook).

Research with terminally ill patients and their patient-designated primary caregivers has suggested that there is broad support for euthanasia and PAS in hypothetical situations involving others in severe pain, but this support drops dramatically in scenarios where the imagined patient seeks termination of life due to the perception of being a burden on the family (Emanuel, et al., 2000). However, only a small minority of sampled patients actively considered these options for themselves, with patient depression being the main motivating factor for interest in euthanasia and PAS. Furthermore, such personal interest in euthanasia or PAS appeared quite unstable with about half of those interested changing their minds over time (Emanuel, et al., 2000).

This research supports the provisions in Oregon's PAS law for multiple conversations between the patient and his or her physician over time. While approximately 17% of terminally ill patients (in Oregon) have talked to their families regarding PAS (Tolle, et al., 2004), there is no mandated provision in the Oregon law to protect the family to ensure that they are supportive of the idea of PAS over time, or that all other resources that could be brought to bear to help the family and support the patient have been exhausted.

> Despite caregiver's support for euthanasia and PAS, less than 20% of those who deemed euthanasia or PAS ethical would be wiling to personally help their family member end their life. This may reflect anxiety about prosecution and uncertainty about committing these actions reliably. But it also may reflect the emotional burden of actually performing euthanasia or assisting with suicide. As a family whose relative had repeatedly asked for suicide assistance states, performing euthanasia or PAS may not be a fair burden to place on the family (Emanuel, et al., 2000, p. 2465).

The indictment of poor end-of-life care in the United States has been well documented (Field & Cassel, 1997), so one must consider the degree to which euthanasia or physician-assisted suicide would still be considered if sufficient palliative care for the patients and the family had been in place throughout the entire trajectory of the illness, not just as an option during the terminal phase.

New Directions in Palliative Care

Traditional medicine seeks to eliminate the underling causes of illness within an individual patient, while palliative care, utilizing a multidisciplinary approach, seeks to eliminate or minimize the physical, psychosocial, and spiritual burden of life-limiting and terminal illnesses while recognizing that the burden is experienced and carried by both the patient and the family (National Consensus Project for Quality Palliative Care, 2004). Palliative care has long been the model for home-based hospice care. Its integration with inpatient care has rapidly expanded in the last decade (Morrison, Maroney-Galin, Kralovee, & Meier, 2005). In the summer of 2006, both the American Medical Association and the Accreditation Council for Graduate Medical Education approved of a new medical subspecialty in hospice and palliative medicine (see www.aahpm.org), thereby moving palliative care closer to its ideal of being integrated with curative treatment from the time of diagnosis of a life-threatening condition (National Consensus Project, 2009). While the family's voice is more readily heard in the context of palliative care and represents a significant advance over traditional medical care, the individualistic assumptions embedded in current models of surrogate decision making at the end of life still prevail in palliative care.

For instance, training physicians for palliative medicine emphasizes the importance of taking time to communicate with families during decision-making meetings focused on goals of care (Fineberg, 2005; Tulsky, 2005), but such communication commonly occurs with a view of the family as a collection of individuals. Communication training for physicians, therefore, has largely focused on dyadic communication skills between the physician and separate family members, with special attention given to the formal health care proxy. The clinical and research literature on palliative care has paid limited attention to the accumulated body of empirical data assessing dimensions of family systems functioning (e.g., cohesion, flexibility, and communication) (Olson, 2000). It has also taken full advantage of the family therapy literature which includes techniques for intervening in unhealthy family system dynamics (e.g., multidirected partiality) (Boszormenyi-Nagy, et al., 1991) that are readily adaptable to facilitate family decision making during goals of care family conferences. Thus, while palliative care ostensibly does a better job than traditional medicine of including the voice of the family system in end-of-life decision making, until research, clinical practice, institutional policies, procedures and laws take full stock of the intricate web of interpersonal family dynamics in which end-of-life care decision making is embedded, the vision of the patient and the family as the true focus of palliative care will be stymied.

Chapter 12

Ethical and Legal Issues in End-of-Life Decision Making

Madeline Jacobs

Since the 1970s, a series of court decisions fueled nationwide debate and discussion around end-of-life care, resulting in a national consensus regarding patient autonomy. These cases highlight the importance and difficulties in balancing the interests of individuals with those of the general public and have shaped and defined the ethical landscape around end-of-life decision making.

Futility and Substituted Decision Making

In 1976, the country was embroiled in a heart wrenching debate about Karen Ann Quinlan, a 21-year-old woman in New Jersey who suffered irreparable brain damage and ended up in a persistent vegetative state (PVS) after mixing alcohol with prescription medications on an empty stomach. Because her physicians disagreed with her parents' decision to have Karen disconnected from a respirator that was maintaining her body, the case ended up in the court system. Eventually, the New Jersey Supreme Court's ruling in the Quinlan case established the right of family of a dying, incompetent patient to let that individual die by disconnecting life support. After more than 10 years in a nursing home, Karen Quinlan died of pneumonia.

The case of Nancy Cruzan, in Missouri, was very similar, except the life-sustaining treatment was a feeding tube.

The rulings in the case of Nancy Cruzan (see sidebar) further solidified the rights of competent patients to accept or reject any life-sustaining treatment including artificial hydration and nutrition. In addition, the Supreme Court ruling in the Cruzan case established that individual states had the right to regulate standards of evidence for end-of-life decisions. Missouri requires clear and convincing evidence of a patient's wishes to be demonstrated before life-sustaining treatments can be removed, as do New York and Florida. This standard of evidence usually requires written or explicit verbal statements substantiating the patient's wishes.

On January 11, 1983, Nancy Cruzan suffered irreversible brain damage from a car accident that resulted in her falling into a persistent vegetative state. For years, at an annual cost of $130,000 paid for by the state, she was sustained by a surgical feeding tube. After 4 years, when it became clear that there would be no change in her condition, her parents and husband asked doctors to remove the tube. This request was refused by medical providers who did not agree with the family's choice. In court hearings Cruzan's family presented a case around their claims that she would not want to live in such a condition. The case went all the way to the U.S. Supreme Court, which upheld Missouri State law requiring clear and convincing evidence of what an incompetent person would want. The court also ruled that living wills were constitutional, on the foundation that a patient has the right to withhold consent from medical treatment, and no medical treatment can be performed on any competent patient without his or her concession to it.

On December 14, 1990, 7 years after her accident, and only after the State of Missouri withdrew from the case and the family's attorney and state-appointed guardian filed separate briefs, did a judge authorize the feeding tube to be removed and Cruzan died.

The Terri Schiavo case illustrates a worst-case scenario about conflict escalating out of control. In 1990, Schiavo, a 27-year-old woman, collapsed and lost consciousness. Resuscitation efforts failed to awaken her and although she suffered brain damage from lack of oxygen, she was able to breathe on her own and consequently put on a feeding tube. After many years of trying multiple types of therapy, her husband accepted the medical judgment that Schiavo had suffered irreparable brain damage and would never improve or regain consciousness. He asked to have her feeding tube removed. Schiavo had not left any written wishes for her treatment in this kind of situation, but as her legal proxy in the State of Florida, there was always a clear legal basis for allowing her husband to make decisions on his wife's behalf (substituted decision making). Unfortunately, her family disagreed with his decision to end life-sustaining treatment. Indeed, they made it clear that they would never come to that conclusion and even began accusing the husband of having abused their daughter and causing the original injury, a claim unsupported by any evidence. The involvement of the press and ultimately the political system (Gov. Jeb Bush, Pres. George W. Bush, and Sen. Bill Frist), as well as the Supreme Court, turned this private tragedy into a public circus.

All three of these cases deal with the issue of withdrawing treatment in situations with an incapacitated patient who has left no written or legal documentation of her treatment preferences for being kept alive in a coma and the conflict and disagreement that can result.

Futility and Stakeholder Interests

The increase of conflict around the issues of futility has transformed the work of hospital care teams. How do these conflicts arise? Why are there some stakeholders ready to think that the patient is dying while others remain adamant that curative care must be provided and will be helpful?

Joseph Fins, a bioethicist and palliative medicine specialist, writes, "Many futility disputes are often a product of miscommunication between doctor, patient, and family. Families who demand care believed by physicians to be futile are often operating upon different assumptions than practitioners because the clinicians have done an inadequate job of communicating basic information about diagnosis, prognosis, and remaining therapeutic or palliative options."

The issue of futility is especially difficult because the visual evidence that the body is in the last stages of life is not always easily recognized by untrained laypersons. The patient may look like he or she is improving or strong enough to benefit from further curative treatments, when in reality systems are shutting down. Patients are also known to rally a bit and perk up around those they love.

Quill suggests that overly optimistic prognostication may lead families to push for life-sustaining technologies rather than palliative care or hospice care. In the case of Schiavo, "experts" kept providing her parents with "proof" of therapies that might work or testimony that kept their hope alive that their daughter was still somewhere inside that damaged brain and body. Frist, who also happened to be a physician, disputed the diagnosis of PVS using a short videotape of Schiavo as evidence. This inappropriate and simply false information provided a tragic misconception about Schiavo's likelihood of recovery. Autopsies after Schiavo's death proved that her brain was severely damaged beyond repair and all sensory function had been destroyed by the oxygen deprivation.

Fins (2006) suggests that physicians need to do a better job focusing on the goals of care and communicating with patients and families. "The highway of aggressive medical treatment runs fast, is heavily traveled, but can lack landmarks and the signage necessary to know when it is time to make for the exit ramp....These signs are there and it is your responsibility to communicate them to patients and families."

For example, many of the technologies currently used in the course of routine hospital care, such as cardiopulmonary resuscitation (CPR), were created to save lives on the battlefield. Instead of stabilizing young soldiers so they could recover and go on to lead productive lives, these technologies are used routinely to bring old and ill bodies back from the dead. Patients and families are typically not fully informed about the pain and suffering caused by CPR techniques, the post-CPR process, and the mortality rate of survivors. Indeed, most patients in the final stages of their lives do not ever leave the hospital after being resuscitated.

Advance Care Planning

In 1990, Congress passed the Patient Self-Determination Act (PSDA) which requires many Medicare and Medicaid providers (hospitals, nursing homes, hospice programs, home health agencies) to give adult individuals, at the time of inpatient admission or enrollment, certain information about their rights under state laws governing advance directives. This information includes:

1. the right to participate in and direct their own health care decisions,
2. the right to accept or refuse medical or surgical treatment,
3. the right to prepare an advance directive, and
4. information on the provider's policies that govern the utilization of these rights.

The act also prohibits institutions from discriminating against a patient who does not have an advance directive. The PSDA further requires institutions to document patient information and provide ongoing community education on advance directives.

Five years later, in 1995, the SUPPORT study found that only 47% of the physicians surveyed knew when their patients preferred to avoid CPR. In addition, 46% of do not resuscitate (DNR) orders were written within 2 days of death. Most disturbingly, the SUPPORT study intervention, which included enhanced opportunities for communication around goals of care, failed to improve end-of-life communication and planning.

The publication of these findings galvanized the medical community into finding more effective ways of complying with the legal requirements set forth in the PSDA. Having patients sign a proxy statement, an informed consent, and a DNR as part of a huge stack of admissions papers might comply with the letter of the law; it didn't provide any helpful information or guidance for making difficult treatment and end-of-life decisions. The SUPPORT study proved that the legislation wasn't enough to change practice. Improved training and treatment protocols around treating pain and incorporating communication around goals of care were necessary.

There are multiple stakeholders involved in every health care decision. Families and other parties are often involved in health care decisions. However, based on the PSDA, the competent patient is legally considered the ultimate decision maker. Of course, some competent patients want someone else to make decisions for them, but they must clearly communicate that preference.

In all cases, the physicians must determine whether the patient has the capacity to understand the information necessary to make a decision. When there is conflict about a treatment decision, the role of the physician and/or the ethics committee is first and foremost to defend and protect patient autonomy—the right of the patient to determine how decisions are made and information is shared.

Definitions of Key Advance Care Planning Concepts

Advance directives: There are two types of advance directives.

Proxy/durable power of attorney for health care: A person who has the legal authority to make medical decisions for an incapacitated patient. The authority is assigned through a signed and witnessed proxy statement or durable power of attorney for health care, depending on the state law. Another word for a proxy is *agent* and representing a patient is called *agency*.

Living will: A person's written statement of treatment preferences in the event of incapacity. There are many different forms of living wills.

Cardiopulmonary resuscitation (CPR): The medical procedures used to restart a patient's heart and breathing when the patient suffers heart failure (his or her heart stops). CPR may involve simple efforts such as mouth-to-mouth resuscitation and external chest compression. Advanced CPR may involve electric shock, insertion of a tube to open the patient's airway, injection of medication into the heart, and, in extreme cases, open chest heart massage.

Do not resuscitate (DNR) order: A written order that tells medical professionals not to perform CPR. There are two types of DNRs: Hospital and nonhospital. A hospital DNR is only in effect for the length of the hospitalization and needs to be renewed for each hospitalization. A nonhospital DNR needs to be signed by a physician and reviewed every 90 days. The doctor does not have to sign it every 90 days, and it is assumed to be in effect unless there is evidence to the contrary. Emergency workers are often required to try to resuscitate people who call 911, regardless of whether they have a DNR or not.

Artificial nutrition and hydration: Artificial nutrition and hydration is a form of life-sustaining treatment. It is a chemically balanced mix of nutrients and fluids, provided by placing a tube directly into the stomach, the intestine, or a vein.

Do not intubate (DNI) order: A written order that tells medical professionals not to place someone on an artificial respirator in case of heart failure or cessation of breathing.

Requests to Die and Physician Assisted Suicide

According to WebMD, euthanasia is the intentional termination of life by somebody other than the person concerned at his or her request. Assisted suicide means intentionally helping a patient to terminate his or her life at his or her request. The word *euthanasia* comes from the Greek language and translated into "good death."

Since death is a certainty, trying to ensure a good death would seem like a natural process. However, dying in America is not easy thanks to modern technology and conflicts of values among stakeholders. Although there is now a large foundation of legal opinion clarifying the issues of patient autonomy and the roles of different stakeholders, the issues around euthanasia continue to be debated.

	Requests to Die	Physician Assisted Suicide	Euthanasia	Substituted Judgment or Proxy
Who Decides?	Patient	Patient	Other than patient	Patient, as much as possible
Who Takes Action to End Life?	Other than patient	Patient	Other than patient	Other than patient

The major difference between requests to die and physician-assisted suicide (PAS) is who actually conducts the final action that causes death—the patient or someone else. In physician-assisted suicide, the physician helps the patient obtain the means to die, but the patient is in complete control of the process and takes the actions necessary to cause death—administering the drugs, etc.

Euthanasia can also be used to describe situations in which physicians administer or withdraw specific treatment to cause the death of an incompetent patient. The ideal situation is when a patient has appointed a legal proxy/health care and made his or her preferences for end-of-life treatment clear. Unfortunately, this ideal situation is the exception rather than the rule.

The Debate Around Euthanasia and the Right to PAS

While the law is relatively clear on the right of a competent patient to forego or withdraw treatments, there is still disagreement over whether competent patients have the right to actively end their own lives by medical means. Not surprisingly, these issues evoke impassioned debate. Indeed, some opponents of euthanasia assume that anyone who makes a decision to end his or her life must be, by definition, incompetent. The main issues about which people disagree include:

- **The right to die:** Do people even have the legal right to assistance in dying or committing suicide? There is disagreement over the interpretation of legal precedents and what they mean.
- **The definition and value of suffering and dignity in relation to the value of life:** Is the lack of a right to assisted suicide in essence being forced to suffer? Or is it a

protection against murder and abuse? What is the value of life as patients approach death? Is balancing suffering, dignity, and quality of life against the value of life itself creating a nihilistic death culture or a culture of natural compassion?

- **The slippery slope:** Does euthanasia open the door to the slippery slope of legalized murder? There are well-documented instances of medical abuses in history: Unnecessary hysterectomies provides a major example. What do we need to protect ourselves from and how? Is it valid or necessary to restrict certain rights that would produce a good to protect from a possible harm? Disability groups such as Not Dead Yet see legalizing euthanasia as a dangerous precedent that devalues disabled persons and will lead to abuses that unfairly target the poor and disabled.

- **The role of physicians and the Hippocratic oath:** Does the Hippocratic oath forbid or condone euthanasia? Is it binding or a guideline? How should the medical establishment retain the value of historic ethics and values in the face of changing practice and technologies?

- **Healthcare spending implications:** How should physicians, hospitals, governments, payors, and society at large make decisions about allocation of scarce resources? How does the push for new life-saving technology fit in with today's cost containment efforts?

- **The physician's role:** Is it the physician's role to help the patient experience as easy a death as possible as part of good practice and a lifelong continuum of care? Or is euthanasia "fundamentally incompatible with the physician's role as a healer?"

The Bouvia case highlights the issues of quality of life and autonomy. Who gets to define whether someone's suffering or quality of life is more important than society's imperative to protect people from harm? How is harm defined? For both of these individuals, being powerless to control their own destinies was a fate worse than death.

As we saw in the case of Karen Ann Quinlan, the physicians' discomfort with the decision to withdraw treatment caused a drawn out conflict with her family. Elizabeth Bouvia was force fed based on professional discomfort of physicians, lawyers, and judges with her treatment decision. Even when she was eating, a doctor who felt she might still be trying to starve herself by not eating enough started force feeding her again, against her will.

Jack Kevorkian held patient autonomy as an absolute, and he let patients define the nature of their own suffering. Thus, some of the people he helped complete suicide were suffering from nonterminal conditions that made them feel that life was not worth living, such as a woman who had chronic vaginal-pelvic pain. While public opinion was against him because of his seemingly indiscriminate use of his suicide technologies, Kevorkian trained a national spotlight on suffering not related to terminal illness. He revealed the need for new approaches to treating depression, chronic pain, and other kinds of suffering. Interestingly, Kevorkian was found not guilty in all cases of his involvement in PAS, with the exception when he committed active euthanasia.

As of 2011, active euthanasia was only legal in three countries: the Netherlands, Belgium, and Luxembourg. Assisted suicide is legal in Switzerland and, in the United States, Washington and Oregon.

On October 27, 1997, Oregon enacted the Death With Dignity Act, which allows terminally ill Oregonians to end their lives through the voluntary self-administration of lethal medications, expressly prescribed by a physician for that purpose. The Oregon Death With Dignity Act requires the Oregon Health Authority to collect information about the patients and physicians who participate in the act, and publish an annual statistical report.

Eleven years later, physician-assisted suicide was passed in Washington State. The Washington Death With Dignity Act passed on November 4, 2008, and went into effect on March 5, 2009. This act allows terminally ill adults seeking to end their life to request lethal doses of medication from medical and osteopathic physicians. These terminally ill patients must be Washington residents who have less than 6 months to live.

In December 2008, a Montana district judge ruled in the case of *Baxter v. State of Montana* that Montana residents have the legal right to physician-assisted suicide. On December 31, 2009, the Montana Supreme Court ruled against an appeal by the attorney general of Montana, affirming 4-3 that physician-assisted suicide is not "against public policy" in the state of Montana. Note that these rulings did not represent legislation identifying under what circumstances PAS may be performed in Montana (see chapter 9 in this handbook).

The legalization of PAS in places like Oregon, Washington, Switzerland, Belgium, and the Netherlands creates strict processes and protections around the conditions acceptable to help someone end their lives or do it for them. These systems require aggressive treatments for all kinds of suffering—physical, emotional, and spiritual. Rather than opening the door to the slippery slope of unregulated and out-of-control euthanasia abuses, very few people actually get to the point of completing suicide in the places where it is legal.

When patients are empowered to control their own decisions, they seem to choose against death in most cases. Even Bouvia didn't choose to end her life once she got the power over her own decisions. Even so, her experiences revealed a dismal lack of preparedness on the part of the American medical and payer systems to deal with the disabled and injured among us.

Elizabeth Bouvia suffered from severe cerebral palsy and quadriplegia and was abandoned by her parents as a child because they couldn't take care of her. In 1983, with her physical condition declining, nowhere to live, or means to support herself, Bouvia attempted to end her life by asking a hospital to provide her with morphine while she starved herself.

A court ruled against her, stating that the hospital could not be forced to help her die, and instead she was force fed. Bouvia tried to resist the force feeding by biting through the feeding tube. Four attendants would then hold her down while the tubing was inserted into her nose and liquids pumped into her stomach. Some physicians called this battery and torture, while others claimed that the hospital was right to err on the side of continued life. Bouvia sued to have the unwanted tubes removed from her body. The trial court refused, and she appealed. The appeals court overturned the trial court, ruling that:

> By refusing petitioner the relief which she sought, the trial court, with the most noble intentions, attempted to exercise its discretion by issuing a ruling which would uphold what it considered a lawful object, i.e., keeping Elizabeth Bouvia alive by a means which it considered ethical. Nonetheless, it erred for it had no discretion to exercise. Petitioner sought to enforce only a right which was exclusively hers and over which neither the medical profession nor the judiciary have any veto power. The trial court could but recognize and protect her exercise of that right.

The feeding tubes were removed, but she did not die, and she remains alive as of 2012.

Chapter 13

End-of-Life Decision Making: An Irish Perspective

Dolores M. Dooley

Introduction

During the last decade a national conversation has been under way about death and the process of dying in the 26 counties that constitute the Republic of Ireland. The Irish Hospice Foundation, in collaboration with the Health Service Executive, launched national surveys, telephone interviews, personal interviews with health care professionals and patients, media discussions, and focus groups from across the country discussing death and dying. The research was conducted with a view to ascertaining the views of Ireland's population about topics including: how a "good death" is understood, how hospitals can better deliver end-of-life care, wishes about being informed of a terminal condition, role of families in end-of-life decision making, advance directives, pain management, use or refusal of life-prolonging technologies, and physician-assisted suicide and euthanasia. The results of research are numerous publications designed to be user-friendly and accessible and aimed at informing and educating the Irish public, health care professionals, patients, and families. Educational initiatives continue to come from the Irish Hospice Foundation, as well as courses on death and dying that are now appearing in university course listings, all indicating the national conversation continues.

The discussion of end-of-life decision making in this article refers to what has been referred to as a national conversation about death and dying in the Republic of Ireland during the last decade (Doyle, 2008). The conversations are at national level or in the kitchens of Irish homes and even the pubs in towns and cities. The words of Murray and Jennings, speaking of hoped-for reform in end-of-life-care in the United States, echo efforts to develop Ireland's national conversation among laypeople and professionals alike:

> The next decades should be, we believe, a time of education and soul-searching discussions in communities and at kitchen tables, as well as in health care settings. [...] We must talk about what we dare not name, and look at what we dare not see. We shall never get end of life care 'right' because death is not a puzzle to

be solved. Death is an inevitable aspect of the human condition. But let us never forget: while death is inevitable, dying badly is not (Murray & Jennings, 2005, p. 57).

The Republic of Ireland comprises 26 out of the 32 counties that make up the island of Ireland. The six northern counties (Northern Ireland) come under the jurisdiction of the United Kingdom. The current population of the republic is approximately 4.5 million.

Ethnic and Religious Profile

A decade and a half of in-migration has altered the ethnic and religious landscape of the Republic of Ireland. The 2011 Irish census of population shows the ethnic composition is approximately 88.1% Irish while the percentage of non-Irish nationals was 11.9% of the population. Of the 11.9% non-national population in Ireland, non-Irish nationals from the European Union (EU) comprised 71.0%, while non-EU nationals constituted 29%. According to results of the April 2011 census, Ireland remains predominantly a Catholic country, with over 84% describing themselves as Roman Catholic. However, compared to the 2006 census, the 2011 census results show a significant increase since 2006 of persons self-identifying as Muslim (1.1%), making it the most expansive non-Christian religion. Among others who declared a religious affiliation in the 2011 census are members of Church of Ireland, Presbyterians, Methodists, Jehovah Witnesses, Hindus, Buddhists, and Pentecostal Christians. There was a large group of people who chose the no religion category, a 45% increase on the 2006 census, while other categories such as agnostic and atheist were entered as a written choice on the census by over 7,500 respondents. These details of Ireland's size as well as the ethnic and religious diversity are relevant to ongoing national projects around death and dying that are detailed below. From a more dominantly homogeneous population a decade ago (ethnically and religiously), health care centers now have to develop greater awareness and sensitivity that patients and families may have divergent cultural and religious views about what comprises a good death, how much they wish to be decision makers in treatment choices, the role of the family in such decisions, and where they would wish to die.

Irish Hospice Foundation

During the last decade, the Irish Hospice Foundation (IHF), a national charity set up in 1986, has worked in partnership with the Health Service Executive (HSE) that replaced 10 regional health boards and a number of other agencies and organizations to provide health care for the population in Ireland. The Minister for Health has overall responsibility for the HSE in government.

A 5-year, 2007-2012, Hospice Friendly Hospital program (HFH), funded by the IHF and Atlantic Philanthropy, introduced public consultations; national surveys; and interviews with patients, families, and healthcare professionals with the aim of making end-of-life care central to hospital care and bringing it from the margins to the mainstream of Irish health services. To this end, a series of 22 workshops were conducted and covered a spectrum of ages, disability groups, gay and lesbian groups, the homeless, traveller groups, legal experts, and palliative care groups. These groups presented their views on how challenges of dying, death, and bereavement should be addressed in Ireland. Ten public meetings were also held around the country to facilitate participation in the forum. This extensive exercise was intended as a listening one, designed to identify participants' wishes and aspirations for end of life (Keegan, McGee, Brady, et al., 1999; Weafer, 2004; Weafer, McCarthy, & Loughrey, 2009; Weafer, 2009a; Weafer, 2009b; Quinlan, 2009a; Quinlan, 2009b; Quinlan and O'Neill, 2009; Carroll, 2009; McCarthy et al. 2011.

Weafer's survey of 2004 showed that two thirds of participants wanted to die at home, but more than 70% of people actually die outside their own home: 48% in acute hospitals. An estimated 25% of people die at home, 4% die in hospice, and some 20% die in long-stay facilities (National Audit, 2008/9). Given the high percentage of persons who die in hospital, a national audit of end-of-life care in hospitals was conducted in Ireland 2008-2009. The audit assessed the quality of care provided by Irish hospitals in the last week of life as patients and their families went through the journey of dying, death, and bereavement. This is a first ever national audit of end-of-life care in Irish hospitals, and while the quality of care for people who die in an Irish hospital compared favorably to other hospitals in the United States, the United Kingdom, and France, the main countries for which we comparative data, significant weaknesses were also identified. The National Audit aims to structure reviews of improvements in hospitals against quality standards for end-of-life care with the goal of having hospitals become a more hospitable place to die.

National research analyses give broad indications of what people living in Ireland understand about decision making at end of life, what their hopes are for good dying, what fears they have about the process of dying, and patients' preferences for a family role in end-of-life decision making (Weafer, 2009a, 2009b; McCarthy and Loughrey, 2009; McCarthy, Weafer, & Loughrey, 2010).

McCarthy et al. (2011) utilized the research data to develop eight case-based ethics modules to enhance the decision making capacity of patients, families, and the general public in relation to their own deaths and those of their loved ones.

Understandings of a Good Death

Features of a good death were highlighted in focus groups convened during Weafer's qualitative research for the IHF (2009). These include a fast and peaceful death (preferably in your sleep); being cared for at home, with adequate medical support; no pain or suffering involved; to be conscious and able to communicate; having your family with you when you die; having control over the time and circumstances of one's death; your children reared and independent; with enough time to get your affairs in order; dying with dignity and all that entails. Most respondents (70%) in a national telephone survey agreed with the statement that "every competent person has the right to refuse medical treatment even if such refusal leads to their own death." Most agreement came from those less than 56 years old (McCarthy, Weafer, & Loughrey, 2010, p. 455). That spiritual and religious support would be important drew much agreement (73%), particularly by those more than 65 years old.

Minimal Understanding of End-of-Life Terminology

While there are certain desires for one's dying, the general public as well as Irish legislators are largely unfamiliar with terms associated with end-of-life treatment and care such as advance directives, palliative sedation, artificial nutrition and hydration, and physician-assisted suicide. However, terms such as postmortem, cardiopulmonary resuscitation (CPR), do not resuscitate (DNR), persistent vegetative state, and euthanasia indicated more knowledge perhaps owing to the fact that media discussions in Ireland and TV hospital series from the United States used these terms. The unfamiliarity with end-of-life terminology, in general, is consistent with the Irish Council for Bioethics (2005) findings that the Irish public's knowledge and awareness of various bioethical areas was quite limited. Research over the last decade also showed that death is a topic that is generally discussed by Irish people with reluctance. Conscientious attendance at wakes provides a somber but more intimate occasion to discuss death and dying although a consensus emerged in the research that older people (and to a lesser extent the terminally ill) are more likely to discuss different aspects of death and attend funerals. Quinlan claims there is evidence of a culturally specific Irish attitude to death. There is a frankness about death in the United Kingdom and the United States that is absent in Ireland (Quinlan, 2009a, p. 7).

Being Informed of a Terminal Condition

Most people want to be informed if they have a terminal condition, though differences emerged about whether they would want this information given to them on their own or with someone present, the latter being mostly family (McCarthy, Weafer, & Loughrey, 2010). Quinlan & O'Neill, (2009) conducted interviews with health care practitioners working in 15 Irish hospitals and found that information about diagnoses and prognoses is often shared with families instead of patients (particularly older patients) at end of life.

Pain Management

While pain management is cited by health care professionals as a most important objective, there are constraints on achieving this goal. Patients face difficulties in speaking about their pain and seeking pain relief. This difficulty applies to adults but especially to children. McCracken and Keogh (2009) found that describing pain was not easy for patients, and sometimes a patient, may think he or she will be perceived as a complainer and incur the displeasure of staff. Family members can, at times, obstruct pain alleviation by choosing not to have their loved one receive palliative care. One reason for this reluctance is that they do not want their relative to be told that they have terminal cancer. Family insistence on this matter would not harmonize with palliative care philosophy of honest communication about diagnoses if the patient asks. Patients and families both expressed some reluctance to take up the suggestion of hospice care since the very term, *hospice care* conjures up a place to die and/or a place where their loved one would receive too much pain medication and so be confused or unable to communicate with family. This failure to seek palliative care often means that pain continues needlessly and the moral obligation of carers to provide for the well-being of patients is not met (Quinlan & O'Neill, 2009). Furthermore, clinicians and families claimed that, at times, they had serious concerns about the possibility that adequate pain relief could bring about an earlier demise of a patient, which, in turn, might be interpreted as physician-assisted suicide (McCarthy, Loughrey, Weafer, & Dooley 2009, pp. 462-463). These impediments to pain management pointed to an urgent need for education in effective and ethical pain management as well as education in palliative care for Irish health care professionals and the wider public (McCarthy et al., 2011, pp. 222-223).

Decisions on Life-Prolonging Technologies

A finding in Irish research was the belief in the right of every competent person to refuse medical treatment even if such refusal leads to one's death. The Health Service Executive, in conjunction with medical specialists and laypersons, is currently preparing a set of guidelines on DNAR (do not attempt resuscitation). Hospitals, nursing homes, and long-term care centers have, for years, operated differing practices regarding CPR provision, and the HSE recognised the urgent need for some consistency in practice guidelines. As of this writing, these were scheduled to be available in late 2012. Advance directives (ADs), drawn up by persons with capacity, often can provide indications of circumstances when the person, who later may lose capacity, would wish to refuse CPR. As of this writing (2012), there is no specific legislation in relation to advance directives. Some clinicians view a patient's AD as consultative in assisting end-of-life decision making but the implementation is not legally required (Campbell, 2006). The Jehovah Witnesses have drawn up their own AD form that details the terms of refusal for specific medical treatments (Dooley & McCarthy, 2012, pp. 226-227). The right of adult, competent Jehovah Witnesses to refuse blood is acknowledged under the broad legal presumption that there is an absolute right in a competent person to refuse medical treatment even if it leads to death. A series of Irish court cases mainly involving the refusal of blood for minor children of Jehovah Witnesses make clear that the Irish medical profession will not accept proxy refusal of life-saving procedures where children are concerned. Rather, a determination of the best interests is made by the health care clinician in conversation with the family of a child needing life-prolonging treatment.

In 2007 the Irish Council for Bioethics (ICB) published an opinion document called *Is it time for Advance Healthcare Directives?* Public consultations were organized and submissions sought that informed the preparation of a detailed discussion document on ADs in Ireland, including recommendations for the implementation of ADs. In 2009 the Law Reform Commission (LRC) published a report, *Bioethics: Advance Care Directives,* which recommended that an appropriate legislative framework should be enacted for ADs. This framework would be facilitative in nature and be seen in the wider context of a process of health care planning by an individual. Furthermore, the LRC made clear that the framework for ADs does not alter or affect the current law on homicide, under which euthanasia and assisted suicide are criminal offences (LRC, 2009, p. 101).

In the absence of legislative developments to implement the recommendations of the LRC and the ICB, a Think Ahead Project was launched by the Irish Hospice Foundation. A form has been prepared that encourages and facilitates people to fill in their personal details and other information that could be crucial at some time in the future in ensuring that their wishes or preferences for end-of-life care are known to others: family, general practitioners, hospital services, solicitor, emergency services, etc. Copies of the forms are available at www.thinkahead.ie.

Decisions on Artificial Nutrition and Hydration

One life-prolonging treatment that has proved controversial in Ireland is the provision of artificial nutrition and hydration (ANH). The question asked echoes that in the international literature: Is the provision of ANH a universal obligation or is it a form of medical treatment that is optional depending on the circumstances of a particular patient? An Irish court case, *In Re a Ward of Court* was decided in the courts in 1996 and is relevant to the legal and ethical complexity of deciding when ANH is appropriate ([1996] 2 Irish Reports, p. 79). A 46-year-old woman, Lucy Chamberlain, suffered anoxic brain damage under anesthetic during a routine gynecological procedure 24 years earlier when she was 22 years old. During these 24 years, Chamberlain was in a near persistent vegetative state and lacked capacity and any ability to speak. She was fed through an nasogastric tube and, later, a percutaneous endoscopic gastrostomy tube was inserted. Chamberlain's mother applied to the courts to determine whether it was permissible in Irish law to withdraw the PEG tube. The High Court and, on appeal, the Supreme Court held that it was lawful and it was in Chamberlain's best interests that the ANH should be withdrawn and she should be allowed "to die in accordance with nature with all such palliative care and medication as is necessary to ensure a peaceful and pain-free death" (Law Reform Commission 2009, 22). The Irish courts also declared that, after this judgment, the nonuse of antibiotics for treatment of infections, other than in a palliative way to avoid pain and suffering, was also lawful. The courts also made an order allowing Chamberlain's family to make such arrangements as they considered suitable to admit her to a facility that would not regard the withdrawal of ANH to be contrary to their code of ethics. The case of Chamberlain also clarified the authority of families in determining life-prolonging decisions. The leading Irish authority on the role of families can be found in *Re a Ward of Court* (1996) and is possibly best summarized by Hamilton C.J., a member of the Supreme Court at the time of the Ward case.

> The court's prime and paramount consideration must be the best interests of the Ward. The views of the committee and family of the ward, although they should be heeded and careful consideration given thereto, cannot and should not prevail over the court's view of the Ward's best interest ([1996] 2 IR, 79, p.

106).

Most of the time of course, there is no court—but the strict legal rule is as stated above.

The Irish Medical Council (IMC), the official registration body for medical doctors, offers this position on ANH:

> If a patient is unable to take sufficient nutrition and hydration orally, you should assess what alternative forms are possible and appropriate in the circumstances. You should bear in mind the burden or risks to the patient, the patient's wishes if known, and the overall benefit to be achieved. Where possible, you should make the patient and/or their primary carer aware of these conclusions (IMC, 2009, 20).

The Irish Association of Palliative Care (IAPC, 2011a) claims that currently available evidence is insufficient to make universal guidelines for practice with regard to use of ANH in patients receiving palliative care. Moral and legal arguments are discussed in a variety of legal and ethical contexts in Ireland—arguments for withholding, or withdrawing ANH as well as arguments for the universal moral obligation to provide food (Dooley & McCarthy, 2012, pp. 131-133).

Physician-Assisted Suicide and Euthanasia

Physician-assisted suicide (PAS) and euthanasia are both legally impermissible in Ireland. Under Irish law, any person who deliberately ends the life of another person is potentially guilty of murder. It makes no difference that the person consented to the action or even that he or she requested that this should happen. The law does not permit a person to consent to his or her own death even though Irish law recognizes a competent person's right to refuse life-saving treatment. The right of competent refusal is further reiterated by the IMC (2009). Having acknowledged the Irish legal situation on assisted suicide, the discussion about physician-assisted suicide or suicide with the help of others surfaces in the media at intervals, thus indicating that the national debate continues. The IAPC argues that reasons of public interest and threats to physician integrity are strong justifications for an unwillingness to legally endorse PAS or euthanasia (IAPC, 2011c). There have been no prosecutions of Irish health professionals in relation to either assisted suicide or euthanasia. It is thought that the position taken in the English case of *R v Cox* is likely to be followed in Ireland, effectively prohibiting euthanasia (McCarthy, et al., 2012, p. 319). The debates continue about the differences between a deliberate and intentional act of taking one's life and the omission of treatments to prolong that life. Meanwhile, the IAPC, cognizant of the arguments to support PAS or euthanasia that suffering and inadequate palliative care are often contributing factors, strongly recommends continued development of specialist palliative care services throughout Ireland (IAPC, 2011b).

Conclusion

There is a dawning realization in our culture that the way we treat death and dying is a reality we have too-long ignored. The societal practice of focusing all our skills and expertise on cure fails to address the broad and complex landscape of end of life. This broad and complex landscape is the terrain for the work ahead and explained in the Irish Hospice Foundation's 3-year strategic plan 2012-2015.

Loss, Grief, and Mourning

Introduction to Part 3, Chapters 14 – 20

Chapters 14 through 20 focus on loss, grief, and mourning. The Body of Knowledge Committee defined this major category of thanatology knowledge in this way: **the physical, behavioral, cognitive, and social experience of and reactions to loss, the grief process, and practices surrounding grief and commemoration.**

The chapters in Part 3 focus on loss, grief, and mourning in terms of these indicators: culture and socialization, religion and spirituality, historical and contemporary perspectives, life span issues, the family and larger systems, and ethical and legal issues. Six of the chapters are revised from the chapters that appeared in the first edition. One chapter (15) we brought over unchanged from the first edition.

Chapter 14

Culture and Socialization in Death, Grief, and Mourning

Paul C. Rosenblatt

Among the thousands of world cultures there are great differences in how death is understood and how people are socialized and expected to grieve and mourn. What is meant by the word *"culture"*? "A culture" is a set of beliefs, values, ways of talking, rituals, ways of relating to other people, ways of organizing life, ways of defining self and others—all more or less unique to a particular group. Typically a culture has its own distinctive language and a long history. Of course all humans have a great deal in common, but it is arguably true that everything arises from culture and is given meaning and form by it, including dying, death, and grief.

"Socialization" is embedded in culture and is both the process by which people come to fit their culture and the process by which others around shape them to fit the culture. Socialization, development, and change go on throughout life, because all that happens to them, the people around them, the mass media, and the culture(s) that surround them and that they travel through constantly impact them.

"Culture" and "socialization" are abstractions, concepts that help to focus our attention and summarize things we think we know. They can be useful terms for communicating and thinking, but they can also mislead us into believing we know more than we actually do. So even as this chapter offers ideas about how to think about people dealing with death, the reader should not let the partial truths of this chapter erase personal curiosity, awareness, questioning, doubts, learning, and ways of thinking.

Understanding Culture and Socialization as They Relate to Death

Culture and culture-based socialization are always at work in the areas of death, grief, and mourning. Cultures differ, for example, in what is appropriate in the relationships of a dying person with those who are likely to survive him or her. Thus, from Korean culture there is evidence that, while a mother is dying, her children may not speak in her presence as though she is dying (Rosenblatt & Yang, 2004). But even though they may not talk about her dying, they know she is dying and work to deal with the pending death. In particular, the mother and children work at carrying out intergenerational obligations that would be spread over many years if she were not going to die soon. For example, a dying mother may work to teach a young adult daughter to be a good cook, and adult children may move toward a higher level of achievement and responsibility as a dying gift to their mother and as a token of their respect and obligation.

Following a death, cultures differ substantially in the expressions of emotion that are appropriate. For example, some African-Americans reported feeling that, on the average, African-Americans are more expressive at the moment of death and at the funeral than are Euro-Americans (Rosenblatt & Wallace, 2005b). There are cultures in which grieving people may become mute (e.g., Wikan, 1988, writing about women in Cairo, Egypt). There are cultures where bereaved people may injure themselves at the onset of bereavement or become so enraged as to be dangerous to others (Rosenblatt, Walsh, & Jackson, 1976). There are cultures where sadness and grieving are typically masked by smiles (e.g., Heider, 2011, writing about the Minangkaubau of West Sumatra, Indonesia). These culture-based emotional differences, in fact, all culture-based matters discussed in this chapter, challenge simplistic, ethnocentric notions about grief pathology. If the concept of grief pathology means anything at all, it must be applied with awareness of the culture(s) involved. What is pathology in one culture may be normal, accepted, and even desirable in another.

Often socialization has played a big part and continues to do so in shaping the genders in a culture to grieve in patterns that differ, so one would not find women doing certain things that grieving men do not or vice versa. Among the trends in gender differences across cultures, there are more cultures in which if anyone weeps in bereavement it is a woman and if any one rages in bereavement it is a man (Rosenblatt, Walsh, & Jackson, 1976). But it would be a mistake to take the gender patterns in any specific culture and assume they are universal, or even to assume that they are necessarily always followed in the culture in which one notes the patterns.

Cultures differ widely in which significant family and community members are likely to be present when a person is terminally ill or has died. Related to this cultural practice, cultures differ quite a bit in who counts as the principal mourners when someone dies. In many cultures, the people likely to be present and to express strong feelings may include many more paternal kin than maternal kin, because the large majority of cultural groups around the world have kinship systems centered on the male line. In quite a few cultures, those who would be most heavily involved would include a large extended family or even a clan (e.g., the Hmong, see Fadiman, 1997), rather than the nuclear family that might often be involved in many families in the United States.

Many cultures have a defined mourning period that might last 6 months, a year, or longer, during which the principal mourners are limited in what they can do or what they can wear and in their affective expression (Rosenblatt, Walsh, & Jackson, 1976). For some people, not being able to engage in culturally appropriate mourning is very upsetting and may even be experienced as dangerous to themselves, their family, or the spirit of the deceased. In many cultures with extended mourning periods, the period of formal mourning is ended by a second funeral, which may include ritual handling and disposal of the remains of the deceased (Rosenblatt, Walsh, & Jackson, 1976).

Cultures differ in how the deceased is thought of. A deceased family member may be understood to continue as an active and helpful presence in the lives of surviving family members. But in some cultures the deceased may be seen as dangerous to the living or dangerous if the proper rituals are not practiced. In some cultures these matters may change over the months following a death. For example, shortly after a death people may fear that the deceased will want other family members to die to keep him or her company, but years later the spirit of the deceased may be seen as no longer interested in the lives of the survivors.

Grieving people in many cultures develop stories (narratives) about the person who died, the dying, the death, and the consequences of the death (Rogers, 2004; Seale, 1998). These stories reflect culture and the life experiences that are significant in that culture. For example, in the United States, with its long and harsh history of racism, African-American narratives about a deceased family member may address how the life and the dying of deceased were affected by racism (Rosenblatt & Wallace, 2005a). And the narratives people in a culture develop reflect their belief systems, their understandings of how the human body works, their understandings of where misfortune comes from, and their understandings of the actions of the spirits of the deceased in the lives of the living. For example, Hmong immigrants in Australia (Rice, 2000) who are trying to make sense of child and maternal death may turn to traditional beliefs that the woman carried too heavy a physical load, that she behaved badly toward her parents, that her labor in childbirth was too long and difficult, that the life aura of the mother and baby were imbalanced, or the mother had a chance encounter with a malevolent spirit. Or, to take another kind of example, in some cultures most or all deaths are seen as caused by humans, even deaths that many in the United States would consider deaths by disease, natural causes, or accident. In such cultures, an important part of grief narratives is the identification of who was responsible for the death and why and how that person caused the death (for example, Brison, 1992, describing a culture in Papua New Guinea). However, in some cultures, narratives are not an important part of grieving. In particular, there are cultures where people do not often talk about a death. For example, Turkish family members may not talk about a death with each other and may expect visitors not to mention the death (Cimete & Kuguoglu, 2006). This constraint minimizes the development of shared narratives and perhaps even the development of personal narratives.

Cultures are not monolithic, internally consistent, or unchanging. There could be quite a lot of diversity in a culture in, say, ritual practices at a death, the meaning of dying in a certain way, ideas about how to grieve, or the importance of observing a particular mourning practice. For example, Israeli Jewish culture offers contradictory values about what a good death is (Leichtentritt, 2004). Or, to take another example, Muslims in a small town in the Netherlands are diverse in how they observe the religious injunction to bathe the corpse of a family member (Venhorst, 2012-2013). And cultures change. They may change in contact with other cultures or as their economic and political environments change. But not everyone in a culture changes at the same time or in the same ways, so culture change increases a culture's diversity in how people deal with death. Even within a family there may be substantial differences in views about how to deal with a death or how to grieve. Also, some families have members who have roots in more than one culture. When there is diversity within a culture or family, there may be interpersonal tension or conflict at the time of a death or afterward as the cultural differences in dealing with dying and death play out. There also may be intrapersonal tensions as a person wrestles with internalized competing cultural values about what to believe, what to do, what is proper, and so on (see, for example, Lohmann, 2005, writing about a situation in Papua New Guinea where people in a community are torn between traditional beliefs and recently acquired Christian beliefs). Nor is culture change always in the direction of abandoning traditional ways. In some cultures, people have worked to revive traditional ways. For example, some Muscogee Creek Indians of Oklahoma have revived interest in and participation in ceremonial grounds death rituals (Walker, 2008). Then, too, sometimes what changes is not the cultural practice but the meaning and function of the practice—for example, Edwards et al. (2009) have written about how a particular Maori cultural practice in New Zealand has changed from helping the spirit of the deceased to move to the next world to being a way to recruit support for the most bereaved.

Some thanatologists emphasize the common humanity we all share with regard to dying and death, giving a sense that we are all in important ways the same. Perhaps there is similarity across cultures in certain matters. For example, for most people in the many described cultures around the world a death of somebody close to them has an emotional impact and causes sadness and personal disruption. But there is no good evidence supporting the notion that how people deal with death is the same across cultures (Klass, 1999b). In fact, it is consistent with this chapter and with the crosscultural research literature to assume that there is substantial diversity of cultures in all matters dealing with dying, death, grief, and mourning. Thus, even if it is true that for most people in the many described cultures around the world a death of somebody close to them has an emotional impact and causes sadness and personal disruption, the emotional impacts are quite diverse, the way sadness is expressed is quite diverse, and the personal disruptions are all quite diverse.

Many cultures are minority cultures, surrounded by a dominant culture that may limit their culturally appropriate ways of dealing with death. According to Fadiman (1997), Hmong immigrants to the United States from Laos, for example, may find hospitals resistant to the large clan gathering when a person is dying that is very important in Hmong culture. The local community and police may try to stop them from carrying out important rituals that involve animal sacrifice or four days of drumming and chanting. But if these rituals are not carried out, Hmong grieving may be entangled in anxieties and fears about the spirit of the deceased, what other Hmong think, and a sense of having let down both living and dead. Moreover, the Hmong may be under pressure from hospital authorities to autopsy a body of a deceased relative, but body mutilation has horrifying meanings in Hmong culture. One can argue that despite the demands of a surrounding culture, people in a minority culture need to grieve and dispose of a body their way, that anything less than that violates their human rights and may have dire consequences for the course of their grieving, relationships within the family and community, and the spiritual well-being of surviving family and community members and the deceased.

Relating and Helping Across Cultural Lines

If we want to understand and help people we cannot make the assumption that they are like us or like people from our own culture(s) or that they grieve and mourn the way a textbook or a theory says people do or should (Rosenblatt, 1993, 1997, 2012). The theories and realities offered in psychological and related sciences certainly have their uses, but they are generally embedded in a particular culture and history in ways that should make us very cautious in using them (Gone, 2011). We also should not stereotype people, making assumptions that because they belong to a specific culture we know how they will and should grieve. In any culture, people are diverse. From that perspective, fact sheets or other materials that give a simple characterization of how the people in some culture deal with death can be very misleading (Gunaratnam, 1997; Rosenblatt, 1993, 1997, 2012). We have to be open to, understand, and respect cultural differences in the emotionality of bereavement and in how to understand and make sense of a death. And as part of that, we have to be open to the complexity, diversity, and changing qualities of how people within a culture deal with death.

To be effective, those of us who work with the dying, the bereaved, and their families have to be knowledgeable about culture and ethnicity (Stroebe & Schut, 1998), at the very least because it makes us aware of possibilities. For example, knowing that in Zulu culture there is great stigma about HIV/AIDS and that widows traditionally do not look others in the eye (Rosenblatt & Nkosi, 2007), we will be prepared for that if we are working with a Zulu widow and, perhaps even more, we will be open to that as a possibility in working with anyone, no matter what their culture. But even more we have to develop good skills at understanding the beliefs and realities of the specific people who we hope to help and to respect what they say as valid, important, and appropriate. At the very least that means we need to put aside our assumptions about how people do or should deal with death and be ready to work comfortably and nonjudgmentally with people as they reveal themselves to us in the situations in which we encounter them.

In situations where it is not rude to be curious, it can be useful to ask people what they understand to be true and what they think is appropriate for themselves and for us in relationship with them. If a person thinks and feels primarily in a language other than English, it can be helpful to realize that there are concepts, feelings, relationships, and much else that do not translate well, if at all, into English. Related to this awareness about language differences, it might be helpful to make an attempt to understand key terms in the other person's language, for example, feeling terms. And if the terms do not translate well into English, it could be of great value to develop at least an intuitive sense of their meanings and to engage in conversation that respects those terms. For example, there is a traditional term in Ojibwe, *gashkendam* (McNally, 2000, p. 109), which combines grief, lonesomeness, affliction, dejection, homesickness, and melancholy. Part of providing support to someone who is Ojibwe and who speaks of feeling *gashkendam* following a loss might be to ask the person to help one to understand the term and then for it to become a term that is used in your conversation with each other. But then understanding the language of another might not simply be a matter of learning to translate and learning the meanings of words that do not translate well. Sometimes people do not put their feelings and understandings to words in a direct way. For example, in some cultures, crucial aspects of people's thoughts and communication about the aftermath of a death might not be statements of feeling or memory but something else—for example, proverbs, tales, parables, and culturally meaningful nonverbal gestures (Bagilishya, 2000). Understanding these types of communication too can be difficult but might be important if one is to be of help. Sometimes it is of great help to others if we make an effort to understand their terms and meanings in their own language. In fact, for a would-be helper even to try to learn what might be appropriate to say in another's language upon entering the presence of someone who is dying or grieving might be very helpful. But at the same time, people realize that there are cultural differences and may be tolerant of our attempts to understand and deal with them, even if what we do may be inappropriate or amateurish by their cultural standards.

From the perspective of socialization, a time of need or crisis may be when people most struggle to grow as individuals, whether they want to or not. For example, people who are dying or who are bereaved might hunger for a sense of what is normal and appropriate and how they can best deal with their difficulties, fears, and internal changes. This is a time when some turn to others. It may be a time when they try to learn more about their own culture(s). It is also a time when they might be open to aspects of other cultures; even rather alien ones, that offer something that fits for them. However, it may be unhelpful, alienating, and harmful to try to change people from their socialized, culture-based actions, thoughts, beliefs, and rituals. It may be precisely when people are dying or grieving that they most need to function as they think their culture and socialization tells them to function. In adhering to their own culture and socialization they may find a sense of security, of knowing what is right to do, of giving meaning to all that is going on, and of doing things right by the standards of God or the gods. From that perspective, the socialization that goes on at this time might be as much socialization for the would-be helper from an outside culture as it is for the dying or the bereaved.

Chapter 15

Religion and Spirituality in Loss, Grief, and Mourning

Dennis Klass

Issues in religion and spirituality are inescapable when we grieve and when we try to help the bereaved because religion is about human limitations. To be sure a great deal of what we call religion and spirituality is about claiming political power for one group and denying it to other groups, or about rules that keep the society orderly, or about maintaining ethnic heritage. Still, at their best, religions are about life on the boundaries: the boundaries between myself and others, between meaning and absurdity, between hope and despair, between life and death. Difficult bereavements bring us to the boundary of life and death, and so there the potential meaning of life and the potential meaningless of life becomes clear, the possibilities of both hope and despair are present, the boundary between me and the person who has died as well as the boundaries between me and other mourners become both defined and blurred.

Even though the religious issues might be at the heart of grief, religion may or may not be helpful to people as they try to come to terms with a significant death (Tedeschi and Calhoun, 2006). Grief tests the assumptions about how the universe works and our place and power in the universe (see Landsman, 2002). For some people, their prior religious life proves adequate to the task. They come out of their grief more secure in their faith than when they entered it. A man told me that as he stood in front of his mother's body in the casket asking why, his father quoted scripture to him, "The Lord giveth and the Lord taketh away. Blessed be the name of the Lord." At that moment, he told me, he knew he was called to be a Christian minister. On the other hand, for some people, their prior religious life is not adequate to their grief. I remember sitting in a meeting of bereaved parents when the topic was Where was God when my child died? One woman said that after her child died she lost her faith. Then she added, "But I got a new one that's better." Testing, confirming, modifying, or abandoning prior religion or spirituality is not simply a matter of belief. "Coming to terms with the loss of our assumptive worlds is primarily about learning new ways of acting and being in the world" (Attig, 2002, p. 64; see Klass, 1999, chapter 5 for a fuller discussion of the vicissitudes of faith in individual grief).

The religious rituals, beliefs, and symbols that we find in grief are the same as those that offer guidelines in other aspects of life. A basic religious question, for example, is what is our relationship to our body? All religions offer guidelines on how to dispose of corpses as well as on the moral management of our sex drives. Should the body be preserved to await physical resurrection? Should the enduring bones be separated from the perishable flesh? Should the body be burned because the true self has no further need of it? To take another example, religions offer possible meanings for both physical and emotional suffering. Is suffering positive? Or is suffering negative because happiness is the normative or natural human state? Is it an occasion for participating in Christ's redemptive suffering or to realize Buddhism's First Noble Truth, or is suffering simply to be endured stoically or deadened as much as possible? When the bereaved tap into the rituals, symbols, and beliefs of religions, they do so within the whole context of the rituals, beliefs, and symbols that are woven into their lives and into the communities and cultures in which their lives are set.

There are, of course, many assumptions people make about how the universe works and about their place and power in that universe, and many, many ways by which religious meanings can be symbolized. We are at a very interesting time in human history right now. Most people in other times had access to only one or two religious traditions. If you were European, you were probably Christian. If you were Thai, you were probably Buddhist. With developments in technology of communications and travel, all the world's religious traditions have a voice in modern times. There are many Pentecostal Christians in Mexico City and Tibetan Buddhists in New York City. We have Americans who have never been on a reservation, but for whom Native American rituals are meaningful, and Hindus who find French existentialism fits their life. Our age, then, is characterized by the meeting and mixing of religious traditions in a way that has few historical precedents.

In traditional societies with only one religious tradition, Tony Walter (1994) says religious rituals, symbols, and teachings prescribed the inner experience of the mourner. Prescribe literally means *prewrite*, that is, the community rituals supplied the narrative that was the inner experience of the mourner. With the rise of modernity, however, the old rituals lost much of their power to order the mourners' inner worlds. People in grief today, therefore, have an incredible range of symbols available to them. That means their grief narratives are not prewritten, so they must engage in the difficult task of writing their narratives for themselves. There are, of course, many for whom the rituals still prescribe the inner narrative. For religious leaders, that is at it should be (Grassman and Whitaker, 2006). For others, however, their religious heritage is a grab bag of images from popular culture, a few texts and living examples from grandparents, and some symbols that have helped them make sense of their adolescent struggles, all integrated, more or less, into the radical individualism that permeates American culture (see Bellah, Madsen, Sullivan, & Tipton, 1985).

That means that if we are to take grief seriously, especially if we want to hold ourselves out as experts in helping the bereaved, we need to have a rather good grasp of the symbols by which people find meaning or lose meaning, and the religious traditions that supply those symbols. In this brief chapter we cannot give readers the advanced course in world religions that would be helpful to them, nor can we reduce the world's religions to a few simple formulas. We can, however, think about some problems in the way religion and spirituality are presented in a great deal of the clinical lore about grief, and we can present a method that allows helpers to work with people from many religious traditions and at the same time give themselves a bottoms-up education in the world's religious traditions.

Is There Spirituality Without "Religion?"

We need to spend a few moments looking at the words *religion* and *spirituality*. Spirituality and religion are often defined in opposition to one another, in the clinical lore and popular literature about grief. Religion is thus negatively associated with the external, authoritarian doctrines of Christianity, while spirituality is positively associated with the individual search for truth, meaning, and authenticity (Garces-Foley, 2006). Thus we often hear, I'm spiritual but not religious. This way of defining the terms, however, dates only from the mid-1980s and does not hold up to critical analysis. Lucy Bregman (2006), a scholar in the psychology of religion, says the term *spirituality* is a useful "glow word." She finds that not only has the term *spirituality* become fuzzier rather than clearer over time, but by the beginning of the 21st century, it had been sprung free of any intellectual or cultural context. She notes Unruh, Versnel, and Kerr's survey (2002) of as many empirical and clinical studies as they could find that focused on spirituality. They discovered 92 definitions of spirituality, which they could sort, only with a great deal of effort, into six very disparate categories.

Human service professionals, especially those who base their practice in humanistic psychology, are more likely to distinguish between religion and spirituality than other people do. In both the United States and Ireland hospice, personnel tend to be spiritual while the patients tend to be religious (MacConville, 2006; Garces-Foley, 2006). Thus there may be a real disconnect between those who would help and those they would help.

The conclusion I would draw from this brief look at the claim that there is a spirituality separate from religion is that we need to recognize that spirituality is a religion too. If we use any of the 92 definitions as we work with the bereaved, we are missing most of what the bereaved are experiencing as they stand at the boundary of life and death, meaning and absurdity, hope and despair. Spirituality may be the religion that provides meaning to our lives, but the bereaved we seek to help very well might have religions with different symbols that give meaning to their lives.

Official Religion and Lived Religion

One of the difficulties we face as we try to help the bereaved from religious traditions that are different from our own is the gap between the official version of a religion and the same religion as we find it in bereaved individuals and communities. The problem is a practical one because as we look for the literature that will help us learn about bereavement in a religious tradition, we often find that it is written by religious leaders who are describing the official version or orthodox practice, not what people actually do. The official theology of a religion is only one element of the way grief is narrated or the way grief is expressed. In different cultural settings the same religion often provides very different styles of grief. Unni Wikan (1988), a Norwegian anthropologist, studied mothers whose children had died in Egypt and Bali, both Muslim cultures. Officially, Islam teaches that each death has been predetermined, even predestined, but the teaching is interpreted differently in different cultural settings. In Egypt, emotions are to be expressed, because mental health is damaged if they are held in. Egyptian village women beseech God "to help them through the miseries they see as inescapably grounded in their own human lot... Theirs is a very close and present God, compassionate, just, and forgiving. Should not God not understand that sadness is one thing, subjugation to his will is another?" (Wikan, 1988, p. 459).

Wikan says that in Bali the family, including the mother, try to restrain their emotions and work to maintain a calm composure, especially to those outside the family. "But even among intimates, their reactions will be moderate, and laughter, joking, and cheerfulness mingle with mutely expressed sadness" (p. 452). In Bali, she says, sad or negative emotions are not to be expressed because the emotions can spill from the individual to the community and thus cause the spirit of the individual and of the community to weaken. In the weakened state both the individual and the community would be vulnerable to black magic that causes up to 50% of deaths.

We find the same range of cultural differences within the official versions in all religious traditions. For example, the realization that all things are impermanent forms the basis of Buddhism. The suffering in grief is, for esoteric Buddhism, the beginning of the path that will lead to enlightenment. "All life is suffering" is the First Noble Truth. Yet in many Buddhist cultures, the religious rituals during the dying process and in bereavement are not to realize the Noble Truth. Rather the rituals are to build merit, often by devotion to a Bodhisattva, that can then be transferred to the deceased to help them toward a better rebirth. To achieve enlightenment, Buddhism officially teaches, we have as many lifetimes as we need. Reincarnation, rebirth to another lifetime, is a literal reality. Yet, in Japan, although the doctrine of rebirth remains in the tradition, in fact the dead, even the great founders of the various Buddhist sects, become ancestors and stay a part of the family and so are not reborn. For American converts to Tibetan Buddhism, reincarnation plays almost no part in their grief, and merit plays no role in in how they see themselves helping the bereaved or continuing their own bonds with the deceased (see Goss and Klass, 2005, chapter 2; Goss & Klass, 2006).

The examples from Islam and Buddhism that we have given illustrate how the official teaching of a religion is not a good place to learn about how to help the bereaved from those traditions. We could, had we space, give further examples from all the world's religious traditions.

Beyond the gap between official religious teachings and the way the religion interacts with grief, we also see that there are major historical changes in all religious traditions in terms of some basic themes that come up in bereaved individuals and families. In some cases, when people immigrate from one culture to another, the religion changes in just a generation or two. Bereaved children or grandchildren in immigrant families may have very different religious frames than their bereaved parents or grandparents. There are also significant changes over the centuries. In the Western religious traditions, for example, continuing bonds with the dead are often described in terms of the dead appearing to the living as ghosts. When we look at those accounts over the last 2500 years, we find an incredible diversity as well as a historical development (Finucane, 1996). We find great differences between individuals in any Western tradition, and between subcultures in how the appearances of the dead are described, what the dead expect, and how the living can respond to the dead. Heaven as a place the dead go has also undergone a lengthy historical development (McCannell & Lang, 1988). In clinical work, we often find any individual may hold simultaneously several ways of understanding the deceased's being in heaven and experience their continuing bond with the deceased in ways that may or may not match their ways of understanding heaven. Unless we point it out, the bereaved may feel no contradictions between those views and experiences. When we investigate the official teachings of the religion about afterlife and continuing interactions with the dead, we are likely to find they bear little resemblance to the heaven in which the bereaved hope to rejoin their dead family members or to the active interaction with the dead that the bereaved maintain.

Learning World Religions From the Bottom Up

Amidst all this diversity, how are we to help the bereaved with the religious issues that are so central to grief? I would like to suggest a practical scheme that we can use to help the bereaved in religious/spiritual issues whether they be in our own cultural world or from cultural worlds very different from ours. First I will define the elements we find in religion as it is lived and show that each can be both problematic and helpful in grief. Second, I will look at the relationship of these elements that we can use to locate ourselves within the religious life of the bereaved.

Our definition must be useful in two ways: First, it must be applicable to all the world's religious traditions. Thus, an answer like, Religion is beliefs about God is wrong because not all religions have a god (and some have no god or gods). Further, in most religions, belief is not the most important part (see Smart, 1996). Second, to be useful we need a definition that will allow us better to understand the complexities of people living their everyday inner and interpersonal lives, not just the official teachings (see Chidester, 2002).

A useful definition of religion includes three elements. First, encounter or merger with transcendent reality, that is, the sense that there is something beyond our mundane existence that we can, at least for moments, experience as an inner reality. Second, a worldview, that is, a higher intelligence, purpose, or order that gives meaning to the events and relationships in our lives. Third, a community in which transcendent reality and worldview are validated. We can see this triune structure in many religious traditions. In Islam, for example, Allah is the god who can be found but who cannot be understood by human intelligence, the prophet Mohammed was given the revelation to which humans should conform their lives, and the Ummah is the community of all those who submit to Allah. Buddhism has the three refuges: the Buddha, the Dharma, and the Sangha. Christianity affirms the trinity of God the father who is unknowable in Himself, God the son who is in human form, and God the holy spirit who is the giver of understanding and the under girder of the church. In Chinese religion, which is an amalgam of Taoism and Confucianism, heaven or ti is the unnamable reality, Tao is the ordering principle in nature, and li is the ordering principle by which humans can find harmony within society. In each of these traditions, the sense of the transcendent, finding purpose, and membership in community are all necessary elements of religious or spiritual life.

A significant death can reverberate in each of those elements in both helpful and unhelpful ways. In the first element: If when I pray, I feel close to God who feels like a protective father, who has blessed my marriage, I might very well feel abandoned by that father when the marriage was cut short because He did not answer my prayers that my husband recover from cancer. On the other hand, I might also trust that as God has protected me and my family on earth, He continues to protect my husband who is now with God in heaven.

In the second element: If I believe there is a divinely ordained plan for everything and that nothing happens without a reason, it may be difficult for me to understand any reason for a stray bullet from a fight among drug gangs going through the daycare window killing my preschooler. If, on the other hand, I believe that I have very little control over what happens to me, but I must control how I respond to events, then I might not wonder why my child died, but be very determined to make something good come from it.

In the third element: If I feel like I am alone in my grief, I will have a more difficult time. Crying alone is incredibly painful. Crying with others who are also sad over the death is painful, but also comforting. Communities that cry and remember together are helpful in grief. On the other hand, if members of my family or community keep my grief at a distance, and negatively judge my way of grieving, then the community is unhelpful. I remember a young woman whose child miscarried in the seventh month. Some older women in the church where she had been a very active member kept asking what she had done wrong to make the baby miscarry while the minister kept telling her that the baby's death was God's will and that her tears were a sign of her lack of faith. Needless to say, that community was not helpful to her.

In each element I have given positive and negative examples using only the Western religious traditions because I think those are the traditions with which most readers are familiar. But as we learn how to include religious issues in our care of the grieving in a multicultural and multireligious world, we will have to become acquainted with how these elements interact with grief in the many religions, even the secular religion that believes in spirituality. We have very limited resources for working with multiple religious traditions. Kathleen Garces-Foley's *Death and Religion in a Changing World* (2006) is a good place to begin. The book *Dead but not Lost: Grief Narratives in Religious Traditions* (2005) that I wrote with Robert Goss is another.

These elements are not discrete. They work together. I have found that we can diagram the aspects as follows:

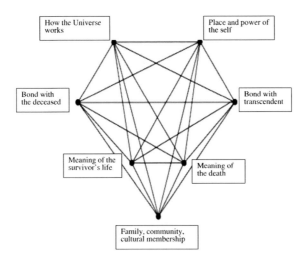

The first element, encounter or merger with transcendent reality, is our bond with the transcendent reality (God in the Western traditions) that is often connected with our bond or continuing bond with the dead person. The second element, a worldview, that is, a higher intelligence, purpose, or order that gives meaning to the events and relationships in our lives, is expressed in our assumptions of how the world works and what place and power we have in the universe. The third element is our membership in a community.

My experience as a professional helping the bereaved is that as a statement in one of the boxes changes, all the others will change. For example, very often as the continuing bond with the deceased is established comfortably in the survivor's life, the bond with the transcendent becomes less troubling, the meaning of a survivor's life becomes clearer, and troubled relationships in the community or family become less of a barrier. To take another example, when the bereaved person's relation to the community changes from alienated to integrated, the bond with the deceased and with transcendent reality feels surer as does the meaning of the survivor's life, and we often see a development in the bereaved person's understanding of the meaning of the death as well as of the dead person's life (see Klass, 1999, chapter 6).

As we grieve or as we work with any bereaved person or group of bereaved people, we can listen closely and understand the content of each of the boxes as they are experiencing them. We can also listen for the content of each of the boxes to which their community's rituals, beliefs, and symbols are pointing them. From what I have said earlier, it should be clear that competent bereavement specialists will be especially attentive to disconnects or discrepancies between the experience of the bereaved person and the expectations of the community.

We do not have to know, then, how Muslims grieve to work with a Muslim individual or family, just as we do not have to know what the Christian, Jewish, Buddhist, Taoist, or whatever, way of grieving. We have already seen that the official guidelines and narrative for the bereaved often have little to do with what bereaved people actually do. All we have to do is to listen carefully and say as best we can how this individual or this family understands how the universe works and their place and power in the universe, the meaning of their lives and the meaning of the death, their bond with transcendent reality and their bond with the deceased, and the meaning for them of their family, cultural, and community memberships. We can learn our world religions, then, from the bottom up, not from the top down. Instead of beginning work with people from traditions different from our own with a stereotyped version of their religion in our mind, we can let the bereaved be our world religions teachers. If we are open and listen carefully we might find that people in our own religious tradition—even if it is spirituality—are quite different from us in how religion interacts with their grief. We might also find that in some significant ways, we and those we would help are alike, even if we are not the same.

Chapter 16

Historical and Contemporary Perspectives on Loss, Grief, and Mourning

Charles A. Corr and Donna M. Corr

This chapter explores some of the many ways in which clinicians, researchers, and scholars have tried to explicate the concepts of loss, bereavement, grief, and mourning, together with examples of some forms of postdeath assistance for bereaved persons.

Some Comments about Language

To begin, it might seem a bit odd that there should be many different understandings and interpretations of experiences that are as basic and as familiar as loss, grief, and mourning. After all, who among us has not encountered some of these experiences in his or her life? Perhaps, however, it is precisely because these experiences are so fundamental in human life that they have been looked at from many different perspectives by scholars and researchers. That may be why there now appear to be altogether too many theories of loss, grief, and mourning to examine in a single chapter. Consequently, here we can only survey some of the most prominent accounts of these subjects.

Before we begin, it might be helpful to note some orienting thoughts. First, losses can take many forms, most of which do not involve death and have been called "nonfinite losses" (Harris, 2011). Second, almost all primary losses of all types are accompanied by secondary losses, although the latter may not be immediately evident. Third, *bereavement* is the term most often applied to the situation of individuals who have experienced death-related losses. Fourth, *grief* is the term that identifies reactions to loss; properly used, this term applies not just to emotional reactions but to all of the human reactions to loss whether they are physical, behavioral, psychological (cognitive or affective), social, or spiritual in nature. Fifth, *mourning* is the term used by some writers to designate all of the intrapsychic and interpsychic processes of coping or learning to live with loss and grief; by others it is restricted to social, public, or ritualized responses to loss. How one understands mourning is critical, but those understandings are complicated by authors who do not explain how they are using this term, who use it in different or inconsistent ways, or who do not clarify whether it is distinct from or equivalent to the term *grieving*. Sixth, cultural, religious, spiritual, social, and individual factors very likely influence how grief and mourning are experienced and expressed (Parkes, Laungani, & Young, 1997; Rosenblatt, 2008). Seventh, outcomes of mourning have been described in many ways, such as regaining equilibrium or the ability to function in healthy ways in life, relearning the world, developing new normals, or reconstructing meaning in life.

It may help to note here that terms such as *recovery*, *completion*, or *resolution* are generally not favored by contemporary scholars since those words may imply a misunderstanding of bereavement and grief or an implicit commitment to a fixed end point for mourning. Even metaphors such as *healing* or *getting through* should be used with caution since they may depict mourning in both helpful and unhelpful ways. Above all, despite their prominence in the public mind and in some forms of professional education, linear, sequential, or fixed stages in mourning have not been favored in most recent thinking on these subjects. This may not be so surprising in light of the following comments from the most well-known proponents of stage-based models (Kübler-Ross & Kessler, 2005, p. 7):

> The stages have evolved since their introduction, & they have been very misunderstood over the past three decades... They are responses to loss that many people have, but there is not a typical response to loss, as there is no typical loss. Our grief is as individual as our lives.

> The five stages...are tools to help us frame and identify what we may be feeling. But they are not stops on some linear timeline in grief. Not everyone goes through all of them or goes in a prescribed order.

Mourning as Detachment

Sigmund Freud was among the first to address these subjects, perhaps best known for comments in, *Mourning and Melancholia* (1917/1961b). By *melancholia* Freud meant what would now be called *clinical depression*, a deviant, complicated, and unhealthy form of mourning. Freud's mature view of normal or uncomplicated mourning seems to have been that it involves a healthy, nonpathological response to the loss of a loved person or object (physical or symbolic). Because one has invested one's psychological energy in such a person or object, there is pain involved in its loss. According to Freud, mourning represents the work involved in uncoupling and achieving detachment or emancipation from the lost object, work that reflects both a desire to hold onto that object and a growing recognition that the object is no longer available as it once was. This work is complex and can take a great deal of time and energy. For Freud, the goal is to withdraw libido (broadly conceived as psychic energy) from the lost object, thereby freeing the ego for new and healthy attachments. This is the *work* of grief. As Freud wrote in *Totem and Taboo* (1912-1913/1961a, p. 65), "Mourning has a quite precise psychical task to perform: its function is to detach the survivor's memories and hopes from the dead." Many have taken the goal of detachment as Freud's last word on the subject, but Siggins (1966) and Rando (1993) have suggested that may overstate or misstate his overall view of mourning.

Acute Grief

In a seminal paper, Lindemann (1944) described typical characteristics of acute grief, including somatic distress, preoccupation with the image of the deceased, guilt, hostility, and alterations in usual patterns of conduct. Many bereaved individuals also adopt traits belonging to the deceased in their behavior. According to Lindemann, grief work involves efforts to emancipate oneself from bondage to the deceased, readjust to an environment in which the deceased is missing, and form new relationships. Individuals who try to avoid the intense distress involved in their experiences of grief may only inhibit and complicate their grief work. For Lindemann, delaying or distorting grief reactions leads to morbid or unhealthy forms of grief.

Attachment Theory and Stages of Grief

Drawing on a variety of perspectives and sources of evidence, attachment theory seeks to explain the development of affectional bonds or attachments between child and parent, and between one adult and another, in both human beings and higher order primates. John Bowlby developed this theory to revise some central tenets of psychoanalytic theory by showing that grief responses are instinctual, adaptational, and valuable for survival. That understanding of grief enabled him to explain both normal and pathological processes of mourning. His views on these subjects appear in early articles (e.g., 1961) and in his three-volume work, *Attachment and Loss* (1969-1980).

Drawing in part on the work of Colin Murray Parkes (1972) with London widows, Bowlby described four general phases seen in the normal, uncomplicated responses of bereaved individuals to the loss of a loved one: (a) numbing, (b) yearning and searching, (c) disorganization and despair, and (d) reorganization. Complicated (that is, abnormal) responses are essentially distortions in onset, degree, or duration. Urges to locate, recover, and reunite with a loved one, along with the anxiety, yearning, anger, protest, and searching that typically accompany them, are not pathological in themselves. They are part of a constructive process of making real (realization) in one's inner world that which is already real in the objective world. Over time, however, healthy mourning leads to accepting the permanence of a death-related loss. If not, something has gone wrong and grief becomes chronic or conflicted.

Tasks in Mourning

Worden (1982, 1991, 2002, 2009) recommended that we think of mourning as an active process involving four tasks, here described in their most recent iteration.

- **To accept the reality of the loss:** This task involves overcoming disbelief and denial of death by acknowledging and accepting the reality of the death.
- **To process the pain of grief:** Productive mourning acknowledges that it is appropriate to experience pain during bereavement as long as the ways in which that pain is experienced are not overwhelming for the bereaved individual.

- **To adjust to an environment without the deceased:** In pursuing this task, bereaved individuals engage in a voyage of discovery to determine the significance of the now-severed relationship, to identify each of the various roles that the deceased played in the relationship, to adjust to the fact that the deceased is no longer available to fill those roles, and often to develop new skills to fulfill roles formerly satisfied by the deceased.
- Worden described a fourth task in different ways: **to withdraw emotional energy and reinvest it in another relationship** (1982, p. 15); **to emotionally relocate the deceased and move on with life** (1991, p. 16; 2002, p. 35); **to find an enduring connection with the deceased in the midst of embarking on a new life** (2009, p. 50). The main point of this fourth task is to encourage bereaved persons to modify or restructure their relationships with the deceased in ways that remain satisfying but that also reflect the changed circumstances of life after a death. This task requires bereaved persons to reconceive their own personal identity, restructure their relationships with the deceased in the light of the loss that has taken place, avoid becoming neurotically encumbered by the past in ways that diminish future quality in living, and remain open to new attachments and other relationships.

Worden's tasks reflect an interpretation of mourning as, in principle, a proactive way of striving to manage one's loss and grief. They depict mourning as involving a set of interrelated tasks requiring effort intended to enable the bereaved person to regain some measure of control over his or her life. Worden (2009, p. 39) wrote that although the tasks of mourning "do not need to be addressed in a specific order, there is some ordering suggested in their definitions." He believes that mourners must accomplish these tasks before mourning can be completed.

The Six "R" Processes of Mourning

Rando (1993) described mourning in terms of six R processes: (1) Recognize the loss—acknowledge and understand the death; (2) React to the separation—experience the pain of the loss; feel, identify, accept, and give expression to all of the psychological reactions to the loss; and identify and mourn secondary losses; (3) Recollect and reexperience the deceased and the relationship—review and remember realistically; revive and reexperience one's feelings; (4) Relinquish old attachments to the deceased and the old assumptive world; (5) Readjust to move adaptively into the new world without forgetting the old—revise the assumptive world, develop a new relationship with the deceased, adopt new ways of being in the world, and form a new identity; (6) Reinvest.

According to Rando, mourners need to acknowledge and gain insight into their losses, experience and express their reactions to those losses, connect with and restructure their former attachments, and find ways to move forward in new modes of living. Rando also drew attention to the many secondary or associated losses that are always involved in an important primary loss. Mention of an assumptive world reminds us that we all function within a set of assumptions concerning what we take to be real about ourselves and about the world around us. The process of reinvestment involves using one's resources in appropriate and rewarding ways both to form a new relationship with the deceased loved one and to develop other or new sources of gratification.

Rando maintained that these six R processes must be undertaken for healthy mourning. They are, she wrote, "interrelated and tend to build upon one another, [although] a number of them may occur simultaneously" (1993, p. 44). Even though they are set forth in a typical order, the sequence is not invariant: "Mourners may move back and forth among the processes, with such movement illustrating the nonlinear and fluctuating course of mourning" (p. 44).

The Dual Process Model

Stroebe and Schut's dual process model (1999, 2010) combines three key elements in its account of coping processes employed by bereaved persons: (1) loss-oriented processes are concerned primarily in coping with loss and involve the intrusion of grief into the life of the bereaved, grief work, and breaking bonds or ties to the deceased, as well as resistance to change in the form of denial or avoidance of restoration changes; (2) restoration-oriented processes are concerned primarily in coping with restoration or going forward with effective living by attending to life changes, doing new things, and denial, avoidance, or distraction from grief; (3) the oscillation between these two processes reflects how grievers change their focus from time to time or even direct attention away from bereavement-related issues.

Note that the term *restoration* as it is used in this model is not about trying to make real once again the mourner's former world of lived experiences (which no longer exists) or the old assumptive world (which has also been shattered or at least rudely shaken by the loss). Rather, it has to do with efforts to adapt to the new world in which bereaved persons find themselves. What is restored, according to this model, is not a past mode of living, but the ability to live productively in the present and future. Thus, both loss-oriented and restoration-oriented processes address issues of coping; the difference between them is centered on their meaning or focus and the model insists that at various times a person coping with bereavement will shift back and forth (oscillate) between them or even take time out from these efforts. The dual process model also suggests that emphases in coping with bereavement may differ from one cultural group to another, one individual to another, and one moment to another.

Meaning Making

Numerous authors have stressed the importance of meaning making for individuals who have suffered a significant loss in their lives. For example, Attig (2000, 2010) has written about relearning the world as a process that involves simultaneously finding and making meaning on many levels. According to Attig, relearning the world includes grieving individually, within our families, and within our communities and cultures, in ways that "engage with several of the great mysteries of life in the human tradition" and that allow us to "make a multifaceted transition from loving in presence to loving in absence" (2001, p. 34).

Similarly, Neimeyer (e.g., 1998, 2000, 2001) has written extensively about the need for bereaved persons to engage in a process of reconstructing meaning in their lives and has asserted that, "Meaning reconstruction in response to a loss is the central process in grieving" (1998, p. 110). Any individual griever may engage in this process at different times, in different ways, and in different connections with his or her culture and community. When a bereaved person finds it difficult to engage in meaning reconstruction or is not able to accomplish this project, as might most often be seen in violent or traumatic bereavements, it has been argued that harmful effects will likely follow. (A contrary view has been offered by Davis, Wortman, Lehman, & Silver [2000] who presented evidence that at least some persons bereaved after a sudden, unexpected death do not attempt to seek meaning in their losses and may be no worse off for that.)

According to Neimeyer (2000, pp. 552-555) meaning reconstruction includes: (1) The attempt to find or create new meaning in the life of the survivor, as well as in the death of the loved one; (2) The integration of meaning, as well as its construction; (3) The construction of meaning as an interpersonal, as well as personal, process; (4) The anchoring of meaning making in cultural, as well as intimate, discursive contexts; (5) Tacit and preverbal, as well as explicit and articulate meanings; (6) The processes of meaning reconstruction, as well as its products.

Holland, Currier, and Neimeyer (2006) extended this point of view by distinguishing between sense-making and benefit-finding as two central forms of meaning making.

Sense-making denotes the comprehensibility of the loss or the survivor's capacity to find some sort of benign explanation for the seemingly inexplicable experience, often framed in philosophical or spiritual terms. Conversely, benefit-finding refers to the significance of the loss and entails the survivor's paradoxical ability to uncover a "silver lining" in the personal or social consequences of the loss, such as enhanced empathy, reordered life priorities, or a closer connection to other people within or beyond the family (p. 176).

Among the conclusions drawn by these authors from their empirical study are the following: (1) "[I]n general, sense-making is a stronger predictor of grief outcomes compared to benefit-finding" (p. 183); (2) These findings "conform to a larger body of empirical and theoretical literature, which challenges the notion that grief unfolds in predictable patterns over time" (p. 183); and (3) "In summary, these results call for more research on the 'multiple meanings of meaning'... particularly around the way in which these interact in adaptation to loss" (pp. 185-186).

Continuing Bonds

Drawing on research with bereaved children, spouses, and parents, as well as other sources, Klass, Silverman, and Nickman (1996) noted the importance for many bereaved persons of efforts to maintain a connection to the individual who has died. By contrast with interpretations of mourning as involving detachment from, letting go of, or forgetting the deceased, this viewpoint reflects the active efforts many bereaved persons make to maintain a continuing bond, an internal representation of or ongoing connection with the deceased individual. This bond is not static but dynamic. It involves negotiating and renegotiating the meaning of the loss over time. It develops in ways that can allow the deceased to remain a transformed or changed but ongoing presence in the inner lives of the bereaved. Connections of this type "provided solace, comfort and support, and eased the transition from the past to the future" (p. xviii).

According to these authors, although "the continuing bond has been overlooked or undervalued in most scholarly and clinical work" (p. xvii) and there has been "little social validation for the relationship people reported with the deceased or absent person" (p. xviii), continuing bonds involve new and altered relationships that reflect "the reality of how people experience and live their lives" (p. xix). They are aspects of normal mourning processes and do not represent psychopathology. Putting stress on continuing bonds in bereavement is, at least, an alternative to (if not a repudiation of) the view that mourning does or should lead to total disengagement from or severing bonds to the deceased.

Resilience

In recent years, George Bonanno (2009) has been the leading proponent of the idea that resilience is the most characteristic feature of the human experience of loss and trauma. He and his colleagues have reported empirical data from both pre-loss and post-loss situations showing that approximately 46% of those in their study exhibited little or no distress following a significant loss in their lives and were able to maintain relatively stable, healthy levels of psychological and physical functioning (Bonanno et al., 2002). In particular, Bonnano (2004) has argued that resilience in the face of loss or potential trauma represents a distinct trajectory from that of recovery, a trajectory in which normal functioning temporarily gives way to threshold or subthreshold psychopathology (e.g., symptoms of depression or posttraumatic stress disorder [PTSD]), usually for a period of at least several months, and then gradually returns to pre-event levels; resilience is more common than often believed, is not a pathological or dysfunctional form of absent grief, and does not lead to delayed grief reactions; and there are multiple and sometimes unexpected pathways to resilience.

Proponents of the concept of resilience in bereavement maintain that grief need not be overwhelming for most people, that the need to talk about loss is not essential for many bereaved people, and that positive emotions and laughter can help. This concept appears to undermine the so-called grief work hypothesis that all bereaved people do or must go through stages in coping with loss. Bonanno's view on this point is that "Grief work processes are appropriate for only a subset of bereaved individuals...most likely those actively struggling with the most severe levels of grief and distress...i.e., those exhibiting either the recovery or chronic symptom trajectories" (Bonanno, 2004, p. 21). This emphasis on resilience also appears to have implications for whether all or many bereaved people—as opposed to a relatively small portion of such individuals—require counseling or therapy to help with their adjustment to loss and grief.

Anticipatory Grief and Mourning

The concept of anticipatory grief was first introduced by Lindemann (1944) and has since been subject to numerous inquiries. In general, anticipatory grief refers to grief experiences that take place prior to but in connection with a significant loss, one that is expected to take place but has not yet occurred—for example, grief that occurs in advance of, but somehow still in relation to, impending death. A forewarning of death is a necessary condition for anticipatory grief, but the heart of the matter is the grief reaction to the anticipated, but not yet actually realized, loss.

Rando (1986, p. 24) originally defined anticipatory grief as, "The phenomenon encompassing the processes of mourning, coping, interaction, planning, and psychosocial reorganization that are stimulated and begun in part in response to the awareness of the impending loss of a loved one and the recognition of associated losses in the past, present, and future." This very broad definition includes both grief reactions and mourning processes. It refers equally to past, present, and future losses. It incorporates a shifting time frame as the dying person moves toward death, and it encompasses the perspectives of both the dying person and his or her survivors to be.

One problem with this definition is that the adjective *anticipatory* would seem to be incorrect since the grief in question is not limited solely to future or expected losses. A second problem is that the noun *grief* is inexact since the definition includes both grief and mourning. For those reasons, Rando (1988) first argued that although the phenomenon of anticipatory grief is real, the term itself is a misnomer. Subsequently, she decided to shift to the phrase *anticipatory mourning* in a later book, *Clinical Dimensions of Anticipatory Mourning* (Rando, 2000).

It seems clear, for example, that when a husband is dying, a wife may realize that she is already without the help he used to give her around the house (a past loss), that she is currently losing the vigorous ways in which he used to express his love for her (a present or ongoing loss), and that with his death she will lose the comfort of his presence and the plans they had for the future together (expected or anticipated losses). Each of these losses may generate its own grief reaction, and each may stimulate a mourning process in which one tries to cope with that loss and its associated grief reactions. However, these experiences need not be inconsistent with maintaining the loving ties that characterize an attachment between two living people.

We might clarify the meaning of anticipatory grief by adopting a narrower definition, one that limits anticipatory grief (and mourning) to reactions (and responses) to losses that have not yet occurred and are not yet in process—that is, to losses that have not yet moved from expectation to reality. If so, reacting to and coping with dying would become the master concepts in predeath experiences of grief and mourning (Corr & Corr, 2000). Prior to death, one might experience anticipatory grief and anticipatory mourning related to losses that are expected to take place in the future, other (nonanticipatory) grief reactions and mourning processes that are associated with existing losses (past and present), and reactions to and coping with the new challenges that inevitably arise during dying. Anticipatory grief and anticipatory mourning may affect the quality of post-death bereavement, but they need not be any more (or less) significant in this matter than all of the other aspects of coping with dying.

There is much that remains unclear about anticipatory grief and mourning. For example, Fulton (2003) has noted his "serious reservations regarding the heuristic value—either theoretical or practical—of the concepts, 'anticipatory grief' and 'anticipatory mourning'" (p. 350). These reservations arise from problems in conceptualizing, defining, measuring, and validating the key concepts. Fulton also argues that much research in this field has depended upon specific understandings of grief and mourning, notably psychoanalytic assumptions that cohorts of bereaved persons will experience a comparable volume of grief and will do so in a linear way. Conflating forewarning of death with anticipatory grief has led some to assume that the latter will inevitably follow the former and will, in turn, relieve the survivor of some share of post-death grief—when, as Fulton rightly insists, they differ in both duration and form.

Disenfranchised Grief and Disenfranchised Mourning

According to Doka (1989, p. 4), disenfranchised grief is "the grief that persons experience when they incur a loss that is not or cannot be openly acknowledged, publicly mourned, or socially supported." To disenfranchise grief is to indicate that a particular individual does not have a right to be perceived or to function as a bereaved person. Thus disenfranchised grief is not merely unnoticed, forgotten, or hidden; it is socially disallowed and unsupported.

Doka (1989, 2002) argued that grief can be disenfranchised in three primary ways: either the relationship or the loss or the griever is not recognized. (Note also that in 1989, Doka added that some types of deaths, such as those involving suicide or AIDS, may be disenfranchising deaths in the sense that they either are not well-recognized or are associated with a high degree of social stigma. In 2002, Doka recast this idea to speak of certain circumstances of death as disenfranchising and to note that ways in which individuals grieve or grieving styles can contribute to disenfranchisement.)

Relationships are disenfranchised when they are not granted social approval. For example, some unsuspected, past, or secret relationships might not be publicly recognized or socially sanctioned. These could include relationships between friends, co-workers, in-laws, or ex-spouses—all of which might be recognized in principle but not in connection with bereavement—as well as relationships that are often not recognized by others as significant, such as those involving extramarital affairs or same-sex relationships.

Losses are disenfranchised when their significance is not recognized by society. These might include perinatal deaths, losses associated with elective abortion, or the loss of body parts. Such losses are often dismissed or minimized, as when one is simply told, "Be glad that you are still alive." Similarly, those outside the relationship may not appreciate the death of a pet or companion animals even though it may be an important source of grief for anyone, regardless of age. Also, society often fails to recognize losses that occur when dementia blots out an individual's personality in such a way that significant others perceive the person they loved to be psychosocially dead, even though biological life continues.

Grievers are disenfranchised when they are not recognized by society as persons who are entitled to experience grief or who have a need to mourn. Young children and the very old are often disenfranchised in this way, as are mentally disabled persons.

Corr (1998, 2002) noted that these three factors (relationships, losses, and grievers) are the key structural elements of bereavement. In addition, Corr argued that the dynamic or functional elements of bereavement (grief and mourning) may also be disenfranchised. For example, a bereaved person might be told by society that the way he or she is experiencing or expressing grief is inappropriate and/or that his or her ways of mourning or coping with the loss and the grief reactions are unacceptable. Some grief reactions and some ways of mourning are rejected because they are unfamiliar or make others in society uncomfortable.

However it occurs, "The problem of disenfranchised grief can be expressed in a paradox. The very nature of disenfranchised grief creates additional problems for grief, while removing or minimizing sources of support" (Doka, 1989, p. 7). Many situations of disenfranchised grief involve intensified emotional reactions (for example, anger, guilt, or powerlessness), ambivalent relationships (as in cases of abortion or between persons who were once but who no longer are lovers), and concurrent crises (such as those involving legal and financial problems). Disenfranchisement may remove the very factors that would otherwise facilitate mourning (such as a role in planning and participating in funeral rituals) or make it possible to obtain social support (for example, through time off from work, speaking about the loss, receiving expressions of sympathy, or finding solace within some religious tradition).

Grieving Styles

Many have claimed that patterns of grief and mourning are essentially related to gender, with men and women grieving (or mourning) in different and contrasting ways. Against this dichotomy, Doka and Martin (2010) have argued that the issue is not really one of gender, but of style. Accordingly, they proposed a distinction between an intuitive grieving style that emphasizes experiencing and expressing emotion versus an instrumental grieving style that focuses on practical matters and problem solving. These contrasting styles are depicted as poles on a spectrum in such a way that many people are likely to occupy the broad middle with mixed or blended grieving styles. Doka and Martin concede that in our society intuitive grieving styles may more often apply to women and instrumental styles to men. However, they caution that these applications are not universal, noting that they likely result from broad patterns of socialization that do not apply universally in rigid ways. Because individuals of both genders have different backgrounds, personalities, and ways of living out their lives, some women are instrumental grievers, some men are intuitive grievers, and many or most bereaved persons adopt some aspects of one or the other grieving style at different times and in different contexts. As a result, this analysis tends to legitimize individuality in coping with loss and grief, even as it identifies shared patterns among various groups of bereaved persons whose members may or may not be of a specific gender.

Prolonged Grief Disorder

What was formerly termed *pathological* or *complicated* grief is currently in process of being replaced by *prolonged grief disorder* (PGD), a phrase that is meant to identify a situation in which a bereaved individual's level of distress and ability to function is extreme, disabling, and persistent. Leading advocates in this area (e.g., Prigerson, Vanderwerker, & Maciejewski, 2008) have proposed that PGD be recognized as a distinct entity within a new DSM category of attachment disorders and have described it as applying to a relatively small group of bereaved individuals who are experiencing chronic and disruptive yearning, pining, and longing for the deceased and who display at least five of the following nine symptoms: "(a) avoidance of reminders of the deceased; (b) disbelief or trouble accepting the death; (c) a perception that life is empty or meaningless without the deceased; (d) feelings of bitterness or anger related to the loss; (e) emotional numbness; (f) feeling stunned, dazed, or shocked; (g) feeling part of oneself died along with the deceased; (h) difficulty trusting others; and (i) difficulty moving on with life" (p. 180). In each case, it is understood that the symptom disturbance characteristic of PGD must cause marked and persistent dysfunction in social, occupational, or other important domains and must last at least 6 months.

Proponents and critics of the concept of PGD recognize that it will be necessary to clarify its relationship to normal or uncomplicated grief, on the one hand, as well as to traumatic grief and posttraumatic stress disorder, on the other hand. In addition, there are concerns about stigmatizing or pathologizing a normal reaction to loss and finding a place for PGD within existing understandings of grief and mourning.

Challenging the Paradigm

We can sum up the most prominent recent developments in understandings of loss, grief, and mourning by drawing on some ideas articulated by Doka (2011):

1. Grief is not just a matter of reactions to death itself: We need to take account also of secondary losses, anticipated losses, disenfranchised losses, ambiguous and nonfinite losses.
2. Rather than universal stages, grief and mourning are better understood as involving personal pathways as seen in tasks, R processes, and the dual process model.
3. Going beyond affect alone, grief is best seen as including physical, psychological, behavioral, social, and spiritual dimensions, which may be expressed through meaning reconstruction efforts and diverse grieving styles all influenced by developmental and cultural variables.

4. Moving beyond passive coping, contemporary writers emphasize choices in mourning, opportunities for transformation and growth, and resilience.

5. Rather than stressing relinquishing ties, recent scholars have highlighted continuing bonds in the form of revisiting and renewing relationships with the deceased.

6. While recognizing healthy resilience in most grievers, researchers have been increasingly attentive to complicated variants in grief and mourning; efforts to define prolonged grief disorder; and the need for careful assessment to determine if, when, and which interventions are appropriate for individual grievers.

Helping Bereaved Persons

This is a huge topical area, one we can only briefly review here. Perhaps the first thing to say is a motto from some hospice programs to the effect that Bereavement care does not begin with the death, but with an admission. The hospice philosophy is well-known for prizing holistic care for both dying persons and their family members, and for advocating ongoing care for family members and members of the community after a death has occurred. This care should involve avoiding unhelpful messages, providing nutrition, hydration, rest, exercise, and social support, and helping bereaved persons with cognitive, affective, behavioral, and valuational tasks.

Many bereaved persons will do well by calling on their own personal resources. They may also benefit from support offered by family members, friends, members of the clergy, and other community resources who offer to befriend, companion, or walk alongside them. Combinations of self-help and mutual help are also seen in bereavement support groups sponsored by hospice programs and other community agencies.

Funeral rituals are also meant to help bereaved persons, in this case by contributing to three basic tasks: (1) disposing of the body of the deceased in appropriate ways, (2) aiding in making real the implications of death, and (3) assisting in social reintegration and meaningful ongoing living. Whether or not funeral rituals actually do contribute to this task work depends on the rituals themselves; the individuals involved; and a variety of cultural, social, religious, and ethnic variables. Thus, some have argued that memorial rituals without the presence of a body, as is typical in a visitation, viewing, or traditional funeral, serve some of the same purposes in more effective ways and at lower cost. To expand and augment its services, the funeral industry in recent years has developed aftercare programs that seek to meet the needs of their clients and communities by offering what can involve a wide range of informal and formal services that follow (or, in community services, precede) traditional funeral rituals (Weeks & Johnson, 2001).

Worden (2009) offered a helpful distinction between grief counseling or facilitating the work of bereaved persons who are coping with normal or uncomplicated grief and mourning, on one hand, and grief therapy, which designates more specialized techniques used to help people with abnormal or complicated grief reactions, on the other hand. From this point of view, grief counseling may be offered by a wide range of professionals, although it is only fair to note that not all of them may be equally well-informed or competent in this field.

Another point to consider is seen in a controversy concerning the claim that formal grief counseling may not actually be effective and may perhaps even be harmful for some grievers by producing what have been termed treatment-induced deterioration effects (e.g., Jordan & Neimeyer, 2003; Neimeyer, 2000). The empirical basis for that claim has been strongly criticized (e.g., by Larson & Hoyt, 2007), while Gamino (2011, p. 113) offered what he called two fundamental findings:

> First, it is only a minority of bereaved individuals who experience distress of an intensity or duration that warrants professional intervention. Second, when practitioners use sound psychotherapy techniques and empirically-documented treatments to help troubled grievers, results are generally favorable.

Here we see the importance of bridging the gap between research and practice as exemplefied in a recent volume on that subject (Neimeyer, Harris, Winokuer, & Thornton, 2011). For the grief counseling controversy, Gamino (2011) reported that he and a colleague recommend asking a potentially troubled griever two simple questions: (1) Are you having trouble dealing with death? and, if the response is positive, (2) Are you interested in seeing a grief counselor to help with that?

Chapter 17

Life Span Issues and Loss, Grief, and Mourning: Childhood and Adolescence

Kevin Ann Oltjenbruns

Research indicates that the experience of grief after a significant loss changes as life stages vary. Corr (1996) reminds us that developmental processes play an important role in determining how an individual deals with loss, as well as how one's bereavement experience may then influence subsequent development. Further, a person's understanding of the concept of death changes over time, as does the use of particular coping strategies. A primary goal of this chapter is to build an argument that, to be effective in helping the bereaved, we must use a developmental perspective. Examples relevant to childhood and adolescence will be used for illustration purposes.

Given the literally hundreds of resources one could use to draw a broad-brushed perspective of a child's or adolescent's grief, and given the very limited number of pages available to address this extensive knowledge base, I have chosen to minimize the use of specific citations in this chapter. I will use that strategy in those cases where a particular finding has been cited so often that it is now perceived as common knowledge. However, specific references will be used for either quotations or in instances where I feel a concept can be more clearly tied to a particular author or researcher. Further, at the end of this chapter, you will find reference to three books that discuss childhood and adolescent bereavement in more depth and include extensive citations.

Common Manifestations of Grief in Childhood

After studying even a small subset of articles written about grief experienced during the early years, it becomes clear that childhood bereavement is not "a different version of adult mourning but rather one unique to the child's capacities" (Sekaer & Katz, 1986, p. 292). Further, certain manifestations of grief are more likely to occur during various substages as compared to a later time frame. For example, regressive behaviors such as bedwetting or thumb sucking, separation anxiety, fear of abandonment, fear that others close to them will also die, guilt due to magical thinking, and feelings of insecurity are quite prevalent during early childhood. Common outcomes of significant bereavement experience in later childhood are more likely to include learning difficulties, school phobia, social withdrawal, and anger. As time since the death grows longer, particular manifestations shift over time; some are more common in the months immediately following the death, and others may not appear until a couple of years later. Using data from The Harvard Childhood Bereavement Study, Worden and Silverman (1996) discovered that 2 years after a parent's death, there were increased levels of social withdrawal, anxiety, and social problems in the bereaved group of children compared to the nonbereaved control group. Given the power of the longitudinal control group design, the researchers involved in the Harvard study were the first to report a curvilinear relationship between the intensity of certain feelings and behaviors and the length of time since the death.

There are many discrepancies among the findings of various childhood bereavement studies (as there are in those focusing on adults) in terms of outcomes following death of a loved one. It is clear that neither short-term manifestations of grief nor long-term outcomes are universal and that the reader must critically analyze such aspects as participant selection, research design, the source of the information about the child's grief experience—often the parent as compared to the grieving child (Paris, et al., 2009), and what Luecken (2008) refers to as moderators toward resilience. Various protective factors include family cohesion, positive parenting, strong self-concept, and positive self-esteem. Risk factors that increase the possibility of more negative outcomes include the distress experienced by the parent, diminished quality of caregiving, multiple secondary losses, as well as minimal coping resources. One simple example of why the reader must attend to sample selection involves the importance of various influencing factors such as culture. Lopez (2011) summarizes various aspects of adolescent grief and bereavement that may be influenced by culture, such as: perception of the loss, role of the family, expression of grief, and communication patterns. Further complicating our understanding is the fact that there are many myths surrounding our understanding of children and grief (Lancaster, 2011). These include: Children do not grieve, children do not need information, children never need to go to the funeral, and many more. These misconceptions sadly guide many adults' interactions with the bereaved child and ultimately may increase feelings of grief stress levels.

Adolescence. The grief of adolescents is multifaceted, as it is in other life stages. Common reactions include feeling different from one's peers, diminished social competency, loneliness, dysphoric mood, guilt, confusion, anger, sense of powerlessness, inability to concentrate, and acting out behaviors. Birenbaum (2000) studied the most frequently reported children's and teenagers' responses (physical and psychosocial) in anticipation of and after the death of a sibling from cancer. They found differing responses among 3-5 year-olds, 6-11 year-olds, and 12-19 year-olds at different points in time: 2 months prior to the death and 2 weeks, 4 months, and 12 months after the death. Not only did responses change over time, but also there were notable differences from one age group to the other.

When an adolescent's peer dies, many of the deaths are sudden and/or violent (suicides, accidents, homicides). Questions related to why are common given that these situations are regarded as unnecessary and often preventable. These types of deaths frequently exacerbate particular reactions such as fear or anger and may be further complicated by having had no time to prepare for the death. Death of an age-mate typically raises issues dealing with personal mortality—possibly for the first time. Even while engaging in certain dangerous behaviors (e.g., drinking and driving) because he or she feels protected by the personal fable, some young persons begin to more fully understand that they too may die.

Understanding of the Concept of Death

Childhood. Cognitive capacity and understanding of the concept of death varies over time and influences how a child deals with the loss. Within childhood, one discovers significant differences over time. The following summary is not meant to engender a debate as to when one stage ends and another begins but is intended simply to encapsulate major shifts; it highlights a generalization of capacities, rather than an agreement among all researchers.

Early Childhood (2 – 4 Years)	Middle Childhood (4 – 6 Years)	Late Childhood (7 – 11 Years)
• is quite egocentric • thinks in concrete, literal terms • focuses on here and now • believes death is temporary, reversible • does not understand that death is universal • does not understand that dead persons are nonfunctional • believes death is a person	• engages in magical thinking, which diminishes over time • understands that death is irreversible • understands dead people are nonfunctional • begins to understand that death is universal (age 5)	• understands death is final • understands that death is a natural part of life • has increased understanding of future without person who has died • has more realistic understanding of causality of death

An understanding of children's thought processes surrounding death provides important insight into how a child is responding to the loss and can also help guide appropriate support strategies. For example, since toddlers do not understand that death is final and irreversible, they may repeatedly engage in seeking behaviors for the deceased. Helpers, then, must explain numerous times that the loved one is not *ever* coming back. Since that same youngster thinks in concrete and literal terms, it is dangerous to use euphemisms that are confusing such as "grandma is sleeping" or "your father has gone on a long trip." Indirect communication not only confuses the child but also may ultimately undermine trust in persons around him or her and/or trigger a fear response. Not fully understanding the nature of death, young children may conclude that they caused the death, simply by wishing someone would go away. Caregivers must give concrete explanations as to what really happened, at a level children can understand, to let them know that he or she did not cause the other person's death.

Adolescence. Cognitive maturation during adolescence affects their ability to comprehend death and related concepts. Adolescents' increasing capacity to use abstract reasoning and understand symbolism allows them to more fully grasp the meanings of life, death, and time. With the ability to think in the abstract, adolescents become preoccupied with their own thought processes, as well as what others may think of them; as a result, teens often play to an imaginary audience. Young persons dealing with a significant loss, then, may camouflage feelings for fear of being regarded as different and then possibly ostracized by a peer group, thus working against a core age-appropriate issue of developing a sense of belongingness.

Mastering Normal Developmental Tasks Within the Context of Bereavement

The classic work by Erik Erikson (1963) notes that within each normative crisis, there are related developmental tasks. Erikson believed that an individual deals with a series of psychosocial stages or crises during the course of his or her life span. During the life stages of childhood and adolescence, individuals are faced with challenges as they strive to develop what Erikson labels autonomy, initiative, industry (mastery of skill), and a sense of identity. The outcome of each crisis is closely tied to the type of environment or social support that is available to an individual in that stage. Factors inherent to a loss experience may propel a person toward a negative or compromised resolution of a particular developmental challenge.

For example, the normative crisis of late childhood (initiative vs. guilt) involves attempts to develop numerous skills valued by one's own society, self-evaluation skills, self-confidence, and interdependence. Those persons giving grief support must also encourage success in each of these areas. Children should be allowed to continue to live their lives, continue with school, lessons, sports, peer interaction, etc. These activities should not be regarded as a distraction from grief, but rather as work toward accomplishing what needs to be mastered at a particular life stage. Failure to accomplish such developmental tasks may jeopardize mastery of subsequent tasks during later periods. This discussion brings to mind Stroebe and Schut's dual process model of coping. While we may naturally give support to children as they engage in the loss orientation, we must also give support to them to continue with a restoration orientation. This encouragement does not fall exclusively to parents but may also be provided by other caring adults.

The death of a loved one during adolescence is likely to add considerable upheaval to this time of life that is already characterized by ambivalence, struggle, and confusion, making it a different experience than that encountered by grieving children or adults. Erikson would define the key developmental task for adolescents as defining a sense of personal identity. Numerous authors have posited a number of other developmental tasks or core issues, including: refining self-image, feeling comfortable with a sense of belonging, sustaining peer relationships, heightening a sense of mastery and control, defining future directions for one's self, among others. Each of these tasks may become more difficult following a significant loss. For example, the death of one's mother during adolescence can complicate defining a personal sense of self since a parent is often used as a reflection to help define either perceived positive or negative aspects of one's self. After the death of a parent, many adolescents feel pressured to assume some of the responsibilities of the deceased; they may then struggle with accomplishing significant development tasks of individuation and separation from family.

Coping Strategies and the Need for Support

Each individual brings to a crisis situation a variety of coping mechanisms that vary somewhat by life stage, personality, and previous experience. Although some adults would like to spare children the knowledge that a loved one has died and protect them from the ensuing grief, this protection is not helpful. Children need the opportunity to say goodbye, share feelings, and deal with emotions. Adults should be prepared to provide support to children who experience a loss in a developmentally appropriate fashion. Children often derive value from active strategies engaging in dramatic play and sharing memories through artwork. Given that children's language capacity changes over time and they may not be able to articulate what they believe to be true about the loved one's death, the caregiver should be attuned to the various play and artistic activities that may provide insight into children's understanding and concerns.

Coping strategies change as one matures. For example, children often try to derive comfort by seeking comfort from others, denying at times the impact of the loss, adhering to familiar activities and routines, using fantasy to ameliorate aspects of the loss. As they enter adolescence, young persons begin to engage in more effective behavioral coping strategies (e.g., help seeking, problem solving, expressing feelings). A recent study by Brewer and Sparks (2011) summarized a number of coping-related themes that an adolescent sample in the United Kingdom found helpful: expressing emotion, engaging in physical activity, involvement in positive relationships, understanding one's area of competence, developing friendships and social supports, having fun, and developing a sense of humor. Further, adolescents begin to engage in cognitive coping strategies (e.g., search for meaning, positive reappraisal, development of a sense of gratitude in regard to current circumstances, acceptance of the loss). One fairly recent phenomenon in relation to adolescents' strategies for coping involves their turning to the Internet and other digital resources for support (DeGroot 2012; Sofka, 2009; Williams & Merten, 2009). Normal developmental characteristics help one understand why a grieving adolescent may turn to online resources for information about loss and various related outcomes. Adolescents live in a world where they seek information and want to interact with others 24/7. Their imaginary audience may propel them to seek information in a confidential manner so that they will not be regarded as different and not feel so self-conscious. This interest, then, can drive them to the Internet where they may remain anonymous if they so choose. Further, given the amount of time invested in staying connected with others through various social media tools, it is understandable that a main means of communication of one's circumstances, thoughts, and feelings would be through such tools as Facebook or text messaging. In recent years memorials to the individual who has died have become virtual tributes to the deceased and tools for a collective network to share their grief. De Groot (2012) found that communication, particularly with the deceased on Facebook, served two functions: sense making and facilitating continuing bonds (upholding relational continuity with the deceased). There needs to be much more research into the efficacy of these digitally based strategies and whether they help adolescents resolve their grief.

There is growing body of research that delineates that the nature of support from caregivers is a key variable in regard to bereavement outcome for children and adolescents. Lin, Sandler, Ayers, Wolchik, and Luecken (2004) examined many variables that differentiate resilient children and adolescents from those with mental health problems following the death of a primary caregiver. They found that those survivors identified as resilient had surviving caregivers who provided greater warmth and more discipline as compared to those bereaved children and adolescents who experienced various mental health problems following the death. In a related study, Haine, Wolchik, Sandler, Millsap, and Ayers (2006) confirmed the power of positive parenting as a significant interpersonal resource that increased the likelihood of dealing with the loss in a positive fashion. Another study concluded that children who are not supported in early phases of grief could develop serious emotional and behavioral problems. Providing education (and support) to surviving parents is important so that they might learn how to more effectively help their children (Kirwin & Hamrin, 2005).

Facing the death of a loved one may ultimately strengthen available strategies for coping with subsequent stressful events. Dealing with a significant loss may ultimately result in negative emotional or physical consequences or, alternatively, lead to positive outcomes. Despite the many challenges faced as a result of the death of a loved one, many adolescents reported that grief experiences resulted in such positive outcomes, an increased sense of maturity, a willingness to deal with responsibility at a young age, an appreciation for life, an ability to cope with adversity, an increased sensitivity to others, an increase in resilience, a sense of optimism, and a desire to help others in need.

Regrief Phenomenon

As years pass and the bereaved individual moves through later life stages, the context for understanding an earlier loss and adjusting to it changes. Within the shift of developmental capacitates and developmental tasks, an individual who experiences a significant loss will often regrieve the loss at a later time, from a different and more mature vantage point. Individuals may struggle repeatedly with a loss that occurred many years prior. While some persons never do resolve the loss and get stuck in their grief, the regrief phenomenon is a developmentally appropriate processing of the experience from a different perspective than what was possible earlier. As one's cognitive capacity changes, a person often needs to add to what was understood earlier in order to create a fuller meaning of the loss, which then supports one's continuing healing. For example, in a study of 125 children (followed for up to 7 years) following their fathers' deaths as a result of the 9/11 tragedy, Christ (2006) found many examples of revisiting their grief over time, including the expression of grief, questions asked about the death, definition of the loss, and shifting strategies to help come to terms with their grief.

Further, new issues may arise as an individual faces different developmental tasks as he or she progresses through more advanced life stages. For example, as a young woman struggles to refine her sense of identity (a normal developmental task of adolescence), she may need to regrieve her father's death of many years prior. Newman and Newman (1999) stress that "one can review and reinterpret previous stages in the light of new insight and/or new experiences…themes of earlier stages may re-emerge at any point, bringing a new meaning or a new resolution to an earlier conflict" (p. 17).

Summary Remarks

One must wear a developmental lens in order to effectively help someone who is grieving. It is crucial to understand an individual's normal developmental capacities in various domains (e.g., psychosocial, emotional, physical, and cognitive) and to be aware of how those capacities interact with the need to accomplish certain developmental tasks at a particular life stage. This interplay has much to do with how the bereaved person defines the loss and how he or she uses both personal and interpersonal resources in the journey toward healing. Only with that insight can a family member, friend, or helper know the challenges faced by the grieving individual and only when that understanding is available can a person offer help that is meaningful. Just as there are no universals in regard to bereavement outcomes, it is crucial that we understand that there are no absolutes when it comes to most effective intervention strategies. Many have been found to be efficacious for those who have participated. Work by Malone (2012) and Sandler, et al. (2010) are examples of two recent studies.

The primary goal of this chapter was to illustrate, using examples from childhood and adolescence, the importance of becoming grounded in a developmental perspective. For those who would like to continue reading in this area, I would recommend Corr and Balk's edited volume, *Children's Encounters with Death, Bereavement and Coping* (2010); Balk and Corr's book, *Adolescent Encounters with Death, Bereavement, and Coping* (2009); and a textbook, *Death and Dying: Life and Living* by C.A. Corr and D.M. Corr (2013). Each of these resources further synthesizes various theoretical and research perspectives relevant to your understanding of the interface of bereavement and the life stages of childhood and adolescence.

Chapter 18

Life Span Issues and Loss, Grief, and Mourning: Adulthood

David E. Balk

The probabilities for the experience of loss, grief, and mourning increase as a person ages. A scan of worldwide mortality statistics (http://www.who.int/whosis/mort/en/index. html; www.mortality-trends.org) discloses that longevity of life brings with it greater likelihood of multiple losses such as the deaths of parents, siblings, children, grandchildren, and friends. For older adults, dealing with these losses becomes intertwined with problems endemic to aging: degradations in physiological operations, the onset of chronic and debilitating illnesses, and diminished functional performance.

Loss, grief, and mourning during adulthood is the focus for this chapter. The topics covered are (a) various schema for understanding responses to adult bereavement and (b) the impacts of some deaths that adults grieve.

Overall Schema for Understanding Responses to Bereavement in Adulthood

Four schema will be presented about ways to understand responses to bereavement in adulthood: (1) a holistic appreciation of bereavement, (2) rhythms to the bereavement trajectories that adults report, (3) life span development concepts, and (4) cognitive-based coping models.

Schema 1: A Holistic Appreciation of Bereavement

Bereavement affects people behaviorally, cognitively, interpersonally, emotionally, physically, and spiritually. Our understanding of life-span issues and bereavement would be impoverished without this holistic template. Consider two examples: physical and interpersonal consequences. Clinical evidence (Goodkin, Baldewicz, Blaney, et al., 2001; Hall & Irwin, 2001) indisputably demonstrates that a physical response to bereavement is a depressed immune system; coupling immune system difficulties following bereavement to the normal degeneration of major human biological systems as one ages (Moss, Moss, & Hansson, 2001) makes clear the impact that bereavement increases older adults' vulnerability to opportunistic diseases. Another example comes from the interpersonal realm. In an increasingly mobile, secularized society with an aging population, adults face more and more the prospects of dealing with deaths less supported by loved ones than other generations have experienced (Benoliel & Degner, 1995).

Schema 2: Rhythms to the Bereavement Trajectories That Adults Report

Assertions that grieving occurs in psychological stages have been put to rest (Kastenbaum, 2001; Lund, Caserta, & Dimond, 1993). Bereavement trajectories form curvilinear paths, extend indeterminately (Lehman, Lang, Wortman, & Sorenson, 1989), and among adults involve basic groupings: a majority of persons who are resilient, a large plurality that struggles but recovers, and a small minority whose grief goes unabated without intervention (Bonanno, 2006; see also Bonanno, Wortman, Lehman, et al., 2002; Bonanno, Wortman, & Neese, 2004).

Bereavement Trajectories[1]

The great surprise for many persons has been evidence regarding the resilience trajectory. This trajectory marks at least a plurality if not the majority of bereaved individuals. In this trajectory, people return fairly soon to regular functioning following the death of a loved one.

Bonanno asserts that resilience is the most common human response to life crises, even in such devastating events as the atomic bombing of Japanese cities. While resilient people retain "at least a bit of wistful sadness" when bereaved, they quickly return to living productive lives and to loving the persons around them (Bonanno, 2009, p. 8). Bonanno's championing of resilience can be found in some other major research efforts aimed at uncovering the consequences of bereavement, in particular the work of Irwin Sandler and his colleagues (Lin, et al., 2004). News of the resilience trajectory told us the world of bereavement research was being mapped anew.

The second trajectory depicts what many of us have long accepted is true for persons when bereaved. In this trajectory persons move only gradually from intense distress to eventual recovery; it takes at least 2 years to regain one's equilibrium when in this second trajectory. People in this trajectory comprise about 40% of bereaved individuals. Bonanno named this path a recovery trajectory. This trajectory depicts the experience I imagine Freud and Bowlby had in mind when they wrote about grief work and four phases of mourning.

What is not clear yet is whether Bonanno has data that explain (or at least describe) how persons in the recovery trajectory actually do recover. Do they engage in confronting distress, detaching from the deceased, and forming a mental representation of the deceased? When these persons come to counselors for help, are they to be politely told to go it on their own? This issue is of no small matter, as the debate over grief counseling

---

1 The material about bereavement trajectories appeared in *Death Studies* (Balk, 2011b).

has made clear. Bonanno, from what I can tell, considers counseling for persons in the recovery trajectory to be a waste of time (Bonanno & Lilienfeld, 2008).

The third trajectory is what we recognize as complicated grief. People's bereavement overwhelms them, and unless they receive effective intervention, they remain in acute grief for years. People in this trajectory "withdraw from the world and become mired in an endless preoccupation, an insatiable desire to have the deceased person back again" (Bonanno, 2009, pp. 96-97). People in this trajectory comprise 10-15% of bereaved individuals. Bonanno called this path a chronic grief trajectory.

Bereavement Phases

While stages of grieving have fallen out of favor, phases ascribed to grieving, for instance, the phases that Bowlby (1980, pp. 85-96) identified, have retained considerable staying power in thanatology and have become a means for explicating changes over time in adult bereavement. Steeves (2002) noted that Bowlby's phases to grief readily demarcate the narratives whereby adult grievers describe their experiences: numbness characterized the initial few weeks, waves of sadness marked the next few months, and loneliness emerged about the 6th month and lasted thereafter. Reorganization and reorientation, the final phase in Bowlby's phases, could not be found in the narratives. As Steeves (2002, p. 7) put it, "The loneliness did not disappear but seemed to become merely another 'fact of life'".

Using the idea of phases to understand the course of bereavement manifests the human intent to construe meaning out of the chaos of bereavement and establish a rhythm to the temporal processes of grief. Applying the idea of phases to bereavement underscores that "bereavement is so obviously socially constructed" (Steeves, 2002, p. 5). What is clear is that an order can be applied to these narratives, one that disquietingly ends with an enduring loneliness. Steeves suggested that the course of bereavement typically lasts at most 9-12 months for elderly adults; most persons I know dispute that the duration of bereavement is so short-lived. Perhaps Steeves followed his elderly research participants only into the diminishment of their acute grief and the onset of normal grief but did not interview them beyond the first year of their bereavement. Impressive national data indicate that many years after their spouses' deaths, widows commonly had memories of and conversations about their spouses and occasionally became sad and upset over reminders (Carnelley, Wortman, Bolger, & Burke, 2006); what these researchers discovered about the long-term process of grieving a spouse's death suggests the loneliness Steeves reported does extend well past the first 2 years of becoming a widow, but the national data also pointed to personal growth, such as, increases in self-confidence and personal strength, following spousal bereavement. These findings about personal growth are suggestive of reorganization and reorientation.

Schema 3: Life Span Development Concepts

For several decades researchers have studied human development from a perspective that looks at how change over time describes the human lifecycle (Baltes, Reese, &

Nesselroade, 1977). One major contribution from the life span development perspective has been a template provided both for understanding critical life events and for designing interventions pertinent to them (Danish, 1977; Danish & D'Augelli, 1980). To wit, critical life events exhibit several properties, among them, probability of occurrence, sequence, and duration. To illustrate these life event properties, consider the death of a parent:

- There is high probability of the death for an aged parent, but low probability for a young parent.
- In countries with highly developed and accessible medical care, the death of a parent prior to the death of that parent's child is considered to occur in sequence, whereas the death of a child ahead of a parent's death is out of sequence.
- Duration is much trickier as discrete events such as the death of a parent can have temporal repercussions that resonate for months and years, but the notion of duration can be seen with these contrasting examples: the sudden death of a parent in a car accident versus the lingering death of a parent to cancer following several years of treatment, remission, and relapse.

Schema 4: Cognitive-Based Coping Models

Coping is now understood from a cognitive-based perspective. *Cognitive-based* means that human coping involves comprehending implications, planning responses, and evaluating outcomes. Further, events that require coping do not occur in isolation. As Moos and Schaefer (1986) pointed out several years ago, life events are embedded in three sorts of factors: (a) personal and background factors (for instance, one's age, culture, religious beliefs, gender, and previous experiences with loss), (b) event-related factors (for instance, anticipated versus unexpected events, painful versus peaceful deaths), and (c) socioenvironmental factors (for instance, social support systems, accessible health care). Placed into the context of this chapter, consider young parents coping with the death of a toddler:

- Religious beliefs may help the parents find meaning in what seems so inexplicable.
- Preparing for a child's death due to an incurable terminal condition presents a different scenario to finding a child died in her sleep.
- whereas some decades ago bereaved parents were basically overlooked, various support groups such as Compassionate Friends and The Candlelighters have emerged as the product of concerned parents.

Empirical evidence demonstrates that aging does not reduce the ability to use cognitive coping strategies but rather "older persons are increasingly effective in using cognitive strategies in regulating their emotions" (Moss, Moss, & Hansson, 2001, p. 243). The coping models that have gained currency (for instance, Folkman, 1991, 2001; Moos & Schaefer, 1986) emphasize adaptive tasks such as appraising the personal significance of the event, identifying what the event demands, preserving a sense of self-efficacy, reasonably maintaining emotional balance, and upholding interpersonal relations. Empirical research has found "older bereaved persons more likely than younger persons to have engaged in extensive account-making about their loss (searching for a private meaning in the loss) and more likely to have confided these accounts to others" (Moss, Moss, & Hansson, 2001, p. 243).

Impacts of Some Deaths Adults Grieve

In this section we will examine empirical evidence regarding three types of deaths that adults experience: (a) the death of an elderly parent, (b) the death of a child, and (c) the death of a spouse. While the death of an elderly sibling is one of the most likely bereavement experiences for an older adult, little research or clinical attention has been given to sibling bereavement during old age. Such a gap obviously needs to be filled.

The Death of an Elderly Parent

As adults see their elderly parents age and grow more frail, they naturally begin realizing their parents' deaths likely will happen, will occur in sequence (that is, before the deaths of their children), and hopefully will take place without ongoing pain and suffering. Adult children begin to prepare for the deaths of elderly parents and to see these deaths as normative occurrences; it is disputed whether such anticipation mitigates the impact of the loss. Let us look at two issues that empirical research has uncovered about bereavement and the death of an elderly parent: (a) anticipating the death of an elderly parent and (b) the impact of an elderly parent's death upon the self of a middle-aged adult.

Anticipating the death of an elderly parent. The life span concept that events happen either in sequence or out of sequence designates that in postindustrial societies children are expected to out live their parents. Anticipating the death of an elderly parent emerges as frailty becomes undeniable, as cognitive or physical functioning deteriorates, and/or as chronic and debilitating diseases become more pronounced. Two of the more harrowing deteriorations that persons witness as elderly parents age are the onset of senile dementia or the descent into Alzheimer's disease; the loss of the elderly parent under these conditions seems to occur before death itself and aptly has been called ambiguous (Boss, 1999). The strains of taking care of a frail elderly parent suffering from senile dementia or Alzheimer's include financial, emotional, and physical strains (to mention three). For instance, emotional difficulties follow various paths for caregivers following the death of a parent afflicted with Alzheimer's—sorrow for some, clinical depression for others, numbness for others, to cite three examples—and emotional distress increases for caregivers who were already distressed prior to their parent's death (Aneshensel, Botticello, & Yamamoto-Mitani, 2004). Thankfully, senile dementia and Alzheimer's disease are not sure outcomes to aging.

As aging parents become old, their adult children begin to manifest adaptation anxiety (Moss, Moss & Hansson, 2001). Some manifestations of adaptation anxiety include worry over how to provide for parents at their very end of life, how to cope with their parents' actual dying, and how to manage life without their parents. Empirical evidence is mixed about whether anticipating a death proves helpful to grievers: some research concluded that following an elderly parent's death adult children who reported anticipatory grief were better adjusted than persons who did not experience anticipatory grief (Smith, 2005); other research indicated that adaptation anxiety did not make coping with an elderly parent's death any less difficult (see Lund, 1989; Moss, Moss, & Hansson, 2001).

Clinical lore held for quite some time that anticipated deaths rather than sudden deaths were easier on the griever; part of the reasoning was that an anticipated death triggered a process called anticipatory mourning (Rando, 2000a, 2000b). The reality of anticipatory mourning is disputed (Fulton, 2003), and empirical evidence has shown that (a) over time spousal bereavement outcomes may be indistinguishable between sudden and anticipated deaths (Gilliland & Fleming, 1998) and (b) severe psychological costs may attach to an anticipated death that is difficult and drawn out over an extended time (Da Pena, 2002; Diwan, Hougham, & Sachs, 2004; Gibson, Breitbart, & Tomarken, 2006; Grunfeld, Coyle, Whelan, et al., 2004).

Impact of an elderly parent's death on the self of a middle-aged adult. Event characteristics influence the impact on the self of an elderly parent's death. Typically these deaths are expected and considered normative. Acceptance of an elderly parent's death can be confounded if the death involved protracted suffering (Moss, Moss, & Hansson, 2001).However, complicated grief following an elderly parent's death is rare and—as uncovered in other research about traumatizing bereavement (Prigerson, Shear, Bierhals, Pilkonis, Wolfson, Hall, Zonarich, & Reynolds, 1997)—has been associated with anxious attachment bonds. Vaillant (1985), who followed 268 males from adolescence into middle adulthood, concluded that long-term, deleterious effects following parental death were best explained by the ambivalence associated with having been raised by immature, conflicting, and mismatched parents. On the other hand, it needs to be noted that Scharlach (1991) tested for and found no evidence that anxious attachment accounted for unresolved adult grief following a parent's death. In short, links between attachment bonds, complicated grief, and bereavement over deaths of parents are not settled.

Empirical research on a middle-aged adult's sense of self-efficacy following bereavement over spousal death (Benight, Flores, & Tashiro, 2001; Ford, 2006; Solomon & Draine, 1995) has indicated that, as one would expect, positive adjustments are directly associated with greater awareness of self-efficacy; these findings align quite well with cognitive theories of coping discussed earlier (Folkman, 1991, 2001; Moos & Schaefer, 1986). Considerable reassessment of life, renewal of purpose, and extensive reflection on identity and human existence have been found in the lives of adult women following the deaths of their parents (Westbook, 2002). Several authors have noted that the death of an elderly parent accentuates for surviving children the sense of personal mortality (Doka, 1997; Douglas, 1990; Scharlach & Frediksen, 1993; Sherrell, Buckwalter, & Morhardt, 2001).

The Death of a Child

Through his in-depth ethnographic research Dennis Klass (1988) has disclosed in rich, intimate detail the phenomena of parental grief as manifested in the lives of bereaved parents who participated in self-help groups. A theme suffusing his research is that bereaved parents redefine their sense of identity and their relationship to others because of their experience of bereavement. For the majority if not all the parents Klass studied, their dead child was an ongoing presence in their lives. While the impressive longitudinal research that Silverman and Worden (1993), (Worden & Silverman, 1996) conducted with bereaved children contributed to the acceptance of continuing bonds following bereavement, it was primarily Klass who noted that bereaved adult parents, defying judgments of clinical pathology, found solace in enduring attachments to their deceased children. Klass (1999) argues that enduring attachments with their dead children sensitized the adults to transcendence; the dead children served for the bereaved parents the same function that saints and bodhisattvas provide in Catholicism and Buddhism (see also Goss & Klass, 2005).

One thing we have learned from other research looking at bereavement involving children and parents is the central role that consistent parenting plays in the long-term adjustment of children following a death (Kirwin & Hamrin, 2005; Tein, Sandler, Ayers, & Wolchik, 2006; Worden, 1996). As noted earlier, Vaillant's extended longitudinal work with 268 males showed the impact on unresolved grief and difficult life adjustments for individuals raised by immature, conflicting, and mismatched parents.

An area of growing clinical and research interest involves the bereavement responses of grandparents (DeFrain, Jakub, & Mendoza, 1991-1992; Gardner, Scherman, Efthimiadis, & Shultz, 2004; Hayslip & White, 2008; Winston, 2006). Grandparents typically yield to the grief of others (Moss, Moss, & Hansson, 2001); further, whereas bereaved parents' attention centered on the dead child, bereaved grandparents' attention focused on the suffering of their own children—that is, on the parents of the dead child (Ponzetti, 1992). Grandparents' own grief typically gets overlooked. Overlooking grandparent grief illustrates a form of disenfranchisement (Doka, 1989). Ignoring the role of grandparents in the lives of families during bereavement does not match the cultural experiences of many groups of people—whether in the culturally rich amalgam that is the United States or in the rest of the world. For instance, African-American grandmothers raising AIDS orphans do so often at great personal cost, and their coping strategies include reliance on deep religious faith (Winston, 2006).

Two forms of deaths of children are early pregnancy loss and sudden infant death syndrome. We look first at early pregnancy loss.

Early pregnancy loss is one form of bereavement over death of a child that has been overlooked on the whole. Epidemiologists report the rate of early pregnancy loss due to miscarriage ranges between 14-20% (Hutti, 1992; Kilier, Geller, & Ritsher, 2002; Klein, Stein, & Susser, 1989). The term *miscarriage* refers to the unintended, spontaneous end of a pregnancy resulting in fetal death. We use the terms *miscarriage* and *early pregnancy loss* interchangeably.

There is some variance in what clinicians and researchers accept as the duration of pregnancies that end in miscarriages: 14-16 weeks gestation to as high as 26+ weeks (Kilier, Geller, & Ritsher, 2002; Neugebauer, Kline, O'Connor, et al., 1992; Shapiro, 1988). Time at which pregnancies end in recognized miscarriage is undergoing some downward shifts as medical technology enables awareness of fetal life to be gained earlier than previously possible (Cecil, 1994; Wilcox, Weinberg, O'Connor, et al., 1988).

The medical literature is replete with understanding of the physical complications involved with miscarriage. These complications involve maternal and fetal risk factors (for instance, polycystic ovaries and embryonic chromosomal abnormalities) (Mishell, 1993; Rai, Backos, Rushworth, & Regan, 2000). Of singular importance for thanatologists is that "studies concerning psychological distress in the aftermath of (an early pregnancy) loss event are sparse" (Kilier, Geller, & Ritsher, 2002, p. 131).

Three categories of psychological distress following early pregnancy loss primarily have been noted: depression, trauma, and grief. Various researchers have emphasized the importance of depressive symptoms that fall below the level of clinical depression or what is sometimes termed *psychiatric caseness*. As Kilier, Geller, & Ritsher (2002, p. 133) wrote, "Failing to reach the threshold for caseness does not imply that an experience has had no significant impact on the person's subjective distress and social functioning." The prospect for major depressive disorder following miscarriage was found to be 2.5 times greater than a community control group exhibited (Neugebauer, Kline, O'Connor, et al., 1997), and episodes of minor depressive disorder were found in 5.2% of women who had miscarried as compared to 1% in women in the community.

Anxiety is another psychological outcome noted less frequently but recently given more attention; intrusive thoughts and images as well as traumatizing flashbacks are major manifestations of anxiety and of yearning for what has been lost (Brier, 2004; Neugebauer, Kline, O'Connor, et al., 1997). As Brier (2004, p. 14) noted, women whose pregnancies have ended in miscarriage will find that intrusive thoughts that defy control aggravate "the increased likelihood of reexperiencing symptoms of trauma (i.e., flashbacks, nightmares) which represent the person's attempt to 'take-in' the stressful elements of their pregnancy loss."

Some persons propose a bereavement response of women whose pregnancy ends unexpectedly in the premature birth of their infant (Charles, 2011; Kingma, personal communication, March 3, 2011). The bereavement is said to stem from the loss of various anticipated experiences such as a normal full-term pregnancy. Lamaze classes, baby showers, holding the newborn upon delivery, leaving the hospital with your newborn, and caring for an infant immediately from his or her birth. The health risks of the newborn are also proposed as a source of the mother's bereavement. Premature birth is asserted to be both traumatic and grievous for the woman. Skepticism toward claims of bereavement over premature birth start with bafflement over what seems a narrow, narcissistic focus upon self that ignores both joy and relief that the baby is alive and concern for the baby's continued welfare. Proponents of bereavement due to premature birth invoke both intangible losses and disenfranchised grief as umbrella concepts to address the skepticism they have encountered.

Sudden infant death syndrome (SIDS) is another form of death that claims the lives of young children. SIDS, the unexpected and abrupt death of an infant under 1 year of age, is also called by such terms as *cot death* in the United Kingdom and *crib death* in the United States (Deri-Bowen, 2001). The National SIDS/Infant Resource Center maintains that SIDS kills more infants between 1 and 12 months of age than any other cause (see http://www.sidscenter.org/SIDSFACT.HTM). The greatest incidence of such deaths occurs between the infants' 2nd and 4th months of life, with very few SIDS death occurring in the 1st month of life. The death is associated with sleep and there are no signs that the infant had a medical disorder. However, as of yet no definitive cause for SIDS as been determined. Medical researchers are focusing on central nervous system defects that control heart rate and breathing, on delayed brainstem maturation, on developmental changes during the first 6 months of life that destabilize infants' homeostatic controls, on outside stressors such as becoming overheated, and on brain irregularities that may make infants vulnerable to SIDS.

The sudden, unexpected death of a healthy infant poses a very difficult bereavement for parents (as well as for siblings and grandparents). One of the first items noted in research literature is that such a death violates assumptions about the natural, expected order of events: Children are supposed to outlive their parents (Rando, 1993; Raphael, 1983; http://www.sidscenter.org/SIDSFACT.HTM). Schiffman (2004) reported three prevalent emotional responses to a SIDS death were extreme guilt, anger, and blaming, and confirmed that spouses' communication and emotional support for one another decreased following a SIDS incident.

Raphael's (1983) elegant synthesis of the grief reactions to SIDS remains an excellent source of information on parents' reactions. She notes mothers' and fathers' grief reactions show discrepant coping responses and dyssynchronous patterns of recovery. "The mother tends to be more depressed, withdrawn, more disrupted by her loss. The (father)....takes over protective, management functions, suppresses his feelings, deals with his distress more quickly and cannot understand his wife's continuing preoccupation with (the death)" (Raphael, 1983, p. 260). Citing a study from the late 1970s, Raphael wrote that it took on average a bit less than 4 months for the father to achieve normal functioning but over 10 months for the mother.

According to Raphael, fathers' responses to SIDS tend to be angrier and more aggressive than mothers'. She wondered if the fathers' apparently quick recovery of normal functioning actually masked or camouflaged their intense feelings that they feel very uneasy admitting or exploring. What may be occurring for fathers is what Cook (1988) noted is the double-bind that grieving fathers experience when bereaved: Men have been raised to understand that expressing strong negative emotions is to be kept in check; stemming from this socialization about expression of strong negative emotions is the dilemma in which grieving fathers find themselves: They are expected to comfort their wives, and they are told healthy grieving requires disclosing the distress associated with grief.

A typical coping response to a life crisis (see Moos, 1986) is to seek information about what caused the calamity. "Parents try to find all the information they can about the syndrome" (Raphael, 1983, p. 256), and in this search they are aided by the autopsy and by the other procedures established to ascertain the facts in the case. The hunt for information about SIDS leads parents to the frightening realization that medical research does not know what causes infants to die from SIDS, and increases the parents' dread that they are powerless to prevent such a tragedy from happening again. It is as though caring for their infant was futile, but such a realization does not assuage "the overwhelming nature of parental guilt and blame" (Raphael, 1983, p. 258). It is clear why SIDS would present a risk for complicated grief (Prigerson & Jacob, 2001).

The search for a cause, coupled with the overwhelming parental sense of guilt, can militate against the parents being resources for one another as they cope with their loss. As Moos and Schaefer (1986) noted, a key adaptive task in coping with a life crisis is to maintain interpersonal relationships, but Raphael (1983, p. 259) reported some husbands and wives become estranged as they look for what could have led to their baby's death. However, it would be wrong to leave the reader with the impression that marriages are doomed following SIDS. Longitudinal research with 220 parents bereaved following SIDS and other early childhood deaths learned that bereaved parents demonstrated positive signs of healthy adjustment over time to the deaths of their children (Vance, Najman, Thearle, Embelton, Foster, & Boyle,1995).

The Death of a Spouse

Widows comprise the great numbers of persons who have participated in bereavement research and upon whom generalizations have been formed about loss, grief, and mourning. In longitudinal research with widows, Parkes and his colleagues (Glick, Weiss, & Parkes, 1974; Parkes, 1975; Parkes & Weiss, 1995) identified early signs of vulnerability to spousal bereavement. These signs included lower socio-economic status, little time to prepare for a spouse's death, extensive and prolonged yearning for the dead husband, and the coexistence of other stressors, including marital difficulties.

Differences have been noted in the bereavement of younger versus older spouses. One difference involves autonomy and coping with the wider world. Due to feminism and other liberating processes in secular societies, younger widows have been educated and socialized to develop a repertoire of personal skills that succeed in the wider world; however, Moss, Moss, and Hansson (2001, p. 246) noted, "...many older widows (especially) who were raised in simpler times, in smaller and more tightly woven communities, were not encouraged to learn the skills that would assist them in accessing or developing new support relationships outside of the family."

Many researchers have concluded social support provides a major influence on adjustment to the death of a spouse (Impens, 2005; Larman, 2004; Silverman, 2004), although Wolfgang Stroebe and his colleagues (Stroebe, Zech, Stroebe, & Abakoumkin, 2005; Stroebe, Stroebe, & Abakoumkin, 1999; Stroebe, Stroebe, Abakoumkin, & Schut, 1996) have raised several theoretical and empirical issues that question whether social support plays a singular role in bereavement recovery: For instance, social support was of greater benefit for widows when there were emotional attachments involved.

The intensity and duration of grief reactions of younger and older widows vary. For instance, widows under the age of 41 report more depression than do older widows (Larman, 2004). Applegate (1997) found younger widows more vulnerable to depression if they perceived little support from others following their husbands' deaths. Older widows report significantly less depression, less anxiety, and better adjustment over time than do younger widows (Zisook, Schuchter, Sledge, & Mulvihill, 1993).

The death of a spouse plunges many individuals, particularly females, into loneliness because friendships with married couples become awkward without the partner that death has taken (Lund, Caserta, & Dimond, 1993; Moss, Moss, & Hansson, 2001). However, Pinquart (2003) reported there are many more buffers against loneliness for widows than for widowers; one reason is contact bereaved women maintain with children, friends, and siblings. Financial stressors were found to impede widowers in seeking social support; widows with university education, particularly those women with a best female friend, coped well following their husbands' deaths (van Baarsen & van Grolmou, 2001).

Lindemann (1944) noted the physical symptoms of acute grief, among them chills, fatigue, diarrhea, and constrictions in the throat. Longer-term health issues following bereavement emerge directly from the suppression of the immune system, as mentioned earlier. The landmark Institute of Medicine volume examining bereavement considered bereavement poses a serious risk to physical health (Osterweis, Solomon, & Green, 1984). In his well-received book, *Bereavement: Studies of Grief in Adult Life,* Parkes (1987) examined the increased risk for coronary thrombosis among the recently bereaved (spouses, parents, grandparents) and noted two significant points: (a) young widows were more susceptible than any other bereaved group and (b) it was not clearly understood what led to increased mortality among persons who were bereaved. However, dysfunctional behaviors used to deal with the distress of bereavement (for instance, smoking cigarettes, drinking alcohol, abusing prescription drugs) as well as intense emotional reactions (for instance, clinical depression and anxiety) place people at serious risk of physical health problems, including mortality, and are much more likely contributing factors than is bereavement by itself (see also Parkes & Brown, 1972).

Analysis of overall mortality statistics from numerous countries has confirmed that the bereaved are significantly more likely than married persons to die from cirrhosis of the liver, from suicide, from vehicular accidents, from diabetes, from lung cancer, from heart disease, and from leukemia (Stroebe & Stroebe, 1993). The Stroebes (1993) noted that mortality was highest among younger age bereaved groups and was more prevalent among widowers than widows. These gender differences do not match what Parkes (1987) found, but the age differences do fit his findings.

Endemic health problems of old age make bereavement one of many contributing stressors that characterize challenges to the elderly: Examples include a series of chronic debilitating illnesses such as emphysema and arthritis and osteoporosis, forced relocation from one's home, and declining mental capabilities due to senile dementia or Alzheimer's. While severe reactions to the death of a spouse have been linked to younger adults and while the early response to spousal bereavement is more intense for younger adults, the duration of emotional, behavioral, and physical bereavement symptoms last longer among older adults (Moss, Moss, & Hansson, 2001). It is hypothesized that these age differences signal the fact that spousal death is much less a surprise to older adults but also that spousal death sets off an intertwined set of circumstances endemic to being old. As a team of gerontology scholars noted, becoming a widow signals to elderly persons that they have crossed the threshold into being old (Moss, Moss, & Hansson, 2001).

Prolonged dying from chronic, debilitating conditions presents "a new context of dying" (Carr, 2008, p. 425) for adults and raises serious doubts about the applicability of earlier research findings to the contemporary process and experience of adult spousal bereavement. Carr (2008) reported that the strongest predictor of healthy psychological adjustments for bereaved spouses following a prolonged dying "was most closely linked to physical aspects of the death" (p. 429). Anxiety was found much more in surviving spouses whose partner had died in considerable pain, and anger was found much more in surviving spouses when medical negligence or incompetence seemed complicit in the partner's death. The dying spouse's knowledge of and acceptance of impending death and the surviving spouse's acknowledgement that their partner had led a full life "did not predict survivor's psychological adjustment" (Carr, 2008, p. 429).

The basis for these conclusions from Carr about the sequelae of spousal bereavement came from the study known as Changing Lives of Older Couples (CLOC), a comprehensive, prospective study with a matched nonbereaved control group, "enabling comparisons over the course of spousal loss" (de Vries, 2009, p. 680). The CLOC study provided data leading to, among other things, conclusions about (a) bereavement trajectories (Bonanno (2006, 2009), (b) changing realities in the experience of dying (Carr, 2008; Carr, Neese, & Wortman, 2005), and (c) evidence for framing "interventions, policies, and practices to assist older bereaved spouses" (de Vries, 2007, p. 680; see also Carr, Neese, & Wortman, 2005).

Summary Remarks

This chapter on life span issues and loss, grief, and mourning examined bereavement during adulthood. Four schema were presented as ways to understand adult responses to bereavement: (1) a holistic appreciation of bereavement, (2) rhythms to the bereavement trajectories that adults report, (3) life span development concepts, and (4) cognitive-based coping. Empirical evidence was presented regarding three types of deaths that adults mourn: (a) the death of an elderly parent, (b) the death of a child, and (c) the death of a spouse. An important theme to remember is that bereavement in older adulthood is intertwined with problems characteristic of aging: degradations in physiological operations, the onset of chronic and debilitating illnesses, and diminished functional performance.

Chapter 19

The Family, Larger Systems, and Loss, Grief, and Mourning

Alicia Skinner Cook

Death is a family event. It occurs within the context of existing relationships and family dynamics. While grief is often viewed as a personal experience, it occurs in two realms simultaneously—the intrapsychic level and the interpersonal level. Grief occurs in a social context and is embedded in a web of complex relationships. In most societies, the closest relationships and attachments are found in family systems. In some cultural contexts the focus is on the nuclear family, while in others family is defined in broader terms and includes a large network of extended family members for whom there is much interdependence. In contemporary life, the definition of family has become increasingly complex and may include stepparents and other steprelatives, both same-sex and opposite-sex relationships in which partners cohabit but are not married, single-parent and multigenerational households, and a wide range of other family structures. With changing demographics, families will increasingly represent four and five generations as the average life expectancy continues to increase (Galvin, Bylund, & Brommel, 2004).

Family Systems Theory

Each family is unique and is an entity that is greater than the sum of its individual family members. According to family systems theory, families are characterized by wholeness or unity. Central to this theory is the notion that one cannot understand individual behavior in isolation, emphasizing the importance of understanding one's responses in the context of the social group(s) to which one belongs. While the experience of grief is a personal event for individuals, it is also a systems event for families.

To understand any particular family system during the time of loss, one must look at individual family members, their relationships to each other, and their relationships and interactions with other individuals and systems outside the family. Family systems are made up of subsystems illustrated by marital, sibling, and parent-child relationships. The death of a family member can have a powerful impact not only on the family system but also on the subsystem(s) of which that individual was a part (Cook & Oltjenbruns, 1998).

A death causes disequilibrium in the family system, often disrupting a family's functioning and affecting available emotional and physical resources. The death of a spouse may alter the extended kinship network, the death of a child may alter perceptions of the future, and the death of a parent or breadwinner can diminish a family's sense of security (Hansson, Berry, & Berry, 1999).

The effects of especially difficult losses can be transmitted through multiple generations. When secrecy and taboos surround a particular death, families can become more vulnerable to future losses. Genograms are used as a technique for mapping family structures and patterns of interaction (McGoldrick, 2011). They provide multiple types of information about individual family members and relationships between family members in both past and current generations. What is known and what is not known can each yield useful insights. Missing information on cause of death for children in families, for example, can suggest patterns of avoidance after a particularly painful loss and lack of communication about death-related issues. Understanding multigenerational patterns of interaction and communication around loss issues can lead to a better understanding of current family functioning and coping styles.

Grief and the Family Lifecycle

According to Shapiro (1994), "a systemic developmental perspective on the family life cycle crisis of bereavement suggests that the developmental course of all families is inevitably altered by the shattering blow of grief" (p. 278). The timing of a loss in the family lifecycle can be a critical factor in adjustment. Deaths that are untimely in terms of chronological or social expectations are especially difficult. These untimely deaths include early widowhood, early parent loss, and death of a child. Surviving family members may know no individuals within their social networks who have coped with such untimely events and thus have few models for effective coping and support. The death of a child is one of the most painful losses a family can experience. Intense grief can extend over a long period of time as parents try to make sense of a senseless event that defies the natural order of life (McGoldrick & Walsh, 2005).

Timing of a loss can also coincide with other lifecycle changes that pose unique challenges. For example, loss of a spouse can occur near the time of birth of the first child, which is a major transition in itself, or at the time a family is coping with the financial demands and launching issues of adolescents and college-age dependents. Multiple stressors, developmental demands, and related losses can result in overload and influence a family's ability to cope (McGoldrick & Walsh, 2005). Furthermore, these losses have the potential to affect both family relationships and individual development, particularly with regard to the processes of separation and individuation (Cook & Oltjenbruns, 1998).

The Cultural Context of Loss

The experience of grief is affected by the environment in which it takes place. In particular, the cultural milieu influences the manifestations of grief, opportunities for expression, and interpretation of the loss. The community and the larger society also provide the context in which family coping will occur. A family's ethnic and religious values and traditions influence the amount and type of support available to grieving families. Different cultures also have different norms regarding the appropriate length of mourning, beliefs about what happens after death, open displays of emotion, and gender roles (Anderson & Sabatelli, 2007). For example, some traditions encourage outward display of emotion while others reflect the belief that feelings are private and are not to be shown in public.

Societal expectations can also affect who is expected to grieve a loss and under what circumstances. Disenfranchised grief is grief that exists even though society does not recognize one's need, right, or capacity to grieve (Doka, 2002). Pet loss is an example of a significant family loss that oftentimes is not acknowledged by the larger society. Cultures that are highly age-segregated may also deny children opportunities to grieve or say goodbye to a dying loved one. In some cultures, children are an integral part of all family rituals surrounding death, and in others they are rarely included.

Healthy Family Processes Following Loss

Beavers and Hampson (2003) have concluded that the ability to accept loss is at the core of all processes in healthy family systems. Cook and Oltjenbruns (1998) along with other authors have documented the importance of families sharing their loss, maintaining open communication, reorganizing and regaining equilibrium, and effectively utilizing available support systems and external resources.

Sharing the Loss

Funerals, memorial services, and other postdeath ceremonies can serve as meaningful times of coming together of family members to acknowledge and share the loss of a loved one. Imber-Black (2005) observes that every culture has rituals to mark profound losses, acknowledge the life of the deceased, provide support for survivors, and facilitate ongoing life after such loss. Following a loss, families begin a transition process as they cope with their loss. Whether formal or informal, rituals can have therapeutic value following a loss and facilitate emotional healing and family cohesion. Bosley and Cook's (1993) study of bereaved adults found that funeral rituals can be a tool to assist in accepting the reality of the loss; serve as an affirmation of faith, religious beliefs, and/or a philosophy of life; facilitate emotional expression and provide a context for emotional support from family, friends, and the larger community; and to reconnect to a greater sense of family and the integration of personal and family identity.

A ritual is a specific behavior or activity that gives symbolic expression to feelings and thoughts. Actions occurring many months or years after a funeral, such as going through the loved one's personal belongings and taking off a wedding ring, can be considered rituals and have important symbolic significance. Rituals following a loss also provide a context for reminiscence to occur. Rosenblatt and Elde (1990) view shared reminiscence about a deceased loved one as an important aspect of social support. They found in their interviews with adults who had lost a parent that shared reminiscence was common, particularly between siblings, and that it had positive implications for relationships with surviving family members.

Maintaining Open Communication

According to Galvin, Bylund, & Brommel (2004), communication may be viewed as a symbolic, transactional process of creating and sharing meaning. These symbols include words, verbal behavior, and the full range of nonverbal behavior as well as facial expressions, gestures, and spatial distance. The communications within the family are transactional in that family members have an impact on each other. Individual family members communicating within this interpersonal context often develop a shared reality or set of meanings. Open communication both before and after a death allows family members to share deep feelings and create stronger bonds, but family members must be accepting and supportive of the range of feelings that may be expressed. Some types of loss, such as death by suicide, may evoke strong feelings of anger and shame that may be particularly difficult to share with others. Lack of open communication has been shown to increase the possibility of blame, guilt, and conflict (Vess, Moreland, & Schwebel, 1985).

Reorganizing and Regaining Equilibrium

Death of a family member disrupts established patterns of interacting and requires an age-appropriate redistribution of roles and responsibilities. An unanticipated loss may require additional changes such as relocation, changing jobs, or seeking additional employment. Open family systems in which information is freely exchanged with individuals both inside and outside of the system tend to cope better with change. These families have the adaptive capacity to reorganize in new and effective ways that support and acknowledge individual family members while maintaining the functioning of the system as a whole. In contrast, closed family systems tend to be rigid and locked into strictly prescribed patterns. These families have difficulty accepting assistance from outside the system, have few skills or experience with adaptive change, and have difficulty responding to the demands following loss (Cook & Oltjenbruns, 1998).

Effectively Utilizing Support Systems and External Resources

Internal family resources are typically not enough to sustain a family following a traumatic loss, and external systems can offer valuable support to bereaved families. These external systems include extended family and friends, religious institutions, community and mental health services, and formal support groups such as Compassionate Friends (for bereaved parents). Religion and spirituality play a major role in the lives of many families, and churches can often mobilize quickly after a death to offer assistance. Religious institutions also provide time-honored rituals surrounding death that can provide comfort for families and link them with others sharing their belief system (Cook & Dworkin, 1992).

Some families are more at risk than others for having inadequate external support. For example, geographically mobile families may lack strong social networks and links with their new communities and live considerable distance from close family and friends. Other families may have rigid unspoken rules about "dealing with our own problems" that prevent them from reaching out for additional support and professional assistance when it is needed.

Coping: Family-Level Variables

While the study of resilience among individuals has been a focus of research for quite some time, it has only recently been applied to the family as a system. Hawley and De-Haan (1996) support the notion that resilience can be conceptualized at the family level and reflects more than a collection of resiliencies of individual family members. Resilience is demonstrated in response to adversity and allows the family and its individual members to bounce back, thus reaching or surpassing a precrisis level of functioning. Resilience is most likely to be found when protective factors are present and risk factors are minimized. Hawley (2000) cautions, however, that resilience is not a static characteristic in families and can be conceptualized as "a pathway a family follows over time in response to a significant stressor or a series of stressors" (p. 106). Coming to terms with loss as a family unit has no timetable. As the process unfolds, new stressors may appear, internal and system strengths may be discovered, and thus the balance of protective and risk factors may be altered.

A number of protective factors within the context of family relationships have been examined by researchers. For example, recent studies on bereaved children support the efficacy of preventive interventions on strengthening parenting (Sandler, Wolchik, Ayers, Tein, Coxe, & Chow, 2008). Haine and her colleagues (2006) found that positive parenting served as a protective resource for bereaved children. Also, Lin et al. (2004) found that children's resilience was positively predicted by the surviving caregiver's warmth and the ability to provide consistent discipline. Traylor, Hayslip, Kaminski, & York (2003) studied the association between adult grief and family system characteristics. Higher levels of family affect and family cohesion were predictors of fewer manifestations of grief over time.

Risk factors for poor outcomes after loss include internal family factors (e.g., poor communication, conflict in interpersonal relationships) as well as factors related to the loss itself. Sometimes other concurrent stresses are also present that are unrelated to the death such as loss of a job, caring for aging parents, or personal health problems.

Type of death also has implications for effective coping. Sudden, unexpected deaths can be particularly difficult for families because they have no time to prepare for the loss. Sudden deaths may also involve violence, such as in the case with homicide, and therefore involvement with the criminal justice system. Furthermore, individuals experiencing bereavement following violent death by accident, homicide, or suicide have been shown to have difficulty making sense of the loss, and this failure to find meaning can lead to complicated grief symptomatology (Currier, Holland, & Neimeyer, 2006).

In the case of an anticipated death, the challenges are different as families adjust to the changing conditions associated with a particular illness. Families often spend extended periods of time at a medical facility prior to the death of a loved one, interact with a variety of health care providers, and may face complicated insurance and legal issues.

The stresses associated with extended illness, such as financial expenses, can exacerbate already existing interpersonal issues within the family and accentuate tensions. From the time a life-threatening illness is diagnosed, the dying person, together with family members and friends, may begin to grieve. This anticipatory grief is related to the many losses associated with the dying process as well as the impending death itself. An anticipated death, however, does give loved ones the opportunity to say goodbye and draw closure on a variety of concerns (Cook & Oltjenbruns, 1998).

Some illnesses, such as Alzheimer's disease, involve ambiguous losses. In these circumstances, the individual is physically present but perceived as psychologically absent during the later stages of the illness as the person experiences more dramatic intellectual and social decline (Boss, 1991). Watching these changes can be extremely painful for family members who often have a sense of helplessness. Kapust (1982) has described living with dementia as "an ongoing funeral" for the healthy spouse and other family members.

Sudden loss can also involve ambiguity as is the case when the loved one is physically absent but still psychologically present due to lack of confirmation of the death (Boss, 2006). Examples include natural disasters in which remains are not identified and soldiers missing in action. Without proof of the death, family members often maintain hope that their loved one is still alive. They frequently struggle with accepting the death, and the timing of this acceptance may vary among family members. Some adults may become preoccupied with the lost loved one and the search for evidence of the death, thus no longer fulfilling their responsibilities to other family members.

Negative Outcomes

The experience of illness or death can bring family members closer together but it can also cause significant discord. Based on their research findings, Dyregrov and Dyregrov (2008) stated that many couples report increased closeness after a loss while a large number report growing apart; few report that the relationship remained the same. Each individual family member's grief is unique and based on relationship with the deceased, developmental level of the griever, personality and coping skills, prior losses, and a host of other factors discussed elsewhere in this volume. The manifestations and duration of grief of one family member may be quite different than that of another family member. This variability is referred to as *dissynchrony of grief*.

In a similar manner, family members may use different coping mechanisms or *discrepant coping styles* to deal with their loss. Some family members may prefer to grieve in private while others find solace in talking frequently about their loss and openly expressing their emotions. In particular, gender differences can influence the manifestations and style of grieving. Men are more likely than women to avoid grieving situations and use work as a distraction. Distraction can also take a form that is detrimental to the individual's health, such as excessive drinking (Umberson, Wortman, & Kessler, 1992). When grief is expressed, men tend to show anger more than do women (Gilbert & Smart, 1992). In studying couples who had experienced either a fetal or infant death, Gilbert (1989) found that the majority of couples experienced marital discord following the loss. According to the researcher "inconsistencies in beliefs and expectations resulting in a perception of incongruent grieving served as the major contributors to most of these conflicts" (p. 609). These differences in grieving and ways of coping can result in a perceived secondary loss as a result of a change in the predeath relationship.

Unhealthy patterns may also develop as the family reorganizes to meet roles and responsibilities involved in daily living. Parents may be so absorbed in their individual grief following loss of a child that they are unable to reach out to each other or to provide emotional support for their remaining children. In these instances, a surviving child may become parentified and be the one to attempt to care for all other family members, thus compromising his or her own development.

Positive Outcomes of Coping with Loss

Little attention has been given to the positive outcomes of grief. Despite the pain associated with loss, families often report finding meaning in their suffering. Nadeau (2008) in her work on meaning making in families found many families report positive changes following a loss. This growth is often expressed as truths realized or lessons learned.

Positive outcomes can also relate to changed self-perceptions of individual family members such as seeing oneself as stronger and more mature. Three quarters of widowed persons in the Changing Lives of Older Couples study reported that they had become more self-confident as a result of having to manage on their own since losing a spouse (Utz, 2006). Other outcomes relate to changes in interactions with others such as more caring for others, enhanced communication skills, and more openness in sharing feelings (Calhoun & Tedeschi, 1990).

In their interviews with parents 1 to 8 years after the death of a child, Brabant, Forsyth, and McFarlain (1997) found that the majority expressed a fundamental change in themselves, feeling more sensitive and more spiritual as a result of their loss, and also perceiving themselves to be better persons. Most also expressed a change in values, including a desire to help others more and placing a higher priority on family and less on money and work.

Klass (1986) has observed that death creates new bonds in some families as individual members pull together to cope with their shared loss. Surviving a common loss as a family can result in a renewed sense of closeness and cohesion, a better understanding of each other's strengths, and enhanced communication and flexibility.

Summary

Grief typically takes place in the context of a family. While much attention has been paid to individual grief, understanding the impact of death at the family system level is also important. The family often provides the context for healing and variables such as stage of family lifecycle, patterns of family interaction, differences in grief manifestations of individual members, and cultural context will all influence the process. The following healthy family processes after a loss have been identified: sharing the loss, maintaining open communication, reorganizing and regaining equilibrium, and effectively utilizing support systems and external resources. Resilience among grieving families is found more often when risk factors are minimized and protective factors are present. While a variety of factors can lead to negative outcomes of grief in families, many families report positive outcomes as a result of their shared grieving.

Chapter 20

Ethical and Legal Issues and Loss, Grief, and Mourning

David K. Meagher

There are many ethical and legal issues that are often overlooked when confronted with the death of a loved one. Legal issues affected by death include ownership of the remains of the deceased, the decision for conducting an autopsy, the distribution of the deceased's property (execution and probate of the will), implementing plans for the disposal of the body, qualifications of grief support personnel, and the inclusion of bereavement leave within the legal structure of society. However, as Shah and Miller (2010) write, for the most part, "legal consequences of death do not require determining the moment of death with precision. None of these consequences depend on determining death within a matter of minutes or seconds. It is only when death became a prerequisite for vital organ donation that it began to matter exactly when a person died" (p. 542).

Determination of Death

In the past, physicians were limited in their ability to determine the moment of death. The available technology limited the physician to the senses of touch (pulse), vision (movement caused by respiration), and hearing (using a stethoscope). Death was declared when breathing and heartbeat were said to have ceased. In more recent times we have seen a gradual movement to more technologically arrived at decisions about the declaration of death. Both the reports of the Harvard Ad Hoc Committee on Brain Death Syndrome (1968) and the President's Commission for the Study of Ethical Problems in Medicine and Behavioral Research (1981) recommended a set of criteria that may be employed by physicians in the determination of the onset of death in accordance with available medical knowledge and technology. From these reports, the denotation of a patient with brain death has become equated legally to the actual death of a person by U.S. state legislatures and has been upheld by the courts (Rosenberg, 2009).

Death by brain criteria is a clinical diagnosis that can be made when a decision has been reached that there is complete and irreversible cessation of all brain function. Since it is now technically possible to sustain cardiac, circulatory, respiratory and other organ function after the brain has ceased to be alive, a diagnosis of death by brain criteria can be made before the heart beat stops (Phillips, 2005).

However, there is an ongoing debate over the determination of death, particularly over brain death or death determined using neurological criteria, and the relationship between definitions of death and organ transplantation (Smith & Cherry, 2010). Khushf (2010) suggests that the policy for the declaration of death and the harvesting of organs are intertwined. In the United States, there is a dead donor rule (DDR) that makes it necessary to first determine that death has occurred (Smith and Cherry, 2010). "From a legal point of view, not having scientifically valid criteria of cessation of circulation and respiration for declaring death could lead to the conclusion that organ procurement itself is the proximate cause of death. Although the revised Uniform Anatomical Gift Act (UAGA) of 2006 provides broad immunity to those involved in organ-procurement, courts have yet to provide an opinion on whether persons can be held liable for injuries arising from the determination of death" (Verheijde, Rady, & McGregor, 2009, p. 15).

Is it even necessary to declare a patient has died? Miller, Truog, & Brock (2010) write that "transplantation of vital organs has been premised ethically and legally on the dead donor rule (DDR), the requirement that donors are determined to be dead before these organs are procured. Nevertheless, scholars have argued cogently that donors of vital organs, including those diagnosed as 'brain dead' and those declared dead according to cardiopulmonary criteria, are not in fact dead at the time that vital organs are being procured....We challenge the normative rationale for the DDR by rejecting the underlying premise that it is necessarily wrong for physicians to cause the death of patients and the claim that abandoning this rule would exploit vulnerable patients. We contend that it is ethical to procure vital organs from living patients sustained on life support prior to treatment withdrawal, provided that there is valid consent for both withdrawing treatment and organ donation. However, the conservatism of medical ethics and practical concerns make it doubtful that the DDR will be abandoned in the near future. This leaves the current practice of organ transplantation based on the 'moral fiction' that donors are dead when vital organs are procured" (p. 299).

Allowing temporary organ-preservation (TOP) without expressed consent of the patient and/or family is inherently a violation of the principle of respect for one's autonomy (Verheijde, Rady, & McGregor, 2009). Opponents are of the opinion that the UAGA provides the legal authority for TOP while attempts are made to ascertain the wishes of the patient and/or family. TOP, they state, does not violate any legal family interest and protects practitioners and hospitals from any legal liability associated with the procedure (Bonnie, Wright, & Dineen, 2008).

In summary, we accept the physician's decision as absolute and valid. The physician, in this case, is acting both as a medical practitioner and as an agent of the state. The declaration of death is first a medical decision. Even if a person, though appearing to be dead, was still alive, the decision that a patient has died will most likely be a valid one since all interventions cease at the moment a physician declares the person dead. Secondly, this declaration is also a legal one. Once a person is declared dead, a death certificate having been signed to validate the decision, the deceased no longer enjoys the rights and privileges enjoyed before death. The Declaration of Independence, the foundation of the laws of the United States, declared that all are endowed with certain unalienable rights which included the right to life. Each person has a right to his or her life. Each of us is given a life, and it is naturally our own. All legislation subsequent to the Declaration of Independence was enacted, at least in theory, to protect the rights of all members of society. Of course, the laws only protect those living members of a society. Do the deceased have any rights or protections under the law? If not, who, then, possesses the right to act in the name of the deceased? Who owns the body? What rights of the deceased, if any, may this person protect?

Many of the authors of the U.S. Constitution believed that the "right to property" was a kind of summary right; in it were contained all the other rights (Rendell, 2004). The remains of a decedent do not qualify in the ordinary sense as property. A surviving spouse or next of kin does not have a right of ownership over the corpse. However, in the absence of any contrary documents, a surviving spouse or next of kin does have the right to the possession of the body for the purpose of burial or other lawful disposition which they may see fit. The questions of ownership and protection of rights to one's body are particularly important when it comes to the issue of organ and tissue donation.

Organ Donation Debate

Advances in organ transplantation technology and successes of immunosuppressant techniques have resulted in giving a new lease on life to critically ill patients. However, the number of patients waiting for a donor organ far exceeds the number of available donors. By some estimates, 92,000 Americans are waiting for an organ donation, with a name added to the list every 16 minutes. Twelve Americans die every day because a needed vital organ is not available (Harris & Alcorn, 2001). Worldwide numbers of persons waiting for an organ are difficult to ascertain, The Eurotransplant International Foundation (2011) reports approximately 16,000 potential recipients. The Wikipedia Encyclopedia (2006) reports there are more than 2 million patients in China, 50,000 in Latin American countries, and 2,000 in Australia and New Zealand on waiting lists for organs. The need is great; the resources to meet this need are extremely deficient. In the United States, UAGA expressly grants the right to the next of kin to control disposal of the body, in conformity with the common law. The UAGA is a model set of laws regarding a person's gift of his or her body parts after death and has been adopted by most of the U.S. states. It includes provisions that govern how individuals can give their bodies to medical schools and hospitals for various purposes and also has provisions that allow family members to make those decisions. The gift of body parts by an individual or next of kin may not be made if there are indications to the contrary within those who, by law, have a right to be involved in the decision.

Some general components of the UAGA are:

1. No witnesses are required on the document of gift, and consent of next of kin after death is not required if the donor has made an anatomical gift.
2. A gift of one organ does not mean there is a limitation on the gift of other organs after death if there has not been any contrary indication by the decedent.
3. An individual must be at least 18 years of age to be a donor.
4. For the wishes of a deceased to be a donor, document of gift signed by the donor is necessary. If the donor cannot sign, the document may be signed by another individual with two witnesses, all of whom have signed at the direction and in the presence of the donor.
5. If a document of gift is attached to or imprinted on a donor's motor vehicle operator's license, revocation, suspension, expiration, or cancellation of the license does not invalidate the anatomical gift.
6. A document of gift may designate a particular physician or surgeon to carry out the appropriate procedures.
7. Donation does not require waiting for a will to be probated.
8. A donor may amend or revoke an anatomical gift by: a signed statement, an oral statement made in the presence of two individuals, or any form of communication during a terminal illness or injury.
9. A stated wish to be a donor that is not revoked by the donor before death is irrevocable and does not require the consent or concurrence of any person after the donor's death.
10. In a priority listing, the spouse, adult child, either parent, adult sibling, a grandparent, guardian of the decedent, or any other person authorized or under obligation to dispose of the body may make an anatomical gift of all or a part of the decedent's body for an authorized purpose, unless the decedent, at the time of death, has made an unrevoked refusal to make that anatomical gift.
11. If a person proposing to make an anatomical gift knows of an objection to making an anatomical gift by any member of the above-authorized list, the donation may not be made until the objection has been resolved.

Opt-in vs. Opt-out Models

In the United States, the basic structure created by the National Organ Transplant Act (NOTA) of 1984 includes a system of voluntary altruistic donations or also known as an opt-in model (Cutler, 2002). An alternative method is an opt-out model or one known as presumed consent.

The opt-in model is one that depends on having the expressed consent of a donor and/or obtaining the consent of the family after the death of a patient.

In England and Canada, Human Tissue Gift Acts are examples of an opt-in practice. In most situations in both countries, any adult person can consent to be an organ or tissue donor in writing at any time or orally if in the presence of at least two witnesses during the person's last illness. When a person has not given consent under these circumstances, or if in the opinion of a physician, one is incapable of giving a consent by reason of injury or disease and his or her death is imminent, the patient's next-of-kin or the person who is lawfully in possession of the body, may consent on the behalf of the deceased. In any case, consent cannot be given if there is reason to believe that the deceased would have objected (Sperling, 2004).

In contrast, Spain, Israel, and Singapore are examples of countries that have established an opt-out or presumed consent model, which assumes the presence of consent where there is no clear indication that consent has been withdrawn (Voo, Campbell, & de Castro, 2009).

Financial Incentive Donations

A commonly debated alternative system is one that provides a financial benefit incentive for donation. This system would allow for survivor families to receive some financial benefit as a result of the donation. Benefits might include monies to offset funeral expenses or be charitable donations to qualified nonprofit charities in memory of the deceased (Cutler, 2002). Neither UAGA nor NOTA permit the provision of any financial benefit to the organ donor or families and there are no data to suggest a financial incentive system would increase or decrease the number of donations.

Voo, Campbell, and de Castro (2009) address some significant ethical issues with presumed consent. One issue questions whether making the potential donors responsible to indicate their unwillingness to participate disrespects an individual's right to self-determination. For some, the benefit of saving lives outweighs any consideration of autonomy violations.

A second ethical concern for Voo, Campbell, and de Castro (2009) is the role of an impact on the family in the presumed consent model.

Survivor-Family Response to Request

Family members or others responsible for making donation decisions have reported confusion and uncertainty around the moment of the request. Cleiren and Van Zoelen (2002) report that many family members report not knowing or remembering what tests were used to declare their loved one dead. They seemed unaware what questions about brain death to ask a physician. Most did not know that, if the loved one was to be a donor, the body had to be artificially respirated. For some bereaved family members, they contend that no information about brain death was provided, and they cannot recall the moment when consent for donation was obtained. In only a small percentage of cases were donations discussed preceding the death. Family members felt superfluous and ignored afterward. The desire to be informed about the results of the transplanted organs was strong in almost all bereaved (Burroughs, Hong, Kappel, & Freedman, 1998). Some were frustrated that they did not receive information from the transplant coordinator, although this information had been promised. Sque, Long, & Payne (2005) report that the perceived quality of hospital care affected families' donation decision making and appeared to impact on their subsequent grief. Families needed (1) time to understand the information given, (2) care in the way and context that information was shared, and (3) attention to their emotional needs (Dinhofer, 2003).

The National Kidney Foundation (2002), along with a number of other professional organizations working with families of organ donors, has developed a set of care expectations these families have a right to expect. Known as the Bill of Rights of Donor Families, its purpose is to provide members of Organ Procurement Organizations (OPO) and other related associations with a list of services that they should be offering to donor families. Among other recommendations, included in this statement of rights, are a number of actions that are designed to assist the family members with both their decisions and their grief. They are: (1) assuring that their loved one will be treated with respect throughout the process, (2) providing timely information regarding how any donated organs and/or tissues were used upon request and whenever possible, (3) if family members wish, giving an opportunity to exchange communications with individual recipients and/or recipient family members, (4) providing accurate updates on the condition of the recipients if families so request, and (5) providing ongoing bereavement followup support for a reasonable period of time. Included in such support are the provision of: the name, address, and telephone number of a knowledgeable and sensitive person with whom they can discuss the entire experience; free copies of literature about organ and tissue donation; free copies of literature about bereavement, grief, and mourning; opportunities for contact with another donor family; opportunities to take part in a donor or bereavement support group and/or the services of a skilled and sensitive support person (National Kidney Foundation, 2002).

In an effort to prevent grief from turning into distress, many countries have enacted what are know as presumed consent laws. These laws allow transplant coordinators to approach families in an attempt to ascertain the deceased's wishes concerning donation or to seek permission from the families if the wishes are unknown. The most common reason for missed opportunities is the denial of consent by the family. Since the issue of consent regarding giving away one's organs after death implies ownership, family members cannot give away something they do not first own, any more than they can sell it (Cutler, 2002). Voo, Campbell, & de Castro (2009) conclude that presumed consent legislation has not improved the rate of organ donations even in countries with such legislation.

Legal issues of ownership of the deceased's body are not only a component of the organ donation debate. It is also part of the decisions concerning what happens to the deceased's remains. There are legal and ethical issues to consider. The first concerns the needs of the state.

Autopsies

An autopsy may be required in deaths that have medical and legal issues and must be investigated by the medical examiner's or coroner's office. Deaths that must be reported to and investigated by these officials include those that have occurred:

1. Suddenly or unexpectedly, including sudden natural death, sudden infant death syndrome, or the death of a person who was not under the care of a doctor at the time of death
2. As a result of any type of injury, including suicide, homicide, a motor vehicle accident, drug overdose, or poisoning
3. Under suspicious circumstances
4. Under other circumstances defined by law

When an autopsy is required, the coroner or medical examiner has the legal authority to order an autopsy without the consent of the deceased person's family or next of kin. If an autopsy is not required by law, it cannot be performed until the deceased person's family provides permission.

The decision about an autopsy occurs at a difficult time for most families since they have just lost a loved one. Counselors or members of the clergy who specialize in bereavement services may be available to help families through the process. In cases in which an autopsy is not required by law, family members may consider requesting one:

1. When a medical condition has not been previously diagnosed
2. If there are questions about an unexpected death that appears due to natural causes
3. If there are genetic diseases or conditions that they also may be at risk for developing
4. When the death occurs unexpectedly during medical, dental, surgical, or obstetric procedures
5. When the cause of death could affect insurance settlements or legal matters
6. When the death occurs during experimental treatment

When the medical examiner or coroner decides there is a need for an autopsy to be performed and there is a cultural or religious tenet against autopsies, the law supersedes culture and religion. However, it should be expected that, in these cases, any invasion of the body be minimal and that all tissues and organs that have been removed for examination be replaced after the procedure is complete, thus maintaining the bodily integrity required by religious or cultural practice (Klaiman, 2005). The next question to be answered is, What are the legal ways to dispose of the remains of the deceased?

Body Disposal and the Law

In addition to allowing the deceased's body to be harvested for usable tissue and organs in a transplantation program or for medical research, there are three other lawful means of disposing the remains of a loved one who has died: burial, cryonics, or cremation. The most common means of disposal is the burial of the body following a funeral or memorial service. Funerals provide an important rite of passage. Similar to rituals that mark other transitions in life, funerals provide a time for family and friends to celebrate the life of the loved one and share their feelings concerning the loss of this person in their lives. Coming together like this provides a satisfactory environment for mourning and expressing grief.

In addition, funerals are important rituals for the survivors. They affirm one's basic beliefs about life and death and help one through the loss.

Funerary customs comprise the complex beliefs and practices used by a culture to remember the dead, from the funeral itself, to various monuments, prayers, and rituals undertaken in their honor. These customs vary widely between cultures and between religious affiliations within cultures. A question that is often asked is, If a ritual is going to include an open casket viewing, must the body be embalmed? There is no federal law that requires that a body be embalmed prior to burial. In fact, the Centers for Disease Control (CDC) says no public health purpose is served by embalming (Hoyert, 2001). In addition, no state routinely requires embalming. A few states do have laws that require embalming generally:

1. When death occurs from a disease that may put funeral personnel at risk;
2. If the body will be transported by public transportation;
3. If the final disposition will not be accomplished within 72 hours after the death;
4. If the body will be publicly viewed; and
5. If so ordered by the commissioner of health for the protection of the public health (Funeral Consumer Alliance (FCA), 2006).

A supporting rationale for embalming states that it is primarily done to disinfect and preserve the remains. FCA (2006) counters this rationale with the policy that the process does not preserve the body forever; it merely delays the forces of nature. A second supporting position is that without embalming, an open casket viewing would be impossible. The body would become unviewable within a short time. Refrigeration of the body during nonvisitation periods would accomplish the same result as embalming if the viewing period is not too long. The United States is the only country in which embalming has been widely promoted by the funeral industry. It is rarely done in other countries, with no risk to public health. Even visitations are held in those countries without having the body embalmed first (FCA, 2006).

Funerals rank among the most expensive purchases many consumers will ever make. A traditional funeral, including a casket and a vault, may cost $6,000 or more. This expense does not include cemetery costs such as purchase of a grave and labor cost incurred at the time of the burial. Extras like flowers, obituary notices, acknowledgment cards or limousines can add thousands of dollars to the bottom line. The cost of many funerals is more than $10,000.

To protect the purchasers of funeral products and services, the U.S. Federal Trade Commission (FTC) (1994) enforces a set of regulations known as the Funeral Rule. According to the Funeral Rule:

1. One has the right to choose the funeral goods and services he or she wants for themselves or for someone he or she represents.
2. The funeral provider must state this right in writing on the general price list.
3. If state or local law requires a person to buy any particular item, the funeral provider must disclose it on the price list, with a reference to the specific law.

4. The funeral provider may not refuse, or charge a fee, to handle a casket someone has purchased elsewhere.
5. A funeral provider that offers cremations must make alternative containers available.

Each year, Americans grapple with these and many other questions as they spend billions of dollars arranging more than 2 million funerals for family members and friends. The increasing trend toward preneed planning—when people make funeral arrangements in advance—suggests that many consumers want to compare prices and services so that ultimately, the funeral reflects a wise and well-informed purchasing decision, as well as a meaningful one.

With the exclusion of Alabama, which is the only state without any preneed laws, all states have some preneed legislation. However, each and every state's preneed laws are significantly different. Some states require 100% of preneed funds to be placed in trust. Other states merely require the holder of funds to maintain a custodial relationship. Some states require an annual report to be prepared by a certified public accountant. Other states don't require any annual report (FTC, 1994).

After the funeral ritual, a burial service is generally conducted at the side of the grave, tomb, mausoleum, or crematorium, at which the body of the decedent is buried or cremated at the conclusion. According to most religions, coffins are kept closed during the burial ceremony. In Eastern Orthodox funerals, the coffins are reopened just before burial to allow loved ones to look at the deceased one last time and give their final farewells.

In most areas of the country, state or local laws do not require the purchase of a container to surround the casket in the grave. However, many cemeteries require such a container to prevent depressions of a grave. Either a grave liner or a burial vault will be required.

Many families choose cremation as a way to either reduce costs or preserve the environment. Cremation is significantly less expensive than traditional burial rituals. In addition, there are those who believe the land designated as a cemetery could be designated as protected open spaces in a densely inhabited environment. There are a variety of options available to dispose of cremation remains: interment in a family grave, placement in a columbarium, or being kept by the family in the home, to cite some examples. Another choice may be a ritual scattering of the remains over land or water. More recently, cremated remains have been placed in space crafts and sent into orbit. This choice, though, is much more expensive than a traditional funeral and burial ritual.

The U.S. Environmental Protection Agency (EPA) allows for burial at sea of cremated remains. The burial may be by boat or plane and must occur at least 3 nautical miles from land, and each burial of cremated remains be reported to the EPA. At sea includes inland navigable water, but excludes lakes and streams. Scattering cremated remains from a bridge or pier is prohibited under federal law. Cremated remains must be removed from the container or urn before scattering.

A futuristic alternative option may be cryonics. Cryonics is the practice of preserving (freezing) humans or animals that can no longer be sustained by contemporary medicine until resuscitation may be possible in the future. The process is not currently reversible, and by law can only be performed on humans after legal death in anticipation that the early stages of clinical death may be reversible in the future. Cryonics is based on a view of dying as a process that can be stopped in the minutes, and perhaps hours, following clinical death. If death is not an event that happens suddenly when the heart stops, we face philosophical questions about what exactly death is. Some have noted "...few if any patients pronounced dead by today's physicians are in fact truly dead by any scientifically rigorous criteria" (Whetstine, Streat, Darwin & Crippen, 2005, p. 540). Donaldson (1988) has argued that death based on cardiac arrest or resuscitation failure is a purely social construction used to justify terminating care of dying patients.

Ethical and theological opinions of cryonics tend to pivot on the issue of whether cryonics is regarded as interment or medicine. If cryonics is interment, then religious beliefs about death and afterlife come into consideration. Resuscitation is generally deemed impossible because the soul is gone, and according to most religions only God can resurrect the dead. Expensive interment is seen as a waste of resources. If cryonics is regarded as medicine, with legal death as a mere enabling mechanism, then cryonics is a long-term coma with uncertain prognosis. It is continuing to care for sick people when others have given up, and a legitimate use of resources to sustain human life (Whetstine et al., 2005).

Grief: A Normal or Pathological Response

Kleinman (2012) describes grief as a normal response to a loss of something truly vital in one's life. The loss results in an end to a form of living. It requires a transition to a new time and a different way of living. He writes that there is no conclusive evidence to show what a normal length of bereavement is. Diagnosing a response as a major depressive disorder (MDD) is unreliable and potentially harmful to grieving persons. There is a significant difference between what may be described as a normal reaction to loss and that which some bereaved individuals who over time manifest symptoms found in MDD.

Balk, Cupit, Sandler, and Werth (2011) identify some potential problems for a diagnosis of depression in the first 2 months of bereavement. Firstly, they state that labeling grief as a major mental disorder may have an iatrogenic effect on bereaved persons. Secondly, people with disordered grief might be mistakenly treated for major depression. Given that the appropriate treatment for depression and prolonged grief disorder differ, the diagnosis of depression may lead to an inappropriate treatment and interfere with the person's coping with the distress of bereavement. Lastly, they posit that if diagnosed with a MDD within the first 2 months of bereavement, it is likely that many individuals will receive antidepressant medication that has potential negative side effects.

Bereavement Leave

Often, the acuteness of the grief experience makes it very difficult for the bereft to fulfill normal daily activities, such as meeting one's occupational responsibilities (Rando, 2000b). Having the opportunity to take a paid leave from work (bereavement leave) so that one would be able to focus on the felt grief and help others in the family cope would be a very positive support. However, in the United States. there is no automatic right to time off with pay in instances of bereavement of a relative or friend. Any time off with pay is either stated in the company's terms and conditions of employment or decided by the employer at his or her discretion. The Employment Relations Act 1999 does give employees the right to time off without pay, in the event of the death of a dependent. In the legislation, a dependent is defined as a spouse, child, parent, or a person who lives in the same household as the employee other than a tenant, lodger or boarder.

While the U.S. Family and Medical Leave Act provides for 12 weeks of unpaid leave for someone who is caring for a dying family member, the act does not include provisions for bereavement leave. Federal civil service workers, however, may use up to 104 hours (13 days) to make arrangements necessitated by the death of a family member or to attend the funeral of a family member.

Paid bereavement leave is a more common practice in other countries. Specific provisions for a paid bereavement leave are included in part III of the Canada Labour Code. It states that an employee who has been continuously employed in a company for at least 3 consecutive months is entitled to "leave on any normal working day that falls within the 3-day period immediately following the day the death occurred." If the employee has not been employed for the 3-month period, he or she is entitled to the 3-day leave without pay.

A sampling of other countries reveals the following paid leave opportunities:

A. 3, 6, or 8 days in Taiwan depending on the relationship with the deceased;

B. 7 days in Chile;

C. 3 days in China and Luxembourg; and

D. 2 days in Spain.

Ethical-Legal Issue of Research

"The field of bereavement research has lagged behind the disciplines of medicine and clinical psychology in its consideration of ethical issues, and yet the researcher is confronted with unique and complex ethical challenges" (Stroebe, Hansson, Stroebe, & Schut, 2001, p. 12).

Some of the ethical issues are described by Cook (2001). They include issues of recruitment methods employed by the researcher, the timing of the recruitment, issues of informed consent, threats to confidentiality, increase in subject's distress induced by participation, a violation of cultural norms, and unethical application of study findings.

Several of the ethical concerns and responsibilities identified are particularly relevant to the question of how best to link research and practice. Intervention studies can be particularly ethically problematic because of the tension that exists between the need to generate data to inform clinical practice and the potential harm to the bereaved that may result through their participation in research (Genevro, Marshall, & Miller, 2003).

Summary

An examination of the ethical and legal issues of loss, grief, and mourning in a single chapter is a formidable task. There is not enough space within a single unit to completely address the issues presented. The topics examined focused primarily on postmortem issues. Almost immediately after a death has been declared, and often before the person has been so certified, issues of organ and tissue donation arise. The need for donors far exceeds the availability of organs and tissue necessary to save lives. The first concern is to be as certain as one can that a death has occurred. The declaration of death is both a medical and a legal decision. Not only does declaring a person dead bring a stop to all forms of aggressive intervention, but also removes any constitutional rights the deceased had.

We come to the next issue—who, if anyone, now owns the body? Not only does the answer to this question impact on whether an autopsy will be performed and on organ and tissue donor programs but also indicates who has the responsibility to dispose of the decedent's body. The subsequent issue is, once the determination of ownership or responsibility has been made, how might the body be disposed of?

Three additional issues related to the survivors are briefly discussed. These include the debate concerning the inclusion of bereavement in the diagnosis of MDD; a grieving person's rights, if any, to a paid time off from one's job in what is popularly called bereavement leave. Lastly, since the research in bereavement requires subjects who have experienced a loss, what ethical practices should be followed to ensure the subjects are not caused any additional pain and suffering.

Assessment and Intervention

Introduction to Part 4,
Chapters 21 – 27

Chapters 21 through 27 focus on assessment and intervention. The Body of Knowledge Committee defined this major category of thanatology knowledge in this way: **information gathered; decisions that are made; and actions that are taken by professional caregivers to determine and/or provide for the needs of the dying, their loved ones, and the bereaved.**

The chapters in Part 4 focus on assessment and intervention in terms of these indicators: culture and socialization, religion and spirituality, historical and contemporary perspectives, life span issues, the family and larger systems, and ethical and legal issues. Six of the chapters are revised from the chapters that appeared in the first edition. One chapter (27) from colleagues in Israel is wholly new.

Chapter 21

Culture and Socialization in Assessment and Intervention

Ester R. Shapiro

Clinical vignette: Carmen Ruiz was a 32-year-old single Puerto Rican woman and 3rd of 11 siblings when her 50-year-old mother, Gloria, died of breast cancer, leaving Carmen in charge of three younger siblings: Mario, age 24 and a heroin addict, and two half-siblings, Roberto, age 16, and Luisa, age 11. Carmen became her mother's coparent at age 8, when her hard-drinking father died in an accident near home in rural Puerto Rico, and her mother was pregnant with Mario. Gloria Ruiz relocated her family to Boston where, remaining single, she had the two younger children. While older siblings married and had families, Carmen learned little English, her world revolving around her mother and care of their household. With Gloria's diagnosis of stage IV breast cancer, Carmen became her mother's primary caretaker through swift progression of devastating illness reducing her beautiful, sociable mother to agonized skin and bones. At her mother's request, Carmen became the younger children's primary parent, struggling to establish parental authority but thwarted by their rebellion and rejection. Seeking parenting help at our Child Guidance Center, she was referred to a new Family Bereavement Center where I worked. Respecting her request, initial interventions used behavioral parenting counseling techniques to help Carmen set effective age-appropriate limits with her half-siblings. As these relationships improved, Carmen requested help with her own overwhelming grief and family conflicts concerning bereavement. Carmen disclosed her continuing close yet troubled relationship with her mother's spirit, who visited her nightly in dreams and scolded her for not taking proper care of the children. The younger siblings were frightened by Carmen's invocation of their mother's deceased spirit and refusal to change anything in their mother's bedroom. Her older siblings thought Carmen's grief exceeded acceptable cultural and spiritual traditions.

In weekly individual meetings with Carmen supplemented by family consultation sessions with the younger children and extended family, we explored Carmen's current grief in light of her history as designated family caretaker, positively framing her self-sacrifice as a generous contribution to family well-being. At the same time, we identified this moment as a meaningful developmental opportunity, exploring how Carmen might take up aspects of her own, interrupted life course, enjoying the independence and focus on personal goals she made possible for others. At a family meeting, the older siblings noted that Carmen's experience as her mother's coparent and continuing connection with her mother's spirit mirrored her great aunt's relationship to her maternal grandmother. These conversations provided a link to an intergenerational legacy consistent with familial and cultural traditions, while making differences a basis for shared understanding and connection. Using her language for images of relationships, we revisited her relationship with her mother. Carmen requested help understanding her mother's illness, and we reviewed her thick medical chart, translating the English while decoding the high-technology medical treatments. Recognizing that failure to provide translation impacted both her mother's care and her own confusion, Carmen further realized her mother had delayed care, reluctant to face a diagnosis destroying her cherished feminine beauty and social life. As we explored their relationship, Carmen was able to speak up about her frustrations, especially her thwarted needs for a life of her own, first to me and then directly to her mother during her nighttime visits. I coached her to respectfully speak out in her own defense to her mother's spirit, who responded well, becoming more supportive of Carmen and complimenting her parenting. This transformed relationship with her mother's spirit freed Carmen to pursue life interests: She enrolled in English language classes at a local church, began dating, and asked for more household help from both her older and younger siblings.

When I met Carmen Ruiz in 1982, bereavement practice emphasized expressing distressing feelings and decathexis or closure in relationship to the deceased, with little to offer in understanding culturally based experiences of death and grief for diverse U.S. communities whose experiences with loss were also interwoven with impacts of inequalities. In psychiatry, assumptions made by psychoanalysis were being replaced by remedicalization, displacing community mental health perspectives with dehistoricized, decontextualized symptom checklists used in DSM-III to achieve consensus on symptom presentations. I was fortunate to work with colleagues coming out of community-based, social-justice informed approaches to understanding race, culture, community, and bereavement who supported my work applying an intergenerational family development approach to grief as a family process (Shapiro, 1994). Listening to Carmen and other bereaved patients, I drew from my own experiences within an immigrant Cuban Eastern-European Jewish family whose life-course losses were intertwined with political disruptions and diaspora. I also drew from experiences conducting qualitative research on gendered adult development during family lifecycle transitions and from our interdisciplinary community-oriented mental health team that brought in bereavement experts focused on lived experiences of social realities, challenging prevailing psychopathology perspectives and expanding the frame to cultural and sociopolitical considerations. Since that time, I have focused my practice and training efforts on educating culturally and developmentally informed practitioners sensitive to contexts who can address presenting concerns while identifying and mobilizing resources supporting growth even under adverse circumstances. This approach to culture, grief, and growth emphasizes practitioner self-knowledge regarding both personal and professional assumptions regarding death's impacts and mutual learning through collaborative, strengths-based inquiry about the complexity of culture as a resource in facing societal barriers and opportunities as these contribute to death's multifaceted impacts. This approach also allows using the power of intergenerational and life-course perspectives in understanding death's timing and cultural contexts as redirecting shared development and the central role of advocacy for mobilization of multisystemic resources supporting positive shared development (Shapiro, 2007).

This chapter argues that cultural and ecosystemic developmental perspectives on bereavement practice need to be incorporated into a holistic understanding of the intervention knowledge base in thanatology. Paul Rosenblatt, whose qualitative research on culture and grief has spanned 4 decades, argues that, "No knowledge about grief is culture free" (Rosenblatt, 2008, p. 207). LaRoche (2012) notes that segregating culture as if it could be isolated from other aspects of human experience can easily lead to an approach drawing from social stereotypes and be vulnerable to racial profiling. Further, for many of the world's communities, in the United States and globally, understanding relationships between life and death incorporates culturally specific, historically evolving religious traditions (Klass, 1999b). Yet this broad understanding of culture as intertwined with all other facets of death and grief experiences presents challenges in reviewing literatures needed to understand culture and socialization in thanatology interventions. First, because of the diverse settings within which thanatologists practice, culturally meaningful bereavement care needs to consider timing and settings of experiences with death. The reasons for requests for services and their clinical and societal contexts may vary widely, from health care settings grappling with recommendations regarding appropriate end of life in acute, palliative, or hospice care to concerns about potentially burdened or symptomatic bereavement pathways in the immediate aftermath or many years later. We are used to thinking of these pathways in developmental terms for children only, yet culturally informed human development perspectives allow us to appreciate how child, adult, and family processes are interdependent, gendered, and grounded in cultural time and place (Valsiner, 2003, 2012). Finally, social environments are not created equal, and ethnic minorities and socially disadvantaged groups, in the United States and all over the world, live with and die with the consequences of what the health disparities literature terms excess death (Thomas et al., 2011) and barriers to needed resources that are increasingly the focus of health promotion perspectives in thanatology (Fook & Kellehear, 2010; Oliviere et al., 2011).

Using culturally based ecosystemic frameworks as a lens on developmental psychopathology and resilience attuned to social inequalities and cultural strengths, I selectively review culturally sensitive practice literatures offering opportunities to incorporate strengths-based health promotion perspectives as well as problem prevention in interventions. These literature reviews include current literatures on cultural competence in health care and gender-sensitive multicultural counseling, especially the growing literature calling for culturally sensitive end-of-life and bereavement care. Cultural and multicultural counseling approaches view culture as dynamically constructed and emergent in specific intervention contexts and as including the counselor's own culturally based beliefs and values, professional training, and treatment setting. Further, they expand our appreciation of the relevant knowledge base for practice and of the ethical dimensions of practice with communities targeted by inequality (Enns & Williams, 2012). Culturally sensitive care also has to connect to quality care initiatives in health care and community services; building bridges to consensus on best practices in bereavement care compatible with culturally meaningful assessment and intervention more broadly (Bernal & Domenech, 2012; LaRoche & Christopher, 2009). Finally, culturally sensitive practice approaches emphasize institutional and practitioner ethics, accountability and advocacy in recognizing the ways marginalized communities are targets of social exclusion or discrimination, and working actively as advocates for change (Gambrill, 2012; Prilleltensky, 2012; Thomas et al., 2011; Ungar, 2012).

Culturally competent care requires attention to a scientific knowledge base, while expanding our appreciation of where knowledge comes from, incorporating person, family, and community centered perspectives. Such work requires systematic critiques of social or cultural assumptions and ideologies, multimethod and partnership approaches to inquiry that examine patients and communities, uncovering the privilege of their lived experiences and goals, and calling for accountability for changing unjust conditions (Bernal & Domenech, 2012; Enns & Williams, 2012; Gambrill, 2012; Sue & Sue, 2008). Culturally sensitive bereavement care consistent with these frameworks incorporates culturally meaningful health promotion, empowerment, and social justice approaches reducing symptoms of distress and promoting wellness while addressing social inequalities in both exposure to stressors and access to resources.

To address these complexities in culturally sensitive thanatology practice, this chapter integrates interdisciplinary, multicultural counseling, and cultural competence frameworks using synthesis of multidisciplinary ecosystemic developmental models highlighting life-course potential for promoting grief and growth in contexts of resourceful, resilient communities, and collaborative inquiry and intervention approaches emphasizing access to needed resources in achieving person and family-centered goals. Whether we work with individuals or families, we consider intergenerational relationships and social contexts in creating a shared understanding of death, its circumstances, and realistic impacts as well as meanings for what matters most in a transformed life. Through this inquiry, we can partner to cocreate a new, more developmentally favorable ecological niche for facing death and grief, identifying and mobilizing positive coping resources, while supporting attainment of desired goals for change and growth. This selective review also introduces work in cultural adaptation of evidence-based practice (Bernal & Domenech Rodriguez, 2012), while describing implications for thanatology emphasizing constructivist and narrative approaches to transformations of meaning making (Denborough, 2008; Neimeyer, 2012), revised relationships with both other bereaved family members and the deceased as resources in coping with death supporting resilient adaptation (Koenig & Davies, 2003; Silverman, 2000b), multisystemic factors associated with resilience in bereavement responses that can be targeted in bereavement care (Mancini & Bonanno, 2012; Sandler et al., 2008; Shapiro, 2007), and intervention research applying family-centered multisystemic approaches alleviating distress while mobilizing positive coping resources (Kissane & Bloch, 2002; Kissane & Hooghe, 2011; Shapiro, 2012).

Cultural Complexity in Thanatology Practice: Understanding Death and its Impacts in Everyday Life Contexts

Societies have traditionally taken tremendous care with the shared transformation of life into death, because of their responsibility to preserve everyday life's continuity and stability in the face of death's many disruptions. Cultural beliefs and practices concerning death and its aftermath emerge from a cosmology of shared worldviews incorporating death into interdependent, intergenerational lifecycles under highly specific circumstances for everyday survival. Who died, how they died, who remains to mourn and remember them, and what assistance they should expect from their community, are interpreted in light of cultural understandings of death, its timing and circumstances, and its place in connecting the arduous present to an ancestral past and a hoped-for future. The United States is a pluralistic, diverse society, yet dominant assumptions supported by medical and mental health models emphasize decontextualized private experience, individual autonomy, and capacity to overcome all challenges through problem-solving action. Culturally meaningful assessment and intervention in thanatology requires a shared journey of inquiry into the cultural complexity of death's place and its impacts in unique yet interdependent life pathways unfolding in highly specific settings. Further, thanatologists train in multiple disciplines and work in diverse practice contexts. Each discipline and practice setting provides its own guidelines for culturally sensitive care within disciplinary and organizational guidelines for quality care. Cultivating critical thinking, essential to knowledge-based culturally sensitive practice, requires a systematic approach to examining knowledge claims and recognizing the societal and scientific ideologies and economic or prestige incentives underlying them (Gambrill, 2012). Culturally meaningful care cannot be conducted in a vacuum, but rather responds to changing health care and community service systems and current challenges to achieve greater efficacy and equity (Institute of Medicine, 2003).

Ecosystemic approaches to practice (Becvar & Becvar, 2006; Boyd-Franklin, 2003; McDaniel et al., 2005; Ungar, 2012) identify individual, family/relational, neighborhood/community, and sociocultural levels within which to assess relevant qualities of individuals, their relationships, formal and informal institutions, social practices or policies, and their interpretations or meanings contributing to particular adaptive outcomes of interest. **Collaborative practice models** are found in many disciplines, and draw from social constructionist views of change emphasizing the culturally and relationally based nature of subjective reality and the importance of power sharing, especially in contexts of social inequality (Neimeyer, 2009; Pare & Larner, 2004).

Ecosystemic models emphasize the dynamic complexity, interdependence, and contingency/responsiveness to context of adaptive outcomes for any individual, while identifying risks and resources empirically associated with resilient, ordinary and expectable, or problematic adaptation, especially with exposure to adversity. Culturally meaningful practice requires recognition of the multifaceted nature of cultural experience and the enormous range of individual differences and contexts that can create differences in the interpretation of culture within any given family or community (LaRoche, 2012). Using a collaborative approach to ecosystemic practice, clinical assessment and intervention are understood as consultations, constructed through a compassionate, respectful dialogue using an individual and family's own language for their struggles, exploring culturally based assumptions and goals for interdependent development (Boyd-Franklin, 2003; Falicov, 2012; Shapiro, 1994, 2012). This approach draws from relevant research literatures studying cultural protective factors in positive coping with the stresses of acculturation and racism (Boyd-Franklin, 2003); research on developmental pathways resulting in positive and symptomatic adaptive outcomes throughout the life span and emphasizing resilience in coping with adversities such as death, divorce, poverty, exposure to racism, or community violence (Luthar, 2006; Sandler, 2001); psychotherapy research on effective practice emphasizing patient-directed goals, mobilizing supportive relationships and resources within and outside therapy (Prochaska & Norcross, 2009; Gibbs, 2002) and culturally meaningful adaptation of evidence-based practice (Nagayama-Hall, 2001; Bernal & Dominech Rodriguez, 2012). It recognizes the scientifically demonstrated power of the sacred healing arts (Koenig, King, & Carson, 2012), and conducts a culturally sensitive spiritual inquiry as part of a basic assessment.

Ecosystemic dimensions of culture relevant to thanatology must focus not only on death, its circumstances, and meanings, but also on the social resources available for rebuilding disrupted lives in the presence of death and grief. In every society, disparities in available resources due to race, ethnic minority status, gender inequality, or social class differences intersect uniquely to generate the circumstances, consequences, and meanings of death and grief. Culturally informed thanatology practice requires that we consider a society's distribution of stressors, risks, and protective resources exposing some individuals or communities to higher rates of mortality risk while depriving them of access to resources promoting recovery and resilience. Dimensions of culture relevant to thanatology practice include the cultural specificity of spiritual and religious beliefs and practices; an individual's location in immigration/acculturation processes; evaluation of an individual's relationship to dominant cultural resources, beliefs, and practices; and negotiation of individual differences in the interpretation of culture, which may differ by personal style, gender and generation within the same family.

In conducting assessment and intervention from a cultural perspective, the thanatologist joins the ecosystem and has a responsibility to understand him or herself as a potential resource or barrier to successful adaptation, growth, and change. Some authors argue that the medical and mental health fields have themselves become subcultures with their own beliefs and economic interests guiding their prescriptions for responding to death, dying, and grief. In the mental health field, this medicalization of bereavement has led to overemphasizing psychopathology rather than the contextual risks or resources individuals and families experience, and neglect of the culturally meaningful strengths they mobilize in response to contexts of inequality or social exclusion (Prilleltensky, 2012; Ungar, 2012). A strengths-based, goal-oriented inquiry emphasizes the bereaved's own account of their experience and needs, highlighting culturally meaningful goals for life in the presence of grief. These approaches help us consider with each unique individual and family how cultural resources can help transform and repair altered landscapes, economics of survival, relationships and roles, and meanings shattered by a loved one's death and its circumstances.

Clinicians conduct a culturally meaningful appreciative inquiry into death and its impacts, creating a collaborative contract for interventions supporting person and family determined goals. Culturally meaningful thanatology practice:

- Recognizes the practitioner's own location in specific cultures of personal and professional experiences and practice settings and seeks consultation from colleagues supporting rigorous questioning regarding cultural assumptions: *When I first met Carmen Ruiz, I was a secular Jew with hospital training in psychopathology and Spanish fluency; I was able to work from a strengths-based cultural framework with the support of a multidisciplinary team committed to emphasizing cultural and community resources in the face of social oppression.*

- Explores culturally mediated individual experience of death and its impacts using a multidimensional, dynamic understanding of culture as a force organizing roles, relationships, emotions, and beliefs in everyday life, while connecting these to the flow of intergenerational time and to the wider society: *Carmen and her family found it helpful to understand differences in their grief responses as due to different ages and life experiences within the family. We framed Carmen's more extreme grief response as rooted in Puerto Rico's unique synthesis of Catholic, African, European spiritist, and indigenous beliefs in the enduring presence of spirits, as based in an intergenerational family legacy, and as reasonable given her assigned caretaker role after her father's death; these framings helped initiate a new conversation about how best to support Carmen in her grief and new roles while also addressing the needs of the younger siblings and extended family.*

- Conducts a culturally informed appreciative inquiry into person and family experience and goals for life in the presence of death that is compassionate, strengths-based, and accountable to family-determined goals: *Carmen first requested help with more effective parenting. The success of structured behavioral interventions for setting limits at home made the next step possible, in which she requested help with her own deep bereavement and its discordance with that of other family members.*

- Creates a collaborative contract for interventions that closely follows the patient and family's stated goals, applying and adapting appropriate, effective clinical tools: *I followed Carmen's narrative lead in framing the visits from her mother's spirit as dreams and in hearing her distress at her mother's unfair criticisms. I appreciated Carmen's positive contribution as designated coparent going back to her father's death, while using her mother as an example of how someone could grieve and also go on to enjoy a full life, to affirm that Carmen also had these rights. After a coaching session role playing how Carmen could express her frustrations and needs to her mother's spirit, she was able to challenge her mother's criticism respectfully and constructively. Subsequently she reported that her mother's spirit had ceased criticizing and had instead complimented her, saying the children were looking well and gorditos or plump, high praise in a culture concerned about economic survival associating plumpness with good health.*

- Recognizes both individual uniqueness in death and grief responses and their interdependence based on gender, generation, and unique relationships to the dying and deceased: *While Carmen Ruiz felt a deep connection to an intergenerational legacy of continuing spiritual bonds to her deceased mother, her older, less acculturated siblings endorsed that tradition but felt she took it too far, while her younger highly acculturated siblings found these traditions unfamiliar and frightening. Both individual sessions and family consultations were designed to increase positive family communication, mutual understanding, and resolution of conflicts in ways that negotiated differences while enhancing mutual affection and shared support.*

- Explores culturally meaningful resources for positive change, identifying leverage points helping reduce distressing symptoms while also mobilizing relationship and environmental factors associated with positive coping in responding to a loved one's death and coping with its aftermath: *In the Ruiz family, ecosystemic leverage points included:* **at the individual level,** *work with Carmen on her* *developmental history of grief as well as on making progress in adult skills and goals such as speaking out about her needs within the family, learning English, and exploring new intimacies outside the family; **at the familial level,** discussing differences in grief reactions made it possible for the family to negotiate differences and gain greater compassion for Carmen; behavioral interventions created a more stable home environment with age appropriate rules; **extended family and community resources** were mobilized to support Carmen in her new role as parent and in her new life goals.*

Culture, Socialization, and Human Development

The cultural dimension of death and grief has long been the province of anthropologists, who have appreciated the ways a community's rituals and beliefs facilitating the passage between life and death illuminate its beliefs and practices. Moments of social transition are valuable in understanding the workings of culture, because for most of us, culture is part of the atmosphere or ethos of our everyday lives, appearing as natural and unremarkable as the air we breathe or as the solid ground beneath our feet. We are socialized into culture from before birth, through the work of generations anticipating our futures. From birth, we are born neurologically incomplete, formed by relationships with caretakers whose talent for survival we depend on and from whom we learn our place in the world. Valsiner (2012) integrates cultural and dynamic developmental systems framework to articulate four interdependent dimensions of culture generating human development: landscape and the natural world, economic activities for survival, human roles and relationships, and cultural symbols and meanings. Valsiner suggests that human symbolic activity guided by culture allows us to organize and symbolize our understanding of our environments, so that we are both shaped by them and shapers of them. The experience of embeddedness in culture as natural and given is reinforced by continuity in our social environments and by the neurocognitive schemas or working models of relationships we develop for making sense of the world. Yet both the challenges of contemporary life, in which our intergenerational socialization is characterized by discontinuity between the world of our parents and our progeny, increasingly require reflexivity, or the capacity to evaluate or own subjectivity as bounded by our social location so as to adapt with flexibility and agency to a continuing process of change (Enns & Williams, 2012). What appears to be a private, isolated self in Western psychology can best be understood as interdependent and contingent, organized by specific life circumstances, relationships, and shared adaptive goals responsive to changing contexts for development. Our schemas or working models of relationships balance universal human needs for self-assertion and connection, responsive to cultural roles and meanings guiding gendered, intergenerational relationships as we confront specific problems of the family lifecycle (Shapiro, 2008).

Throughout human development, both expected and unexpected lifecycle transitions create disruptions and discontinuities that we bridge by drawing on the relationships, environments, private and shared meanings that offer stability and continuity, ways of making the new and unknown safe and familiar. Cultural anthropologists use the construct of liminality to describe rituals of transition as culturally sanctioned spaces of transformation bridging one state or stage and the next. Cultural death and grief rituals are designed first and foremost to reassure the broader society that a community's life goes on after a member's death. They may not necessarily fit an individual or family's unique needs in response to a very particular death, its circumstances, and its cultural context. In culturally diverse societies, and in traditional societies changing through modernization, the relationship between culturally sanctioned death and bereavement rituals and an individual or family's grief experience may be discordant (Shapiro, 1996). For this reason, thanatologists conducting an assessment and planning an intervention with bereaved families need to understand cultural dimensions relevant to bereavement care as contextual, multidimensional, and unfolding in specific contexts for shared development. Reflexivity, conceptualized by feminist and multicultural counseling as a necessary process for rigorously examining practitioner social location as evoked by client characteristics, becomes an increasingly central dimension in any intervention relationship (Enns & Williams, 2012). Fook and Kellehear (2010) argue that reflexivity becomes particularly important in shifting frameworks towards health promotion in palliative care.

Models of Culturally Competent Practice: Implications for Thanatology

Clinical practice fields are currently developing guidelines for culturally informed practice that vary by discipline and by emphasis. Health care and medicine most often use the term *cultural competence,* while the fields of counseling and psychotherapy more often refer to *multicultural counseling competencies.* There is a great deal of debate in this field about use of the term *competence*, as compared to *cultural humility* better capturing the complexity of culturally informed interventions and the clinician's stance as learner. Other debates include:

1. The importance of ethnic-specific knowledge versus process approaches emphasizing universal principles for contextualizing care;
2. The value of ethnographic approaches in cultural anthropology or crosscultural, comparative psychology versus multicultural counseling models emphasizing both diversity and power inequalities within a single social context; and
3. The relevance of research on effective practice, much of which has not included diverse patient populations nor culturally meaningful dimensions of treatment (Leong & Lopez, 2006; Domenech & Bernal, 2012).

In the field of cultural competence and health care, Arthur Kleinman's work on illness narratives as negotiated meanings has been especially influential (Kleinman, 1990; Fadiman, 1997). Kleinman's recent work emphasizes the moral dimension of patient experiences of suffering, recommending that questions about the patient's own understanding of the illness and its cause also explore what matters to the patient within his or her specific social world. His poignant contribution to the bereavement field (Kleinman, 2012) argues that his experience as a widower, interpreted through the frame of his work, suggests that a biomedical perspective on bereavement psychopathology overlooks the importance of grief experiences as they honor our most important relationships. Carrillo et al. (1999) developed a framework for a patient-based approach to crosscultural primary care incorporating Kleinman's questions into a culturally sensitive clinical interview emphasizing social contexts as well as private meanings. This model teaches skills for negotiation between clinician, patient's and family's explanatory models of illness and its impacts, and the patient's desired agenda for care. This model calls for a social context review of systems exploring economic burdens, migration history, social support, language literacy, and health communication, doing so in ways that are patient-centered and problem-specific. The influence of Kleinman's patient-centered cultural approach is also evident in the American Psychological Association recommended DSM-V guidelines for cultural inquiry.

The most widely referenced models of multicultural counseling (Sue & Sue, 2008) argue for a process-oriented understanding of culture emphasizing clinician self-knowledge, respectful communication, and openness to learning even when one's own personal or professional assumptions are challenged by a unique individual or family. Sue and Sue (2008) present a multidimensional approach to developing cultural competence mapping three components of cultural competence: clinician awareness of attitudes and beliefs, knowledge about cultural groups and their complexity, and clinical intervention skills with knowledge of how to best adapt these to cultural beliefs and preferences. These components of cultural competence operate at multiple levels of individual, professional, organizational, and societal and require specific knowledge about racial and cultural groups. While these models often include major themes in worldviews of Latino Americans, African-Americans, Asian-Americans or Native Americans, they do so to heighten awareness of differences when compared to assumptions made by psychotherapy and counseling practice based on European Americans. These approaches caution clinicians to balance universalist (etic or outsider's view) and relativistic (emic or insider's view) methods by recognizing the ways both individual subjectivity and cultural socialization influence experience. Clinically, they require practicing what Sue and Sue call dynamic sizing, assessing when to generalize and when to individualize interventions, depending on how well a particular group's cultural norms fit a specific individual. Further, different dimensions of culture become relevant in addressing specific challenges or problems. The specific challenges of death and its aftermath may call forth traditional ancestral beliefs in otherwise highly acculturated individuals; may bring deeply religious individuals into a crisis of faith; and may increase diversity within a single family whose members may mourn a death distinctly yet interdependently based on culturally meaningful differences in gender, generation, and acculturation. In any treatment setting, the practitioner's socialization into cultural assumptions, the cultural beliefs and practices of a particular treatment setting, and the person in treatment will cocreate a dynamic, multifaceted cultural context for interventions.

Recent work on cultural competence and evidence-based practice (Bernal & Domenech Rodriguez, 2012; Bernal & Saez-Santiago, 2006; Hwang, 2006; Nagayama-Hall, 2001) also emphasizes the importance of knowing empirically supported treatments relevant to a particular patient's care, while also adapting these in ways that are sensitive to culturally based values and experiences. Nagayama-Hall suggests that sensitivity to issues of interdependence, attention to religion and spirituality, and inquiry into experiences of discrimination are examples of culturally meaningful themes that can reorient empirically supported treatments to increase their cultural competence.

Culturally Meaningful Care in Thanatology: Literature Review

Most of the published literature on assessment and intervention in culture, death, and grief uses an ethnographic cultural approach that considers cultural influences on behavior from a single cultural context, or a crosscultural approach comparing cultural differences across different nationalities (Klass, 1999). Rosenblatt (2008) uses a social constructionist approach to culture, death, and grief that emphasizes the dynamic, coconstructed nature of grief reactions. In the field of thanatology, the greatest progress in establishing guidelines for culturally sensitive care has been made in the field of end-of-life and palliative care. As can be expected given the very different social contexts for health care, the UK and Australian literatures emphasize public health perspectives in which health care in general, and compassionate palliative and hospice care in particular, are seen as human rights and guided by governmentally sponsored systematic guidelines. Richardson and Koffman (2012) explore the role of cultural and spiritual beliefs in end-of-life care, for religious and ethnic minority groups experiencing the end of life in the context of multiple, intersecting social disadvantages. They describe the work of the UK charity Social Action for Health, which conducted community-based participatory research to explore the end-of-life experiences of South Asian immigrants and the role of both culturally meaningful practices and societal experiences of exclusion as important dimensions in the education of practitioners. Evans et al. (2012) reviewed the British literature on cultural competence in end-of-life care and were alarmed by the inconsistencies in definitions and guidelines, suggesting that the field is very much in need of systematic integration. Gysel et al. (2012) reviewed the literature on culture and end-of-life care in seven European countries, noting an overemphasis on the quantitative literature in biomedicine, excluding critical contextual factors meaningful to patient- and family-centered care, and lacking a focus on ethnic minority groups within these national settings. Jones (2005) reviews the qualitative research literature on diversity in end-of-life care, applying a view of culture as socially constructed that emphasizes philosophical differences with Western medicine and bioethics emphasizing patient privacy and autonomy. Jones suggests that family-centered and meaning-making approaches in palliative and hospice care support the specific explorations into relationships, religious beliefs and spirituality, social roles, and values needed in appreciating diversity in end-of-life care.

The U.S. literature on culture and end-of-life care has been growing in recent years, recognizing the ways racial and cultural health disparities in access to quality care can impact patient experiences throughout the treatment process and at the end of life (Kagawa-Singer et al., 2010). Barrett (2001) reviews the multicultural competency literature and its implications for end-of-life care. He highlights the need for self-knowledge of privilege on the part of clinicians, an attitude of respect and openness to learning about the role of cultural differences, their intersection with other factors such as social class or sexual orientation, and their relevance in a particular setting, sensitivity to histories of discrimination and their impact on crossracial relationships, and willingness to consult with and refer to knowledgeable colleagues. He argues that culturally competent clinicians are sensitive to institutional barriers preventing minorities from accessing resources for end-of-life care, and to the need for ethnically and racially diverse practitioners offering consultation and care.

Prigerson et al. (2012) argue that while institutional factors and lack of consistent end-of -life guidelines impact racial and cultural differences in end-of-life care, physician sensitivity to communication with diverse patients and to cultural and contextual factors including experiences with racism and spirituality need further study and implementation. Searight and Gafford (2005) review cultural diversity issues in end-of-life care relevant for family physicians, identifying cultural differences in communication of bad news, in who makes decisions concerning care, and in attitudes toward advance directives and end-of life care. They emphasize the greater diversity in preferences for end-of-life care among ethnic minority patients and their families, including sensitivity to cultures that see direct disclosure of terminal diagnoses as potentially disrespectful or harmful in eliminating hope and causing distress. Many immigrant groups, especially Asian-American and Hispanics, place less emphasis on patient autonomy that they may see as isolating, instead valuing protecting patients from burdens of making treatment decisions that are handled by family members in positions of authority due to age or gender. Ethnic minority patients are less likely to sign advance directives, and family members may view advance directives as giving up on a patient's life, compounded by experiences of discrimination and barriers to access. Preferences for aggressive treatment at the end of life may also stem from different views of suffering and the value of life or from emphasis on filial piety and the importance of elders to family life. Because of the complexity and sensitivity of these culturally based beliefs and communication processes, they stress the importance of asking direct questions concerning these preferences and using trained medical translators.

Koenig and Davies (2003) focus on culturally sensitive care for dying children and their families, identifying "differences that make a difference" including immigration status and different cultural beliefs about medical authority; disclosure of illness status; and ways that culture, ethnicity, and race are distinct from social class. They emphasize the importance of communication and negotiation with families about appropriate care, use of medical interpreters when needed, and explaining medical decision making while taking into account cultural differences in attitudes toward palliative care vs. curative care or in declaration of death. They offer a template for assessing ethnocultural differences in care for children with life-limiting conditions and their families that includes: evaluating the actual language used by the child and family members and their openness to discussing diagnosis, prognosis, and death; determining the locus of decision making and their expectations concerning the child's involvement and the medical team's authority versus shared decision making; considering the relevance of religious beliefs concerning healing, death, and the afterlife; evaluating cultural attitudes toward suffering and expressions of pain; assessing how hope for recovery is regarded and discussed; evaluating desires for control of care and views of family involvement in nursing and supportive care; considering issues of gender, political and historical considerations including immigration history, poverty, and histories with racism and discrimination, and using family and community resources in these evaluations. After the child's death, culturally sensitive assessments need to address expectations for how the body should be approached and handled and preferences for expression and duration of grief.

Summary: Challenges of Culturally Competent Thanatology Practice

In sum, culturally meaningful thanatology practice requires a commitment to personal and professional reassessment in response to the challenges presented by cultural differences in death, dying, and bereavement within a diverse society, for example:

- To appreciate the lived experiences of racism and grief described by African-Americans if we are protected by white-skin privilege (Barrett, 2001; Rosenblatt & Wallace, 2005)
- To understand intergenerational obligations constraining Japanese American bereaved adults, caught between elders expecting obedience and acculturated defiant teens, when we view mature independence as emphasizing individual rights (Hwang, 2012)
- To learn how Latino families bring indigenous and African beliefs into interpretations of Catholicism, when we have learned to label these practices as "primitive" (Falicov, 2012)

The great challenge for practitioners striving to understand another culture emerges both because we take our own cultural understandings for granted and because our power and authority makes it possible to inadvertently overlook or silence the experiences of more vulnerable others. For this reason, most guidelines for culturally informed practice emphasize the practitioner's rigorous self-questioning about his or her own cultural biases in every clinical encounter, because each creates a new unique configuration of clinician, patient, and clinical context. This relationally based self-knowledge is generated through respectful listening and willingness to leave the safe territory of expertise, in order to be educated, humbled, or surprised by what we learn from others about their culturally based experiences with dying, death, loss, grief, renewal, and growth. Families become the experts on their own experiences of death, dying, and grief within culture, and we gain enormously from these opportunities to leave our own cultural comfort zones. We learn how far we can go before we confront the limits of our expertise, and when we need to collaborate with or refer to practitioners with the appropriate linguistic and cultural background. We learn how to explore a bereaved family's own goals for grief, recovery, and growth and to help them mobilize the personal, family, and community resources to do so. Clinical encounters with difference require that we carefully scrutinize our own assumptions in an ongoing conversation with colleagues and with the bereaved families we serve. Using terms such as *collaboration* and *dialogue* emphasize that communication across differences must be centered on knowing the lived experiences and desired goals of others, especially when that knowledge will challenge our own personal and professional assumptions. Through the self-awareness generated by authentic dialogue, we can learn to appreciate how realities we confront in our lives and values we strive to live by shape distinctive pathways for new lives altered by death.

In ecosystemic, collaborative thanatology practice, the culturally meaningful appreciative inquiry initiating an assessment already incorporates important principles mobilizing positive growth, healing, and wellness. Respectful listening sensitive to the ways death and its circumstances have impacted on family members, with an attitude of openness and curiosity about what a family might teach us about their understanding and traditions, creates a climate of relationship support honoring the family's narrative experience. This actively counters the experience of being treated in disrespectful or racist ways due to ethnic minority status and of having relationships sidelined in the interest of high-technology care in many settings. By conducting an appreciative inquiry, we have actively framed a way of listening, learning, goal setting, and planning designed to reduce suffering and distress while also promoting positive developmental processes that mobilize positive adaptation and growth.

Culturally sensitive care requires a creative rethinking of our customary practice training, as we evaluate what we thought we knew for certain and discover the worlds of diverse patients we had little exposure to. It challenges us to learn new dimensions of our own cultural socialization in our own changing family lifecycle, as we encounter diverse individuals struggling with illness mortality and loss. It rewards us with an extraordinary expansion of our worldviews and affirms the vast resources for replenishment available even in the midst of suffering and adversity.

Chapter 22

Religion, Spirituality, and Assessment and Intervention

Kenneth J. Doka

Introduction

One cannot understand life-threatening illness as only a medical crisis. It is a psychological, social, and family crisis as well. Yet, even more than that, it is a spiritual crisis—fraught with existential questions.

This chapter attempts to address, at least in part, those questions. The chapter begins by defining both spirituality and religion and exploring the ways that spirituality and religious faith influence the experience of life-threatening illness, death, and grief. It seeks to offer tools for assessing and utilizing the spiritual strengths of those who face illness and the prospect of death—recognizing that in this final encounter an individual needs to marshal all resources.

Religion and Spirituality: An Overview

Religion and spirituality are often elusive concepts that are difficult to define and differentiate. For example, a New Zealand study of patients and providers found divergent definitions. Some simply equated religion and spirituality. A second group saw spirituality in the nonphysical and extraordinary dimensions of life, while a third group defined it in more humanistic and existential terms (Egan, MacLeod, Jaye, McGee, Baxter, & Herbison, 2011). A Consensus Conference funded by the Archstone Foundation brought together scholars and practitioners from a broad range of fields and disciplines in 2009. The agreed upon definition emerging from the Consensus Conference was that: Spirituality is the aspect of humanity that refers to the ways that individuals seek and express meaning and purpose and the way they experience their connectedness to the moment, to self, to others, to nature, and to the significant or sacred (Puchalski, Ferrell, Virani, Otis-Green, Baird, Bull, Chochinov, Handzo, Nelson-Becker, Prince-Paul, Pugilese, & Sulmasy, 2009, p. 887). The International Workgroup on Dying, Death, and Bereavement defines spirituality as "concerned with the transcendental, inspirational, and existential way to live one's life" (1990, p. 75). Miller's definition is more poetic:

Spirituality relates to our souls. It involves the deep inner essence of who we are. It is an openness to the possibility that the soul within each of us is somehow related to the Soul of all that is. Spirituality is what happens to us that is so memorable that we cannot forget it, and yet we find it hard to talk about because words fail to describe it. Spirituality is the act of looking for meaning in the very deepest sense; and looking for it in a way that is most authentically ours (1994).

To Miller, spirituality is inherently individual, personal, and eclectic. Religion, however, is more collective. Religion is a belief shared within a group of people. Miller again offers a lyrical perspective:

Now religion works in a very different way. While spirituality is very personal, religion is more communal. In fact, if you take the words back to its origins, "religion means that which binds together," "that which ties things into a package." Religion has to do with collecting and consolidating and unifying. Religion says, "Here are special words that are meant to be passed on. Take them to heart." Religion says, "Here is a set of beliefs that form a coherent whole. Take them as your own." Religion says, "Here are people for you to revere and historical events for you to recall. Remember them." Religion says, "Here is a way for you to act when you come together as a group, and here's a way to behave when you're apart" (1994).

Thus while spirituality is very personal, a person's spirituality may very well be shaped by an individual's religious beliefs. Yet, because of the individual nature of spirituality, religious affiliation is not likely to be the sole determinant of spiritual beliefs. Often developmental outlooks, personal experiences, and cultural perspectives will join with religious beliefs in shaping an individual's spirituality.

However, whatever these beliefs are, they are likely to be challenged by life-threatening illness, dying, and death. As stated earlier, a life-threatening illness is an existential crisis. The encounter with the possibility or even the probability of death raises a series of questions. Why do I have this diagnosis and why now? Is life worth this suffering, treatment, and uncertainty? Is it consistent with my belief system, my spirituality to cease treatment or forego certain types of treatment? If I recover what did I learn, what will I take, and what will I do with this experience? If I die, did my life have meaning, and how do I wish to die, and what will happen after? Death brings similar questions: Why did this person have to die—now or in this way?

A life-threatening illness or death then is a reachable moment—a time where one's spirituality looms large. Because the assumptive world is now called into question a person is able to be reached—that is, to consider other ways to examine his or her spirituality. That spirituality may offer answers and reassurance, breeding resilience. Or that spirituality may seem empty now leading to an existential despair or a new quest for a deeper spiritual sense that can sustain one in this crisis.

Religion and Spirituality: Complicating and Facilitating Factors

Research has indicated that religion and spirituality can both facilitate and complicate responses to life-threatening illness and grief. In reviewing this research, it is well to link both terms as the operational definitions of spirituality and religion vary considerably among the researchers. Nonetheless, this research has indicated that spirituality and religion can have positive roles in assisting individuals who struggle with life-threatening illness or grief.

For example, research has supported the fact that religion and spirituality can assist persons in finding a sense of meaning in the illness (Siegel & Schrimshaw, 2002). Often the diagnosis of a life-threatening illness challenges an individual's assumptive world as the person struggles with attempting to make sense of the illness. Later in the illness, individuals may seek to make sense of their suffering, their death, or their life. In summation, life-threatening illness strikes at the totality of the person—not just his or her physical well-being but also his or her psyche, social relationships, and spirituality

Throughout this existential endeavor, religious and spiritual perspectives can offer meanings. Religious and spiritual perspectives may reassure persons with life-threatening illness that their illness is part of a larger plan or that the illness experience may offer lessons to self or others. Even with death, there is some evidence that religious and spiritual beliefs may minimize fear and uncertainty (Siegel & Schrimshaw, 2002). In short, spiritual and religious perspectives can assist individuals in making sense of the illness.

It may also allow a sense of a larger connection. Even in the inherent existential isolation of an illness, there may be a sense that a god or some higher power will sustain and protect. This connection may be more tangible as well. Many individuals may benefit from the social support available through the ministries of a chaplain, clergy, spiritual advisor, ministry team, or even within the larger faith community. The sense that one is not alone—others are caring, visiting, and praying seems to provide benefit (Siegel & Schrimshaw, 2002; Townsend, Kladder, & Mulligan, 2002).

Religious and spiritual practices and beliefs may even enhance health. Most spiritual belief systems suggest either abstinence or moderation in certain behaviors such as alcohol or tobacco use. Such practices and beliefs may discourage inappropriate coping techniques throughout the course of the illness or subsequent grief. Spiritual and religious beliefs also may enhance coping by encouraging self-esteem. Most religious and spiritual systems stress the inherent worth of the individual. Such beliefs may be especially important in a life-threatening illness or in grief where self-blame may loom large and self-acceptance is threatened. There is also some speculation that spiritual and religious beliefs may have physiological benefits such as lowering blood pressure or enhancing immune function though here the research has shown some inconsistency (Dane, 2000; Lin & Bauer-Wu, 2003; Miller & Thoresen, 2003; Olive, 2004; Sephton, Koopman, Shaal, Thoresen, & Spiegel 2001; Stefanek, McDonald, & Hess, 2005).

Religious and spiritual beliefs also may influence an individual's sense of control. In a time of life-threatening illness, an individual may feel that he or she has little or no control. Religious and spiritual beliefs may reaffirm a sense of personal control. Self-efficacy can be expressed in a number of ways. Individuals may have a sense of interpretive control— that is the ability to find meaning or benefit from the experience. They may have a sense of vicarious control—leaving the illness in the hands of a higher power. In some cases, the control may be of a predictive nature, perhaps believing that God will cure them or be with them throughout this experience.

Yet, this discussion also demonstrates the ways that religious and spiritual beliefs may complicate the response to a life-threatening illness or grief. For example, a person with life-threatening illness may be convinced that he or she may be cured by a divine intervention. If death ensues, such an individual or other family members may become immobilized, unrealistic in decisions, or even despondent.

Certain religious or spiritual beliefs may serve to increase rather than decrease death anxiety or complicate grief. For example, fears over divine judgment or uncertainty in an afterlife may not offer comfort to a dying person. The certainty with which religious and spiritual beliefs are held as well as the nature of such beliefs is a factor in the reasons that the relationship of religiosity and spirituality to death anxiety is inconsistent (Neimeyer, 1994). Moreover, religious and spiritual perspectives can sometimes conflict with medical practices and advice. For example, some spiritual systems such as Christian Science may eschew any medical treatment while others such as the Jehovah Witnesses may prohibit certain medical practices such as blood transfusions or blood-based therapies. In other cases, a fatalistic spirituality may inhibit health-seeking behaviors or adherence to a medical regimen. It is little wonder that Pargement, Koenig, Tarakeshwar, and Hahn (2004) found in a longitudinal study that certain types of religious coping such as seeking spiritual support or believing in a benevolent god were related with better health while other spiritual coping behaviors and beliefs such as a perspective of a punishing god or religious discontent were predictive of declines in health.

Religious and spiritual beliefs also may be evident in reactions to illness. For example, anger could be directed toward god. There may be anger that one has the disease or that the disease has come at an inopportune or unfair time. Guilt may be clouded by a moral guilt—a belief that this illness is a punishment for some transgression. Fear and anxiety, as mentioned earlier, can also have a religious or spiritual root, as one may fear the wrath of God in this world or the next. There may even be an existential sense of abandonment—a sense that one is facing the crisis alone, alienated from god. In all of these cases, religious and spiritual beliefs may intertwine with psychological and affective reactions to the illness.

Spiritual Tasks in Life-Threatening Illness

Throughout the illness, an individual may have to cope with distinctly spiritual tasks. In an earlier work (Doka, 1993b), I proposed, building on the work of both Weisman (1980) and Pattison (1978), that life-threatening illness can best be viewed as a series of phases. These phases are the prediagnostic, diagnostic, chronic, terminal, and recovery phases. In any particular disease, individuals may jump from one phase to another. For example, in some cases, a successful removal of a tumor may place an individual right into a recovery phase with virtually no chronic phase. In another disease, diagnosis may be immediately followed by a steep and inexorable decline toward death. In each phase, there were distinct medical, psychological, social, and spiritual tasks.

For example, with the first two phases, the prediagnostic and diagnostic phases, individuals had to deal with the diagnosis of a life-threatening illness. As Weisman (1980) notes that even when the diagnosis is expected or feared, it still comes as a shock, creating a sense of existential plight where one's very existence is threatened. Often it is a life divide. Even if the person survives the encounter, it often will be seen as a turning point wrought with implications that follow for the rest of life.

Here the spiritual issue is incorporating the present reality of illness into one's sense of past and future. Questions such as, Why did I get this disease, now? loom large here. An individual now struggles to make sense of the disease and of the new reality of his or her life. Spiritual and religious beliefs may offer an answer to these questions or at least provide direction for further quest.

The chronic phase centers around the time of treatment. Here the individual must not only cope with the disease but also the burdens and side effects of treatment. Often as persons continue such treatment, they may resume some of their prior roles—returning to work or functioning within their families. Often, this time is lonely. The crisis of the diagnosis is now past, so family, friends, and other social support may not be as available. This phase can also be a time of great uncertainty as individuals cope with the ambiguities of both the disease and treatment.

In the chronic phase, suffering may become a major spiritual issue. Why am I suffering through this disease and treatment? Is it all worth it? Persons will often look to their religious or spiritual beliefs to make sense of this suffering. Their beliefs may vary. Again some may see the suffering as retribution for sins in this or another life. Some may even find comfort, believing that suffering now may offer recompense or even purification that will mollify God or better prepare them for an afterlife. Others may see suffering as random. Still others may see their suffering as a learning experience allowing greater empathy. Others may see it as sacrifice, offering it as a way to gain a greater connection to God or others. Such beliefs can strongly influence patients' receptiveness to pain management (Doka, 2006).

Not everyone dies from life-threatening illness. Many individuals may fully recover, resuming their lives, and others may face long, even permanent, periods of remission. Yet, the encounter with disease leaves all types of residues. Individuals may have an enhanced sense of their fragility, feeling that they are living under a sword that can strike at any time (Koocher & O'Malley, 1981).

There also are spiritual residues. Individuals may struggle with a sense of the bargain. It is not unusual for persons to make spiritual commitments and promises in a cosmic deal to surmount the illness. Now that they have recovered from this threat, individuals may now feel they have to fulfill their promises. A failure to fulfill such commitments may loom large should a person experience a relapse or even encounter another disease.

There may be other spiritual changes as well. Some individuals may move closer to their religion or become more spiritually aware and active. Others may feel alienated either from their god or their spiritual community. Some may actively seek a new spirituality, perceiving that their past beliefs did not serve them well in this crisis.

During the course of a life-threatening illness, patients and their families will have to make critical ethical decisions about care. How long should active medical treatment persist even if it is perceived as futile? When should treatment cease, and who should be empowered to make such determinations? Should the patient receive artificial hydration and nutrition? Can treatments be withheld, or if administered, withdrawn? Is assisted suicide ever a valid ethical choice in life-threatening illness?

Health professionals have long realized that religious and spiritual systems play a significant role in the ways that patients and their families make end-of-life decisions and resolve ethical dilemmas (Koenig, 2004). As patients and their families struggle with these decisions, they often turn to their religious and spiritual values, and even to their clergy or spiritual mentors, for guidance.

In the terminal phase, the goal of treatment moves from extending life or curing the individual to a strictly palliative goal. In this phase, individuals often struggle with three spiritual needs (Doka, 1993a; 1993b). The first is to have lived a meaningful life. Individuals may assess their life to find a sense of meaning and purpose. Here individuals may struggle seeking forgiveness for tasks unaccomplished or for hurtful acts that they may have committed. Life review and reminiscence therapy can assist individuals in achieving a sense of meaningfulness. Individuals may struggle with a second goal—to die an appropriate death, however that experience is individually defined. A final spiritual need is to find hope beyond the grave: The individual needs a sense that life will continue— in whatever appropriate way is supported by the person's spiritual understanding. This sense of continuity can include living on the memories of others, in the genes of family members, within one's community, in the creations and legacies left, in a sense of eternal nature (that is, that one returns to the cycle of life), in some transcendental mode, or in an afterlife (Lifton & Olsen, 1974; Doka 1993b).

Spirituality and Grief: After the Death

Families, too, may cope with similar spiritual issues. Even after the individual dies, the family may still spiritually struggle, trying to reconstruct their own faith or spiritual system that may have been challenged by that loss (Doka, 1993a). There may be very significant spiritual issues as individuals experience grief. Bereaved individuals may experience a number of spiritual reactions. There may be a loss of faith. Individuals who are grieving may have a spiritual or cosmic anger—alienating them from sources of spiritual strengths such as their beliefs, rituals, faith practices, or their faith community. They may experience a sense of moral guilt—or a belief that the death of the deceased is due to some moral failing or sin that is now being punished.

As in illness, spirituality can be both facilitating and complicating. It may allow a sense of meaning—that this loss fulfills some purpose or is part of a cosmic plan. Spirituality can offer a sense of connection—a belief that the deceased is now safe or happy or a belief that even entertains a possibility of future contact or reunion. Spiritual beliefs and practices can even allow a continuing connection—through, for example, prayer, veneration of ancestors, or some other form of contact.

Yet, not all beliefs or practices are facilitating. Some beliefs may disallow or disenfranchise the normal feelings of grief as indicating a lack of faith. Other beliefs may trouble the bereaved. For example, a survivor of a completed suicide who feels that a person who commits suicide faces eternal damnation may find such a belief complicates grief.

Assisting Individuals and Families at the End of Life: Utilizing Spirituality

Since spirituality is so central as individuals and their families struggle with later life, it is important that holistic care includes spiritual assessment. The Consensus Conference suggested a threefold process that included a quick spiritual screening to assess whether the illness has created a spiritual crisis, a spiritual history to understand the patient's needs and resources, and a full spiritual assessment completed by a board certified chaplain (Puchalski, Ferrell, Virani, Otis-Green, Baird, Bull, Chochinov, Handzo, Nelson-Becker, Prince-Paul, Pugilese, & Sulmasy, 2009). Based on the results of such a process, spiritual intervention can become another component of care.

While there are a variety of tools to assist spiritual histories and assessment (Hodge, 2005; Ledger, 2005), the key really is to engage both the individual and family in an exploration of their individual and collective spiritual histories. The goal is to understand the collective and individual spiritual journeys. Do they identify with a particular faith? Do they actively practice that faith—engaging in public and private rituals and practices? Do they belong to a church, temple, synagogue, or mosque? How important is their faith system in making decisions?

Such an assessment should go beyond religious affiliation. It might be worthwhile to explore with individuals when and where they feel most spiritually connected. What practices they utilize when they're stressed, anxious, or depressed? What are the stories, prayers, or songs that offer spiritual comfort? Such approaches may allow a larger exploration of the very distinct ways that individuals find meaning and hope. An assessment may yield information on spiritual strengths that an individual possesses, themes within an individual's spirituality (such as grace, karma, fate, or retribution etc.), and experiences that have tended to challenge that person's spirituality. Occasionally, such an assessment may uncover forms of spiritual abuse—spiritual beliefs or practices or behaviors of spiritual mentors that have resulted in a sense of spiritual alienation.

Once an assessment of spirituality is made, individuals can be encouraged to connect with their spiritual strengths. Often, this connection involves their clergy, chaplains, spiritual mentors, or members of their faith community. Clergy, chaplains, and other spiritual mentors can play an important supportive (and sometimes an unsupportive) role as an individual responds to a life-threatening illness, death, or grief. Their visits throughout the illness may be valued. Clergy, chaplains, and other spiritual advisors may be sought as an individual or family member responds to the spiritual questions inherent in the experiences of grief and illness. Despite the importance of ministry to the ill, the dying, and bereaved, many clergy reported little formal seminary education on dealing with dying patients and their families (Doka & Jendreski, 1985; Abrams, Albury, Crandall, Doka, & Harris. 2005).

While clergy, chaplains, and other spiritual mentors play an important role, faith communities also can play a critical role. Often, such communities can offer spiritual comfort and connection; visits, calls, cards and letters that show support and ease isolation; and assistance with tangible tasks such as cooking, home maintenance, transportation, and caregiving. Spiritual beliefs and practices also may be sources of strength. A person's spiritual beliefs may be critical in making meaning throughout an illness and for family, after the death. Often a simple question such as, How do your beliefs speak to you in this situation? can engage the person in spiritual exploration. It may also be useful to investigate the ways that the individual's beliefs assisted and helped the person make sense of the experience in earlier crisis. There may be situations where the individual's beliefs seem inadequate or dysfunctional.

Spiritual practices such as prayer and meditation also may have a role in the illness. At the very least, intercessory prayer (that is the prayer of others) is a tangible sign that the individual is not facing this crisis alone. It offers family and friends a tangible thing to do—reaffirming a form of vicarious control in an unsettled time. Individuals who are struggling with physical illness often use prayer as a form of coping (Ribbentrop, Altmaier, Chen, Found, & Keffala, 2005). There is some evidence that prayer and meditation do affect physical health in a number of ways including lowering stress levels and blood pressure (*Mayo Clinic Health Letter*, 2005). Schroeder-Sheker (1994) has even pioneered the field of musical thanatology, using spiritual music as a way to ease the transition to death.

Rituals also can be a source of comfort to both the ill or dying patient as well as family. Many faith traditions that have rituals for the sick and the dying, such as the Roman Catholic Rite for Anointing of the Sick (popularly known as *Last Rites*) or rituals at the time of death such as washing or preparing the body.

Individuals who do not have distinctive rituals as part of their tradition may be invited to create one at the time of death. These rituals can include acts such as lighting a candle, anointing the dead person, and joining in prayer or meditation, singing a spiritual hymn or song, or in other, individual ways saying a final goodbye to mark the transition from life to death. Rituals work well in these liminal or transitional moments—offering participants a way to acknowledge loss and transition.

Certainly rituals after the death such as funerals can be critically important to families and others as they cope with loss. Funerals can allow mourners a sense of reality of death, a chance to ventilate feelings, meaningful actions in a disorganized time, opportunities to remember the deceased, bring together supportive others, and interpret the death according to their own philosophical or spiritual background (Rando, 1984). The value of funerals can be enhanced when mourners have opportunities to plan and participate in the ritual (Doka & Jendreski, 1985). Moreover rituals can be utilized therapeutically throughout the mourning process (Martin & Doka, 2000).

Conclusion: The Challenge of Spiritual Support

Spiritual support can be a challenge. Many health professionals have little specialized training in spirituality. Moreover, there may be concern lest one impose his or her own spirituality upon a patient or family member. Sometimes out of respect for the diversity and individuality of a person's spiritual beliefs, health professionals may be reluctant to enter into conversations involving religion or spirituality. Thus, there often is temptation to leave these issues to chaplains, clergy, or other spiritual mentors. Such delegation to spiritual mentors is unlikely to suffice. Spiritual concerns arise throughout the entire experience of the illness. Patients and families will choose when, where, and with whom they will share these spiritual concerns. These choices may not always fit into neat organizational charts or job descriptions. They are the responsibility of the team.

Nor can these spiritual concerns be neglected. Holistic care entails that spiritual concerns both are acknowledged and validated. A true respect for spirituality means that such concerns and struggles need be addressed by every professional. Spirituality therefore cannot be ignored. Death, after all, may be the ultimate spiritual journey.

Chapter 23

Historical and Contemporary Perspectives on Assessment and Intervention

Robert A. Neimeyer and John R. Jordan

Historically, care for the dying and the bereaved has been the responsibility of family members and their community. People have traditionally sought comfort from those who knew the deceased and shared the loss. However, in keeping with the greater complexity of modern life, these informal supports have been supplemented in recent decades by a cadre of volunteers and professionals who offer some form of counseling and guidance for people who have experienced loss. For example, in some countries such as the UK, support networks have grown to include well-coordinated organizations of trained volunteers who provide outreach to the recently bereaved under the aegis of groups like Cruse, which organizes national and regional conferences to share developments in theory, research, and practice. In the United States, the growth of organizations such as the Association for Death Education and Counseling provides for similar dissemination of knowledge and skills among professional counselors, coupled with certification programs to ensure their familiarity with recent theories and research. In Australia, government-funded bereavement care is becoming even more fully integrated into the national landscape, especially in the aftermath of natural disasters such as bushfires and floods that have devastated whole communities. Finally, in recognition that bereavement care is a crucial element of end-of -life care, networks of bereavement care services throughout the world are growing to extend the compassionate engagement of oncology and hospice services beyond the terminal patient to family members. This chapter offers a brief review of some of the key concepts that guide these more formal caregiving efforts, with a focus on the diagnosis and treatment of problematic grief responses of adults following the death of a loved one. It is divided into four sections: (1) historical perspectives, (2) contemporary perspectives on assessment, (3) interventions, and (4) evidence-based practice.

Historical Perspectives on Assessment and Intervention

Foundational Concepts of Normal and Complicated Grieving

Perhaps inevitably, efforts to understand problematic grief lead to questions about the boundary between normal and complicated responses. Indeed, the issue of what constitutes normal grief, and whether there is any form of grief response that should be pathologized, is one that is still contested within thanatology (Hogan, Worden, & Schmidt, 2006; Neimeyer, 2006a; Prigerson & Maciejewski, 2006). Similarly, important debates have developed about the similarities and differences between grief and depression, and the merit (or problems) involved in changing the diagnostic categories of the Diagnostic and Statistical Manual (version V) to reflect a new understanding of bereavement-related depression (Wakefield & First, 2012; Wakefield, Schmitz, First, & Horwitz, 2007; Zisook & Kendler, 2007). While the potential for losses to be devastating has been the subject of human reflection for thousands of years, the scientific study of bereavement can be dated to the work of Sigmund Freud (Freud, 1957). His idea that healthy mourning required *decathexis* (the withdrawal of emotional energy from the deceased), while pathological bereavement involved a failure to psychologically let go of the deceased, has profoundly influenced both professional and public views of what is to be expected in mourning (Stroebe, Schut, & Stroebe, 2005). Subsequently, most major 20th century bereavement theorists have set forth variations on this theme of decathexis (Bowlby, 1980; Lindemann, 1944; Parkes, 1996).

The key process in this conceptualization is grief work (*trauerarbeit* in Freud's terms), which assumes that mourning entails experiencing and expressing the difficult thoughts, emotions, and memories that have been triggered by the loss (Stroebe, Gergen, Gergen, & Stroebe, 1992). Seen from this broad psychodynamic perspective, grieving has been viewed as a process of painfully reviewing or working through and then letting go of the attachment to the deceased by way of confrontation with the reality of the death and emotional catharsis of the resulting emotions. From this perspective, assessment of the grieving process involves judging the extent to which this grief work has been accomplished (or avoided), and interventions are designed to facilitate the resolution of the attachment by assisting in this necessary labor. Failure to confront the reality of the loss, as well as failure to perform the psychological work involved in letting go, have been viewed as the core of a pathological grief response. Note that this viewpoint emphasizes the largely intrapsychic nature of grieving, with pathological grief residing within the psychological skin of the mourner.

Building upon this foundation, the 20th century also saw the emergence of various stage and task models of bereavement. Beginning with the popularity of Kubler-Ross's book, *On Death and Dying* (Kubler-Ross, 1969), stage and task theories have been widely accepted by the professional community as well as the public. Typically, stage models suggest that mourners begin in a state of denial of the reality of the loss, and move through a series of unwelcome emotional phases of adaptation marked by anger, bargaining, and depression before achieving some form of acceptance or resolution. Alternatively, other theorists emphasize the necessary activities of grieving, such as the need to accept the reality of the death, experience the pain of the grief, and adjust to an environment in which the deceased is missing (Worden, 2002; Worden & Winokuer, 2011). Correspondingly, the failure to progress through the stages or tasks implies unfinished grief work, and interventions are designed to facilitate resolution of this uncompleted activity.

Recent Challenges to the Traditional Grief Work Model

These traditional views of mourning are being challenged on many fronts in contemporary thanatology. For example, longitudinal studies of bereavement adaptation fail to provide much support for a model of stages of emotional response to grief (Maciejewski, Zhang, Block, & Prigerson, 2007). One recent study of a large cohort of bereaved individuals suffering the death of a loved one by natural causes found that acceptance of the death, presumably the final stage of adaptation, actually was the predominant response of survivors from the earliest weeks of loss, with depression and yearning being the strongest of the negative indicators of grief-related distress across 2 years of bereavement, while symptoms of denial and anger occurred at consistently low levels. In contrast, for those whose loved ones died by accident, homicide or suicide, disbelief did predominate in early weeks, with anger and depression eclipsing yearning for the loved one across much of the grieving period (Holland & Neimeyer, 2010). Such findings argue against the relevance of one-size-fits-all models of mourning, as well as for the importance of evaluating popular models against actual data on adaptation to loss.

Furthermore, research has called into question the necessity of confronting and working through a loss for all mourners. For example, researchers present compelling data that suggest that, at least after spousal loss, not everyone appears to go through a painful process of depression and mourning. Some spouses seem to begin coping well within a matter of weeks, and some even experience apparent relief following their partner's potentially lengthy illness or a long but conflictual marriage (Bonanno, 2004; Bonanno, Wortman, & Nesse, 2004; Wortman & Silver, 1987). Such findings argue that traditional models of grief have underestimated people's resilience in the face of loss, and indeed more recent empirical studies suggest that many normal grievers will adapt well to loss over a period of several months, with or without formal grief counseling (Currier, Neimeyer, & Berman, 2008) (particularly after more normative losses such as the death of a partner/spouse in later in life).

Likewise, the idea that decathexis is central to the process of grieving is being challenged by theorists who argue that the establishment of ongoing bonds with the deceased is both healthier and more normative across human cultures than the notion of detachment from the deceased (Klass, Silverman, & Nickman, 1996; Rubin, 1999). While refinements are emerging in the types of continuing bonds with the deceased that may be adaptive or pathological (Field, Gao, & Paderna, 2005), the field appears to be moving away from the earlier view that successful mourning necessarily involves a relinquishment of the emotional attachment to the deceased. Instead, evidence suggests that maintaining an emotional bond with the loved one may be comforting or distressing, depending on such factors as how far along survivors are in their bereavement (Field & Friedrichs, 2004), whether they have been able to make sense of the loss (Neimeyer, Baldwin, & Gillies, 2006), and perhaps their level of security in important attachment relationships (Stroebe & Schut, 2005). Accordingly, theorists espousing a two-track model of bereavement (TTMB) (Rubin, Malkinson, & Witztum, 2011) advocate assessing difficulties occurring on both the track of biopsychosocial functioning (e.g., depression, anxiety, work performance) and the track of the relationship to the deceased (e.g., how the loved one is held in memory, residual feelings in the relationship, ritual practices for maintaining his or her presence in the mourner's life). This two-track assessment then permits careful targeting of problems in both domains in the context of grief therapy.

In the wake of growing skepticism about traditional models of mourning, other new theories also have been proposed. One such model is the dual process model of coping with bereavement formulated by Stroebe and Schut (Stroebe & Schut, 1999, 2010), which argues that normal grief involves an oscillation between confronting the loss (loss orientation) and compartmentalizing it so that the mourner can attend to the life changes necessitated by the death (restoration orientation). This increasingly influential departure from traditional thinking describes mourning as a cyclical rather than linear and stagelike process, as the mourner repeatedly revisits the loss and its associated emotions, strives to reorganize the relationship to the deceased, and to take on new roles and responsibilities necessitated by a changed world. This formulation also extends our understanding of pathology by suggesting that the inability to distract oneself from or avoid grief may be as much a sign of pathology as the inability to confront it. It is important to note, however, that although recent research documents engagement in both loss-oriented and restoration-oriented stressors on the part of bereaved people, just what constitutes the optimal balance and timing of focusing on each remains to be determined (Carr, 2010).

Yet another important theoretical development is the emergence of a meaning reconstruction approach to grief (Neimeyer, 2011a; Neimeyer, Burke, Mackay, & Stringer, 2010). In this perspective, bereavement is viewed as challenging the survivor's self-narrative, the basic organization of life events and themes that allows people to interpret the past, invest in the present, and anticipate the future (Neimeyer, 2006b, 2001). Although the meaning systems on which people rely to negotiate life transitions are often resilient, providing resources that promote adaptation, recent research documents that a painful search for meaning in the near aftermath of loss forecasts more intense grief months and years later, whereas the capacity to find significance of the loss predicts greater long-term well-being and resilience (Coleman & Neimeyer, 2010). Attention to this quest for meaning may be especially critical in cases of traumatic loss, such as suicide, homicide, and fatal accidents, where an inability to make sense of the death appears to mediate the impact of these violent as opposed to natural deaths on the subsequent adaptation of the survivor (Currier, Holland, & Neimeyer, 2006), perhaps especially in the case of suicide bereavement (Jordan, 2008; Jordan & McIntosh, 2011). Likewise, studies of parents who have lost a child have documented that a struggle to make sense of the loss accounts for considerably more of the intensity of the parents' grief than such objective factors as the passage of time, the cause of death, or the parents' gender (Keesee, Currier, & Neimeyer, 2008). Investigations that trace just what meanings the bereaved find in their experience are therefore particularly useful (Park, 2010), such as those that suggest the generally salutary role of spiritual meaning making in predicting less intense grief after tragic loss (Lichtenthal, Currier, Neimeyer, & Keesee, 2010). Nonetheless, other recent research suggests that spiritual coping is no panacea for profound grief, as longitudinal study of people mourning the homicide of a loved one suggests that high levels of complicated grief symptomatology earlier in bereavement forecast later spiritual struggles, whereas neither positive nor negative religious coping predicted subsequent grief (Burke, Neimeyer, McDevitt-Murphy, Ippolito, & Roberts, 2011; Neimeyer & Burke, 2011). Taken alongside the accumulating evidence for the role of sense making and benefit finding in bereavement adaptation (Neimeyer & Sands, 2011), such findings argue for the relevance of meaning-making strategies in grief therapy, a point to which we will return.

Lastly, although social support has generally been acknowledged as important by most grief theorists (Stroebe, Stroebe, Abakoumin, & Schut, 1996), the failure to grieve successfully has traditionally been understood as a problem contained within the individual mourner. However, recent approaches have begun to focus on the transactional nature of mourning at levels ranging from family processes (Walsh & McGoldrick, 2004) to cultural discourses about bereavement (Dennis, 2011). This view suggests that the meaning of the loss for an individual cannot be separated from the family, community, and societal meanings ascribed to death and loss and the resulting social responses to the mourner. This more systemic approach recognizes that the bereaved must adapt not only to a world where the deceased is no longer physically available, but also where many other altered aspects of the postloss interpersonal landscape must be confronted. While these changes have clear intrapsychic components, they also intimately involve the interactions that mourners have with other people, who provide approval and support for or disapproval and withdrawal from the bereaved based on the fit of the mourner's coping style with their altered networks (Neimeyer & Jordan, 2002). Beyond this focus on the broader social context, exacting qualitative research on the relational negotiation of grief within families has begun to document their dynamic regulatory processes, such as cooperation in maintaining a bearable distance from the acute pain arising from the loss of a child, while also safeguarding the child's memory (Hooghe, Neimeyer, & Rober, 2012).

In short, developments in bereavement theory are beginning to change our understanding of what constitutes an expectable response to loss, and with it, our view of what constitutes pathological grief. This shift toward a more complex and refined understanding of the heterogeneity of the grief response is particularly important for assessment and intervention, the topics to which we shall now turn.

Contemporary Perspectives on the Assessment of Grief

Complicated Grief: Symptomatology and Diagnosis

Currently, the mental health community, as represented by the current edition of the Diagnostic and Statistical Manual of the American Psychiatric Association (DSM IV-R), does not officially recognize any pattern of grief as pathological. Bereavement is viewed as a life problem that may need clinical attention, but it is not, in and of itself, a mental disorder. Instead, difficulties adjusting to a loss must be diagnosed in terms of depression, anxiety, or other disorders, such as posttraumatic stress disorder (PTSD). This official position notwithstanding, a great deal of evidence has accumulated over the last 15 years that supports the diagnosis of one particularly pernicious response to bereavement, alternately termed *complicated grief* (CG) (Shear et al., 2011b) or *prolonged grief disorder* (PGD) (Prigerson et al., 2009)[1]. Table 1 summarizes criteria for this condition, adapted from those put forward by the two major work groups contributing to the literature and summarizing existing research.

Table 1. Diagnostic Features of Complicated Grief

1. Duration of bereavement of at least 6 months
2. Marked and persistent separation distress, reflected in intense feelings of loneliness, yearning for or preoccupation with the person who has died
3. At least 5 of the following 9 symptoms experienced nearly daily to a disabling degree:
   - Diminished sense of self (e.g., as if a part of oneself has died)
   - Difficultly accepting the loss on emotional as well as intellectual levels
   - Avoidance of reminders of the reality of the loss
   - Inability to trust others or to feel that others understand
   - Bitterness or anger over the death
   - Difficulty moving on or embracing new friends and interests
   - Numbness or inability to feel
   - Sensing that life or the future is without purpose or meaning
   - Feeling stunned, dazed, or shocked by the death
4. Significant impairment in social, occupational, or family functioning

Adapted from H. G. Prigerson, et al., 2009 and M. K. Shear et al., 2011a.

The criteria for CG essentially describe a combination of intense and prolonged separation distress regarding the deceased, along with signs that the mourner's adaptation socially and psychologically have been compromised by the death. Note that the diagnosis refers to symptoms experienced by the mourner, regardless of the circumstances of the death, which may or may not be sudden or violent. A considerable amount of empirical research has demonstrated that the presence of CG is associated with elevated rates of psychological distress, physical illness, and social dysfunction (Lichtenthal, Cruess, & Prigerson, 2004; Prigerson et al., 2009; Prigerson, Vanderwerker, & Maciejewski, 2008). Moreover, the CG diagnosis has been shown to cohere as a symptom cluster, to differ sufficiently from major depression and posttraumatic stress disorder to be legitimately considered a separate diagnostic category (Prigerson & Maciejewski, 2006) and to predict deleterious health outcomes even once depression and anxiety symptoms are taken into account (Bonanno et al., 2007). Although a good deal of converging evidence supports the validity of this conceptualization of complicated grief, it is worth underscoring that it does not exhaust the ways in which bereavement can be complicated. For example, in addition to increasing the risk of protracted and disabling grief per se, loss of a loved one to homicide greatly elevates the risk of clinically significant posttraumatic stress and depressive symptomatology in mourners, which also deserve careful evaluation (McDevitt-Murphy, Neimeyer, Burke, & Williams, 2011). Similarly, research indicates that complicated grief following suicide can be compounded by a keen sense of abandonment or rejection, shame and stigma, concealment of the cause of death, blaming, and self-destructiveness in the survivor (Jordan & McIntosh, 2010). Such findings underscore the importance of a broad-gauge clinical assessment strategy that includes but is not limited to complicated grief as an orienting framework for possible intervention. We will return to this topic after introducing several relevant risk factors for CG below.

Risk Factors for Complicated Grief

Bereavement outcome research over the last 40 years has identified a number of factors that forecast the development of prolonged and intense grieving. In a recent review of this literature, Burke and Neimeyer (2012) considered 43 studies of prospective risk factors, that is, features of the mourner, the social system, or the death itself that preceded the loss of the loved one, and were associated with heightened or chronic grief in its wake. Risk factors that emerged as most salient included being a spouse or a parent of the deceased, low levels of social support, an insecure attachment style on the part of the mourner, high levels of predeath marital dependency, preexisting psychological problems such as a disposition toward depression or anxiety, and discovering the body (in cases of violent death) or dissatisfaction with death notification. Inasmuch as CG is conceptualized

---

1 Note that these two terms are functionally equivalent, with the former emphasizing the complication of a normal course of bereavement, and the latter emphasizing a chronic state of intense grieving that disrupts functioning over a period of months or years. For clarity, we will adopt the nomenclature of complicated grief in this chapter.

as an attachment-based disorder, with symptomatology indicative of separation distress and preoccupation with the deceased (Prigerson, et al., 2009), it is understandable that mourners who are vulnerable to feeling abandoned and alone, who suffer from excessive anxiety or obsession, and who lose a security-enhancing or care-providing relationship, under conditions of minimal support, and perhaps in circumstances that leave them struggling with posttraumatic imagery, would be especially prone to the development of CG.

In addition to these confirmed risk factors, studies further suggested several potential risk factors predictive of intense and disabling grief (Burke & Neimeyer, 2012). These included such circumstantial or demographic conditions such as being female, being young, belonging to a minority group, having less education, little income, prior losses, or losing a child of any age to a violent, sudden death. Unfortunately, few of those conditions are modifiable in the context of therapy, though several point to the sort of health care disparities that argue for a social justice orientation to bereavement care (Molaison, Bordere, & Fowler, 2011). Other potential risk factors identified could be more amenable to psychological treatment, such as low family cohesion; a struggle to find meaning in the loss; and negative interpretations of the mourner's self, life, future, or his or her grief symptoms themselves. Fortunately, these are some of the psychosocial factors targeted for intervention by evidence-based approaches to grief therapy, a topic to which we will turn after considering the assessment of grief in a bit more detail.

Self-Report Measures of Grief Symptomatology

A number of paper and pencil measures for the assessment of the grief response have been developed. Although widely used, early scales such as the Texas Revised Inventory of Grief (Faschingbauer, 1981) and the Grief Experience Inventory (Sanders, Mauger, & Strong, 1985) have a questionable psychometric foundation (Neimeyer, Hogan, & Laurie, 2008). Several newer bereavement measures offer the promise of more psychometrically valid and clinically useful tools. These include the Hogan Grief Reaction Checklist (Hogan, Greenfield, & Schmidt, 2001), the Core Bereavement Items (Middleton, Burnett, Raphael, & Martinek, 1996), the Grief Evaluation Measure (Jordan, Baker, Matteis, Rosenthal, & Ware, 2005), and the Inventory of Complicated Grief (ICG) (Prigerson & Jacobs, 2001). Of particular interest is the ICG, which has been developed as a measure that specifically taps into the symptoms of CG outlined in the proposed diagnostic criteria. A number of specialized bereavement measures have also been created for specific types of losses, including suicide (Barrett & Scott, 1989), sibling loss (Hogan & De Santis, 1992), and perinatal loss (Toedter, Lasker, & Alhadeff, 1988).

Beyond these assessments of grief symptomatology, additional new measures have been constructed and validated to assess key processes posited by contemporary models of bereavement. These include the Inventory of Daily Widowed Life (Caserta & Lund, 2007) to measure orientations toward loss vs. restoration in the dual process model (Stroebe & Schut, 1999, 2010), the Two-Track Bereavement Questionnaire (TTBQ)

(Rubin, Malkinson, Koren, & Michaeli, 2009) to evaluate biopsychosocial symptoms and relationship to the deceased in terms of the TTMB (Rubin, et al., 2009; Rubin, et al., 2011), and the Integration of Stressful Life Experiences Scale (Holland, Currier, Coleman, & Neimeyer, 2010) to assess struggles in meaning making in response to loss, the focus of the meaning reconstruction approach (Neimeyer, 2011a; Neimeyer, 2011b; Neimeyer & Sands, 2011). All of these measures show promise as assessment tools in both clinical and scientific contexts.

Clinical Assessment of Response to Bereavement

Whether or not self-administered questionnaires are used in bereavement counseling, a thorough evaluation of the mourner's experience, symptomatology, social and family relations, and styles of coping can inform treatment. Factors to consider include:

1. **Clients' narratives of the death and their reactions to it.** This factor encompasses the trajectory of any illness and circumstances of the death, clients' participation (or lack of it) in the end-of-life or dying process, the funeral, and the subsequent experience of living without the deceased. Of particular relevance are clients' perceptions of how prepared they were for the death, as well as any aspects of the death that were horrifying or terrifying for them, as these could suggest traumatic as well as grief responses.

2. **An exploration of the meaning of the loss for the mourner.** This factor is obviously a broad topic, and facilitating discovery of the meaning of the loss can be a central goal of grief counseling itself. Topics might include the role of the deceased in the mourner's life, the changes that the loss is bringing about in the mourner's psychological and interpersonal world, and the degree to which the coherence of the mourner's assumptive world has been challenged. Useful questions to explore these topics might include: What sense did you make of what was happening at that time? How has the significance of the loss changed for you over time? Were there any spiritual or philosophic beliefs that helped you cope with this loss? Were these beliefs themselves challenged or changed by the loss, and if so, how? How have you changed as a person as a result of this loss? A broader frame for a meaning reconstruction interview can be found elsewhere (Neimeyer, 2002a).

3. **Clients' own evaluations of their responses to loss.** Asking, Is there anything about the way that you are responding to this loss that especially concerns you? can alert the clinician to a range of less obvious problems, such as the client's sensed failure to function in other important relationships (such as with children), as well as acute problems such as suicide ideation. It can also help bring to light aspects of grieving that might be disallowed and hard for the griever to acknowledge or accept, such as anger or guilt. Alternatively, inquiring how a trusted friend or family member would describe how the client is handling the loss can reveal additional problems at interpersonal levels (My wife would say I'm cutting off from her.) as well as at intrapersonal levels (She's worried about

my anger). Finally, if the client is seeking therapy some months or even years after the loss, it can be helpful to ask how he or she is doing now compared to a few months ago. Concerns are raised when the client seems to be in a frozen, protracted state of grief or deteriorating, and are assuaged when he or she can acknowledge ongoing distress, but also identify clear signs of progress.

4. **An assessment of the ethnic, cultural, religious, gender-based, and social class factors that affect the mourner's experience of the loss.** These assessments often give a sense of the implicit grieving rules to which the survivor is striving to conform. Some avenues into such topics could include asking whether there are ways in which others outside the family just don't seem to understand the client's response to the loss, what sort of advice the client is receiving from them and whether it fits for him or her, or what healthy grieving would look like, and where he or she got that idea. This approach could segue naturally into therapeutic questioning of whether these implicit standards and expectations work for the client, and if not, what would. It can also be valuable to inquire about the client's perceptions about how other people from his or her social reference groups (work colleagues, church or religious community, ethnic tradition, etc.) would typically handle such a loss as theirs.

5. **The quality of perceived social support from family and intimate others.** This factor includes the degree to which mourners feel understood by essential others in their grief and the amount of interpersonal strain or abandonment that has occurred around the loss. Also important is an assessment of the mourner's interpersonal skills and willingness to elicit social support from others in their network, which again could suggest targets of intervention. Assessment of the client's coping fit with other members of their family, the general norms in the family about the sharing of psychological distress, and the family's shared or conflicting narratives about the reasons for the death and the impact of the death on the family and its members can reveal important information about the mourner's perception of communal support or alienation. Family-level assessment and intervention, while beyond the scope of this chapter, can be a vital part of facilitating healing in clients after the death of a family member (Kissane, Lichtenthal, & Zaider, 2007; Kissane & Lichtenthal, 2008). Likewise, it is not simply the absence of social support that may be problematic, but also the number of actively negative interactions with one's social network that may impact bereavement outcome (Burke, Neimeyer, & McDevitt-Murphy, 2010).

6. **The psychiatric history of the mourner.** Of particular relevance are major affective disorders (depression and bipolar disorder), posttraumatic stress disorder, and substance-abuse problems. If the mourner has a positive history for psychiatric disorder, follow-up should investigate whether he or she has received treatment for the problem, its success, and any signs of the disorder(s) reoccurring within the context of the grief.

7. **The stability of the mourner's life situation,** including health, employment, marital and family relationships, and living arrangements. In addition to buffering or exacerbating bereavement distress, these domains of living can themselves be affected by the client's response to the death, contributing to secondary losses and additional stressors of considerable clinical significance.

8. **The quality of clients' past relationships,** both in their family of origin and in subsequent relationships. Of particular importance are close relationships with attachment figures, and relationships that may have been abusive, traumatizing, or characterized by abandonment. These relationships can prime the client to experience bereavement in similar terms, reinforcing a longer-standing sense of the futility of intimacy, the inevitability of loneliness, or the danger of investing emotionally in another.

9. **The coping skills possessed by mourners.** Both ability to confront the reality of the loss when necessary and to take a timeout from grief to make necessary changes in their world play a part in emotion regulation following loss. Also significant are clients' previous coping methods when faced with emotional injuries and losses, with particular attention paid to coping efforts that are self-defeating or self-destructive (e.g., substance abuse, suicidal behavior). The manner in which the mourner has adapted to earlier life losses can also suggest personal, social, and spiritual resources that could be useful in dealing with the current loss.

10. **The mourner's expectations about counseling and how it might be of help.** Previous experiences with therapy (whether bereavement related or not), and their perceived helpfulness or unhelpfulness, can give therapists a sense of what the client has, and has not, found helpful in the past, and hence what might be offered or avoided in the present treatment.

Interventions for Bereavement

Interventions for bereavement are offered in a great variety of contexts and can take a still greater variety of forms. Here we will touch on some of these settings and strategies, focusing particularly on interventions that have a coherent theoretical base and are informed by both basic and applied research on grief and grief therapy.

Contexts of Intervention

Hospice and palliative care. In the United States and many other Western nations, hospices and palliative care settings (especially those associated with oncology) routinely provide some type of bereavement follow-up with families that have received services (Chochinov & Breitbart, 2009). Hospices are probably the largest providers of professional bereavement care in the United States. The typical hospice offers a range of services for the bereaved, especially over the 1st year. These services may include individual grief counseling; various kinds of bereavement support groups, sometimes oriented to the community in general as well as family members of hospice patients; grief education;

social support programs; expressive arts therapies; grief camps for children; and sometimes family bereavement programs (Connor & Monroe, 2011). Although programming across different hospices is eclectic and creative, many settings are moving toward some form of evaluation of their services to address the calls for greater medical accountability in the institutions in which they are situated.

Community organizations and bereavement programs. Especially in North America, a variety of institutions and groups provide bereavement support, including funeral homes, churches, hospitals, and social service or bereavement agencies, with the great majority of these providing, at a minimum, facilitated bereavement support groups. Some cities have freestanding bereavement agencies that offer a wide range of services, one example being the Wendt Center for Loss and Healing in Washington, DC (http://www.wendtcenter.org/). Likewise, there are many self-help organizations that usually have formed around a particular type of loss. Some examples are the Compassionate Friends for parents who have lost a child (Klass, 1999a), TAPS for military families who have lost an active duty member of the military (http://www.taps.org) and Heartbeat (http://heartbeatsurvivorsaftersuicide.org/index.shtml) and Friends for Survival (http://www.friendsforsurvival.org/) for people bereaved by suicide.(Jordan & McIntosh, 2011). Other organizations, such as Widow to Widow in the United States (Silverman, 2005) and Cruse Bereavement Care in the UK offer home visitation or drop-in services, with the latter being particularly impressive in its goal to provide support services to any interested bereaved person in the country (Parkes & Prigerson, 2009). Most agency-sponsored support groups are conducted by a mental health professional or clergyperson, whereas self-help groups are typically facilitated by lay volunteers, many of whom are themselves survivors of similar losses who have received variable degrees of training for their role. Very few controlled studies of the effectiveness of the typical community-based grief support group have been conducted. Nor has there been much standardization of the models used to guide these types of groups, although recent popular criticism of grief counseling has increased pressure to demonstrate its value (Konigsberg, 2011).

Children's bereavement centers. One particular variant of the community support model is the Dougy Center in Portland, OR (www.dougy.org), a pioneering children's bereavement service. The Dougy Center offers developmentally attuned play or discussion support groups for bereaved children of all ages, plus parallel groups for parents. The program has been extensively replicated in the United States and around the world, and has inspired other dedicated services such as the Highmark Caring Place centers for grieving children throughout Pennsylvania (http://www.highmarkcaringplace.com/cp2/index.shtml). Such agencies are widely accepted as a valuable form of bereavement care for children, although again, formal studies of the efficacy of these programs appear to be lacking at this time.

Disaster services. A variant of the support group model is Critical Incident Stress Debriefing (CISD) or Management (CISM) (Mitchell, 1983). This procedure employs a structured protocol for a group meeting (typically a single session) after a traumatic event, such as a natural disaster or a terrorist attack. Participants are encouraged to recount their experience with the distressing situation and are offered information about the nature of the posttraumatic response. Originally developed for emergency response workers such as police and fire personnel, this form of intervention has been widely adopted by organizations involved with disaster response, such as the American Red Cross. More recently, however, CISM has been criticized as lacking in empirical support and possibly even being harmful for some participants (Gist & Lubin, 1999; Litz, 2004). Partly in response to this concern, contemporary bereavement work in the aftermath of natural or humanmade disaster tends to be more sustained and multifocal, offering extended and varied forms of instrumental, socioemotional, and ritual support for those losing loved ones (Kristensen & Franco, 2011).

Online support. An important and accelerating form of bereavement support is the development of online resources for the bereaved (Stroebe, Van Der Houwen, & Schut, 2008). These resources have the advantage of helping mourners find assistance when there is a paucity of face-to-face resources within their own geographical area. They also provide nonjudgmental support and much more availability than traditional bereavement support groups, while affording the mourner the anonymity of the Internet. This combination may be particularly important for people whose face-to-face support networks are sparse or actively harmful to the mourner (Feigelman, Gorman, Beal, & Jordan, 2008). In addition to listservs or online support groups, these resources may provide reading lists, inspirational narratives, suggestions for coping, and links to other online services. Examples of these types of resources might include GriefNet (http://griefnet.org/) and Open to Hope (http://www.opentohope.com/). It is important to note that the value and potential problems of using the Internet as a resource for psychological and social support have begun to be evaluated. Nonetheless, it seems very likely that utilization of this medium will increase in coming years.

Techniques of Grief Therapy

As might be expected of an interdisciplinary field like thanatology, which is situated in a great variety of settings; serves a great range of bereaved individuals and families; and addresses losses due to stillbirth, cancer, accident, and homicide among other causes, the techniques of grief therapy are diverse in form and function. Here we sample from the nearly 100 such practices documented by Neimeyer (2012) to illustrate the range of methods available to professional (and in some cases volunteer) helpers. Many of these techniques are integrated into the empirically informed therapies described in the following section. Readers interested in specific instructions for each technique and an illustration of its use in the context of an actual case study are encouraged to consult Neimeyer (2012) for details.

Framing the work. Fundamental to most forms of grief therapy is the practice of presence, that is, the fearless willingness to sit alongside clients, validating, clarifying, and exploring their feelings and needs in the wake of grievous loss. As one expression of this approach, the therapist can help clients cultivate mindfulness about their own grief responses, which implies heightened abilities to observe their thoughts and emotions without reifying or attaching to them, while practicing self-compassion. More specialized techniques are built on this foundation, as therapists discern opportunities to address a specific need that becomes evident as therapy progresses.

Modulating emotion. Especially when the pain of loss is fresh, or when one is confronted by regrieving triggers like significant anniversaries, holidays, and reminders, learning to regulate one's level of emotional arousal in bereavement can be essential. Monitoring the intensity of grief in a daily log takes a step in this direction, which is furthered by meditative practice, exercises to discriminate grief from other significant emotions, and sometimes, when bereavement-related depression is unremitting, appropriate medication. In combination with some of the strategies reviewed below, this can help mourners dose their grief, acknowledging the loss in the terms of the dual process model without relinquishing restoration.

Working with the body. Grief is an embodied experience, so that listening to how loss is held at bodily levels—as an emptiness in the heart, a constriction in the throat, a churning in the abdomen—can inform us about the felt sense of our grief as well as what we need to heal. Practices ranging from qi-gong through movement therapies to symbolic body drawings can promote awareness and give direction to healing action.

Transforming trauma. Some component of trauma may be subtly present in all deaths, but it is often vividly so when a loved one has died suddenly, and especially by suicide, homicide, or fatal accident. It is important to note that by trauma, we are referring to the clinical syndrome of PTSD, whether it is present at a syndromal or subsyndromal level in the individual. Bereavement-related PTSD includes clear evidence of more than just emotional upset at the loss. Clients who are traumatized show signs of intense autonomic arousal (difficulty sleeping, irritability, etc.), report psychological and physical experiences of reliving the trauma, and make efforts to avoid being triggered back into reliving this flashback experience because of its horrifying or terrifying nature. For example, a person who has lost a loved one to suicide may report having intrusive and horrific images of their loved one hanging by a noose, and they may be unable to control when or where these images arise. Consequently the person may avoid going into a room where the suicide happened precisely to avoid having these images evoked. It is also important to recognize that the mourner does not need to have been an eyewitness to the death scene to develop traumatizing images of the sights and sounds involved in the dying process of their loved one.

Specialized experiential and exposure-based therapeutic techniques that involve slow and systematic retelling of the loss narrative in the presence of compassionate witnessing, sometimes aided by procedures such as eye movement desensitization reprocessing (Shapiro & Forrest, 2004) to facilitate mastery of troubling imagery and emotion, can usefully supplement a focus on separation distress in such cases.

Changing behavior. Confronting the death of a loved one can be immobilizing and pose myriad social, personal, and occupational obstacles to engaging our changed lives.

Techniques such as behavioral activation can help counteract depressive shutdown, just as assertion skills can be useful in constructing boundaries and bridges with people in our social worlds. Devising action plans for balancing attention to internal and external realities and managing predictably difficult times can help restore some sense of behavioral competence when it is sorely needed.

Restructuring cognitions. Catastrophic thinking about the loss can promote helplessness, which can be gently disputed and restructured through the use of cognitive therapy procedures. This work can usefully be pursued at the level of clients' surface-level automatic thoughts or at the level of deeper schemas bearing on their sense of lovability, abandonment, or justice that are activated by the loved one's death. Clinical experience seems to confirm the truism that each loss that we experience reverberates in one way or another with previous losses. Likewise, catastrophic losses seem to reactivate for mourners their deepest concerns about themselves and their world, issues that often have their foundation in developmentally earlier schemas about the self and the world (Kauffman, 2002a).

Finding meaning. For clients struggling to make sense of the loss or their lives in the wake of it, a wide variety of techniques can be of assistance. These techniques include various forms of directed journaling to enhance meaning making and benefit finding; use of loss characterizations to explore their postbereavement identities; metaphorical and spiritual interventions; and numerous forms of narrative work that document, validate, and extend the literal and symbolic stories of clients' lives and losses.

Integrating the arts. Literal language often fails to convey the deep emotional significance of loss, as well as the prospect of lasting love and transformation. Expressive arts therapies can help fill this void, using photography, montage, music, sand tray, memorial work, poetry, or creative intermodal approaches that combine several of these methods.

Renewing the bond. At the heart of bereavement distress is the yearning to reaffirm or reconstruct the bond with the loved one that has been challenged by death. Practices of introducing the deceased to others through our stories about them, using guided imagery to invoke their ongoing presence in our lives, fostering deeply meaningful symbolic conversations with them using letter writing or an empty chair, and pursuing their legacies in our lives in both words and photographs help repair and restore such bonds in sustainable form.

Revising goals. Profound losses portend change, as we relinquish or redefine goals previously linked to the loved one's physical presence in our lives, and project ourselves into an altered future. A variety of procedures for goal-setting can assist us in this process, whether at the broad level of envisioning a changed self or at the specific level of how we will engage in self-care or confront a particularly difficult circumstance, such as getting through the holidays.

Grieving with others. The death of another can isolate us, mark us as different, disrupt the usual way in which we connect with others in the family, workplace, or broader social world. For this reason, the careful cultivation of communication with others in the home, a support group, or work setting is as important as securing personal time for reflection and renewal. Techniques to facilitate this communication include tools for soliciting different forms of instrumental and emotional support, negotiating when to talk with a partner about a shared loss and when not to, creative therapeutic games to facilitate disclosure and sharing with children, and workplace study circles that help reintegrate a bereaved employee. Importantly, virtual, Internet-based resources, and computer-mediated communication with others who have suffered similar loss can extend communities of concern beyond those we can access in person.

Activism and transforming the negative into the positive. For some mourners, comfort and meaning in a loss can be found in becoming active in efforts to make something positive or redemptive emerge from the death. One common form of this activism is trying to help others who have suffered a similar loss or working to prevent others from having to go through a similar experience. Examples might include raising funds to help prevent the type of cancer that ended the life of a loved one, working to prevent the violence and homicide that led to the death of the loved one, or becoming a facilitator of a bereavement support group for people who have experienced the suicide of another.

Ritualizing transition. Finally, it is often helpful to mark our healing journey symbolically, constructing private or communal ceremonies of transition or inclusion, commemorating significant days or events, identifying linking objects, and placing our personal suffering in broader frames of significance. Practices such as launching memory boats, tracing a labyrinth or grief spiral, or joining a barefoot walkabout can promote these ends.

Evidence-Based Practice in Grief Therapy

The last decade has witnessed a spirited (and sometimes contentious) debate within thanatology regarding the efficacy of grief counseling (Jordan & Neimeyer, 2003; Larson & Hoyt, 2007). Recent reviews of bereavement interventions for both adults (Currier, Holland, & Neimeyer, 2008) and children (Currier, Holland, & Neimeyer, 2007) call into question the practice of routinely offering therapy to all bereaved people, as those who are left untreated ultimately improve to similar levels. Such findings underscore the considerable resilience of many people in the face of loss (Bonanno, 2004), and suggest that an appropriate stance of thanatologists would be to study the everyday competencies that permit people to surmount loss, rather than presume that therapy is a universally applicable response to ordinary life transitions. However, the same research also documents that therapy is indeed measurably effective in mitigating the suffering of at-risk groups suffering traumatic loss (e.g., the death of a child or violent death bereavement) and is particularly efficacious when it is offered to those persons with clinically significant symptomatology (e.g., complicated grief, depression or anxiety disorders) (Neimeyer & Currier, 2009). Thus, there is evidence that grief therapy can provide much to those who most need it. Our optimism about the field of grief counseling is reinforced by the burgeoning collaboration between clinicians and researchers in developing and documenting new models of treatment that are demonstrably effective in randomized controlled studies (Sandler et al., 2005). In this closing section we will discuss five such approaches that draw on many of the models and methods reviewed earlier in this chapter.

Complicated grief therapy (CGT). One research-informed model of treatment has been devised by Shear and her colleagues (Shear, Frank, Houch, & Reynolds, 2005), which draws on the dual process model of Stroebe and Schut (1999) to both foster accommodation to the loss and promote restoration of life goals and roles. The former entails procedures for revisiting or retelling the story of the death in evocative detail, while promoting cognitive and emotional mastery of the experience; engaging in imaginal conversations to rework the attachment relationship to the deceased; and reviewing both pleasant and troubling recollections related to the deceased to help the client consolidate a more positive memory of their life together. In addition, in keeping with the restoration focus of the DPM, clients review and revise life goals to align them with the changed circumstance of their lives. Sixteen sessions of CGT was found to be far more effective than interpersonal psychotherapy in alleviating complicated grief symptomatology, although clients showed improvement in both conditions.

Cognitive behavior therapy (CBT). Likewise, Boelen and his associates (Boelen, de Keijser, van den Hout, & van den Bout, 2007) drew on a cognitive-behavioral model of complicated grief to formulate a two-phase treatment featuring cognitive restructuring and sustained exposure exercises. Cognitive interventions used familiar procedures to identify, challenge, and change negative automatic thoughts in the course of grieving. Exposure treatment entailed inviting clients to tell the story of their loss in detail followed by a homework assignment to write down all of the internal and external stimuli— ranging from specific memories to people and places—that they have tended to avoid, and used the results to construct a hierarchy of situations that were confronted imaginally and behaviorally in the remaining sessions. Results indicate that 12 sessions of treatment in the cognitive-behavioral conditions outperformed a supportive condition, and that exposure interventions were especially effective in ameliorating grief symptomatology. A recent meta-analysis of the literature on interventions using similar CBT methods supports their general efficacy, although it is unclear whether they are more effective than other existing therapies when investigator allegiance is taken into account (Currier, Holland, & Neimeyer, 2010).

Meaning-making approaches. Recently, Lichtenthal and Cruess (2010) studied a narrative intervention for bereavement, drawing on meaning-oriented models that emphasize the role of sense making and benefit finding in the wake of loss (Neimeyer, van Dyke, & Pennebaker, 2009). Randomizing participants to 1 of 4 conditions—emotional disclosure (ED), sense making (SM), benefit finding (BF), or a control (CC) condition—

they requested that bereaved participants write for three, 20-minute sessions over the course of a week about either their deepest thoughts and emotions related to their loss (ED), making sense of the event by exploring its causes and place in their lives (SM), any positive life changes that came about as a result of their loss experience (BF), or simply the room in which they were seated (CC). They found evidence that writing about the loss experience was more efficacious in reducing grief 3 months postintervention than writing about a neutral topic. The novel BF meaning-making intervention appeared especially beneficial. Significant treatment effects on depressive and PTSD symptoms also emerged, especially among those in the BF condition. An additional randomized controlled trial of an Internet-mediated writing therapy featuring prompts for perspective taking regarding the loss reinforces these general conclusions (Wagner, Knaevelsrud, & Maercker, 2006).

Family-focused grief therapy (FFGT). Kissane and his associates have devised a family-focused intervention, practiced as a brief four- to eight-session intervention for distressed relatives of patients receiving end-stage treatment in palliative care settings (Kissane & Bloch, 2002). As an alternative to the individualistic orientation of the other research-tested therapies described above, theirs is based on an assessment of family functioning, defined in terms of members' self-reported levels of cohesiveness, expressiveness, and capacity to deal with conflict. Importantly, Kissane and his colleagues offered professional therapy only to those families whose family processes placed them at risk for poor bereavement outcomes; supportive families that enjoyed high cohesion and conflict-resolving families that dealt with problems through effective communication were judged as inappropriate for intervention. Therapy concentrated on telling the story of the illness and related grief while enhancing communication and conflict resolution. Although a randomized comparison of FFGT with treatment as usual produced equivocal effects, significantly greater improvement in general distress and depression, though not social adjustment, was shown by the 10% of FFGT-treated family members who were most troubled at the outset of treatment. Importantly, members of sullen families characterized by muted anger and a desire for help showed the most improvement in depression as a result of FFGT. In contrast, hostile families marked by high conflict actually did *worse* in FFGT than in the control condition (Kissane et al., 2006). Results therefore suggest the utility of family-level bereavement intervention, but only when discretion is exercised in the recruitment of those most likely to benefit (highly distressed and sullen families) and to avoid offering treatment to those who would fare as well or better without it (functional and hostile families).

The Family Bereavement Program (FBP). Finally, in what is perhaps the best designed example of a theory driven and evidence-based bereavement intervention, Sandler and his colleagues have developed the Family Bereavement Program (Sandler et al., 2003; Sandler et al., 2008). Building on the idea of reducing known risk and strengthening known protective factors for parentally bereaved children, the program provides parallel group experiences for children or adolescents and their parents that increase positive interactions, increase active coping behaviors, and decrease negative appraisals of the loss and the inhibition of bereavement-related emotional expression. To their credit, Sandler and his colleagues have meticulously studied the impact of the intervention using a randomized control trial design coupled with longitudinal follow-up and have found positive program effects as far out as 6 years after treatment (Sandler et al., 2010). The researchers have also begun a pioneering effort to translate the research findings and intervention into real world clinical settings where this evidence-based program can be adapted for use in a variety of organizations providing services to bereaved families (Ayers, Kondo, & Sandler, 2011).

In summary, a variety of experiential, cognitive-behavioral, narrative, and family-focused methods are being developed and have been found to hold promise in the treatment of bereavement-related distress. Prominent features of these demonstrably effective treatments include (a) their grounding in contemporary, research-informed models of grief; (b) their tendency to screen for significant levels of distress or complicated grief as a criterion for treatment; (c) inclusion of oral or written retelling of the loss experience, often in evocative detail; (d) the learning of adaptive coping skills to help the mourner live in the changed, postloss world; and (e) typically the prompting of some form of meaning making, in the form of consolidation of positive memories, cognitive restructuring of fatalistic thoughts, integration of the loss into one's self-narrative, or finding of unsought benefits in terms of personal growth, reordered life priorities, and the like. Our hope is that such factors, in combination with the novel procedures featured in some of the therapies (e.g., directed imaginal dialogues with the deceased or writing of letters to the loved one or to hypothetical others who have experienced a similar loss), may represent the formation of a new wave of more sophisticated, evidenced-based, and effective interventions for bereavement-related distress. We believe they will continue to inspire experimentation with new models and methods in order to enrich and deepen the scope of grief counseling in the years to come.

Chapter 24

Life Span Issues and Assessment and Intervention

David A. Crenshaw

Sound intervention strategies need to be based on a careful assessment of developmental and life span issues in children and adults. To be effective, intervention requires the evaluator to forego all preconceived notions of what the child or adult need but rather to assess the intervention needs of this particular child or adult at this specific point in time in the context of current life circumstances.

A key question guiding assessment at all stages of the lifecycle is whether grief is proceeding along a healthy path or whether it is taking a pathological turn that requires professional assistance. In the former instance, professional intervention is typically not needed as individuals and families turn to their family, friends, spiritual advisors, and the community for support. In the latter case, it is crucial to assess whether the grief has developed into complicated bereavement or even traumatic grief or has led to clinical symptoms of depression or anxiety or posttraumatic stress syndrome (PTSD) (for a thorough discussion of assessment issues in the case of traumatic grief in children see Balk & Corr, 2009; Cohen, Mannarino, & Deblinger, 2006; Doka & Tucci, 2008; Webb, 2010).

An important issue to be explored at any stage of life is the meaning of death for an individual. Children, particularly during adolescence, as well as adults can struggle intensely to reconcile death as a natural part of life, and the meaning of a particular death also needs to be understood in each individual case (Langs, 2004).

In recent research greater emphasis has been placed on resilient trajectories following extreme adverse events including death and losses taking many forms in both children and adults (Bonanno, 2012). A resilience trajectory was defined by Bonanno (2012) as a relatively stable pattern of adjustment over time in spite of experiencing an extreme adversity. These resilient outcomes are far more common than originally thought and provide a cogent reminder of the pitfalls of pathologizing and underestimating the resilient spirit and remarkable capacity for repair in human beings.

Assessment

Issues for Children

Children vary in their concepts of death and in their abilities to undertake grief work. Research suggests that if children experience the death of a parent prior to age 5, it is more likely to be traumatic due to their inadequate cognitive and emotional resources to handle a loss of such magnitude (Lieberman, Compton, Van Horn, & Ghosh Ippen, 2003). It should not be assumed, however, that this outcome will always be the case. Rather the assessment should be based on a thorough developmental evaluation of the child with generous input from parents, teachers, day care providers, or other caregivers.

A child whose developmental progress has been halted or derailed as a result of a death of a family member or other important person may require professional intervention. A starting point is to do a developmental history with input from family, school, and other caregivers. Important background data can be gathered by a counselor well-versed in developmental assessment of young children. Counselors who are trained in doing developmental play assessments with young children can gather important data regarding cognitive, as well as emotional and behavioral functioning by direct observation of the child's spontaneous play. The child's response to directives from the therapist to engage in structured play tasks can expand the observational data such as using the puppets create a story about a puppy who is sad or they may be asked to do an individual play genogram developed by Eliana Gil (Gil, 2003), or the magic key projective fantasy drawing (Crenshaw, 2008).

Changes in the child's functioning immediately following a death are expected but if problems persist and developmental progress is impeded intervention may be indicated. School-age children will be able to collaborate more fully in the assessment process due to their greater verbal facility and cognitive skills but input from the family and school will still be essential since children may not be fully aware of some of the psychological and behavioral changes observed by adults after a death.

Adolescent Issues

Teens typically have more cognitive and emotional resources to understand death and to grieve the death of someone important to them, but they are also at a vulnerable age, particularly if the loss was preceded by attachment insecurity in the adolescent (Fagundes, Diamond, & Allen, 2012). If the life of someone important, particularly a peer, is snuffed out at the time they are beginning to claim a life and identity of their own, the emotional impact can be devastating. It can cause anxiety, insecurity, and fear of taking risks. Changes in adolescents following a death may take the form of acting-out behaviors such as increased alcohol or illicit drug use, reckless behavior such as unsafe driving, or engaging in unsafe sex. This type of response is particularly likely with boys but occurs in girls as well. Adolescent girls are at increased risk of symptoms of anxiety and depression or other symptoms of internalizing disorders that include eating disorders or self-harming behaviors (Little, Sandler, Wolchik, Tein, & Ayers, 2009). Balk (2011a) identified adolescent cores issues related to bereavement during three stages: (1) early adolescence, (2) middle adolescence, and (3) late adolescence. Balk also described the regrief phenomenon in adolescence whereby grief is revisited as development proceeds and emotional reminders of a previous loss triggers a new wave of grieving.

Young and Middle-Age Adults

In adult life significant changes or disruptions in family and social relationships subsequent to the death of a relative or close friend would signal a need for further assessment and possibly intervention. Increased alcohol use, abuse of prescription or illicit drugs, dramatic deterioration in professional or occupational performance would be important indicators of the need for more careful exploration along with the more obvious signs of clinically significant degrees of anxiety and depression. An important study of college students found that avoidant emotional coping style predicted complicated grief and severity of PTSD symptoms following a traumatic loss (Schnider, Elhai, & Gray, 2007). This study supported the long-held belief that facilitating emotional expressions of grief in counseling leads to healthier outcomes than achieved by persons who cope by avoiding the expression of emotional responses.

Issues for the Elderly

The elderly command a special concern. Close and meaningful attachments are a crucial buffering and protective factor in the lives of people at any age but become especially critical in the elderly. When important ties are disrupted by death, the emotional devastation in an elderly person may be compounded by other stressors such as economic strain, poor health, loneliness, or other prior losses. The incidence and prevalence of depressive symptoms and suicide risk increase, with advancing age (Bahr & Brown, 2012).

The risk of suicide needs to be carefully considered at any stage of life in the face of a devastating loss, but it becomes especially important to evaluate in the case of the elderly, especially if they live alone, are in poor health, suffer from ego despair, or manifest other risk factors such as alcohol abuse. The presence of clinical depression or any prior history of mood disorder or suicidal ideation or attempts would be further indicators of risk and need for careful assessment by a licensed mental health professional.

Important ethical issues arise if technological advancements allow us to extend life but in the process we strip the elderly of their humanity and dignity (see Kastenbaum, 2004a, 2004b for a fuller discussion of these issues).

Interventions

Four forms of interventions will be described as they relate to life span issues: (1) death education; (2) bereavement support; (3) individual, family or group counseling; and (4) professional caregiver support.

Death Education

In societies where death is treated as a taboo or unmentionable topic, death education plays a crucial role in preparing children especially for the possible deaths they will face as they advance through childhood, including the death of pets, perhaps grandparents, other relatives, in some cases a friend or perhaps a teacher. Becker (1973) delineated the many ways in which people avoid awareness of death. Becker viewed this denial as emotionally detrimental in that people unable to confront the fact of their own mortality are unable to appreciate life and live fully. Parents should be encouraged to fully utilize opportunities afforded to teach toddlers about death by capitalizing on their natural curiosity. They often ask questions about dead insects or birds, and they can be helped to see that death is a natural part of life and as basic to all living things as birth and growing older. Toddlers should be given simple and direct explanations in response to questions about death. The death of a family pet affords an opportunity, although painful, for children to learn in a natural way about death. Children in the age range of 3 to 6 will need help to differentiate the true versus the fantasy causes of events, especially the painful ones in their lives.

School-age children and adolescents should feel free to approach the trusted adults in their lives when they have questions about the mysteries of death. It is not uncommon that children go through phases of fear of death. As they continue to advance in their cognitive and emotional development they began at around age 9 to understand death in a more complex way. They begin to understand that death is not reversible, that it is inevitable and universal. These abstract concepts are hard for younger children to grasp because they have a limited capacity for abstract thought and concepts. It is not just children and adolescents who shy away from discussing death.

It is astounding that even in the current age when so many other taboos have vanished there are plenty of adults who do not feel comfortable talking about death. Death for many adults is a subject to be tucked away and visited only when forced to by circumstances beyond their control. There is still great potential for increasing the coping capacities of children and adults throughout the life span for handling death by expanding our educational efforts not only through formal death education courses but in parent and teacher training.

Bereavement Support

Throughout the life span the primary intervention for most bereaved children, adults and families is some form of bereavement support. The majority will receive this support from their families; church, synagogue, or mosque; their school; or the larger community. Young children will primarily receive it from their families although the parents may seek advice from their religious advisers or counselors as to help children through the grieving process. Older children and adolescents often receive support from school counselors and in the case of sudden or traumatic death many schools have organized crisis support teams to offer counseling immediately after the death to those who are affected. Resources for adults and the elderly are available often through support groups organized within the community by church organizations, the bereavement support programs offered by hospice, or the local mental health association. Often support groups are available for children and adults of various ages and also by the type of death. Suicide survivor groups, and groups for parents who have lost children, or for surviving siblings are available depending on the size of the community. A good example of a community support for survivors of traumatic death is Bo's Place in Houston (Walijarvi, Weiss, & Weinman, 2012). Bo's Place is an 8-week, curriculum-based traumatic death support group program to help family members who have experienced a death in the family by suicide, murder, accident, or sudden medical problem.

Individual, Group, or Family Bereavement Counseling

While most bereaved do not need or seek professional counseling there are circumstances that may require such intervention that can take the form of either individual, group, or family counseling conducted by a mental health professional and/or certified grief counselor. Sudden and traumatic deaths are prime examples of the types of bereavement that may in some cases require professional intervention. While such an event would be stressful at any point in the life span they exert a particular toll on children, adolescents, and the elderly. Children are vulnerable because their development is still in progress and they may lack adequate cognitive, emotional, and social resources for coping with such a stressful event and may result in developmental arrest in one or more domains. Groundbreaking work by Cohen, Mannarino, & Deblinger (2006) led to an empirically derived treatment model that addresses childhood traumatic grief (CTG). Childhood traumatic grief is defined as a condition in which the trauma symptoms interfere with the child's ability to undertake the normal grieving process. The CTG treatment program addresses both trauma and grief symptoms and includes a parental treatment component. Bereaved children tend to be more amenable to less invasive treatment interventions that include therapeutic play, narratives, metaphors, symbol work, drawing, and storytelling strategies (Crenshaw, 2005; Crenshaw, 2008).

As mentioned in the assessment section, adolescents may require professional intervention depending on the circumstances of the death and many other variables including their prior loss history, preexisting psychiatric conditions, and their developmental vulnerability related to their need to move away emotionally from their families and begin the process of making a life and a separate identity. Sudden death can shatter the life assumptions of the bereaved at any stage of the lifecycle but the blow suffered to the adolescent's sense of omnipotence and invulnerability is particularly shocking.

Adults are not exempt from traumatic or complicated reactions to death that under such circumstances may require professional counseling intervention or treatment by a licensed mental health professional. Young adults who are most likely to be faced with the death of a young child are particularly at risk because this loss may be the most stressful bereavement of all. A child facing the death of a parent or a parent confronting the death of a young child represent some of the most anguishing and heartbreaking of all human experiences. Adult bereavement can be complicated in the case not only of traumatic death but when the relationship of the bereaved and deceased person was highly conflicted or highly dependent (insecure attachment). In the later case, the bereaved adult may suffer a loss of identity as well as anxiety and depression.

The loss of loved ones, which is a universal human experience, increases in frequency as we age, along with the decline in physical vigor and increased poor health. Since social isolation is a concern for the elderly bereaved, group and community support are a helpful adjunct to any individual counseling. The involvement of other family members in the counseling may strengthen the social support network available to the griever.

Professional Caregiver Issues

Caregivers and professional counselors face their own inevitable losses, and it is necessary that they adequately attend to their own grief issues in order to be effective in providing bereavement support and counseling to others. As caregivers and counselors go through life the number of losses in both their personal and professional lives accumulates and the distance to their own death diminishes. This realization may make it hard to hear the continuing sad stories of the bereaved, especially the horror narratives of the traumatically bereaved. It is imperative that professional counselors and caregivers counterbalance the inherent stress of work with the bereaved by providing adequate care and consideration to themselves. (See chapter 40 in this handbook.)

The caring and support of family is a crucial balancing force, along with healthy lifestyle habits of regular exercise, adequate nutrition, engaging hobbies, as well as sufficient rest and relaxation. In addition the support of colleagues and the availability of supervision or consultation with more experienced colleagues are essential. When counselors are working with families who have experienced the heartrending death of a child or traumatic death of any nature it may create anxiety in the counselors since it can heighten their own since of vulnerability. Trauma tends to shatter beliefs and assumptions that the world is a safe place and counselors are not exempt. In the wake of major disasters or terrorist attacks, counselors will be particularly challenged for they will have the same concerns for their own safety and the safety of their families at a time when they are attempting to make themselves emotionally available to their clients. It would be especially critical in disaster work for the counselors and caregivers to attend to their own sense of woundedness and to draw on the support of their team of colleagues. No one should do this work as a lone ranger.

Chapter 25

Assessment and Intervention in the Family and Larger Systems

Jennifer L. Matheson

Grief and loss can impact not only the individual but an entire family system as well as larger systems such as neighborhoods, communities, schools, businesses, and countries. Recent national and international disasters such as school shootings, war, and natural disasters like hurricanes, tsunamis, floods, and earthquakes have brought to light the importance of grief assessment and interventions on a larger scale.

The experience of family or group grief has similarities and differences to grief experienced by an individual. Clinicians have found that in some ways, group grief can create an environment for additional support and a sense of belonging but can also complicate the bereavement process as individuals grieve in different ways and go through different processes. Walsh and McGoldrick (2004) have endorsed a systemic approach to family grief that understands "the chain of influences that reverberate throughout the family network of relationships, including partners, parents, children, siblings, and extended kin" (p. 6). Others agree that grief occurs in two areas at the same time: the individual level and social or interpersonal level (Cook & Dworkin, 1992). Therapists may be called to help with families or larger systems such as communities that have experienced traumatic loss. Regardless, therapists who are comfortable using an eclectic approach to treatment and intervention will likely find the best results (Lattanzi-Licht & Doka, 2003). Increasingly in recent years, experts in the area of family bereavement have also depended on strength-based, competency-based, and resiliency approaches as a key element to effective intervention and treatment (Hemmings, 2005).

Research suggests that not all people and groups who have experienced significant grief pursue treatment for symptoms. Those with normative patterns of grief rarely feel the need for formalized treatment, though they may explore the types of support that are available in their communities. When grief is complicated by other stressors, however, it is often the job of clinicians to assess for grief-related problems and provide interventions to relieve chronic or acute symptoms. The needs of the family or the group are crucial, and interventions aimed at the whole family or larger system often depend on an accurate assessment of clinical need. While many assessments are available for individuals, few have been designed explicitly for families and large groups.

General Considerations of Assessing and Treating Families and Larger Systems

There are general, overarching issues that should be explored when planning or executing an intervention for families or larger systems dealing with grief and loss. The first key issue is the meaning a family or community makes of the loss event. Nadeau (1998) identified factors that can enhance or inhibit the process of family meaning making. Some enhancers are family rituals, the frequency of contact among members, and openness of members to share their meaning. On the other hand, things that can inhibit the process include secrets, incompatible beliefs, and the level of fragility of relationships in the family. Regardless of the intervention, it is important to incorporate ways to help people explore meaning making at different points in their coping process and allow for wide variations in the meaning people make of a loss event.

In addition to meaning making, those who assess for grief symptoms and provide interventions for families and larger systems should consider all manner of diversity such as gender and cultural differences. Researchers have noted that currently embraced interventions may fall short of addressing the varied needs of all bereaved people because of the limited populations who have been studied in the past (Breen & O'Connor, 2011). While there is some evidence to suggest that, in general, men may cope with bereavement better than women, research suggests that gender differences in bereavement outcomes are few and small (Hayslip, Allen, & McCoy-Roberts, 2001). Of the few studies that show any differences, one study indicated that women may prefer individual, couple, or family therapy or support groups, whereas men may benefit more from talking with friends and families (Rich, 2000). Women may be more confrontive and expressive in their grief than men (Stroebe, 2001). Another publication suggested that women's grief in general has more of an intuitive pattern where men's is instrumental, but that a better model is to weave both into a comprehensive model that addresses both types (Martin & Doka, 2000). Overall, having some sensitivity to the needs of clients based on individual gender differences may be helpful to improving assessment and treatment outcomes.

Finally, and equally important, the cultural and spiritual makeup of a family or community should be considered when planning an intervention. While some elements of grief are nearly universal, people from different religions, ethnic, or cultural backgrounds may have different ways of experiencing, expressing, and ritualizing loss events. Developing sensitivity to these differences can help those who assess and treat loss symptoms. In addition, respecting the individuality of families and communities by including them in the planning of any interventions is a good way to ensure their particular religious or cultural needs will be met.

Theories That Guide the Assessment and Treatment of Grief in Families and Larger Systems

For individuals, families, and communities, the process of bereavement can be understood from a wide range of theories that incorporate issues of attachment, coping, and loss (Williams, Zinner, & Ellis, 1999). One theory that may help guide the assessment and treatment of grief symptoms in families and larger systems is family systems theory. This theory encompasses a broad set of interventions used to treat families and larger systems in general and can be applied to the assessment and treatment of groups of people experiencing significant loss and grief. According to Nichols and Schwartz (1998), "Working with the whole system means not only considering all the members of the family, but also taking into account the personal dimensions of their experience" (p. 8). Therapists who are trained in family systems theory are often trained to use an eclectic approach that may include a number of key models of therapy. These models include Cognitive-Behavioral Family Therapy, Structural Family Therapy, Narrative Therapy, Internal Family Systems, Solution-Focused Brief Therapy, Psychoanalytic Family Therapy, or Experiential Family Therapy. These models are often paired with the available models of treatment for bereavement to treat grief in families and groups. Regardless of the clinician's theory of choice, however, how a family or group experiences grief will depend on their individual, family, social, cultural, and spiritual context (Stokes, 2005). These contextual issues also must be included in any thorough assessment and may serve as either resources or stressors that must be considered in treatment.

Bowlby's attachment theory is another that often underlies interventions for bereaved families and larger systems. According to Stroebe, Schut, and Boerner (2010), "A basic theme of the theory is that persons who have experienced (lack of) dependability and consequent (in) security in their early childhood relationships will subsequently remain influenced by this in forming, maintaining and—importantly here—relinquishing relationships" (p. 260). One example of a bereavement theory based in attachment theory is that of continuing bonds. The developers of the theory of continuing bonds, Klass, Silverman, and Nickman (1996), were among the first scholars to question psychoanalytic beliefs that the bereaved should relinquish their ties to the deceased person for maximum adaptation (Stroebe et al.).

Most of the theories that address grief and loss at a larger systems level deal with tragic or traumatic losses that larger groups experience together. This larger systems level may be church communities, workplaces, neighborhoods, communities, states, or entire countries. Many of the theories on grief that exist for individuals can be applied to larger systems as well. In general, trauma theory is prevalent in helping people understand what happens when a community or larger system grieves, mostly because community grief usually follows a tragedy or traumatic event. Most people who experience a larger systems level loss are resilient, though many may have both acute and long-term stress reactions (Williams et al., 1999). Learned helplessness is often replaced by learned resourcefulness (i.e., Antonovsky, 1990). According to Antonovsky, the community has found a way to make sense of the event with the help of targeted interventions that help make the event manageable and make resources available for recovery. The theory suggests that these communities heal also because they find meaning by reframing the event as a challenge. Regardless of the theory used, most use Miller's and Steinberg's (1975) long-standing notion of community grief that specifies, "having options, a plan of action, or a knowledge of how to cope gives strength to an otherwise traumatized community" (in Williams, et al., 1999. p. 14).

Assessment of Needs

Few formal assessment instruments exist to measure the severity of grief being experienced by families and larger systems. When families present with grief or bereavement, therapists can encourage parents to invite children to the session as long as the information will not be too sensitive or complex to discuss in front of children (Hemmings, 2005). According to Stokes (2005), assessment provides "clarity and an understanding of how individuals within the family are experiencing the bereavement" (p. 29). Stokes adds that the assessment should aim to establish the impact of the death for this family at this time living in this community. Other determinants of grief that should be assessed include: who the person was in relation to them, the nature of the attachment, strength of the attachment, security of the attachment, ambivalence of the relationship, conflicts with the deceased, mode of death, historical antecedents, personality variables, social variables, rituals, and concurrent stressors (Parkes & Weiss, 1983). Stokes also suggests beginning with a genogram that has a number of advantages in a bereavement assessment including recording who is in a family, previous losses, past coping strategies, and key family transitions that may have an impact on bereavement. Assessing both the risk factors of a family and the elements of resilience are important. It is important when children are present in a family to include them in the assessment, but to use activities and language at a level they can comprehend. After the assessment phase is complete, therapists should be prepared to recommend family work, individual work, or a combination of both. Being explicit with families about what the therapist notices as areas needing attention, and providing some information about what specific interventions may be used, can help families feel safer and more grounded in treatment.

For larger systems, a few key questions can help guide the assessment of need for grief and bereavement services (Williams et al., 1999). Those questions include,

- What is the community's history of similar losses?
- What is the community history in general?
- What is the nature of the losses experienced by this community?
- To what extent was the event normalized?
- To what extent does the community have the support it needs?
- What are the cultural practices, beliefs, rituals, and customs that can help or interfere with healing?

- In what ways has the community found meaning in the event?

These questions can help determine what interventions would be most effective in any given community at any given point in time.

Family Interventions

There is a wide range of interventions that can work with families who are grieving. These techniques come not only from the family therapy field but from psychology, social work, counseling, pastoral counseling, and other fields of mental and spiritual health disciplines. Some of these approaches would fall under the category of family support, especially in cases where the grief and loss issues are less complicated, whereas family therapy would be indicated in situations where the symptoms of grief are beyond what is usual and expected or when grief is complicated by other factors.

One program that has been found to be effective is called the family bereavement program (FBP) (Sandler, Ma, Tein, Ayers, Wolchik, Kennedy, & Millsap, 2010). The FBP incorporates separate groups for various members of a family: children, teens, and adult caregivers. The program's aim is to change risk and protective factors for bereaved children (Sandler, Ayers, Wolchik, Tein, Kwok, Haine, et al., 2003). Researchers describe the FBP as a cost-effective and brief model for highly stressed families whose parents learned to sustain their learned behaviors of emotional warmth and positive discipline with their children after a parental loss event (Hagan, Tein, Sandler, Wolchik, Ayers, & Luecken, 2012).

Family support from caring peers and professionals is undoubtedly an important part of healing from loss. Family support is indicated in cases when symptoms and experiences of grief and loss are considered within a normative range during assessment or if families choose this form of intervention. National organizations have formed grief centers solely for the purpose of providing grief support and aftercare to individuals and families. Some of the most well-known and national organizations include The Compassionate Friends and Partnership for Parents. In addition, other support groups are available through smaller organizations such as local hospice programs, The Dougy Center, Growth House Inc., GriefShare, SHARE Organization, MISS Foundation, Rainbows, and UNITE. The Internet is an excellent resource to help families locate these organizations and groups near their homes.

Besides interventions that follow a family systems perspective, family support for grief and loss may come in the form of bibliotherapy (Briggs & Pehrsson, 2008; Goddard, 2011; Koehler, 2010). Bibliotherapy is the use of literature for therapeutic intervention and has been used for decades to help people identify with characters or situations in the hopes that it will lead to increased insight into their own situation. It can be used as a form of or in conjunction with family therapy, or it can be used in a family support role. Providing a list of books that are helpful for different types of families, a range of ages, and a range of issues can be helpful. For some, reading in itself can be calming, relaxing, and comforting. Fiction, nonfiction, plays, or poetry can be helpful and can be used individually, between couples, or by entire families to create an atmosphere of support and healing.

While family support is indicated for the majority of families who are coping with loss, family therapy may be indicated for families who experience unresolved or complicated grief. Experiential techniques have been combined with Family Systems Therapy by a number of scholars as a way to bring people together around a common, pleasurable task that has the capacity to increase enjoyment and decrease inhibitions (Gil, 1994). These interventions have been used with families and larger systems, partly to make the treatment of grief more relevant and inclusive of children (Hemmings, 2005). Treatment providers who offer these forms of intervention during times of bereavement "emphasize caring for all members of a family, including children" (DeSpelder & Strickland, 2005, p. 365). Children often have more limited ability and interest in communicating solely through verbal means. Besides providing a way to integrate children into the assessment and treatment of family grief, family play therapy can be highly effective as a way for individuals and groups to begin to heal from symptoms of grief.

Experiential Family Therapy is an eclectic grouping of theories and techniques that emphasizes the here-and-now experience of clients with an emphasis on increasing sensitivity and feeling expression (Nichols & Schwartz, 1998). Many experiential family therapy techniques can be effectively applied to problems related to grief and bereavement in families (Mason & Haselau, 2008). These techniques include activities such as psychodrama; role playing; play therapy; and dance, music, and art therapies. Research has shown that experiential methods such as sandplay are effective in the reduction of complicated grief symptoms among families (Xu & Zang, 2011). These techniques are useful because they access multiple parts of the human brain so that each individual can experience the intervention from their own set of skills and needs. They are flexible enough to be able to be used by multiple age groups or generations at the same time.

Family play therapy is a related theory that can be used with families and larger groups who are dealing with grief and loss issues. Eliana Gil and others (see Lowenstein & Herlein, 2012) have written about the use of play therapy with families, extending the work of classical play therapy with children to the family and larger system. One example of a family play technique is the use of puppets to help families tell a story together, assessing their process, interactions, and the content of the stories to help them work through issues (Gil, 1994). The technique "stimulates communication and demonstrates how a family mobilizes toward a goal or task" (p. 46). It helps put families at ease, allows them to have fun, encourages them to be spontaneous, and can be used during the assessment phase to examine family functioning. This technique also encourages symbolic communication in that families can use it as a way to speak in code, especially about difficult, painful, and sensitive topics that often exist in times of grief and loss.

Various forms of art therapy such as drawing a family tree, family portrait, or self-portrait are useful in treating families with complicated grief symptoms. Sand tray techniques where families can express their thoughts and feelings through the use of miniatures may also be effective. Therapists can also help families create a memory jar or box of items and stories that relate to their deceased loved one (Way & Bremner, 2005). Games such as The Talking, Feeling, Doing Game as well as feeling cards (which clinicians can make themselves with basic paper and markers) can be a fun and engaging way to help families talk not only about their thoughts or behaviors, but their feelings as well. Finally, some techniques are not only effective, but they are also very inexpensive and require no specialized or costly materials and supplies. These techniques may include storytelling activities and other drawing or writing tasks that only require paper and markers, or pencils.

Regardless of the intervention, it is always important to remind clients about the individual nature of grief and that family members can be both supportive during the grief process and also create challenges for one another when the processes do not match well in terms of type of things such as individual expressions of grief and length of time grieving.

Larger Systems Interventions

Community grief is a complex process that may take months or years to fully resolve (Williams et al., 1999). Community tragedies occur when one or more members of a group die unexpectedly. These losses can involve many or few, but the larger the number of people who die or are injured, the wider the impact on the community. Besides death and injury, these tragedies can also include destruction to property, relocation, unemployment, and short- and long-term health risks (Williams, et al.). The more unexpected the loss, the more severe the grief and loss experience. These experiences can be an opportunity for growth and bonding or an ongoing crisis for a community. Swift, targeted, caring interventions are needed to help communities cope and recover.

The effective resolution of community grief is needed for the loss to become a reality within the identity of the community. While it would be normal for some residual pain to exist, the outcomes that come from effective community grief recovery can become a shared history that evokes enhanced feelings of closeness and pride. Support groups for communities and larger systems are available to help these large groups cope with losses. Children's programs are available through many of the above organizations, but also through individual communities and schools (discussed more below). These programs help children cope in a group setting in their own personal ways. Hospitals, churches, community mental health, and other community-oriented organizations also often develop grief support groups that are either ongoing or are developed in response to particular community crises. Support groups exist all over the world and are easier to find than ever, thanks to the Internet. Experts believe that in order for these types of centers and groups to be most effective when a community or larger system is coping with loss, these mechanisms should be in place prior to the loss event (Williams et al., 1999). Procedures can be activated and followed through more effectively so as to help restore community functioning as members heal.

In addition to group support, there has been a growing popularity of online Internet resources for bereaved families and individuals such as Bereaved Families Online, griefnet. org, caringinfo.org, Grief and Healing Discussion Page, Sidelines National Support Network, and Grief Watch. While most experts agree that face-to-face treatment is the foundation of grief therapy, the use of technology can decrease the literal space between service providers and clients when necessary (Stubbs, 2005). It also allows for interventions to occur on a larger scale when multiple lines are open and utilized at once. Phone and email support for bereaved individuals and communities can be used from the very earliest points of an intervention when geography or other logistics make it impossible to be in the same location. When this service comes in the form of a phone help line, it affords the potential client anonymity, control, immediacy, ease of contact, and accessibility. Email support has been used since the early 1990s and offers many of the same benefits as phone contact. Of course, these methods that do not have the advantage of face-to-face contact have the obvious disadvantages of having neither nonverbal cues nor the ability to see the expressions and hear the finer nuances of a conversation.

Schools can be a crucial point of support for individual or groups of children who have been bereaved, albeit at times inconsistent (Abdelnoor & Hollins, 2004). Silverman and Worden (1992) reported that children who received support at home and at school following the death of a parent had fewer problems than children who did not have the school support. But staff and teachers often feel unprepared for how to respond to bereaved children (Rowling, 2005). Short- and long-term interventions both inside and outside of the classroom should be planned ahead of time. Schools should incorporate training for teachers and administrators as well as form partnerships with outside agencies and the families of the school's students to prepare for present and future needs in the area of grief and loss. Facilitators can be trained early in bereavement support so that short-term interventions can be provided on the school grounds as soon as they are needed. Schools may also benefit from asking the students for input on what they want or need in the short- and long-term. Schools must be prepared for the long-term needs of the students and staff, not only for the crisis intervention activities that are sometimes needed.

In cases of community mourning complicated by issues such as trauma, violent crime, and terrorism, there are a few models of intervention widely used with groups. The most widely used and studied is called critical incident stress management (CISM) (Everly & Mitchell, 1999). CISM has been cited as the standard of care for intervention of crisis situations and originated as a treatment for police, paramedics, and firefighters who provide assistance in emergencies (Gamino, 2003). While this approach has been questioned for its lack of empirical evidence and for possible iatrogenic results (Gist & Lubin, 1999; Litz, 2004), CISM remains a widely accepted form of treatment for individuals and groups who have experienced a critical incident that overwhelms their "usual coping mechanisms resulting in psychological distress and a disruption in adaptive functioning" (Gamino, 2003, p. 125). CISM is a seven-component program of stress management. Group members come together after a traumatic event and discuss what happened to them, the thoughts and reactions they have had, and the symptoms they are dealing with. Then they learn that many of their symptoms are normal and they are not alone in facing them, and finally are given time to wrap up and develop a plan for any needed future action. CISM interventionists are trained in precrisis preparation, individual crisis intervention, large group demobilizations or informational briefings, critical incident stress debriefing' defusing, family/organizational consultation, and follow-up referral. One meta-analysis of eight prior studies indicated that CISM was effective in providing "comprehensive crisis response capabilities that cover the entire crisis spectrum from precrisis planning through acute crisis and post crisis interventions" (Everly, Flanner, & Eyler, 2002, p. 180). Another review of prior research on CISM found that it is "one effective way to address the adverse psychological distress that may result from such events. Although CISM interventions are sometimes thought to be only relevant to the needs of emergency services personnel (Litz, Gray, & Adler, 2002), these CISM studies document their efficacy with a variety of victims groups worldwide with significant outcome domains such as improved safety, enhanced care, sustained productivity, and dollar cost efficiencies. Most of these studies reported significant helpful outcomes..." (Flannerly & Everly, 2004, p. 326).

For a shorter term intervention, one element of the CISM model is helpful. The critical incident stress debriefing (CISD) can also be used with groups after a traumatic event (Everly & Boyle, 1999). CISD is a structured group discussion of a crisis that lasts somewhere between 1 and 3 hours and is implemented no less than 24 to 48 hours after the incident occurred. This model is not therapy but instead is meant to help achieve closure on the event, if possible. It also provides an opportunity to reach out to people who otherwise might not attend a longer term intervention and to provide needed information and referral sources. CISD has been found to be an effective crisis intervention in one meta-analyis of five prior evaluation studies (Everly & Boyle).

Finally, Kalayjian's (1996) seven-stage model of community healing may be helpful to community leaders. It begins with a preassessment before the intervention is implemented that includes exploring the dynamics of the community, to whom the event occurred, who are the survivors, community preparedness, and what is the overall civic climate of the community. They do an onsite assessment to determine community strengths and weaknesses, resources, and motivation for change. Next the community's response to the event is evaluated and a plan for services is developed. The plan is implemented; then an evaluation of the intervention is completed. To conclude, the community leaders modify and reevaluate the intervention for possible changes when it is implemented again in the future.

Conclusion

In the assessment and treatment of grief in families and larger systems, many techniques can be effective and used in multiple contexts that embrace and honor the cultural, spiritual, gender, and familial needs of the group and individual members. Regardless of the intervention and how eclectic a therapist is in her or his interventions, the relationship with the clinician continues to be thought to be one of the most important factors for short- and long-term positive outcomes. This relationship must be filled with a sense of trust and the notion that the therapist understands the individual's and group's issues in order for treatment to be effective.

One benefit to doing family or larger systems therapy on issues of grief is that it is less likely that the individuals will feel isolated and alone in their grief. Interventions that involve whole families or whole groups enable people to embrace the individual nature of grief and create a less isolated, lonely environment. On the other hand, the complication present in treating families or groups who are experiencing significant grief is that all members will grieve at their own pace and in their own way. Helping members to honor the ways in which others grieve can be therapeutic for families and larger groups. According to Thirsk and Moules (2012), "The timing of interventions needs to be carefully contemplated, and decisions about what type of interventions are offered should be reflective of what the family most needs *at that time*. Furthermore, if grief is indeed a lifelong and life-changing experience, then the evaluation of whether or not interventions are useful needs to take into account this longevity, and not only focus on the immediate 1-2 years after the death or after the counseling. …Families can be significant supports to each other not only before and after counseling, but they can also be instrumental in achieving change and healing *during* counseling. …Grief is not something that is escapable and thus as helping professionals, we have the obligation to continue to challenge and question our practices to do the best by the families we serve" (p. 120).

Chapter 26

Ethical and Legal Issues in Assessment and Intervention

Jackson P. Rainer

To effectively address death from the perspective of ethical and legal issues in assessment and intervention, attention must be given to end-of-life issues. As T.S. Eliot wrote, "... the mind of God in me shows what it is time to move on to and what it is time to let go of. What we call the beginning is often the end, and to make an end is to make a beginning; the end is where we start from" (1936, p. 86). Advances in managing and treating acute, life-threatening illnesses have led to greater longevity and have brought a lengthening of the typical dying trajectory giving the individual a prolonged period of disability. This change in dying and disability causes ethical and humane concern about the prospect of longer, medicalized, and impersonal deaths. Individuals in contemporary society are progressively more interested in a greater degree of self-determination in the dying process. With the current health care crisis and the high cost of end-of-life care, economics further confounds the proposition of self-determination.

The Centers for Disease Control and Prevention note that the average life expectancy in developed countries, such as the United States, has risen to 78.5 years in 2009 (CDC, 2011). Gains continue to be made in the average life expectancy primarily because of changes in the causes of death. Despite continued problems with the health care system of the United States, advances in medicine and public health have led to the diminishment of infectious disease as a primary cause of death. Now, degenerative diseases that occur more frequently in adulthood, such as cancer, heart disease, and stroke, have emerged as the leading causes of mortality. Progress has been made at a slower rate in the treatment of these diseases, and current research involves more speculation about how the body may be able to repair the damage it does to itself through malady and aging. Molecular biology, genetics, and stem cell research hold great promise in significantly extending average life expectancy, which baby boomers heartily embrace.

That being said, quality of life has emerged as important an issue as longevity. High-profile cases, such as Karen Ann Quinlan (In *re Quinlan*, 1976), Nancy Beth Cruzan

(*Cruzan v. Director, Missouri Department of Health,* 1990), and most recently Terri Schiavo (*In re: the guardianship of Theresa Schiavo,*1998) brought public attention to the fact that medical technology has advanced to the point where it can sustain life even when the individual is in a persistent state of unconsciousness with no hope of recovery. In the recent past, Floridian Terri Schiavo's case brought public attention to the private matter of extension of life and definition of death. In 2003, the relatives of Schiavo, a young woman who in 1990 suffered a brain injury and exhibited no further cognitive function, had a serious dispute about her treatment that triggered actions by officials of all three branches of Florida's state government (*Schindler v. Schiavo*, 2003). Her primary caregiver wished to remove her feeding tube in order for nature to take its course. Advocates of her continued care rejected the argument that cessation of life support, prohibited in all other situations, was acceptable when physical or cognitive limits were defined as extreme.

In an earlier and similar case, the Quinlan decision allowed the parents, on their daughter's behalf, the authority to refuse unwanted medical treatment, in this case mechanical ventilation. Even without this treatment, she lingered for another 8 years while receiving artificial nutrition and hydration. Now more than 40 years later, the wake of this court decision helped medical health care teams to be forthright in the withdrawal or withholding of life-sustaining treatments under similar circumstances where there is apparent meaninglessness of existence without consciousness. The Cruzan case then reified the legal precedent that an incompetent, terminally ill individual could forego life-sustaining treatment (with the decision of a surrogate). However, the Cruzan case led to the decision that states also hold the right to set evidentiary requirements for surrogate decision makers. In Missouri, the state can demand clear and convincing evidence that the stated action is what the individual would have wanted if competent. The judgment led to the use of advance directives to protect the self-determination of individuals who have reached a point in their illness when they are no longer about to make their own care decisions (Wachter & Lo, 1993). As in the Quinlan, Cruzan, and Schiavo cases, the use of life-sustaining medical interventions becomes an issue when patients are no longer competent to participate in decisions about their care. An advance directive is a means of stating personal preferences for medical treatment while still mentally capable and in anticipation of a time when one will no longer be as capable. Since treatment decisions in these situations may be morally charged, costly, contested, and counter to the wishes of the patient, the use of an advance directive as a means of extending the autonomy of patients when they are incompetent has evoked considerable interest (Emanuel, Barry, Stooeckle, et.al, 2012).

Even with established legal guidelines, the uncertainties demonstrated by these exemplary cases makes the following question figural: What is the ethical frame in which such cases should be judged? (Soldini, 2005). In each circumstance, there is an ethical dilemma regarding the definition of death. Historically, before the development of intensive care, an individual was declared dead when breathing and circulation stopped. However, such traditional concepts of death are now problematic because an individual's breathing and circulation can be sustained on life support after all cerebral functions are permanently lost, as occurred in the Quinlan, Cruzan, and Schiavo cases. All were in persistent vegetative states. In Florida statutes, a persistent, vegetative state is defined as a "permanent and irreversible condition of unconsciousness for which no recovery is possible" (Koch, 2005, p. 376). Those seeking Schiavo's continuance argued that her condition was only end stage and terminal when hydration and nutrition were removed. Her life might have continued for years had her care continued, as it had in the Quinlan case.

Out of this question, criteria for brain death were written, amplified, and are now widely accepted: It is defined as "irreversible loss of functioning in the entire brain, both cortex and brainstem" (Lo, 2000, p. 178). This designation is known as whole-brain death, also defined as "permanent cessation of the functioning of the organism as a whole" (Bernat, 1992, p. 21). Most states have adopted the Uniform Determination of Death Act as an effective ethical definition of death. It declares, "Any individual who has sustained either (1) irreversible cessation of circulatory and respiratory functions, or (2) irreversible cessations of all functions of the entire brain, including the brain stem. A determination of death must be made in accordance with accepted medical standards" (Furrow, 1991, p. 1034).

Symbolically, the moment of death is no longer momentous. Deathbed scenes throughout history have held cosmic drama in the expunging of weakness and sin, purification of the soul, and redemption, all which occurred close to the moment of dying. This concern for dying in grace carried over to rites for disposition of the body and for religious customs that would protect the dead on their journey into the afterlife. While this tradition persists, there is less theatricality due to the blurring of the terms *brain death, clinical death,* and *persistent vegetative state.* Now, the graying of the population and slow decline from multiple chronic conditions frequently result in cognitive and communicational impairments before death. Nevertheless, people are encouraged to bring their own beliefs and values to the end-of-life situation prior to the loss of capacity.

Psychologist James Bugental says that in our humanity, we have two fundamental givens. He says, "Humans have the capacity of acting or not acting, and humans have choice" (1984, p. 543). It is out of our choices that meaning is created. Choice and control are vital to personal sanity, even in the presence of death. In contemporary society, families and patients must wrestle with medical advances and hard choices. The traditional understanding of the Hippocratic oath acknowledges that in some circumstances medical treatment is futile and has no reasonable possibility to "cure, ameliorate, improve, or restore a quality of life that would be satisfactory to the patient" (Haley, 1996, p. 571). With the advent of medical technologies, however, it has become the slogan of many physicians and medical practitioners, as well in society at large, to keep the patient alive at all costs. This option is not necessarily the best decision or the only choice.

While the metaethical principles of beneficence, nonmaleficence, justice, and fidelity all apply as they might in any studied dilemma, the principle of autonomy has more weight during death assessment and intervention. Three terms must be defined. *Autonomy* is a fundamental concept in the law that proclaims the right of individuals to act on their own, to make decisions, and to determine their fate. *Consent* is a legal term indicating an agreement regarding something to be done. It is known to be an act of reason following deliberation. Consent offers an alternative to submission and is one of the derivatives of autonomy. As noted earlier, an *advance directive* is a legal document consisting of two elements: a living will and a durable power of attorney for health care. A living will is an advance directive to the physician regarding the dying individual's feelings about the use of life-support equipment or other extraordinary measures to sustain life. It is recognized as a legal document in all states. However, the use of living wills is still not widespread and applies only to a narrowly defined range of circumstances. It is easily rescinded even though it indicates the individual's thoughts regarding heroic care. The durable power of attorney is a document appointing a caregiver as health care proxy who is legally designated to make decisions about treatment and medical care. There are state-by-state restrictions on the enactment of the document, oftentimes requiring the aid of a notary or lawyer to draft and execute (Rainer & McMurry, 2002). A third type of directive is a do not resuscitate (DNR) order, also known as a no code. The DNR conveys a physician's order that a dying individual should not receive cardiopulmonary resuscitation if the patient stops breathing and/or the patient's heart stops beating. All three advance directives are based on the concept of autonomy and ensure continuity of decisions made while the individual is competent in the event of later loss of decisional ability.

Autonomy affirms the right to make decisions, consent describes the process of making decisions, and advance directives ensure continuity of decisions across time. Advance directives take the elements of decision making from the presumed moral authority of the medical practitioner and place them into the consumer-driven perspective of health care where the individual assumes the responsibility of choice. Dying is no longer a matter simply between a patient and a physician. It is expanded to include intimates, family, and community, all subsumed under the legal definition of surrogate. Over time, the value laden concept of quality of life has replaced the more difficult to define phrase "death with dignity." However, the primary question revolves around constitutional guarantees of a right to life. At the same time it does not allow clinicians to end a sustained life, even by artificial means. The landmark Quinlan, Cruzan, and Schiavo cases are benchmarks of the great dissonance between the law and clinical practice.

Because it declares the right of an individual to act in his or her personal best interest, autonomy is basic to health care decisions. An individual need not submit to treatment and can knowingly consent to or refuse treatment. It is a fundamental right that enables each person to be treated as an individual rather than as a part of a collective. The concept of autonomy and its practical translation allows the individual to make informed treatment decisions that are consistent with personal culture, values, and belief systems.

Consent is an autonomous act that gives permission for a specific therapy, treatment, or procedure to be performed. Included in consent must be information of the risk–benefit ratio of the treatment. Ideally, consent is not a static event but an ongoing process that involves clear communication between the individual and the health care provider. "To perform a procedure or treatment on a patient in the absence of consent constitutes abuse and subjects the one who performs the procedure to charges of abuse or assault. Consent to perform procedures on patients who lack the ability to provide consent lies with a guardian appointed by the local court. Parental consent is required in order to treat children and juveniles" (Lamers, 2005, p. 111).

Informed consent is the voluntary decision made by a person with decisional capacity who is cognizant of all relevant facts. The implication stands that the person who grants consent is truly informed about the subject and is capable of making a decision based on facts. The individual must understand the problem, treatment alternatives, and possible outcomes, including side effects, costs, and timing. Veiled language, euphemisms, and poor vocabulary are clinically discouraged, though are actively used in many aspects of death-related care. Truly informed consent is explicit and includes a written, signed, and dated legal document. Implicit consent is inadequate in end-of-life and death-related care. Without a record that necessary facts were revealed and discussed, there is no sense that the individual was able to make critical decisions regarding the course of treatment or care.

Any discussion of the ethics of death care regarding assessment and intervention must consider those who will speak for the deceased, particularly when there is disagreement among those in the person's intimate system. Despite the growth of the hospice movement in the United States in the past 30 years, more than 50% of American die in hospitals and long-term care facilities (Beckwith, 2005). This mortality statistic implies a continuing cultural distance from death. As a result, the dying process of a loved one can be a difficult family experience that can test even the closest family relationships. Family caregivers provide more than 80% of all home care services, yet receive no formal training or support for their roles (Beckwith, 2005).

Such caring brings focus to the metaethical principles of beneficence and nonmaleficence. Beneficence refers to the notion of doing good, while nonmaleficence directs the clinician to do no harm in the process. To many families and health care teams, death still translates as failure. For family caregivers, this stance may lead to increased isolation, misunderstanding, and feelings of abandonment when their loved one dies. When family members are spread across the country and geographic dispersion is added to the multiple derivations of families, e.g., stepfamilies and civil unions, the intimate system often will delay and postpone decision making until an emergency forces the issue. Differing belief systems, interests, lifestyles, experiences, and codes of ethics come into play by the committee of family members obligated to make death-related decisions, potentially causing conflict. Family members may disagree about the type of care that should be provided. There may be disagreement of the disposition of the body or of funeral rites. However, the most common issue is related to the settlement of the deceased's estate.

It is well-documented that most couples and families do not want to discuss death. Despite the compelling reasons for advance directives and their professional and public endorsement, they "...are infrequently used" (Emanuel, Barry, Stoeckle, et.al, 2012). Regretfully, at the point when there is no avoiding the subject, the patient is unable to participate in the conversation because of being too ill or sedated. Decision making then falls to the surrogate or to unprepared family members. The potential for strained communication is mitigated if clinicians provide timely clinical and prognostic information and offer continuous psychosocial support to all involved in the death discussions. Effective communication includes sharing the burden of decision making with other family members. The shift from individual responsibility to a patient-focused consensus permits the family to understand, even with great reluctance and sadness, how to proceed in the most caring and beneficent way.

Again, the notion of advance directives comes into play. These documents should be considered equally important to the dying person and to family members following the death. It should be noted by the clinician, though, that a complication of the advance directive process can add pressure to a family. Some individuals will indicate they want their family's wishes to take precedence over their own previously stated wishes, in the belief that the family will do what is best (Sehgal, Galbraith, Chesney, Schoenfield, & Lo, 1992).

A final advance directive to be discussed is the last will and testament, a legal document stating the individual's wishes for the settlement of the estate after death. A will is the best way to determine the distribution of personal belongings and assets, to provide for family needs regarding underage children, to plan wisely for taxes, and to make charitable contributions. Only by having a will can the individual be assured that personal wishes will be carried out after death.

The fundamental meaning of the word *care* is "to grieve, to experience sorrow, to cry out" (Rainer & McMurry, 2002). To care for another is an invitation to enter into that person's pain and suffering. There are few right answers in the ethics of assessment and intervention at the time of death. The complexity of the time is marked by its fluidity and developmental nature. During impending and actual death, there is a progressive loss of social convention and a diminished expectation and capacity for efficiency. Clinicians are obligated to provide instrumental aid and psychosocial support through the significant, difficult, and intimate life transition.

Death is a unique experience for each person, bringing multiple possibilities of ethical dilemmas. There is no substitute for the power of presence of the clinician. Professionals working to assess and intervene in this stage of grief will find a high degree of systemic confusion and must serve to balance fears with openness and anxieties with trust.

Chapter 27

On Bereavement Interventions: Controversy and Consensus

Simon Shimshon Rubin, Ruth Malkinson, and Eliezer Witztum

How to help people deal with the loss of a loved one is a matter of concern shared by individuals, families, communities, and societies. With scientific and clinical advances in the field of thanatology, our ability to describe and specify variations and dimensions of the bereavement response has grown dramatically (Malkinson, 2007; Malkinson, Rubin & Witztum, 2000; Rando, 1993). Theory, research, and clinical experience have deepened our appreciation of the lifelong impact of bereavement on the survivors.

This chapter on the value of intervention postbereavement has three parts. We open with controversies and consensus involved in diagnosis and intervention. We then move to a consideration of assumptions regarding assessment and intervention via the prism of the Two-Track Model of Bereavement (Rubin, 1999). Finally, we utilize case material to further clarify the extent to which intervention following loss is based on bereavement-related concepts and cannot be adequately measured without attention to these themes.

Appreciating the pervasive impact of bereavement upon an individual or family, however, is far removed from thinking that intervention is called for. In the words of a deceased colleague: Although [grief and] mourning involves grave departures from the normal attitude to life, [in most cases] it never occurs to us to regard it as a pathological condition and to refer it to medical [psychological] treatment. We rely on its being overcome after a certain lapse of time, and we [generally] look upon any interference with it as useless or even harmful. If one removes the brackets, what is left is a direct quotation from Freud's 1917 work *Mourning and Melancholia*.

Almost a century later, it is possible to read in the scientific literature on the efficacy of bereavement intervention as well as in the professional discussions advocating against the inclusion of a bereavement diagnosis in the DSM5, strong echoes of Freud's theoretical assertions (Lancet, 2012). Many who disagree, however, challenge the idea that grief is almost never pathological or maladaptive or that intervention is typically useless or even harmful. Promoting a grief diagnosis may have the potential to identify problematic responses to loss early and thus promote assistance that can mitigate suffering following loss and bereavement. It is possible to agree or disagree with all of the above, but the relevant question is, Do we have sufficient data to assist us to determine how to proceed? This question is particularly important with regard to intervention.

The controversies surrounding the value of bereavement counseling and psychotherapy stem from a number of sources. One source draws from differences in adherence to what is valued in a rigorous approach to the measurement of bereavement difficulties. This measurement rigor includes specification of criteria for when to call something helpful and choices of outcome measures and populations (Kleinman, 2012). Differences in the choice of paradigms in outcome research also contribute. Some studies privilege the efficiency of treatment models with strict selection and control criteria (Weston, Novotny, & Thompson-Brenner, 2004). Others follow the efficacy of intervention models that seek to measure intervention outcome as it is practiced in the real world (Seligman, 1995; Shedler, 2010). The use of meta-analytic statistics in reviews of benefit following bereavement interventions include a variety of subsets of these studies in their analyses, and they provide us with important information (Allumbaugh & Hoyt, 1999; Jordan & Neimeyer, 2003; Kato & Mann, 1999). Nonetheless, the impact and value of bereavement interventions remains open to discussion and debate (Larson & Hoyt, 2007). While we are much more knowledgeable than we were 15 years ago, a conceptual and operational paradigm shift may be required to provide some of the individual information still required to intelligently address the issues involved (Currier, Neimeyer, & Berman, 2008; Rubin, Malkinson, & Witztum, 2008).

The consensus among researchers, practitioners, and the bereaved themselves is that there is no one right or universal way to experience and respond to loss (Neimeyer, Kesee, & Fortner, 2000; Parkes & Prigerson, 2009; Rubin, Malkinson, & Witztum, 2012). Given that perspective, should intervention be offered when the bereaved is suffering but may or may not meet criteria for serious dysfunction? On the basis of current literature, it appears that providing some form of counseling or psychotherapy for all the bereaved and all bereavements has not been shown to be effective (Currier et al, 2008; Schut, 2010). When bereavement interventions are targeted for particularly difficult bereavements, the utility and effectiveness of psychological interventions emerge strongly (Gamino, 2011).

The Two-Track Model of Bereavement stresses the significance of joining a perspective on biopsychosocial functioning with one attending to the nature of the reworked relationship to the deceased following interpersonal loss (Rubin, 1981, 1999, 2012; Rubin et al, 2012). This framework allows us to better consider whether what is being assessed, discussed, and measured for both diagnosis and intervention outcome studies following bereavement is sufficiently sensitive to the specificity of the bereavement process. It is relevant for assessment, intervention, research, and theory (Rubin, Bar Nadav, Malkinson, Koren, et al., 2009).

The Two-Track Model of Bereavement and Bereavement Intervention

Part 1: Theory and research. What is and what should be the evidence for bereavement intervention? Simply put, it should be based on bereavement-related responses and bereavement-related difficulties. Bereavement challenges people to find a way to continue their lives following loss while dealing with the thoughts, feelings, and imagery that accompany adjusting to the reality that a loved one has died. As a model that attends to both biopsychosocial functioning (Track I) and the ongoing relationship to the deceased (Track II), the Two-Track Model advances a bifocal perspective. The model joins attention to function and dysfunction (present in all the studies reviewed by Currier and colleagues) with attention to the relationship with the deceased following loss (not present in the studies reviewed).

Renegotiating the psychological relationship to a significant person who has died requires accommodating to a changed interpersonal reality vis a vis the deceased. Prior to the loss, the relationship had involved connection as well as interpersonal interactions (or the possibility of interactions) to this highly significant person. After loss, the relationship will continue on only in the hearts and minds of the bereaved. This adjustment takes time. The process of adjustment and mourning the loss of the beloved and the reality that had been is often painful. It can be a wrenching experience marked by dramatic changes in functioning, but the grief process is not isomorphic with changes in functioning (Bonanno, 2009). An adaptive response to bereavement will generally balance attention to the challenges of life with a flexible but ongoing connection to the deceased.

When difficulties in the response to loss occur, they typically reflect some degree of interdependence as well as independence of the tracks of the bereavement response. Early in bereavement, the interdependence is manifest. In cases of complications of grief, however, difficulties may be manifest predominantly on only one of the tracks. Thus, even in the absence of biopsychosocial difficulties, we cannot assume the bereavement response is adaptive without information on the preloss and postloss experience of the relationship with the deceased. If biopsychosocial functioning is adaptive and adequate and yet memories of the deceased are avoided or superficially accessed, one can speak of positive outcome only with regard to Track I. If the relationship and bond with the deceased are accessible without significant difficulties, with indications of emotional support, connection and growth, the relationship to the deceased and its meaning for the bereaved are proceeding well. However, it there are indications of dysfunction in biopsychosocial functioning, one may speak of difficulties on Track I domains requiring assessment and possibly intervention. The memories of a relationship and the bond to the deceased may be set aside and deactivated, but this type of response is quite different from finding a way to retain a connection to the significant person who has died alongside involvement with life and relationships with others. Attending to both spheres of the bereavement response are shown in Figure 1.

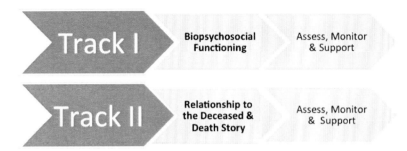

Figure 1: The Twin Tracks of the Two-Track Model of Bereavement

Having presented what we understand bereavement-related interventions need attend to, we now return to the comprehensive review of bereavement outcome of Currier et al. (2008). In the 61 studies they reviewed, of the eight domains of outcome measurement, seven were clearly related to track I's biopsychosocial functioning. The measures assessed general distress, depression, well-being, relational functioning/social adjustment, physical health, anxiety, and trauma. The remaining domain of grief and how it was measured was unspecified in the review (Currier et al, 2008). The design of the studies as well as the results of the meta-analytic summaries reflect a bias drawing from a medical model or pathology perspective. This emphasis by researchers and clinicians focuses on the biopsychosocial elements of bereavement and can miss a significant part of what bereavement, grief, and adaptation to loss involve.

The relationship to the deceased as central to bereavement outcome is not a new development. Prior to the adoption of the continuing bonds paradigm (Klass, Silverman & Nickman, 1996; Rubin, 1996), the earlier emphasis in bereavement was on grief and mourning as a process of detaching oneself from emotional investment in the deceased (Balk, 2011c; Freud, 1917/1957; Rubin, Malkinson, & Witztum, 2000). In other words, the relationship to the deceased and its psychological representations have been a focus of bereavement theorists and clinicians for close to a century. Discussing why this central axis has not been sufficiently incorporated into the assessment of the bond to the deceased and its place in assessing response to loss, recovery, and complications of bereavement would take us too far afield. Suffice it to say that this state of affairs is highly problematic and underscores why the Two-Track Model of Bereavement can be of assistance here (Rubin, 1999; Rubin et al. 2009, 2012).

Of course, we are not the only ones to critique the state of bereavement outcome studies. Somewhat surprisingly perhaps, after reviewing the evidence for bereavement interventions, Currier, Neimeyer, and Berman themselves call into question the relevance of the data from the 61 research studies they have analyzed (2008). They do this by questioning the choice of outcome measures, which they describe as manifesting "an overreliance on generic measures of psychopathology or general functioning that are insensitive to the manifestations of bereavement adaption...most warranting attention in therapy" (Currier et al, 2008, p. 656). In other words, the study of bereavement interventions' utility does not use measures most suited to the study of bereavement.

Narrowly focusing on the extent of behavioral difficulties and symptoms of various types following bereavement is valuable to a point. Its predominance, however, restricts the understanding by professionals and laypersons alike, of what is unique to bereavement. Without such understanding, bereavement remains a source of major psychological stress not fundamentally different from any other (Rubin, 1999; Rubin, et al., 2008). The unchallenged predominance of biopsychosocial functioning as a criteria for bereavement outcome is illustrated by a series of research studies aimed at identifying what components of bereavement response influence how professionals and nonprofessionals evaluate bereavement difficulties. In all of these studies, participants were asked to evaluate brief case descriptions and answer questions about the stories.

Overall, research participants evaluated problematic responses to loss affecting the biopsychosocial realm as being of serious concern, whereas difficulties in the ongoing relationship to the deceased were typically not seen as significant or as warranting intervention in and of themselves (Asmar-Kawar, 2001; Rubin & Schechter, 1997; Wiener-Kaufman, 2001). This bias is reflected even more sharply in a recent research study focused on meaning making (Halevi, 2012). Here, the contribution of meaning-making difficulties was assessed by linking it to either difficulties in how one managed one's life (related to the Track I axis of bereavement outcome in the Two-Track model) or to how one managed the relationship to the deceased (Track II). The results were consistent. In cases where biopsychosocial functioning was compromised, meaning-making difficulties added to the perceived severity of the problems—but only when bound up with how the bereaved viewed his or her own postloss world (Track I). When difficulties in meaning making were centered on the relationship to the deceased or the loss event, their effect on evaluation of response to loss was insignificant (Halevi, 2012).

Succinctly put, while relationship to another is what initiates bereavement, grief and the loss response, laypersons as well as most professionals respond similarly—as if the relationship to the deceased is neither central or of particular significance. This bias remains 15 years after the publication of Continuing Bonds and its adoption as the predominant conceptual model in bereavement today (Klass, Silverman, & Nickman, 1996; Rubin, 1999; Rubin et al., 2012; Stroebe, Gergen, Gergen, & Stroebe, 1992).

Larson and Hoyt published a very thoughtful review and analysis of the "empirical foundations of the new pessimism" (2007). Their article is more than a critical review of both individual and meta-analytic research studies published at the time of their review and their shortcomings. It is also a very strong critique of the way that trends in the science of bereavement have undergone a transformation from modest or unconfirmed evidence to becoming fact and accepted thinking. As a field, we need to be attentive to the significance as well as to the limitations of our data. We turn now to a case study to further illustrate what we mean by assessment, intervention, and research issues based on the Two-Track Model of Bereavement.

Part 2: Clinical perspectives. In the following case material, we set forth an example of assessment and intervention that conveys the significance of the continuing impact of loss and bereavement.[1] In working with clients, the use of strategic interventions as well as judicious use of the letter-writing technique can assist the progression of psychotherapy. The case under discussion was conceptualized as bereavement-related difficulty. It is, however, important to remember that health care professionals and therapists working from a focus on biopsychosocial functioning alone could conceptualize and intervene in this case without attaching overarching significance to the relationship to the deceased or specific bereavement-related issues.

Iris was a 60-year-old widow and mother of three, who broke her hand in a home accident. Soon thereafter, she complained of anxiety, reported decreased appetite, sleep difficulties, but no other mood difficulties. Due to her broken hand, she had difficulties in day-to-day activities. She was referred for evaluation and possible psychotherapy. Information about her past included the following: Iris was born in Israel to parents of Turkish background. She was the youngest of eight children. Iris felt she had missed opportunities in life (e.g., minimal education) and reported that she felt bitterness and anger toward her parents whose parenting choices had held her back in life. Iris married young to get away from home and initially stated that she had enjoyed a good life with her husband, Moshe, who was a financially successful man. She had undertaken to get a degree at the Open University and was successful. Almost 10 years earlier, however, her husband Moshe became ill with cancer and died. Over time, there were additional losses: a brother who died 1 year later and a sister who died 5 years after that. Upon further discussion of her past, the impact of the loss, and areas of difficulty that emerged after her husband's death, a more complex picture emerged. As will be seen below, the therapist (EW) believed that the primary source of difficulties here were bereavement-related.

On assessment, Iris's difficulties would probably not have met criteria for the variants proposed for a DSM5 diagnosis of complicated or prolonged grief (e.g., Prigerson, 2008; Shear, Simon, Wall, Zisook, et al. 2011). Nonetheless, assessment with the Two-Track Model highlighted that bereavement-related issues were present, and both tracks were problematic. Iris's feelings of anxiety, coupled with difficulties in sleeping and functioning at home, represented elements of biopsychosocial functioning difficulty that are characteristic of Track I. Later on, more of her sadness would emerge as important as well. On Track II, the relationship to the deceased, Iris reported that when she thought of her relationship to Moshe prior to his death as well as the circumstances of the death, she had predominantly sad memories. It soon emerged that she felt ambivalent toward him, with the sense that Moshe had left her with a "mess of a life." She also felt strong

1 This case illustration is shortened and adapted from the extended case discussion and presentation on strategic therapy and letter writing from Rubin, Malkinson, and Witztum's volume *Working with the Bereaved: Multiple Lenses on Loss and Mourning* published by Routledge (2012).

yearning and longing for him. Her loneliness was augmented by the additional losses of her siblings.

Iris's response to loss did have elements of complication (Rubin et al., 2008) and prolongation (Prigerson et al., 2008). The triggering event had been Iris's broken hand, which had effectively shattered her reconstructed postloss life. The damage effectively excluded her from her previous work and stimulated her feelings of fragility and helplessness. It had reconnected her with how she felt after her husband had died. Then she had felt that her life had come apart. She felt ignored by the extended family, financially threatened on the verge of bankruptcy, and emotionally depressed and anxious. These feelings had never gone away, but they were more pronounced again now.

The therapist's formulation placed grief and difficulties in adapting to her multiple losses as a central issue. The losses of her husband and the support he provided, followed by additional loss of brother and sister, were painful and now reactivated. At the outset of the treatment intervention, EW openly expressed his sympathy and communicated empathic responsiveness. He also shared his formulation that placed bereavement-related difficulties at the heart of her current plight despite the many years that had elapsed since then. Additionally, he explained about letter writing and how he thought it would assist Iris in reorganizing her thoughts and emotions related to the loss of her husband.

As part of the therapy, Iris was asked to write to Moshe in order to reopen and continue her long-frozen dialogue with him. In this way, she could make him aware of her struggles and her feelings. Iris agreed. In the first session following the assessment, Iris began writing. Her initial letters interwove the personal with the family's narrative. A major influence on her response to her loss related to business complications involving the nuclear, extended, and business family. After her husband's death, it turned out that much of his business had been based on oral agreements and that many business associates who owed him money denied their debts. Many of them had even claimed that he had owed them money. As she explained in her letter to him, her way of honoring and maintaining Moshe's reputation made her reluctant to declare bankruptcy.

By the fourth session, encouraged to do so by her therapist, Iris wrote for the first time about the anger she felt toward Moshe because of the disorganized way he had run his business. The absence of written and organized record keeping was devastating. One consequence was that her children argued bitterly about whether or not to pay the father's supposed debts. Some of these were undoubtedly false, but which ones? Years later, these issues continued to reverberate within the family.

The reopening of the inner dialogue within Iris and the dialogue with her husband allowed for change and growth. For example, Iris discussed in therapy the difficult interpersonal dynamics that developed between her and Moshe's family after his death due to the financial problems. The result was sad estrangement from this side of the family and her own feelings of being rejected. She thought that his family was ungrateful to Moshe and his help over the years, and she was angry with them. Direct work on the relationship with her husband continued and found its way into dreams that directly and indirectly featured him and reflected her longing for him. She shared her wish that he visit her in her dreams. The focus on the relationship to her husband at this stage of treatment was accompanied by intense emotions, but also with a sense of progress and readiness to reduce the frequency of sessions.

In one of the later sessions, Iris shared the emotional upheaval she experienced as the 10th anniversary of Moshe's death approached. She hinted to the therapist that she wished to cope with the upcoming event by herself. In the following session held a month later, Iris described her experience of the memorial service. She wished to share a special dream with EW. In her dream, she had been walking in her garden, which was full of blooming yellow flowers. She added, "Daffodils are my favorite flowers." The dream was so vivid for her that when she awoke, she ran to the garden to check if the daffodils had indeed bloomed. Together with the therapist, Iris concluded that blooming of the daffodils represented her return to life. She said that for the first time after a long period, she felt more optimistic.

This brief vignette reflects how bereavement-related difficulties may reverberate and resurface years after the event. The circumstances of her husband's death and her dependence on him had resulted in anxiety, ambivalence, and strong, but suppressed, negative emotions including anger, guilt, remorse, and disappointment. Over time, she had returned to functioning although of a more limited range that had been the case preloss. With the breaking of her hand and the changes in her lifestyle that followed, she reentered and reexperienced the emotions that had characterized the initial years following her husband's death. The biopsychosocial elements (Track I) of difficulty included anxiety, somatic complaints, and difficulties investing in life tasks, and ultimately, a sense of dysphoria. As for the relationship with the deceased (Track II), she initially suppressed her ambivalent and conflicted feelings toward her husband, who had left her alone and with a financial mess that reverberated interpersonally and within the famjly. She continued to feel yearning and longing for him. The symptoms of each track were handled strategically—the first with cognitive restructuring and the second with continuous letter-writing homework and use of metaphors to express her feelings. Iris responded well to the interventions and soon overcame the resurgence of anxiety and feelings of dependency that were manifest at the outset of therapy. She regained her functioning and, in a relatively short time, succeeded in becoming more assertive. She was able to create a space for herself as well as resume working.

In this case, the significance of the relationship to the deceased was both the major source of difficulty and the major key to the intervention. During the years following her husband's death, Iris had managed to reach a relatively high level of functioning. It is highly likely, however, that had one been assessing the nature of her ongoing relationship to Moshe, her bereavement response would have been seen as problematic in that area. The case of Iris is not one that would generally make its way into the research or outcome literature on the effectiveness of bereavement intervention. It is, nonetheless, a case that reflects the efficacy of bereavement interventions and the value of including the bifocal perspective central to the Two-Track Model of Bereavement in our thinking about bereavement intervention and outcome.

Conclusion

The loss of a significant relationship is a highly involved and multidimensional experience. The opportunity to share one's experiences and interact with others can assist in the reworking of the life narrative (Silverman, 2000a). In many cases, but certainly not all, these interactions serve to encourage and reconnect the bereaved to his or her own grief, to a fuller appreciation of who the deceased was and could have been, and also to the ongoing living fabric of one's connections to one's fellows. In Western society today, self-help as well as structured interventions have a role to play in providing support. Bereavement interventions serve to provide social support even as they span a very broad range from nonspecific support to highly specialized interventions for specifically defined difficulties (Currier et al. 2008; Kato & Mann, 1999).

The recent American Psychological Association's resolution on the effectiveness of psychotherapy is not a statement on the effectiveness of intervention following bereavement. Nonetheless, it included three points relevant to our own discussion. These are: (a) the value of evidence-based practice ("the integration of the best available research with clinical expertise in the context of patient characteristics, culture and preferences" [APA Task Force on Evidence Based Practice, 2006, p. 273], (b) the importance of a working definition of psychotherapy ("Psychotherapy is the informed and intentional application of clinical methods and interpersonal stances derived from established psychological principles for the purpose of assisting people to modify their behaviors, cognitions, emotions and/or other personal characteristics in directions that the participants deem desirable" [Norcross, 1990, p. 218-220], and (c) the focus of treatment ("...include problems in living, conditions with discrete symptoms that are identifies as or as related to illness or disease, and problems of interpersonal adjustment.") Painting with a wide brush, the document states: "The general or average effects of psychotherapy are widely accepted to be significant and large [APA, 2012]." We are not yet able to make comparable statements about the value of bereavement interventions overall, nor of their value with regard to the relationship to the deceased and the circumstances of the loss.

The literature to date, however, does identify consensus on the value of intervention under conditions of traumatic and violent bereavements, for select populations, where prolonged or complicated responses are present (Currier et al, 2009; Gamino, 2011). Losses where social support is minimal fall under this category as well (Doka, 2002). To these, we add subjectively perceived traumatic losses that also increase the risk of maladaptive responses to loss (Rubin, et al., 2012). For the future, interventions need to be examined for their impact on well being, their ability to shorten the period of suffering, their reworking of the relationship to the deceased, their attention to the nature of the ongoing relationship to the loss event and to the deceased, and for their success to facilitate positive change and growth. Under those conditions, we expect that the controversies on the effectiveness of intervention will narrow and additional areas of consensus will emerge.

Ultimately, we unequivocally support providing assistance to the bereaved who are interested in such help, by persons who are trained in bereavement and with proper attention to issues of competence and ethical responsibilities. These forms of assistance are generally assumed among licensed health care professionals but need not be limited to them. Despite this support, we believe that the research and outcome literature have not yet provided us with the necessary data to fully support or seriously challenge our perspective.

Traumatic Death

Introduction to Part 5, Chapters 28 – 33

Chapters 28 through 33 focus on traumatic death. The Body of Knowledge Committee defined this major category of thanatology knowledge in this way: **sudden, violent, inflicted, and/or intentional death, shocking encounters with death.**

The chapters in Part 5 focus on traumatic death in terms of these indicators: culture and socialization, religion and spirituality, historical and contemporary perspectives, life span issues, the family and larger systems, and ethical and legal issues. All of the chapters are revised from chapters that originally appeared in the first edition of the handbook.

Chapter 28

Culture, Socialization, and Traumatic Death

Jeffrey Kauffman

Trauma uniquely resists formalization. This constraint is true of individual, cultural, and social trauma. Caruth (1996) argues that traumatic events are inherently incomprehensible because at the core of trauma is forgetting. Blanchot (2000) and Krystal (2002) carry this issue further, suggesting that the most traumatic aspect could not be experienced, but is intensely dissociated, continuing to happen until it can, if possible, be remembered, or otherwise, lived with, in one way or another until one dies. One is frozen in the moment of traumatization. The disruption of memory in trauma is corollary to the disruption of self. The core of traumatic death remains dissociated and incomprehensible, but its consequences are life-defining. Trauma is a remarkable response of the human organism, in which the cohesion of the self is shattered, producing a diversity of symptoms and other life redefining consequences. Caruth argues that traumatization is being possessed by an image or event. And, what the image or event means is "being *possessed* by the ravages of the self violated by or *exposed* to a traumatizing death." While trauma is outside the realm of meaning, persons who have been traumatized may present differently than the usual posttraumatic stress disorder (PTSD), with just about any of a wide spectrum of mental health disorders, such as bipolar disorder, major depression, addictive disorder, borderline personality disorder, somatic symptoms, phobias, dissociative disorder, schizoaffective disorder, and anxiety disorder. Traumatization releases a monstrous upheaval within. Trauma consequences vary widely or, as we say more technically, trauma is plastopatholic.

Plastopatholic designates that traumas do not result in a uniform symptomatology, but that the pathology is highly variable; the psychopathology of traumatic grief has a high level of plasticity to it. Disturbances of traumatic grief savage the soul in such a way that, while dissociation may be rampant and self-loathing, shaming, self-blame may be typical, the forms these symptoms take are molded around the history of life experiences in diverse ways. Traumatic grief disrupts the capacity to experience oneself. It disrupts the continuity of time, based in the continuity of one's experience of oneself. The power of trauma to cause fragmentation and compromised self-healing efforts, leaves the traumatized griever unable to maintain the normalcy of self-experience, developing diverse disorder patterns. Plastopathic means the collapse of boundaries or destabilization of boundaries between one pathology and another.

Human Relationships and Identity

Van der Kolk observes that traumatized persons avoid intimate relationships (1987, p. 3). Relationships may be sought, but they tend to be turbulent, and emotional intimacy is usually not possible. The grief from a traumatic death is especially socially alienating. The sense of safety and self-belief are fragile, and, while the survivor of a traumatic experience of death may aggressively pursue goals in the social world, he or she lives on the thin ice of the vulnerability of the traumatized self to disintegrate, to be abandoned in extremis, to flee in terror, reliving being helpless to stop the catastrophe. The traumatized, in the extreme that characterizes the condition, "have no self, no 'me,' no individuality." (van der Kolk, 1987). Young and Erickson (1989) see trauma as disrupting the sense of continuity, leaving one alienated and isolated. The trauma disturbs experience so severely that the pre- and posttraumatic self are discontinuous. The disruption of the temporal continuity of experience disrupts one's connection to oneself and to others. "Victims of extreme social violence often have difficulties relating to family members and to the community at large" (Suárez-Orozco and Robben, 2000, p. 43). Traumatic death may impair one's capacity to experience social support, where safety normally would be found.

Special Social and Cultural Concerns

Bioarchaeological research shows that throughout the history of our species, interpersonal violence, especially among men, has been prevalent. Cannibalism seems to have been widespread, and mass killings, homicides, and assault injuries are also well-documented in both the Old and New Worlds. No form of social organization, mode of production, or environmental setting appears to have remained free from interpersonal violence for long (Walker, 2001).

Trauma and Modernity/Postmodernity

Bracken (2002) emphasizes the sociocultural context of traumatic death, with a special concern that those who work with victims of wars, mass violence, and natural disasters, put aside their culture-bound assumptions and be open to the unique languages in which other cultures experience traumatic death. He writes, "The current discourse on trauma is simply inadequate to grasp the complexity of how different human beings living in different cultures respond to terrifying events" (Bracken, 2002, p. 8). Bracken suggests that the psychological concept of trauma is culture-bound specifically by the postmodern occurrence of an "economic and cultural shift to an intense form of consumer capitalism," which defines our "contemporary experience of trauma, distress and alienation" (Bracken, 2002, p. 14). This understanding may be too narrow a causal attribution, as economic influences are one of many key dimensions that define our culture.

Young takes a more radical approach, arguing that, "During the nineteenth century, a new kind of painful memory emerged. It was unlike the memories of earlier times in that it originated in a previously unidentified psychological state, called 'traumatic,' and was linked to previously unknown kinds of forgetting called 'repression' and 'dissociation.'" (Young, 1995, p. 3). This argument takes trauma as a "new kind of painful memory" that originates in our sociocultural world in the 19th century. His argument is basically that the emergence of this new psychological language signifies a new way of experiencing; but this approach seems to overstate the point, for a trauma by any other name is a trauma. Nonetheless, a new age of traumatic death with mass killings and savagery seems to have been repeatedly erupting since the French Revolution.

Young sees not just the concepts as new, but also the phenomena identified as sociocultural constructs. Trauma theory is, then, itself sociocultural evidence of the emergence of a new condition that Young traces to a new 19th century sensitivity to and perception of the suffering of traumatic grief, a sanctioning that comes to recognize a particular disruption of memory and identity on all levels of human organization. Trauma is not just culturally diverse; it is, according to Young, an historically bound phenomena of our culture.

Friedman and Marsella (1996, p. 11) report that accounts of "emotional reactions to extreme stress have been noted by historians and literary authors for 4,000 years..."; however pre 19th century reactions to devastating events may not have had the particular meaning that trauma as hysteria has in the work of the 19th century psychologist Janet. The difference between Janet's (1978) work on hysteria and the trauma theory that has emerged in the last quarter of the 20th century are late 19th and late 20th century reflections of trauma in an age that is particularly dissociative and where the social and cultural symbolics in which traumatic death was assigned a meaning are not functioning very well. In this 19th and 20th century phenomena called trauma there is a psychological sensitivity to and awareness of the disturbances in which a psychic injury is inflicted from outside.

We can look at trauma theory as itself a sociocultural reaction of modernity, to an urgency in a culture that, perhaps since the French Revolution (Fritzsche, 2004), has been traumatized. This view of trauma as a sociocultural construct takes trauma to be a specific name for an experience that was emerging in the West in the 19th century, that is, that modernity and postmodernity are "an age of trauma." Bracken, echoing Janoff-Bulman (1992), argues that in the contemporary world, "the experience of horror calls into question the basic order of the world" (Bracken, 2002, p. 3).

The world of posttraumatization, for Bracken, is the onset of a sociocultural world in which, while traumatic death narratives are more abundant than ever, traumatic death becomes socioculturally more pervasively alienated. Farrell (1998) makes the interesting argument that trauma is a "strategic fiction that a complex stressful society is using to account for a world that seems threateningly out of control" (as cited in Bracken, 2002,

p. 3). The very conceptualization of trauma in modern times is, by this light, a self-expression of the traumatization of the social world, an assumption or construct intended to control a world whirling out of control, by recognizing it, and by way of the imagination, developing strategies intended to manage it. Suarez-Orozco and Robben write that "the twentieth century brought us some of the most barbaric episodes of large-scale violence and trauma" (2000, p. 1). The 20th century has been, globally, an age of traumatic death. This fact is highly consequential, as traumatic death becomes more intense at the beginning of the 21st century. In the 21st century death is traumatizing on a global scale, and Americans are notably fearful.

Collective Trauma

In *Everything in its Path,* Kia Erickson introduces a concept of collective trauma, describing how a traumatized community "gradually realizes that the community *no longer exists* as an effective source of support and that *an important part of the self has disappeared"* (Erickson, 1976). The loss of self may be a consequence of the loss of community. Davoine and Gaudilliere argue that "historical and social traumas" (2004, p. xxiii) have a pervasive effect on individuals and on the culture or society as a whole. They also assert eccentrically, that historical-cultural trauma is the root of "madness." But, it may not be so eccentric. Traumatic disturbances embodied in a culture may instill psychological disorder in the culture. They suggest that madness is a consequence of sociocultural traumatic events.

Suarez-Orozco and Robben argue that collective trauma targets "the body, the psyche, as well as the social order." The sociocultural context "intertwine[s] psychic, social, political, economic and cultural dimensions," in an affliction of massive trauma. (2000, p. 1). Cultural identity is shaped by traumatic death, as the trauma is encoded into cultural narratives that are transgenerationally transmitted (Suarez-Orozco and Robben, 2000). A group subjected to traumatic deaths receives "an indelible mark upon their group consciousness, marking their memories forever and changing their future identity in fundamental and irrevocable ways" (Alexander, 2004, p. 1). In traditional societies traditional symbolics, practices, and rituals respond to collective trauma to secure collective identity and the stability of meaning (Alexander, 2004). These are, it is generally recognized, less available, less powerful and less consequential in the posttraditional world and do not adequately serve the social reintegrative function of premodern posttraumatic sociocultural practices. Major traumatic deaths shape a deeply interior aspect of collective reality. Traumatic exposure violates the most private interior of psychic and sociocultural being.

Alexander, following Herman (1992) and many others, argues that the restoration of collective psychological health is in "lifting societal repression and restoring memory" (Alexander, 2004, p. 7). Remembering is only a starting place toward restoration, though, especially regarding collective death traumas; remembering is a defiance of sociocultural and political powers that ignore, disavow, or derealize historical collective traumatic deaths.

Trauma and Moral Responsibility

Alexander elaborates upon a social construct theory of trauma, by bringing in a very significant moral dimension. "By constructing cultural trauma.... social groups, national societies, and sometimes even entire civilizations not only cognitively identify the existence and source of human suffering but 'take on board' some significant responsibility for it" (Alexander, 2004, p. 1). This responsiveness to trauma is not an American strong suit. Alexander's account of the genesis of cultural moral consciousness of trauma begins in the act of recognizing the occurrence or presence of trauma, and, once recognized, it becomes the conscience of the culture, a moral call for a just healing. The concepts of justice and healing sometimes are, with regard to trauma, closely related.

Cultural Diversity

PTSD is a culture-bound concept, though aspects of it are found in non-Western cultures; these aspects are found through the eyes of Western cultural and psychological assumptions. If societies construct reality, traumatic death will have a different meaning and will be a different experience, in different socially constructed realities. Below I say more about such difference, but at the outset note that this notion of cultural distinctions implies that our own social construct of traumatic grief expresses something specific about our own culture.

Friedman and Marsella summarize the basic question about the universality and cultural diversity of trauma by writing that "while a universal neurobiological response to traumatic events most likely does exist, there is room for considerable ethnocultural variation in the expressive and phenomenological dimensions of the experience, especially among comorbidity patterns and associated somatic, hysterical, and paranoid symptoms and experiences... If more sensitive cross-cultural research and clinical methods are used in the study of PTSD, ethnocultural variations may emerge with greater regularity and clarity" (2004, p. 107). Notice that the explanatory categorization system used here is Western psychology. Friedman and Marsella say the universal response *most likely* exists. In this argument, a universal response is implied by the trauma reaction being basically neurobiological and assuming that the neurobiological is not evolutionarily affected by cultural factors. Also, we may infer from this account that variations between cultures are on the level of experienced meaning. There is not enough research that attempts to phenomenologically describe the experienced meaning of traumatic death crossculturally. Most authors interpret non-Western behavioral languages of traumatic grief in Western psychopathological terms, and not in terms of experienced meaning.

Kirkmayer claims that the major difference in non-Western cultures are in the somatic and dissociative expressive languages of some cultures. He questions the accepted view that trauma is an anxiety disorder. He argues that "the symptomatology of PTSD overlaps with affective, somatoform, dissociative and anxiety disorders" (Kirkmayer, 2001, p. 131) and suggests that trauma is closely associated with depression and "some degree of enduring loss" that is grief. He says that crossnational and crosscultural studies of somatoform disorders indicate three problems for existing nosology. These problems are, "(a) the separation of somatoform disorders from anxiety and mood disorders reflects distinctions between physical and emotional distress that are not made in other cultures; (b) in many cultures, somatic symptoms and attributions commonly are used as idioms of distress to convey a wide range of personal and social concerns that may or may not indicate individual psychopathology; (c) the nature of physical symptoms varies cross-culturally with ethnophysiological theories, illness models, and previous illness experience" (Kirkmayer, 2001, p. 132f).

Robben and Suarez-Orzco approach the problem of describing traditional cultures on their own terms, asserting, "Traditional, non-industrial societies have often sought to collectivize the social injuries of massive trauma. They have created healing rituals, religious ceremonies communal dances, and revitalization movements, and have restored symbolic places" (2000, p. 22). They argue that due to repeated exposure to trauma the Navajo developed a ritual. "The Navajo Enemy Way ceremony represents the culture's ritualized attempt to cleanse returning warriors from the deleterious impact of war trauma and to help.... reintegration into peacetime Navajo society" (2000, p. 24). Friedman and Marsella claim that what one culture experiences to be traumatic, another may appraise to be a rite of passage, as in the case of the Navajo. Fairbank et al. (1995, p. 24) suggest that in societies that provide stable and safe social bondedness, vulnerability to traumatization is reduced. Such considerations as these need more study. Traumatic death in our culture may be on the rise, and our culture's rituals and norms may be hard-pressed to integrate and symbolically transform traumatic death.

The Flourishing of Temporary Memorials

Memorials at the site of roadside fatalities have appeared in all corners of the world for thousands of years. They first appeared in the United States through the influence of Mexico in the 18th century and were called descansos, resting places—even though they were not burial places (Doss, 2012). Today there is great increase in these roadside memorials. Doss suggests that this increase expresses "an obsession with issues of memory and history and an urgent desire to express and claim those issues in visibly public contexts" (p. 2). In our culture today this surge in temporary memorials may also express a heightened anxiety about remembering and a traumatic sensitivity specific to and indicative of our time; these memorials may be read as signs of the time. They are occurring with increasing regularity not just in America, but throughout the world (Weir 2012.)

Contemporary sociocultural meanings of traumatic grief, the loss of a living bond with the past, the privatization of death, and other ways in which traditional meanings of death have been deracinated, prompt a particular need for public recognition of a death, making hallowed the random, anonymous place where a roadside death occurred. Placing a roadside memorial is an act of connecting and bringing one's presence to and sanctifying the place of a loved one's violent death, an act of reaching out to the deceased in an effort to make meaning of the utter meaninglessness of the vehicular homicide or other senseless act that occurred.

Ann Cvetkovich calls these memorials "repositories of feelings and emotions embodied in material form and narrative context" (2003). The objects used to construct the memorial expresses an emotional story. The memorial is a construct that contains the emotional reality of the overwhelming traumatic grief. The memorial is an expression of remembering and feeling, where there is only a terrible inner vacuum. Typically the material that makes up the memorial are flowers, real or plastic; a wreath; a handwritten message; a photo of the deceased; a date; a name or initials; a cross; and perhaps a personal item. The items express a connection to the loved one who died there and represent being with the loved one in that lonely place by the wayside.

In *No Place to Die: The Poetics of Roadside Sacred Places in Mexico* (Weir, 2012), Weir notes that the exact location of a person's death is important in Mexican roadside memorials, and this is certainly a factor in roadside memorials more generally, as the death and the memorial transform the landscape into a text of traumatic grief. Weir, like numerous other commentators, sees the meaning of roadside memorials in the *force* of emotions. This recurring emphasis suggests that the phenomenon of roadside memorials contains, in the simple objects present, the power of traumatic grief emotions. Wolf sees these memorials to be "tears and prayers made visible" (Wolf, 2008).

In some states these memorials are banned and in others a permit is needed, such as in Virginia. The state installs the memorial and leaves it up for two years. This taking over converts the explicit function of the memorial into a driver safety program. On Virginia's markers the most prominent words are "Drive Safely." This bureaucratization of roadside memorials deprives the mourner of vital personal meaning in creating the memorial and constructing it of objects that help negotiate the death and relationship with the deceased.

Roadside memorials are one type of temporary memorial flourishing in contemporary America, part of a wider memorialization boom that Doss calls memorial mania. There are also increasing numbers of spontaneous traumatic grief memorials that mobilize social groups, in what Brennan calls a "transmission of affect" (Brennan, 2004 p. 15), a mass hysterical outpouring of traumatic grief. The most memorable of these was the spontaneous memorials that covered Manhattan and Ground Zero in the wake the Sept. 11, particularly in front of fire stations, where candles, messages, and objects were assembled, expressing gratitude and an array of traumatic grief symptoms, marking the entire physical and social landscape a traumatized zone. These spontaneous temporary memorials express a desperate effort to make sense and find meaning in the loss of the assumptive worlds of normalcy, predictability, and safety (Kauffman, 2002b). When proximity to the site of the World Trade Center was accessible, it was sanctified and claimed by the traumatic grief of the entire community, becoming a temporary memorial by the objects placed there, vigils performed there, and the community bonding there, a site of traumatic grief mobilized by these memorial acts into a sanctified place of healing.

Spontaneous community expressions of traumatic grief through temporary memorials have occurred frequently in contemporary America. Within hours at Columbine High School where two students gunned down 15 students and teachers, the campus became an overflowing grief-drenched site, with mounds of memorial objects growing to 4 feet deep, with personal notes, balloons, stuffed animals, religious items, origami cranes, sneakers, soccer balls, shirts with messages, votive candles, and more; venders, crowds, and television crews contributed to making it a frenzied traumatic grief space, a memorial circus flooded with traumatic anxiety. These are but two of a great number of spontaneous community-cohesive memorial events at sites of murders and accidents, such as the site where a mother drowned her two children in a car in a lake, where TWA flight 800 crashed, where Matthew Sheppard was murdered by homophobics, and at the Johnson Space Center after the Columbia disaster. This brief list shows a variety of events that draw people together in creating a spontaneous temporary memorial of material objects and sites of vigils. These are spontaneous memorials of grieving communities in the wake of traumatic deaths that have public meaning.

Temporary memorials are not always site-specific to the death, such is in the case of memorial decals in the rear window of cars, where the driver is bearing witness to the loss, displaying the memorial publicly as an insignia of grief and memory. In all types of temporary memorials a mourning-negotiation seeking to give meaning to the overwhelming emotional wound of traumatic death is involved.

Internet and Traumatic Grief

The Internet has become a valuable resource and networking place in the field of traumatic grief, as it has in so many aspects of life. Persons experiencing traumatic grief may find therapy, support, information, and a place for memorials. Communities may find a place to meet and talk after a traumatic loss. Professionals may find training programs, research and clinical information, including information about the Internet and traumatic grief. Sofka coined the term *thanatechnology* to name the thanatology resources available on the Internet. In addition to social support sites, she recognizes sites for the grieving as "narrative, commemorative, expressive, and experiential" (Sofka,1997).

Online support groups provide similar benefits to traditional support groups, reducing isolation, information sharing, and education. Gary and Remolino (2010) note that there are, however, no set standards for interaction, crisis management, or training of group leaders, if there are group leaders. Online support groups also emerge in reaction to specific traumatic events. After school shootings [referring to unspecified events they studied between 1997 and 1999], for example, students and others affected have gone online to try to understand these school tragedies, to reach out to others, to learn how to make schools safe, to cope with school violence, to handle grief reactions, and to recognize danger signs of violence in high-risk youth. Once the shock wore off and the grieving began, online support groups for loss were overwhelmed in the days and weeks following many of the school shootings. New members, either from the local area of the shootings or from among television viewers, joined veteran online support group members to seek support and to express anger, outrage, and other emotions. Dialogues were strained, and many members seemed to experience inhibition when disclosing intimate feelings (Gary and Remolino, 2000).

Other limitations of online groups they cite are anonymity breaches, differing stages of group development and phases of grief among members, hoax perpetuations, limited feedback, and lack of accountability.

By the beginning of the 21st century online support groups are a regular occurrence after a public event of traumatic grief. For example in the aftermath of 2007 Virginia Tech and 2008 Northern Illinois University shootings "nearly 90% of students joined a shooting related *Facebook* group, 80% used instant messaging to discuss shootings and more than 60% discussed trauma on their *Facebook* walls" (Vicary & Fraley, 2010). While this online communication contributed to a sense of connection, Vicary and Fraley did not find any long-term benefit from these activities. Online support groups are a developing medium of support for traumatic grief and come with benefits and risks. These risks need to be better understood to help minimize risk.

Aboujaoude has noted "that because almost every significant event is recorded and turned into web images and videos, we are repeatedly exposed to traumatic, sad and fear-inducing events whether we wish to be or not" (quoted in Humphreys, 2011). If a traumatized person does not feel sufficient control over the experience, this exposure can be retraumatizing. The traumatized vulnerable need to exercise care to be safe in an age of ubiquitous electronic images of trauma.

Cognitive behavior therapy (CBT) has developed online treatment modalities, and CBT, the most researched approach to psychotherapy, usually has an evaluation component built in. An example of this online treatment and research is the work of Wagner, Knaevelsrud, and Maercker who developed and evaluated the efficacy of a short-term Internet-based CBT program for bereaved people suffering complicated grief. They concluded that, "Participants in the treatment group (N = 26) improved significantly relative to participants in the waiting condition on symptoms of intrusion, avoidance, maladaptive behavior, and general psychopathology, and showed a large treatment effect. Follow-up results show that this improvement was maintained after 3 months" (Wagner, Knaevelsrud, & Maercker, 2006, p. 429). Numerous other Internet-based treatments also report decreased trauma symtomotology. Here is an example of another such study. Interapy: The Effects of a Short Protocolled Treatment of Posttraumatic Stress and Pathological Grief Through the Internet examines the effectiveness of an online standardized treatment of posttraumatic stress and pathological grief, and the authors report that "participants improved strongly from pre- to posttreatment on posttraumatic stress and pathological grief symptoms and in psychological functioning. These improvements were sustained during the follow-up period. Moreover, 19 of the 20 participants were clinically recovered after treatment" (Lange, Schrieken, et al., 2000, p.

175). The efficacy of online psychotherapy programs such as this for traumatic grief and the optimism and meaning of these outcomes, however, needs greater scrutiny.

Surfing the Net for Medical Information about Psychological Trauma: An Empirical Study of the Quality and Accuracy of Trauma-Related Websites (Bremner, Quinn, Quinn, and Veledar, 2006) cautions against the quality of information about trauma available on the Internet. Of the 72 sites evaluated based on searching *psychological trauma*, *stress*, *PTSD*, and *trauma*, 82% did not provide a source of their information, and 41% did not use a mental-health professional in the development of the content. Ratings of content (e.g., accuracy, reliability, etc.) were 4 (2 SD) on a scale of 1 – 10, with 10 being the best. There were similar ratings for the other variables assessed. These findings suggest that although abundant, websites providing information about psychological trauma are often not useful and can sometimes provide inaccurate and potentially harmful information to consumers of medical information...This study shows that websites related to psychological trauma are not providing appropriate information.

Mobile Internet technology is also employed in crisis situations to provide treatment and guidance to victims at a remote disaster site where onsite help is not available or to network among colleagues (Fan, Yang, et al., 2009).

Training programs for professionals in traumatic grief may also be found on the net. Here are some examples: http://www.nctsn.org/category/affiliated-resources/website-and-online-resources at the National Child Traumatic Stress Network. The University of Maryland School of Social Work offers an interactive training in CBT for child traumatic grief at http://ebpexchange.wordpress.com/2008/09/11/childhood-traumatic-grief-ctgweb-online-interactive-training/, and a website called Trauma Recovery offers CBT training programs at http://trauma-recovery.net/2011/11/01/3-online-training-programs-about-traumatic-stress-and-interventions-high-quality-free-and-convenient/ Since the 1990s (Sofka, 1997) memorial sites have been appearing online, and there are now many. For traumatic grief, where personal narratives are especially prone to be silenced in shame, new digital modes of expression provide new memorializing opportunities. Content typically includes photos, music and videos, stories from family and friends, and a guest book, which may be especially meaningful in dealing with complications of traumatic grief.

Chapter 29

Religion, Spirituality, and Traumatic Death

Gerry R. Cox

Religion and Traumatic Death

Sociologists generally view religion as the way in which peoples put their beliefs into practice. Religion is something that people do. Death is not a private event, nor is it only a psychological event. The rituals of religion help us to recognize, understand and process our beliefs about dying and death. The challenge of traumatic death often causes those providing social support to be even more involved in religious rituals. Those who provide social support do so by attending the wake or visitation, funeral, cemetery rituals, the meal afterwards, donating to favorite charity, bringing food for the grieving, visiting or simply sending a personal sympathy note. For many religious organizations, death rituals are quite predictable. As an example, Roman Catholic practices are very similar from one church to another, from one region or nation to another, from one year to another year.

Using religion to manage traumatic death can produce both positive and negative outcomes. Positive religious outcomes would include feeling connected with God, finding comfort and assurance in God's love and care, seeking God's aid in overcoming anger and/or seeking forgiveness, perceiving God as a source of strength in time of need, and attempting to find control through God's grace and help. This positive religious outcome allows one to better accept and adjust to the traumatic loss. Negative religious outcomes would include questioning God's love and mercy, feeling abandoned by God, feeling punished by God, questioning what I did wrong to make God punish me, and feeling confused or dissatisfied with God. Those who experience positive religious outcomes will exhibit fewer negative symptoms and psychological stress. Negative religious outcomes could lead to depression, lowered quality of life, and other negative psychological symptoms. For the religious person, death can bring out the frailty of faith, and it can detach us from any promise or hope that can lead to despair and hopelessness leaving a dark cloud on our remaining days (Aden, 2005). Koenig (1997) found that negative religious coping led to greater depression and lower quality of life. Death is both natural and mysterious and activates a complex mixture of emotions, thoughts, behaviors, and changes like no other experience in life (Richards, 2001). Rituals/ceremonies evoke a cognitive means of making sense of our traumatic losses.

For the Australian Aboriginals, ceremonies are sacred and secret at the same time. Elders hold knowledge that is crucial for survival, and this knowledge is kept secret because it only has meaning when it is spoken by the ceremonial elder to an initiate in a way that affects every aspect of his being (Randall, 2003). As in Native American religion, the Aboriginal religion does not separate the spiritual from the practical. After a traumatic event, a Lakota might go to the hills for spiritual renewal. For the Hopi, their sacred place would be the land of the red rocks, a place with a deep, reverent connection to their ancestor spirits as well as those of animals and plants (Aitchison, 1992). For the Australian Aboriginals, there are also many sacred sites. The Katatjuta, or Olgas', located in the Northern Territory; Uluru, or Ayers Rock, located in the center of Australia; and even Mother Earth in her entirety is sacred. Like American Indians, the Aboriginals think that the destruction of sacred sites causes illness and even death among elders (Voigt & Drury, 1997). American Indians and Aboriginal peoples both manage traumatic death through rituals and ceremonies. The destruction of culture, the loss of tradition, and the influence of modern society has made it much more difficult for these groups of people to manage traumatic deaths. For the Navajo or Diné, grief is private with public grief viewed as harmful while therapists often view lack of public expression as negative; for the Navajo, it is not, and grief assessment should include the entire family or clan rather than focus upon the individual (Rubin, Malkinson, & Witzum, 2012).

For all religions, ritual and ceremony are basic. Hindus use elaborate cremation ceremonies that involve the entire community, African villagers engage in a series of mourning rituals that often last for weeks, Jewish traditions require burial within 24 hours but require a 7-day mourning vigil or shiva, Irish-Catholics hold wakes that include humor and sadness from stories about the deceased in a long practiced ritual (Biziou, 1999).

While the rituals and ceremonies vary immensely, all religions use them to help manage traumatic death. The Chinese both detach and maintain connections with the deceased. Traditional Chinese farewell rituals are designed to assist the deceased in terminating their relationship with this world and their passage to the next with spiritual guides offering prayers during the wake, the funeral, burial service, and every 7th day from the date of death times 7 (Cheung, Chan, Fu, Li, & Cheung, 2006). Cheung and colleagues report that the Chinese, unlike those of a Judeo-Christian background, typically link death to ghostly actions, to painful death, and to judgment in hell as punishment for any wrongful act that the person may have committed during his or her lifetime (Cheung et al., 2006). Buddhists suggest that death is inescapable, that life is short, that the young and healthy may die before the old and infirm, that as sheep are taken to slaughter one moves closer to death with each step, and that rebirth leads to suffering and death (Klein, 1998). Dying and death are viewed as a religious opportunity in the process of dying and rebirth, while traumatic death, depression, suicide, desperation, or fear can put the person at risk in the process (Klein, 1998). For all groups, rituals aid those who are grieving. Christians, Buddhists, American Indians, and many other groups after experiencing a traumatic loss engage in rituals such as creating a sacred place, journaling or story-telling, drawing or writing, humor, music, art, creative experiences, and ritualistic prayer to aid their coping with loss. For example, a Buddhist family might create a sacred place in a room or less-often used portion of the home containing pictures; trophies, and other artifacts from the person's life; candles and other sacred items; and items from the deceased person's life. Christians might include icons, crucifixes, rosary beads, and other religious items as well as the other items used by Buddhists. Such ritualistic acts allow us to keep the deceased close and to allow us to remain spiritually with them.

Spirituality and Traumatic Death

In recent years, there has been a trend to speak of spirituality rather than religion. What might have been described a generation or so ago as a religious person is now described as a spiritual person. As science and secularism have grown in society, the use of the term *spiritual* has replaced the term *religious*. People who do not even attend church can now be considered to be spiritual.

Catholic theologian Matthew Fox describes spirituality as the search for one's roots (Fox, 1981). Rabbi and scholar Earl Grollman suggests that being embraced by a loving community is fundamental to Jewish spirituality (Grollman, 2000). Morgan suggests that spirituality is the human quest for meaning (1993).

The role of spirituality in grief is to offer the grieving ways to express their grief, to share their grief, and to bring them back from the chaos of traumatic death. Klass argues that losing, finding, or relocating spiritual anchors in the aftermath of personal devastation—a process that requires reconstructing one's life when the foundations of what was thought trustworthy was broken—is the basis of spiritual life (1999a). Rituals allow the expression of our spirituality and aid our grief. Golden suggests that rituals provide a way to release the chaos (1996). Golden suggests that ritual activity is intended to connect with our pain and grief and allows us to move out of ordinary awareness and into the experience of grief in a safe way for a period of time (1996).

Elisabeth Kübler-Ross argues that each human has four quadrants: physical, intellectual, emotional, and spiritual. A quadrant is literally "each of four parts of a circle, plane, body, etc. divided by two lines or planes at right angles." (See http://askoxford. com.) The spiritual quadrant, which is based upon love we receive from others, sustains us through time and helps us through the windstorms of life that are all of the tragedies of our lives (Kübler-Ross, 1991). Not only does spirituality allow us to express our grief, but it also allows us to grow through meditation, reflection, prayer, and ritual expression.

Spiro suggests that if there are no rituals or ceremonies to appease the dead, then the living can turn fear into anxiety, and the bereaved can come to feel or be the victim of overwhelming hostility (1967). He also says that Jewish culture reflects the same ambivalence as other cultures between the desire to hold onto the dead and the desire to get rid of them as soon as possible, and that while immediate burial gets rid of the body as soon as possible, mourning rites and ceremonies guarantee the perpetuation of the dead (1967). By contrast, Buddha preached a religion devoid of ritual and suggested that the intense self-effort required to manage the end of suffering was in our hands (Smith, 1994).

Death is considered a natural occurrence within life, something to be accepted rather than feared. Parkes sees grief as the cost of love (2011). He also suggests that the root cause of grief is separation anxiety, which reflects a continuing and powerful desire to search for and cling to the lost person (2011). American Indians reduce separation anxiety by maintaining a continuing relationship with the dead. Rather than disconnecting with the dead, America Indians continue to have a relationship with them. From the American Indian perspective, death is not a defeat. It is not the result of an offense against God or some other deity but, rather, the common fate of all.

Almost universally, tribes make provisions for a spirit journey, whether for a single burial or for a group burial (Atkinson, 1935). Tribal groups did not abandon their dead but provided them with ceremonies and dignified disposal.

Many spiritual practices exist for all cultures. Disposing of the dead is a universal spiritual practice. Nowhere are losses of tradition in cultural practices more evident than in the realm of funeral practices. The European immigrants to the United States, Australia, and elsewhere have lost their own traditions and have attempted to destroy the traditions and practices of those whom they conquered. (From the indigenous perspective, the people who invaded the Americas, Australia, New Zealand, etc., are immigrants who conquered native peoples and destroyed or at least tried to destroy their cultures and religions.)

Golden (1996) suggests that the rituals of Potlatch Ceremony of the Athabaskan tribes of the Northwest North America allow the entire community and not just the grieving family to move from grief into a more joyous ceremony. Thompson argues that while grief is very personal and intimate and, therefore, somewhat isolated, that research supports that collective grieving is mutually supportive and, while it can be divisive, it generally aids individual grieving (2009). The dominant U.S. culture, lacking grief rituals like the Potlatch, makes grief to be private and, paradoxically, places obstacles to connect to the grief within (Golden, 1996). Adams (2002) suggests that after traumatic death, the spiritual challenges are not given sufficient attention, but rather the clergy are given the job of attending to religious rituals at the time of the funeral, burial, or cremation and that spirituality is often a low priority in family life (2002). Jupp argues that as faithful and observant Catholics approach the end of their lives, a common cause of concern is what will happen if their children and those close to them are not religious (2008). The community of believers in their congregation will hopefully provide them with the rituals that they desire.

All cultural groups develop patterns to manage death as a community. People wash and prepare the body. Family and friends mourn the loss. Some wear mourning clothes.

All cultures engage in mourning practices. Some cremate, and some bury the deceased. The deceased is assisted on his or her journey by song, laments, eulogies, gossip, laughter, joking, conversing with the dead, appeal to spirits, appeals to God, dancing, prayer, and ritual. Some cultural groups drop tradition because they become too sophisticated, cultured, religious, or educated to follow the "old ways." Spirituality and rituals that are not used are soon forgotten. Generally, most immigrants to the United States have deliberately rejected and long-since forgotten their traditional ways.

America Indian Spirituality

The values of American Indians are reflected in their spirituality. Although all Indians do not think alike (McMaster & Trafzer, 2004), the sacred is an important part of this world. The sacred is reflected through symbols in music, dance, silence, meditation, rituals, and ceremony. Encounters with the sacred evoke deep emotions and behavioral transformations. Music, dance, drama, art, and sculpture inspire spiritual engagement while providing explanations for why things such as birth, existence, and death occur. Each of the hundreds of indigenous nations has a diverse, rich, heritage of forms of spirituality, expressions, and traditional narratives (Tinker, 2004).

Evil also is embellished with meaning. The ultimate evil is often portrayed as death. The world is a violent, dangerous place, and yet, spiritual worlds evoke images of peace and harmony. The sacred gives meaning and purpose to human existence.

Spiritual empowerment originates from ritual, sharing with family and community, and living according to the model of spirituality of the group. All cultures have rites of passage for marriage, adulthood, aging, and death. Stories are told of children dying, engaging mythic monsters in combat, and challenging spirits in battle. In funeral rites, the newly dead are often thought to be in an in-between state. The dead are respected as ancestors; such ancestors also are feared as a potential source of death for those who live. Rituals that manage dead spirits are developed to cope with grief and loss. Artistic expression is also used to aid with loss.

Spirituality and America Indian Values

A single American Indian religion cannot be identified. Nonetheless all religions and spiritual orientations have similarities. American Indians believe they dwell in a world filled with spirits; birds carry messages, animals tell tales, rocks speak, and spirits roam the earth. Communication with mysterious beings is available to all. Dreams and visions provide messages or instructions that all may receive as a gift from the spirits. The dead remain a part of our lives. According to Jupp, continuing bonds allow for a widow to remarry while still retaining a relationship with her dead husband (2008). As Attig (2001) suggested that we can continue to love in the absence of our loved ones, Dennis Klass views the continuing relationship with the deceased as a way not only to recognize their death and to mourn them, but also to continue the bond with the deceased and give meaning and validation to our relationship with them (Klass, 2001). All life has a purpose/

meaning; each person exists for a reason, and lives trying to identify what that reason may be. Visions, dreams, rivers, rocks, animals, birds, and spirits can give messages to be listened to. Cultures with oral traditions can travel back as far as the chain of memory will allow. In a world filled with spirits, the past provides a guide to the present. Storytellers' tales of animals that talk, of spirits that roam the earth, of rocks that have messages both instruct and entertain those who listen. Storytellers play a drum, sing, and dance as they weave their tales, while masks, costumes, regalia, and performances mark their stories. Such rituals serve a spiritual role of aiding us in our spiritual journey of grief (Richards, 2001).

All of us face losses. One's spirituality can be an important component in that learning process. Attig suggests that intellectual/spiritual coping helps us through concepts and beliefs to orient us to reality (1995). Death is natural and mysterious. Traumatic death is not natural, but it does create mystery. Why did it occur? How did the person die? While losses are constant in life, traumatic death is not.

The person who is grieving a loss may ask others questions that are painful and confronting when they are in pain. We need to listen to the pain of our loved ones without judging or lecturing on the rightness or wrongness of their reactions (McKissock, 1998). Papadatou calls for a renewed focus on relationships as dying and death are social affairs that are shared by family, friends, and professionals (2009). After suffering a loss to a violent act, we may suffer dramatically over the loss of a favorite toy, a pet, or the loss our house to a fire or other disaster and show little emotion over the death of a loved one. Our public reaction to the loss does not necessarily reflect the magnitude of the loss. Our grief for the toy or pet or even our grief for a person who was distant from us may be an outlet for other losses that occurred long ago (Gilbert, 1999). When grieving the loss of a loved one to a violent death, the loss of a pet may be more than we can handle. Little losses become big losses. Fleming and Buckle suggest that picking up the pieces is exhausting, painful, and continues indefinitely, but that we must engage in regeneration (Buckle & Fleming, 2011). We may or may not understand this process, but we need to try to understand the process of loss and growth to be able to cope with violent death.

Chapter 30

Historical and Contemporary Perspectives on Traumatic Death

Lillian Range

Traumatic deaths may contain elements of (a) suddenness and lack of anticipation; (b) violence, mutilation, and destruction; (c) preventability and/or randomness; (d) multiple deaths; and (e) the mourner's personal encounter with death (Rando, 1993). Traumatic deaths could be due to war, suicide, homicide, accidents, sudden infant death syndrome, terrorism, pervasive epidemics, genocide, and natural disasters. Traumatic loss differs from nontraumatic loss in the psychological impact (Kauffman, 2002a). How people historically understood and how they understand responses to traumatic death diverge in some cases and converge in others.

As early as 1920, psychodynamic theory addressed the issue of traumatic death. In *Beyond the Pleasure Principle*, Sigmund Freud (1920, 1975) developed the psychodynamic idea that humans have two instincts, both derived from broad, all-pervading biological principles. One instinct, eros or libido, involves sexuality or love; another, thanatos or aggression, involves death or self-destruction. Aggression turned outward causes war, murder, etc.; and, aggression turned inward causes melancholy, depression, suicide, and destructive habits such as smoking. According to psychodynamic theory, traumatic deaths that have a human component (such as murder) are a manifestation of the aggressive instinct.

After a traumatic death, people may respond by developing annihilation anxiety (an exaggerated fear of their own death) or a repetition compulsion (intrusive thoughts, images, nightmares, etc., of the death). Psychodynamic theory posits that annihilation anxiety comes from an unconscious fear that I caused the death by wishing for it; therefore, I feel guilty. Repetition compulsion is an attempt to achieve analgesia or excitement, which reduces my emotional pain. These responses may occur because I feel a heightened sense of personal vulnerability to suicidal or homicidal impulses.

Psychodynamic theory emphasized the critical importance of childhood conflicts. Thus, traumatic death may correspond in its essential features to some early childhood trauma or conflict-laden fantasy. The individual would then misperceive current reality in terms of the childhood conflict and respond as he or she did in childhood. Alternatively, traumatic death may lead an individual to turn away from current reality and unconsciously seek gratification in the world of fantasy. The individual would then develop psychological symptoms based on the childhood conflicts (Arlow, 2004). Psychodynamic theory would posit that traumatic death overwhelms the person's ability to handle instincts, particularly the aggressive instinct. Historically, psychodynamic theory was precursor to other theories that also addressed the issue of traumatic death.

An outgrowth of psychodynamic theory, attachment theory began with a monograph summary of a report for the World Health Organization in 1951. Bowlby (1969, 1982) emphasized the importance of attachment to the mother, particularly during the second half of the first year of life, when the relationship is developing. Three social conditions introduce complications into the grieving process: the loss is socially unspeakable, the loss is socially negated, and the loss occurs in the absence of a social support network (Worden, 1991). Traumatic deaths are often unspeakable (e.g., suicide), socially negated (e.g., homicide), or situated in the absence of a social network (e.g., aftermath of Hurricane Katrina). Therefore, traumatic deaths can threaten the attachment bond even more than other losses, thereby damaging the person's ability to make subsequent secure attachments. Psychodynamic and attachment theories emphasized early life events, and laid the groundwork for other ways to understand traumatic deaths.

In the late 1950s, behavior theory emerged as a reaction to the psychodynamic theory prevalent at the time. Associated with Russian scientist Ivan Pavlov, and American scientists B. F. Skinner, Joseph Wolpe, and Albert Bandura, behavior theory understood psychological problems based on classical and operant conditioning, emphasizing the role of associations and contingencies in shaping human responses and adaptation. Behavior theory stressed the importance of commitment to the scientific approach, including testable hypotheses, measurable outcomes, replication, and innovative research strategies that allow rigorous evaluation of specific methods (Wilson, 2005). Behaviorism initially focused solely on observable behavior, rejecting all cognitive mediating processes. Newer revisions of behavior therapy, associated with scientists such as Aaron Beck and Albert Ellis, however, recognized the importance of cognitive mediating processes (Beck, 1976; Ellis, 1962). Bandura (1969, 1974) unequivocally identified the fundamentally important place cognition plays in learning and maintaining behavior. Thus, cognitive/behavioral theory posits that environmental events influence behavior depending on how the individual perceives and interprets them. For cognitive/behavioral theorists, whether or not a death is traumatic depends on how the individual interprets it.

For example, a person might react with learned helplessness to the sudden, unexpected death of a loved one, and subsequently develop depression. In this case, cognitive/behaviorists would stress current determinants of the depression rather than possible historical antecedents. The cognitive behaviorist would note faulty perceptions and interpretations of the death, poor coping skills, impaired communication, maladaptive habits, and self-defeating emotional conflicts. A cognitive/behavioral therapist would examine how the traumatic death impacted the person's beliefs about self, other people, and the world. Along with psychodynamic and attachment theories, cognitive/behavioral theory stressed individual responses to traumatic death.

In contrast, systems theory focused on the entire family unit. In the 1950s, Murray Bowen (1985) and others began focusing on the family when treating disorders such as schizophrenia, with the view that illness in the person is the product of a total family problem. In the family systems view, traumatic death disrupts the equilibrium of the family unit, particularly if the death is of the breadwinner, the parent in a young family, or the head of the clan. Traumatic deaths send an emotional shock wave through all family members, even those who were not close to the deceased person, disrupt family equilibrium, and cause breaks in communication between family members. However, one type of death commonly considered traumatic, suicide, would not necessarily be considered traumatic death from a systems view. Suicides are commonly followed by prolonged grief and mourning reactions, but not necessarily an emotional shock wave unless the person who died played an essential role in the family.

Psychodynamic, attachment, cognitive/behavioral, and systems theories laid the groundwork for contemporary theories. Arising out of existential theory, newer theories addressing traumatic death include narrative/constructivism and terror management.

Existentialism arose among a number of psychologists and psychiatrists in Europe in the 1940s and 1950s as a different way to understand humans than the prevailing psychodynamic theory. Associated with Ludwig Binswanger and Medard Boss in Europe, existentialism was introduced to the United States in 1958 with the publication of *Existence: A New Dimension in Psychiatry and Psychology*, edited by Rollo May, Ernest Angel and Henri Ellenberger. Existentialism asks fundamental questions about the nature of being human, and identifies four ultimate concerns: death, freedom, isolation, and meaninglessness. Existentialists note that death is unavoidable, and at the deepest levels humans respond to this knowledge with mortal terror. A core conflict is between awareness of inevitable death and the simultaneous wish to continue to live.

To existentialists, any death plays a major role in internal experience, haunting the individual as nothing else can (May & Yalom, 2005). To cope with this terror, individuals erect defenses against death awareness. These defenses are based in denial, and include an irrational belief in being personally special and having an ultimate rescuer. Any death reminds people of their own mortality, but a traumatic death fundamentally challenges their denial and causes them to be terrified.

To help people confronted with traumatic death, an existentialist would strive to understand their current life situation and fears. The therapist would focus on personal responsibility for their own lives, such as by saying "You mean you won't face the death instead of you can't." The therapist would emphasize life choices, helping persons recognize that they themselves must generate and choose among options. The goal would be to help persons who have experienced traumatic death live life authentically, being open to nature, others, and self.

According to existentialists, human beings spend much energy trying to transcend personal experience. The confrontation with mortality that arises in traumatic death may have the negative effect of blocking transcendence efforts, pushing survivors to anxiety or despair. Alternatively, the confrontation with mortality that arises in traumatic death may have the positive effect of being an impetus to live life more completely and fully, with increased mindfulness. Traumatic deaths can motivate survivors to choose how to bear the ensuing suffering and focus on the positive aspects of the experience. In this case, survivors might count their blessings and let go of the petty concerns that previously held their attention.

One outgrowth of an existential understanding of traumatic death, constructivistic/ narrative theory, stresses people's basic assumptions about the world and themselves. These assumptions typically include believing that the world is predictable, controllable, meaningful, fair, safe, and benevolent, and that, generally speaking, other people can be trusted (Janoff-Bulman, 1992). Assumptions of a benevolent world and a worthy self provide tremendous comfort. Traumatic deaths are out of the ordinary, directly experienced, and seem to threaten survival and self-preservation. In traumatic deaths, individuals confront their own mortality, recognize their fragility as physical creatures, and recognize that the traumatic death does not readily fit their longstanding, fundamental, comfortable assumptions about themselves and the world (Corr, 2005). Traumatic deaths can shatter a person's assumptive world.

An early proponent of constructivistic/narrative theory, Ronnie Janoff-Bulman, focused on grief, mourning, and bereavement following the traumatic death of a loved one. Janoff-Bulman (1992) maintained that a person who is unable to reconstruct or reinvent a new assumptive world is vulnerable to pathological grief, mourning, and bereavement, and may manifest the dissociative symptoms characteristic of posttraumatic stress disorder. Dissociative symptoms involve a disruption in the usually integrated functions of consciousness, memory, identity, or perception. For example, the person may be unable to recall important personal information (dissociative amnesia), have two or more distinctively different personalities (dissociative identity), or have persistent or recurrent feelings of being detached from his or her own mental processes or body (depersonalization).

Constructivistic/narrative theory notes that immediately after a traumatic death, survivors may be confused about what exactly happened. They ordinarily need to review the events in detail and may be frustrated and dismayed by having insufficient information to formulate a coherent account of the experience. Nevertheless, a starting point in placing the experience in the context of one's life is developing a basic narrative that includes some plausible causal explanation. The person who loses someone from traumatic death needs to achieve a sense of cognitive mastery and reestablish a sense of safety and control for the future. The process of forming an account of a traumatic death includes the questions, What happened? and How did it happen? (Landsman, 2002). Because traumatic deaths fall outside cognitive schemas, violate assumptions, or shatter illusions, they are especially likely to lead to a crisis of meaning.

Traumatic loss also disrupts the continuity of the person's self-narrative, undercutting the associated sense of identity. Faced with such profound invalidation, the person struggles to attribute sense to the tragedy, find something of value in the loss, and reconstruct a new, viable sense of self as protagonist (Niemeyer et al., 2002).

Another outgrowth of existentialism, terror management theory, was inspired by the writings of cultural anthropologist Ernest Becker, who synthesized ideas from the natural sciences, social sciences, and humanities to formulate what he hoped would become a general science of humanity (1971). Terror management theory (Greenberg, Solomon, & Pyszczynski, 1997) posits that humans, because of their sophisticated cognitive capacity, experience self-consciousness. As a byproduct, people are burdened not only with the knowledge that their existence will inevitably end and but also the recognition that they can never fully anticipate or control potentially lethal events. This knowledge, juxtaposed with a predisposition for survival, creates the potential for debilitating terror. To cope with the terror, people construct cultural worldviews, humanly created symbolic conceptions shared by group members that give the acculturated individual a credible and security-providing depiction of reality. Cultural worldviews give meaning, order, and permanence to existence; provide a set of standards for what is valuable; and promise some form of either literal or symbolic immortality to those who believe in the cultural worldview and live up to its standards.

Cultural worldviews promise literal immortality in their explicitly religious aspects that directly address the problem of death and promise heaven, reincarnation, or other forms of afterlife to the faithful who live by the standards. Cultural worldviews promise symbolic immortality by enabling people to feel part of something larger, more significant, and more eternal than their own individual lives through connections and contributions to their families, nations, professions, and ideologies. Cultural worldviews emphasize the psychological separation between humans and nature through a wide variety of cultural practices, such as eating with utensils, avoiding public nudity, and creating cultural artifacts, such as Stonehenge or the Sistine Chapel. Cultural worldviews buffer against anxiety, thereby facilitating day-to-day functioning. People devote a substantial proportion of activity to maintaining faith in their own cultural worldview and the belief that they are personally meeting or exceeding the standards of that worldview. By heightening the tendency to turn to their cultural worldview, traumatic deaths greatly intensify efforts to maintain personal faith and self-esteem.

According to terror management theory, people turn to their cultural worldview when facing the crisis of traumatic death. Different cultures mold their members' experiences differently, but all cultures provide order, stability, meaning, and personal enduring significance (Pyszczynski, Solomon, & Greenberg, 2003). Research indicates that making death momentarily salient, such as by asking people to remember the death of a loved one, increases liking for members of one's own cultural group and increases hostility for people who are members of a different cultural group. Any threat to cultural worldview, such as the mere existence of people with different cultural beliefs, makes people especially likely to respond by derogation, attempts at assimilation, or annihilation. Traumatic deaths would be especially likely to have this effect.

From the perspective of terror management theory, the traumatic deaths that result from a terrorist attack make two blows on mortality salience. First, those who suffer a terrorist attack, such as the 9/11 plane crashes into the World Trade Center in New York City, experienced spectacularly vivid and gruesome images of death and destruction. Experiences such as these render personal vulnerability and potentially imminent mortality profoundly salient. Second, an accompanying symbolic blow was the brutal assault on major cultural symbols. The destruction of cherished symbols severely undermined the functional integrity of the psychological shield than enabled people to feel secure. Thus, terrorism heightened the explicit and implicit thoughts of death that a secure belief in a cultural worldview ordinarily served to quell (Pyszczynski et al., 2003).

Exposure to traumatic death breaches the boundary of the self, inflicting a sense of profound and enduring peril. Psychologically, this violence attacks value and meaning, resulting in feeling unsafe, distrustful, and extremely guarded. In traumatic loss the person experiences persistent panic about helplessness and annihilation and believes that there is no safe future. No safe future means that no future is imaginable, a dilemma that is intense and overwhelming (Kauffman, 2002).

Reactions to the traumatic death are multifaceted, encompassing a wide range of powerful emotions, cognitive distortions, physical health problems, and psychosocial difficulties (Bonanno & Kaltman, 2001). Although most people experience such reactions mildly or moderately and return to preloss levels of functioning relatively soon (Bonanno, Moskowitz, Papa, & Folkman, 2005), around 10–15% go on to suffer from more disabling or pathological grief reactions (Prigerson et al., 1995). Complicated grief includes intense longing and searching for the deceased, intrusive thoughts of the deceased, purposelessness and futility, numbness and detachment, difficulty accepting the death, lost sense of security and control, and anger and bitterness over the death. Many bereavement researchers and theorists now believe that complicated grief is different from depression (Newson et al. , 2011; Prigerson et al., 1995), and the empirical and clinical literature on complicated grief is expanding rapidly.

Different theories may define traumatic deaths somewhat differently; stress personal history or current circumstances; and focus on individual, family, and/or culture. All recognize, however, that individual reactions are unique and personal needs vary for individuals who lose a loved one to traumatic death.

Chapter 31

Life Span Issues and Traumatic Death

Karolina Krysinska and David Lester

The experience of death has changed dramatically over the centuries. Life expectancy has increased tremendously, and this phenomenon, together with the decline in extended families sharing the same residence, has resulted in people today having less experience of death of any kind. For example, in one parish in London in the 1580s, for every 100 babies born, about 70 survived to their 1st birthday, 50 to their 5th, and only 30 to their 15th (Forbes, 1970). Life expectancy in the United States rose from the 40s in 1900 to the 70s in 2000 (Lamb, 2003).

In the United States, wars have not occurred on American soil since the Spanish-American War of 1898-1902. The Civil War in 1861-1865 resulted in roughly 215,000 battle deaths, and the Spanish-American War in only 385 battle deaths.[1] On the other hand, natural disasters have continued to take lives, although not to the extent as those in the past. The most lethal earthquake (in San Francisco in 1906) resulted in about 500 deaths, the most lethal hurricane (in Galveston, TX, in 1900) resulted in roughly 7,000 deaths, and the most lethal set of tornadoes (in the South in 1884) resulted in about 800 deaths (Lamb, 2003). More recent disasters have not come near to breaking these records, and so traumatic death from these sources has become less common over the years.

In other parts of the world, of course, wars and disasters still account for deaths in large numbers. In these traumatic deaths, those of all ages can be victims and, in wars, children can even be perpetrators. However, there are few statistics available on the involvement by age in these traumatic deaths, although www.child-soldiers.org reported (March 27, 2006) that there were up to 300,000 children actively involved in armed conflicts. Epidemics of disease such as AIDS have also had a disproportionate effect by age, in some countries leaving a large proportion of children orphaned, while other catastrophes (such as famines) can result in higher mortality in children than in adults. However, accurate numbers on the impact of these events are not obtainable.

---

1   The attack on the World Trade Center in New York City on Sept. 11, 2001, resulted in 2,948 deaths.

Accurate data on the incidence and experience of traumatic death are available primarily for suicide and homicide.

Homicide

The Victims

The incidence of homicide shows interesting trends. Lester (1986) found that the peak rate for being a victim of murder was most often being an infant in the 1st year of life, closely followed by being a young adult (25-34 years of age). Those nations with a peak rate for infants were, surprisingly, primarily nations in Western Europe such as Austria, Denmark, England and Wales, Germany, Norway, and Switzerland.

Even in the United States, the distribution of the murder rate by age is bimodal, with a secondary mode for infants. For example, in the year 2000 (www.who.int), the highest rates for being a murder victim for men were 20.9 per 100,000 per year for men aged 15-24, 16.2 for men aged 25-34, 10.2 for men aged 35-44, and 9.8 for infants. For women, the highest rate of being murdered was for infants (7.4), followed by women aged 25-34 (4.1)

These data suggest that more modern nations manage to suppress the murderous impulses of adults toward one another, but are less successful in suppressing the murderous impulses of parents and other adults toward children. Since stepchildren are murdered at a higher rate than children in intact homes (Daly & Wilson, 1996), the high rates of divorce and remarriage may be responsible in part for the high risk of being murdered for infants.

The majority of victims of homicide are male. Lester (1986) found that this mortality statistic was so in almost every nation. Interestingly, Lester and Frank (1987) found that in the United States, babies of both sexes are murdered at the same rate. The sex difference in victimization appears only after the age of 1. For the 1st year of life, the sex of the baby does not affect its risk of being murdered.

The Murderers

Just as the risk of being murdered is greatest for those aged 15-24, so the rate of murdering is greatest in youths of that age. In the United States in 2002, the rates of being a murderer by age ranged from 26.8 per 100,000 per year for those aged 18-24 to 1.4 for those aged 50 and older (www.ojp.usdoj.gov/bjs). The high rate of murdering by youths accounts for the fact that the proportion of youths aged 15-24 in the population is a very good predictor of the nation's homicide rate (Holinger, 1987). Mortality statistics indicate that African-American males in particular are more likely than other persons to be the perpetrators and victims of homicide among youth and young adults in the United States (Kochanek, Xiu, Murphy, Minino, & Kung, 2011).

Suicide

Fuse (1980) described three patterns in the distribution of suicide rates by age: (1) in the Hungarian pattern, the suicide rate increases with age; (2), in the Japanese pattern, the major peak is in old age but there is a minor peak in young adulthood; and (3) in the Scandinavian pattern, the suicide rate is an inverted U-shape with a peak in middle age. These labels for the patterns are not the best (for example, the pattern in most nations varies by sex), but these are the most common patterns found.

Lester (1982) and Girard (1993) found that the level of economic development was critical here. The suicide rates for men peak in old age for almost all nations. For women, the peak rises from 55-64 to 75+ as the economic development of the nations decreases until, for the poorest nations, the peak is found in women aged 15-24. In the United States in 2000 (the latest year with data available on www.who.int), the suicide rates peaked at 42.4 for men aged 75 and older and at 6.7 for women aged 45-54.

Rising Youth Suicide Rates

Recent decades have witnessed a number of claims of rising suicide rates in the youth of the world, sometimes in particular ethnic groups such as African-Americans or the Maoris in New Zealand. With the exception of India and China, this increasing youth suicide rate is found primarily in male youths and not in female youths (Eckersley & Dear, 2002; Pitman, Krysinska, Osborn, & King, 2012). Furthermore, often other age groups have higher suicide rates than youths. For example, Lester (1998) noted that, although suicide rates had risen in black males aged 15-24 in the United States, their rates were still lower than the suicide rate of black males aged 25-34. Not all nations experienced this increase in youth suicide. For example, the suicide rate for men aged 15-24 in Japan dropped from 40.9 in 1960 to 15.8 in 2000, in contrast to the United States where the rate rose from 8.1 in 1960 to 17.0 in 2000.

To explain the rising youth suicide rates in some nations, many commentators claim that the lives of youths have become increasingly stressful and unpleasant (e.g., Eckersley, 1993). Eckersley and Dear (2002) saw the high rate of suicide in youths as "the tip of the iceberg of suffering," arguing that the majority of youths today have a harder time developing identity and attachments than they did in times past.

In contrast, Lester (1990) used Henry and Short's (1954) theory of suicide to argue that, as the quality of life improves, suicide becomes more common (since there are fewer external sources to blame for one's misery, and the responsibility is internalized). Thus, the rising youth suicide rate, Lester argued, was a result of the improving quality of life for the youth. Indeed, worldwide, suicide rates are strongly associated with the quality of life in nations—the higher the quality of life in a nation, the higher the suicide rate.

Differences in the Circumstances of Suicide By age

The motives and circumstances for suicide differ for younger and older suicides (Leenaars, 1989). Younger suicides are often reacting to interpersonal conflicts, whereas elderly suicides are often reacting to personal problems. Maris (1985) found that younger suicides (in their teens and 20s) more often had experienced suicide in their families, more often had divorced parents, had lower self-esteem, and more often killed themselves out of revenge. Lester (1994a) noted that older suicides use guns and hanging more than younger suicides, more often have an affective disorder (whereas younger suicides more often have a personality disorder), have experienced less recent stress, and are less motivated by interpersonal conflicts. Young people might also be particularly vulnerable to the impact of portrayal of suicide in the media, including suicide-related information on the Internet and information about suicide methods (Hawton, Sauders, & O'Connor, 2012; Pitman et al., 2012).

Lester (1994b) found that the major theories of suicide differed in how appropriate they were for particular age groups. For example, Binswanger's (1963) theory was more appropriate for the elderly suicides, while theories of Jung (1974), Murray (1981), and Sullivan (1956) were less appropriate. Binswanger's theory of suicide views the potential suicide as preoccupied with the past, detached and cut off from the future, living an empty and meaningless existence, experiencing dread and fear. In these circumstances, suicide becomes a meaningful event and an act of liberation. These themes seem to be more appropriate for the elderly than for younger adults.

Suicide in the Very Young

Traditionally, medical examiners and coroners did not classify deaths of those under the age of 15 as suicides, but this practice has changed in recent years as clinicians have documented suicidal behavior in younger and younger children (Pfeffer, 1986). For example, Leenaars (1996) presented the case of a suicide attempt in a 4 year-old boy who tried to hang himself. Orbach described family dynamics centered round "an irresolvable problem" that might be related to suicidality in children (Orbach & Iohan-Barak, 2009). Solution of an irresolvable problem might be beyond the child's capacity, not attainable because, as soon as a problem is solved, a new problem emerges, or because the possible solutions are limited or unrealistic. It may also happen that the problem is disguised as a child's problem, while the real source of the problem, is another family member or the problem is a result of a constellation of family factors.

The Impact on Survivors Across the Life Span

Those who experience the suicide of a loved one are called *survivors,* and the variation of suicide rates with age affects survivors of different ages. Countries that have a higher youth suicide will more often leave parents bereaved, while countries with a high suicide rate in the elderly will more often leave children bereaved. Since survivors are at increased risk of suicide, this has important implications for the suicide rate of later generations.

Many studies on the grief process after suicide are conducted with heterogeneous groups of survivors, typically individuals in different kinship relationships with the deceased, such as parents, children, other relatives, and acquaintances. The research usually focuses on detecting similarities and differences between the psychosocial sequelae of different types of deaths (Jordan & McIntosh, 2011a). There has been only a limited number of studies looking at the grief process in different age groups and virtually no longitudinal studies looking at the impact of suicide on the subsequent development of child and adolescent survivors. For example, two types of reactions have been observed in children whose parents died by suicide: (i) anger, hostility, and deviance, and (ii) sadness, guilt, and withdrawal (Cain & Fast, 1996). No follow-up studies have tracked the developmental trajectories and impact of these two types of reactions on psychosocial adjustment, and psychopathology in later life remains unknown (Cerel & Aldrich, 2011).

Adult Suicide Survivors

The majority of studies have looked at the impact of suicide on adults, mostly the parents of children and adolescent suicides and the spouses of suicides (Jordan & McIntosh, 2011b). Suicide bereavement in these groups shares many similarities with reactions following other types of death, although some themes, such as feelings of guilt, responsibility, and blame for the death and feelings of rejection and abandonment by the deceased, seem to be more prominent in suicide survivors. As more suicides among adults occur in men than in women, the majority of spouse survivors are women. No studies have looked specifically at suicide bereavement in adult men, although it has been found that bereavement increases suicide risk in widowers, especially if the wife (or partner) died by suicide (Agerbo, 2005).

Similar to parents who have lost a child in an accident or as a result of a chronic illness, parent survivors often experience death-causation guilt, that is, guilt for what was done or not done to prevent the death, child-rearing guilt related to their parenting style, and illness-related guilt linked to the regrets for not providing best care for the child or not being present when the child died. Parents bereaved by suicide are also sometimes blamed by others and held accountable for the child's death, are less-liked, and are perceived as more emotionally disturbed than other bereaved parents (Jordan & McIntosh, 2011b). Experience of a suicide of an adult child increases the risk of mental health problems in older survivors and increases their suicide risk (Waern, 2005). On the other hand, biographical accounts indicate that adult survivors of a parent's suicide (including the suicide of an elderly parent) often struggle with feelings of abandonment, guilt, and anger; concerns about their own suicide risk and the risk of suicide in their families; and issues related to identification with the deceased parent (Stimming & Stimming, 1999).

Child Suicide Survivors

In general, the grief reactions of children and adolescents under the age of 18 who have lost a family member or a friend to suicide seem to be comparable to the grief experienced by adolescents affected by other types of deaths (Cerel & Aldrich, 2011). Nevertheless, studies conducted in clinical samples show that youth survivors of family suicide might show behaviors such as substance abuse, suicidal ideation and behavior, and interpersonal aggression. Survivors of sibling or peer suicide might experience traumatic grief reactions, adjustment problems, depression, and posttraumatic stress disorder (Melhem et al., 2004). The family dynamics of young suicide survivors before and after the death (especially the resulting turmoil and psychopathology), the adolescent's perception of the death, and the manner in which the suicide was communicated to them seem to be important factors impacting their ability to cope with the loss.

The Impact of Traumatic Death on Survivors

There has been little research on the grief process and possible posttraumatic stress in those of different ages, primarily because the same psychological tests are not appropriate for those of varying ages. What little research exists suggests that the grief associated with trauma is similar in children and adults (Melhem, et al., 2004). Repeated exposure to traumatic experiences appears to protect children from adverse outcomes (Garbarino & Kostelny, 1996) but, again, comparative studies of children and adults have not appeared. A study by Pfefferbaum, et al. (2006) on the reactions of children in Kenya after the 1998 bombing of the American Embassy in that nation reported that posttraumatic stress was associated with physical exposure to the bombing, stress from other negative life events, the type of bomb-related loss and subsequent losses, associations that would be expected in adults exposed to the same trauma.

Regarding the impact of suicide on the survivors, there seems to be a gap between personal accounts of individual survivors and the narratives of clinicians working with the bereaved versus the outcomes of research studies (Grad, 2011). The former indicate the uniqueness of bereavement after suicide. They focus on the experience of guilt and shame, social stigma and isolation, as well as the desperate search for the meaning of the death by the bereaved and his or her increased risk of suicide. The latter often find more similarities than differences among different groups of the bereaved in regards to major themes and the trajectory and duration of bereavement.

In an attempt to explain the differences observed in clinical practice and research studies, Jordan and McIntosh (2011a) have proposed a framework encompassing various levels of grief reactions. According to this framework, in suicide bereavement one can recognize (i) reactions present in bereavement after all types of death, such as sorrow and a yearning to be reunited with the deceased; (ii) reactions characteristic for bereavement after unexpected deaths, such as shock and a sense of unreality about the death; and (iii) elements of bereavement after violent deaths, such as the trauma of finding a mutilated body and a shattered illusion of personal invulnerability. In addition to these shared reactions, suicide survivors experience features that seem unique to suicide bereavement, such as anger at the deceased for "choosing" death over life and a feeling of abandonment.

Discussion

For suicide and homicide, causes of mortality for which many nations keep accurate statistics, it is easy to show variations in their rates over the life span. There is less information as to how the meanings, motives, and circumstances of these acts change over the life span. Although a few trends were noted for the act of suicide, acts of murder have not been studied in depth. Future research should explore how the phenomenon of murder varies with age and, in addition, endeavor to collect more accurate data on the experience of other forms of traumatic death by age. Comparative studies by age of grief and posttraumatic stress after traumatic loss are also scarce, and this is another area that needs to be explored in the future.

Chapter 32

The Family, Larger Systems, and Traumatic Death

David A. Crenshaw

The Impact on the Family System of Traumatic Death

The wake of traumatic loss can reverberate through a family system for multiple generations (Kaplow, Saunders, Angold, & Costello, 2010; Schonfeld, 2011). Attachment researchers have found that unresolved grief and trauma reduces the flexibility of adults to access information about childhood and hampers their ability to reflect upon such information in a coherent manner and reduces their likelihood of raising securely attached children (Siegel, 2012). Trauma disrupts the emotional life of the family and in some respects may halt the family's lifecycle progress. In a family, for example, whose father died in a drive-by shooting, the children may be acting like much younger children 7 years later as if they were trying to turn the clock back to the time before the trauma occurred.

While the effects of the trauma may be registered in each family member in different ways, typically no one completely escapes the impact. At the same time as the family system is deeply affected by the devastating blows of trauma events, it also contains the healing forces often referred to as posttraumatic growth that potentially enable its members to resume full participation in life in due time (Bonanno, 2012).

The Family Systems Approach to Reconciling to a Traumatic Loss

Families who have suffered a traumatic loss can't realistically expect to fully return to the preloss state. A more reasonable expectation is that they can reconcile to the traumatic loss and gradually resume full participation in life, but such events cause families to be forever changed. We should not assume that the family will be changed in a pathological way. The process of reconciling to such a devastating loss may strengthen the family's ties and deepen the inner resources of the individual family members leading to posttraumatic growth in the family (Berger, 2009). The art of family systems work is to conceptualize and intervene within a relational framework. Important relational questions are pursued such as, Who within the nuclear family and the extended family was most affected by the trauma events? or What changes have been observed by other family members as a result of the traumatic loss and who else in the family has been most affected by those changes? Additional questions to pursue would include Who is most worried about the most affected members in the family? and Who in the family is having the hardest time right now? These relational questions stem from the assumption of family systems theory that changes in one or more family members will impact the homeostasis (stability) of the entire family unit, and this issue needs to be carefully considered and sensitively understood in planning interventions in the family.

An example may be helpful in illustrating the ripple effect of change within the family. If an inner-city family living in an economically deprived neighborhood suffers the trauma of their 17-year-old son dying in a shooting on his way to school, his 13-year-old sister may soon develop separation anxiety and refuse to leave the house, even to go to school. It would be logical to assume that the younger sister fears leaving her house and going to school because of the murder of her brother while he was on his way to school. By asking relational questions, however, it is learned that while those fears are part of the explanation of her symptoms, it is only part of the story. It soon becomes apparent by pursuing the trauma effects on different family members, that the daughter's main worry is about her mother who has been clinically depressed since her brother's death. She is afraid to leave her mother alone in the house. Further exploration leads to the revelation that her worst fear is that her mother might commit suicide if she were left alone. If the daughter's symptoms had been viewed simply as part of a posttraumatic stress disorder (PTSD) without the relational component the main underpinning to her fears would not have been addressed.

Thus, the family systems approach to traumatic loss honors the centrality of relationships and attachments in our lives and the focus is on the family unit as a whole. The goal is to determine who else in the family is connected or affected by the traumatic event. A valuable resource for all who work with traumatic loss in the family context is *Living Beyond Loss: Death in the Family, Second Edition* (Walsh and McGoldrick, 2004).

Families need education about trauma issues so they can be enlisted as an ally and a partner in trauma treatment. Recent research highlights the important role of families in coping with traumatic death including helping members find meaning in the loss (Davis, Harasymchuk, & Wohl, 2012). Families who are able to find congruent and shared meaning in the wake of devastating loss are more likely to experience posttraumatic growth.

The Trauma-Focused Treatment Approach for Children and Families

An empirically derived treatment model for childhood traumatic grief (CTG) has been developed that includes a parental treatment and family sessions as well (Cohen, Mannarino, & Deblinger, 2006). The CTG model builds on the groundbreaking work of

Pynoos and Nader (1990) in helping children and families exposed to traumatic death. CTG is defined as a condition in which the trauma symptoms such as intrusive images and memories interfere with the ability of children to negotiate the normal grieving process. The treatment model includes addressing both grief and trauma components and involves separate sessions for the children and the parents but some family sessions as well to facilitate sharing of the trauma narrative within the potentially healing context of the family. The treatment protocol is relatively short-term (approximately 16 sessions).

A recent attempt to build on the solid foundation of the work of Cohen, Mannarino and Deblinger to develop strategies for children and families who have suffered multiple traumas and losses and who may require a more extended treatment intervention is described in the current author's previous writing (Crenshaw, 2005). The strategies consist of projective drawing and storytelling strategies that offer clinicians tools to deal with such seriously impacted youth and families. These techniques offer the advantage of approaching the trauma events gradually in the relative safety offered by symbolism and metaphor.

Mass Trauma and Death—When the Unthinkable Happens

The events of Sept. 11 and the more recent impact of Hurricane Katrina reminds us in a shocking and horrifying way that trauma can occur on a massive scale even on our own soil, not necessarily in some distant part of the world. Such events are so horrifying they are unthinkable.

Kastenbaum (2004) notes that mainstream thanatology has focused its efforts on improving the understanding, care, and social integration of people who are exposed to life-threatening illness or bereavement, but that in light of the large-scale disasters the world has recently witnessed, it may now be time to expand the vision, scope, and mission to include large-scale death. He discusses the 9/11 terrorist attacks as an example of mass death with complex correlates and consequences. A useful reference for counselors involved in mass disasters is the book, *Mass Trauma and Violence: Helping Families and Children Cope* (Webb, 2004). The book describes a range of effective interventions to help children and families cope with major traumatic experiences such as community violence, war, and terrorist attacks.

Issues Faced by Survivors

The 9/11 terrorist attacks led to a number of studies of the effects on survivors but has resulted in more questions than answers. In a review of the studies by Eisenberg and Silver (2011), the researchers concluded that the emotional impact for most children, except those who witnessed or suffered direct losses from the attack, were transitory. Similarly, Bonanno and colleagues (2010) concluded from a review of the research that among youth, while elevated symptoms are common in the immediate aftermath of a high-impact disaster (first few months), chronic elevations in symptoms rarely exceed 30% of the youth sampled. The likelihood of increased psychopathology is found with preexisting vulnerabilities or actual direct exposure. Bonanno and colleagues stated that a combination of risk and resilience factors, including contextual factors and personality, also are contributing factors.

Of course, the severity of the trauma, what is sometimes called in the research the *dose gradient*, is a crucial factor (Crenshaw, 2013). When former Ugandan child soldiers were studied, for example, only 27% exhibited no signs of PTSD (Klasen, Oettingen, Daniels, Post, Hoyer, & Adam, 2010). These researchers found that perceived spiritual support (the belief that God had not abandoned them) was a significant contributor to resilience in these children and adolescents and in fact nearly doubled the likelihood of a resilient outcome.

Issues Faced by Rescue Workers

Those who courageously and selflessly rush to scenes of mass disasters or terrorist events to help others are faced not only with physical dangers but mental health risks as well. A study of disaster workers following 9/11 found that perceived safety is an important factor in health and the ability to work after traumatic exposure to disaster events (Fullerton, Ursano, Reeves, Shigemura, & Grieger, 2006). The study examined symptoms of PTSD, depression, and perceived safety in disaster workers 2 weeks after the 9/11 terrorist attacks. The findings indicate that perceived safety was lower in those workers with greater exposure and was associated with greater symptoms of intrusion and hyperarousal but not avoidance, depression, and peritraumatic dissociation.

Another study suggested the advisability of assessing and following up the partners of rescue workers at the scenes of disasters (Pfefferbaum, Tucker, North, Jeon-Slaughter, Schorr, Wilson, & Bunch, 2006). They evaluated 24 female partners of firefighters who helped in recovery efforts with the terrorist bombing in Oklahoma City. The partners were assessed 43 to 44 months later. Most of the participants with postbombing symptoms suffered from preexisting conditions. 40% met both intrusive reexperiencing and hyperarousal criteria. More than half met the criteria for hyperarousal criteria on at least one measure. These researchers recommend that partners of disaster recovery workers be assessed for mental health and physiological consequences related to their indirect exposure since these symptoms may persist years after the event, even in the absence of a diagnosable psychiatric condition.

An important study of first responders to the disaster of Hurricane Katrina included 1,382 people who were assessed at point one, 6 to 9 months after the disaster, and then again at point two, 13-18 months after the hurricane (Osofsky et al., 2011). The results revealed that 10% of the responders had significant levels of PTSD, 25% reported significant levels of depression, more than 40% reported increased alcohol use, and 41% reported increased conflict with their partner. A statistically significant decrease in the symptoms of PTSD or depression was not found after 18 months following Katrina.

Issues Faced by Counselors

Counselors intervening in disasters now have some guidelines to intervention called psychological first aid based on evidence-informed principles. Hobfoll and his colleagues (2007) assembled a worldwide panel of experts on intervention with victims of mass disaster and identified five empirically supported principles to guide intervention. The five principles are promoting (1) a sense of safety, (2) calming, (3) a sense of self and community efficacy, (4) connectedness, and (5) hope. In addition, eight core actions are included in *Psychological First Aid: Field Operations Manual* (Brymer, Jacobs, Layne, Pynoos, Ruzek, Steinberg, et al., 2006). The eight core actions are contact and engagement, safety and comfort, stabilization, information gathering, practical assistance, connection with social support, information on coping, and linkage with collaborative services (Allen, Brymer, Steinberg, Vernberg, Jacobs, Speier, & Pynoos, 2010). The perception of providers undergoing the training in psychological first aid was that they gained confidence in working with both children and adults in disaster situations. Effective training and evidence-based guidelines can help to combat the stress of this challenging work.

Counselors are human beings with their own history of loss and perhaps trauma and concerns for their own safety and that of their families at the same time they strive to be fully emotionally available and responsive to the victims of disasters. This complex phenomenon presents both a unique challenge and an occupational hazard. *Compassion fatigue* is the term elaborated by Figley (1995a) as a variant of secondary trauma occurring in those helpers who become emotionally overwhelmed in their efforts to provide comfort, compassion, and support for others facing traumatic stress. Figley (1995) defined compassion fatigue (CF) "as the formal caregiver's reduced capacity or interest in being empathic or bearing the suffering of clients and is the natural consequent behaviors and emotions resulting from knowing about a traumatizing event experienced or suffered by a person" (p. 7). Figley views CF as consisting of two components: secondary trauma and job burnout (Adams, Boscarino, & Figley, 2006).

It is crucial that those who do this heroic work make a priority of self-care that involves maintaining a life balance. Aspects of such life balance include giving and receiving nurture and support in loving relationships, the joy of engaging in passionate hobbies and a variety of relaxing interests, eating properly, getting adequate rest, and exercising regularly. (See Webb, 2004, for other self-care suggestions).

Chapter 33

Ethical and Legal Issues in Traumatic Death

David K. Meagher

Introduction

Events in the recent past have resulted in the need for grief counselors to become more knowledgeable of the impact of trauma on the grief process. Human-caused events such as the bombing of the federal building in Oklahoma; the terrorist attack on the World Trade Center in New York and the Pentagon building in Washington, DC on Sept. 11, 2001; the underground bombings in London, England, on July 7, 2005; and the train bombings in Madrid, Spain, on March 11, 2004, are not alone in demonstrating the need to prepare more effective trauma-grief support personnel. Natural events such as the 2004 Indian Ocean tsunami, Hurricane Katrina of 2005, the Haitian earthquake in 2010, and the 2011 earthquake and tsunami in Japan have also resulted in populations in need for trauma support resources.

The purpose of this chapter is to introduce the reader to a number of legal and ethical issues around the diagnoses of, treatment strategies for, and research into trauma and traumatic grief. In addition, a brief discussion of the rights of the victims of traumatic deaths will be presented. An awareness of the issues should provide sufficient motivation to those skilled in grief counseling but not in trauma support to further their studies and training prior to offering assistance to individuals who have experienced a traumatic event.

Definitions

A first step in a discussion of the ethical and legal issues in traumatic death must be the task of arriving at universal definitions of trauma, traumatic death, and traumatic grief. This agreement is necessary in order for there to be:

1. Objective criteria for assessing a response to a loss;
2. Reliable means of identifying needs of the affected individuals;
3. Valid instruments for data collection; and
4. The development of effective intervention techniques.

Trauma is defined as a "direct personal experience of an event that involves actual or threatened death or serious injury, or other threat to one's physical integrity; or witnessing an event that involves death, injury, or a threat to the physical integrity of another person; or learning about unexpected or violent death, serious harm, or threat of death or injury experienced by a family member or other close associate" (APA, 2000, p. 461).

It may be said that trauma is defined by the experience of the individual. Allen (1995) writes that there are two components to a traumatic experience: the objective and the subjective. "It is the subjective experience of the objective events that constitutes the trauma…" (p. 14).

Traumatic event is an experience that causes physical, emotional, psychological distress, or harm. It is an event that is perceived and experienced as a threat to one's safety or to the stability of one's world. The response to such an event must involve disorganized or agitated behavior (APA, 2000).

Traumatic grief is defined as a response to a loss that included the elements of sudden, perhaps horrific, shocking encounters. Traumatic grief is one in which the griever, in addition to reacting to the loss of a loved one, "…is preoccupied with the scene of the trauma, wishes to avoid reminders of the event, and is hypervigilantly aroused by and oriented to threat, danger, or the return to a similar threat" (Jacobs, 1999, p. 16).

"When the circumstances of a loved one's death are traumatic (as in cases of death through homicide, suicide, or disfiguring accident) or when the loss itself violates the 'natural order' (as in the untimely death of children or young adults), then additional challenges to the survivor's adaptation arise beyond those associated with bereavement *per se*. As with the basic impact of bereavement, these (challenges) can be observed on both biophysical and psychosocial levels" (Neimeyer, 2002b, p. 936).

Although virtually all deaths may be perceived as personally traumatic, five factors are usually considered necessary for the diagnosis of traumatic death:
1. Suddenness and lack of anticipation;
2. Violence, mutilation, and destruction;
3. Preventability and/or randomness;
4. Multiple deaths; and
5. The surviving mourner's personal encounter with death, where there is either a significant threat to personal survival or a massive and/or shocking confrontation with the death and mutilation of others.

In addition to the above definitions, the professional literature also includes other syndromes describing difficult responses to death loss. Prigerson, Horowitz, Jacobs, Parkes, Asian, et al. (2009) employ the term *prolonged grief disorder* (PGD) for a loss response associated with significant impairment. It is the position of these authors that PGD is often referred to as complicated grief, traumatic grief, or complicated grief disorder. These responses are different from major depressive disorders in the Diagnostic Statistical Manual of Mental Disorder (DSM) and the International Statistical Classification of Diseases and Related Health Problems (ICD).

Pathological grief has been defined as a grief response that becomes a threat to the health and well-being of the person. Within this model, inhibited grief, delayed grief, or chronic grief are the defining elements.

Complicated grief or complicated bereavement is often the term used to describe a person's failure to accept the fact of the loss (Rando, 1993). Complicated grief brought on by the death of a significant other may evoke a traumatic grief syndrome (TGS). TGS, according to Neria and Litz (2003), is a pathological response to the loss of a significant other. TGS, these authors posit, is comprised of two sets of symptoms: separation distress symptoms and traumatic distress symptoms.

The DSM IV (American Psychiatric Association (APA), 2000) lists five basic criteria for posttraumatic stress disorder: the stressor event, a reexperiencing of symptoms, avoidance behavior, a numbing of general responsiveness, and arousal. The disturbance must cause clinically significant distress in significant areas of life (APA, 2000).

Although differences between PTSD and TGS have been reported in the literature (Courtois, 2004; Davis, 1998), these differences are more theoretical than empirical in nature. Clearly, "more exploration of the overlap between trauma and loss is needed, including the processes involved, the nature of the responses, and theoretical or conceptual notions that might link these two areas of study addressing some of the most difficult experiences that we, as humans, must endure" (Green, 2000, p. 14).

Legal Issues

A major legal problem inherent in the area of traumatic grief is a lack of agreed-upon definitions that permit the development of reliable and valid tools of diagnoses and assessment.

Misdiagnosis and inappropriate techniques of intervention can cause harm to the grieving person. Incidents of harm are considered a major reason for the institution of malpractice suits against trauma specialists and grief counselors.

If there are not clear distinctions between traumatic grief syndrome and posttraumatic stress disorder, as inferred earlier, then the chances of a misdiagnosis and subsequent inappropriate intervention techniques are increased. Significant overlap in the signs and symptoms of normal grief, traumatic grief and posttraumatic stress syndrome make it very difficult to arrive at a valid diagnosis.

Other legal issues that will be discussed with ethical concerns later in the chapter include:

1. Diagnosis and treatment of children;
2. The rights of victims of traumatic deaths, including the rights of crime victims; and
3. Informed consent issues in trauma research.

When Pitman and Sparr (1998) write that the use of PTSD as a diagnosis of a psychological disorder has severe diagnostic reliability and validity, they might have also been describing issues of TGS. They identify common errors leading to both the overdiagnosis and underdiagnosis of PTSD. The following table outlines these errors.

PTSD Diagnoses Errors

Overdiagnoses Errors	Underdiagnoses Errors
Failure to separate expectable emotional distress from the mental disorder	Characterization of PTSD symptoms as normal reactions to a traumatic event
Applications of fewer criteria than are required for the proper diagnosis	Basing opinion on inadequate, open-ended interviews without an adequate attempt to explore details of the traumatic event and subsequent symptomatology
Failure to consider the contribution of earlier, unrelated traumatic events to the client's illness	Idiosyncratic thresholds for diagnosis.
Failure to diagnose preexisting psychopathology	Failure to acknowledge that the diagnosis of PTSD may be made despite the presence of major vulnerability factors
Failure to identify a positive family history of mental disorder that may point to another etiology	Mistaking predisposition for preexisting psychopathology
	False attribution of the client's symptoms to other life events

(Pitman & Sparr, 1998, pp. 2-3)

Diagnostic Issues

The need for valid, reliable instruments of assessment is substantial. Although Baldwin, Williams, and Houts (2004) support the use of current PTSD diagnostic tools, they do remind the diagnostician that the assessment scales are based primarily on subjective descriptions by the victim. Since many symptoms are self-reported, diagnoses often rely on a client's description of a traumatic event experience. Failure to review all of the client's symptoms may lead to a form of diagnostic error called *confirmatory bias* (Koch, 2001). Knowing that the client experienced a traumatic event, a counselor may conclude, without a complete examination, posttraumatic syndrome disorder.

Simon (1995b) raises the legal issue of the objective validity of the instruments. It is his position that both the psychological and physiological scales designed to objectify the diagnosis of PTSD are based on subjective accounts. With regard to the physiological measures, the results may indicate the presence of a general stress response not connected to a traumatic experience (Simon, 1995b).

Questions concerning the ability to distinguish among the varied responses to a loss need to be answered so that appropriate necessary forms of intervention may be utilized. The issue becomes more clouded when the concepts of complex posttraumatic stress disorder (CPTSD) and disorders of extreme stress not otherwise specified (DESNOS) symptoms not addressed by a PTSD diagnosis, is added to the mix of possible trauma responses. Instruments designed to diagnose PTSD may not reveal the complexities of CPTSD/DESNOS (Courtois, 2004).

A number of problem areas reducing the reliability of assessment instruments to diagnose CPTSD/DESNOS have been identified. They include:

1. Difficulties in controlling affective impulses;
2. Issues associated with maintaining attention;
3. Changes in self-perception;
4. Significant changes in a person's belief system;
5. Inabilities to trust or feel close to others;
6. Onset of medical problems affecting all major body systems; and
7. Feelings of hopelessness and a lack of belief that others can understand them or their suffering (Courtois, 2004, p. 414).

Ethical Intervention Issues

Certain issues are both ethical and legal in nature. For example, confidentiality is both an ethical concept that often serves to protect the client or patient and a legal term that refers to a client's statutory right to have confidential information protected. National and state mental health associations have developed and continue to refine ethical standards in an attempt to create a model code of conduct to ensure the protection of patients' rights. These standards are also promulgated to provide guidance for the profession and help prevent patient exploitation and impairment of therapists' judgment.

Two issues critics raise concerning the effectiveness and timing of trauma counseling (Dyregrov, 2004) are:

1. What determines the need for professional assistance? and
2. Does professional assistance help (empower) or harm (disempower) a person experiencing a traumatic reaction to a loss?

There have been several strategies offered for defining the limits of professional assistance. They range from not intervening unless the affected individual requests help to offering immediate debriefing assistance with or without long-term follow-up. Any strategy of intervention must have, at a minimum, the following goals:

1. Normalizing the situation,
2. Minimizing recovery time,
3. Reducing distress,
4. Restoring functioning, and
5. Mobilizing resources (Dyregrov, 2004).

Dyregrov and Regel (2012) address the question of the timing of interventions. They suggest that in place of what is termed *watchful waiting* a more proactive earlier intervention tailored to the needs of clients may be more beneficial.

When selecting a treatment strategy, issues of age, severity level, type of trauma response, and acuteness of the response must be taken into consideration. Overall, the most highly recommended techniques are anxiety management, cognitive therapy, exposure therapy, and psychoeducation (Dyregrov, 2004; Marotta, 2000).

Maguire (1997) suggests a recovery bill of rights for trauma survivors encompasses four major areas of legal and ethical concerns: (1) personal authority... the right to manage and direct one's recovery; (2) personal boundaries ...the right to have one's person respected and to be permitted to accept or reject any and all suggestions for treatment; (3) communication... the right to clear explanations and respect for one's feelings; and (4) intervention...the right to choose one's own counselor, to expect that the counselor is trained in trauma treatment, and he or she will abide by the laws and ethics of confidentiality. Clients should expect that they would be taught skills that lessen the risk of retraumatization.

It is essential that grief counselors identify best practices for providing trauma loss services. The counselor must develop practice guidelines so as to demonstrate not only the effectiveness but also the ethics of the practice.

The Council for Accreditation for Counseling and Related Standards (CACREP) has developed a set of standards for counselors involved in the theory and practice of traumatology. Five general guidelines to assist counselors to be in compliance are:

1. Know the organizations and government agencies and their purposes.
2. Understand the major principles of trauma counseling.
3. Provide trauma counseling only to the extent of one's competence.
4. Develop knowledge and practice competencies in disaster response, trauma counseling, and crisis intervention if one is planning to train others to practice.
5. Recognize that disaster and trauma counseling is a growing specialty that needs research and study to insure outcome-based practices (Webber & Mascari, 2009).

Intervention With Children

Children who have experienced a traumatic event present special legal and ethical issues, and what little information is available is sometimes contradictory. For some, terrorism is not a discrete event for children. It is a continuous stressor. This position holds that children who develop PTSD after exposure to terrorism often continue to manifest symptoms of PTSD over time, even though the terrorist threats are no longer present (Street & Sibert, 1998). Fremont (2004) suggests using the term *continuous stress syndrome* for children. However, Henry, Tolan and Gorman-Smith (2004) found no differences between pre- and post-September 11 in children in symptoms of traumatic grief or PTSD; specifically on measures of child anxiety, depression, and feelings of safety. PTSD diagnostic measures may not fully capture the spectrum of posttrauma symptom among children (D'Andrea, Ford, Stolbach, Spinazzola, & van der Kolk, 2012).

There are many serious methodological problems inherent in, and specific to, research on children and trauma: (1) current diagnostic formulations of PTSD may not be operationally sound when applied to children as they lack age-appropriate diagnostic sensitivity and specificity; (2) symptom characteristics unique to PTSD can affect reliability and validity estimates of trauma measures; (3) few studies of trauma and children have utilized control groups, and specific, trauma-related studies have assessed effects on small, unique samples making generalization difficult; and (4) few treatment outcome studies incorporate designs with adequate empirical rigor to explore effectively the respective influence of possible moderator variables (e.g., race, age, or gender) or mediator effects (e.g., treatment compliance or family support (Cook-Cottone, 2004).

D'Andrea, et al., (2012) suggest "...the need for the development of a construct, *developmental posttraumatic adaption,* that could serve as a basis for diagnosis (in children and adolescents) if research supports specific cutoffs for a categorical distinction between clinically significant symptoms and normative levels of developmental posttraumatic adaptation (p. 191).

The signs and symptoms of PTSD in children can vary dramatically with respect to the severity, chronicity, and number of symptoms (Chibbaro & Jackson, 2006; Faust & Katchen, 2004). Professional interveners must distinguish between an unanticipated single event and repeated exposure characterized by massive denial, psychic numbing, and personality problems. These manifestations may be consistent with classic PTSD symptoms (Cook-Cottone, 2004; Faust & Katchen, 2004). The professional caregiver/ counselor must modify the treatment employed, especially with the child's grief reactions. Grief work must be conducted prior to addressing the PTSD reaction and the processing of grief should be revisited periodically.

When becoming involved with children who are experiencing signs of a traumatic response, or when designing studies to involve direct contact with children, consideration must be given to their attention span, level of development, and literacy skills. Of course, working with children requires consent of the child and informed consent of an adult caregiver. The child's consent is not sufficient to begin intervention or data collection but it should be necessary to begin the process. Even assuming that parents or guardians make decisions that are in the best interests of their children does not absolve counselors or researchers of their responsibility to ensure that no harm is caused by the intervention.

Cunningham (2003) cautions potential interveners not to ask children to participate in a trauma study that is not in the best interest of the child. Such studies should be used when the information cannot be gained in any other way. If a child is still at risk, the appropriate social services consistent with local ordinances should be notified.

Other Ethical Considerations

Trauma events do not leave a great deal of time or resources for negotiations between a caregiver and a client about the types of assistance wanted or required. However, those impacted by a trauma event should not be expected to accept intervention strategies that do not meet their needs. It is the responsibility of the intervener to be attuned to the cultural needs and developmental concerns of the client. Assistance offered must be independent of any political agenda and be calibrated to the people and demands in each unique situation (Flanagan, 2007).

Trauma intervention plans require a flexible approach that counters assumptions and biases about victims, assures a favorable ethical cost-benefit ratio, and improves the benefit to the survivors of traumatic stress (Newman, Risch, & Kassam-Adams, 2006).

Victim/Survivor Rights

Unlike many other countries, the United States does not have a national legislated set of legal rights for trauma or crime victims. A constitutional amendment to protect the rights of crime victims was introduced into Congress in 2003; however, the proposal was referred to committee and never returned for a vote.

Every state has a victims' bill of rights. These rights generally include the rights associated with criminal cases and deal with issues of protection, intimidation, notification, victim input at bail hearings, plea bargaining, sentencing, parole, the use of victim trauma as evidence, and due process rights. What remains unaccomplished is any comprehensive cataloging or interpretation of these cases. As a result, it is unclear whether there can be any certain prediction about how victim rights will eventually be interpreted in the criminal justice system (Young, 1997).

A summary of rights that have been suggested include the rights to be:

1. Treated as human beings, not as evidence;
2. Provided with information about case status and what to expect at trial;
3. Evaluated as to the onset of any psychological trauma the victim may be experiencing;
4. Permitted to have someone present at the trial on whom the victim can count for emotional support;
5. Informed and consulted with about potential plea bargain or diversion procedures; and
6. Given the opportunity for input into proceedings when possible, including the opportunity to make a victim impact statement (Kilpatrick, 1986; Jackson, 2003).

A few states have enacted measures allowing victims to recover damages resulting from acts of terror. These measures generally allow victims and their families to recover damages for emotional distress and any other relief that the local or state courts may deem necessary. Kilpatrick and Resnick (1993) suggested guidelines for criminal justice and victim service professionals that can increase their understanding of, and development of policies related to, the mental health treatment of crime victims include:

1. Trauma victims and their family members may experience immediate, short-term, and long-term trauma-related mental health problems that require treatment;
2. Considerable individual variations exist among trauma victims in the types of psychological injuries they are likely to sustain and how long it will take them to reconstruct their lives, with or without treatment;
3. For many victims, elimination of trauma-related psychological injuries might not be a realistic treatment goal. Rather, helping victims to learn to cope is the main objective; and
4. At times of stress (including criminal justice system-induced stress), victims are likely to have exacerbations of psychological injuries.

The international community has agreed to the 1985 UN Victims' Declaration that includes the following statements relevant to this discussion.

1. The right to be treated with respect and recognition.
2. The right to be referred to and receive adequate support services.
3. The right to give input to any decision making.
4. The right to protection of physical safety and privacy.

Research Issues

A complete discussion of all the legal and ethical issues of trauma research is beyond the scope of this chapter; a brief look at some of the more prevalent issues will be presented.

Methodologies to help subjects tell their stories in a respectful manner need to be created. Instruments designed for a trauma study should be developed and employed. Trauma research should be grounded in the needs of the study participants, to help them receive more effective service. Seven trauma research principles are outlined below:

1. The research must adhere to all standards for the ethical treatment of research subjects including informed consent, voluntary participation, confidentiality, and anonymity;
2. The research should be gender, culturally, and developmentally sensitive in its design and conduct;
3. The researchers must be prepared to provide appropriate referral or treatment of participants who are identified as being in crisis or needing a mental health intervention;
4. The researchers must treat research subjects with respect, attend to their privacy interests, and chose methodologies that are not unduly demanding of their time;
5. Those conducting the study should communicate and distribute research results in language and formats which are accessible to practitioners, clients, policy makers, and legislators;
6. In designing and conducting the study, the researchers need to identify the implications of their findings for legislative and policy reforms and work cooperatively with community partners to communicate those implications to relevant officials;
7. The researchers should consider the potential for unintended consequences of laws, policies, and programs as well as the benefits (Cunningham, 2003, p. 3).

Summary

Before strategies of intervention or research of trauma response can begin, there must be an agreement on what is being treated or studied. Clear distinctions must be made among normal grief, complicated grief, traumatic grief syndrome, and posttraumatic stress disorder. Many legal problems arising from trauma intervention programs evolve from what is sometimes perceived as the subjectivity of the employed measures of diagnoses.

In addition to the need for agreed-upon bases for professional actions, there are special areas of concern when children are the object of support and study. Informed consent and privacy issues may be more problematic when children are involved.

A number of factors influencing trauma response have not been addressed; i.e., the impact on victims when experiencing difficulties with such organizations as the U.S. Federal Emergency Management Agency, Social Security Administration, insurance companies, and/or banks. In addition, studies of the grief responses of family members who have lost a loved one in an act of capital punishment or other socially stigmatized ways may reveal unique legal and ethical considerations. While studies addressing these issues were not found in the literature, the professional caregiver must be cognizant of their potential influence on traumatic grief.

Death Education

Introduction to Part 6,
Chapters 34 – 39

Chapters 34 through 39 focus on death education. The Body of Knowledge Committee defined this major category of thanatology knowledge in this way: **formal and informal methods for acquiring and disseminating knowledge about dying, death, and bereavement.**

The chapters in Part 6 focus on death education in terms of these indicators: culture and socialization, religion and spirituality, historical and contemporary perspectives, life span issues, the family and larger systems, and ethical and legal issues. All the chapters in Part 6 are revised from chapters that originally appeared in the first edition of the handbook.

Chapter 34

Culture, Socialization, and Death Education

Lynne Ann DeSpelder and Albert Lee Strickland

As the television camera was turned off, the interviewer turned and asked quietly: Why are Anglo funerals so serious? Answering this question requires cultural competency, that is, the ability to explore, consider, and respond appropriately to cultural differences. An individual's values, beliefs, and worldview are significantly influenced by his or her culture. Culture can be defined as "all that in human society which is socially rather than biologically transmitted" (Marshall, 1994, p. 104; see also Brenneis, 2002; Erickson, 2002). Many different elements go into making people who they are; culture is just one of these elements (Weaver, 2005). It is nonetheless a key influence in guiding thinking and shaping behavior (Weaver, 2005).

Reading this chapter, you have an opportunity to add to your knowledge and gain skills relative to culture, socialization, and systems for dealing with death. In Greek mythology, Thanatos was the personification of death. Our word *thanatology*, the study of death, is a linguistic heir of the Greek term. Within the realm of thanatology, cultural competence implies being knowledgeable about the cultural scripts that influence persons in a given culture, being informed about cultural differences, and being able to ask culturally sensitive questions that acknowledge another person's belief system and values regarding death and dying, end-of-life choices, and grieving (Hayslip, Patrick, & Panek, 2011, p. 294).

Because of our mortality, death has an important role in shaping the organization and experience of life. A person's cultural identity is developed through a process termed *socialization,* a topic that is touched on in several other chapters in this handbook. The process of socialization involves a variety of influences, beginning with the family and extending to the mass media and the global transcultural environment. Although the primary phases of socialization occur during the years of childhood, this process continues lifelong. How we are socialized is significantly tied to the fact that we will one day die (Settersten, 2002).

As Italian thanatologist Francesco Campione (2005) points out, death is not only a topic for reflection, study, and research; it is also an existential problem, which touches every aspect of human existence and every field of knowledge. Kastenbaum (1993, p. 75) says that, although the term thanatology is usually defined as the "study of death," it is perhaps better defined as "the study of life with death left in."

One of our jobs as thanatologists is to provide our clients and students with materials to deepen their intellectual understandings about death. At the same time, we must strive for a balance between the cognitive and the affective aspects of death education. Both the intellectual and the emotional aspects of death apply to our endeavors (DeSpelder, 2006; DeSpelder & Strickland, 2004). Further, death education takes place across the life span. Socialization experienced in childhood and adolescence is not enough to meet the demands of the adult years (Settersten, 2002). In a fast-paced and ever-changing world in which life spans seven or more decades, individuals must prepare for successive resocialization as they move through adult life (Settersten, p. 34). *Re-socialization*, a term that refers to the "uprooting and restructuring of basic attitudes, values, or identities," occurs when adults take on new roles that require altering or replacing their existing values and modes of behavior (Goodman, 1992, pp. 84-85; see also Etzioni, 2000). Examples of occasions that may necessitate such secondary socialization include starting a new job, getting married, having children, and surviving the death of a mate. Widowhood involves changes in many areas of life, as new roles and activities are taken on (Silverman, 2004).

Attitudes that we bring from our cultural experiences reflect practices that are a familiar part of our heritage. Paying attention to how people use language reveals a great deal about personal as well as cultural attitudes toward death. By becoming aware of the metaphors, euphemisms, slang, and other linguistic patterns that people use when talking about death, we can appreciate more fully the range of attitudes and responses elicited by encounters with death, dying, and bereavement (DeSpelder & Barrett, 1997).

Take our television reporter. Notice that she used the word *Anglo*. Considering her word choice, her name, and her appearance, you might guess that her background is Hispanic. Her use of the word *serious* also deserves attention.

Cultural competence depends on the ability to listen and gather information. Consider the reporter's question. What kind of response might you give to gain a better understanding of her heritage? It is best to get information before framing a response. Thus, a useful question is: What has been your experience with Anglo funerals? It is doubtful that she is talking about a British Anglo-Saxon funeral. More likely, she is asking about North American Caucasian funerals as contrasted to rituals of her own family or ethnic group. By matching her language and using the term *Anglo* in response, she is likely to give you more specific information.

She describes two recent deaths, one of a Caucasian colleague and the other of a family member. The contrasts between the two funeral ceremonies were quite perplexing to this young woman. The Caucasian funeral was a Protestant service held at a mortuary. The reporter talked about her experience at the visitation and funeral for her colleague. She arrived at the mortuary to find the deceased's body in a small, empty room. Walking through the door, she noticed a condolence book set out for her to sign. She did so, briefly viewed the body, and left. During the funeral, the family sat behind closed curtains, cut off from the view of the casket and the mourners sitting in the public portion of the funeral chapel.

The funeral for her uncle was held in his parish church (Catholic) in an area of Miami populated mostly by Cuban immigrants. The funeral itself was preceded by several days and nights of viewing at a funeral home where family members, including small children, visited. Cuban music played in the background, and central to the gathering were jokes, laughter, and stories about the deceased. Laughing and crying together, the family visited with other members of the community who came to pay their respects.

As she talks about the differences in the funeral rituals, her use of the word *serious* is placed in context. Now we have much more information about the cultural differences that spark her curiosity. As you imagine the contrast between these two gatherings, it makes sense that, to the reporter, one seemed to be more serious (solemn and staid) than the other.

Death is a universal human experience, yet, as this example illustrates, our response to it is shaped by our cultural environment. Understanding attitudes toward death, our own as well as others, is an essential component of death education (DeSpelder, 1998). Consider the terms used to describe thanatology, and death education in particular, in Japan. Thanatology is usually translated as shiseigaku. Shi means death, sei means life, and gaku means learning or study. Thus, shiseigaku literally means the study of death and life. Many scholars prefer the word shiseigaku, and this word is often used in books and articles. Some people translate thanatology as shigaku. That means simply the study of death. The main death education organization in Japan is called Seitoshi wo Kangaeru Kai, which translates as the Association for Thinking About Life and Death. Thus, in this case, life comes first. The Japanese translation of the phrase *death education* also has variety. Some translate it as seitoshi no kyoiku, meaning the education of life and death. The internationally known Dutch expert on Japanese thanatology Alfons Deeken (1999), uses the words shi eno jyunbi kyouiku, meaning *preparatory education* for death. Some use the words, shi no kyoiku, meaning the education of death. Recently, it seems schoolteachers prefer the words, inochi no kyoiku. This phrase translates to *the education of life.* Inochi means life. Inochi no kyoiku includes not only topics about death and bereavement, but also topics about the birth of life, the preciousness of life, life stages, and so on. With this usage, the word *death*, or shi, is omitted from the description of life and death studies among schoolteachers at the elementary and secondary school levels (personal communication, K. Iakeuchi, Reitaku University, Chiba, January, 2006). Perhaps this phrasing makes death education more acceptable in the Japanese school system?

Learning how people in different cultures relate to death in their lives can shed light on our own attitudes and behaviors. However, there is no formula or recipe that can be applied to understanding a particular cultural group. While generalizations about beliefs and practices might be helpful guides, the map is not the territory. Culture does not consist of rigid principles that dictate behavior (Weaver, 2005). Do not assume that all individuals of a particular religion, race, or cultural or national group share the same beliefs. Each person is unique. Norms can be used only as a guide. They are not a substitute for individual assessment. Operating with a stereotype or generalization in mind can block an authentic understanding of a particular individual or family's attitudes, beliefs, and practices. Relying on stereotypes will trip you up.

When you hear a generalization about a cultural group, ask yourself how this might help you understand a particular individual or family. Understanding culture requires knowledge of how an individual defines his or her heritage. The Barrett inferential model points out that this heritage may be better understood by exploring factors such as cultural associations, spirituality, and social class (Barrett, 1998, pp. 88-91; DeSpelder & Barrett, 1997, p. 68). Research on African-American death customs shows that, even within particular cultural groups, there is tremendous diversity. The African-American experience, as an example, is more heterogeneous than homogeneous. Thus, skin color is not the determining factor in matters of death, dying, and bereavement (Barrett, 1995a). Other factors include geographic location, rural or urban setting, family influences, and the number of generations from immigration to a particular country.

Consider the power of social class. The celebrations around the dead in Mexico, el Día de los Muertos, seem more fully embraced by the poor. The Mexican government has instituted a program in the city of Oaxaca to interest the middle and upper class in the traditions of their ancestors. As noted in the African-American research, the affluent in a culture are more likely to move away from their communities of origin, thus becoming less traditional. The poor are more likely to follow traditional practices.

Different religions and religious affiliations shape spirituality in different ways. The more conservative the religious experience, the more conservative and traditional will be the attitudes, beliefs, and values that ultimately affect behavior. More conservative believers can be characterized as the keepers of the tradition. They hold to old ways of relating to death, dying, and funeral rites. Some conservative or traditional believers, for example, object to practices such as autopsies and tissue or organ donation.

In central California and other areas of the United States, where there is a large Hispanic population, the impact of the number of generations from immigration can be seen also in the celebration of el Día de los Muertos (Lomnitz, 2005, p. 467). Many second- and third-generation individuals and families are rediscovering the elements of the celebration that their parents and grandparents had left in the old country.

The study of dying, death, and bereavement compels us to look at our own stories, as well as the stories of our neighbors, both locally and globally, with the aim of comprehending not only the diverse social and cultural influences on our understanding of death, but also our personal mortality.

People sometimes talk or write about *death in the United States*, but this phrase conceals what, in fact, are many different ways of death, reflecting attitudes, beliefs, and customs of culturally diverse groups. In describing families from the United States, Olson and DeFrain (2006, p. 32) remind us that "tremendous diversity exists among people who are commonly grouped together."

The extent to which people identified as belonging to a specific cultural group maintain distinctive attitudes and practices varies widely, both between different subcultural or ethnic groups and among people who share a particular heritage. In a cosmopolitan world, individuals may find themselves wrestling with the dilemma of seeking to maintain their cultural distinctiveness while also taking steps to broaden the conventional terms of what it means to be a member of their culture. When a person's opinions or views differ markedly from those commonly held within his or her culture, this divergence can lead to cultural dissent from majority views. For example, influenced by body disposition practices in a global context, an individual might opt for cremation instead of burial, despite the latter being the strongly held preference and conventional practice within his or her own cultural group. Such choices reflect the fact that today's societies are increasingly homogeneous (similar) across cultures and heterogeneous (diverse) within them (Sunder, 2001, pp. 497-498).

Nevertheless, ethnicity and other cultural factors often have an impact on such matters as methods of coping with life-threatening illness, the perception of pain, social support for the dying, behavioral manifestations of grief, mourning styles, and funeral customs. A comparison of bereavement customs among ethnic and other cultural groups in the United States shows that, "while adapting partly to Western patterns, these groups also adhere to the bereavement procedures of their own cultures" (Stroebe & Stroebe, 1993, p. 201; see also Eisenbruch, 1984; Goss & Klass, 2005, pp. 92, 188; Hayslip & Peveto, 2005; Howarth, 2007, pp. 227, 266; Sanders, 2002).

African-American funerals and mourning practices illustrate how traditional customs can persist despite the passage of time and changed circumstance. Elements of traditional West African practices retain their importance for many African-Americans (Barrett, 1995a; Barrett, 1995b). This cultural persistence is evident in customs such as gathering at the gravesite to bid godspeed to the deceased and referring to funerals as a *home-going* ceremony honoring the spirit of the deceased. Roediger (1981, p. 163) says such customs "grew from deep African roots, gained a paradoxical strength and resilience from the horrors of mid-passage, and flowered in the slave funeral—a value laden and unifying social event which the slave community in the United States was able to preserve from both physical and ideological onslaughts of the master class."

Similarly, Spanish-speaking people in northern New Mexico continue to practice traditional forms of *recuerdo,* or remembrance, which memorialize the dead and comfort the bereaved. Presented as a written narrative or ballad, the recuerdo tells the story of a person's life in an epic, lyrical, and heroic manner. This story telling is a kind of farewell, a leave taking or la despedida, on behalf of a deceased person. Such memorials frequently contain reminders of the transitory nature of life and express the notion that life is on loan from God for only a short time, that we are only shadows. Korte (1995-1996. p.

254) says, "The wisdom of the culture has provided many termini [points on the journey] where family, friends, and community may take their leave and depart from a deceased person." The poignant beauty of the recuerdo, given to the bereaved family and often published in local newspapers, suggests that life has meaning because there is death.

Another source of meaning making is children's literature. Many classic children's stories and fairy tales depict death, near deaths, or the threat of death (Tatar, 2002). There are "tales of children abandoned in woods; of daughters poisoned by their mothers' hands; of sons forced to betray their siblings; of men and women struck down by wolves, or imprisoned in windowless towers" (Windling, 2001, p. 227). Death has often had a place in children's stories, and this fact is especially true of the earliest versions of familiar stories that parents and other adults share with children. Children in the United States taught to read with textbooks such as *McGuffey's Eclectic Readers* found that death was presented as tragic, but inevitable, and many of the death-related stories conveyed a moral lesson (Lamers, 1995). In the 19th century, the violence in children's stories was usually graphic and gory so that it would make the desired moral impression (Marvin, 2000). The manner in which death is presented in children's stories communicates cultural values. Consider, for example, the contrasts between the European and Chinese versions of the tale of *Little Red Riding Hood.*

In the Western version, Little Red Riding Hood goes by herself to visit her grandmother, encounters the wolf, and is tricked into believing the wolf is her grandmother (Orenstein, 2002). In the traditional version of the story, the wolf eats Little Red Riding Hood, but she is saved by a woodsman who kills the wolf and slits its stomach, allowing Little Red Riding Hood to emerge unharmed. In more recent versions, Little Red Riding Hood's screams alert the woodsman, who chases the wolf, and then returns to announce that she will be bothered no more (the killing of the wolf occurs offstage and is not mentioned) (Morel, 1970, pp. 11-13).

The Chinese tale of *Lon Po Po* (Granny Wolf) comes from an oral tradition thought to be over 1,000 years old. In this version of the story, three young children are left by themselves while their mother goes away to visit their grandmother. The wolf, disguised as Po Po (Grandmother), persuades the children to open the locked door of their house. When they do, he quickly blows out the light. By making perceptive inquiries, however, the oldest child cleverly discovers the wolf's true identity and, with her younger siblings, escapes to the top of a ginkgo tree. Through trickery, the children convince the wolf to step into a basket so they can haul him up to enjoy the ginkgo nuts. Joining together, the children start hauling up the basket. But, just as it nearly reaches the top of the tree, they let the basket drop to the ground. The story says, "Not only did the wolf bump his head, but he broke his heart to pieces" (Young, 1989, p. 27). Climbing down to the branches just above the wolf, the children discover that he is "truly dead." Unlike the European version, which has a solitary child facing the threat of the wolf by herself and ultimately being saved by someone else, the Chinese folk tale emphasizes the value of being part of a group effort to do away with the wolf.

Although death is fundamentally a biological fact, culturally shaped ideas and assumptions create its meaning. This cultural influence is borne out in the experiences of Hindus living in England who encounter cultural imperatives related to their customary death rituals. In India, where there are few undertakers or funeral directors, funeral arrangements are usually made by the deceased's family. Cremation is a public event, and a principal mourner lights the sacred flame of the funeral pyre. In Britain, the body is placed inside a coffin and concealed from view inside the cremator, which is operated by employees of the crematorium. "For the mourners there is neither the smoke to sting their eyes, nor the fire to singe their hair, nor the smell of burning flesh to bring the poignant immediacy and reality of the experience to their consciousness" (Laungani, 1996, p. 198). Living in a different cultural environment, some Hindus in England feel that they are socially constrained to give up a communal and spiritual ceremony and, in its stead, are left with an anonymous, individualistic, materialistic, and bureaucratic procedure.

The examples given illustrate the multicultural nature of modern societies and the resulting challenges to traditional cultural identities. Such challenges apply not only to members of immigrant populations, but to people generally. Social scientists point out that diversity of identity is growing along with increasing globalization, such that most people worldwide now develop a bicultural or hybrid identity that "combines their local cultural identity with an identity linked to elements of the global culture" (Arnett, 2002, p. 774). The cosmopolitan nature of life is transforming a rigid conventional understanding of socialization. "Where a child grows up now matters less than in the past in determining what the child knows and experiences" (Arnett, 2002, p. 782 ; see also Buchholtz, 2002).

People tend to acquire their learning about dying and death on an ad hoc basis; that is, in a disorganized and impromptu fashion. Formal education about death is offered through courses, seminars, and the like, but these avenues of socialization are not part of most people's experience. *Tactical socialization* refers to strategies that palliative care staff or hospice caregivers, for example, use to informally teach people about death and dying (Mesler, 1995). Such strategies involve an intentional effort to change or expand an individual's or family's perceptions and behaviors relative to some aspect of their social world.

Just as societies have a natural interest in the way the educational system is organized to provide services to individuals, they also have an intrinsic interest in such matters of public policy as procedures for legally defining and making a determination of death, rules governing organ donation and transplantation, ways of classifying different modes of death into socially useful categories, the manner in which investigative duties are carried out by coroners and medical examiners, and the criteria that apply to performing autopsies—to name just a few aspects of the death system; that is, the elements of a society that have an impact on how people deal with dying and death (Kastenbaum, 2009, pp. 77-88; see also Doka, 2003a; Hayslip, 2003, p. 35; Kastenbaum, 1989; Kastenbaum, 1996, p. 113). These various aspects of public policy are sometimes interrelated, mutually affecting one another and differing between nations. For example, in recent decades, new legal and administrative procedures for defining death had to be created when modern medical technologies led to organ transplantation.

Kastenbaum says: "We may think of the death system as the interpersonal, sociophysical, and symbolic network through which an individual's relationship to mortality is mediated by his or her society" (2009, p. 104). According to Kastenbaum, the components of a death system include people (for example, funeral directors, life insurance agents, weapons designers, people who operate slaughterhouses, as well as people who care for the dying), places (for example, cemeteries, funeral homes, battlefields, war memorials, disaster sites), times (for example, memorial days and religious commemorations such as Good Friday, anniversaries of important battles, Halloween), objects (for example, obituaries, tombstones, hearses, the electric chair), and symbols (for example, black armbands, funeral music, skull and crossbones symbols, language used to talk about death).

How the death system functions varies among different societies and at different times in the same society. The functions of a death system include:

1. Warnings and predictions about potentially life-threatening events (for example, storms, tornadoes, and other disasters, as well as advice to specific individuals, such as doctors' reports of laboratory results or mechanics' warnings about faulty brakes)
2. Preventing death (for example, emergency and acute medical care, public health initiatives, antismoking campaigns)
3. Care of the dying (for example, hospice, home health aides, trauma workers, family caregivers)
4. Disposing of the dead (for example, funerals and memorial services, cemetery plots, memorialization processes, identification of bodies in disasters)
5. Social consolidation after death (for example, coping with grief, maintaining community bonds, settling estates)
6. Making sense of death (for example, religious or scientific explanations, support groups, poetry and consolation literature, last words)
7. Killing (for example, capital punishment, war, hunting, raising and marketing of animals)

In practice, there are many interconnections and mutual influences among these functions. It is clear from this brief listing, however, that the elements composing the death system touch on virtually every aspect of social and individual life. As you study the various topics related to dying and death, you may find it worthwhile to keep in mind how they fit into the death system. As Kastenbaum says, "Everything that makes a collection of individuals into a society and keeps that society going has implications for our relationship with death" (Kastenbaum, 2009, p. 104).

The concept of the death system is a helpful model for contemplating how death shapes the social order and, in turn, our individual lives. Technology, in the form of the digital online universe, has had a significant impact on the death systems of societies worldwide, as people create Web-based memorial sites, blog about grief, stream funerals online, offer support to the bereaved, and launch novel initiatives with respect to death education (Sofka, Cupit, & Gilbert, 2012). As a network of people, places, and times as well as objects and symbols, the death system affects our collective and personal relationships to mortality in many ways. Thus, again, we see that culture is influential in shaping attitudes and practices with respect to the range of elements that relate to dying, death, and bereavement.

Diversity in death attitudes, customs, and death systems can benefit society as a whole by making available a broader range of resources for coping with death. Yet it also presents challenges in pluralistic societies. When everyone in a society shares essentially the same attitudes, beliefs, and customs, there are known and socially accepted ways of dealing with death and grief. Cultural diversity may jeopardize this comforting situation because there is less agreement among the members of a society about which practices are socially sanctioned for managing death and minimizing existential dread (Mellor, 1993, pp. 12-13, 18-19; see also Littlewood, 1993; Mellor & Schilling, 1993). Uncertainty about the social norms for dealing with death is apparent, for example, when individuals at funerals are anxious about how they should act or what they should say to the bereaved. In today's cosmopolitan societies, people find themselves in situations where socially sanctioned rites for dealing with dying and death are in flux.

Remember our reporter and her question about Anglo funerals?

Becoming culturally competent, can give greater understanding of and connection to people whose customs are unfamiliar to us. Instead of making a judgment that a funeral is "serious" as our TV reporter did, we might understand that socialization, culture, and death systems produce different actions and reactions to dying, death, and bereavement. Becoming culturally competent allows each of us to better understand our own lives and to better serve diverse populations.

Chapter 35

Religion, Spirituality, and Death Education

Robert G. Stevenson

Every person and society holds certain things to be of value. Death, both in its nature and its rituals, has long been an area where there are clear personal and societal values. However, there is a lack of agreement on many of these values. There seems to be a need for a dialogue that can foster both awareness of these values and greater understanding of differing points of view.

There is a relative new discipline that examines the origins of such values. It is known as *consciousness studies.* This discipline is based on the premise that the meaning given to an object comes from subjectivity. That is, the meaning we give to a thing comes from internal thoughts and it is each person's internal reality that enables the person to decide if a thing matters and, if it does, to what degree it matters (Black, 2011). To understand this internal reality in each person requires input from both science and religion since, after all, values come from each source sometimes what each source says about particular values can be quite different. Taking this idea into schools, which are being asked increasingly to teach values can be quite a challenge. However, the school may well be an appropriate place for providing information that can allow such a dialogue to begin. Part of such values education would be education about death. Nowhere is examining the role of values more important than in teaching about death. This curriculum would include the way death as a concept is viewed in a society as well as an examination of the rituals and beliefs and the role they play in trying to understand what death means to each of us. In schools, parts of this examination can take place in history class, or in biology class, or in a type of course referred to simply as death education.

This chapter examines the connections among death, religion, and spirituality and suggests a need to include all three—death and spirituality and religion—in an education program. The vehicle for such inclusion would be death education. Death education has been defined as "instruction that deals with death, dying, grief and loss and their impact on the individual and on humankind" (Stevenson, 1984). It has also been defined as:

education about death that focuses on the human and emotional aspects of death. Though it may include teaching on the biological aspects of death, teaching about coping with grief is a primary focus (Wikipedia, 2011).

Such instruction can be formal, through texts, courses, conferences, workshops and/or lectures/sermons. It can also be informal, through life experience, observation or something as simple as a parent's use of a teachable moment. Formal death education may contain components dealing with religion and spiritual beliefs as they relate to death, to life after death, and/or to the grief process. Instruction may also include lessons on scientific findings and the way in which they can cause one to view death. These units and their effects can be studied and evaluated.

In contrast, informal death education can vary widely from incident to incident. It can occur during or after any loss. By its nature, this informal death education may include religious beliefs, rituals, statements, or spiritual exercises. It may even consist of watching scenes in a cartoon, a movie, or on the evening news. Religious or spiritual beliefs and traditions are often used at such moments in an attempt to soften the blow of a loss. However, it is also possible that in individual informal situations, for some people, none of these things will be present and they must try to deal with the event and any accompanying feelings alone.

Death education takes place on many levels and in many contexts. It can be found in secondary schools, undergraduate and graduate college curricula, professional development programs, as well as in religious teachings. It may even be needed at the elementary school level.

Children are exposed to death at home, at school, and in the media. It has been estimated that approximately 4-7 percent of children experience the death of a parent by the time they are sixteen years old. Others will experience the death of a sibling, a grandparent, or other family member. The death of a loved one affects not only the child, but also has a ripple effect on the rest of the children in the classroom. Alternately, the class as a whole may experience the death of a member of the school community (e.g., teachers or staff) or the death of an individual in the media (e.g., Michael Jackson). In other cases, children may be exposed to the media reports of a national or global tragedy (e.g., the earthquake in Haiti). Children who experience death will have a range of reactions in a variety of settings, including school, where they spend much of their time. Thus, schools are a critical setting for children who are dealing with death and loss. Talking to children about death is a common problem faced by educators who are confronted with children's questions. It is a challenging subject and one that is often ignored and avoided (Talwar, 2011).

Talwar stated that (1) schools are a critical setting for children who are dealing with death and loss and (2) that some educators encounter problems when speaking with children about death.

Farther along the education graduate spectrum, studies of graduate students find they have needs in this area that are still unmet. Even those who are preparing to enter the schools as counselors seem to benefit from taking courses that cover such material. One study found that graduate students studying in the field of counseling benefitted from a death education course in three areas: (1) a greater openness in discussing death and death-related issues, (2) an increased understanding of death, and (3) a reduced personal fear of death (Harrawood et al., 2011).

Despite the certainty of Talwar and others and the findings of Harrawood et al., when the students are adolescents, or younger children, the place of death education is still a cause of active debate. It is sometimes assumed that, when the students are adults, there would be less difficulty merging the topics of science, religion, and spirituality with death education because these students are able to choose whether they wish to pursue this avenue of investigation and are operating at a higher intellectual level. However, even for adults the topic can be sensitive. In one New Jersey college, the chair of the sociology department refused to allow any text to be used that spoke of religion when discussing death and the grief reaction of a community or an individual to a death.

In formal death education courses, the connection shared by death education, religion, and spirituality can appear obvious because the common areas of interest are numerous. However, recognizing this connection is not always the case. When teaching a course on death, grief, and loss to sociology and psychology majors and student nurses at the college referred to above, one instructor was denied permission to select for the students any text on death and/or grief that referred to religion, even indirectly. His supervisor stated that the study of religion and spirituality had no place in an objective examination of death, loss, or grief. He believed that religion and science were two separate and distinct fields and that neither field was needed to understand the other. For that reason, the supervisor rejected two texts that were being used in many death education classes at that time. Each of the texts had a chapter that mentioned religion (Vernon, 1970; Bender, 1974). Students often brought up issues linked to religion, but found no references within the approved course texts. The course was intentionally limited in its ability to address the needs of the whole person. It is now possible for a defense of such inclusion to be made using consciousness studies, formalized in the 1980s, as a basis for that part of the curriculum (Black, 2011).

How can the needs of the whole person in relation to death, loss, and grief be addressed if religion and spirituality are excluded even though people have spiritual needs? Hospital chaplain Carole Smith-Torres (1985) examined this question when she addressed Spiritual Care of Patients at a Columbia-Presbyterian Symposium in New York City. She spoke of the need to work with the whole person. She expressed agreement with the earlier work of Fish and Shelly (1978) who said that, "Man is a physical, psychosocial, and spiritually integrated being, created to live in harmony with God, himself and others" (p. 33). If people are meant to life this way, issues related to the end of life impact each of these aspects of humanity as well. One need not personally hold such beliefs to understand that there are many people who do. It is possible to see that there will be many students who will be unable to fully grasp the meaning of death, dying, and grief if the issues related to religion and spirituality are never addressed.

Mwalimu Imara (1980), a hospital chaplain, worked with Elisabeth Kübler-Ross in Chicago, during the time when she was engaged in developing her five-stage model of dying. In a 1980 interview concerning death education, he described a concept known as *authentic religion*. His research found that belief in a particular religion did not, by itself, necessarily influence the way in which a person dealt with death or with grief. He stated that it was authentic religion that described what it takes to be a "real" person. Imara defined authentic religion as one that provides answers to the following three questions:

1. Who are you? This question is answered by relationships, not through a single title or job description. Authentic religion helps the individual form his or her self-identity.
2. What are your priorities in life? Every religion requires its members to set and follow priorities. Those who believe in authentic religion take their life priorities from that faith.
3. What is it that makes sense out of life/death? To be a whole person one must make choices and be willing to face the consequences of those choices.

Imara's work led him to conclude that authentic religion, because it helped the person to answer important life questions, was a key to coping with death, loss, and grief.

Spirituality has been defined as the name given to issues related to the nonmaterial aspects of life (Morgan, 1993). It involves a quest for answers to the questions posed by life and by death. If that is the case, then Imara's concept of authentic religion describes a quest that is part of spirituality. People who are able to use religion to answer the three questions identified by Imara (1980) were said to have authentic religion. People with this authentic religion have found a way to answer the questions that life and death pose to everyone. As a group, they had less anxiety about, and less fear of, death. These people were better able to cope with loss and to move through the grief process to recovery. If religion can offer such a seemingly effective way of coping with death and grief, how does one justify omitting it from any curriculum that addresses those topics?

Before examining the relationship that exists between religion/spirituality and death education, it is important to remember the many forms of death education and the variety of contexts in which education about death occurs. One now must also look at loss education. Formal death education courses, having become broader to cover more of the types of loss and grief that impact students, have evolved and are now a part of some guidance seminars that deal with loss and grief. What had once been referred to as death education is now subsumed into learning about loss and developing ways to cope with its effects. If death will one day touch every life, so too does loss, of which a death is but one example. Loss education may well be the name that will eventually be given to curriculum that was once called death education.

To discuss the connections of death education, religion, and spirituality, it is necessary to start with an operational definition of each. In this reading, religion is defined as codified belief in the transcendent in an integrated system that is oriented toward helping people find meaning and purpose in life (Gladding, 2011). Spirituality is defined as a unique, personally meaningful experience of a transcendent dimension that is associated with wholeness and wellness (Gladding, 2011). The chief difference between the two terms is that religion is defined as a *set of beliefs,* and related practices, which can provide meaning, while spirituality is defined as an ongoing *quest to find meaning.* The two concepts are not precisely the same but they are interwoven. In simple terms, one can say that religion is external, while spirituality is internal (Gamino, et al., 2003). Religion addresses the group while spirituality is individual. Gilbert (2002a) says, "The function of religion is to build the person spiritually" (p. xiv). Now science is added to this mix. Like religion, science provides a set of beliefs and is external. Some see the relations of science and religion as adversarial with religion—in the area of evolution, for example. However, others say that the two can work with each other and that it need not be an either/or choice of which set of beliefs will be presented.

Religious orientation does go beyond science in that it can be described as either intrinsic or extrinsic. Those people with an intrinsic orientation tend to see religion as an end in itself, while those with an external religious orientation use religion as a means to an end (Allport & Ross, 1967). Either orientation can influence the behavior and feelings of those facing death or the coping of survivors after a death. This insight would appear to make religious orientation an integral part of any examination of attitudes toward death.

Religion and spirituality can influence the content and organization of death education courses, programs, and workshops. Science is already there when one asks What happens when someone dies? or What causes a death? In terms of content, religious beliefs and practices are often included in:

- definition of the moment of death
- views of the afterlife
- funeral rituals
- the role of ritual
- the grief process
- ethical issues (such as euthanasia, suicide, or abortion)

Religion has been one of the means used to examine these topics. It has also provided some people with answers to the questions that the study of these topics can raise (Stevenson, 1993). Sigmund Freud linked death and religion by claiming that, for early man, death was "natural, undeniable and unavoidable" (1915/1959) and that the basis of religion is an attempt by man to lessen his terror of death (Hardt, 1979).

Young people have at least as many questions as adults about these issues. Religion has provided many with answers to these questions, but how might the different teachings of different religions and the values they hold be included in a death education or loss education course? How can educators avoid offending the beliefs of some while describing the beliefs of others?

Religion in a Pluralistic Society

Religious institutions have always provided a type of death education, even if it was not, as yet, labeled such. Diversity of religious belief, or the lack of such belief, in our pluralistic society makes it difficult to generalize about the impact of religion in the education of young people about death. Christians may view death as a transition to eternal reward. They may also see it as punishment for sin. Some Christians have attributed their feelings of guilt to a traditional religious portrayal of death. On the other hand, their faith can also offer comfort in times of grief. Jesus said, "Blessed are those who mourn for they shall be comforted" (Matthew 5:4). The comfort is said to come through the belief that Jesus is the resurrection and the life and that one who believes in him "will live, even when he dies" (John 11:25). The reaction to any of these individual statements can vary among individuals—becoming a source of comfort, suffering, or a combination of both.

Science defines death as "the permanent cessation of all life functions" (Miriam Webster, 2011). However, Eastern religion speaks of death as a transition in which the life force moves on to a new plane of existence or another life in this world. Eastern faiths, such as Hinduism, Buddhism, or Taoism do not speak of personal salvation. There is common ground with Western faiths, however, in religious teachings about death. In general, religious belief offers explanation for events that may otherwise seem incomprehensible, such as, Why did he have to die? Science might answer that the reason was because something made the body unable to live (illness, accident, advanced age). Religion offers belief that can help calm fears regarding the fate of the deceased (heaven, reunion with Brahma, movement to a new physical form through reincarnation) and through ritual (wakes, shiva, cremation, graveside services) and can be a source of communal strength. In addition, when one feels hopeless, religion can be a source of hope...hope that the deceased in now beyond this "vale of tears" and that those who mourn may one day be reunited with their loved one. Religion generally offers the belief that life continues in some form after the event of physical death and may help the bereaved to move on with their lives.

The roles of family and religion must both be taken into account when working with bereaved individuals. When death education is offered in schools, it is not done in isolation. Teachers must try to be conscious of the many influences in the lives of their students. Cultural, regional, and religious differences must all be acknowledged if death education is to be truly responsive to the needs of students (Stevenson, 1993).

In a secular environment, even in American secondary schools where it is required to preserve the separation between church and state, there is clearly a difference between teaching religion and teaching *about* religion. There are numerous courses that traditionally teach about religion. Social studies include information about deities of the ancient world (Egypt, Greece, and Rome), the beliefs of the Hebrews, the rise of Christianity in the

Roman Empire, the teachings of Mohammed and the rise of Islam, the Renaissance, the Reformation, and the beliefs of Europeans who emigrated to the New World seeking religious freedom. World cultures classes describe the teachings of Hinduism, Buddhism, and Islam in order to understand their role in the cultures they have helped to create and to shape. In humanities classes, the *Bible*, the *Torah*, the *Quran*, and other religious texts are studied as keys to understanding human values and beliefs (Stevenson, 1993).

Death education courses in schools present religious information related to death and grief in much the same way. Zalaznik (1979) created a curriculum that used student writings, guest speakers, and/or group discussion to cover the beliefs of a variety of religions. An earlier high school curriculum, started in 1972, used religious sources, along with secular sources, to address student questions in units entitled Death and Beyond, Death and Ritual, and Why Do People Die? (Stevenson, 1972). The inclusion of religion in these courses is consistent with the use that young people have made of religion since long before death education courses existed. It has been shown that students use religion to:

- provide a framework to discuss death (Mills et al., 1976)
- confront and cope with the fear of death (Hardt, 1979; McHugh, 1980)
- answer questions about death and what happens "after we die" (Grollman, 1967; Mills, 1976; Stevenson, 1993)
- understand the religious origins and role of many death-related rituals (Grollman, 1967; Vernon, 1970)

These uses of religion are not relegated to young people alone. One study of the elderly in rural communities showed that they used religion to "render the world intelligible" (Tellis-Nayak, 1982). If these uses of religion to understand death-related issues continue throughout the life span, surely religion should be included in any course attempting to discuss the topics in which religion plays such an important role.

Treatment of Controversial Issues

Even if religion is used by individuals to help them understand the world in which they live and cope with the crises they face in that world, the inclusion of religion in death education is still seen by many as controversial. It should be noted that death education itself is still seen by many as controversial. In an amazing piece of writing, combining partially correct information (selectively chosen) and personal opinion, Blumenfeld stated that death education was being used "in virtually every public school in America for at least the last fifteen years" (1999, p. 1). That is simply not true, unless one defines death education as never mentioning the word *death*. The reason for such gross overstatement is to raise concern in parents, and it can create a split between parents and educators. Blumenfeld particularly attacked the inclusion in death education of the topic of reincarnation—implying that such teaching was the reason for the killings at Columbine High School.

Blumenfeld's article first appeared on the Internet in 1999. It is still, in the second decade of the 21st century, being circulated as if it were written only yesterday. The

Internet gives such articles a life of their own, with little or no way for an individual to check their validity or how current the information may be.

There is yet another reason why teaching about religion and spirituality belong in a curriculum that deals with death and other losses. It has been pointed out that the modern denial of death may be a result of the decline in the belief in personal immortality (Kovacs, 1982). It has also been stated that religious belief in an afterlife can provide support to the bereaved and that the secularization and deritualization of grief deprives individuals of the solace such rituals may provide (Brennan, 1983). Denial of death has been shown to be ineffective for adolescents in dealing with death-related issues and/ or the grief process (Stevenson, 1984). In attempting to prolong their use of denial in dealing with death and bereavement, some adolescents engage in risk-taking behavior to prove to themselves the validity of their belief in their own personal immortality. It is this sort of affirmation of personal belief that is taking the place of traditional belief concerning an afterlife. Both Hostler (1978) and Yalom (1980) attribute increased risk-taking behavior to adolescent attempts to preserve the coping mechanism of denial. The belief that adolescents should "learn to deal with bereavement and grief on their own" (p. 284) when developing coping skills is not borne out by the facts and may be itself a contributing factor to the increase in potentially self-destructive adolescent behavior (Stevenson, 1993).

Religion and Spirituality as Controversial Issues

If educators are to avoid negative pressure being brought to bear on their courses when religion or spirituality are discussed, it may be helpful to have a procedure in place in advance for dealing with these issues as controversial issues. There are a variety of policies and practices in schools for dealing with controversial issues when one looks beyond the United States and Canada to other countries and cultures. However, it seems that in the United States there has been the greatest need for a policy that allows controversial issues, such as religion or spirituality, to be included in death education. One school district's approach will be used as an illustration of what can be done.

There is an existing policy that has been in place for over 40 years in one school district in New Jersey. It is a policy that can be used to fit this situation. This policy, approved by the River Dell Regional Board of Education, defines a controversial issue as a question in which,

> ...one or more proposed answers...arouse strong reaction in a section of the citizenry...The immediate cause of this reaction may be personal belief or interest, or allegiance to an interested group. The most critically controversial questions are those characterized by current importance and by group opinions and interest (River Dell, 1970, p. 4).

Religion and spirituality each fits this definition. Personal beliefs will be addressed if religion and spirituality are addressed. Interested groups can include all organized faiths, as well as persons who do not believe in a higher power, or those who do not want any mention of religion in public schools. In a time of increasing diversity it also allows for inclusion of Asian religions and philosophies, such as Hinduism, Buddhism, Shinto, and others.

The decision whether a particular question should be a matter for school study is made by the board of education, through approval of the course of study. When a potentially controversial issue arises unexpectedly, the educator is guided by five key questions.

1. Is this a question of timeless importance? Questions related to death, suffering, life after death, and the quality of life have been asked by people since the beginning of recorded history. Religion and spirituality have played a key role in providing answers to these questions.

2. Are the students mature enough to deal with this question? With religion and spirituality, as with any other topic in education, it is important that the topic be addressed in a way that is age-appropriate.

3. Do answers to this question help meet student needs? A balanced presentation of religious values and teachings that can have an impact on the lives of students can be beneficial to the students involved.

4. Is consideration of this question compatible with the purposes of the school? Public schools in the United States are charged with educating the whole child. With the importance of religious and spiritual belief in the developing lives of children (as described most significantly by C.G. Jung and by other contemporary researchers), it would be difficult to meet this charge if the major role of religion and spirituality in the life of each child were to be ignored.

5. Is the teacher prepared for the responsibility of dealing with this question? The question of "adequate" preparation is a tricky one. Rather than state specific characteristics of such preparation, the policy states the following, "The wise teacher avoids going into a controversial topic which is beyond his or her own depth (of understanding). A student would be better uninformed about a question than misinformed about it" (Stevenson, 1993, p. 286).

The following list of suggestions can serve as a basis for procedures to apply with courses that include religion in a death education curriculum. It is based on a similar list of points related to teaching about religion in public schools developed by the Public Education Religious Studies Center (PERSC) of Wright State University, Dayton, Ohio, (Smith, 1981). In any procedure for including religion and spirituality in death education courses/programs in secular institutions, it is suggested that in the United States:

- A public institution may sponsor the study of religion, but not the *practice* of religion.
- A school may expose students to all religious views, but may not *impose* any particular view.
- The approach to religion is one of *instruction*, not one of *indoctrination*.
- The function of instruction is to *educate* about religions, not to *proselytize* any one religion.

- The approach of death education to religion is *academic*, not *devotional*.
- Death education courses/programs in a secular context should study what *people do believe.* These courses/programs should not teach students what *people should believe.*
- Death education courses/programs should strive to increase student *awareness* of the beliefs and the role(s) of religion, but should not press for *acceptance* of any one religion, or even religion is general.
- Death education courses/programs seek to *inform* students about a variety of beliefs, but should not seek to *conform* to any one belief (Smith, 1981, p. 65).

Policies and procedures, such as those cited above, may assist death educators to avoid unnecessary controversy if they decide to include religion and spirituality in a curriculum. To not include religion or spirituality because these are potentially controversial issues implies that these topics are either not important, or that they are important, but schools and educators are unable to discuss them in an objective manner. As a consequence, students may believe that:

- such topics are not important enough to be considered by students, or
- such topics are too difficult for educators and schools and are therefore beyond the ability of students to comprehend.

The existence of a policy on the treatment of controversial issues, by itself, shows there are educators and boards of education that believe some questions lack one correct answer and that these questions are of such importance that they still deserve to be addressed throughout society, including schools.

Death Education in Religious Schools

One might think that curricula dealing with death, loss, and grief would already be in every religious school. The worry that a discussion of religion, or religious values, in public school may undermine the influence of religious advisers need not be an issue in this environment. In most religious schools, there would be a clear central focus—the core beliefs of the religion that supports the school—and students would not necessarily have to confront beliefs contrary to their own. However, there can be concerns here as well. In one parochial high school, for over a year after a teenage student had died by suicide, the faculty members were prohibited from speaking about the death with any students. They were not to even use the word *suicide* in the presence of students. The principal, a psychologist herself, believed that this discussion would increase the likelihood of other suicides. What resulted was emotional chaos as everyone tried to cope with the death, and with the suicide that caused it, without the ability to actually speak about it directly. It was only when an outside speaker was brought in to address the faculty on a professional development day that the silence was finally broken.

In a nearby community a parochial elementary school father had a psychological breakdown. He killed his children and his wife with a knife. He then stabbed himself multiple times. The principal visited every class and spoke about the deaths of their friends and classmates. However, she then cautioned the students not to speak about this to "the little ones." The principal then went to grades 1 through 3 and told those students that the family had moved away. This principal's approach created a situation where children in the same family could not speak to each other. Some of the children asked their parents, Why did Sister lie?

Each of these cases could be viewed as an exception that had no connection to death education. However, the point is that we cannot assume that all religious schools address issues related to death and grief. In these schools there is a place for prayer. The faith of these students allows prayer to be used as a way of coping with a loss and in most religious schools the underlying theology of the sponsoring religion allows comments, such as, They have gone to be with God, to be made in all sincerity. Yet, some of these schools believe that death education had no place.

The main point here is that in religious schools, as in any other institution, death education needs to be offered in an age-appropriate, planned manner. The presence of religious faith, by itself, does not guarantee that the topic will be dealt with in a professional and caring way.

Death Education in Clergy Education

It was stated above that, it might be assumed that, when the students are adults there would be less difficulty merging the topics of religion and spirituality with death education because these students are able to choose whether they wish to pursue this avenue of investigation. Religion offers many definitions for, and explanations of, death. It has been identified in ways that range from death as the wages of sin to death as the ultimate step in reunion with God. These broad differences in meaning must be understood by clergy if they are to be able to assist their followers in ways that take personal spirituality and religious differences into account. An issue for clergy, especially those serving as chaplains in a medical or military setting, is the ability to help individuals deal with the need to cope on some level with the problems posed by loss and by suffering. When the death education is offered in the context of a particular faith system, there is not as great a concern about offending the beliefs of others as might exist in a secular context. Pastoral counseling typically includes discussion of helping others to deal with loss and/or suffering, and death education is a part of such preparation.

While pastoral counseling in general may be more attuned to psychological responses to loss and suffering than was the case some years ago, there are clergy/spiritual advisers who receive a broader preparation that acknowledges differences in belief and tries to prepare the clergy to assist individuals whose religious practices or spiritual beliefs they may not share. That group consists of military and hospital chaplains. For chaplains, the possibility of death and the reality of suffering and grief are constantly present. These possibilities affect the individuals whom they are trying to assist. These affected individuals hold a wide variety of beliefs that may come from different religious traditions. They may also have very different ways of relating to the spiritual dimension in their lives. In this context death education takes a different approach.

In a study of practicing chaplains, Sakurai (2006) examined the themes the chaplains themselves found to be important in their pastoral roles. The responses showed that 84% saw "attending to suffering" as the major theme in their work. They then saw inviting the individual to share his or her story or dialogue as the next most important theme (59%). Any professional death education programs aimed at assisting chaplains, with the very diverse beliefs of this client base, would do well to share personal stories as a starting point.

Reverend Richard Gilbert, a director of Chaplaincy Services, has studied the role of spirituality in helping individuals to face illness and loss. He offers the following common threads that chaplains can use to carry on in the face of suffering and grief. His points seem to parallel the questions identified earlier by Imara (1980) (and listed previously). Gilbert sees these common threads as:

- the person's understanding of God/his or her beliefs (creed)
- the person's sense of the transcendent in his or her life
- the role of the religious leader/spiritual adviser
- the symbols identified as important by the individual
- how this set of beliefs/practices engages the individual
- the way(s) in which this religion/set of beliefs helps the individual to determine the meaning of life, suffering, and death
- the ritual(s) that may be beneficial to individuals coping with personal loss and suffering (Gilbert, 2002a)

These common threads shared by most religions should also be a component of any professional death or loss education program for clergy. Chaplain education programs have already begun to broaden their approach with greater numbers of Muslim chaplains training for service. In 1999, Georgetown University, a Jesuit Roman Catholic institution, named Imam Yahya Hendi as the first Muslim college chaplain in the United States (Petersen, 2011). In 2011 he is trying to help that institution solve the lawsuit that has resulted from values in conflict. Georgetown is being sued to remove all religious symbols from its buildings since they offend the values and beliefs of Muslims. Fuad Rana was a student on the search committee that brought Hendi to campus. He said the university was terrific in its recognition and response to the growing needs of the Muslim community, and Hendi's presence was invaluable in that response. "Having an imam is a great resource in terms of providing a link between students and campus ministry, and offering support and developing programs that students couldn't do otherwise," Rana says. "I'm sure there are students on campus today who could not imagine what it was like without an imam on campus" (Petersen, 2011, p. 1). Now, because the university has been unable to reconcile different values and cultural beliefs, Hendi is in the center of a legal case that will may have far-reaching consequences. If actions are taken without looking at underlying values, this can be the result.

Some of the points mentioned above may also be included in death and loss education programs in the schools where, too often, the spiritual dimension is omitted. When such omission happens, the rituals and coping styles of grieving individuals can become more difficult for young people to comprehend (Cox, Bendiksen, & Stevenson, 2002; Gilbert, 2002b; Gilbert, 2006). The Georgetown situation shows that a failure to examine such values can lead to problems for adults and for the institutions as well.

Religious Values and Society

Traditionally, religion has fulfilled several functions in society. It has been a kind of social glue that provided people with a common set of values and beliefs that helped to develop a sense of community. It can give people a sense that life and death have some larger meaning or purpose. Religion reinforces most of the norms of a society. In addition, religion can provide help during major life events or periods of change by assisting people to face, and to deal with, these events and the stress that accompanies them (Robertson, 1977).

Religious values can provide a sense of belonging to those who share those values. They have provided some with a feeling of security when one is confronted with the reality of personal mortality or the death of loved ones. Finally, religious values have been shown to give to some a sense that life has meaning…even a life of suffering. This last function of religious values in society is of increasing interest to educators and parents at a time when schools are being asked to take a more active role in stemming a rising tide of adolescent suicide. Schools are being asked to take on values education to place greater emphasis on life and its relationships. Death education can assist in meeting this challenge.

A simple goal of all education is, or should be, to have students accept as fact the belief that each of us is responsible for the consequences of his or her actions (Stevenson, 1983). A decision about an act being right/wrong or good/evil is essentially a value judgment. Gordon and Klass (1979) saw such value judgments as one of the major goals of death education. They saw this death education goal as "defining value judgments raised by issues related to death." They cautioned that educators would need to be aware of their own values and personal beliefs and to understand the complexity of the issues involved to be able to present all sides in a clear, straightforward manner (Gordon & Klass, 1979). Even if we were to decide that religion, religious values, and spirituality had no place in death education, how can anyone be sure of the personal values (religious and otherwise) that educators may be using to create and implement lesson plans? If we first set guidelines for discussion of values, including religious values and discussion of religion as these apply to death education, there is a greater chance to approach such values in a conscious manner.

A conscious understanding of our values and those of others can give us a greater feeling of control over our lives. Such an understanding, to be complete, must include religious values and the spiritual questions asked about the meaning of life and death. In some cases, discussion of values is said to be limited to humanistic values. However, since humanism is seen by some as becoming more and more like a religion in its own right, adopting humanistic values may not solve the situation. It may merely add a new dimension to it.

Summary

Death is a topic about which individuals and societies hold strong values. One vehicle to facilitate communication about these different ideas and values is formal death education. Death education, defined earlier as "instruction that deals with death, dying, grief and loss and their impact on the individual and on humankind," exists to provide individuals with information. Those who take such courses/programs typically want such information to (1) better understand themselves and others and (2) to make informed decisions related to issues in their lives, including loss and grief. Religion and spirituality, as well as the lack of any formal religious belief, play a role in the lives of most people. Since no decision can be better than the information upon which that decision is based, it is necessary to include all relevant areas in any course/program that seeks to educate students about death, loss, and/or grief and their impact on a person's life. To try to have a meaningful curriculum about death and grief without examining the role played by religion/spirituality means that such a curriculum is consciously omitting a body of important information on this topic. Anthropological interpretations of religion have generally held that the supportive effects of religion and spirituality on a culture outweigh disruptive consequences (Barra, et al., 1983). The possible pitfalls in adding religion and spirituality to death education can be addressed in advance of their inclusion in a curriculum. By creating appropriate policies and procedures for the inclusion of this important information, death education students will be better equipped to examine death, loss, and grief in the context of their impact on the whole person.

Chapter 36

Historical and Contemporary Perspectives on Death Education

Illene Noppe Cupit

It could be easily said that death education began as soon as human beings realized the boundaries of their own life spans. Death education, or the formal and informal study of issues pertaining to dying, death, grief, and loss, has been a significant part of folklore, oral traditions, rituals, literature, art, and, of course, religion, throughout history. How death was understood paralleled the historical and social institutions of a particular culture anchored into a specific time. Greek mythology, the changing nature of the understanding of the universe in relation to humanity's place within, the black plague of Europe in the 14th century, a Western shift emphasizing individualism over communal thinking, world wars, and changes in life expectancy may serve as organizing frameworks for understanding how both life and death was known (Cruz, 2010). And these factors give perspective and meaning to why contemporary death education is so important to a global citizenry.

Generally speaking, prior to the 20th century individuals learned early on in life that people died. They also learned what behaviors and ideas were expected in the face of death and derived a concept of the afterlife from religious teachings and secular responses. Death was acknowledged as a fact of life, and a scant few were shielded from it for very long. In fact, during the latter part of the 19th century, childrens' mourning kits containing the accoutrements of funeral and ritual (e.g., black armbands) could be purchased to teach young girls how to properly execute the behaviors associated with death rituals (Stearns, 2010). What a perfect blend of American capitalism and death education!

The history of death education has been viewed primarily through a Western/ European lens. According to Stearns (2010), knowing the history of thanatology is important because how death was and is currently known has gone through a number of profound changes that we, as a society, have yet to completely understand. This complex evolution in thinking may especially be the case with regard to the cultural revolution heralded by the information age.

The social historian Philippe Aries (1981) described how Western concepts of death approximated sociohistorical events. Thus, the cultural view of death prior to the Middle Ages was shaped by the attitudes of knights and monks, into a "tamed death." This notion was simple death, orchestrated by the dying person him- or herself, publicly acknowledged and ritualized as a known aspect of life on this earth. Death was viewed not as much about personal loss, but more as a part of the natural order of things. Death education during this period most likely took the form of learning via observation the appropriate rituals and behaviors accompanying the deathbed scenario. This form of death changed during the Middle Ages, when self-awareness and religion's emphasis on a judgment day led to a focus on death of the self. Death education, in the form of religious teachings, reflected the emphasis on living life in preparation of the afterlife and eternal salvation. The concept of dying well (known as *Ars moriendi)* was heralded during this time in Christian-based handbooks outlining deathbed rituals. Another change in death attitudes occurred during the 18th century. In tandem with the Industrial Revolution and trends toward social secularism, romantism, and spiritualism, the mourning and memorialization of the death of significant others became central to the concept of death. Proper mourning behavior, typically different for males and females, was an important aspect of learning about death and dying. Whereas Aries (1981) concedes that these past themes reflect an acceptance of death, he notes that significant demographic trends and historical events in the 20th century changed how people related to death. People lived longer, became increasingly mobile, and were more easily distanced from immediate contact with death. Death, dubbed by Aries (1981) as "denied and forbidden," became wrapped in a conspiracy of silence, at least in Western society (Aries, 1981). Perhaps the most significant death education lesson learned was that this subject was neither to be acknowledged nor studied. Although Freud wrote of death and grief in *Mourning and Melancholia* (1917/1959), death as a topic of teaching and learning was largely nonexistent. Too culturally toxic for conversation, death was not formally discussed until individuals were directly confronted with the death of their loved ones or the impending death of themselves. Uneducated, fearful, and poorly socialized into the multifaceted aspects of issues such as dying, grieving, and legal aspects of death, stress from dying and death was compounded by cultural ignorance.

Perhaps then, it was inevitable that the need for education about death would emerge during the latter half of the 20th century. Death education as an articulated focus of study is traditionally dated to Herman Feifel's (1959) landmark publication, *The Meaning of Death,* an edited set of articles that sought to remove the taboo of honest discussion about death. It was from such humble beginnings that the multidisciplinary field of thanatology arose (the study of death and dying) evolving into books, journals, courses, workshops, and Internet offerings throughout the world. Because the field of thanatology is so new, death education has undergone significant transformation in a relatively short period of time, approximately 50 years. This chapter will provide a brief road map of death education, with a discussion of its informal and formal aspects particularly with respect to higher and professional educational contexts (where the "movement" began). The current status of death education (and speculation of the future) will be examined, particularly with regard to the profound influences of the Internet on "the way we do death." Death education specific to different periods of the lifecycle will be discussed in chapter 37 in "Life Span Issues and Death Education."

There are three main themes that will be used as the overarching conceptual framework for understanding death education: (1) the definition and articulation of the field, (2) pedagogy and death education, and (3) the current and future concerns of death education.

The Definition and Articulation of Death Education

Death education involves an interdisciplinary approach. A true understanding of what death means for contemporary societies stems from examining death through an historical lens, through the perspectives of other cultures and belief systems, and through individual and shared meanings. Even political events, environmental factors, and economic policies impact the ways in which we "do death." In the United States, our death education can be affected by debates on health care, in Sub-Saharan Africa it may be the rampant HIV/AIDS crisis, and in the Mideast it could be the loss of life due to violence and war. The content of death education is holistic, as its four central dimensions engage the intellectual (cognitive), affective (emotions), behavioral (actions of people in death-related situations), and personal and social values (Corr & Corr, 2013).

From its earliest days to the present, death education is recognized as occurring both in formal and informal settings. At the informal level, death education occurs whenever there is a teachable moment that spurs conversation and discussion about death. Unless a family's communication is completely closed, children are exposed to such talks when a pet or grandparent dies, when there is a death affecting a classroom, or when newsworthy events make such discussion unavoidable. Many adults engage in these informal discussions as well, stimulated by a movie, current events, family crises, a child's questions, or an issue arising in a professional setting as when a coworker dies. Such spontaneous discussions rely on attitudes and knowledge arising from religious teachings and past exposure to death and dying. Unfortunately, with little education, misconceptions and misinformation could be the result of such conversations. In cultures where death is more accepted as a fact of life, many informal death education opportunities are available as children and adolescents participate in deathbed vigils and funeral rituals, and sadly are not shielded from the traumas of war, famine, and interpersonal violence. The latter, by the way, is also a tragic fact of life for U.S. children living in impoverished inner cities where children learn early that when somebody dies in a drive-by shooting it means the person is not coming back.

The formal aspects of death education center on educational goals and objectives, a curriculum, and assessment/evaluation. Its history has been traced to the first few college courses that were created in the 1960s, such as Robert Fulton's course at the University of Minnesota, and Robert Kastenbaum's course at Wayne State University, with new course offerings subsequently appearing in departments of psychology, religion, and sociology (Pine, 1977). Their number has mushroomed to the point that virtually every college campus now offers some form of thanatological coursework (Doka, 2003). Death education also can be found at primary and secondary grade levels, although the extent to which younger students are exposed to information is difficult to gauge, as it typically does not appear as a standalone subject but rather is integrated into other course content as a module (Doka, 2003b). The work of Kubler-Ross (1969) highlighted the need for death education for the medical profession and was of particular interest to nurses, who thirsted for guidance in the care of patients who were dying of chronic degenerative diseases.

Although the goals of those first death education courses varied, their major focus was to create an environment where it was safe for participants to discuss a culturally taboo topic. Additionally, they were designed to promote values clarification, reflect on the experience of death as structured by cultural and social forces, promote understanding of the processes of grieving and dying, prepare citizens for politically informed decisions, and promote professional development (Corr & Corr, 2003a; Leviton, 1977; Pine, 1977). Leviton (1977) aptly noted that the thematic glue of the goals of death education were improve the quality of life and living as well as dying, an emphasis that remains central to the field today. Thus, thanatology can be defined as "the study of life with death left in" (Kastenbaum, 2004, p. xviii).

According to Leviton, the value of education about death and dying would be to improve communication amongst those whose death is imminent and their loved ones, help students to become more aware of measures that could be taken to prolong life with quality, and to be able to recognize and cope with the symptoms of grief. Leviton's (1977) perceptive and prescient writing also called for measurable and testable means for death education's learning outcomes. The most apparent of these approaches has been in the assessment of death education as a means toward the reduction of death anxiety through increased knowledge (Durlak, 1994). Although research does suggest that students do gain increased knowledge about topics in thanatology, such as funeral rituals, theories of grief and mourning, the process of dying, and life span issues in death and dying, research also indicates that the goal of lowering anxiety about death and dying is only partially successful (Durlak, 1994; Maglio & Robinson, 1994,). However, an evaluation of how courses on palliative care and end-of-life issues for Hungarian medical students was more encouraging with fear of the death of significant others and fear of the dying process significantly lowered as a result of taking the course (Hegedus, Zana, & Szabo, 2008).

As a testimony to the farsighted vision of the pioneers (dubbed by Pine in 1977) of death education, the goals and learning outcomes of contemporary courses in death education have not changed significantly from those of the recent past. Rather, what has changed is the virtual explosion of materials available to students and scholars. Scholarly and trade books on topics of death and dying regularly appear, instructors have an increased array of textbooks from which to choose, including several now in their 7th, 9th and 11th editions (e.g., Corr, & Corr, 2013; DeSpelder & Strickland, 2011; Kastenbaum, 2012, respectively). Journals and newsletters (e.g, *Omega: The Journal of Death and Dying; Death Studies; Mortality; The Forum: Newsletter of the Association for Death Education and Counseling*) provide recent theoretical and empirical work in thanatology, and of course, the Internet abounds with websites related to a cornucopia of topics in the field. Professional organizations such as the International Work Group on Death, Dying, and Bereavement, the Association for Death Education and Counseling, and the Hospice Foundation of America were formed during the 1970s and 1980s and currently enjoy respect as major contributors to knowledge in the field. Included in their missions is the promotion of education about death and dying. As the recognition (and sensationalism) of the importance of knowledge of death has grown, informal death education now regularly occurs from information provided in newspapers, television, the movies, and the Internet. Death, still a taboo topic, has nonetheless become the quirky darling of the media (as in witnessed in several television shows with euphemistic titles such as *Six Feet Under, Pushing Up Daisies,* and *Go On*).

Pedagogy and Death Education

Cognitive and affective components of death education

The holistic features of death education provide students with opportunities to explore the subject both on intellectual and affective planes. A death educator needs to know if students are taking a course in thanatology as a requirement, to satisfy their intellectual curiosity, or to help them work through a personal issue. For a number of students, all three of these motivators may be operating.

Over the years, two major teaching methodologies evolved. One is didactic, involving the dissemination of knowledge, and the other is experiential, providing a focus on affective factors, While the didactic method, emphasizing lecture, reading, and discussion of content-driven material promotes increased cognitive awareness, Durlak's (1994) and Maglio and Robinson's (1994) meta-analysis of death anxiety indicated that it is the experiential method, with a focus on personal reflection, or a combination of didactic and experiential methods, that aids in reduction of death anxiety. Students' knowledge, behavioral, and affective changes with respect to death-related issues are tied to the type of education received.

Death Education as Interdisciplinary and Multidisciplinary

The first contemporary death educators recognized the need to draw knowledge and approaches from a number of different perspectives, a multidisciplinary approach that involved fields as diverse as philosophy, religion, anthropology, history, psychology, and sociology (Corr & Corr, 2003; Noppe, 2010). The early courses frequently drew upon guest speakers from a number of disciplines as a way of ensuring the inclusion of differing perspectives (Morgan, 1987). That tradition continues today (Wass, 2004) and ensures creative collaboration across disciplinary units. However, as thanatology has evolved into its own specific field of study, it has also developed a scholarly and pedagogical tradition that is inherently interdisciplinary in nature, the creation of an orientation that integrates the wisdom and approaches of many traditional fields into its own framework. Once considered experimental or renegade, courses in death education now are viewed as legitimate on most college campuses and may even be part of the requirements for general education or for a major. A survey of the syllabi of recent thanatology courses by Noppe (2007) indicated that the most common topics were medical ethics, funerals, process of dying, crosscultural perspectives, death and public tragedy, hospice, spiritual issues, bereavement and grief, and children and death. The increase in death education that is seen in higher education has not necessarily been true for lower grade levels, although there is little research to confirm this assertion. It can only be a speculation that most of the death education that takes place at lower grade levels is informal.

The "New" Pedagogy of Death Education

The teaching of death and dying has always demanded a certain degree of creativity from instructors. However, as undergraduate education has recently enjoyed an upsurge in interest in enhancing the effectiveness of teaching and learning via new classroom experiences, many ideas have been adapted in death education courses. From the earliest days of college courses in death and dying, instructors recognized the value of experiential learning. Activities and projects have been greatly expanded in contemporary courses, ranging from cemetery analysis, visits to funeral homes and interviews of funeral directors, examining children's literature on thanatological content, and student-initiated research projects that may be presented at professional conferences. *The Forum* even has a regular feature article on teaching thanatology. Recently, service learning, wherein students perform volunteer work relevant to the course topic and simultaneously engage in related academic activities, offers many rich experiential opportunities for thanatology students and has been demonstrated by Basu and Heuser (2003) as an effective learning tool in death education.

Perhaps the most significant pedagogical change in thanatology courses has been increased involvement of the computer as a tool for teaching and learning (Cupit, Sofka, & Gilbert, 2012). Fifty years ago, the early thanatologists could not have possibly envisioned the information age of the new millennium. Today, thanatology courses are offered online, sources of material are studied from a variety of websites, and students have access to materials from sites physically remote but readily accessible in their virtual state. The Internet has also been a wellspring of resources for informal death education, particularly Facebook, where postings and information sharing amongst "friends" leads to the sorts of death-related discussions (particularly when there is a tragic death) that can bring comfort and knowledge as well as misinformation and cruel jokes (Cupit, Sofka, & Gilbert, 2012). Even online gaming and video games, particularly those that involve killing or warfare, may play a role in informal death education (Simpson, 2011). In chapter 37, such use of the Internet, particularly with respect to the impact on adolescent and young adults, is further explored. (See Chapter 42 of this handbook.)

On the formal level, the number of online death education courses has mushroomed (Cupit, Sofka, & Gilbert, 2012). These courses open up accessibility to a wider, potentially global population utilizing original source materials in ways that were not available in the past either to students or instructors. In addition, communication barriers between student and scholar interaction fall away as e-mail and Internet discussion sites offer a level playing field for intellectual interchange. Both didactic and experiential components can be included in such courses leading to a flurry of creative pedagogical methods. Inherent to course effectiveness of such sensitive content, however, is the need to build a sense of community online that is perceived as a safe place to explore issues, cultural differences, and values (Gorman, 2012).

Current Issues and Future Concerns of Death Education

The early years of death education typically saw survey courses that were part of a liberal arts curriculum. Professional fields such as medicine, social work, and mental health saw little in terms of formal course work; rather death education occurred in workshops and extracurricular events that largely were one-shot affairs. Many of these modules of death education were driven by nursing educators, who as frontline caregivers felt the a great need to learn how to help the dying, although palliative care issues are still inadequately covered in undergraduate nursing curricula (Mallory, 2003). The inadequacies of the health care system to care for the dying, the right-to-die movement, and other public policy concerns have led to increased demand for such education. The Association for Death Education and Counseling and the Hospice Foundation of America have been at the forefront in trying to expand death education, by offering webinars focused on topics such as children's grief, loss, and public tragedy, and ethical dilemmas at the end of life. Adult and continuing education courses have also reached out to professionals and the general public. However, most of the material is integrated within the basic curriculum and in workshops with few full courses offered (Dickinson, 2002; Wass, 2004). In addition, medical textbooks offer limited coverage of material pertaining to end-of-life care (Rabow, Hardie, Fair, & McPhee, 2000). Nursing education is more progressive and thus more courses that increasingly are a blend of classroom and online learning are successfully offered (Kavanaugh, Andreoni, Wilkie, et al. 2009). Some specialties such as emergency medical services do not, for the most part, offer death education, and for those that do, the units are taught by instructors with no formal training (Smith & Walz, 1998). Also needed is more course work and workshops in medical schools that examine and teach strategies to cope with dying patients to medical students (Williams, Wilson, & Olsen, 2005). This development may reflect a new trend in professional training that emphasizes more of a holistic approach, including care for the caregiver.

Today, death education has expanded into professional and graduate education. Graduate level programs, such as the master's level programs at Brooklyn College in New York, Hood College in Frederick, MD, and Marian University in Fond du Lac, WI, and certification programs, as offered by the Association for Death Education and Counseling, are valuable in helping to develop death educators for medical and mental health professionals. Clinical psychologists are also recognizing that they may play a significant role in treating individuals facing end-of-life issues, although opportunities are sparse for training in death and dying content, clinical assessment, the understanding of evidence-based practice, and supervised practica (Haley, Larson, Kasl-Godley, & Neimeyer, 2003). A recent study by Ober, Granello, and Wheaton (2012) of 369 mental health professionals reported that more than half of their sample had no formal course work on grief.

A second issue that has received more extensive discussion among death educators involves recognition of the need to understand the influence of culture and race on the dying process (Crase, 1987; Surbone, 2008). In death education, this requirement means going beyond treating varying cultural practices and beliefs toward death as interesting oddities. Rather, it involves examining how culture and diversity permeate the social construction of the dying process, the meaning of death, spirituality and religiosity, and moral and ethical issues at the end of life. In addition, global studies have become increasingly important in higher education in the United States, and death education has responded to such international trends. Learning about how death education is taught in other countries can lead to an important crossfertilization of ideas in the teaching of multicultural content and teaching techniques. Faculty from American universities who have the opportunity to teach death and dying abroad, learn a greater appreciation for the role of culture in end-of-life issues and may be more effective in imparting that approach in their death education courses in the United States (Shatz, 2002). Study abroad programs that include death education as part of the curriculum also provide rich opportunities for students to learn about death and dying in other cultures (Cupit, 2011). As the United States becomes increasingly diverse, and as more student-faculty and student-student interactions take place online within a global classroom, understanding the impact of culture on values and cognitions about death and dying will do much to diminish miscommunication and disenfranchisement (Cupit, Sofka, & Gilbert, 2012; Noppe, 2004). Bordere (2009) named such understanding *cultural consciousness*. Fortunately, there are a number of death educators who have worked hard to infuse their courses with materials that recognize that we cannot homogenize thanatology (DeSpelder, 2009; Fowler, 2008; Ruffin, 2010).

A third issue concerns the continued presence and role of the Internet in death education. There is no doubt that both formal and informal learning will continue to evolve and expand at an incremental pace. As new tools and technologies emerge, death educators will have to keep up with the latest trends and learn how to effectively translate their materials and instructional tools to an online environment (Cupit, Sofka, & Gilbert,

2012). Death educators will also have to be attuned to cultural differences as students reach across the globe. These educators will need to be sensitive to students' coping with time differences, different styles of communicating and learning, and offering online activities that will effectively educate the next generation of thanatologists. Educating the educators to teach in an online universe should be a major aspect of graduate education.

Kastenbaum (1977), in an early examination of death education, raised a number of important questions regarding educational techniques, the qualifications and motivations of the death educators themselves, expectations of and by students, and the dangers and benefits of such courses. We should not become complacent about such issues just because three decades have passed and death education is legitimized on most campuses. Thus, the three major trends of the future are dependent upon a focus and emphasis on a pedagogy that relies on what is known as *evidence-based practice*. According to Balk (2007), evidence-based practice refers to the mutual interaction between researchers and practitioners to inform one another so that researchers can evaluate what are the most effective methods in clinical practice, and practitioners can inform researchers about the important issues that need to be evaluated. Evidence-based practice is increasingly being applied to medical and clinical work. In education, the call for evidence-based practice in the classroom is now being heard. Known as the scholarship of teaching and learning or SoTL, this type of research is essential for determining if the classroom methods and goals of educators are being met. This need for evidence-based practice may be especially true for death education courses because of its holistic, interdisciplinary focus (Noppe, 2008). Death educators will need to know if the ways in which they deliver their content, the ways in which they assess student learning, and the ways in which they devise experiential exercises meet their intended purpose—and this evaluation of achieving course objectives may be especially true for online course work. In all fields of higher education, and for death educators who train in more informal settings, the same tenets apply: Death education involves knowing the research, understanding its usefulness, and translating it into educational action (Wass, 1995).

Conclusion

In a relatively short period of time, death education has changed in terms of its number of course offerings, its broadening beyond traditional liberal arts curriculum into graduate and professional education, recognition of the significance of a multicultural perspective, and increased reliance on electronic media for teaching, learning, and scholarship. Yet, the central motivation behind the creation of such educational experiences remains the same—the belief that as more is learned about dying, death, and loss, the greater the potential for enhancement in the quality of living.

Chapter 37

Life Span Issues and Death Education

Illene Noppe Cupit

Learning about death, reflecting on personal and cultural values, and understanding one's own emotions and those of others with regard to death and dying are lifelong tasks. Hopefully people fill their typical days with the chores and joys of living, but there are junctures during the lifecycle when the need to know and to be knowledgeable about death are central. Whether the teachings about death are experiential, handed down in cultural or family lore, learned through media interactions, or formally taught in a classroom, all humans are continuous recipients of death education from childhood until old age. How such death education is received is influenced by gender, social and cultural context, life experiences, and religious orientation. Most significantly, the life span demands and associated normative developmental tasks impinging on an individual are important to the design and effectiveness of any educational experience in death and dying. The purpose of this chapter, therefore, is to examine how the ways in which death education may be enhanced when it is placed within the context of human development

Death Education and the Normative Death Issues of the Life Span

Erikson (1968) presented the life span as a series of psychosocial issues and tasks that confront individuals from birth until death. These issues (or crises) appear throughout the life span, but one issue takes on a particular salience at each stage of the life span—for example, trust during infancy. As Erikson (1968) insightfully noted, these developmental tasks are embedded within cultural context, so that the entry into adulthood and the tasks associated with childhood and adult life will vary with social structure. It is helpful, therefore, to link the awareness and meanings of death with the major developmental tasks of each stage. In addition to developmental tasks, conceptual understandings of death framed by overall cognitive development and individual experiences, such as the death of a parent or a sibling, greatly influence the meaning of death throughout the life span.

Early Childhood and Death Education

During the early childhood years, death education typically and appropriately is taught in informal ways. However it is taught, death education for children must be contextualized in terms of how their death concepts evolve from early to later childhood. Nagy (1948) suggested that children initially perceive death to be a transitory, reversible phase where the dead exhibit limited life functions. During a second phase, death is perceived as a person such as a bogeyman, who may be outsmarted by a fast and clever child. Finally, toward childhood's end, a mature concept of death evolves, which involves a consensual agreement amongst adults of a particular culture and religious background as to what death means. In the Judeo-Christian traditions of the Western world, a mature concept of death incorporates the principles of universality, inevitability, nonfunctionality, causality, and noncorporeal continuation (separation of body and soul, with the soul continuing on). During the developing conceptualizations of death, a major source of education, which may be spontaneous, comes from the behaviors of adults, both verbal and nonverbal, and from the real and fantastic deaths portrayed in the media (Wass, 2003). Aside from their modeling of behaviors, parents and teachers in the early grades are a major source of information about death in the ability (or inability) to answer spontaneous questions and offer reassurance to their children about their fears and anxieties. These are known as teachable moments (Corr & Corr, 2003a), typically arising out of a death-related situation (e.g., the family dog dies) and they may catch adults off guard. Many adults are uncomfortable with such discussions, unaware of the developmental differences in death conceptions, and are at a loss as to what words to use to explain death to young children. Stammering through or avoiding such a conversation teaches children much about the taboo nature of death. In such cases, books specifically designed to guide children through the concept of death, paying mind to how death concepts differ from adults' concepts, have been helpful in breaking the ice (see Corr & Corr, 2013). Parenthetically, one aspect of adult death education is how to explain death to young children. A key feature of such explanations is providing adults with the developmentally appropriate words to use with young children. Schaefer (1988) suggests that adults can tell children that it is a sad time, that death refers to the time when "a person's body stops working and will not work any more" (p. 132). Referring to death as sleep, going on vacation, or passing away is misleading, confusing, and ultimately frightening to young children.

Of course, one of the most potent death educators during the early childhood years is experience. Recent work has suggested that an early acquisition of a mature understanding of death occurs when the child has experienced a death of a loved one (Silverman, 2000a; Silverman & Kelly, 2009), experienced a life-threatening illness (Bluebond-Langner, 1978), or has lived in an environment rife with death and violence (Barrett & DeSpelder, 1997). Unfortunately, in many areas throughout the world, children are quickly reminded of how easily one can die from heinous slaughters, natural calamities, or rampant disease such as HIV/AIDS (Richter, Somai, Zuma, & Ramsoomar, 2008). Perhaps the best form of education is what Corr and Corr (2013) call effective communication that occurs *prior* to a death. In the absence of an immediate crisis, such effective communications provide an attitude of preparedness in an environment of calm. It involves active listening to what the child needs to know, not overexplaining the issue, clarifying their understanding, and speaking honestly and in language that they can understand. It may mean that adults have to admit I do not know.

Children also learn much about death through the media. Television, video games, and movies provide much exposure to death-related content. For example, Cox, Garrett and Graham (2005) content analyzed 23 death scenes from animated Disney films. They concluded that many of the classic films distort the depiction of death, and recommend that discussions between children and their parents could be a positive consequence of viewing such films.

Not all media events are detrimental to a child's death education. In April 2010, public television premiered a special created by the Sesame Workshop entitled "When Families Grieve" *(http://www.pbs.org/parents/whenfamiliesgrieve/)*. The intent of this workshop was to provide a model dialogue about death for parents of young children. In addition to the television special, Sesame Street made a number of online and printed resources available. Unfortunately, no assessments of the effectiveness of educational components of this ambitious project are available. The workshop does provide a link to bereavement camps, which are another valuable resource for the education of parents and their grieving children. Many camps have as one of their primary goals to normalize their grief experience through providing information and discussions of what is normal in the grieving process (Noppe, Hames, & Schreiber, 2010) within a friendly camp setting.

Few formal death education programs exist for young and elementary schoolchildren because teachers may be unprepared for such lessons, because of the concern that it may do more harm than good, and because of the belief that this topic is better taught in the home (Wass, 1985; Shackford, 2003). However, mental health professionals who work with children in the schools have been increasing their calls for more formal school-based death education for children (Aspinall, 1996; Shackford, 2003). Such concerns have been voiced abroad as well. In Ireland, a survey of parents and educators of children aged 5-12 years generally supported the idea that death education should be taught in schools, particularly with appropriate teacher training. As is true in the United States, the mixed message stemmed from teachers' concerns that parents would abdicate responsibility for the children's death education if this school-based teaching were to happen (McGovern & Barry, 2000).

Adolescence and Emerging Adulthood

Formal types of death education may be seen in middle school and high schools, although such coursework is relatively uncommon. The material may be integrated as units within other subjects (health education is a favorite) or may appear as independent courses in the curriculum (Corr & Corr, 2003a). Stevenson (2009) notes that in countries other than the United States, death education, even the formal type, is mostly available outside of school. Death education programs for adolescents tend to focus upon proactive education (i.e., providing information prior to the occurrence of a death), intervention when a crisis occurs, and long-term support (postvention). The foundation of such proactive programs are rooted in death educators' ability to actively listen to the adolescent, showing acceptance of his or her feelings, and respecting the adolescent's ability to find solutions to his or her own problems (Corr & Corr, 2013.) Educators themselves need to be trained to learn how to discern which of their students, facing a death-related crisis, might be having an especially difficult time coping with their intense emotions (all the more so during adolescence). These teens might be at risk for failing in their schoolwork. Their social relationships may suffer. Significant changes in these behaviors may be at-risk indicators that active intervention is necessary, a tricky challenge because many adolescents do not trust adults enough to bare their grieving souls. Furthermore, there are significant individual differences in physical and emotional maturity that can affect the degree to which social support systems treat the adolescent as an adult or a child when it comes to crisis events such as death. In this regard, culture must also be considered, as in some countries an adolescent can be functioning with adult responsibilities and expectations (Stevenson, 2009).

Death educators also must recognize that whereas adolescents clearly have a mature concept of death, what concerns them about death is linked to the developmental tasks of this period of the life span. Developmental tasks involving identity development, increasing independence from the family, and increasing reliance on peers for support and socialization intermingle with sophisticated use of technology and the media, biological maturation, and the demands of a complex, global society. It is not surprising that adolescents' thoughts of death may be manifested in risk-taking behavior, and a fascination with death in music, television, and on the Internet (Noppe & Noppe, 1997; Sofka, Cupit, & Gilbert, 2012). However, because this developmental period is associated with life-affirming activities, with an underlying assumption that adolescents are not as vulnerable as children when it comes to death, there may be little social support available or it may be short term. We tend to disenfranchise grieving adolescents. Unfortunately, many adolescents actively avoid seeking help from adults, particularly those whom they do not know; they may seek isolation, or may receive faulty advice and misinformation from their peers. Thus they do not have the opportunity to learn that what they are experiencing in their grief is normal.

Bibliotherapy might be particularly useful for the grieving teen. For example, Markell and Markell (2008) offer a most interesting and creative way to teach children and adolescents about loss and death—through the use of the popular Harry Potter series. Sofka (2012a) found that there are a number of contemporary books, written for teens and young adults, that explore a variety of death-related issues such as dying and death of the self, the death of a significant other, and even explorations of the paranormal.

She recommends that future researchers investigate whether such books enhance an adolescent's knowledge and understanding of end-of-life issues and facilitate a change in their beliefs or behavior. In addition, she offers perceptive recommendations regarding the use of literature for death education for adolescents including training for librarians and parents about resources on these scary topics. These recommendations would also include resources found on the Internet.

For many adolescents and young adults, death frequently occurs in a sudden and tragic way through suicide, vehicular accidents, and homicide (Hayslip & Hansson, 2003; Noppe & Noppe, 2009). As a result, death education may be framed by crisis and occur within the context of peer grief support groups or counseling sessions run by school psychologists or guidance counselors. Aside from work on suicide prevention, attending to the acute grief needs often are primary goals of those running such groups (Corr & Corr, 2003) and as such, are not a part of continuing instruction (Wass, 2003). In addition, educators frequently are at a loss as how to handle information during public tragedies—they may even be required by administrative personnel to minimize exposure of the news to their students (Noppe, Noppe, & Bartell, 2006).

It is only a slight exaggeration to suggest that many sources of information about death pale in comparison to the amount of information available to adolescents via social media, websites, and other online materials (Sofka, 2009, 2012b; Sofka, Cupit, & Gilbert, 2012). The Internet may serve primarily as a social networking resource; a place for group support, blogging, and posting heartfelt memoirs to a lost loved one. However, there is much education, for better or worse, that accompanies the time spent in these endeavors. As Cupit, Sofka, and Gilbert (2012) point out, many informal lessons about dying and death occur via use of websites that offer postings from grieving individuals, memorial tributes, letters to the deceased, or information about loved ones facing a life-threatening illness. In the privacy of their rooms, the adolescents can find solace and learn much about the multifaceted aspects of dying and death (e.g., end-of-life decision making, funeral rituals, controversies regarding assisted suicide). Furthermore, the Internet is a valuable resource in exploring global concerns regarding thanatological issues. Adolescents may be more savvy and tolerant about the richly diverse approaches and belief systems of death and dying across the globe, although this possibility is not empirically verified. The concern, however, is that there is no stopping of the malicious sites that provide misinformation and communications that could be potentially harmful. This concern is where death educators play an important role. Ideally included in any high school education about information literacy would be lessons on determining what sites could be misleading or potentially harmful. It is here that an environment of trust between school personnel who have received death education training becomes valuable.

Formal courses in death and dying are found on virtually every college and university campus in the United States (Doka, 2003b) and are well-received by students. These courses are taught in a variety of different departments by faculty from a number of disciplinary perspectives (e.g., psychology, sociology, religious studies). Although the content of these courses may vary, they usually cover material on dying, bereavement and grief, funeral customs, and medical issues. These courses have become increasingly popular over the past two decades (see chapter 35). Many college courses are now being offered online, reaching a broader group of students in the United States and abroad. In addition to being intellectually engaging, students may find such courses helpful in their coping with personal crises. College death educators must respond to the fact that approximately 22-30% of traditionally aged college students are in their first year of suffering the loss of a significant other (Balk, Walker, & Baker, 2010). As in the adolescent years, young adults encounter death most often through sudden and traumatic ways (Cupit, Servaty-Seib, Parikh et al., in review). In addition, the very real prospect of going to war or seeing friends sent to life-threatening political hotspots and normative deaths of grandparents and pets make such courses valued.

The developmental tasks of the college years may have undergone a change in the past two decades. Taking an Eriksonian perspective, Arnett (2000, 2004) characterizes the years 18 – 29 as a period of emerging adulthood. This period in between adolescence and adulthood is defined by transitional lifestyles in terms of residence and education, lack of role constraints, and continued identity exploration and self-focus. College instructors of death education courses need to be aware of the anxieties created by the instability and transitory characteristics of this period of the life span. Young adults live in very challenging times—job prospects are poor, they have much to juggle at one time, and are delaying marriage and family until their late 20s. If they are death anxious, they may not find relief from their thanatology courses (Durlak, 1994), or they may question the value of going to school and find coursework not personally relevant to their immediate lives (Cupit et al. in process). Educational opportunities may be provided by several thanatological organizations. The National Students of AMF (www.studentsofamf.org) is a grief support network for college students. This organization also provides training and an annual conference whereby information about death and loss is presented to the attendees (primarily college students and personnel working in student services).

Not all emerging adults are found on college campuses. A number of them are currently serving in the military or are returning veterans. Awareness of mental health issues amongst military personnel has increased over the past several years, as the number of mental health problems, suicides, and highly publicized violent acts by veterans have become an almost daily feature in the news. Yet, to date, few opportunities for death education are available for mental health counselors working with military personnel, or for those overseas or at home who may have been traumatized by all of the death and destruction they had witnessed (Christian, 2006). One notable exception is in the organization Tragedy Assistance for Survivors (TAPS, www.TAPS.org) that offers webinars and other education programs on death and loss.

Adulthood and Middle Age

The period of the life span between emerging adulthood and old age covers many decades, and there is much variability in the ways in which life is negotiated. The normative tasks of adulthood and middle age involve commitment—to relationships (including children), to work, to belief systems, and to remaining active and engaged in continued growth or generativity (Erikson, 1968). Such commitments have profound implications for end-of-life decision making, clarifying values regarding death, and nurturing others with regard to their own quest for understanding. It is no small task in a society that still harbors death phobia. The need for information leads many adults to seek out both formal and informal ways of learning about death.

In terms of career development, those interested or involved in work in the medical field may receive formal instruction in death. Once notably lacking in the professional curricula such information is increasing (Chapter 35, Dickinson 2007; Wass, 2004). In health care education, material on death and dying typically does not appear in stand-alone courses, but rather is integrated as modules in larger courses or as a part of a clinical internship (Dickinson & Field, 2002). Dickinson (2007) notes that course work in death for medical personnel is still limited in time devoted to the topic and in the depth that is given. Course modules, webinars, online courses, and professional development workshops, often associated with conferences, such as the annual conference of the Association for Death Education and Counseling, are offered for individuals who see themselves encountering death issues in the workplace, such as nurses, social workers, educators, hospice workers, funeral directors, and clergy. More also needs to be offered to human resources departments in all types of places of employment on how to help grieving coworkers. Such training ostensibly could be offered in graduate managerial programs as well. The need for such death education is increasing, because as the demography of developed and developing nations shifts toward a larger proportion of older people with longer life expectancies, many adults seek out training and careers in the health care professions. In the United States, pressure to move to managed health care systems demands an educated citizenry in order to make informed political and personal decisions. Medical personnel, mental health therapists, missionary workers and others who travel to parts of the world that have been devastated by the HIV/AIDS crisis (e.g., South Africa), war (e.g., Afghanistan), or natural disaster (e.g., Haiti) need to learn how to work with large populations or traumatized and bereft children and adults (Gupta, 2008; Lewis, 2008).

As the adult years involve increasing responsibilities in family and work, many adults seek out information about death and loss in order to know how to provide for their families in the case of an untimely accident or terminal illness. In their parenting role, adults may desire to learn something about how to discuss death with their children. The market has certainly responded to such demand, as witnessed by a surge in the number of publications about death intended for children and adults. Online courses and educational materials make such information accessible to ever more people (Cupit, Sofka, & Gilbert, 2012). In addition, some adults may face the tragic loss of a child (Hayslip & Hansson, 2003), and support groups, such as Compassionate Friends, frequently have speakers who offer education as well as comfort.

These issues will continue on into the middle adulthood years, but as parents die and as the possibilities for life-threatening illnesses such as heart disease and cancer increase, the awareness of one's own mortality moves to the forefront (Hayslip & Hansson, 2003; Corr & Corr, 2013). As people age, they must learn how to adjust and cope with the constraints (and opportunities) related to this time in their lifecycle (Heckhausen, Wrosch, & Schultz, 2010) potentially leading to an increased desire to learn about dying and death. Aside from the career-related workshops and seminars, middle-aged adults rely upon informal death education such as from the media, books, and the Internet to enhance their understanding about death. Most baby boomers fit this demographic, encouraging the media to respond to concerns about their increasing encounters with dying and death with articles in newspapers and magazines, discussion groups in book clubs and churches, public radio programs and movies, and television shows that explore these issues in serious and comedic venues. Admittedly not all of these sources provide accurate information in a sensitive, effective manner, but they nonetheless open possibilities for dialogue and exposure to issues that were considered taboo not so long ago.

Older Adults

That older adults must frequently confront death is a given as they increasingly experience the loss of their friends and spouses (Hayslip & Hansson, 2003). Thus, encountering death, to the point of bereavement overload, can lead to a framework of life wherein death and loss predominate. Despite the obvious association between aging and death, older adults are given few opportunities for education about end-of-life issues and death other than the popular modalities discussed above. The literature on death anxiety (Fortner & Neimeyer, 1999) suggests that relatively speaking, older adults do not necessarily manifest high levels of death anxiety. Yet, as Wass (2004) notes, many older adults do express concerns and fears about dying and death. Fortner and Neimeyer's (1999) meta-analytic study of the aged and death anxiety found higher levels of death anxiety in older adults who were in relatively poor physical and mental health. Death educational content specifically geared to the developmental issues of the aged, such as coping with pain and negotiating the medical system, aspects of widowhood, or the dying process may help to alleviate some of these worries (Wass, 2004). Furthermore, many older adults are genuinely interested in the topics covered in death education. Learning about various funeral customs, differing religious beliefs about death, and perspectives on grief and loss can be favored topics in community workshops and university outreach programs for retirees. For example, Doll (2006) reports on the success of a human development and aging (including thanatological content) college course that involved older adults from a local retirement community. Learning in retirement programs, now being offered by many institutions of higher education, may be a valuable mechanism for offering courses in death and dying. In addition, hospice nurses and volunteers may be particularly effective in providing one-on-one educational experiences for older adults. Wass (2004) suggests that nursing home personnel and family members be taught how to communicate more effectively about death-related issues to older adults. Grief in an aged population may also involve the loss of an adult child, a grandchild, or sibling, and should be addressed in death education programs for those who work with the elderly.

The Efficacy of a Life Span Approach to Death Education

Teaching and learning implies change and development, and death education is no exception. Given that the goals and content of death education vary as a function of the developmental needs of its recipients, it is not surprising that a clear and consistent picture of the efficacy of the pedagogy of death has not emerged. Relevant to the developmental needs of the intended audience, death educators face the decision of how to measure the effectiveness of their educational program. How do you know, for example, if preschoolers have benefited from a teachable moment when a class pet dies? Is it enough to report anecdotally that the children are more considerate of one another subsequent to the discussion (Hopkins, 2002), or should they have advanced toward a more mature concept of death?

Most of the research on the effectiveness of death education assesses content and death anxiety, especially in college courses. For younger age groups, few systematic assessments using psychometrically sound instruments exist. For the adult courses, those that emphasize content in a lecture style format are more likely to encourage cognitive changes, whereas those that focus on experiential dimensions that provide opportunities for learners to process their own personal understandings show modest success in modifying feelings and attitudes (Durlak, 1994).

Assessment of death education for professional development tends to focus on the adequacy of preparation of materials for medical and mental health personnel (Dickinson, 2007; Chapter 33). Given the inadequacy of intervention efforts in communication among physicians and patients (SUPPORT, 1995), longitudinal research needs to be continued on the relationship between education and intervention efficacy.

Wass (2004) points out that data need to be obtained about the preparation received by death educators, as well as standards and guidelines that would serve to improve the quality of death education for grief counselors, many of whom work with children and adolescents. Given that death education occurs across the life span in a variety of formats, systematic assessment on the interaction of pedagogical techniques and age-related needs of learners, known as the *scholarship of teaching and learning* would further advance the field (Noppe, 2007). As death education increasingly becomes an online endeavor, it is imperative that the efficacy of such courses, in terms of best practices, delivery of content, and student learning outcomes be carefully assessed (Cupit. Sofka, & Gilbert, 2012).

Life Span Death Education: Present and Future Needs

Age-related concerns about death and dying are normative but also reverberate to the rhythms of a rapidly changing world. In order to maximize its humanistic potential, death education and death educators must be responsive to contemporary issues and how these affect youth, adults, and the aged. For example, death educators should consider how to teach death to youngsters who are coming of age in a world of increased globalization, terror, and violence that confront them daily on television, the Internet, and in their personal lives. Death educators need to learn the characteristics of emerging adults, and how emerging adulthood plays out on an international level (Cupit & Servaty-Seib, in press). Death educators must learn how to effectively use the Internet and electronic technology, particularly for those populations (e.g., adolescents and young adults) who rely on such technology as primary sources of information. The development of educational programs responsive to the needs of middle-aged and older adults, many who are living longer, healthier lives in age-segregated communities away from families of origin, will become of increasing importance in the future. And finally, a pressing issue will consider who are to be the next generation of death educators and how are they to be trained, as the field of thanatology itself matures.

Regardless of how the many questions of death education evolves in the future, there is consensus that death education is needed and important for all ages—an important component of life-long learning in all senses of the term.

Chapter 38

The Family, Institutional/Societal Systems, and Death Education

Kathleen R. Gilbert and Colleen I. Murray

The intent of this chapter is to provide information on the ways in which families educate their members about death and orient them to ways to behave in situations associated with death. In addition, we will address ways in which institutional/societal systems, such as the media, broadly defined, also serve to educate. Consistent with Corr and Corr (2003a), we define the term *death education* as efforts to educate on any topic that is somehow death-related. This notion includes both formal and informal educational efforts regarding dying, death, grief, and bereavement.

The development of an understanding of death is a meaning-making process (Gilbert, 1996; Nadeau, 2001; Neimeyer, Prigerson, & Davies, 2002), and this process of making meaning begins early in life. We come to an understanding of death and how we should respond to it through what is an essentially collaborative meaning-making process with others. Through interaction with others, our subjective interpretations of death are confirmed by others and given an objective reality (Berger & Luckman, 1966), which we come to view as real because significant others reinforce its reality. The family and larger systems are integral parts of this social construction of reality (Gilbert, 1996), and we will explore its role in death education.

The Family as a Death Education System

Our family is the first source of death education we encounter in our lives, and its influence continues throughout our lives. It serves as a—many would say the—primary force in initially shaping our worldview and then contributes to the way in which we encounter and comprehend new information throughout life. This shaping occurs in many ways: formally and informally, directly and indirectly, in concert with other sources of death education. It occurs obviously through such socially recognized rituals as funerals and memorials, but less obviously through small rituals like bedtime prayers or, in the old days, watching one's father remove his hat when a funeral cortege passed. Everyday activities within the family also contribute to the family's education of its members (Keeley

& Baldwin, 2012). A family that easily deals with issues of death likely will produce individuals who are less fearful of death than a family in which death is only spoken of in hushed and fearful tones, if discussion is permitted at all (Weber & Fournier, 1985). The family that struggles to deal with loss and complicated grief may present members with pathways to resilience or withdrawal. Attempts to shield children from an adult's pain still result in nonverbal messages indirectly conveyed to the child. Regardless of a family's approach to death education, in every case, an essential role of the family is to convey, both verbally and nonverbally, information about death—that is, to serve as sources of death education.

The Family an Agent of Death Education

The family contributes to each member's acquisition of cultural norms and expectations while also leading them to adapt their behavior to fit those norms. Typically, we think of this influence in terms of values, standards, beliefs, and appropriate behaviors associated with those values, standards, and beliefs (Day, 2010). Acquiring such socialization allows family members to function within society.

An example of this informal education is the way in which children often are socialized along gender lines toward different male and female roles. According to Doka and Martin (2001), boys and girls are informed in different ways, leading them toward approaching death and grief differently. Boys engage in team play, with interactions centered around activities. They are encouraged to view relationships in a hierarchical rather than col-laborative way and focus on control of their emotions. Girls, on the other hand, are en-couraged to be more cooperative, have more empathy for others, to share confidences, and to be more supportive of others. The result is different, resulting in complementary approaches to life and death and to grief that generally follow along lines fitting each gender role. Recent work in Canada found these patterns continue into adulthood, with bereaved fathers demonstrating more focus on work and task-focused coping (Alam, Barrera, D'Agostino, Nicholas, & Schneiderman, 2012). In contrast, bereaved mothers used more child-focused coping and were more actively nurturing the relationship with their surviving children.

This educational process occurs most obviously in children's early years. Less obvious, and less studied, is death education that takes place across time as family forms shift and change when members join, leave, and create new families. Yet, this process continues throughout life, as members respond to the needs to fulfill new roles within their family as it evolves over time. One of the authors of this chapter (KG), having grown up in a family whose death-related behavior was heavily influenced by its Eastern European heritage, was shocked when attending the funeral of her grandmother-in-law, to see, among other alien sights and experiences, Mammaw dressed in a negligee in the casket. She was not "waked" for long hours, with coffee provided in the basement of the funeral home. Instead, the family held a viewing that lasted 2 hours, in the evening. Although there were similarities, many aspects of the funeral and its aftermath were different, requiring that she (KG) be quickly tutored on role-appropriate behavior. The other author (CM) grew up in a rural family that routinely took photos of family members in the casket after death. These served as reminders of the actual loss and a source of comfort. Only when she enrolled in her first graduate course in thanatology did she realize that other students found this to be a bizarre practice since the topic had never come up in interactions outside the family prior to this exchange. A practice that had been common during the advent of the camera for mailing to those family members who lived too far away to attend the funeral had fallen into disuse as family mobility changed, cameras became commonplace, and visual images were out of step with the focus on remembering the deceased as they had been—active and vibrant.

Talking about death in the family. Family members attempt to anticipate questions, concerns, and needs when they prepare for an impending death-related event, such as a funeral. This preparation is most obvious with children, but, as noted above, continues through the life of the family. In terms of children, and depending on the family, parents might talk with their child about what to expect and how to behave, they may provide coaching, or they might simply tell the child to behave, not ask questions, and not act out. Some parents might choose not to involve the child or refuse to answer questions. In adulthood, couples might rehearse appropriate ways to respond. The film *The Funeral* (Hosogoe & Itami, 1984), demonstrates such rehearsal clearly as a bereaved daughter and her husband watch instructional films to prepare for their roles as bereaved family members in her father's Buddhist funeral.

Children's books about death and loss along with other media may be used as a resource by parents who wish to supplement their own knowledge base as they address their child's questions (Carney, 2003-2004). Portrayals of parents in these books can be used as models or standards (by children or parents) as to how they should interact, educate, or help children cope with death (Corr, 2006-2007). These types of information exchange may be planned, possibly in response to a death or in anticipation of a death in the family. They may also happen spontaneously, in response to some sort of triggering agent or event. Losing a pet (Kaufman & Kaufman, 2006) or hearing someone discussing a death can be such an event or agent. The death of a pet can be a particularly difficult loss for a child, and parents must be sure not to trivialize the death (Kaufman & Kaufman, 2006) as they discuss it with their child.

In addition to children's books on death, family members may refer to informational books on death, dying, loss, and grief for their own use or as a resource to help other family members. Increasingly, websites and other Internet resources serve as informational resources (Sofka, 2012a). In addition, other media, like television programs (Charkow, 1998) or films (Cox, Garrett, & Graham, 2004-2005) might be used as a planned or spontaneous triggering agent for discussion.

Families also can be involved in the direct and indirect death education of adolescents. In addition to informal education during teachable moments (e.g., after a vehicle-related death of a peer, or the media reporting of soldiers' deaths in war, or suicide of a celebrity) they can share in death education that combines school instruction with family discussions. Waldrop and her colleagues (Waldrop, Tamburlin, Thompson, & Simon, 2004), found that the addition of family discussions to school activity increased students' comfort level with the idea of organ donation. Although the study looked only at students' response to the discussions and did not look at family changes, it would be interesting to learn about effects of the discussions on the larger family, that is changes in comfort level in discussing death, the effects on the discussions, or any end-of-life decisions that were made by others in the family.

Modeling of death-related behavior. Another way in which families teach their members about how to behave when they are confronted with death is through the modeling of appropriate behavior associated with death, essentially serving as role models for family-approved behavior. Young children, in particular, learn by example, and significant others in the family become role models for how to behave in situations associated with death. In this modeling, the family members serve as examples of the norms and behaviors associated with death.

Families and learning styles. Family members often try to adapt their informal or formal teaching about death to the needs of each child, considering the child's cognitive level and needs. One factor families may consider is the child's learning style (e.g., whether a child learns best through visual, auditory, or tactile experience). Dozens of theories have been proposed on the learning styles of individuals, and there is much debate among psychologists and neuroscientists as to where general education tailored to the learning style of the child has any effect on learning (cf. Pashler, McDaniel, Rohrer & Bjork, 2008). There is a lack of systematic research on this issue as applied to families and to death education in particular. Although some family members may share a style of learning, there is no evidence that there exists an overall family learning style. Studies of learning and death education would need to consider the adult's own learning style as it may impact the presentation of death education to younger family members. A parent who learns best visually or through touch may encourage the child to view the body in the casket and feel the hand of the deceased to better understand how death differs from life. Others who don't share this style may be uncomfortable with such an approach. Regardless of the particular learning style or method of presentation, an understanding of death includes both cognitive and affective components.

Families Making Meaning: Collaborative Death Narratives in the Family

From the family systems perspective, the critical process that underlies all interaction in the family is the process of meaning making (Nadeau, 2001). It is important to note that the family's involvement in the attribution of meaning is embedded in the broader culture and society (Gilbert, 1996) and is a process that is ongoing throughout the existence of the family. As family members encounter new information in their environment or are faced by situations when old meanings no longer fit, they test their theories and use other family members as a reality check on what things mean and how one should respond. If family members find their own views confirmed by others in the family, these views are given objective reality—what they perceive comes to be seen as reality because significant others also see it that way (Berger & Luckman, 1966; Thomas & Thomas, 1928). If their views are challenged, they may question their views, that of their family members', or both (Gilbert, 1996). The death of a child in the family, for example, may result in radically different perspective on the meaning of the loss and the implication for family members. Parents may feel a need to protect the surviving children, may feel overwhelmed by their own grief, or may perceive the other children as unaffected by the loss. The children may end up with a distorted view of their sibling's death, its meaning for them, their culpability in the death, and the legitimacy of their own rights as a griever (Schwab, 1997). During periods of uncertainty, stress, or the terminal illness of a family member, informal education from voluntary, recurring experiences with small talk or the creation of rituals can lead to a sense of security, reassurance, and calming for children (Keeley & Baldwin, 2012). It can strengthen family identity (Baxter & Braithwaite, 2006). Members can socially construct meaning of the loss by generating, renegotiating, or even resisting change in everyday interactions (Hollander & Gordon, 2006).

Mutually validated views facilitate communication, provide structure and meaning to family interactions, and serve as the basis for familial coping behavior (Reiss, 1981). However, the various family systems and larger systems in which we live may result in family members holding contradictory or competing views on appropriate beliefs and behaviors associated with death. This discrepancy in views can be seen most clearly with children of divorce, who may face contradictory views from their parents in each of their households. An example would be when religious beliefs are a key source of disagreement and conflict in the divorce. These children could then find themselves pulled between two different and conflicting belief systems about death and the afterlife and might find the views and expectations of their parents, now untethered from each other, changing and evolving away from each other over time.

Most authors in Western cultures have made the assumption that optimal family education about death includes open communication, emotional disclosure, and sharing of experiences (Hooge, Neimeyer, & Rober, 2011). However, recent empirical studies have not demonstrated that this sharing of emotions results in bereavement recovery (Meads & Nauwen, 2005; Zech & Rimé, 2005). Avoidance and not expressing grief may, in some situations, add to adult resilience by providing a distraction from the death (Boelen, van den Hout, & van den Bout, 2006). In those families where anger and hostility commonly occur during interactions, communication between the members may not effectively facilitate death education or grieving. Extroverts may benefit more from social support than introverts, and those whose personalities tend toward neuroticism may not reap the benefits of making sense or finding benefits from loss that can occur for others (Boyraz, Horne, & Sayger, 2012).

Decision making in the family. The same potential for conflict or collaboration on attributed meaning may be found in families dealing with a variety of decisions that are made in the family: choices made about end-of-life care, advance care planning discussions, wakes, funerals, and periods of mourning. These decisions come with significant transitions in the family's life course and are associated with high stress (White & Klein, 2007). In her study of end-of-life decisions, Gauthier (2005) found that family concerns were an important factor in the decision making of terminally ill patients. Increased dependence, the need to relocate to be near family, decisions made to accommodate the needs of family caregivers, the economic burden on family, concerns about a lack of communication were all social concerns that were associated with family function. Interestingly, the study did not identify family factors that positively affected end of life decision making, but it may be that the participants saw the focus of the study on impediments to easy decision making.

Rituals as a tool for dealing with death. Rituals often become more valuable to the family during times of loss. Rituals are composed by metaphors, symbols, and actions that are packaged in a highly condensed, time and space-bounded, dramatic form to establish and maintain family identity (Imber-Black, 2004). Family rituals serve five functions within families: relating, issues of expressing and maintaining relationships; changing, transitions for self and others; healing, recovery from relationship betrayal, trauma, or loss; believing, voicing beliefs and making meaning; and celebrating, affirming deep joy and honoring life with festivity (Imber-Black & Roberts, 1992).

In their overview of cultural variations in approaches to end-of-life decisions as well as associated rituals, Searight and Gafford (2005) described a wide range of approaches to decision making in the family, even to the extent of whether or not the dying person should be involved in the decision-making process or even if he or she should be informed that a decision needed to be made. In a world that allows greater mixing of culturally diverse individuals and the blending of cultures in families, issues of meaning may become intense at these times (Klessig, 1992).

Death Education in Institutional/Societal Systems

Just as the family plays a role in death education, so too do societal and institutional systems. From our general society and our personal communities, we are exposed to information and beliefs about dying, death, and bereavement through formal and informal means. In addition, we learn about responses and practices surrounding death-related events from various social institutions.

Although they are a key source of death education, and the principal venue for formalized death education, the role of educational institutions (i.e., schools and colleges) as well as religious organizations will not be addressed in this chapter. The ways in which death education plays out in these more common sources of death education are addressed in greater depth in other chapters in this text. Instead, we focus primarily on the role of media as a source of death education. We will address traditional forms of media (i.e., print and broadcast), but will place more emphasis on the role of the Internet in death education, as it incorporates elements of earlier forms of media and includes the unique aspect of interactivity and bidirectional communication among members of the Internet community. An example of how the Internet is being incorporated into death education at the time of the publication of this text then will be presented.

Media and Death Education

Print media. Books and other printed materials are readily available resources for death education. As noted earlier in this chapter, these resources can be used either directly, as a tool for discussion of death, particularly with children, or as a source for detailed information on death, dying, and bereavement. Schuurman (2003-2004) has identified a selection of high-quality texts that can be used for a variety of audiences so they may talk with children. Other resources, like self-help or professional texts, articles in newspapers and news magazines, pamphlets, and circulars may be used for both informal and formal death education, both for adults and for children. An excellent example of a journalistic resource for adults is the article by Klein (2012) mentioned earlier. The difficulty is in selecting high-quality resources that meet the specific needs of the reader.

Often, when a major loss event occurs, journalistic and other publishing sources will produce death-related articles and other materials. Examples range from personal accounts to depictions of the response to natural disasters, like hurricanes and related flooding and human-made disasters, like the mass shooting at a movie theater in Aurora, CO, in 2012. A more personal and relatable example of the first is "The Long Goodbye," (Klein, 2012), addresses issues of difficult end-of-life decisions the author had to make through his parents' dying process, as well as his own progression through grief and life review that resulted from his parents' failing health and death. Articles such as this one can be an informal death education resource, but could be used for guided student discussion in a formal death education course.

Public television. Public television has had a long history of developing and presenting content that addresses death and dying. PBS, with its inherent educational mission, has provided death education programming over the years. Many of these programs continue to be available for purchase or immediate play and have accompanying educational materials for download on the PBS website. "Dealing With Death" presented under the In the Mix banner, is an example. This program, directed at teens and with its own website, has a companion discussion guide, for use in formal death education. Studies have been conducted on the effects of death-related content in educational service programs. In the case of Sharapan's (1977) study of death content on "Mr. Roger's Neighborhood", for example, letters from families indicated that they engaged in discussions of death-related themes after viewing the show.

Death education in news media. Journalists engage most frequently as informal death educators. Newspapers and magazines publish stories of individuals who have been diagnosed with a life-threatening or terminal condition or have coped with the death of loved ones. Narratives of these stories often are selective and serve a social purpose. Following the Oklahoma City bombing, the narrative that developed was one of brave, highly resilient Midwesterners. Levine's (1996) content analysis of news media reports showed that any contrasting story line was seen as somehow abnormal.

Similar to the media stories of deaths of common people, the death of a public figure often takes on more significance in the media than the simple recognition and memorializing of an individual. These celebrity deaths often become media events (Hearsum, 2012; Water, 2010), providing opportunities to present an inspiring death narrative, as well as implied rules for ways in which the bereaved should behave (Thomas, 2008). The impact of the coverage of these deaths can extend over decades. We, the authors of the chapter, still can remember childhood images of President Kennedy's funeral in 1963 and the admiring observations of television commentators as they talked about Jackie Kennedy's behavior. The message was that contained, reserved, tear-free mourning was socially desirable while any overt display of grief was, by implication, wrong.

Television and, to a lesser extent, radio news can have a uniquely intense emotional impact, and concern has been raised about the coverage of death and grieving in the news media (Gamino, 2005). Of particular concern are images of violence as news content and the coverage of personal details. The phrase "If it bleeds, it leads" is said to describe and define the guiding rule of television news. Graphic images sell programs and sensationalistic stories have a longer shelf life. Violent images are used in news coverage to portray consequences of events and, as education about death and that which is valued in the society, the portrayal of those who should receive sympathy and support, those who deserve to die, who should receive our attention if missing, are all part of a possibly unintended educational process.

Saylor and his colleagues (Saylor, Cowart, Lipovsky, Jackson, & Finch, 2003) studied elementary students' media exposure to images of the 9/11 terrorist attacks. Even though the children in their study were in South Carolina and did not know anyone directly affected by the attacks, evidence of effect of television viewing of *both* positive and negative images resulted in higher levels of symptoms of posttraumatic stress disorder (PTSD). Thus, the exposure to trauma-related media images appeared to have been the trigger for higher symptoms, regardless of valence of the images. They did note that the children who developed symptoms may have been predisposed toward developing them. Saylor and his colleagues also found that the media balanced positive and negative images, so it was not that the children were exposed to primarily negative images. Therefore, the situation may be more complex than simply searching for a simple solution to negative effects.

TV and Film (fictional). Fictional death scenes in film and on television can trigger strong emotion, can emotionally engage the viewer, and can serve as a tool for discussion of death and dying. Schiappa and her colleagues (Schiappa, Gregg, & Hewes, 2004) examined the effect that college students' viewing of a television show, "Six Feet Under," had on the death attitudes. They found that viewing the program adversely affected death attitudes among students, a finding consistent with earlier studies. On the other hand, concerns among students about what happens to the body after death seemed to have lessened. As discussed earlier, television viewing is a common tool for parents to use as they address their children's questions about death. Perhaps the goal, then, should not be to desensitize people to death through the use of television but to help them explore their attitudes and beliefs.

Criticisms of fictional depictions of death, dying, and grief in the media include the fact that images presented of death are unrealistic. Meyer (2005, p. 3) looked at major films and identified several distortions: narrative shortcuts that advance the story of the revenging hero, often after the death of an innocent; a primary focus on the violent act itself; consequences that are commonly abbreviated and edited to include only glimpses, or are verbally or visually implied; in some films, violent consequences are shown in graphic and gory detail; on television, where the Federal Communications Commission, viewer complaints, and advertisers' concerns limit the range of options, images of death may be sanitized.

Cox, Garret and Graham (2004-2005) examined the depiction of death in Disney films and found the depictions of death were also unrealistic and often accompanied by some sort of moral message. Because of this moral message, they recommend that children should view these films under parental supervision, as the children may need to process, among other things, the idea of someone "deserving" to die.

The Internet. The Internet holds a unique status as a medium for communicating information regarding dying, death, and grief. Indeed, it holds a unique capacity for transmitting all other media discussed here—and more. It is possible to acquire all of the information available through print and broadcast media through the Internet. In addition, an ever-expanding variety of resources for both formal and informal death education is also available. Universities and colleges now provide online death and dying courses and professional organizations like ADEC offer webinars that provide needed information and provide continuing education units for professional advancement. Informal death education is available from a variety of resources. Open to Hope (Horsley & Horsley, 2012) and Griefnet (Lynn & Rath, 2012) are examples of resources that are directed primarily at a lay audience, providing material authored by scholars in the field, written with bereaved readers and their supporters in mind. A casual search of the Web provides an astonishing array of informational resources: static Web pages; chat rooms; bulletin board systems that may include online support groups; Web logs (i.e., blogs), which are personal web pages established by individuals to tell their personal story or to address concerns of personal interest; video diaries; podcasts; audio recordings or videos; and online book and media stores. Given the organic, growing nature of the Internet, this list may provide only a subset of available resources at the time that you are reading this chapter.

As with any form of information exchange, the quality of these resources is a concern. The information may be inaccurate or biased, information that is developmentally inaccurate or culturally insensitive, websites that are not user-friendly or are poorly designed—these can all make the use of the Internet for death education problematic, especially when used for informal death education. Sofka's (2012a) guide to evaluating the quality of informational websites is a useful tool and one we highly recommend.

Death Education, the Internet, and Returning Military Personnel

With the end of the Iraq war and the drawing down of the war in Afghanistan, military personnel are returning home, many with significant challenges. One that has received considerable attention in the media is what has been described as a suicide epidemic (c.f. Mulrine, 2012). Military personnel typically have a lower suicide rate than is found among the general population; this prevalence rate is not true for current military/veterans who have seen active duty in Iraq and Afghanistan (Kang & Bullman, 2009). Although Kang and Bullman argue that the rates do not reach epidemic proportions, others have expressed greater concern (c.f. Kuehn 2010), principally because of gaps in care provided to military and veterans and in the willingness of military personnel to avail themselves of resources (Kuehn, 2009).

Death education, as it focuses on suicide risk and suicide prevention, may prove useful in meeting the needs of returning military and veterans. At present, potential contributing factors and their role in suicide risk are hypothesized, but the evidence for their role is still uncertain (Kuehn, 2010).

Various forms of media noted earlier in this chapter serve an educational purpose for returning military and their families and many of them are available through the Internet. Also, as noted earlier, heavy dependence on news media may result in a skewed and sensationalistic view. A resource that has been established by the U.S. Department of Defense, Military OneSource (www.militaryonesource.mil), provides clear, straightforward information that is well-sourced and written for a lay audience. In addition, the website of Tragedy Assistance Program for Survivors (TAPS, www.taps.org) has been established to serve as a resource for survivors of the death of military personnel. It is, however, not as extensive as Military OneSource; it serves primarily as an access point for finding care and support.

Conclusion

Both the family and societal systems contribute to the education of family members with regard to death and behavior related to it. They make this contribution through the sharing of information, and in maintaining a structure in which collaborative meaning about death can come to be known. The societal/institutional system also contributes to the knowledge of individuals about death and related behaviors. Images of death, dying, and grief presented in the media are only partially realistic, intended to move a storyline forward, and to serve a larger purpose. Thus, caution should be taken in using these as resources for death education, in formal settings or in the family. The Internet can be seen as a cornucopia of information on dying, death, grief, and bereavement, allowing access to other forms of media for both formal and informal death education.

Chapter 39

Ethical and Legal Issues in Death Education

Carla J. Sofka

Perceptions of ethical and legal issues related to death education are quite polarized. This chapter will summarize ethical and legal issues related to death education from a range of perspectives. Literature can be categorized into contributions from two camps of authors: the advocates or believers (widely published thanatology scholars, death educators, and experienced clinicians affiliated with hospice or thanatology-oriented areas of practice) and the critics (stories published in the mass media or by conservative columnists). The absence of literature representing a third camp—the skeptics—is surprising.

Death education, once called a nasty little secret by vocal critic Phyllis Schlafly (1988), has been in the public eye for many years since Schlafly's scathing exposé and the video she helped produce with the Eagle Forum of Colorado that aired on 20/20 on September 21, 1990. Death education has also been described as an *edufad* (McKeever, 1999). Patrick Vernon Dean (1995), a death educator and advocate, was grateful to the critics for breaking the alleged silence about death education. Death education efforts continue on many levels as do the debates and discussions about ethical and legal issues connected with them.

Ethical Issues

Merriam-Webster Online (2012) defines *ethics* as "a set of moral principles or values, or a guiding philosophy," and *ethical* as "involving or expressing moral approval or disapproval as well as conforming to accepted professional standards of conduct." Ethics and ethical issues are relevant to death education from personal and professional points of view. Significant differences exist in personal and professional perceptions of the appropriateness and value of death education.

One must be mindful that remarkable variations in personal values about these topics are influenced by factors including, but not limited to, individual differences in age, life experience, cultural and religious/spiritual background, and differences in political perspectives and other societal factors. Corr (1984) notes the importance of the valuational dimension of death education—the role of death education in identifying, articulating, and affirming basic values that influence human lives and death-related issues in society. While some persons assume that fundamental values can be separated from everyday interactions with life and death (Corr, 1984), death educators must respect that "individuals bring to their educational programs experiences that have emerged from a diversity of social, cultural, and religious backgrounds" and "provide for an appreciation and utilization of individual differences" (International Work Group on Death, Dying, and Bereavement, 1992, p. 63).

There are legitimate concerns about death education that focus on (a) when does death education occur, (b) to whom and under what obligations does death education occur, (c) where does it occur and by whom it is taught, (d) what content is included, (e) how death education opportunities are delivered, and (f) how the outcomes of death education efforts are evaluated. These factors will be used to structure this examination of ethical issues related to death education.

When Does Death Education Occur?

What event might prompt an individual to seek out an opportunity for death education? Why might death education efforts be initiated to reach a specific audience? Corr and Corr (2013) note that death education can occur in three ways: formal education, informal education, and teachable moments.

Opportunities for formal or planned education are affiliated with organized instruction at levels ranging from K-12, college courses, professional and postgraduate education, in-service trainings, or workshops for clients or the general public (Corr, 2004; see also chapter 37 in this handbook). Significant concerns arise when participants are minors. If a death education opportunity is sought out by an adult capable of informed consent to participate, ethical issues may arise if the teacher is not competent or if there is a negative reaction to the course by a participant. Materials for use in death education exist for individuals of all ages, including children's books and young adult fiction that can be used in a variety of ways (Berns, 2003/2004; Markell & Markell, 2008; Sofka, 2011).

Informal education, often unplanned, is provided by parents or within family or social group interactions (see chapter 38 in this handbook). Informal education is a lifelong process of lessons learned as a result of personal experiences, the experiences of others, or exposure to thanatology-related issues through the media or travel (Corr & Corr, 2013).

Opportunities for informal education also arise as a result of teachable moments: unanticipated events in life that provide educational insights and lessons for personal growth (Corr & Corr, 2013). These moments often combine a need for support with opportunities for education about life and death. Silverman (2000a) also advocates for wisely using teachable moments in the lives of children to promote competence in dealing with loss and grief.

To Whom and Under What Obligation Does Death Education Occur?

Who is the intended audience and what are the obligations of death educators to the intended audience? The answer to these questions varies tremendously depending on the setting and the intended goals and content. Ethical issues often come into play when the target audience includes minors, when parents have not been involved in the planning, or when parental consent has not been secured prior to their children's participation.

Death education efforts for children may be a necessity in light of the situations involving loss and grief that are commonly experienced by children in our society. At what age is it appropriate for children to participate? Developmental levels of children and the readiness for children and adolescents to deal with death education topics should be carefully assessed (Gibson, Roberts, & Buttery, 1982). A child may be involved in death education at an early age due to a teachable moment combined with the presence of an adult who is comfortable discussing relevant topics and skilled at communication using age-appropriate language (e.g., Brent, 1977-78). Death education efforts for children with special needs and adults with developmental disabilities must also be tailored to account for developmental and cognitive challenges (Hoover, Markell, & Wagner, 2004/2005; Kauffman, 2005). Markell (2009) and Stevenson (2010) provide detailed discussions of death education as potential interventions for children and adolescents.

Participants of any age may have negative reactions to a death education effort. Kübler-Ross and Worden (1977-78) reported that adults attending death education workshops were people who, for professional or personal reasons, wanted to come to grips with death. The relationship between personal experience with loss and participation in death education opportunities merits consideration.

What information about students should be considered prior to their participation (Gibson, Roberts, & Buttery, 1982)? Are there contraindications for participation? Using data collected from death education classes over a span of 20 years, Brabant and Kalich (2008-2009) documented that the number of students with personal grief issues enrolled in these courses were "both substantive in number and consistent across time" (p. 15). Their findings support the following suggestions documented in previous literature that it is the responsibility of the instructor to (1) anticipate and be sensitive to the death-related experiences of their students and (2) be skilled in counseling and crisis intervention techniques or identify skilled professionals to be available for follow-up with participants for whom the experience triggers a need for support and/or access to community resources (Doka, 1981-82; International Work Group on Death, Dying, and Bereavement, 1992; Leviton, 1977). Brabant and Kalich (2008-2009) also discuss the relevance of the Code of Ethics of the Association for Death Education and Counseling (http://www.adec.org/Code_of_Ethics/1725.htm) for death educators who utilize experiential exercises in their teaching, noting the importance of respecting the student's right to determine the degree to which he or she self-discloses and the need to separate evaluation of the student from any consideration of self-disclosures made within the course. They also encourage educators to carefully consider how to ensure the confidentiality of students who self-disclose about personal experiences.

Cook, Oltjenbruns, and Lagoni (1984) explored a fascinating issue: Do death education programs have a ripple effect on individuals who do not even attend? These authors noted that "death education programs appear to serve as stimuli for death-related thoughts and conversations that extend beyond the boundaries of the instructional setting" (p. 189). Identification of these types of ripple effects and the mechanisms by which they operate is an important topic for future research.

Where Does Death Education Occur? By Whom Is it Taught?

The answers to the questions Where does death education occur? and Who is the teacher? have a significant impact on whether ethical issues are present. Key issues of debate include the implications of the setting, how the teacher is related to the student, and the qualifications and characteristics of the death educator.

Some believe that death education should not occur in schools but in the home (Noonan, 1999). Some advocate for death education within the context of religious education, health education, or family-life education (Crase, 1981; Moore, 1989; Somerville, 1971). Death education is increasingly occurring in community-based settings, through the media, and online (Cupit, 2013; Cupit, Sofka, & Gilbert, 2012; Gilbert & Murray, 2013). One's views about the appropriate setting for death education are largely influenced by the valuational component of death education previously defined (Corr, 1984). At the center of this debate is the following question: Does instruction that instills critical thinking (instead of values clarification) undermine parental authority? This important question remains to be empirically explored.

Dean (1995) found that parents and teachers, with very few exceptions, share the goal of acting in the best interests of the children. Family-life educators have been noting the importance of death education for many years, and it should be noted that life education, of which content on loss, death, and grief is included, is commonly occurring in schools in Japan (Yomiuri, 1998) and Taiwan (Wong, 2003). The view held by Dean (1995) of the parent-teacher relationship as a meeting of the minds rather than the battleground envisioned by Schlafly (1988) can guide the development of effective death education partnerships in the schools.

These partnerships can be facilitated by: (1) considering the readiness of the community and the compatibility with community value systems when selecting and/or developing appropriate curriculum materials and (2) identifying strategies to deal with moral, ethical, cultural, and religious/spiritual considerations based upon the societal and family context of students (Gibson, Roberts, & Buttery, 1982; Leaman, 1995; Markell, 2009; Stevenson, 2010). Common concerns raised by parents and community members about death education initiatives can be effectively managed by proactively involving them in the planning stages and monitoring for reactions once the initiative has been completed (Gibson, Roberts, & Buttery, 1982; Leaman, 1995; Silverman, 2000). Death education should be viewed as an ongoing process throughout the lifecycle, with responsibility shared by the home, church, other community agencies, and the schools.

The most common forums for death education on a daily basis are the print, electronic (radio, television, and online), and entertainment media. Most death professionals can readily give examples of times when the media proved a great resource, but also recall situations where individuals impacted by tragedy have been revictimized by the media during the time that they or their situation was newsworthy.

Informational support is a valuable resource that is often eagerly sought out during times of crisis or tragedy (Sofka, 2012a), and the media provides timely information of importance to the public. Stories involving thanatology issues that are sensitively and accurately written (1) can validate and normalize an experience or reaction, (2) provide valuable information about resources designed to address unmet needs, and (3) educate the public about ways to support those impacted by these events. Stevenson (1990) also notes that the media can inform the public about the benefits of death education.

The role of the entertainment media must also be recognized, and we are all recipients of death education when we begin to watch cartoons or Disney movies. Exposure has the potential to influence children's conceptions of death as well as opportunities to talk about what they have seen with peers or adults (Cox, Garrett, & Graham, 2004-2005). While the accuracy of the information gained in some cartoons is questionable (e.g., Wile E. Coyote's ability to cheat death), wonderful vehicles for death education have evolved (e.g., "Mr. Roger's Neighborhood", "Sesame Street"). According to Bader (2001), the entertainment media can also put death in the public eye, potentially influencing the way that the general public perceives death professionals.

Death education in the media can have benefits, but at whose expense? It is not difficult to find horrific examples of the insensitivity and unethical behavior by reporters and the media outlets that disseminate the stories. The media can skirt dangerously close to or cross the line of appropriateness in the process of educating the public. Books about media ethics note the fundamental conflict between the public's right to know and an individual's right to privacy (Kieran, 1997) and the challenges inherent in accountability of the media to members of the public (Pritchard, 2000).

Additional concerns involve the impact on people who are contacted by the media and the impact on viewers who are exposed to the images and content of a media report. What is the impact of media contact and the subsequent coverage that occurs on survivors of the deceased? How does exposure to crisis, tragedy, and death in the media impact individuals who have a similar experience in their past? Does repeated exposure to this content desensitize individuals to thanatology issues over time? Since research exploring the impact of exposure to images of catastrophe has identified responses ranging from increased stress and vicarious trauma (e.g., Kaplan, 2008; Propper, Stickgold, Keeley, & Christman, 2007) to transforming the viewer in a positive, prosocial manner (Kaplan, 2008), death educators have a responsibility to carefully consider how to wisely use these resources in death education efforts.

As previously noted, community death education opportunities are becoming more common and occur through local health care organizations (particularly hospice programs), senior centers, adult education programs, or even through community education offerings of local department stores. Another significant ethical issue involves the qualifications and characteristics of the death educator. Who is motivated to promote and teach death education? Some may join the field due to its popularity (Pine, 1977). Leviton and Kastenbaum (1975) wondered what kind of person is tapped to teach death. Since some death educators may self-select into this role, it is important to note that the experience of a significant loss in one's life may result in the desire to become a death educator.

There may be times when the personal lives of death educators have an impact on their professional roles and responsibilities. Noppe (2004) poignantly describes having a pedagogical out of body experience (described as being the recipient of her own death education, p. 4) while dealing with her mother's illness, death, and coping with her grief. She notes that death educators are "ultimately the survivors of our own lessons" (p. 4). Manis and Bodenhorn (2006) recognize the importance of examining the meaning making of life and death on a personal and professional level to maintain personal well-being, and Stillion (as quoted in Bordewich, 1988) believes that death educators must have training in handling their own feelings about death, dying, and loss. One's personal experience must be used without negative consequences to the students or the course, such as becoming upset or overinvolved or imposing one's own values and style (Engel, 1980-81). Wass (1995) wisely notes that personal experiences are helpful, but "they do not transform us into death educators" (p. 334).

The literature has also identified characteristics that are important for death educators to possess: (1) thorough knowledge about thanatology and the willingness to be a life-long learner in light of a constantly changing knowledge base; (2) basic knowledge about scientific study to the extent that the educator becomes an educated consumer of the research, determines its usefulness, and translates research into educational action; (3) appropriate training as a death educator to acquire competencies and techniques that are necessary for effective teaching; (4) the ability to integrate knowledge about loss with a student's developmental level; (5) sensitivity and availability to the individual needs of trainees who are intellectually challenged and/or emotionally affected by the content of the training; (6) basic communication skills and the specialized group facilitation skills required to lead discussions, raise appropriate questions, involve participants by establishing an atmosphere of trust and respect, and handle group dynamics when highly emotional or controversial topics are discussed; (7) the skill to help individuals with death-related problems and the ability to guide them to professional helpers should the need arise; and (8) responsibility and integrity, including the courage to admit when there are no clear answers or when one is ignorant (Stillion, as quoted in Bordewich, 1988; Crase, 1989; Wass, 1995; Papadatou, 1997). This author believes that *I don't know* are, in some cases, the three most important words to be able to say to students.

While the number of opportunities for continuing education/distance education about death and grief has greatly increased, the limited availability of adequate death education opportunities among the initial curriculum offerings of teachers and health professionals while earning their original degree remains a concern. Wass (1995) noted the need for systematic training and screening of death educators at all levels, but expressed concern that there is no mechanism in place to stop the individuals who enter the field (most often at the continuing education level) possessing none of the requisite knowledge, skills, and characteristics. Theoretically, anyone can teach a workshop or course to a group of unsuspecting adults as long as the participants don't ask for educational credits or want proof of the instructor's credentials (Wass, 1995). Therefore, settings offering death education opportunities have a responsibility to the students/ participants to make sure that the educator is experienced and competent. Brabant and Kalich (2008-2009) "encourage further discussion on both the ethical considerations in teaching death education at the college level as well as the development of practical guidelines and training prerequisites for those who teach these courses" (p. 16).

What Content Should be Included?

Gibson, Roberts, and Buttery (1982) noted that one of the goals of death education is "to assist individuals in the process of clarifying values related to social and ethical issues" (p. 17). The list of value-laden issues published in the early 80s is still relevant in the 21st century: euthanasia, abortion, capital punishment, and prolonging life by artificial or extraordinary means. In 1982, the following value-laden question was significant: Am I doing things that may cause me or others to die unnecessarily and prematurely? (p. 17). At the present time, this statement would need to be modified: Am I being exposed to things that are out of my control that might cause me or others to die unnecessarily and prematurely? If one lives in an urban area, the news often includes descriptions of children and youth who were killed by stray bullets or murdered by a parent or abuser. Do we as a society have an obligation to provide these murdered victims' siblings and friends with information and resources for coping with these tragic deaths and the fear that these tragedies might instill?

Three current textbooks commonly used in death education courses note in some manner a variety of value-laden issues such as suicide; euthanasia; abortion; capital punishment; quandaries posed by modern medicine and its complex technologies at the end of life as well as throughout the life span (reproductive technology, assistive technology during times of physical trauma); and other societal and global issues such as terrorism, disasters, nuclear warfare, epidemics, famine, malnutrition, genocide, and dislocation of populations (Corr & Corr, 2013; DeSpelder & Strickland, 2011; Kastenbaum, 2012). The appropriateness of including these topics in the curricula of students at various levels of education must be carefully considered. It is crucial to develop strategies to monitor the well-being and safety of students and guarantee access to appropriate resources for assistance should suicidal ideation or other types of psychological distress be experienced by participants in death education.

Regardless of the topics being included, the material must be current, accurate, and based on sound empirical research when the content merits a scientific focus. Death educators have an ethical obligation to stay current on new developments, even though this can be a daunting and time-consuming challenge. Dennett (1998) states: "Information technology has multiplied our opportunities to know, and our traditional ethical doctrines overwhelm us by turning these opportunities to know into newfound obligations to know" (p. 87).

How Should Death Education Opportunities be Delivered?

Ethical issues can also arise based on how death education opportunities are delivered and how the content is taught. While a review of the literature exploring the connection between death education and death anxiety is beyond the scope of this chapter, it must be noted that participation in a death education opportunity may result in increased anxiety about thanatology-related issues. Literature describing the impact of experiential learning vs. didactic teaching methods raises an interesting issue for debate: Is it ethical to use pedagogical strategies that increase anxiety about thanatology-related topics? The answer to this question seems to depend upon whether the participants are capable of managing the resultant anxiety, if resources are available to help participants deal with any negative consequences (Leviton, 1977), or if the educator can skillfully process role plays without turning a class discussion into a therapy session (Barton & Crowder, 1975).

In her pioneering work with computer-assisted resources for death education, Lambrecht (1991) provided death educators with innovative resources. The changing face of educational technology, particularly the prevalence of online opportunities for death education, is creating new ethical issues. A wide range of courses for students, professionals, or consumers is offered by colleges, universities, and Web-based training companies. In his discussion of social and ethical concerns regarding online learning and teaching, Brey (2006) asks a question that can be applied to online death education: Can social and cultural values be successfully transmitted in computer-mediated education? While it is wonderful to see death education becoming so accessible, this and numerous questions need to be asked and examined through sound empirical research.

Now that online teaching is proliferating, how does a death educator prepare to offer a death education opportunity online? What competencies are required to successfully implement death education opportunities that use educational technology? Death educators are encouraged to consult the growing body of literature about e-learning and web-based pedagogy for guidance (e.g., Cole, 2001; Salmon, 2003; Cupit, Sofka, & Gilbert, 2012). Continuing education opportunities about e-learning and web-based pedagogical workshops should be included at thanatology conferences and should be available online. Death educators can gain insight about online learning and distinguish between effective and ineffective strategies for Web-based teaching by participating in an online course.

One must carefully consider how existing online resources are used in death education efforts since there is no guarantee that information on a Web-based resource is accurate or reliable, and instructors have a responsibility to make sure that content utilized in death education courses meets these criteria. Consumers of online information need to become educated consumers of electronic resources (Lozano-Nieto, Guijarro, & Berjano, 2006), and students should be provided with resources to help them gain information literacy skills (e.g., Sofka, 2012b).

There are also significant differences between classroom dynamics and the dynamics of interactions in a virtual classroom. How does the absence of face-to-face interactions (between the instructor and students as well as between fellow students) influence the experiences of the students as well as the desired educational outcomes? Drawing on this author's experiences, the absence of nonverbal cues in a virtual classroom provides a simple but powerful illustration. In death education courses, it is not uncommon for students to disclose personal experiences, an act that involves some degree of emotional risk taking. Moderators are responsible for creating and maintaining a safe environment in which this type of disclosure can take place (Gorman, 2012; Salmon, 2000).

How does a moderator create and maintain this safety in a virtual classroom, where it is not possible to gauge the immediate reactions of classmates to the information that has been shared? Misperceptions can and will take place in online discussions, particularly during conversations that are asynchronous (e.g., do not occur in real time). Moderators must carefully monitor all postings for content that could be misinterpreted or content that may startle, shock, or upset other students in the class. While it is important to try to anticipate issues or situations that may create discomfort for the author of a posting or among fellow students when they read a posting, it is impossible to predict them all.

Another situation that can prove to be awkward is the inevitable posting to which few students (or no students) respond. The moderator has the ultimate responsibility to make sure that at least he or she posts a response and that efforts to facilitate discussion are consistently made in a timely manner. Gorman (2012) provides a comprehensive discussion of strategies to create a safe space for student learning in online death education offerings.

Cultural and ethical issues can arise during distance education efforts when international students are enrolled in the course (Anderson & Simpson, 2007). Language barriers may impact the degree of active participation of a student expected to communicate using a second language. Do the participation grades of students for whom English is not their native language suffer as a result of cultural differences in teaching and learning? It is important to make sure that international students are not unfairly penalized for being a stranger in a strange online land.

Ethical issues can also relate to the timeframe and timing of a death education offering. For traditional courses, it is important to schedule the course in a time slot that provides access to the instructor in a timely manner after the class ends. Opportunities for follow-up once the course is completed may also need to be considered. Time-limited death education opportunities, such as brief workshops or those provided via distance education, may present special challenges. If an instructor does not live nearby, have arrangements for contact via phone or e-mail been made? Who does the follow-up if a student experiences difficulties after a workshop or course is completed? Has the instructor made arrangements with local resources to be available? Is each distance-education student aware of local resources that can assist should the need arise? Dunn (2005) notes professional and ethical considerations and challenges related to the provision of counseling services to distance students. Administrators responsible for the scheduling and oversight of these courses and workshops must be aware of these special considerations.

How Are Outcomes Evaluated?

The evaluation of death education efforts has always presented challenges to death educators. Scholarly literature provides guidance with this task (Durlak, 1978-79; Durlak & Reisenberg, 1991; Papadatou, 1997), including guidelines for ethical issues related to thanatology research (Cook, 1995; Cupit, 2012). Research about the impact and effectiveness of death education must be conducted, particularly for courses involving students who have personal experience with loss (Balk, 1995). Alternative educational programs such as large-scale symposiums involving a variety of events and media coverage are generally not evaluated (Waldman & Davidshofer, 1983-84). Longitudinal outcome studies must also be considered since a significant limitation involves the absence of information about the long-term impact of death education on participants' professional roles (Durlak, 1978-79).

In recent years, death education through the use of "thanatechnology" (Sofka, 1997) such as distance education initiatives and continuing education via webinars, podcasts, and training DVDs has proliferated. However, the impact of the use of these strategies for death education is largely undocumented. As a result of the changes in the way that death education is being delivered, one must consider the possibility that the outcomes of the educational process may also change. Is online death education effective? Are continuing education and distance education strategies that rely on independent study methods and the use of new technologies resulting in the acquisition of the required professional knowledge and skill-based competencies?

The evaluation of death education efforts that utilize thanatechnology presents multiple challenges (Cupit, Sofka, & Gilbert, 2012). Death educators need to consider how to best evaluate their courses and these new educational tools using valid and reliable measurement strategies (e.g., Mehrotra & McGahey, 2012; Vai & Sosulski, 2011). It is also crucial for death educators to work collaboratively on empirical tools and share results as quickly as possible to facilitate the comparison of outcomes. Web-based resources provide opportunities for expedient dissemination of information, provided that the intellectual property rights that guide online publications are respected.

Death educators must also consider the following questions: How does an instructor evaluate skill-based competencies when the student has not been involved in face-to-face opportunities for direct observation and assessment? In addition to the ethical issues of academic integrity and honesty when written work and exams are submitted online, do written responses on an exam accurately reflect one's ability to effectively apply knowledge and skills in a real-world situation?

Death educators have an obligation to consider these issues and to conduct research that will either confirm that the use of technology does not compromise the desired educational outcomes or challenge death educators to consider whether online education is an appropriate method to gain skill-based competencies. The use of both online and traditional strategies may be required. Research comparing perceptions of the quality of online and traditional learning and the reasons why students prefer one type of learning environment over the other suggests that there is reason for offering more hybrid courses, that is, courses combining face-to-face and Internet interaction (Hannay & Newvine, 2006). Regan and Youn (2008) note that the rapid developments in technology that is used to teach clinical skills through Web-based learning environments "be tempered with careful planning, evaluation, and research concerning the most effective and ethical methods for delivering this type of education" (p. 111). Ethical issues regarding the education and training of clinicians who provide services via an online environment to individuals dealing with issues of dying, death, and grief also demand increased focus by death educators and mental health professionals (Gamino, 2012; Sofka, Dennison, & Gamino, 2012).

Full discussion of the multiple factors that have an impact on death education is beyond the scope of this chapter. For additional information about the impact of culture, socialization, religion/spirituality, life span issues, and the family and larger systems on death education, consult chapters 34-38 in this handbook.

Legal Issues

The distinction between ethical and legal issues related to death education appears to be a subtle one. The remainder of this chapter will focus on the following legal issues regarding death education: intellectual property rights and copyright issues, liability issues related to a negative outcome resulting from a death education opportunity, and the certification of death educators.

Intellectual property rights and copyright issues are relevant to all educators. The American Association of University Professors (AAUP) notes that these already complex issues have been further complicated by the significant growth of distance education (AAUP, 2012). Death educators have a responsibility to be familiar with not only the laws that govern these issues but also the policies and procedures governing these issues at his or her host institution. Useful summaries of matters to address in distance education policy and contract language are available from the AAUP website at http://www.aaup.org/AAUP/issues/DE/. Faculty are advised to clarify with administrators whether a faculty member retains copyright ownership of works that are created or if those works become the property of the institution and to get any agreements about ownership in writing. The development and use of new technologies always leads to uncertainty about these issues, so a wise educator with an institutional affiliation should take note of these suggestions in a proactive manner (AAUP, 2012).

Death educators must also be mindful of intellectual property rights in relation to preexisting materials that are utilized in death education courses. Death educators who taught before the advent of Blackboard, WebCT, and other online course support resources will recall that concerns about a visit from the "copyright police" could be avoided by honoring fair use policies through library reserve or preparing readings packets after securing permissions through one's institution or the staff at the local copy shop. Resources are available to help educators learn about copyright law as it relates to print, video, music, websites, and other expressive content that can liven up in-class and online teaching (e.g., Blanke, 2002; Starr, 2010; U.S. Copyright Office, 2009). Being vigilant about citing sources on course materials, PowerPoint slides, or any materials disseminated to students not only keeps you in good standing with the "copyright police" but demonstrates academic integrity and provides good role modeling for students.

In our litigious society, it is possible for death educators and the institutions in which death education occurs to be held accountable for a negative outcome that could be connected with involvement in a death education opportunity (e.g., an attempted or completed suicide after participating in a suicide prevention program; exacerbated symptoms of mental illness—depression, anxiety, post-traumatic stress—following involvement in a death education opportunity). It is important to possess the requisite knowledge and skills, ensure parental involvement of minors in the planning process, and identify strategies for being aware of the loss histories of participants in death education opportunities (which can be particularly challenging for community-based workshops or professional trainings). At a minimum, reactions to the content and process of the death education experience should be monitored. Prior to the start of a death education opportunity, mechanisms for follow-up or a process for referrals to resources for support that participants may need following completion of the death education opportunity should be in place and should be communicated clearly to participants. Evaluation of all death education efforts should occur to assess the effectiveness of the death education opportunity and to assist in identifying potentially problematic situations. Legal counsel should be involved in the review of informed consent documents that describe potential risks/potential for harm and in the creation of any relevant disclaimers. Creating a process to document the accountability of death educators has occurred in the form of certification efforts for over 20 years.

Wass (2004) noted the topic of teacher competence as particularly relevant to discussions of legal issues and death education. Do death educators have the knowledge and skills required to facilitate death education efforts that are effective?

Do they understand basic group dynamics, and are they able to create psychologically safe environments within the classroom? Is there a need to develop competencies for death educators in general or within various disciplines involved in death education? There is also a need to obtain data on death educators regarding their preparation, their competencies, continuing education that has been completed throughout their careers, and to whom they are accountable.

One strategy for assessing the competencies of death educators is the process of certification (Zinner, 1992). Thanatology-related certification has become available from a variety of sources (e.g., a Certification in Thanatology or Fellow in Thanatology from the Association for Death Education and Counseling, various certificates from the American Institute of Health Care Professionals/the American Academy of Grief Counseling, the National Center for Death Education, the American Grief Academy, Marian University, Maria College, and King's University College). Several institutions of higher education have created degree programs in thanatology (e.g., King's University College and Hood College) or concentrations in thanatology within other degree programs (e.g., Brooklyn College and Marian University). However, many of these options represent the completion of educational training designed to enhance knowledge and/or to indicate competence in the provision of services or support to those in crisis, the dying, or bereaved. Certificates allow individuals to label themselves as being certified in relation to a particular knowledge base, competency, or skill area, but are not equivalent to being licensed with the affiliated legal powers and liabilities. In addition, certification processes may not adequately evaluate the pedagogical skills of death educators. How do death educators gain pedagogical skills? What is the best way to assess the competencies and effectiveness of death educators once they are certified? These questions merit ongoing attention.

Conclusion

Implementing effective opportunities for death education that adequately and respectfully address the ethical and legal issues outlined in this chapter is a task that would present challenges for even the most experienced death educators and the organizations in which death education opportunities are delivered. Wass (1995), a respected death educator and scholar, stated: "I have tried for the past fourteen years to become a good death educator. I am still trying" (p. 334). May we all, with humility and grace, accept the fact that the knowledge base for thanatology is constantly growing and willingly adopt Wass's philosophy of lifelong learning as we strive to become the best death educators that we can be.

Three Overarching Indicators Within Fundamental Knowledge of Thanatology

Introduction to Part 7, Chapters 40 – 42

Chapters 40 through 42 focus on three overarching indicators: professional issues, resources, and the Internet. The Body of Knowledge Committee defined professional issues in this way: **factors that affect professionals' training, abilities, and responsibilities in providing care.** Resources **involve materials, organizations, and groups of individuals that facilitate knowledge acquisition. Ideas and materials are based upon the findings of empirical research and theoretical synthesis that add to the knowledge base.** The Body of Knowledge has yet to address the influence and function of the Internet.

The authors of these three chapters have synthesized information sources that cut across the six major categories of dying, end-of-life decision making, loss, grief, and mourning, assessment and intervention, traumatic death, and death education. Chapters 40 and 41 are revised from the contributions that appeared in the first edition of the handbook. Chapter 42 is wholly new and reflects the growing awareness of the pervasive influence and power of the Internet in matters thanatological.

Chapter 40

Professional Issues and Thanatology

Carol Wogrin

The field of thanatology has changed dramatically over the past few decades. Medical advances that enable us to keep people alive in the face of life-threatening illnesses create a vast array of challenges and responsibilities for the professionals providing care. Models of care for the dying have developed significantly since the start of the modern day hospice movement with the establishment of St. Christopher's Hospice by Cicely Saunders England in 1967, as discussed in detail in chapters 3 and 5. Efforts to provide palliative care in countries across the globe have steadily increased, particularly over the past couple decades. Development of the theoretical understanding of the grief process, as described in chapters 16 and 23 brought about a fundamental paradigm shift that consequently altered clinical practice. Such rapid change in the field over such a relatively short time span places significant responsibility on the caregiver to keep his or her knowledge base up to date, including general knowledge of the field of thanatology and the body of knowledge specific to his or her own discipline and area of practice with in the field.

When providing end-of-life and bereavement care, professional caregivers need to possess in-depth knowledge, experience, and skills in order to be able to attend to a wide variety of specific and often complicated circumstances (International Work Group on Death, Dying, and Bereavement, 2006). While the volume of information has grown significantly, as has the knowledge base in many areas, the foundational skills required in order to provide optimal care to the dying and the bereaved remains the same. In a report by the Institute of Medicine (Field & Cassel, 1997), the authors identify the requirements of professionals who provide care at the end of life. These requirements include strong interpersonal skills, along with clinical knowledge and technical proficiency that is informed by scientific evidence, values, and personal and professional experience. This report stresses the responsibility that health care professionals have for educating themselves and the larger community regarding good care for the dying and their families.

Areas identified that are important to professional preparation across disciplines include the following.

Interpersonal skills and attitudes, including:
- listening to patients, families, and other members of the health care team
- conveying difficult news
- understanding and managing patient and family responses to illness
- providing information and guidance on prognosis and options
- sharing decision making and resolving conflicts
- recognizing and understanding one's own feelings and anxieties about dying and death
- cultivating empathy
- developing sensitivity to religious, ethnic, and other differences

Ethical and professional principles, including:
- doing good and avoiding harm
- determining and respecting patient and family preferences
- being alert to personal and organizational conflicts of interests
- understanding societal/population interests and resources
- weighing competing objectives or principles
- acting as a role model of clinical proficiency, integrity, and compassion

Organizational skills, including:
- developing and sustaining effective professional teamwork
- understanding relevant rules and procedures set by health plans, hospitals, and others
- learning how to protect patients from harmful rules and procedures
- assessing and managing care options, settings, and transitions
- mobilizing supportive resources (e.g., palliative care consultants, community-based assistance)
- making effective use of existing financial resources and cultivating new funding sources

It is critical that clinicians stay current in their knowledge base in the rapidly growing field of thanatology. As models of care for the dying have evolved over the past few decades, so too has the field's understanding of the grief process and needs of the bereaved. Chapter 16 discusses the shift in the theoretical framework from understanding grief as a process oriented toward disconnecting from the deceased to one that recognizes the importance of continuing bonds with the deceased. This shift in thinking subsequently alters the ways in which we approach intervention with the bereaved. We are only beginning to understand the ways in which the professional community can support the bereaved, including identifying who benefits from what kind of intervention as discussed in chapter 23. To date there are as many questions as there are answers.

While important, keeping up to date on current understanding and empirically based recommendations for practice can be very challenging to do. There presently exists a significant gap between research and clinical practice (Bridging Work Group, 2005; Devilly, Gist, & Cotton, 2006). Many practitioners regard much of the available research as holding little relevance for their work. Likewise, many researchers believe that clinical practice has little to contribute to the scientific study of bereavement (Bridging Work Group, 2005). Given the expanding field, including issues such as the evolving empirical evidence that challenges assumptions about effective strategies for caring for the bereaved, as discussed in chapter 23, this gap is particularly problematic. In recent years, efforts to address this gap are increasing. One such example is work by Neimeyer, Harris, Winokuer, and Thornton (2011). The chapters of their book *Grief and Bereavement in Contemporary Society: Bridging Research and Practice* pair researchers and clinicians, with the specific intent of bringing the research and clinical domains closer together. Of note, though, Neimeyer and Harris (2011) report that the attempt to do so was not entirely smooth or without its challenges, with doubt being expressed by professionals on both sides of the dialogue regarding such efforts.

An example of an area where both practice and research have been developing along somewhat parallel and nonintersecting tracks is that of community crisis response to traumatic death. Hospices and bereavement professionals are often called to support organizations and larger communities when traumatic deaths occur. The bereavement needs of people in the immediate aftermath of public tragedy have aspects that are unique to this sort of event. Those who will respond to these requests have a responsibility to have appropriate training in crisis response as well as the knowledge and experience to adapt the intervention to the type of trauma being addressed (Homan, 2005). Training in crisis response can be obtained from several different organizations including the International Critical Incident Stress Foundation (www.icisf.org), the American Red Cross (www.redcross.org), and the National Organization for Victims Assistance (www.nova.org) (Homan, 2005).

However, there is a gap between clinical practices and the growing body of empirical data that challenge the beliefs and assumptions surrounding the intervention strategies. Devilly, Gist, and Cotton (2006) examined the literature involving psychological debriefing. They identify significant disagreement between clinicians who employ models of crisis management and the research data regarding the effectiveness of these models. They conclude that while the serious literature of psychology and related disciplines has increasing evidence that brings into question the effectiveness of traditional debriefing practices, information flowing to consumers about debriefing has been almost solely in the domain and control of intervention proponents. As a result, there are conflicting bodies of information, one presenting objective, refereed, independent assessments of measured efficacy, and another, which is dominated by a social movement attempting to argue those accumulating data away. The fact that the discrepancy is intensifying over time is a troubling indicator of a schism between research and practice, with academic psychologists becoming detached from the realities of application and practice, and many practitioners becoming progressively more estranged from the empirical underpinnings of their discipline (Devilly, Gist, & Cotton, 2006).

Crisis response in communities is merely one example of the prevalent gap between research and practice in the field of thanatology. In the time to come, it is the responsibility of both researchers and practitioners to close this gap. Efforts will need to include recognition of how much each group has to learn from the other, as well as the development of collaborative models for sharing information, increasing theoretical understanding, and investigating the effectiveness of various interventions (Bridging Work Group, 2005).

In addition to maintaining an up-to-date knowledge base, good communication skills are fundamental to the role and responsibility of the professional caregiver. These skills include the ability to use active listening and empathic understanding of an individual's internal and social world (International Work Group on Death, Dying, and Bereavement, 2006). In order to communicate effectively and responsibly, as discussed in chapter 7, the caregiver must have a solid understanding of and pay close attention to issues of culture. Culture informs a person's beliefs and values surrounding illness and death, the experience of pain, beliefs about sharing information about dying, the interpretation of the ethical imperative for truth telling, and practices around care and disposal of the body (Koenig and Gates-Williams, 1995). It is extremely important that professionals working with death and grief have an awareness of the influence of culture on their own beliefs, values, and biases as well as maintaining an awareness of cultural beliefs and values in the people to whom they are providing care. As medical advances result in increasingly more options for treatment, and therefore choices to be made, it is important for caregivers to have an understanding of the interplay between culture and the ethics of caring when working with the dying, their families, and the bereaved.

Practitioners working in the field of thanatology also have responsibility to develop expertise in understanding the dynamics of the caregiver/client relationship. Throughout the remainder of this chapter, the term *caregiver* is used exclusively to refer to professional caregivers.

Working with the dying and bereaved is not something that people do simply because they can't find another job or because it's an easy way to keep a roof over their head and food on the table. Rather, people elect to work in the field for a variety of personal and professional reasons, but generally central to the choice is the belief that the work is meaningful and the experience of the work being rewarding. Professionals who work in the field know what a gift it is for people to allow them into their worlds at such difficult and important times, allowing caregivers to share in some of the most meaningful and intimate moments of their lives. Every day, professional caregivers to the dying and the bereaved are reminded of the transient nature of life, and consequently the importance of appreciating and making use of the life we have while we have it. However, with the rewards come some significant challenges and responsibilities. Caregivers have a responsibility to their patients, clients, and to themselves to understand and attend to the dynamics of the caregiving relationship and the impact this relationship has on the patient as well as on him- or herself. While many professional issues for caregivers are common to most service professions, some issues take on particular importance when working with matters surrounding death, and others are unique to the field of thanatology. The remainder of this chapter will explore the concepts involved and their application to practice.

The challenge to the professional is to be aware of a number of factors that comprise a therapeutic relationship. These factors include the inherent power and authority of the caregiver; the vulnerability of the client; the opportunity to help; the potential to harm; the feelings, behavior, and perceptions of the client; the professional's own feelings and behavior; and the impact these can have on the client (Sheets, 1999). Daily, thousands of nurses, social workers, psychologists, physicians, counselors, clergy, nursing assistants, physical therapists, volunteers, and many others provide care to those who are suffering and in need. These professionals must negotiate a delicate interplay between the needs and expectations of the patients with their own unspoken needs and expectations (Arbore, Katz, & Johnson. 2006).

An understanding of the therapeutic relationship relies, in part, on the professional caregiver having an understanding of self and what he or she brings to the relationship. When working with death and grief, it is important that the professional be aware of his or her own relationship to death and personal values and belief system about death, grief and mourning. Personal experience of death and significant loss will influence such awareness, values, and beliefs. It is helpful to spend some time thinking about one's own experiences. Professionals should ask themselves the following questions.

- What are the significant losses that I've experienced?
- How did I react and how did those around me react?
- What have I learned about death and grief from my experiences?
- What are my religious and/or spiritual beliefs about death?
- What are my cultural beliefs and assumptions about the expressions of grief, e.g., that it is respectful and "strong" to stay contained and keep a stiff upper lip or that it is respectful to the deceased and healthy to emote intense emotion?
- Based on my experiences, what do I believe and what assumptions do I make about what people need from others as they cope with grief and loss?

When working with issues surrounding death, the professional caregiver is working with people during some of the most emotionally charged and vulnerable times in their lives. In order to offer the kind of support, understanding, and empathy that is needed when someone is dying or coping with the death of a loved one, a professional needs to be emotionally open and willing to get very close to intense and difficult emotions. Because death and grief are universal, caregivers likely have experienced the death of people they love and/or have had other significant losses, as well as knowing they will face the death of people they love. They could easily find themselves in the position of the person they are working with. The personal feelings of the professional may easily be tapped into when coming up against the feelings of the other person. Tapping into one's own feelings can serve as the basis for empathy, but can also run the risk of confusing one's own feelings with those of the client. Because of this possibility, it is imperative that caregivers work diligently to be aware of their own feelings so that they don't confuse their own needs with those of the client or patient.

Being aware of one's own feelings can help caregivers make appropriate and responsible choices in interactions with clients. Personal feelings of the caregiver, referred to as countertransference in the mental health fields, may manifest in many ways, including feelings of nervousness, anxiety, or anger, and can help a person connect with those who suffer. By viewing countertransference as a tool for understanding the patient, the dynamic in the relationship and oneself, rather than as an obstacle, a professional can become a better helper to those for whom he or she provides care (Arbore et al., 2006). However, at times it can be very difficult to remain truly present with a person who is suffering or in intense levels of emotional pain. In an attempt to feel emotionally safe, or cope with their own feelings of helplessness, helpers may retreat from the pain of their clients, by becoming "professional" or objective. This manner of coping often manifests as distancing or aloofness. By remembering that simply our presence and caring can be a healing experience for our patients, we can often sustain ourselves during those emotionally challenging situations (Arbore, et al., 2006).

It is helpful to those in the caring professions to recognize countertransference responses to suffering. Abore et al. (2006) offers a list of responses that are common but unhelpful.

- Helplessness (Caregivers may distance themselves by becoming over or under-involved.)
- Shame and embarrassment (Caregivers may look the other way and not see the suffering.)
- Denial and the wish for it to go away (Helpers may convince themselves that talking about it, seeing it, will contribute to or increase the pain or suffering.)
- Anger and hostility (If unaware of their own anger at the disease or the inability to change things, helpers can displace anger into the helping situation.)
- Sorrow (Deep sorrow can make it hard for the helper to maintain a connection because of being too involved in one's own suffering.)
- Restlessness (Caregivers may impose their own agenda, letting it take precedence over the needs of the client.)

Professional Boundaries

In addition to understanding one's own experiences, feelings, and other reactions, a professional caregiver must develop an understanding of the dynamics of a professional-client/patient relationship. First and foremost is the importance of understanding the concept of professional boundaries. The concept of boundaries is an important one to anyone in any kind of professional caregiving situation or position, but never more so than when working with death and grief. Boundaries can be defined simply as the margins of appropriate behavior (Gutheil & Gabbard, 1998) or as the lines we draw to help us define our roles and interactions in relationships (Leurquin-Hallett, 1999). The establishment of clear boundaries is designed to create an atmosphere of safety and predictability and allow for a therapeutic connection between the practitioner and the client (Gutheil & Gabbard, 1998; Sheets, 1999). These boundaries can be expressed in physical, social, or psychological terms (Martsolf, 2002).

Ethical guidelines for practice help establish the line around appropriate behavior that one should not step over. Where this line is drawn is defined by many different factors, including the discipline within which a person practices, the setting a person practices in, e.g. a facility versus home care, or city versus a small rural area, as well as one's culture. It is the responsibility of the professional to establish the boundaries at the outset of the relationship and maintain them for the duration of the relationship. The rules for appropriate behavior usually include guidelines for contact, including how much, how often, and method; types of information to be shared; physical closeness; and the setting in which the interactions may occur (Martsolf, 2002). There is an inherent power dynamic in caregiving relationships that makes issues of ethical practice and clear boundaries particularly important. Simon (1995a) offers five principles regarding the establishment of boundaries. First is the rule of abstinence—a professional must abstain from personal gratification at the client's expense. This principle is the foundation on which the other principles rest. Working with the dying and the bereaved is often personally gratifying to the professional as he or she is in the role of offering support at a time when it is needed acutely and in a position of helping diminish or alleviate suffering. However, in keeping with this principle, any gratification for the caregiver should come from accurately understanding and then appropriately meeting the needs of another person. It is imperative that the action and communication always be oriented toward the client's needs, and that the client is never asked, in any way, to attend to the emotional needs of the professional caregiver. Second is the duty to neutrality— not to interfere in a client's personal relationships. When working with the dying, in hospice or other settings, caregivers may work with people over long periods of time and frequently in times of crisis or other emotionally demanding times. While crisis can bring people closer together, it can also exacerbate the differences in coping styles or perhaps longstanding conflicts in families. When caregivers offer a listening ear and the therapeutic relationship grows it can be seductive for the caregiver to be in the position of the "chosen one," the confidant, the one who understands. While it is important to offer a listening ear and emotional support, the caregiver must also keep an eye to not encouraging the patient to lean on him or her as a way to avoid working things out between family members, stepping into a position that should be occupied by available family members or other social supports, or in taking sides in family conflicts. Adherence to the first principle helps in maintaining the second. Third is the promotion of client autonomy and self-determination. It is important for the professional to recognize and support a patient's strength and competence, regardless of his or her physical decline from illness and the consequent losses, and not encourage dependence because it makes the caregiver feel important. Fourth is the fiduciary relationship, the contract with the client that the professional will serve to protect. There is a contract between the patient and caregivers that mandates the professional to uphold recognized standards of care. Also, the fact that the client/patient is paying for services, directly or through his or her insurance, helps create a power dynamic in the caregiving relationship. Payment for services means that there is a skill or expertise that the relationship is oriented around. Those who provide the expertise are in the position of power and authority, and that position must be treated with care and respect. Fifth is the respect for human dignity. In order to respect the human dignity of a person who is dying or bereaved, professionals must do their best to understand a client's cultural view, his or her values and belief system, and base interactions on this understanding.

Whether due to blatant disregard for ethical principles on the part of the caregiver, carelessness, or lack of understanding, inevitably there will, at times, be problems with maintaining professional boundaries. Boundary transgressions can be understood in two important ways: as boundary crossing and boundary violations (Gutheil & Gabbard, 1998; Sheets, 1999). Boundary crossings are "brief excursions across boundaries that are often inadvertent or thoughtless" (Sheets, 1999, p. 657). When recognized, the boundary crossing must be pulled back from and the implications and consequences evaluated (Sheets, 1999, 2000). Boundary violations occur when there is confusion between the needs of the professional and the needs of the client. These violations can be in the form of excessive personal disclosure on the part of the professional, reversal of roles, accepting personal favors, or sexual misconduct. Boundary violations make up the highest number of complaints to the Ethics Committee of the American Psychological Associaton (Knapp & Slattery, 2004). Boundary violations and boundary crossings may not be recognized by the client or the professional until the development of harmful consequences (Sheets, 1999). Most practitioners understand the more obvious and clear boundary violations, such as engaging in sexual relations with a client. However, there are other more subtle boundary violations and crossings that are not always as clear, such as sharing personal information that shifts the focus from the needs of the client to the needs of the caregiver, or visiting clients outside of work hours. With these violations it is more common or easier for practitioners to justify their actions as being in the interest of the client.

One of the important methods that help maintain clear boundaries is to have clearly spelled out goals for care and a plan for the achievement of those goals. When the delivery of care stays directed toward the goals and care plan, boundary violations are less likely to occur (Martsolf, 2002). For example, when professionals are working for hospice as a member of an interdisciplinary team, focusing on the benefits and strength of a team and the role the different team members have in meeting the physical, emotional, and spiritual goals of care will help avoid the risk of one person slipping into a special position and functioning as if only he or she can meet the needs of an individual or family.

There are a number of reasons to guard against boundary crossings, some of which may be less obvious and others are easier to justify as being in the best interest of the client. When working with people with life-threatening illnesses, professional relationships can get very close. Long-term illnesses and the treatment protocols for many conditions, whether in a clinic, hospital, nursing home, inpatient hospice, or home care, result in professionals and patients spending a lot of time together over long periods of time. As the relationships develop and difficult, as well as pleasurable, life experiences are shared, familiarity and potentially deep connections develop. Unlike in social friendships, however, in a close professional-patient relationship there should not be a reciprocity that includes the sharing of the professional's concerns and problems, which would burden the patient (Peteet, Ross, Medeiros, Walsh-Burke, & Rieker, 1992). Over involvement can also result in decreased objectivity in decision making and in adequately keeping one's own feelings in check (Docherty, Miles, & Brandon, 2007). Another problem inherent in shifting to the role of that of a friend can lead to making promises you can't keep (Taylor, 1998). For example, if boundaries are crossed and a friendship develops in a relationship with someone who is ill and receiving treatment that will end, or with a family member of a terminally ill person, the implication or expectation is that the friendship will continue after the professional role ends. However, the work demands on the caregiver continue, new patients will need attention, and the caregiver may find himself or herself less inclined to make the time for an ongoing relationship. Or, the patient who is used to the relationship revolving around their needs may feel burdened, betrayed, or violated when the professional begins to expect the reciprocity of support for his or her own problems that is typical of a friendship.

Often times, professionals who cross the appropriate boundary and enter into a social relationship rationalize their choice, maintaining that the situation is unique and that, for one reason or another, it is in the best interest of the client/patient, or what the client wants. However, these relationships tend to be exploitive; they cross the boundaries of ethical practice, serve the needs of the practitioner, and impair his or her judgment. The practitioner's power and client's vulnerability carry over from the professional to the personal relationship. When the shift occurs, a practitioner's power remains but is no longer checked by professional rules of conduct (Kagle & Giebelhausen, 1994).

An important issue in a caregiving relationship that is often very challenging for professionals is that of self-disclosure. In end-of-life care, where relationships may be long-term, very close in nature, and often take place in homes, there may be an inclination on the part of the caregiver to share details of his or her own life as part of sharing himself or herself in his or her work. The problem with self-disclosure, regardless of how insignificant it seems or whether it is information specifically requested by the patient, is that it shifts the attention from the patient to the caregiver, and in the long run, does not serve the patient.

With the changes in the health care delivery system over the past couple decades, health care is more often provided in community settings and homes, which increases the possibility of blurring boundaries between patient and professional caregiver and between professional and social activities (Martsolf, 2002). Knapp and Slattery (2004) identified three specific concerns for professionals who deliver services in client's homes. First is that boundary crossings are more likely to occur when services are provided in homes rather than institutions. Second is that the nature of home-based services provides a professional with more opportunities to act out or step outside professional boundaries, and third is that people working with clients in their homes are more likely to drift into a more social relationship rather than maintaining a strictly defined professional one. Because of these challenges, the importance of professional training and ongoing supervision can't be overestimated. That said, not all disciplines view supervision similarly, and it is not always easy to get people to embrace the practice (Firth, 2011).

It is important to highlight that the type of community in which a person practices warrants attention, as it has a bearing on the way in which a person must think about boundaries. The theory and understanding of professional boundaries has, to some degree, been developed with an eye to urban and more densely populated suburban areas. The idea that a professional's personal life can be kept completely separate from professional-client relationships assumes a level of anonymity and control on the part of the professional that does not exist in rural or geographically isolated areas. In rural areas where the professional will see clients in the grocery story, attend the same church, have children in the same class at school, and serve on the same community committees, the practitioner has less control over what's known about his or her own life (Helbok, Marinelli, & Walls, 2006). In sparsely populated areas there is not the luxury of referring a client to another professional whose personal life does not overlap with that of the client. In these settings, the importance of addressing boundary issues with clients takes on a new form. Informed consent is of importance in a new way, with the professional discussing with the client the implications and limits of meeting in social settings and finding a way to keep the professional relationship separate, establishing clearly with a client at the beginning of the relationship the rules for in-office and out-of-office boundaries (Helbok et al., 2006). Issues of confidentiality and dual relationships all need to be carefully addressed.

It is imperative that a professional always engage in conscious self-monitoring, to be sure that he or she doesn't inadvertently cross boundaries or fail to notice if he or she begins shifting from giving good compassionate care based on the needs of a client, to a relationship in which his or her own needs and personal gratification are moving to the fore. There are red flags, or warning signs, in a caregiver's behavior that are easy to spot when paying attention (Sheets, 1999; Taylor, 1998). These include:

- excessive self-disclosure on the part of the professional caregiver, including discussing personal problems or aspects of intimate life
- beliefs on the part of the professional that he or she is the only one who can meet the client's needs
- giving out a home phone number and encouraging patients to depend on him or her instead of working with other members of the health care team
- repeated or lengthy calls to patients outside of working hours
- inviting patients or families to join him or her in activities outside work
- selective communications, where the professional reports selectively on a client's behavior, gives double messages, provides care with a level of secrecy
- buying gifts for or accepting gifts from patients or families
- lending money or personal belongings
- failure on the part of the professional to seek supervision when the professional is aware of a risk or occurrence of a boundary crossing or violation

Risks Inherent in the Work

While the work of caring for the dying and the bereaved is very rewarding, there are ways that working with this population is uniquely challenging and can have an impact on the caregiver. Professionals must develop high levels of self-awareness and appreciation of the stressors inherent in this work in order to avoid suffering from the various stressors.

Part of the risk inherent in the work has its basis in empathy. Empathy can be defined as the therapist's "ability and willingness to understand the client's thoughts, feeling, and struggles from the client's point of view" (Rogers, 1980, p. 85). Offering support to someone who is dying or coping with the death of a loved one requires a professional to be willing to get very close to intense and difficult emotions and develop an empathic understanding of an individual's internal and social world (International Work Group on Death, Dying, and Bereavement, 2006). Technological advancement over the past couple decades has increased our understanding of the neurophysiological aspect of empathy and shed new light on our understanding of why empathy can pose risks.

Drawing from work of researchers in the 1990s, Rothschild (2006) examines explanations for what makes it possible to vicariously feel what another person is feeling. An important finding was the identification through the use of brain scans of what are now called *mirror neurons*. Brain scans revealed that, not only do specific portions of our brains light up when we perform various activities or have certain emotional experiences, these same portions light up when we observe someone carrying out an activity or expressing emotion. In other words, on a neurological level we are wired to react as if an observed experience of another were our own.

It is not surprising, then, that when engaged empathically with someone who has experienced a trauma or perceived threat, we respond as if we were also being threatened. The portion of our nervous system that regulates the fight or flight response will be activated. We become hyper alert, with increased heart and respiration rate, elevated blood pressure, and dilated pupils; blood is shifted to the skeletal muscles so they are ready to react. When the threat is passed, another portion of the nervous system slows everything down, including heart rate and respiration, and sends blood away from the muscles and to the internal organs. However, when neither flight nor fight is possible, the brain continues to sound the alarm, resulting in persistent symptoms of stimulation, and hallmark symptoms of PTSD: hypervigilance, exaggerated startle response, and difficulty falling or staying asleep.

The phenomenon of synchrony between people, including responses such as synchronized heart rates between therapists and clients, as tension in sessions is raised and lowered is well-documented (Rothschild, 2006). This nervous system synchronicity is a central component to somatic empathy. The experience of being able to lower the anxiety level of a client by slowing down one's own breathing is a familiar experience to many practicing clinicians (Rothschild, 2006). Anyone who has spent time listening to the experiences of the bereaved, knows the traumatic quality to many of the stories. Significant loss poses a threat to the attachment system, and hence, to one's sense of safety and security. Due to this threat, clients are likely to be in a state of arousal when sharing their stories of suffering and trauma. Therapists empathically joined with them are likely to be as well. The challenge to the therapist is to be consciously attuned to his or her own somatic state and develop the skills of being able to bring himself or herself down from the aroused state at the end of a session and end of a day. This attention to one's own response to therapeutic empathy is likely a critical factor in managing the stresses inherent in the work over long periods of time.

Over the past couple decades, there has been a growing understanding of the effect that working with the suffering of others can have on the caregiver (Figley, 1995; Meadors & Lamson, 2008). In her work on stress of professional caregivers, Vachon (2004, p. 992) states, "Not only do patients and their families suffer distress when confronting terminal illness, but so do those who care for them. The professional who cares and empathizes with patients and their families can experience significant stress in response to working with dying persons as well as in response to the death of particular patients." She goes on to note that the stress may be due to a variety of internal factors, such as previous or current life experiences, personal death experience, too much emotional investment in patients without sufficient replenishment over too long a time, or from feelings of powerlessness and lack of control in the health care system.

If professional caregivers fail to develop adequate professional boundaries, as discussed earlier, or adequately attend to their own states and skills to manage these boundaries, two different forms of caregiver stress may develop. The professional may experience burnout or compassion fatigue. While these terms are sometimes used synonymously, they are actually somewhat different, and it is helpful to be aware of the risks of both.

Burnout

Systems issues in the workplace can place a person at risk of high levels of stress, resulting in burnout. These stressors include high demands placed on individuals, unrealistic expectations of workload, limited or inadequate resources, or limited professional support. Burnout can be defined as a state of physical, emotional and mental exhaustion, depersonalization, and reduced personal accomplishment caused by long-term involvement in emotionally demanding situations (Maslach,1982). The emotional demands are usually caused by high expectations combined with chronic situational stress (Pines & Aronson, 1988).

Burnout tends to be high when professionals perceive a low level of control over the care they provide, whether that's due to authoritarian supervisors, lack of input into policies that govern a person's job, or being given more responsibility or higher work volume than a person feels like he or she can handle (Maslach, 1982). Hospice and palliative care staff, specifically, were found to experience increased stress when workloads were unrealistic, level of involvement in decision making was low, and social support was not available (Vachon, 2004). In her study on occupational stress in caregivers for the terminally ill, Vachon (1987) noted that despite her expectations that much of the stress experienced by caregivers would be related to their interactions with patients, she found that this expectation was not the case. Most of the stress experienced was attributed to the work environment and occupational role rather than the direct work with dying patients and their families.

Compassion Fatigue

Elements of burnout can be seen in all professional settings. A unique form of it, labeled compassion fatigue, is directly linked to people in caregiving professions (Joinson, 1992). Compassion fatigue can be defined as a pattern of tiredness and emotional depletion from too much caring and too little self-caring (Ochberg, 1998). Other terms for the concept include compassion stress, secondary traumatic stress, or vicarious traumatization. Figley (1995, p. 7) defines the concept of secondary traumatic stress as "the natural consequent behaviors and emotions resulting from knowing about a traumatizing event experienced by a significant other—the stress resulting from helping or wanting to help a traumatized or suffering person." Working with the dying and the bereaved is emotionally demanding work. Hospice workers, palliative care professionals, and others who provide care for people with life-threatening conditions frequently come up against high levels of suffering in the people they care for. Professional work that is centered on the emotional suffering of clients includes absorbing information that is about suffering. Absorbing the information about suffering often includes absorbing that suffering itself as well (Figley, 1995, 2002).

Figley (1995b) contended that therapists who have enormous capacity for feeling and expressing empathy—in short, the most effective therapists—are the ones who tend to be at highest risk of being adversely effected by the experiences of their clients, since they are the most likely to absorb the pain and traumatization of their clients. More recently, researchers are challenging this formulation, suggesting that it is not empathy, per se, that causes compassion fatigue, but rather, what a person does with the empathy they experience.

Considering the view that we respond empathically on a physiological level to the clients we sit with, Rothschild (2006) asserts that the problem in terms of compassion fatigue seems to be not one of too much empathy, but rather, the inability to turn it off when done. Therefore, caregiving professionals are at particular risk of developing compassion fatigue if they are exclusively focused on the suffering of others and unaware of the state of their own body and mind. This notion is supported by various findings that a high level of empathic engagement serves as a protective practice for clinicians who worked with traumatized clients, providing it was in conjunction with a high level of self-awareness and clarity about interpersonal boundaries, enabling the therapist to get very close without confusing the clients' experience with his or her own (Harrison & Westwood, 2009; Weininger & Kearney, 2011).

Strategies for Avoiding and Managing Compassion Fatigue

There is a growing body of literature addressing strategies to help avoid developing or to ameliorate caregiver stress. However, there is limited empirical examination of the efficacy of teaching these strategies (Paris & Hoge, 2010), and the evidence that does exist is somewhat equivocal. The primary characteristic that does receive consistent empirical support is that of self-awareness (Harrison & Westwood, 2009; Kearney, 2009; Rothschild, 2006; Wicks, 2008). Likewise, strategies that foster the development of self-awareness, such as mindfulness meditation and reflective journaling, have received empirical support as well (Shapiro, Astin, Bishop, & Cordova, 2005; Harrison & Westwood, 2009). These findings are in keeping with the paradigm for compassion fatigue described by Rothschild (2006). If a person is self-aware, including of his or her somatic responses, there is a much greater likelihood that he or she will be able to avoid patterns that lead to chronic stress. Heightened self-awareness will also play an important role when working with the bereaved in terms of managing the task of keeping personal losses and difficult emotions separate from those of clients.

Woven through the literature on self-care is a range of cognitive and behavioral approaches. While empirical support for the effectiveness of these strategies is limited, they are ones that make a certain amount of intuitive sense. They can be divided into three categories: professional, personal, and organizational strategies. It is reasonable to believe that these strategies are more effective if employed by a therapist with a good level of self-awareness. It is also feasible that inattention to the variable of self-awareness is a factor in the sometimes contradictory research findings on efficacy.

Professional strategies include those aimed at a person's professional identity and activity. An important strategy is the development and maintenance of clear professional boundaries (Pearlman & Saakvitne, 1995; Rourke, 2007). These limits include both interpersonal boundaries, which provide a protective function by helping professionals not take on the suffering of their clients as their own, and boundaries that help to keep a clear line between work and home. Professionals able to set time limits on their work and keep their work life separate from their home life manage their stress much more effectively over time (Ablett & Jones, 2007; Becvar, 2003; Davies et al., 1996; Meadors & Lamson, 2008).

Because of the nature of many of the stresses in our work, it is important to have social support from colleagues. Workplace support is important because it is our colleagues who understand the rewards of the work and the reasons we are in this field. So, too, are they the ones who best understand the losses and related stress we experience in this context (Davies, et al., 1996; Papadatou, 2002; Vachon, 2007).

The second category is that of personal strategies. Having a number of ways to nurture oneself is necessary to counterbalance the affects of the stresses inherent in work with the dying and the bereaved. Practices that develop self-awareness, such as meditation, journaling, or psychotherapy are of high importance. Time away from work needs to be used to focus on things other than attending to the suffering of others. Social supports in one's personal world, separate from work, are important because they allow people to develop aspects of themselves that are not about caregiving (Figley, 2002a). Behaviors that support physical, emotional, and spiritual health are central to preventing or managing compassion fatigue (Becvar, 2003; Holland & Neimeyer, 2005; Joinson, 1992; Meadors & Lamson, 2008). These nurturing strategies include adequate rest; nutrition; exercise; and activities such as meditation, journaling, and developing a strong social network. Spiritual well-being may be enhanced through activities such as spending time in nature or engaging in a religious practice. Humor offers another way of reducing the effects of stress (Ablett & Jones, 2007; Welsh, 1999).

Finally, organizational efforts to develop systems for staff support are important (Davies et al., 1996; Figley, 2002a; Meadors & Lamson, 2008). Thompson (2011) makes a strong case for attention to the role that organizational issues play in caregiver stress, as it is impossible to adequately address systems issues on a person level. Additionally, it is important to attend to both formal organizational support, such as adequate leave time, supervision, and ongoing educational trainings, as well as informal support, such as the development of an organizational culture that values staff relationships, promotes job satisfaction, and recognizes the need to attend to the stressors inherent in the work (Maasdorp, 2011). Without this support from organizations and institutions, it is too easy to overtly or covertly frame caregiver stress as a weakness in the individual rather than as a normal response to problems in the system or in the work.

Chapter 41

Resources and Research in Thanatology

Melissa Bell, Gordon Thornton, and Mary Lou Zanich

It is vital for certified thanatology professionals of all kinds to keep abreast of current research and be familiar with important resources provided by national and local organizations in the field. For clinicians, such resources may be an adjunct to counseling. For instance, a self-help group experience might add to individual therapy, and written materials can provide the foundation for psychoeducational aspects of therapy. For educators, such resources may aid in teaching about dying, death, and bereavement. Moreover, individuals who are facing a crisis in dying or bereavement often seek out educators to recommend resources that might be helpful.

A few provisos must be noted. First, the purpose of this chapter is primarily to identify organizational resources expected for professionals who have a basic foundational knowledge about thanatology; these resources will be organized around the basic competency categories that structure this handbook. Also, the emphasis will be on organizational resources on the national level in the United States; it goes without saying that professionals need to be familiar with local resources. Lastly, it is important for certified thanatologists to be aware of, and use the resources provided in, texts/journals published in the areas of death and dying. Although the chapters throughout this handbook cite a wealth of books and articles, a nonexhaustive list of text and research resources is included within the competency categories below. Some these resources are included because of their status as modern classics in the field.

Dying

Organizations

Alzheimer's Association (www.alz.org) supports advocacy and research to find prevention methods, new treatments, and, ultimately, a cure for Alzheimer's disease. The association provides referrals, an online network for caregivers, and support groups.

The American Childhood Cancer Organization, (www.acco.org) website contains information on resources, awareness and advocacy, and research. The organization offers free books on childhood cancer to families, patients, educators, and caregivers. ACCO advocates for increased research, including less toxic treatments for children. This website hosts The Candlelighters, an international organization established in 1970 by parents of children suffering from cancer. In aiding children with cancer the website offers information and support to children with cancer, childhood cancer survivors, their families, and health care providers.

Center to Advance Palliative Care (CAPC) (www.capc.org) provides resources for palliative care program development and expansion. The website includes information for health care professionals including information on certification, education, fellowships, and professional organizations. It also provides links to recommended journals and other publications.

Children's Hospice International (CHI) (www.chionline.org) supports the inclusion of children and adolescents into hospice care. The website provides information on the Children's Hospice International Program for All-Inclusive Care for Children and their Families (CHI PACC). The program was developed with the involvement of CHI and provides a model of care that addresses the needs of children with life-threatening conditions and their families. CHI publishes *Home Care for Seriously Ill Children: A Manual for Parents* and *Interdisciplinary Clinical Manual for Pediatric Hospice and Palliative Care,* both of which can be ordered through the website.

HIV/AIDS has multiple websites. The CDC National Prevention Information Network (www.cdcnpin.org) provides references, referrals, and information. The Elton John Aids Foundation (www.ejaf.org) funds research and education. The Gay Men's Health Crisis (gmhc.org) offers a variety of programs for men, women, and children that include education and outreach programs, a hotline, and counseling services.

Hospice Action Network (HAN) (www.hospiceactionnetwork.org) is a legislative advocacy group for hospice care. HAN seeks to mobilize hospice advocates to increase influence in policy making for improved access to hospice and palliative care and to represent end-of-life issues. The website provides information for the media and congress as well as providing an online legislative advocacy center for the public.

Hospice Foundation of America (HFA) (www.hospicefoundation.org) offers "leadership in the development and application of hospice" providing programs for professionals (who are dealing with dying and grief on a personal or professional basis), disseminates information to the public, and publishes work on dying and grief. An annual teleconference, "Living with Grief," educates professionals on a variety of topics in thanatology and may provide continuing education credits. The organization's website also has a listing of the *Living With Grief* books and videos published by HFA. A monthly newsletter, *Journeys,* is distributed to those experiencing grief as a way to offer support and guidance. HFA's website provides information on subjects such as: myths about dying, what to expect before and after death, pain, and hospice. Information designed specifically to assist caregivers is also provided.

International Association for Hospice and Palliative Care (IAHPC) (www.hospicecare. com/) provides resources to advance hospice and palliative care on an international level. The website includes information and links to fellowships to support professionals to travel to developing nations to teach about hospice and palliative care, scholarship programs, education, international organizations, and publications. The website also includes a recommended reading list and policy and advocacy tools. IAHPC provides a free online newsletter.

The mission of **Make-A-Wish Foundation of America** (www.wish.org) is to make wishes come true for children between the ages of 2½ and 18 who have life-threatening, but not necessarily terminal, illnesses. Thousands of children's wishes have been turned into reality. Professionals in the medical field, parents, and the children themselves may refer a child for consideration. The foundation's website allows a search for local chapters.

National Hospice Foundation (NHF) (www.nationalhospicefoundation.org/home.cfm) is a supporter of the quality and research goals of the National Hospice and Palliative Care Organization. The website includes information about caregiver resources and special programs related to pediatrics, veterans, and professional education. The website also provides access to information related to advance care planning, living wills, advance directives, and financial planning. NHF produces a newsletter called *Giving Matters*, which is available online.

The **National Hospice and Palliative Care Organization (NHPCO)** (www.nhpco.org) is dedicated to increasing the availability of hospice care and improving end-of-life care for terminally ill patients and their families. Its underlying philosophy is to ensure health care, pain management, and emotional support to patients along with their families. Members of NHPCO include hospices, palliative care programs, bereavement programs, researchers, home health agencies, and health care consultants. The NHPCO website allows individuals to find local hospice programs, palliative care programs, bereavement programs, and grief therapy.

Super Sibs (www.supersibs.org) provides support and grief resources for siblings of children living, dying, or deceased due to cancer. The site includes a Sib Spot that offers age-specific activities as well as information related to specific diagnoses. The site also contains information for medical and psychosocial professionals, parents and guardians, grandparents, religious and spiritual leaders, friends and neighbors, and educators. The organization has a donation-based program that provides scholarships to high school seniors who have had a sibling with cancer. The monthly newsletter *SibBlast* can be received via e-mail.

Research, Books, and Other Resources

In *Awareness of Dying,* Barney Glaser and Anselm Strauss (1965) provided the foundation for four types of communication patterns (closed awareness, suspected awareness, mutual pretense, and open awareness) common in those confronting death.

On Death and Dying is the classical work by Elizabeth Kübler-Ross (1969). Reporting transcript data from dying patients, the book describes stages of the dying process, i.e., denial and isolation, anger, bargaining, depression, and acceptance.

In *Living With Life Threatening Illness: A Guide for Patients, Families, and Caregivers,* Kenneth Doka (1993) considers the dynamics that affect people living with a life-shortening illness. Five distinct phases are proposed: prediagnostic, acute, chronic, terminal, and recovery.

In *The Private Worlds of Dying Children*, Myra Bluebond-Langner (1978) describes children with leukemia and their understanding of their illness. Potential changes in self-concept and recognition of the seriousness of their illness for these children are outlined.

End-of-Life Decision Making

Organizations

Caring Connections (www.caringinfo.org) offers information and support for advanced care planning including talking with health care providers and with loved ones who are facing end-of-life decisions. The website includes information on various aspects of financial and advance planning, as well as information on advance directives that are specific to each state. Links to hospice care in specific geographical areas are also provided. There are special sections for employers and caregivers.

Children of Aging Parents (CAPS) (www.caps4caregivers.org) provides information, referrals, and support, including support groups, to caregivers. In addition, the organization offers educational workshops and conferences for professionals and caregivers. CAPS assists the formation of new, CAPS-affiliated groups and provides training and support to those groups.

Compassion and Choices (www.compassionandchoices.org) works to improve end-of-life care including pain control, advance directives, and physician assistance in dying. In addition to education so that the dying and their families understand options and rights, the group is actively involved in the legal and legislative arena. Compassion and Choices has as its vision a society where everyone receives state-of-the-art care at the end of life and a full range of choices for dying in comfort, dignity, and control. This nonprofit organization has over 60 chapters.

Both **Donate Life: Make Organ and Tissue Donation Your Way of Life** (http://donatelife. net) and the U.S. government's website for organ donation (www.organdonor.gov)

provide valuable information about organ donation. The Donate Life website notes that many people die each day waiting for organ transplantations. Sections on frequently asked questions and myths and facts about donation dispel common misconceptions. The site provides organ donor cards and special information for minority donations.

Five Wishes is a booklet (available at www.agingwithdignity.org/5wishes.html) that serves as a living will documenting how individuals wish to be treated if they are not able to make their own end-of-life decisions due to a serious illness. It takes into account an individual's medical wishes, while also attending to his or her personal, emotional, and spiritual needs. Additionally, it encourages preplanning for funerals. Approximately 10,000 organizations in the United States offer copies of *Five Wishes*, such as churches, hospices, hospitals, and law offices. The website allows access to a nondownloadable copy of *Five Wishes*; the booklet may be ordered online. The website also allows individuals to search for states that recognize *Five Wishes* as a legal document. *Five Wishes* is written in layman's terms and may be signed at home.

The **National Kidney Foundation (NKF)** has incorporated the former National Donor Family Council (www.kidney.org/transplantation/donorFamilies/index.cfm) as a subsection. Donor Families provides support and advocacy to families of deceased organ/tissue donors and assistance to health care professionals working with these individuals. NDFC publishes a newsletter called *For Those Who Give and Grieve*, which provides information on organ/tissue donation and offers grieving families the chance to memorialize a donor through stories, poetry, and pictures. The newsletter also has a Donor Family Friends column, which utilizes a pen pal system that allows grieving families to offer support to other families having a similar experience. NDFC also has the Patches of Love Quilt, the National Donor Family Quilt, that allows a donor's relatives to be memorialized in a unique way. Finally, the website provides a listing of books as well as links to bereavement websites.

Research, Books, and Other Resources

The **SUPPORT** study (1995) documents the difficulties in the medical field with end-of-life issues. Even after intervention, there were still shortcomings in communication, frequency of aggressive treatment, and hospitalized deaths.

Loss, Grief, and Mourning

Organizations

American Widow Project (www.americanwidowproject.org) connects military widows to one another to promote healing. The site contains access to resources, including a DVD, newsletter, list of scholarships and grants available to military survivors and their families, and a hotline staffed by a military widow. Social events are planned to connect widows in person.

Bereaved Parents of the USA (BP/USA) (www.bereavedparentsusa.org) is a self-help group for bereaved parents, grandparents, and siblings who are suffering after the death of a child. The organization's website provides information on the grief process and produces a newsletter called *A Journey Together*, which discusses bereavement. Local chapters hold monthly meetings, and these meeting times and locations may be found on the website. BP/USA also offers those grieving over the loss of a child the opportunity to attend workshops on grief and rebuilding life. Finally, a special page is dedicated to links to helpful resources.

Center for Loss in Multiple Births (CLIMB) (www.climb-support.org) was founded by and for parents who have experienced the death of one or more children during a multiple pregnancy, at birth, or in childhood. The organization is intended for families, caregivers, and organizations whose goal is to provide support and comfort to parents who have lost a child of a multiple pregnancy. The organization is volunteer-run and provides services to the United States, Canada, and other countries. CLIMB provides a newsletter every three months with personal stories and updates, articles, and information.

The Compassionate Friends (TCF) (www.compassionatefriends.org) has 600 support groups across the United States with the mission of helping bereaved families following the death of a child. These local chapters have monthly meetings to offer support and the opportunity to work on grief issues. TCF's website provides chat rooms where the bereaved can offer support, help each other deal with grief, and provides resources and information on grief. TCF also has a pen pal program for grieving siblings of children who died. A monthly newsletter, phone calls, and home visits are used by the local chapters to reach out to people grieving over the death of a child. *We Need Not Walk Alone* is TCF's bimonthly magazine that discusses grief issues. There is also a national conference that includes workshops, siblings' program, and a 2 mile Walk to Remember. During TCF's Worldwide Candle Lighting program, candles are lit around the world for 1 hour on the second Sunday in December in remembrance of children who have died.

GriefHaven (www.griefhaven.org) is an organization for parents who are grieving the loss of a child. The website contains a chat room for grieving parents and links to resources including support organizations and groups, grief specialists, funeral preplanning, and recommended books and other literature. The organization provides free newsletters for parents and siblings.

Grief's Journey (www.griefsjourney.com) website concentrates on bereavement for the loss of a spouse or life partner. It provides links to resources on various topics including legal, health, and financial information as well as information on how to perform do-it-yourself tasks and projects that one's deceased spouse or life partner may have managed. There are also sections on coping with special days and parenting after the death of a spouse or life partner.

March of Dimes (www.marchofdimes.com/baby/loss.html) focuses on grieving due to the loss of a baby through miscarriage, stillbirth, or after birth. The website contains links to state-level March of Dimes chapters and information on the *Hurt to Healing* literature.

MISS Foundation (www.missfoundation.org/index.html) is an international organization that provides crisis and long-term support to families after the death of a child; the foundation also participates in legislative activities and advocacy. There are sections on the website intended for professionals, families, bereaved children, and groups. Website information is available in English and Spanish. Information about The Kindness Project, started by a member of MISS as an avenue to help resolve grief through random acts of kindness, is available on the website.

The **National Alliance for Grieving Children (NAGC)** (www.childrengrieve.org) provides a network for communication between children's bereavement professionals to facilitate the sharing of resources that support grieving families. The website includes a national database on children's bereavement support programs. NAGC also offers online education, webinars, online discussions, and an annual symposium on children's grief. A section for help within schools and access to an archive of the organization's newsletter are also provided.

National Funeral Directors Association (NFDA) (www.nfda.org) offers educational programming, including online learning, podcasts, webinar and home study programs, as well as events for professionals. The website includes links for professionals and for the general public. A special section for grief resources contains information on more specific types of loss such as the loss of a child or teen. A funeral home locator and a digital version of the NFDA publication *The Director* are available online.

National Students of AMF (Actively Moving Forward) Support Network (www.studentsofamf.org) is an organization that connects grieving college students to one another through a supportive blog and other events. The organization has National Students of AMF Campus Chapters on college campuses nationwide. The organization also seeks to raise awareness of the needs of grieving college students and supports the annual National College Student Grief Awareness Week.

National SUID/SIDS Resource Center (The National Sudden Unexpected Infant Death/ Sudden Infant Death Resource Center (www.sidscenter.org/Bereavement/index. html) contains a section on bereavement support. The website provides resources for families, friends, children, and providers including literature and links to resources and organizations.

Sesame Street Workshop (www.sesameworkshop.org/what-we-do/our-work/dealing-with-grief-30-detail.html?print=1) provides families and grief care providers nationally with outreach kits, When Families Grieve (available in both English and Spanish). One of the kits is intended for the general public while the other is intended for military families. The kits contain DVDs, books, and family activities.

SHARE: Pregnancy and Infant Loss Support, Inc. (www.nationalshare.org) is a national organization committed to helping individuals who have experienced the death of a baby through miscarriage, stillbirth, or infant fatality. The organization's website provides a directory for local SHARE support groups, as well as information on the grief process, funeral services, and on how to honor and remember a baby. This website also offers a chat room and message board. A separate page displays current research on miscarriage, stillbirth, and support to parents after losing a baby as well as upcoming research on these topics asking for participants. For professionals, a listing of resources is offered and training is provided. Finally, SHARE publishes a bimonthly newsletter called *Sharing* for bereaved parents.

Tragedy Assistance Program for Survivors (TAPS) (www.taps.org) is a national organization that provides information and support for bereaved individuals who have lost a loved one serving in the armed services. TAPS has a tollfree hotline (800-959-8277) staffed with trained crisis intervention professionals to help these individuals with their grief. Additionally, TAPS also has a survivor network that connects people who have experienced the death of a loved one while in the armed services. The Annual National Military Survivor Seminar and Good Grief Camp for Young Survivors were established by TAPS in order to "remember the love, celebrate the life, and share the journey" through workshops and support groups. TAPS' website offers a chat room for bereaved individuals where they can share experiences with one another. Finally, TAPS publishes *A Kids Journey of Grief, TAPS Edition* as well as *TAPS Quarterly Magazine*.

Twinless Twins (www.twinlesstwins.org) provides supportive services to twins (and siblings of all multiple births) who are experiencing the loss of their twin through death, estrangement, or in-utero loss. The organization offers regional activities and national conferences. The website includes links to recommended books, other relevant organizations, and crisis support.

Research, Books, and Other Resources

Sandler and his colleagues (2003) assessed the effectiveness of a **Family Bereavement Program**. The child/family intervention used age-appropriate groups and was designed to reduce risk and increase positive factors. Findings indicated improvement in parenting, individual risk, and protective factors.

The efficacy of **family therapy** with consideration of family styles was supported by Kissane and Hooghe (2011). Both authors also noted the resilience of mourners and the importance of natural support.

General support for a **Kübler-Ross stage model of grief** was found by Maciejewski, Zhang, Block, & Prigerson (2007). Although highly criticized by ADEC professionals, the study did validate some common reactions such as disbelief, yearning, anger, and depression to bereavement.

In ***Disenfranchised Grief: Recognizing Hidden Sorrow*** (1989), Ken Doka (editor) coined the term *disenfranchised grief* as grief that is not recognized or sanctioned. In his follow-up edited book, *Disenfranchised Grief: New Directions, Challenges, and Strategies for Practice* (2002), Doka refined and elaborated on the concept.

Grief Counseling and Grief Therapy by J. William Worden (2009) provides a wide range of information on clinical intervention and assessment of bereavement. Besides arguing for a distinction between counseling and therapy for the bereavement, Worden describes four basic tasks for coping with the mourning process, i.e., accept the reality of death, process the pain of grief, adjust to the environment without the deceased, and find an enduring connection with the deceased in the midst of embarking on a new life.

The Grieving Child (2003) by Helen Fitzgerald is written as a guide for parents. Based on her experiences with bereaved children, the book has practical advice appropriate for parents and professionals.

In the ***Handbook of Bereavement Research*** (2001), Stroebe, Hansson, Stroebe, and Schut provide a theoretical and empirical base for understanding various facets of bereavement including the methodology and ethics or research, bereavement consequences, coping with bereavement, and intervening in the coping process.

Helping the Bereaved College Student (2011) by David E. Balk examines the prevalence of bereavement among college students, discusses what bereaved college students say they want and need, and offers several firsthand accounts in the form of vignettes. The book is written primarily for professionals who are in positions to help bereaved students (college counselors, student services personnel, and campus ministers, for instance). The book is written in a style that is accessible to students. Numerous exercises (such as workshops and training seminars) are presented in detail. Campuswide policies adopted by some universities to assist bereaved students are offered verbatim.

Life and Loss: A Guide to Help Grieving Children (2000) by Linda Goldman provides a wealth of information about bereaved children. A variety of childhood losses are addressed. Grief work in children and a range of grief resolution techniques are discussed.

In ***Meaning Reconstruction and the Experience of Loss***, Robert Neimeyer (2001) outlines the challenges to the bereaved in finding meaning after a death. The griever's assumptive world as well as self and relationship attachments to the deceased will often need to be reconfigured.

Conducting **child bereavement groups** and child grief camps are mainstays of hospice programs (Connor & Monroe, 2011). Two noted nonhospice child bereavement programs are the Dougy Center: The National Center for Grieving Children and Their Families (www.dougy.org) and Highmark Caring Place (www.highmarkcaring place.com).

Living With Loss Magazine (www.bereavementmag.com) is characterized as a support group in print for bereaved individuals. Grief professionals and individuals experiencing grief contribute articles, poetry, and stories to the magazine.

Resilience in coping with a death is recognized in most normally bereaved individuals. Research by George Bonanno and his colleagues (2002; 2005) has provided empirical support for this concept.

Assessment and Intervention

Research, Books, and Other Resources

The **Center for the Advancement of Health** (www.cfah.org) has the goal of "translating health research into effective policy and practice." The Grief Research: Gaps, Needs and Action Project was designed to observe and report on bereavement and grief research with the goal of improving research and care with a focus on the use of research to guide intervention strategies. One report from the project reported on the state of bereavement research, guidelines for improving research, and the use of research in clinical practice (Center for the Advancement of Health, 2004), and a report from the project's Bridging Work Group (2005) examines the gap separating bereavement practitioners and researchers.

Bereavement intervention with children was studied by Currier, Holland, and Neimeyer (2007). The research questioned the effectiveness of such intervention despite the fact that earlier intervention with the inclusion of distressed children showed positive outcomes.

Using **Complicated Grief Treatment (CGT)** Shear, Frank, Houck, and Reynolds (2005) found that the treatment was effective in a randomized controlled trial. Although not as effective as CGT, interpersonal psychotherapy also resulted in improvement.

Grief and death anxiety measures are other resources for assessment. The Grief Experience Inventory by Sanders, Mauger, and Strong (1985) is a 135-item self-report questionnaire. It is designed to measure 17 dimensions of grief and also has a social desirability rating. The inventory is available from Department of Psychology, Hood College, Frederick, MD. The Hogan Grief Reaction Checklist (Hogan, Greenfield, & Schmidt, 2001) is a 61-item questionnaire designed to measure grief reactions after the death of a child. Six dimensions of grief are delineated in the checklist. The death anxiety scale by Templar (Templar, 1970) is a 15-item true or false scale with scores from 0 to 15. The threat index: provided forms (Tip) (Epting & Neimeyer, 1984) has 40 bipolar dimensions. Examinees choose from the poles to identify their present self and their attitudes toward death. The difference between the selections for self and death indicates death anxiety. The Collett-Lester fear of death scale (Collett & Lester, 1969) consists of ratings of disagreement/agreement on 36 statements. The measure provides scores for four dimensions of fear: death of self, death of others, dying of self, dying of others.

Grief and Bereavement in Contemporary Society: Bridging Research and Practice (Neimeyer, Harris, Winokuer, & Thornton, 2011) contains chapters that are coauthored by a researcher and a clinician. A wide variety of losses are discussed within a theoretical, practice, and research context.

Therese A. Rando in a variety of books such as *Treatment of Complicated Mourning* (1993) and *Grief, Dying and Death: Clinical Interventions for Caregivers* (1984) describes theoretical and clinical approaches to issues in bereavement including her theory about coping with loss that includes recognizing the loss, reacting to the separation, recollecting and experiencing the deceased and the relationship, relinquishing the old, readjusting to move adaptively, and reinvesting.

Organizational Resources: Traumatic Death

Organizations

AirCraft Casualty Emotional Support Services (ACCESS) (www.accesshelp.org) is a national organization that provides volunteer peer grief support and resource information to those who have survived or lost loved ones in air disasters including commercial, private, helicopter, and military air disasters, and those who lost loved ones in the World Trade Center and the Pentagon terrorist attacks. ACCESS has a hotline and provides disaster response training for crisis responders. Newsletters from the organization are available online.

American Association of Suicidology (AAS) (www.suicidology.org) is dedicated to research, information dissemination, and prevention of suicide. Members of AAS include mental health care providers, researchers, crisis intervention centers, school employees, and suicide survivors. AAS provides certification to crisis intervention centers and crisis workers. A directory of local survivor support groups is offered; AAS also sponsors a Healing After Suicide Conference. The organization's website offers pages on how to identify and assist a suicidal individual, as well as links providing more in-depth information on suicide and prevention resources. Many publications are offered by AAS including, *Suicide and Life-Threatening Behavior* (bimonthly journal), *Newslink* (members' newsletter), *Surviving Suicide* (survivors' newsletter), and a *Directory of Suicide Prevention and Crisis Intervention Agencies in the U.S.*

American Foundation for Suicide Prevention (www.afsp.org), along with a focus on preventing suicide and raising awareness, provides support to individuals who are mourning a suicide loss. A directory of local chapters is available on the website as well as information on training that AFSP provides to those who facilitate or plan to facilitate suicide bereavement groups for adults. Together with the Suicide Prevention Resource Center, AFSP developed After a Suicide: A Toolkit for Schools. A copy can be downloaded online.

Concerns of Police Survivors (COPS) (www.nationalcops.org) is a national organization that provides assistance to families of police officers who have been killed in the line of duty. COPS communicates with the surviving family members six times during a year; peer support is available. Membership is extended to the spouses, children, parents, siblings, significant others, and coworkers affected by the death of a police officer while on duty. The National Police Survivors' Conference takes place each May, which allows law enforcement survivors to work on grief and to share information. Also, the COPS Kids/Teens Program and Summer Camp are offered to children who are grieving over the loss of a parent. During these programs, the children receive support and guidance from professionals. COPS' Annual Wilderness Experience is designed for surviving children between the ages of 15 to 21; this program is designed to increase self-esteem. Among COPS' many programs are: annual retreats, which include activities and grief counseling, offered for surviving parents, spouses, siblings, adult children, and in-laws; supplying volunteers who will attend the trial of the accused and provide support to the victim's family; and financial assistance to the victims' children for therapy to work on grief issues surrounding the death of a parent. COPS' publications include a quarterly newsletter and a handbook entitled *Support Services to Surviving Families of Line-of-Duty Death.*

Crisis intervention training is available from the Red Cross (www.redcross.org) through its mental health disaster training, from the International Critical Incident Stress Foundation (www.icisf.org). There is controversy about the effectiveness of crisis/critical incident interventions; however, many professionals have provided those services.

Friends for Survival (www.friendsforsurvival.org) is a national outreach organization that provides resources for survivors of suicide and to professionals who work with those who have been impacted by suicide. Friends for Survival provides monthly newsletters (available online in electronic form), monthly educational and supportive meetings, referrals, and training programs.

Grief Recovery After a Substance Passing (GRASP) (grasphelp.org) is mainly for nonprofessionals and provides resources to individuals and families who have lost a loved one due to substance abuse or addiction. The website provides a directory of local chapters and information on starting other local chapters.

Mothers Against Drunk Driving (MADD) (www.madd.org) is an organization dedicated to ending drunk driving, providing support to victims of drunk drivers, and educating the public about drunk driving. There are approximately 600 local chapters of MADD. Extensive information may be located on the website concerning the grief process after losing a loved one in a drunk driving accident, posttraumatic stress disorder due to witnessing the traumatic event, and physiological consequences of the accident and how to cope. Also online discussion forums are provided on MADD's website to allow victims to have a space to talk to others who are experiencing similar situations. Local chapters offer support groups. Victims may be provided with a victim advocate who assists with the legal and court issues by providing information (e.g., on steps to execute in order to receive a crash report, victim's rights, attorneys, and the legal system, etc.), working on the impact statement with the victim, and accompanying the victim to court. Victim advocates are also a source of emotional support and may also help victims seeking financial services from the Crime Victims Compensation Fund. MADD publishes *MADDvocate*, a magazine designed for victims of drunk driving and for victims' advocates.

National Fallen Firefighters Foundation (www.firehero.org) is dedicated to honoring and remembering firefighters who died in the line of duty and providing support for survivors. Activities include a memorial weekend for families, coworkers, and the public to honor firefighters who died in the line of duty during the year, and a survivor's weekend for families to interact with trained grief counselors. The foundation provides support programs for survivors including a lending library, grief brochures, and a Fire Service Survivors Network.

National Organization for Victim Assistance (NOVA) (www.try-nova.org) offers information, support, and advocacy for victims of violent crimes and their survivors. NOVA offers a 24-hour tollfree hotline called the National Crime Victim Information and Referral Hotline that provides crisis counseling, advocacy, referrals to local programs, and information for violent crime victims and survivors. NOVA's website offers victims and survivors essential information on crime, the steps to take following a crime, and possible trauma caused by a violent crime. NOVA has also created the National Community Crisis Response Team, a multidisciplinary team that goes to sites affected by a catastrophic event, and the Hostage Family Project, designed to help meet the needs of families of Americans who have been taken hostage. The membership of NOVA includes violent crime victims and survivors, mental health professionals, researchers, and legal professionals. To assist victim advocates in helping victims and survivors, NOVA publishes *Directory of Victim Assistance Programs and Resources in the United States*; *Directory of National Programs Serving Survivors of Crime, Crisis and Trauma*; and the *Directory of International Programs Serving Survivors of Crime, Crisis and Trauma*. NOVA offers an annual conference, training seminars, and workshops.

Parents of Murdered Children (POMC) (www.pomc.com) is a national organization providing assistance, crisis intervention, and referrals to local chapters for those grieving due to the murder of a child. Members include those who are grieving as well as the professionals who support them. POMC local chapters provide monthly meetings, connect members through telephone contact, discuss grief, and arrange for murder survivors to be accompanied to court. POMC's website offers a Forum of Hope, which allows members to share thoughts, emotions, and experiences with other individuals also grieving the loss of a loved one to murder. Also, the website provides individuals the opportunity to ask questions of various experts, such as a forensic pathologist, bereavement specialist, homicide detective, judge, funeral director, chief counsel, forensic scientist, or criminal profiler. Helpful information is also offered on the website about writing a victim's impact statement, and information is provided for professionals about the problems facing murder survivors. POMC offers other programs including: a self-help weekend developed to help murder survivors grieve and rebuild a new life; The National Murder Response Team, established to help and support communities following a violent murder; *Survivors*, a triannual newsletter offering important information to murder survivors; and training for mental health professionals, social workers, doctors, nurses, ministers, teachers, lawyers, and law enforcement personnel on murder survivors and the consequences of murder.

Survivors of Violent Loss Resources (www.svlp.org/home.html) offers support to those who are experiencing grief after a traumatic loss such as homicide, suicide, drunk driving, or terrorist attacks through the Survivors of Violent Loss Program. SVLR provides consultation and training services as well.

United States Department of Veterans Affairs Bereavement Counseling (www.vetcenter.va.gov/Bereavement_Counseling.asp) offers bereavement counseling to family members of armed forces personnel, reservists, and National Guardsman who died while on duty. Services are provided at local centers or can be provided in the family's home. The website contains contact information for services.

Research, Books, and Other Resources

Suicide and Life Threatening Behavior publishes articles on research, theory, and clinical practice that are concerned with self-inflected deaths.

Linda Goldman's *Breaking the Silence: A Guide to Helping Children With Complicated Grief—Suicide, Homicide, AIDS, Violence and Abuse* (2002) focuses on violent deaths in the lives of children and is a guide to helping children with complicated grief.

Surviving: When Someone You Love Was Murdered (1989) written by Lulu Redmond, a past president of the Association for Death Education and Counseling, has practical information on the grief associated with a death by homicide and on assessment and therapy guidelines and other suggestions for professionals.

Edwin Shneidman was a pioneer in the study of suicide and suicide prevention. He was noted for his groundbreaking work on suicide notes, *Clues to Suicide* (1968) with Norman Farberow. Shneidman coined terms such as *psychological autopsy* and *psychache* as methods for understanding suicidal behavior.

TAPS (Tragedy Assistance Program for Survivors) magazine is a quarterly publication that provides professionally written articles for the bereaved, highlights of TAPS events, news of TAPS events, and encouragement and support to bereaved military personnel and their families.

Death Education

Organizations

The **Association for Death Education and Counseling** (www.adec.org) is an international, multidisciplinary professional organization. Its purpose is to promote excellence in research, theory, and clinical practice in the areas of death education, care of the dying, and bereavement counseling.

The **Center for Disease Control and Prevention** (www.cdc.gov/index.htm) provides information on many health-related issues including suicide. In particular, the CDC's National Center for Health Statistics (www.cdc.gov/nchs) summarizes overall death and mortality rates for the United States.

Growth House (growthhouse.org) provides access to books, blogs, podcasts, and videos about end-of-life care, palliative medicine, and hospice care. The material is intended for both the general public and for professionals. Resources can be accessed free of charge online.

The **International Work Group on Death, Dying, and Bereavement** (IWGDDB) (www.iwgddb.com) consists of professionals from around the world. IWG develops and publishes policy statements regarding thanatology issues.

PBS Kids Dealing With Death (pbskids.org/itsmylife/emotions/death/index.html) is a site for children and their parents that addresses issues such as understanding grief, funerals and memorials, when a friend is grieving, pet loss, and other issues related to death. True Tales on the website are stories of other children who are dealing with grief.

Research, Books, and Other Resources

Death Studies is a professional journal that publishes articles on bereavement counseling, research, education, care of the dying, and ethics. Contributors include professors, clinicians, nurses, and medical doctors. Book reviews and News & Notes are special sections in each issue.

Omega—Journal of Death and Dying provides articles on terminal illnesses, dying, and the grief process. Among the contributors are professors, medical doctors, and funeral directors. Along with the journal *Death Studies,* this journal is recognized for scholarship on issues related to death and dying and serves to assist mental health professionals in working in crisis management.

Death and Dying, Life and Living (2012) by Charles Corr and Donna Corr provides comprehensive coverage of the field of thanatology. A popular textbook in thanatology, the authors' analyses of statistical data to illustrate trends, the wealth of resources provided, and the thoughtful synthesis of research and practice are strengths of the book. Based on the hospice philosophy, the book also has a good description of the four tasks (physical, psychological, social, and spiritual) of the dying person. Since 2002 the book has been one of the required readings for the ADEC certification examination.

In *Explaining Death to Children* (1967) and other books such as *Talking about Death: A Dialogue Between Parent and Child* (1990) and *Living When a Loved One Has Died* (1977) Earl Grollman has encouraged professionals and laypersons to recognize and to educate children about death, dying, and bereavement.

Growing Through Grief: A K-12 Curriculum to Help Young People Through All Kinds of Loss (O'Toole, 1989) is a manual in age-appropriate sections with over 120 handouts for educators or professionals working with bereaved children.

The Last Dance: Encountering Death and Dying (2010) by Lynne DeSpelder and Al Strickland is a popular college text for courses on death and dying. The text provides a broad range of topics in thanatology and gives rich cultural information. Since 2002, the book has been one of the required readings for the ADEC certification examination.

Principles and Practice of Grief Counseling (Winokuer & Harris, 2012) is an introductory textbook for grief counseling integrating information from research, theory, and practice.

The Psychology of Death by Robert Kastenbaum and Ruth Aisenberg (1992) was the first broad comprehensive book on thanatology.

ADEC Ethics Code (www.adec.org) details a comprehensive set of ethical standards for thanatologists engaged in clinical practice, research, and teaching.

CMI Educational Institute (www.cmieducation.com) conducts seminars across the United States as the nonprofit American Academy of Bereavement (AAB). AAB is dedicated to providing education for professionals and general public on topics concerned related to thanatology, especially bereavement.

Online courses and programs are available from many sources (such as National Center for Death Education at www.mountida.edu). It is important to note that the quality of these educational programs may vary greatly and that the qualification of the faculty and the objectives of the program should be investigated before enrollment.

Talking to Children About Death is a 14-page, patient informational publication from the Clinical Center of the National Institutes of Health, (www.clinicalcenter.nih.gov/ccc/patient_education/pepubs/childeath.pdf). The document includes a list of recommended books for parents and for children.

Concluding Remarks

As the field of thanatology continues to develop, additional resource materials will become available. The resources listed above attempt to capture the most important and relevant organizations in the field today. With the passage of time, such organizations may disappear, change, or be subsumed; new organizations will be added. It behooves the practitioner to explore the Internet on his or her own in an attempt to stay current. This proviso is especially true with regard to the professional literature appearing in books and research studies. Such a surfeit of resources is one sign of the maturity of the field of thanatology and the body of knowledge produced by its professionals.

Chapter 42

Thanatology in the Digital Age

Anne M. Smith and Corinne Cavuoti

Background Information

The Internet and digital/electronic technologies available today provide unprecedented access to information and support for people coping with illness and loss. Since the advent of the Internet in 1982, the human–computer interaction (HCI) has redefined individual relationships, social interaction, and global consciousness. The Internet provides unlimited access to information on any topic including issues surrounding death that were once considered taboo. The use of the Internet for death-related information and education has expanded to include loss-specific multifaceted websites, social networking for support, interactive counseling, artistic expression, blogging, cyber memorials, and postmortem continuing bonds. The methods and capabilities of access to the Internet also continue to advance rapidly. In the past decade, the idea of personal computing has advanced from the desktop computer to laptop computers, cell phones, tablets, and a variety of handheld devices. Similarly, the software programs available have expanded from basic programming to advanced social media, face-to-face interactions, cell phone apps, live streaming of events, video/digital storytelling along with instantaneous access to information 24 hours a day, 7 days a week. The newest development of cloud technology centralizes information. By using cyber storage, cloud technology allows greater sharing of information at greater speed. The cloud also allows dissemination of information to all personal devices making information and connectivity completely portable (Huang, Guo, Xie, & Wu, 2012, p. 39).

The technological advancements of the digital age affect the global perspective and social construct of dying, death, and bereavement. Before exploring the influence of technology on grief response and mourning rituals, it's relevant to examine the social issues surrounding use of the Internet. Undoubtedly, online access to information and communication is reshaping the way the world interacts. The 2012 *Global Information Technology Report (GITR): Living in a Hyperconnected World* describes the changing economic opportunities and human interaction as well as the challenges and risks associated with growing global hyperconnectivity. Hyperconnectivity is described as having the following attributes: "super-fast connectivity, always on, on the move, roaming seamlessly from network to network, wherever we go—anywhere, anytime, via any device" (Biggs, 2012, p. 47). The GITR (Biggs, 2012) acknowledges the constant need to reassess and redefine the measurement and impact of connectivity to reflect the changing trends and technologies. Since the 1990s there have been questions regarding inequitable availability to the Internet and information and communication technologies (ICTs).

The inequities are attributed to unbalanced access to service and technology along with limited access to training and education. "Persistent gaps between developed and developing nations, as well as gaps domestically along socioeconomic, geographic, educational, racial, and gender lines" initially described the digital divide (Epstein, Nisbet, & Gillespie, 2011, p. 92). Access remains a primary concern; however, the newest smart phones and handheld devices provide opportunity to connect to the Internet without the costly need for home Internet service (Modares, 2011). As availability to connect changes, focus shifts to address other aspects of the divide. Over the past two decades, a more complex interpretation of the division has evolved.

Defining the digital divide has created much debate. In addition to understanding the impact of access, discussion continues regarding age and generational affect on usage. Prensky (2001) coined the phrase *digital native* to describe the generation of students born into the digital age compared with *digital immigrants,* those adapting to a new technology (p. 1). This concept of the *digital divide* has been widely accepted in both the popular and academic arenas affecting research, funding, and educational direction (Graham, 2011). Brown and Czerniewicz (2010) caution against presuming age-related digital literacy to avoid marginalizing those who are labeled immigrants and promoting those labeled natives to an elevated status. Inherently present in the divide and labeling is the "apparently insurmountable gap between them [digital natives] and the less technologically literate older generations" (Bennet & Maton, 2010, p. 322). In recent research, it is suggested that there is a range of user knowledge and ability that spans across the age barriers (Bennett & Maton, 2010; Epstein, Nisbet & Gillespie, 2010; Modares, 2011).

The expansion of the Internet demands the digital divide be understood as both ability to access and level of user knowledge and skill. There are many methods of access to the Internet and gradations of user ability that cross the lines of age, education, and economic status. As we move forward in the digital age, both the technology and the individual user profile will change. Prensky (2009) reconsidered the label of *digital native* suggesting *digital wisdom* to be more descriptive of the *digitally enhanced human* (p. 1). In 1997 Sofka identified the potential of Internet resources in the field of thanatology describing the new genre as *thanatechnology* (p. 553). As we consider thanatechnology today, it is critical that we understand access and availability to the Internet as well as the digital wisdom of its users.

All cultures have norms of expected behavior in response to dying, death, and bereavement. These death-related practices are part of each society's death system defined by Kastenbaum (1972) as the "sociophysical network by which we mediate and express our relationship to mortality" (as cited in Sofka, Cupit, & Gilbert, 2012, p. 6). The system is a means of defining the culturally acknowledged and accepted code of behavior. When life-altering events occur, these norms dictate the communal response and support to those experiencing such events (Corr, Nabe, & Corr, 2009). Undoubtedly, online connectivity is a vital tool in providing and enhancing the availability of individual and social support. Sofka, Cupit, and Gilbert (2012) describe a thanatechnological death system enhancing the traditional model to incorporate the impact of the Internet and HCT technology. The thanatechnological model acknowledges global connectivity and incorporates a crosscultural approach to defining the death system (p. 10-11). Looking forward, a thanatechnological model including hyperconnectivity can redefine social norms in response to death, enhance personal death awareness, and affect global consciousness regarding death and loss. This chapter will explore the impact of the Internet and HCTs on the field of thanatology.

Thanatology in the Digital Age

Death-related losses challenge the bereaved to cope with living in a new world. The newly bereaved often describe their new world as foreign, unpredictable, and threatening. A death, illness, or traumatic event has shattered their assumptive world.[1] Attig (2001) further defines the experience of loss as diminishing our sense of wholeness and connection to the people in our lives, our community, and the world at large. A death or traumatic event may cause an individual to question the meaning of life, the meaning of the loss, and the meaning of the future. Social connectivity is central to the meaning of life and plays an important role in meaning reconstruction after loss. In a struggle to relearn the world and find meaning, the bereaved may alter past connections and struggle to embrace new, supportive connections. Social interaction and reconnection to family, friends, and community are consistent staples of support for the bereaved.

The Internet provides access to social connectivity. The connectivity is private, available 24 hours, enables sharing with others experiencing a similar loss with the option for anonymity (Gilbert & Horsley, 2011). A bereaved person can assess his or her individual needs and self-modulate postloss reconnection. Through multifaceted websites such as Open to Hope, GriefNet, and Compassionate Friends, information and education is widely available. Individuals are able to navigate through resources privately as they determine what is helpful to them. These sites contain a broad spectrum of support options ranging from education to qualified counselors and groups for support.

---

1   A "conceptual system, developed over time that provides us with expectations about the world and ourselves" (Janoff-Bulman, 1992, p. 5).

Mourners also have opportunity to hold online conversations connecting with others experiencing specific types of losses (Horsley & Horsley, 2012, p. 309). Many sites also include memorials, blogs, and other means for creative expression. All of these options can be utilized from any device, anywhere, at any time.

Grief and mourning are experienced within a social construct of death. The positive impact of social support is shown repeatedly across bereavement studies. In his work with bereaved college students, Balk (2011d) found that grievers look for a safe place for expression, comfortable situations, and compassionate, supportive people in their lives. As the bereaved begin to redefine their lives and rebuild a self-narrative, the social component of their identity is critical to positive reaffirmation of life (Neimeyer, 2010). Similarly, a study examining Internet support groups for bereaved parents following the loss of a child to suicide, reports a safe and open place to connect to other parents was a "quintessentially important element to group membership" (Fieigelman, Gorman, Beal, & Jordan, 2008, p. 241). Findings from a recent Pew Internet study (Hampton et al., 2011) indicate people using the Internet regularly report having closer ties, discussion confidants, and less sense of isolation In addition to the growing number of young people online, 79% of adults report using the Internet and 59% report using social networking sites (SNSs). Over half of the SNS users are over the age of 35. Of note, 2012 reports state 53% in the 65+ age group utilize the Internet and/or e-mail, and 69% reported owning a mobile phone (Hampton, Goulet, Rainie, & Purcell, 2011).

The explosive use of SNSs expands the capabilities of the Internet in the social support arena. A SNS is a website designed to facilitate networking usually based on shared interest, service, or activity. There are many different types of SNSs, each maintaining a different focus of connection. For example, Facebook and Google+ are social-networking platforms, LinkedIn is a professional network, Instagram is designed to share photos, and Pinterest is a virtual pin board to display ideas or interests. Each of these platforms has a resource within the site for grief education and/or support. The most successful of these networks is the social-networking site, Facebook. Started in 2004, Facebook has grown to a worldwide membership of approximately 955 million. Briefly, a Facebook page consists of a personal profile defined as a "summary of who you are, what you've been doing and your interests" (newsroomfb.com, 2012). A "friend" is someone connected to another through Facebook, usually an established friend or acquaintance outside of the SNS. Each Facebook user has a timeline used to "post" comments, photos, or video clips. Friends can read and respond to material posted on each other's timelines. If desired, private messaging can be done through the user's profile as well. In addition to individual timelines, businesses or organizations have "pages," that also allow for interaction for those who are linked to the page through the "like" option. There are many Facebook pages devoted to bereavement such as The Grief Toolbox, Grief Journeys, and GriefShare, where those connected can post and respond to others experiencing loss. In comparison to other Internet users, those who use Facebook regularly reported higher levels of social support (Hampton, et al., 2011).

Facebook and other SNSs may create an opportunity to customize support to accommodate self-identified social needs and technical capabilities. Neimeyer (2003) warns against a one-size-fits-all type of support suggesting that clinicians direct attention to accommodating the individual's personality traits, history, and coping styles. Use of the Internet early in the grieving process may promote self-determination as the user explores various support options. The *Pew Internet Report: Social Networking and our Lives* (Hampton et al., 2011) is a study comparing SNS users to Internet users not involved with networking sites. Researchers found Facebook users have a significantly higher level of social support and are also twice as likely to believe that people can be trusted. Through Facebook, a user can post information, emotional status, and reach out to friends at any time for support. The user is eliciting the support, and in response friends begin a dialog that fosters connection to the bereaved. Each post creates another web of connection, all initiated by the timeline creator. Similarly, memorials can be created on a user's timeline or on a community page to commemorate the deceased. A deceased user's timeline can also be a means to communicate to the deceased. Many bereaved SNS users speak to deceased loved ones through their SNS page, and by doing so, encourage friends to comment and speak to the deceased as well. Memorials promote a community of support that can be ongoing in response to users' needs.

In addition to social networking, Twitter, Yammer, and other social messaging sites (SMSs), or microblogging, offer a venue to post the "status" of one's emotions and perceptions. A status update, also known as "tweeting," is generally a short statement (140 characters or less) posted to reflect the user's mood, an event, or general personal status. Status reporting forces a succinct snapshot of the emotional status of the writer or a brief report of information. The update goes to all friends often initiating an instant response and support. According to recent reports, 15% of adults online use SMSs to post status updates, up from 11% in 2011 (Hampton, et al., 2011). These forums for communication and support are becoming added tools for support of the bereaved.

As an example, the case of Barbara illustrates the potential of Facebook, SNSs, and SMSs to meet the individual needs of the bereaved. Barbara and her husband, Rob, were married for 22 years and have one child. Barbara is the sole financial support for the family, and Rob was a stay-at-home father. Rob was diagnosed with brain cancer at age 48 and died 5 years later at the age of 53. Barbara started her Facebook entries on the day of her husband's death. Barbara describes herself as a disciplined person and values her ability to solve problems and remain in control. Barbara's coping style is an important element to understanding how she processes her grief. Martin and Doka (2010) describe coping styles as a "continuum from intuitive to instrumental" (p. 71). Intuitive grievers cope through affective expression, while instrumental grievers cope using problem-solving techniques and activity. Barbara is a blended griever, largely instrumental, but uses affective coping techniques as well. Six weeks after her husband's death, Barbara attended a bereavement support group. She described feeling overwhelmed by the group process and unable to "focus on her own grief story." Using Facebook offered a way to express her feelings, pace her reconnection, reach out for support as needed, and memorialize her husband:

> July 31, 2010
> Barbara: My husband Rob passed away this morning after a courageous 5-year battle with brain cancer. He was the love of my life and a wonderful father. Funeral arrangements will be posted. (35 comments ranging from 7-31, 9:36 a.m. to 8-2, 12:37 p.m.)

The user, Barbara, displayed a picture of the deceased, prior to his illness, as a memorial. In the same entry, there is an expression of her loss as she begins to explore the reality of the death. Barbara posted to her timeline within hours of her husband's death because she "had to do something." A second post offered information for friends regarding funeral arrangements. Both posts reflect her need to remain active and use her problem-solving coping skills. And, in turn, there are compassionate comments helping her feel connected and supported.

> December 23, 2010
> Barbara: Many of you have been there for me this year. Whether a kind word, a "like," a message, a visit, coffee, dinner, a movie, a phone call—all of these expressions of friendship and caring helped me through some very dark days. This Christmas will be filled with great memories and some sadness, but I know my angel is smiling down on us. Merry Christmas to all. (24 "likes" and 7 comments ranging from 12-23, 6:49 p.m. to 12-24, 12:39 p.m.)

The following post was addressed to the deceased with pictures of him over the years with their child.

> October 7, 2011
> Barbara: Pics from the first 21 years—our baby is all grown up!
> (30 responses and comments)

Of note, in the two entries above, Barbara is posting at Christmas and her daughter's birthday. She has self-identified her need for additional support and initiated a chain of supportive comments and "likes." She also shared her concept of a continuing bond with the deceased. The positive response to continuing the relationship allowed her to post additional pictures and talk about her husband openly on her timeline.

> November 20, 2011
> Barbara: Today would have been Rob's 54th birthday. It's been 16 months since he left us and the pain of missing my best friend and partner of 24 years just doesn't seem to be getting any easier to handle. It feels like yesterday that he was holding my hand, making me laugh uncontrollably, driving me crazy changing channels on the remote, telling me the awful dinner I cooked was delicious,

telling me I was the most beautiful woman in the world even when I looked my worst and marveling over having created such a beautiful and talented daughter. I know he is in a better place and happy but sometimes it is little consolation for those he had to leave behind. Happy Birthday in Heaven to the love of my life—love never dies. Photos of deceased included.

(34 "likes" and 21 comments ranging from 7:54 a.m. to 3:53 p.m.)

The above entry includes several important components of Barbara's grieving process. It is a memorial to Rob's birthday with photos and celebration of his life. In celebrating, she continues to have him in her life. At this time, Barbara began to use "love never dies" as a memorial to her husband—the phrase reappearing on additional posts, pictures, written cards, and status posts. Barbara also acknowledges her struggle with reconstructing her identity describing who she was as seen through the eyes of the deceased. In reading this post, one can see the challenges she faces to regain her sense of identity. The supportive comments encourage her continuing bond with the deceased and offer additional social connection as others share their bond as well. At this time, Barbara decided to meet with a bereavement counselor. Jordan and Neimeyer (2003) posit that in addition to the type of intervention, the timing of grief support may contribute to successful outcome. The individual's grieving process may include a "critical window of time" for optimum response to intervention (p. 774). The interaction on the Internet allowed Barbara to assess her needs and engage in counseling at a time when she felt supported and open to counseling.

> January 8, 2012
> Barbara: Spent several hours today sorting and arranging 7,000 pics on my computer, and found this very first pic when Rob and I were dating. Love this. (Attached to first picture of couple together) (25 "likes" and 12 comments).

> January 31, 2012
> Barbara: Today is a year and a half since Rob had to leave us. Miss his handsome face every day. (Attached to photo of deceased) (21 "likes" and 12 comments)

> March 25, 2012
> Barbara: Hosted a widows group of 15 at my house tonight and met some lovely people that can really relate to each other. The last people didn't leave until after midnight so I guess it was a success. (21 "likes" and 2 comments)

> May 6, 2012
> Barbara: My gardening project for today—think it turned out pretty. (Picture of gravesite decorated with flowers) (31 "likes" and 4 comments)

The Facebook entries demonstrate Barbara's positive movement in the grieving process. She is able to acknowledge her continuing bond with her husband, while moving forward with her life. In addition, her involvement in the widow's group enables her to develop a sense of meaning and build on her new identity.

The Internet continues to grow and provide potential for the bereaved to remain connected as they cope with the loss of a loved one. The SNS and SMS options can be a tool for grievers to begin the process of reacclimating to a world without the deceased. An individual can begin to reconnect with friends online at a comfortable pace as they explore options and evaluate their need, if any, for further support. Online communication and resources are shaping the way we respond to loss and socially support the bereaved.

Social media is also utilized for community support. The recent shootings in a movie theater in Aurora, CO, resulted in 12 deaths and more than 50 seriously injured. There was an immediate response with posts on Facebook, tweets on Twitter, and sites being started to support the families. The response has become part of the culture—a way to connect and support not only an individual or family, but a community as well. Leeat Granek, a health psychologist studying grief response, states there is a "trend where people are going online to express grief...it's the same as getting together with people when you used to go over to someone's house with a casserole" (Tucker, 2012, p. 1).

The Internet can also play an important role in the reduction of social isolation and disenfranchisement. Disenfranchised grief refers to losses that are not socially sanctioned. This type of grief is not recognized, validated, or publicly mourned. Disenfranchised grief may leave the bereaved vulnerable for greater difficulty coping with loss and may contribute to "factors that may facilitate or impair grief resolution" (Doka, 2002, p. 18). There are three different types of disenfranchised grief: the relationship is not socially acceptable, the loss is not deemed significant enough to warrant a grief reaction, and exclusion of the griever. If a person is excluded from the right to grieve, there will be little or no social recognition of his or her sense of loss or need to mourn (Doka, 2002). The elderly population is often perceived as "having little comprehension of or reaction to the death of significant others" (Doka, 2002, p. 13). The elderly are often excluded from discussions and rituals concerning loss, and this neglect is especially true in cases of nursing home residents. For those residing in nursing home facilities, bereavement can be especially troubling because of the residents' sense of isolation and estrangement from their former life connections.

The use of digital technology can be a way for the elderly to reconnect to people and places. A recent news report followed nursing home residents given iPads (tablet computer devices) with Internet access. Through the iPads, the residents were able to access information and connect to the outside world (Adlersberg, 2012). For example, nursing home residents are using web mapping service applications, such as Google Maps, on their iPads allowing visual access to the places that are familiar. These map locations can be connected to a television screen in the nursing home facility. "A few taps on the screen and a resident can be right back home in a few seconds" (Adlersberg, 2012, p. 1). Nursing home staff reports using the iPad reanimates residents who were passive and uninvolved (Adlersberg, 2012). One resident reported that using the iPad to connect to the Internet allowed her to shop online with her family and plan a Mother's Day brunch. This involvement in the family planning of an important day made the resident feel like part of the family even though she couldn't be physically with them. Referring to re-involvement using the computer, one resident stated, "My family asks my opinions, now they ask me questions; they respect me in a different way" (Aldersberg, 2012, p. 1). The use of the Internet to stay connected to family and friends can be an essential tool in decreasing residents' isolation and loneliness, especially during bereavement.

Pet loss has also been identified as a form of disenfranchised loss. Many pet owners often feel embarrassed and isolated by their loss. There are many websites and Internet pages such as ASPCA (aspca.org) and the Association for Pet Loss and Bereavement (aplb. org) that offer information and support. In addition there are virtual pet cemeteries and blogs that provide posting and creative opportunities for bereaved pet owners. Through the Internet, they are able to locate other bereaved pet owners to share their experiences diminishing loneliness, isolation, and despair.

The Internet and ICTs may also affect the global consciousness regarding death, dying, and bereavement. Through the Internet, we are exposed to events unfolding in real time. Videos, photos, and personal accounts of catastrophic disaster, pandemics, and death-related events may inspire global unification and encourage immediate response. During a disaster, the inability to communicate and share information is one of the greatest problems. ICTs offer a means for more effective communication and organization as people join together to take action. The social media's representation of death-related events also affects compassion towards grievers.

What are the factors that affect a global response to the pain and suffering of other human beings? The *Oxford Dictionary* defines empathy as having the ability "to share and understand the feelings of another person." Compassion is defined as "concern for the suffering of others" (Oxforddictionaries.com). In order to feel compassion for another, people must be able to connect and relate to the experience. Often, the failure of people to respond to the pain of others is directly related to their inability to understand and relate on a variety of social levels (Cikara, Bruneau, & Saxe, 2011). The Internet includes many different venues that foster empathy and a collective response. The social media integrates information across the world sharing live coverage, humanitarian efforts, and personal accounts. In addition video-sharing sites, such as YouTube and photo-sharing sites, such as Instragram have a powerful impact on empathic response.

Laituri and Kodrich (2008) have identified the following characteristics of Internet technology and communication that pertain to disasters and death-related experiences. Online media facilitates global communication, conveys a sense of urgency, enhances dissemination of information, provides instantaneous information, and fosters a sense of global community. The online disaster response community then unites to provide financial support; public creation of blogs, pictures, and video recordings; and message boards providing information for survivors. Informal social networks of communication develop providing firsthand accounts of death-related experiences and disasters. Local victims of an event often volunteer to collect and distribute data in text, blogs, videos, pictures, maps, and chat rooms (Laituri & Kodrich, 2008).

Images of traumatic world events such as the 2001 terrorist attacks on the World Trade Center in New York, Hurricane Katrina in New Orleans, and the earthquake in Haiti, provide opportunity for global communities to relate to the experience of others, express empathy for victims, and respond. Survivors also have the opportunity to express their grief by telling the story of their loss.

In 2010, Haiti was devastated by a 7.0 earthquake that resulted in 316,000 deaths, 300,000 people injured, and 1 million people left homeless. According to the U.N. News Service, the international community united in an outpouring of support to assist the survivors and their families. Much of the support was orchestrated through the Internet. As an example of online disaster support, the Red Cross continues relief efforts and communication for those affected by the 2010 earthquake. The site provides links to Facebook, YouTube, LinkedIn, Twitter, and other social networks to allow survivors to continue to talk online about their lives and experiences in relation to the earthquake. The Red Cross site encourages continued connection for those affected by the disaster as a source of support across the globe (redcross.org.uk).

The Internet and online communication also has the capacity to raise awareness and foster unity on a global level. After the Sept. 11, 2001 attacks on the World Trade Center, there was a response of support and empathy reflected in e-mail messages across the world. In addition, the online reporting, videos, etc., began a global dialog that reflected questions about mortality, terrorism, and global connectivity. The IIE Solutions headquarters, which hosts social community websites, provided a forum for international comments. A quote from Germany from the REFA staff (World Confederation of Productivity Science) stated:

> The German society is shocked by the brutal murdering of innocent people. The families who were unbelievably hit will be in our minds for a long time. REFA staff and members will do everything that is in our hands to contribute to connecting people and cultures to benefit each other (http://solutions.iienet.org p. 33).

A member of the IAI Technical Information Center in Israel stated:

> My colleagues and I are shocked beyond belief—this despite the fact that as Israelis we have become accustomed to living daily beneath the threat of terror against innocents. Accustomed but not inured (http://solutions.iienet.org p. 32).

Another quote from South Africa stated:

> I was not directly affected by the events but was totally shocked by what I saw. My sympathies go out to the innocent people who were involved, and we will continue to pray that life will return to normal for all of you in the United States (http://solutions.iienet.org, p. 33).

In addition to the support at the time of the 9/11 attacks, the Internet continues to be an important resource for the survivors and victims' family members. There are

Internet sites such as voicesofseptember11.org dedicated to providing support for those affected by the 9/11 event. This site memorializes the victims through the 9/11 Living Memorial Project described as an "online interactive tribute commemorating the lives and preserving the stories of 9/11/2001" (voicesofseptember11.org). Included on this site is a short documentary film, *Voices*. The film contains interviews with family members of 9/11 victims and tells the story of their unified support and resilience. This site is also linked to Facebook and Twitter allowing the support to be easily accessed from any device and portable.

These are examples of how online communication surrounding catastrophic world events can shape perspective and response to death-related experiences. The Internet provides the opportunity for the world to witness events in real time as well as create a global dialog in response. This type of interaction may play a role in creating a broader sense of empathy leading to greater compassion worldwide.

Although the social support is often positive, there can be negative aspects to social media support. For some grievers, the lack of privacy may create further distress as their emotions online can often be made public leaving them feeling exposed and violated. There is also the potential for disturbing online behavior. Some posts may be insensitive or offensive to the bereaved. Overexposure of a loss can also be upsetting to the survivors. After the shooting at Virginia Tech in April 2007, a professor at the university stated,

> Our tragedy had become a product to be sold, with a slick computer-graphic lead-in on every channel, and, of course, a point of leverage for those arguing for either greater or lesser availability of guns (Wittkower, 2012, p. 2).

These unintended consequences must be considered when using the Internet for support or education pertaining to death, dying, and grieving.

The Internet continues to enhance, modify, and challenge the social mores surrounding dying, death, and bereavement. As we explore the impact of thanatechnology on grief and mourning response, we must remain attentive to user knowledge and ability as well as Internet availability and access. The online response to loss and grief is evident on an individual, community, and global level. In fact, the first response to a death or traumatic event often appears online through messaging, social media, video recording, etc. The use of social media has become an important aspect of the grief response. The social media encourages and supports self-determination on an individual level and engages people on a community/global level. Reviewing the impact of the Internet after the terrorist attacks on 9/11, De Vries and Moldaw (2012) suggest that the Internet has the power to "extend the boundaries of who is allowed or expected to participate in the mourning process and alter the face and shape that mourning assumes" (p. 136). There is a wealth of thanatological information, education, and support available through the Internet. The growing methods and opportunity to connect to others is changing how we respond and utilize support. The challenge is to utilize the growing hyperconnectivity to best help those coping with dying, death, and bereavement.

ADEC Code of Ethics

Introduction [1]

Membership in ADEC commits members and student affiliates to comply with the standards of the ADEC Code of Ethics. A lack of awareness or a misunderstanding of an Ethical Standard is not itself a defense to a charge of unethical conduct.

The Preface and Basic Tenets are explicative and provide aspirational goals to guide thanatologists toward the highest ideals. Although the **Preface** and **Basic Tenets** are not themselves enforceable rules they should be considered by thanatologists in arriving at an ethical course of action. Most of the Ethical Standards are written broadly, in order to apply to thanatologists in varied roles, although the application of an Ethical Standard may vary depending on the context. The Ethical Standards are not exhaustive. The fact that a given conduct is not specifically addressed by an Ethical Standard does not mean that it is necessarily either ethical or unethical. The Ethics Code applies across a variety of contexts, whether in person or by postal service, telephone, Internet, and/or other electronic transmissions.

In the process of making decisions regarding their professional behavior, thanatologists must consider this Code of Ethics in addition to the applicable laws and professional board regulations that they are subject to. If this Code of Ethics establishes a higher standard of conduct than is required by law or other codes, thanatologists must meet the higher ethical standard. If thanatologists' ethical responsibilities conflict with law, regulations, practice standards, or other governing legal authority, thanatologists make known their commitment to this Code of Ethics and take steps to resolve the conflict in a responsible manner.

Preface

The Association for Death Education and Counseling (herein referred to as the Association), founded in 1976, is an international, professional organization dedicated to promoting excellence in death education, care of the dying, and bereavement counseling and support. Based on quality research and theory, the Association provides information, support, and resources to its multicultural, multidisciplinary membership, and, through it, to the public.

The Association envisions a world in which dying, death, and bereavement are recognized as fundamental and significant aspects of the human experience. Therefore, the Association, ever committed to being on the forefront of thanatology, provides a home for professionals from diverse backgrounds to advance the body of knowledge and to promote practical applications of research and theory.

Recognizing the impact that death education and/or grief counseling can have upon the lives and well-being of people, the following is the Code of Ethics of the Association for Death Education and Counseling, adopted by the membership of the Association, and subscribed to by all who hold membership in the Association.

Basic Tenets

1. Death education and grief counseling are based upon a thorough knowledge of valid death-related data, methodology, and theory rather than stereotypes or untested hypotheses. Thus, the practice of death education and/or grief counseling requires knowledge of current thanatological literature.

2. The member strives to understand his or her death-related feelings and experiences and the ways in which these may impact his or her thinking and work in the field.

3. The member takes care to know the student or client. Good education and counseling are based upon an understanding of, and a respect for, the student's or client's cultural background, developmental status, perceptions, and other individual differences and needs.

4. The member neither exploits nor deceives others, but strives to improve the health and well-being of the individual and society. Fees, if charged, conform to an available schedule, consistent with comparable services. Research conforms to standards for human participation (as the Commission on Rights of Human Subjects has currently established).

5. The member serves in an advocacy role to assist the individual or society to cope with death-related issues. The member intervenes to prevent exploitation of the student or client and is obligated: (a) to be available to the student or client; and (b) to educate or counsel regarding rights, responsibilities and options with their possible consequences.

6. The member strives to present various views of a death-related question, indicating the member's own values if appropriate, and respecting the student's or client's choice among alternatives.

7. Recognizing that conflicts over the needs of the individual, family, institution, community, or society might arise, the member includes in his or her ongoing relationship, when appropriate, discussion of confidentiality and primary responsibility to the individual, to the family, to the institution, to the community, or to society.

8. The member recognizes his or her own limitations in meeting individual needs, and has available adequate consultation and referral resources. The member assesses the efficacy of his or her referral system by obtaining feedback from the referee, the referral resource, and knowledgeable consultants.

9. The member works to promote greater understanding among lay persons and professionals of dying and death so that each member of society can achieve a more satisfying life and personal acceptance of death.

Ethical Standards

I. General Conduct

The Association is committed to defining and maintaining high standards of professional service and conduct. Members are responsible for keeping the Association informed about developments of new knowledge and improvements in skill development

Members continually strive to improve themselves, their professions, and the Association through diligent efforts to improve professional practices, services, teaching, research, and the preparation of professionals.

Ethical behavior among members and their associates, both members and nonmembers, is expected at all times. When a member becomes aware of another person's violation of ethical standards, the member attempts to rectify the situation. If the situation continues without a satisfactory ethical resolution, the member pursues the issue through appropriate channels.

D. Members provide their professional services to anyone regardless of race, religion, gender, sexual orientation, socio-economic status, or choice of lifestyle. When the member cannot render service, the member makes an appropriate referral.

E. Members do not use their professional relationships to further their personal, political, religious, or business interests.

F. Sexual relationships with clients, students, and/or their significant others is unethical.

G. Members refrain from multiple relationships if (1) such relationships could reasonably be expected to impair the objectivity, competence, or effectiveness of the member in performing his or her responsibilities; or if (2) such relationships otherwise risk exploitation or harm to the person(s) with whom the professional relationship exists or formerly existed.

H. Members avoid conflicts of interest that interfere with professional discretion and impartial judgment. If a real or potential conflict of interest arises, members take reasonable steps to resolve the issue in a manner that reflects the best interests of the person(s) served.

I. Members neither offer, seek, nor accept payment of any kind for referrals.

II. Competence

A. Members continually strive to attain higher levels of competence. Each member is obliged to pursue continuing education and professional growth in all possible and appropriate ways, including participating in the affairs and activities of the Association and pursuing learning activities that lead to professional certification and licensure when available.

B. When called upon to deliver professional services, members accept only those positions and assignments for which they are professionally qualified.

C. Members are aware of the limits and boundaries of their professional competence and in no way represent themselves as having qualifications beyond those which they possess. Each member is responsible for correcting any misrepresentation other persons may make regarding that member's professional qualifications.

D. Members provide only those services and utilize only those techniques for which their training and experience qualifies them.

E. Members do not engage in professional activities when it is likely that personal problems or impairment may prevent them from performing such activities in a competent manner. In such situations, members seek appropriate professional consultation and assistance toward resolution of the situation. If the member is unable or unwilling to remedy personal conditions that may jeopardize the welfare of the member's clients, it is ethical for another member or other professional person to intercede and assist the member in taking remedial action.

III. Responsibilities to Those Served

A. The primary obligations of members are to respect the integrity of and to promote the welfare of clients and students.

B. When members believe that a client's or student's condition indicates that there is a foreseeable, serious, and imminent danger to the client, to the student, or to others, members take immediate, reasonable, and prudent action and/or inform appropriate authorities in accordance with applicable legal mandates. Consultation with other knowledgeable professionals is highly encouraged.

C. Members are free to consult with other professionals about clients and/or students provided that the consultation does not place the consultant in a position of conflict of interest and providing that all concerns of privacy, informed consent, and confidentiality are met appropriately.

D. In providing professional services to clients or students, members neither violate nor diminish their legal and civil rights.

E. Members who offer services, products or information via electronic transmission inform their clients and students of the risks to privacy and the limits of confidentiality.

F. Members take reasonable precautions to protect the confidentiality of clients/students in the event of the member's termination of practice, incapacitation or death. (1) Members insure confidentiality of client/student records; (2) Members either transfer client/student records to another professional, or assure secure storage of the records; (3) Clients/students or their legal guardians are informed about the termination of practice and about the transfer/storage of records.

IV. Responsibility to Others

A. Ethical, respectful and considerate behavior is expected of members at all times among and between professional associates, whether they are members or nonmembers.

   B. Members respect the confidences colleagues share with them during the course of their professional relationships and transactions unless confidences transgress legal and ethical mandates to disclose.

   C. Members who have responsibility for employing and/or evaluating the performance and achievements of others fulfill those responsibilities in a timely, fair, considerate, and equitable manner on the basis of clearly enunciated criteria. Members share their evaluation of a person with the person evaluated.

   E. Members maintain familiarity with the network of professional and self-help systems in the community and assist clients to avail themselves of those resources as appropriate.

   F. Members know and take into account the traditions and practices of other professional groups with whom they work and cooperate fully with those groups.

V. Responsibility to Employers

   A. Members clarify and establish interpersonal relations and working agreements with supervisors and subordinates especially in matters of professional relationships, confidentiality, distinctions between public and private material, maintenance and use of recorded information, and work load accountability.

   B. Members inform employers of conditions that may limit their effectiveness.

   C. Members submit regularly to professional review and evaluation.

   D. Members accept only those assignments that are within their competency.

   E. Members are responsible for on-going continuing education and development of their expertise and the expertise of their subordinates. Continuing Education and staff development should address current knowledge and emerging developments in the field.

   F. Members work to improve the employer's policies, procedures, and effectiveness of services.

   G. Members use employer resources only for purposes for which they were intended.

   H. Members neither engage in nor condone illegal or discriminatory practices.

   I. When employer demands require members to violate ethical principles, members clarify the nature of the conflict between the demands and the principles, inform all parties of members' ethical responsibilities, and take appropriate action consistent with prevailing ethical standards.

VII. Responsibility to Society

   A. Members work to prevent and to eliminate discrimination against any person or group on the basis of age, color, race, gender, sexual orientation, lifestyle, religion, national origin, marital status, political belief, or mental or physical disability.

   B. Members act to ensure that all persons whom they serve have access to the resources, services, and opportunities they require.

C. Members clarify whether they speak as individuals or as representatives of an organization.

D. Members provide their appropriate professional services in public emergencies.

E. Members interpret and share with the public their professional expertise regarding issues affecting the welfare of the society.

VIII. Confidentiality and Privacy

A. Members regard as confidential all information arising in the course of the professional relationship. Consideration for the client welfare is an abiding concern of members.

B. Members inform clients about the limits of confidentiality in a given situation.

C. Members obtain informed client consent prior to recording or allowing third party observation of their activities. Members inform clients about the purpose of recording/observing, who will have access to the recording and under what conditions, and the disposition of the recording. Client consent for one purpose is not valid for another or different purpose.

D. Members shall disclose confidential information when members believe there is clear and imminent danger to the client or to others, and that the danger can be alleviated or avoided by disclosing the information. In such circumstances, members are encouraged to consult with other knowledgeable professionals.

E. When members disclose confidential information without client consent, they do so only with appropriate others and only for compelling reasons.

F. Members safeguard written and recorded information about clients and are alert to potential threats to confidentiality in duplications processes, in use of computer equipment, and in electronic mail and facsimile transmission.

G. In those rare instances when members may disclose information, they disclose only that which is relevant within the context of the incident.

H. Members adequately disguise clinical and other material they use in teaching, writing, and public speaking in order to preserve client anonymity; an alternative is to obtain adequate prior client consent.

I. Members who have professional relationships with minor children assure them proper confidentiality. Members exercise careful judgment and respect applicable laws when discussing those children with their parents or guardians.

J. Client information received in confidence by one agent or agency is not forwarded to another without the client's written consent.

K. Members take into account an individual's capacity to give consent or to refuse care/treatment. Members thoroughly and scrupulously assess the client's relevant abilities and capacity to make decisions. Members exercise careful judgment regarding confidentiality and privacy regarding those individuals who fall below the threshold of decisional capacity.

Death Educators and Trainers

This section addresses those thanatologists who, on either a full-time or part-time or an occasional basis, function as a death educator or provide death education or training in any way to others.

DE-I. Responsibility to Others

    A. Members in charge of programs establish learning experiences that integrate academic study and supervised practice. Such programs develop student skill, knowledge, and self-understanding.

    B. Members orient students to program or learning expectations, basic skills development, and, when appropriate, to employment prospects prior to admission.

    C. When a program or learning experience has a focus upon self-disclosure, self-understanding or growth, members ensure that potential students are made aware of this fact before they enter the program or begin the experience.

    D. Members who employ exercises and simulations which draw upon participant thoughts, feelings, and memories must ensure that appropriate professional assistance is available to participants during and following those learning experiences.

    E. When a student is expected to disclose relatively intimate or personal information about themselves as part of their learning experience, educators and supervisors shall not evaluate the student based upon such self-disclosure. The degree of self-disclosure will be respected without coercion or punitive measures.

    F. When a program or learning experience has a focus upon self-disclosure, self-understanding or growth, members ensure the confidentiality and privacy of information shared in this setting.

    G. Members make students aware of professional ethical responsibilities and standards.

    H. When members function as educators, they maintain high standards of scholarship and objectivity. Members present information fully and accurately, and they provide appropriate recognition of alternative viewpoints.

DE-II. Standards of Professional Competence

    A. Members assuming educative functions do so within their professional competence.

    B. Members teach only in areas in which they have received professional preparation.

    C. Members engage in continuous study and professional development in order to insure that they provide instruction based on the most current information available in the profession.

    D. Members accurately cite or credit those authors and researchers whose work the member is presenting.

Grief Counselors/Therapists

This section refers to those thanatologists who, either on a full time or part-time or an occasional basis, function as grief counselors/therapists providing thanatology-related clinical services to others.

GC-I. Responsibility to Those Served

A. When members receive a referral, they actively seek all available, pertinent information from the client, legal guardian, or referral source, with appropriate written consent.

B. When a member is contacted by an individual who is receiving services from another agency or colleague, the member carefully considers the client's needs before agreeing to provide services. Members should (1) discuss with potential clients the nature of the client's current relationship with the other service provider and the possible risks and benefits of entering into a new professional relationship; (2) seek consent for exchange of information when it would be beneficial to the client. All resources utilized by the client should be documented appropriately.

C. Before members enter into professional relationships with potential clients, members inform clients/legal guardians about their expertise, techniques and other practices that may be used and that may affect the client's well being. Members clarify client/legal guardian goals and the purpose and expectations of the services they provide.

D. Clients/legal guardians are informed verbally and in writing at the time of the first interview about the limits of confidentiality as stipulated by law, regulation, or organizational process.

E. Prior to initiation of services, members notify clients/legal guardians of all financial responsibilities assumed by client/guardian or counselor. Fees for services, and any changes, must be identified and agreed to prior to services rendered. As a portion of their professional activities, members are encouraged to provide pro-bono or reduced fees to clients who experience financial constraints/difficulties.

F. Members make appointments with relatives or collateral of clients only when clients have given their permission, unless an emergent situation requires another course of action. In this case, members consider legal and ethical implications and seek consultation before proceeding.

G. When members agree to provide services to clients at the requests of third parties, the nature of each of the relationships of the involved parties is clarified, accepted by all, and documented as such. Any limitations to confidentiality will be noted as well.

H. Members keep records and other information related to clients confidential for at least the number of years determined by laws in the member's state, province or country of practice.

    I.   Members should seek professional consultation whenever such consultation is in the best interests of those served.

    J.   If members determine that they are unable, or no longer capable of providing a particular service, they carefully prepare the client and assist in making appropriate arrangements for continuing care when necessary. The client's well being is of primary concern; therefore, every attempt is made to ensure that the client does not feel abandoned and that possible adverse effects are minimized. All efforts to this end should be documented.

GC-III. Responsibility to Others

    A.   Grief counselors/therapists do not solicit the clients of others.

    B.   Grief counselors/therapists fully cooperate with professionals who treat former clients of that provider.

    C.   Grief counselors/therapists are encouraged to offer their expertise in the geographical community in which they live and to take part in collaboration and interdisciplinary teamwork when working in a hospital or school environment.

Researchers in Thanatology[2]

This section refers to those thanatologists who, either on a full time, part-time or an occasional basis, function as researchers in thanatology-related subject areas.

RT- I. Responsibility to Institutions

    A.   When institutional approval is required, members provide accurate information about their research proposals and obtain approval prior to conducting the research.

    B.   Members conduct research in accordance with approved research protocol.

RT-II. Responsibility to Research Participants

    A.   When obtaining informed consent, members inform participants about the purpose of the research, expected duration, and procedures; and about their right to decline to participate and to withdraw from the research study without penalty.

    B.   When members conduct research with clients/patients, students, or subordinates as participants, members take steps to protect the prospective participants from adverse consequences of declining or withdrawing from participation.

    C.   When research participation is a course requirement or an opportunity for extra credit, the prospective participant is given the choice of equitable alternative activities.

    D.   Members may dispense with informed consent only (1) where research would not reasonably be assumed to create distress or harm and involves (a) the study of normal educational practices, curricula, or classroom management methods conducted in educational settings; (b) the use of anonymous questionnaires, naturalistic observations, or archival research for which disclosure of responses would not place participants at risk of criminal or civil liability or damage their financial standing, employability, or reputation, and confidentiality is protected; or (c) the study of factors related to job or organization effectiveness conducted in organizational settings for which there is no risk to participants' employability, and confidentiality is protected or (2) where otherwise permitted by law or federal or institutional regulations.

E. Members provide a prompt opportunity for participants to obtain appropriate information about the nature, results, and conclusions of the research, and they take reasonable steps to correct any misconceptions that participants may have of which the members are aware. If scientific or humane values justify delaying or withholding this information, members take reasonable measures to reduce the risk of harm.

F. When members become aware that research procedures have harmed a participant, they take reasonable steps to minimize the harm.

RT-III. Responsibility in Reporting and Publishing Data

A. Members do not fabricate data.

B. If members discover significant errors in their published data, they take reasonable steps to correct such errors in a correction, retraction, erratum, or other appropriate publication means.

C. Members do not present portions of another's work or data as their own, even if the other work or data source is cited occasionally.

D. Members take responsibility and credit, including authorship credit, only for work they have actually performed or to which they have substantially contributed

(1) Principal authorship and other publication credits accurately reflect the relative scientific or professional contributions of the individuals involved, regardless of their relative status. Mere possession of an institutional position, such as department chair, does not justify authorship credit. Minor contributions to the research or to the writing for publications are acknowledged appropriately, such as in footnotes or in an introductory statement.

(2) Except under exceptional circumstances, a student is listed as principal author on any multiple-authored article that is substantially based on the student's **research**. Faculty advisors discuss publication credit with students as early as feasible and throughout the research and publication process as appropriate.

E. Members who review material submitted for presentation, publication, grant, or research proposal review respect the confidentiality of and the proprietary rights in such information of those who submitted it.

---

1. Portions of this Code of Ethics are based on the "Ethical Principles of Psychologists and Code of Conduct" (*American Psychologist*, 2002, *57*, 1060-1073), which is the copyrighted property of the American Psychological Association. While the American Psychological Association has given permission to ADEC to utilize the APA Code of Ethics, APA has in no way advised, assisted, or encouraged ADEC to utilize the APA Code of Ethics. APA is in no way responsible for ADEC's decision to utilize the APA Code of Ethics, or for any actions or other consequences resulting from such use by ADEC.

2. Ibid.

References

Abdelnoor, A., & Hollins, S. (2004). How children cope at school after family bereavement. *Educational and Child Psychology*, 21, 85-94.

Ablett, J., & Jones, R. (2007). Resilience and well-being in palliative care staff: A qualitative study of hospice nurses' experience of work. *Psycho-Oncology*, 16, 733-744.

Abrams, D., Albury, S., Crandall, I., Doka, K., & Harris, R. (2005). The Florida clergy end-of-life education enhancement project: A description and evaluation. *American Journal of Hospice & Palliative Medicine*, 22, 181-187.

Adams, D.W. (2002). The consequences of sudden traumatic death: The vulnerability of bereaved children and adolescents and ways professionals can help. In G.R. Cox, R.A. Bendiksen, & R.G. Stevenson (Eds.), *Complicated grieving and bereavement: Understanding and treating people experiencing loss* (pp. 23-40). Amityville, NY: Baywood Publishing.

Adams, D.W., & Deveau, E.J. (1987). When a brother or sister is dying of cancer: The vulnerability of the adolescent sibling. *Death Studies*, 11, 279-295.

Adams, D.W., & Deveau, E.J. (1995). *Beyond the Innocence of Childhood, Volume 3: Helping Children and Adolescents Cope with Death and Bereavement*. Amityville, NY: Baywood Publishing.

Adams, R.E., Boscarino, J.A., & Figley, C.R. (2006). Compassion fatigue and psychological distress among social workers: A validation study. *American Journal of Orthopsychiatry*, 76, 103-108.

Aden, L.H. (2005). *In life and death: The shaping of faith*. Minneapolis, MN: Augsburg Books.

Adlersberg, J. (2010). *Ban "heartened" by scale of global response to help Haiti quake victims*. Retrieved from http://www.un.org.

Agerbo, E. (2005). Midlife suicide risk, partner's psychiatric illness, spouse and child bereavement by suicide or other modes of death: A gender specific study. *Journal of Epidemiology and Community Health*, 59, 407-412.

Ai, A.L., Park, C.L., & Shearer, M. (2009). Spiritual and religious involvement relate to end-of-life decision-making in patients undergoing coronary bypass graft surgery. *International Journal of Psychiatry in Medicine*, 38, 113–132.

Aitchison, S. (1992). *Red Rock Sacred Mountain: The canyons and peaks from Sedona to Flagstaff*. Stillwater, MN: Voyageur Press.

Alam, R., Barrera, M., D'Agostino, N., Nicholas, D.B., & Schneiderman, G. (2012). Bereavement experiences of mothers and fathers over time after the death of a child due to cancer. *Death Studies*, 36, 1-22.

Alexander, J. (2004). Towards a theory of cultural trauma. In. J. Alexander, R. Eyerman, B. Giesen, N. Smelser, & P. Szomoka (Eds.). *Cultural trauma and collective identity*. Berkeley, CA: University of California Press.

Alexander, I.E., & Alderstein, A.M. (1958). Affective responses to the concept of death in a population of children and early adolescents. *Journal of Genetic Psychology*, 93, 167-177.

Allen, B., Brymer, M.J., Steinberg, A.M., Vernberg, E.M., Jacobs, A., Speier, A.H., & Pynoos, R.S. (2010). Perceptions of psychological first aid among providers responding to hurricanes Gustav and Ike. *Journal of Traumatic Stress*, 23, 509-513.

Allen, J. (1999). *Coping with trauma: A guide to self-understanding.* Arlington, VA: American Psychiatric Association.

Allport, G.W., & Ross, J.M. (1967). Personal religious orientation, and prejudice. *Journal of Personality and Social Psychology, 5,* 432-443.

Allumbaugh, D.L., & Hoyt, W.T. (1999). Effectiveness of grief therapy: A meta-analysis. *Journal of Counseling Psychology, 46,* 370-380.

Amella, E.J., Lawrence, J.F., & Gresle, S.O. (2005). Tube feeding: Prolonging life or death in vulnerable populations? *Mortality, 10,* 69-81. doi:10.1080/13576270500031089.

American Association of University Professors. (2012). *Copyright, distance education and intellectual property issues.* Retrieved from http://www.aaup.org/AAUP/issues/DE/.

American Medical Association. Policy E-2. 21 *Euthanasia,* 1996.

American Psychiatric Association. (2000*). Diagnostic and Statistical Manual of Mental Disorders: DSM-IV-TR.* Washington, DC: Author.

American Psychological Association. (2012). *A resolution on the recognition of psychotherapy effectiveness.* Washington, DC: Author.

Anderson, B., & Simpson, M. (2007). Ethical issues in online education. *Open Learning: The Journal of Open and Distance Learning, 22,* 129-138.

Anderson, S.A., & Sabatelli, R.M. (2007). *Family interaction: A multigenerational developmental perspective.* Boston, MA: Allyn & Bacon.

Aneshensel, C.S., Botticello, A.L., Yamamoto-Mitani, N. (2004). When caregiving ends: The course of depressive symptoms after bereavement. *Journal of Health and Social Behavior, 45,* 422-440.

Antonovsky, A. (1990). Pathways leading to successful coping and health. In M. Rosenbaum (Ed.), *Learned resourcefulness: On coping skills, self-control, and adaptive behavior* (pp. 31-63). New York, NY: Springer-Verlag.

Applegate, J. K. (1997). *Ambivalence toward the spouse as related to the grief of widows in the second year of bereavement.* (Unpublished doctoral dissertation). University of Kansas.

Arbore, P., Katz, R.S., & Johnson, T.A. (2006). Suffering and the caring professional. In R.S. Katz & T.A. Johnson, *When professionals weep* (pp. 13-26). New York, NY: Taylor & Francis.

Aries, P. (1981). *The hour of our death* (H. Weaver, Trans.). New York, NY: Knopf.

Arlow, J.A. (2004). Psychoanalysis. In R. Corsini & D. Wedding (Eds.), *Current psychotherapies* (7th ed., pp. 15-51). Belmont, CA: Thompson/Brooks/Cole.

Arnett, J.J. (2000). Emerging adulthood. A theory of development from the late teens through the twenties. *American Psychologist, 55,* 469-480.

Arnett, J.J. (2002). The psychology of globalization. *American Psychologist, 57,* 774-783.

Arnett, J.J. (2004). Emerging *adulthood: The winding road from the late teens through the twenties.* New York, NY: Oxford University Press.

Asmar-Kawar, N. (2001*). Perceptions of loss among Jews and Arabs: Culture, gender and the Two-Track Model of Bereavement.* (Unpublished master's thesis). Tel Aviv University.

Aspinall, S.Y. (1996). Educating children to cope with death: A preventive model. *Psychology in the Schools, 33,* 341-349.

Atkinson, M.J. (1935). *Indians of the Southwest.* San Antonio, TX: Naylor.

Attig, T. (1995). Respecting the spirituality of the dying and the bereaved. In I. Corless, R.B. Germino, & M.A. Pittman-Lindeman (Eds.). *A challenge for living: Dying, Death and Bereavement* (pp. 61-78). Burlington, MA: Jones and Bartlett.

Attig, T. (1996). *How we grieve: Relearning the world.* New York, NY: Oxford University Press.

Attig, T. (2000). *The heart of grief: Death and the search for lasting love.* New York, NY: Oxford University Press.

Attig, T. (2001). Relearning the world: Making and finding meanings. In R.A. Neimeyer (Ed.), *Meaning reconstruction & the experience of loss* (pp. 33-53). Washington, DC: American Psychological Association.

Attig, T. (2002). Questionable assumptions about assumptive worlds. In J. Kauffman (Ed.), *Loss of the assumptive world: A theory of traumatic loss* (pp. 55-68). New York, NY: Brunner-Routledge.

Attig, T. (2010). *How we grieve: Relearning the world* (2nd ed.). New York, NY: Oxford University Press.

Aviad, Y. (2001*). The social construction of children's responses to the loss of a parent: Evaluating the contributions of the Two-Track Model of Bereavement and relationship to the surviving parent.* (Unpublished master's thesis). University of Haifa.

Ayers, T., Kondo, C.C., & Sandler, I. (2011). Bridging the gap: Translating a research-based program into an agency-based service for bereaved children and families. In R.A. Neimeyer, D.L. Harris, H.R. Winokuer & G. Thornton (Eds.), *Grief and bereavement in contemporary society: Bridging research and practice* (pp. 117-135). New York, NY: Routledge.

Azaiza, F., Ron, P., Shoman, M., & Gigini, I. (2010). Death and dying anxiety among elderly Arab Muslims in Israel. *Death Studies, 34,* 351-364. doi:10.1080/07481181003613941.

Bader, J.L. (2001, June 10). Death be not bad for ratings. *The New York Times,* Section 4, p. 2.

Bagilishya, D. (2000). Mourning and recovery from trauma: In Rwanda, tears flow within. *Transcultural Psychiatry, 37,* 337-353.

Bahr, S.S., & Brown, G.K. (2012). Treatment of depression and suicide in older adults. *Cognitive and Behavioral Practice, 19,* 116-125.

Balboni, T.A., Vanderwerker, L.C., Block, S.D., Paulk, M.E., Lathan, C.S., Peteet, J.R., & Prigerson, H.G. (2007). Religiousness and spiritual support among advanced cancer patients and associations with end-of-life treatment preferences and quality of life. *Journal of Clinical Oncology, 25,* 555- 560.

Balk, D.E. (1995). Bereavement research using control groups: Ethical obligations and questions. *Death Studies, 19,* 123-138.

Balk, D.E. (2001). College student bereavement, scholarship, and the university: A call for university engagement. *Death Studies, 25,* 67-84.

Balk, D.E. (2007). Bridging the practice-research gap. *The Forum, 33*(1), 3-4.

Balk, D.E. (2011). Adolescent development and bereavement: An introduction. *The Prevention Researcher, 18* (3), 3-9.

Balk, D.E. (2011). A shot across the bow. *Death Studies, 35,* 565-569.

Balk, D.E. (2011). *Helping the bereaved college student.* New York, NY: Springer Publishing.

Balk, D.E. (2011). Does coping with bereavement occur in stages? In K.J. Doka & A.S. Tucci (Eds.), *Beyond Kübler-Ross: New perspectives on death, dying and grief* (pp. 45-60). Washington, DC: Hospice Foundation of America.

Balk, D.E., & Corr, C.A. (Eds.) (2009). *Adolescent encounters with death, bereavement, and coping.* New York, NY: Springer Publishing.

Balk, D.E., Cupit, I.N., Sandler, I., & Werth, J. (2011). Bereavement and depression: Possible changes to the diagnostic and statistical manual of mental disorders: A report from the scientific advisory committee of the Association for Death Education and Counseling. *Omega: Journal of Death and Dying, 63,* 199-220.

Balk, D.E., Walker, A.C., & Baker, A. (2010). Prevalence and severity of college student bereavement. *Death Studies, 34,* 459-468.

Baltes, P.B., Reese, H.W., & Nesselroade, J.R. (1977). *Life-span developmental psychology: Introduction to research methods*. Monterey, CA: Brooks/Cole.

Bandura, A. (1969). *Principles of behavior modification*. New York, NY: Holt, Rinehart & Winston.

Bandura, A. (1974). Behavior theory and the models of man. *American Psychologist, 29*, 859-869.

Barra, D.M., Carlson, E.S., Maize, M., Murphy, W.I., O'Neal, B.W., Sarver R.E., & Zinner, E.S. (1993). The dark night of the spirit: Grief following a loss in religious identity. In K.J. Doka and J.D. Morgan, (Eds.) *Death and Spirituality* (pp. 291-308). Amityville, NY: Baywood Publishing.

Barrett, R.K. (1995a). Contemporary African-American funeral rites and traditions. In L.A. DeSpelder & A.L. Strickland (Eds.), *The path ahead: Readings in death and dying* (pp. 80-92). Mountain View, CA: Mayfield.

Barrett, R.K. (1995b). Psychocultural influences on African-American attitudes toward death, dying, and funeral rites. In J.D. Morgan (Ed.), *Personal care in an impersonal world: A multidimensional look at bereavement* (pp. 213-230). Amityville, NY: Baywood Publishing.

Barrett, R.K. (1998). Sociocultural considerations for working with blacks experiencing loss and grief. In K.J. Doka & J.D. Davidson (Eds.), *Living with grief: Who we are, how we grieve* (pp. 83-96). Philadelphia, PA: Brunner/Mazel.

Barrett, R. (2001). Recommendations for culturally competent end-of-life care giving. *Virtual Mentor: American Medical Association Journal of Ethics*. Retrieved from http://www.ama- assn.org/ama/pub/category/6824.htm.

Barrett, R.K., & DeSpelder, L.A. (1997, June). *Ways people die: The influence of environment on a child's view of death*. Paper presented at the annual meeting of the Association for Death Education and Counseling, Washington, DC.

Barrett, T.W., & Scott, T.B. (1989). Development of the grief experience questionnaire. *Suicide and Life-Threatening Behavior, 19*, 201-215.

Barton, D., & Crowder, M.K. (1975). The use of role playing techniques as an instructional aid in teaching about dying, death, and bereavement. *Omega: Journal of Death and Dying, 6*, 243-250.

Basu, S., & Heuser, L. (2003). Using service learning in death education. *Death Studies, 27*, 901-927.

Battin, M.P., van der Heide, A., Ganzini, L., van der Wal, G., Onwuteaka-Philipsen, B.D. (2007). Legal physician-assisted dying in Oregon and the Netherlands: evidence concerning the impact on patients in "vulnerable" groups. *Journal of Medical Ethics*, 33:591-597.

Baxter, L.A., & Braithwaite, D.O. (2006). Family rituals. In L. Turner & R. West (Eds.), *Family communication: A reference for theory and research* (pp. 259-280). Thousand Oaks, CA: Sage Publications.

Beauchamp, T.L., & Childress, J.F. (2001). *Principles of medical ethics* (5th ed.). New York, NY: Oxford University Press.

Beavers, W.R., & Hampson, R. (2003). Measuring family competence: The Beavers Systems Model. In F. Walsh (Ed.), *Normal family processes: Growing diversity and complexity* (pp. 549-580). New York, NY: Guilford Press.

Beck, A.T. (1976). *Cognitive therapy and emotional disorders*. New York, NY: International Universities Press.

Becker, E. (1971). *The birth and death of meaning* (2nd ed.). New York, NY: Free Press.

Becker, E. (1973). *The denial of death*. New York, NY: Free Press.

Beckwith, S. (2005). When families disagree: Family conflict and decisions. In K. Doka, B. Jennings, & C. Corr. *Ethical dilemmas at the end of life*. Washington, DC: Hospice Foundation of America.

Becvar, D.S. (2003). The impact on the family therapist of a focus on death, dying, and bereavement. *Journal of Marital and Family Therapy, 29*, 469-477.

Becvar, D.S., & Becvar, R. (2006). *Family therapy: A systemic integration*. Boston: Allyn & Bacon.

Bellah, R.N., Madsen, R., Sullivan, A.S., Swidler, A., & Tipton, S.M. (1985). *Habits of the heart: Individualism and commitment in American life.* Berkekey, CA: University of California Press.

Bender, D.L. (Ed.) (1974). *Problems of death.* Anoka, MN: Greenhaven Press.

Benight, C.C., Flores, J., & Tashiro, T. (2001). Bereavement coping self-efficacy in cancer widows. *Death Studies, 25,* 97-125.

Bennett, S., & Maton, K. (2010). Beyond the 'digital natives' debate: Towards a more nuanced understanding of students' technology experiences. *Journal of Computer Assisted Learning, 26,* 321-331.

Benoliel, J.Q., & Degner, L.F. (1995). Institutional dying: A convergence of cultural values, technology, and social organization. In H. Wass & R.A. Neimeyer (Eds.), *Dying: Facing the facts* (pp. 117-141). Philadelphia, PA: Taylor & Francis.

Berg, C.A., Wiebe, D.J., Beveridge, R.M., Palmer, D.L., Carolyn D. Korbel, C.D., Upchurch, R., Swinyard, M.T., Lindsay, R., & Donaldson, D.L. (2007). Mother–child appraised involvement in coping with diabetes stressors and emotional adjustment. *Journal of Pediatric Psychology, 32,* 995-1005.

Berger, J. (2009). The posttraumatic growth model: An expansion to the family system. *Traumatology, 1* (1), 63-74.

Berger, P., & Luckman, T. (1966). *The social construction of reality.* New York, NY: Doubleday.

Bernal, G., and Domenech Rodriguez, M. (2012). *Cultural adaptations: Tools for evidence-based practice with diverse populations.* Washington, DC: American Psychological Association.

Bernal, G., & Saez-Santiago, E. (2006). Culturally centered psychosocial interventions. *Journal of Community Psychology, 34,* 121-132.

Bernat, J. (1992). How much of the brain must die in brain death? *Journal of Clinical Ethics, 3,* 21-26.

Berns, C.F. (2003/2004). Bibliotherapy: Using books to help bereaved children. *Omega: Journal of Death and Dying, 48,* 321-336.

Besser, A., & Priel, B. (2007). Attachment, depression, and fear of death in older adults: The roles of neediness and perceived availability of social support. *Personality and Individual Differences, 44,* 1711-1725.

Biggs, P. (2012). Emerging issues for our hyperconnected world. In S. Dutta & B. Bilbao-Osorio (Eds.) *The global information technology report 2012: Living in a hyperconnected world* (pp. 47-56). Retrieved from: http://www3.weforum.org/docs/Global_IT_Report_2012.pdf.

Binswanger, L. (1963). *Being in the world.* New York, NY: Harper & Row.

Birenbaum, L.K. (2000). Assessing children's and teenagers' bereavement when a sibling dies from cancer: A secondary analysis. *Child: Care, Health and Development, 26,* 381-400.

Biziou, B. (1999). *The joys of everyday ritual: Spiritual recipes to celebrate milestones, ease transitions, and make every day sacred.* New York, NY: St. Martin's Griffin.

Black, D.M. (2011). *Why things matter: The place of values in science, psychoanalysis and religion.* London, UK and New York, NY: Routledge.

Black, R.E., Bhan, M.K., Chopra, M., et al. (2009). Accelerating the health impact of the Gates Foundation. *The Lancet, 373,* 1584-185.

Blackhall, L.J., Murphy, S.T., Frank, G., Michel, V., & Azcn, S. (1995). Ethnicity and attitudes toward patient autonomy. *Journal of the American Medical Association, 274,* 820-825.

Blanchot, M. (2000). *The instant of my death.* (Trans.) F. Morgana Stamford: Stamford University Press.

Blanke, J.M. (2002, June). To copy, or not to copy, that is the quandary: An introduction to copying under the copyright law. Paper published in the proceedings of the ASCUE Conference, Myrtle Beach, SC. Retrieved from http://fits.depauw.edu/ascue/Proceedings/ 2002/index.asp#.

Blevins, D., & Papadatou, D. (2006). The effects of culture in end-of-life situations. In J.L. Werth, Jr., & D. Blevins (Eds.), *Psychosocial issues near the end of life: A resource for professional care providers* (pp. 27-55). Washington, DC: American Psychological Association.

Bluebond-Langner, M. (1978). *The private worlds of dying children*. Princeton, NJ: Princeton University Press.

Blumenfeld, S.L. (2011). *Death education at Columbine High*. Western Journalism Center: WorldNetDaily. com.

Boelen, P.A., van den Hout, M.A., & van den Bout, J. (2006). A cognitive-behavioral conceptualization of complicated grief. *Clinical Psychology: Science and Practice, 13*, 109-128.

Boelen, P.A., de Keijser, J., van den Hout, M., & van den Bout, J. (2007). Treatment of complicated grief: A comparison between cognitive-behavioral therapy and supportive counseling. *Journal of Clinical and Consulting Psychology, 75*, 277-284.

Bonanno, G.A. (2004). Loss, trauma and human resilience: Have we underestimated the human capacity to thrive after extremely adverse events? *American Psychologist, 59*, 20-28.

Bonanno, G.A. (2006). *Research that matters – 2006: New findings on loss and human resilience*. A symposium presented at the Annual Conference of the Association for Death Education and Counseling, Tampa, FL.

Bonanno, G.A. (2009). *The other side of sadness: What the new science of bereavement tells us about life after loss*. New York, NY: Basic Books.

Bonanno, G.A. (2012). Uses and abuses of the resilience construct: Loss, trauma, and health-related adversities. *Social Science & Medicine, 74*, 753-756.

Bonanno, G.A., Brewin, C.R., Kaniasty, K., & LaGreca, A.M. (2010). Weighing the costs of disaster: consequences, risks, and resilience in individuals, families, and communities. *Psychological Science in the Public Interest, 11*, 1-49.

Bonanno, G.A., & Kaltman, S. (2001). The varieties of grief experience. *Clinical Psychology Review, 21*, 705-734.

Bonanno, G.A., & Lilienfeld, S.O. (2008). Let's be realistic: When grief counseling is effective and when it's not. *Professional Psychology: Research and Practice, 39*, 377-380.

Bonanno, G.A., Moskowitz, J.T., Papa, A., & Folkman, S. (2005). Resilience to loss in bereaved spouses, bereaved parents, and bereaved gay men. *Journal of Personality and Social Psychology, 88*, 827-843.

Bonanno, G.A., Neria, Y., Mancini, A., Coifman, K., Litz, B., & Insel, B. (2007). Is there more to complicated grief than depression and posttraumatic stress disorder? A test of incremental validity. *Journal of Abnormal Psychology, 116*, 342-351.

Bonanno, G.A., Wortman, C.B., Lehman, D.R., Tweed, R.G., Haring, M., Sonnega, J., Carr, D., & Neese, R.M. (2002). Resilience to loss and chronic grief: A prospective study from pre-loss to 18-months post-loss. *Journal of Personality and Social Psychology, 83*, 1150-1164.

Bonanno, G.A., Wortman, C.B., & Nesse, R.M. (2004). Prospective patterns of resilience and maladjustment during widowhood. *Psychology and Aging, 19*, 260-271.

Bonnie, R.J., Wright, S., & Dineen, K.K. (2008). Legal authority to preserve organs in cases of uncontrolled cardiac death: Preserving family choice. *Journal of Law and Medical Ethics, 36*, 741-751, 610.

Bookwala, J., Coppola, K.M., Fagerlin, A., Ditto, P.H., Danks, J.H., & Smucker, W.D. (2001). Gender differences in older adults' preferences for life-sustaining medical treatments and end-of-life values. *Death Studies, 25*, 127-149.

Bordere, T. (2009). Culturally conscientious thanatology. *The Forum, 35*(1), 3-4.

Bordewich, F.M. (1988). Education: Mortal fears. *The Atlantic, 262*(2), 30-32, 34.

Bosley, G.M., & Cook, A.S. (1993). Therapeutic aspects of funeral ritual: A thematic analysis. *Journal of Family Psychotherapy, 4*, 69-83.

Boss, P. (1991). Ambiguous loss. In F. Walsh & M. McGoldrick (Eds.), *Living beyond loss* (pp. 164-175). New York, NY: W.W. Norton & Co.

Boss, P. (1999). *Ambiguous loss: Learning to live with unresolved grief*. Cambridge, MA: Harvard University Press.

Boss, P. (2006). *Therapeutic work with ambiguous loss: Loss, trauma, and resilience.* New York, NY: W.W. Norton & Co.

Boston, P., Bruch, A., & Schreiber, R. (2011). Existential suffering in the palliative care setting: An integrated literature review. *Journal of Pain Symptom Management, 41,* 604-618.

Boszormenyi-Nagy, I. (1987). *Foundations of contextual therapy: Collected papers of Ivan Boszormenyi-Magy, M.D.* New York, NY: Brunner/Mazel.

Boszormenyi-Nagy, I., Grunebaum, J., & Ulrich, D. (1991). Contextual therapy, In A.S. Gurman & D.P. Kniskern (Eds.), *Handbook of family therapy, Volume II* (159-186). New York, NY: Brunner/Mazel.

Bowen, M. (1985). *Family therapy in clinical practice.* Northwale, NJ: Jason Aronson.

Bowlby, J. (1961). Processes of mourning. *The International Journal of Psycho-Analysis, 42,* 317-340.

Bowlby, J. (1969, 1982). *Attachment and loss.* New York, NY: Basic Books. [Vol. 1, *Attachment*; Vol. 2, *Separation: Anxiety and anger*; Vol. 3, *Loss: Sadness and depression.*]

Bowman, K.W., & Singer, P.A. (2001). Chinese seniors' perspectives on end-of-life decisions. *Social Science & Medicine, 53,* 455-464. doi:10.1016/S0277-9536(00)00348-8.

Boyd-Franklin, N. (2003). *Black families in therapy: Understanding the African American experience* (2nd ed.). New York, NY: Guilford Press.

Boyle, D.K., Miller, P.A., & Forbes-Thompson, S.A. (2005). Communication and end-of-life care in the intensive care unit: Patient, family and clinician outcomes. *Critical Care Nursing Quarterly, 28*(4), 302-316.

Boyraz, G., Horne, S.G., & Sayger, T.V. (2012). Finding meaning in loss: The mediating role of social support between personality and two construals of meaning. *Death Studies, 36,* 519-540.

Brabant, S., Forsyth, C. J., & McFarlain, G. (1997). The impact of the death of a child on meaning and purpose in life. *Journal of Personal and Interpersonal Loss, 2,* 255-266.

Brabant, S., & Kalich, D. (2008-2009). Who enrolls in death education courses? A longitudinal study. *Omega: Journal of Death and Dying, 58,* 1-18.

Bracken, P. (2002). *Trauma, culture,. Meaning and philosophy.* London, UK: Whurr Publishers.

Braun, U.K., Beyth, R.J., Ford, M.E., & McCullough, L.B. (2008). Voices of African American, Caucasian, and Hispanic surrogates on the burdens of end-of-life decision making. *Journal of General Internal Medicine, 23,* 267-274. doi:10.1007/s11606-007-0487-7.

Braun, K.L., & Nichols, R. (1996). Cultural issues in death and dying. *Hawaii Medical Journal, 55,* 260-264. Retrieved from http://www.hawaiimedicaljournal.org.

Braun, K., Pietsch, J., & Blanchette, P. (Eds.) (2000). *Cultural issues in end-of-life decision making.* Thousand Oaks, CA: Sage Publications.

Breen, L.J., & O'Connor, M. (2011). Family and social networks after bereavement: Experiences of support, change and isolation. *Journal of Family Therapy, 33,* 98-120. doi:10.1111/j.1467-6427.2010.00495.x.

Bregman, L. (2006). Spirituality: A glowing and useful term in search of a meaning. *Omega: Journal of Death and Dying, 53,* 5-26.

Bremner, J.D., Quinn, J., Quinn, W., & Veledar, E. (2006) Surfing the net for medical information about psychological trauma: An empirical study of the quality and accuracy of trauma-related websites. *Medical Informatics & the Internet in Medicine,* Vol. 31, 227-36. Retrieved from http://www.ncbi.nlm.nih.gov/pubmed/16954059.

Brennan, A.J. (1983). Paper presented at the children and death conference, Columbia-Presbyterian Medical Center, New York, NY.

Brennan, T. (2004). *The transmission of affect.* Ithaca, NY: Cornell University Press.

Brenneis, D. (2002). Some cases for culture. *Human Development, 45,* 264-269.

Brent, S.B. (1977-78). Puns, metaphors, and misunderstanding in a two-year olds' conception of death. *Omega: Journal of Death and Dying,* 8, 285-293.

Brewer, J.D. (2011). Young people living with parental bereavement: Insights from an ethnographic study of a UK childhood bereavement service. *Social Science and Medicine,* 72, 883-290._

Brey, P. (2006). Social and ethical dimensions of computer-mediated education. *Journal of Information, Communication, and Ethics in Society,* 4, 91-101.

Bridging Work Group. (2005). Bridging the gap between research and practice in bereavement: Report from the Center for the Advancement of Health. *Death Studies,* 29, 93-121.

Brier, N. (2004). Anxiety after miscarriage: A review of the empirical literature and implications for clinical practice. *Birth: Issues in Perinatal Care,* 31, 138-142.

Brierley, J., & Larcher, V. (2011). Organ donation from children: time for legal, ethical and cultural change. *Acta Paediatrica,* 100, 1175-1179.

Briggs, C.A., & Pehrsson, D.E. (2008). Use of bibliotherapy in the treatment of grief and loss: A guide to current counseling practices. *Adultspan Journal,* 7, 32-42.

Brison, K.J. (1992). *Just talk: Gossip, meetings, and power in a Papua New Guinea village.* Berkeley, CA: University of California Press.

British Red Cross. (2012). *Haiti earthquake 2010.* Retrieved from http://www.redcross.org.uk/What-we-do/ Emergency-response/Recovering-from-disasters/Haiti-earthquake-2010.

Brown, C., & Czerniewicz, L. (2010). Debunking the 'digital native': Beyond digital apartheid, towards digital democracy. *Journal of Computer Assisted Learning,* 26, 357-369.

Brown University, the Center for Gerontology and Health Care Research. *Facts on dying.* Retrieved from http://www.chcr.brown.edu/dying/factsondying.htm.

Brymer, M., Jacobs, A., Layne, C., Pynoos, R., Ruzek, J., Steinberg, A., Vernberg, E., & Watson, P. (2006). *Psychological First Aid: Field operations guide* (2nd ed.). Los Angeles, CA: National Child Traumatic Stress Network and National Center for PTSD.

Buchholtz, M. (2002). Youth and cultural practice. *Annual Review of Anthropology,* 31, 525-552.

Buckle, J.L., & Fleming. S.J. (2011). *Parenting after the death of a child: A practitioner's guide.* New York, NY: Routledge.

Bugental, J., & Bugental E. (1984). A fate worse than death: the fear of changing. *Psychotherapy,* 21, 543-549.

Bullock, K. (2006). Promoting advance directives among African Americans: A faith-based model. *Journal of Palliative Medicine,* 9, 183-195. doi:10.1089/jpm.2006.9.183.

Bureau of Justice Statistics. (2012). *Correctional populations in the United States in 2010.* Retrieved from http://bjs.ojp.usdoj.gov/index.cfm?ty=pbdetail&iid=2237.

Burke, L.A., & Neimeyer, R.A. (2012). Prospective risk factors for complicated grief: A review of the empirical literature. In M. Stroebe, H. Schut, P. Boelen & J. Van den Bout (Eds.), *Complicated grief: Scientific foundations for health care professionals.* Washington, DC: American Psychological Association.

Burke, L.A., Neimeyer, R.A., & McDevitt-Murphy, M.E. (2010). African American homicide bereavement: Aspects of social support that predict complicated grief, PTSD, and depression. *Omega: Journal of Death and Dying,* 61, 1-24.

Burke, L.A., Neimeyer, R.A., McDevitt-Murphy, M.E., Ippolito, M.R., & Roberts, J.M. (2011). Faith in the wake of homicide: Religious coping and bereavement distress in an African American sample. *International Journal for the Psychology of Religion,* 21, 289-307.

Burroughs, T.E., Hong, B.A., Kappel, D.F., & Freedman, B.K. (1998). The stability of family decisions to consent or refuse organ donation: Would you do it again? *Psychosomatic Medicine,* 60, 156-162.

Burt, R.A. (2005). The end of autonomy. In *Improving end of life care: Why has it been so difficult? Hastings Center Special Report* 35(6), S9-S13.

Butler, R.N. (1963). The life review: An interpretation of reminiscence in the aged. *Psychiatry, 26,* 65-70.

Butler, R., & Lewis, M. (1982). *Aging and mental health.* St. Louis, MO: Mosby.

Byock, I. (1997). *Dying well. The prospect for growth at the end-of-life.* New York, NY: Putman.

Byock, I. (2004). *The four things that matter most: A book about living.* New York, NY: Free Press.

Calhoun, L.G., & Tedeschi, R.G. (1990). Positive aspects of critical life problems: Recollections of grief. *Omega: Journal of Death and Dying, 20,* 265-272.

Cain, A.C., & Fast, I. (1966). Children's disturbed reactions to parental suicide. *American Journal of Orthopsychiatry, 47,* 196-206.

Campbell, E. (2006). The case for living wills in Ireland, *Medico-Legal Journal of Ireland,* 12(1), 2-18.

Campione, F. (2005). *Manifesto della Tanatologia* [Manifesto of Thanatology]. Bologna: Cooperativa Libraria Universitaria Editrice Bologna.

Cantor, N. (2005). *Making medical decisions for the profoundly mentally disabled.* Boston, MA: MIT Press

Caralis, P.V., Davis, B., Wright, K., & Marcial, E. (1993). The influence of ethnicity and race on attitudes toward advance directives, life-prolonging treatments, and euthanasia. *Journal of Clinical Ethics, 4,* 155-165. Retrieved from http://www.researchgate.net/journal/1046-7890_The_Journal_of_Clinical_Ethics.

Carnelley, K.B., Wortman, C.B., Bolger, N., & Burke, C.T. (2006). The time course of grief reactions to spousal loss: Evidence from a national probability sample. *Journal of Personality and Social Psychology, 91,* 476-492.

Carney, K.L. (2003-2004). Barklay and Eve: The role of activity books for bereaved children, *Omega: Journal of Death and Dying,* 48, 307-319.

Carr, D. (2008). Factors that influence late-life bereavement: Considering data from the Changing Lives of Older Couples study. In M.S. Stroebe, R.O. Hansson, H. Schut, & W. Stroebe (Eds.), *Handbook of bereavement research and practice: Advances in theory and intervention* (pp. 417-440). Washington, DC: American Psychological Association.

Carr, D. (2010). New perspectives on the Dual Process Model (DPM): What have we learned? What questions remain? *Omega: Journal of Death and Dying,* 61, 371-380.

Carr, D. (2011). Racial differences in end-of-life planning: Why don't Blacks and Latinos prepare for the inevitable? *Omega: Journal of Death and Dying,* 63, 1-20. doi:10.2190/OM.63.1.a.

Carr, D., Neese, R., & Wortman, C. (Eds). (2005). *Spousal bereavement in late life.* New York, NY: Springer Publishing.

Carrillo, E., Green, A., & Betancourt, J. (1999). Cross-cultural primary care: A patient-based approach. *Annals of Internal Medicine,* 130, 829-834. Retrieved from http://www.annals.org/cgi/reprint/130/10/829.pdf.

Carroll, B. (2009). Forum on end of life. *Studies: An Irish Quarterly Review,* 98, 457-472.

Carter, B.S., & Sandling, J. (1992). Decision making in the NICU: The question of medical futility. *Journal of Clinical Ethics,* 3(2), 142-145. Retrieved from http://www.researchgate.net/journal/1046-7890_The_Journal_of_clinical_ethics.

Caruth, J. (1996). *Trauma exploration in memory.* New York, NY: Ballantine Publishing Group.

Casarett, D. (2006). Understanding and improving hospice enrollment. *LDI Issue Brief* 11(3), 1-4. Retrieved from http://www.upenn.edu/ldi/issuebrief11_3.pdf.

Caserta, M.S., & Lund, D.A. (2007). Toward the development of an Inventory of Daily Widowed Life (IDWL): Guided by the dual process model of coping with bereavement. *Death Studies,* 31, 505-535.

Cassel, E.J. (1982). The nature of suffering and the goals of medicine. *New England Journal of Medicine, 306,* 639-645.

Cecil, R. (1994). Miscarriage: Women's views of care. *Journal of Reproductive and Infant Psychology, 12,* 21-29.

Center for the Advancement of Health. (2004). Report on bereavement and grief research. *Death Studies, 28,* 491-575.

Center to Advance Palliative Care. (2012). *Palliative care in hospitals continues rapid growth trend for 11th straight year according to latest analysis.* Retrieved from http://www.capc.org/news-and-events/releases/.

Centers for Disease Control. (2012). *Deaths: Preliminary data for 2010.* Retrieved from http://www.cdc.gov/nchs/data/nvsr/nvsr60/nvsr60_04.pdf.

Centers for Disease Control. (2012). *Health, United States, 2010 with special features on death and dying.* Retrieved from http://www.cdc.gov/nchs/data/hus/hus10.pdf.

Centers for Medicaid and Medicare. (2006). *Hospice conditions of participation.* Retrieved from http://www.access.gpo.gov/nara/cfr/waisidx_04/42cfr418_04.html.

Cerel, J., & Aldrich, R.S. (2011). The impact of suicide on children and adolescents. In J.R. Jordan & J.L. McIntosh (Eds.), *Grief after suicide* (pp. 81-92). New York, NY: Routledge.

Cerminara, K. (2009). Three female faces: The law and end-of-life decision making in America. In J.L. Werth, Jr., & D. Blevins (Eds.), *Decision making near the end of life: Recent developments and future directions* (pp. 95-118). Philadelphia, PA: Routledge.

Charkow, W.B. (1998). Inviting children to grieve. *Professional School Counseling, 2,* 117-122.

Charles, C. (2011). *Grief after premature birth: A look at the intangible loss of a full term pregnancy.* Unpublished manuscript, Brooklyn College of the City University of New York.

Chaudhuri, J., & Chaudhuri, J. (2001). *A sacred path: The way of the Muscogee Creeks.* Los Angeles, CA: UCLA American Indian Studies Center.

Chen, I., Kurz, J., Pasanen, M., Faselis, C., Panda, M., Staton, L.J., O'Rorke, J., et al. (2005). Racial differences in opioid use for chronic nonmalignant pain. *Journal of General Internal Medicine, 20,* 593-598.

Cheung, P.K.H., Chan, C.L.W., Fu, W., Li, Y., & Cheung, G.Y.P. (2006). Letting go and holding on: Grieving and traditional death rituals in Hong Kong. In C.L.W. Chan & A.Y.M. Chow (Eds.), *Death, dying, and bereavement: A Hong Kong Chinese experience* (pp. 65-86). Hong Kong: Hong Kong University Press.

Chibbaro, J.S., & Jackson, C.M. (2006). Helping students cope in an age of terrorism: Strategies for school counselors. *Professional School Counseling, 9,* 314-321.

Chidester, D. (2002). *Patterns of transcendence: Religion, death, and dying* (2nd ed.). Belmont, CA: Wadsworth.

Children's Rights Task Force of the Midwest Bioethics Center. (1995). Health care treatment decision making guidelines for minors. Midwest Bioethics Center Task Force on Health Care Rights for Minors, 11(4). Minors' Rights in Health Care Decision Making Kansas City, MO.

Chochinov, H., & Breitbart, W. (Eds.). (2009). *Handbook of psychiatry in palliative medicine.* New York, NY: Oxford University Press.

Chochinov, H.M., & Cann, B.J. (2005). Interventions to enhance the spiritual aspects of dying. *Journal of Palliative Medicine,* 8 Suppl 1:S103-115.

Christ, G.H. (2006). Providing a home-based therapeutic program for widows and children. In P. Greene, D. Kane, G.H. Christ, S. Lynch, & M.P. Corrigan (Eds.), *FDNY crisis counseling: Innovative responses to 9/11 fire fighters, families, and communities* (pp. 108-211). New York, NY: John Wiley and Sons.

Christakis, N.A., & Iwashyna, T.J. (2003). The health impact of health care on families: a matched cohort study of hospice use by decedents and mortality outcomes in surviving, widowed spouses. *Social Science & Medicine, 57,* 465-475.

Christian, J. (2006). Grief and combat related losses: Helping wounded veterans grieve. *The Forum, 32,*8.

Cicirelli, V.G. (1997). Relationship of psychosocial and background variables to older adults' end-of-life decisions. *Psychology and Aging,* 12, 71-83. doi:10.1037/0882-7974.12.1.72.

Cicirelli, V.G. (2000). Older adults' ethnicity, fear of death, and end of life decisions. In A. Tomer (Ed.). *Death attitudes and the older adult: Theories, concepts, and applications* (pp. 175-191). New York, NY: Brunner-Routledge.

Cicirelli, V.G. (2001). Personal meanings of death in older adults and young adults in relation to their fears of death. *Death Studies,* 25, 358-366. doi:10.1080/713769896.

Cicirelli, V.G. (2002). Fear of death in older adults: Predictions from terror management theory. *Journal of Gerontology,* 57, 358-366. doi:10.1093/geronb/57.4.P358.

Cicirelli, V.G., MacLean, A.P., & Cox, L.S. (2000). Hastening death: A comparison of two end-of-life decisions. *Death Studies,* 24, 401-419.

Cikara, M., Bruneau, E.G., & Saxe, R.R. (2011). Us and them: Intergroup failures of empathy. *Current Directions in Psychological Science,* 20, 149-153.

Cimete, G., & Kuguoglu, S. (2006). Grief responses of Turkish families after the death of their children from cancer. *Journal of Loss and Trauma: International Perspectives on Stress and Coping,* 11, 31-51.

Cleiren, M., & Van Zoelen, A.J. (2002). Post-mortem organ donation and grief: A study of consent, refusal, and well-being in bereavement. *Death Studies,* 26, 837-849.

Cohen, J., Mannarino, A.P., & Deblinger, E. (2006). *Treating trauma and traumatic grief in children and adolescents.* New York, NY: Guilford Press.

Cohen, S.R., Mount, B.M., Bruera, E., Provost, M., Rowe, J., & Tong, K. (1997). Validity of the McGill Quality of Life Questionnaire in the palliative care setting: A multi-centre Canadian study demonstrating the importance of the existential domain. *Journal of Palliative Medicine,* 11, 3-20.

Cole, R.A. (2001). *Issues in web-based pedagogy: A critical primer.* Westport, CT: Greenwood Publishing Group.

Coleman, R.A., & Neimeyer, R.A. (2010). Measuring meaning: Searching for and making sense of spousal loss in later life. *Death Studies,* 34, 804-834.

Collett, L.J., & Lester, D. (1969). The fear of death and the fear of dying. *Journal of Psychology,* 72, 179-181.

Connor, S.R. (1992). Denial in terminal illness: to intervene or not to intervene. *The Hospice Journal,* 8, 1-15.

Connor, S.R. (1998). *Hospice: Practices, pitfalls and promise.* Washington, DC: Taylor and Francis.

Connor, S.R. (2009). *Hospice and Palliative Care: The essential guide.* New York, NY: Routledge.

Connor, S.R., Elwert, F., Spence, C., & Christakis, N. (2008). Racial disparity in hospice use in the United States in 2002. *Palliative Medicine,* 22, 205-213.

Connor, S.R., Lycan, J., & Schumacher, J.D. (2006). Involvement of psychologists in psychosocial aspects of hospice and end-of-life care. In J.L. Werth, Jr., & D. Blevins (Eds.), *Psychosocial issues near the end of life: A resource for professional care providers* (pp. 203-217). Washington, DC: American Psychological Association.

Connor, S.R., McMaster, J.K. (1996). Hospice, bereavement intervention and use of health care services by surviving spouses, *HMO Practice,* 10, 20-23.

Connor, S.R., & Monroe, B. (2011). Bereavement services provided under the hospice model of care. In R.A. Neimeyer, D. Harris, H. Winokuer & G. Thornton (Eds.), *Grief and bereavement in contemporary society: Bridging research and practice* (pp. 325-337). New York, NY: Routledge.

Connor, S., Pyenson, B., Fitch, K., & Spence, C. (2007). Comparing hospice and non-hospice patient survival among patients who die within a 3-year window. *Journal of Pain and Symptom Management,* 33, 238-246.

Cook, A.S. (1995). Ethical issues in bereavement research: An overview. *Death Studies*, 19, 103-122.

Cook, A.S. (2001). The dynamics of ethical decision making in bereavement research. In M.S. Stroebe, R.O. Hansson, W, Stroebe & H. Schut (Eds.), *Handbook of bereavement research: Consequences, coping, and cure.* (pp. 19-142). Washington, DC: American Psychological Association.

Cook, A.S., & Dworkin, D.S. (1992). *Helping the bereaved: Therapeutic interventions for children, adolescents, and adults.* New York, NY: Basic Books.

Cook, A.S., & Oltjenbruns, K.A. (1998). *Dying and grieving: Lifespan and family perspectives* (2nd ed.). Dallas, TX: Harcourt Brace.

Cook, A.S., Oltjenbruns, K.A., & Lagoni, L. (1984). The "ripple effects" of a university sponsored death and dying symposium. *Omega: Journal of Death and Dying*, 15, 185-190.

Cook, J.A. (1988). Dad's double binds: Rethinking fathers' bereavement from a men's studies perspective. *Journal of Contemporary Ethnography*, 17, 285-308.

Cook-Cottone, C.P. (2004). Childhood posttraumatic stress disorder: Diagnosis, treatment, and school. *The School Psychology Review*, 33, 127-139.

Corr, C.A. (1984). Helping with death education. In H. Wass and C.A. Corr (Eds.), *Helping children cope with death: Guidelines and resources* (pp. 49-73). Washington, DC: Hemisphere Publishing.

Corr, C.A. (1991). A task-based approach to coping with dying. *Omega: Journal of Death and Dying*, 24, 81-94.

Corr, C.A. (1992). A task-based approach to coping with dying. *Omega: Journal of Death and Dying*, 24, 81-94.

Corr, C.A. (1996). Children, development, and encounters with death and bereavement. In C.A. Corr & D. Corr (Eds.), *Handbook of childhood death and bereavement* (pp. 3-28). New York, NY: Springer Publishing.

Corr, C.A. (1998). Enhancing the concept of disenfranchised grief. *Omega: Journal of Death and Dying*, 38, 1-20.

Corr, C.A. (1999). Children, adolescents, and death: Myths, realities, and challenges. *Death Studies*, 23, 443-464.

Corr, C.A. (2002). Revisiting the concept of disenfranchised. In K.J. Doka (Ed.), *Disenfranchised grief: New directions, strategies, and challenges for practice* (pp. 39-60). Champaign, IL: Research Press.

Corr, C.A. (2004). Teaching courses on death, dying, and bereavement. In G.R. Cox & T.B. Gongaware (Eds.), *The sociology of death and dying: A teaching resource* (pp. 23-32). Washington, DC: American Sociological Association.

Corr, C.A. (2005). Coping with challenges to assumptive worlds. In J. Kauffman (Ed.), *Loss of the assumptive world: A theory of traumatic loss* (pp. 127-138). New York, NY: Brunner-Routledge.

Corr, C.A. (2006-2007). Parents in death-related literature for children. *Omega: Journal of Death and Dying*, 54, 237-254.

Corr, C.A. (2011). Strengths and limitations of the stage theory proposed by Elisabeth Kübler-Ross. In K. J. Doka & A.S. Tucci (Eds.), *Beyond Kübler-Ross; New perspectives on death, dying and grief* (pp. 3-16). Washington, DC: Hospice Foundation of America.

Corr, C.A. (2012). Physician-assisted suicide, aid in dying, and hospice. In K.J. Doka, A.S. Tucci, C.A. Corr, & B. Jennings (Eds.), *End-of life ethics: A case study approach* (pp. 127-139). Washington, DC: Hospice Foundation of America.

Corr, C.A., & Balk, D.E. (2010) *Children's encounters with death, bereavement and coping.* New York, NY: Springer Publishing.

Corr, C.A., & Corr, D.M. (2000). Anticipatory mourning and coping with dying: Similarities, differences, and suggested guidelines for helpers. In T.A. Rando (Ed.), *Clinical dimensions of anticipatory mourning: Theory and practice in working with the dying, their loved ones, and their caregivers* (pp. 223-251). Champaign, IL: Research Press.

Corr, C.A., & Corr, D.M. (2003). Death education. In C.D. Bryant (Ed.), *Handbook of death & dying* (Vol. 1, pp. 292-301). Thousand Oaks, CA: Sage Publications.

Corr, C.A., & Corr, D.M. (2003). *Handbook of death and dying. Vol. 1: The presence of death*. Thousand Oaks, CA: Sage Reference.

Corr, C.A., & Corr, D.M. (2013). *Death and dying, life and living* (7th ed.). Belmont, CA: Wadsworth.

Corr, C.A., Doka, K.J., & Kastenbaum, R. (1999). Dying and its interpreters: A review of selected literature and some comments on the state of the filed. *Omega: The Journal of Death and Dying, 39*, 239-259.

Corr, C.A., Nabe, C.M., & Corr, D.M. (2003). *Death and dying, life and living* (4th ed.). Belmont, CA: Wadsworth.

Corr, C.A., Nabe, C.M., & Corr, D.M. (2009). *Death and dying, life and living* (6th ed.). Belmont, CA: Wadsworth.

Courtois, C.A. (2004). Complex trauma, complex reactions: Assessment and treatment. *Psychotherapy: Theory, Research, Practice, Training, 41*, 412-425.

Cox, C., & Monk, A. (1993). Hispanic culture and family care of Alzheimer's patients. *Health and Social Work, 18*, 92-100.

Cox, G.R., Bendiksen, R.A., & Stevenson, R.G. (2002). *Complicated grieving and bereavement: Understanding and treating people experiencing loss*. Amityville, NY: Baywood Publishing.

Cox, M., Garrett, E., & Graham, J.A. (2004-2005). Death in Disney films: Implications for children's understanding of death. *Omega: Journal of Death and Dying, 50*, 267-280.

Craig, E.L., & Craig, R.E. (1999). Prison hospice: an unlikely success. *The American Journal of Hospice and Palliative Care, 16*, 725-729.

Crase, D. (1981). Death education within health education: Current status, future directions. *Journal of School Health, 51*, 646-650.

Crase, D. (1987). Black people do die, don't they? *Death Studies, 11*, 221-228.

Crase, D. (1989). Development opportunities for teachers of death education. *The Clearing House, 62*(9), 387-390.

Crawley, L., Payne, R., Bolden, J., Payne, T., Washington, P., & Williams, S. (2000). Palliative and end-of-life care in African American communities. *Journal of the American Medical Association, 284*, 2518-2529. doi:10.231/JIM.0b013e3181c87db3.

Crenshaw, D.A. (2005). Clinical tools to facilitate treatment of childhood traumatic grief. *Omega: Journal of Death and Dying, 51*, 239-255.

Crenshaw, D.A. (2008). *Therapeutic engagement of children and adolescents: Play, symbol, drawing, and storytelling strategies*. Lanham, MD: Jason Aronson.

Crenshaw, D.A. (2013). A resilience framework for treating severe child trauma. In S. Goldstein and R.B. Brooks (eds.), *Handbook of Resilience in Children*, (2nd ed.) (pp. 309-327). New York, NY: Springer Publishing.

Cronen,, V.E., Pearce, W.B., & Changsheng,, X. (1989). The meaning of 'meaning' in the CMM analysis of communication: A comparison of two traditions. *Research on Language and Social Interaction, 23*, 1-40.

Cruz, L. (2010). Death may be eternal: Historians are not. *The Forum, 36*, 6-7.

Cruzan v. Director, Missouri Department of Health, 497 DS 261 (1990).

Csikai, E.L., & Chaitin, E. (2006). *Ethics in end-of-life decisions in social work practice.* Chicago, IL: Lyceum Books.

Cunningham, A. (2003). Principles and guidelines for research with vulnerable individuals and families. *Research from the Centre for Children & Families in the Justice System.* London, ON, Canada, 1-8.

Cupit, I. Noppe. (2011). *Teaching that matters: International death education.* Presented to the 33rd Annual Conference of the Association for Death Education and Counseling, Miami, FL.

Cupit, I. Noppe, & Servaty-Seib, H.L. (in press). Bereavement and grief for U.S. college students: A call for global extension. In H. Shanun-Klein & S. Kreitler (Eds.), *Studies of grief and bereavement.* Hauppauge, NY: NOVA Publishers.

Cupit Noppe, I., Servaty-Seib, H.L., Parikh, S.T., Walker, A.C., & Martin, R. (in review). College and the grieving student: A mixed-methods analysis.

Cupit, I., Sofka, C.J., & Gilbert, K.R. (2012). Death education. In C.J. Sofka, I.N. Cupit, & K.R. Gilbert (Eds.) *Dying, death, and grief in an online universe: For counselors and educators* (pp. 163-182). New York, NY: Springer Publishing.

Currier, J.M., Holland, J., & Neimeyer, R.A. (2006). Sense making, grief and the experience of violent loss: Toward a mediational model. *Death Studies,* 30, 403-428.

Currier, J.M., Holland, J.M., & Neimeyer, R.A. (2007). The effectiveness of bereavement interventions with children: A meta-analytic review of controlled outcome research. *Journal of Clinical Child and Adolescent Psychology,* 36, 253-259.

Currier, J.M., Holland, J M., & Neimeyer, R.A. (2008). Making sense of loss: A content analysis of end-of-life practitioners' therapeutic approaches. *Omega: Journal of Death and Dying,* 57, 121-141.

Currier, J.M., Neimeyer, R.A., & Berman, J.S. (2008). The effectiveness of psychotherapeutic interventions for the bereaved: A comprehensive quantitative review. *Psychological Bulletin,* 134, 648-661.

Cutler, J.A. (2002). Donation benefit to organ donor families: A current debate. *Proceedings (Baylor University Medical Center)* 15, 133-134.

Cvetkovich, A. (2003). *An archive of feelings trauma and sexuality in lesbian public cultures.* Durham, NC: Duke University Press.

Daly, M., & Wilson, M. (1996). Violence against stepchildren. *Current Directions in Psychological Science,* 5, 77-81.

D'Andrea, W., Ford, J., Stolbach, B., Spinazzola, J., & van der Kolk, B.A. (2012). Understanding interpersonal trauma in children: Why we need a developmentally appropriate trauma diagnosis. *American Journal of Orthopsychiatry,* 82, 187-200.

Dane, B. (2000). Thai women: Mediation as a way to cope with AIDS. *Journal of Religion and Health,* 38, 5-21.

Danish, S.J. (1977). Human development and human services: A marriage proposal. In I. Iscoe, B.L. Bloom, & C.C. Spielberger (Eds.), *Community psychology in transition.* New York, NY: Halsted.

Danish, S.J., & D'Augelli, A.R. (1980). Promoting competence and enhancing development through life development intervention. In L.A. Bond & C.J. Rosen (Eds.), *Primary prevention of psychopathology* (vol. 4). Hanover, NH: University Press of New England.

Da Pena, E. (2002). *Subjective experiences of daughters as caregivers of their frail elderly parent(s): An exploratory study.* (Unpublished doctoral dissertation). Alliant International University.

Davies, B., Clarke, D., Connaughty, S., Cook, K., MacKenzie, B., McCormick, J., O'Loane, M., & Stutzer, C. (1996). Caring for dying children: Nurses' experiences. *Pediatric Nursing,* 22, 500-507.

Davies, B., Reimer, J.C., Brown, P., & Martens, N. (1995). *The experience of transition in families with terminal illness.* Amityville, NY: Baywood Publishing.

Davis, J.A. (1998). Providing critical incident stress debriefing to individual and communities in situation crises. *American Academy of Experts in Traumatic Stress, Inc.* Retrieved from http://www.aaets.org/arts/art54.htm.

Davis, C.G., Harasymchuk, C., & Wohl, M.J. (2012). Finding meaning in a traumatic loss: A families approach. *Journal of Traumatic Stress, 25,* 142-159.

Davis, C.G., Wortman, C.B., Lehman, D.R., & Silver, R.C. (2000). Searching for meaning in loss: Are clinical assumptions correct? *Death Studies, 24,* 497-540.

Davoine, F., & Gaudillié, J-M. (2004). *History beyond trauma: Whereof one cannot speak: therefore one cannot stay silent.* (Trans.) S. Fairfield. New York, NY: Other Press.

Day, R. (2010). *Introduction to family processes* (5th ed.). New York, NY: Routledge.

Dean, P.V. (1995). Is death education a "nasty little secret"? A call to break the alleged silence. In L.A. DeSpelder and A.L. Strickland (Eds.), *The path ahead* (pp. 322-326). Mountain View, CA: Mayfield Publishing.

Deeken, A. (1999). Evolving Japanese perspectives on death and dying. *Budhi: A Journal of Ideas and Culture* (pp. 215-232). Quezon City, Philippines: Office of Research and Publications School of Arts and Sciences, Ateneo de Manila University.

DeFrain, J.D., Jakub, J.K., & Mendoza. B.L. (1991-1992). The psychological effects of sudden infant death on grandmothers and grandfathers. *Omega: Journal of Death and Dying, 24,* 165-182.

DeGroot, J.M. (2012). Maintaining relational continuity with the deceased on Facebook. *Omega: Journal of Death and Dying, 65,* 195-212.

Delgado, M., & Tennstedt, S. (1997). Puerto Rican sons as primary caregivers of elderly patients. *Social Work, 42,*125-134.

Denborough, D. (2008). *Collective narrative practice: Responding to individuals, groups, and communities who have experienced trauma.* Adelaide, Australia: Dulwich Centre Publications.

Dennett, D.C. (1998). Information, technology, and the virtues of ignorance. In R.N. Stichler and R. Hauptman (Eds.), *Ethics, information, and technology readings* (pp. 79-94). Jefferson, NC: McFarland & Company, Inc.

Dennis, M.R. (2011). Popular culture and the paradigm shifts in grief theory and therapy. *Death Studies,* in press.

DePaola, S.J., Griffin, M., Young, J.R., & Neimeyer, R.A. (2003). Death anxiety and attitudes toward the elderly among older adults: The role of gender and ethnicity. *Death Studies, 27,* 335-354. doi:10.1080/07481180302904.

Deri-Bowen, A. (2001). Cot death. In G. Howarth & O. Leamann (Eds.), *Encyclopedia of death and dying* (pp. 121-123). New York, NY: Routledge.

DeSpelder, L.A. (1998). Developing cultural competency. In K.J. Doka & J.D. Davidson (Eds.), *Living with grief: Who we are, how we grieve* (pp. 97-106). Philadelphia, PA: Brunner/Mazel.

DeSpelder, L.A. (2006). Desu edyuke-syon no shimei [The mission of death education] (K. Takeuchi, Trans.). In S. Hinohara, A. Deeken, & J. Mizuno (Eds.), *Otona no inochi no kyoiku* [The death education for adults] (pp. 111-133). Tokyo, Japan: Kawadeshobo Shinsha.

DeSpelder, L.A. (2010). Cultural competence: Teaching strategies. *The Forum, 35* (2), 15.

DeSpelder, L.A., & Barrett, R.K. (1997, December). Developing multicultural competence. *The Director, 64,* 66-68.

DeSpelder, L.A., & Strickland, A.L. (2004, January/February/March). The life of a death textbook and its authors. *The Forum, 30* (1), 8-9.

DeSpelder, L.A., & Strickland, A.L. (2011). *The last dance: Encountering death and dying* (9th ed.). Boston, MA: McGraw-Hill.

Devilly, G.J., Gist, R., & Cotton, P. (2006). Ready! Fire! Aim! The status of psychological debriefing and therapeutic interventions: In the workplace and after disasters. *Review of General Psychology*, 10, 318-345.

de Vries, B. (2007). Advancing the field of spousal bereavement: The art and science of research. *Death Studies*, 31, 679-783.

de Vries, B., & Moldaw, S. (2012). Virtual memorials and cyber funerals: Contemporary expressions of ageless experiences. In C.J. Sofka, I. Noppe Cupit, & K.R. Gilbert (Eds.) *Dying, death, and grief in an online universe* (pp. 135-148). New York, NY: Springer Publishing.

Dichter, M., Turnbull, K., Hitchins, C., & Zelek, M.E. (Eds.). (2011). Getting the deal through labour & employment in 43 jurisdictions worldwide. *Law Business Research*, (p. 5).

Dickinson, G.E. (2002). A quarter century of end-of-life issues in U.S. medical schools. *Death Studies*, 26, 635-646.

Dickinson, G.E. (2007). End-of-life and palliative care issues in medical and nursing schools in the United States. *Death Studies*, 31, 713-726.

Dickinson, G.E., & Field, D. (2002). Teaching end-of-life issues: Current status in United Kingdom and United States medical schools. *American Journal of Hospice & Palliative Care*, 19, 181-186.

Dinhofer, L. (2003). *The differences in grief responses and outcomes between organ and tissue donor families*. (Unpublished master's thesis). Brooklyn College of the City University of New York.

Ditto, P.H. (2006). What would Terri want? On the psychological challenges of surrogate decision making. *Death Studies*, 30, 135-148.

Ditto, P.H., Druley, J.A., Moore, K.A., Danks, J.H., & Smucker, W.D. (1996). Fates worse than death: The role of valued life activities in health-state evaluations. *Health Psychology*, 15, 332-343.

Diwan, S., Hougham, G.W., & Sachs, G.A. (2004). Strain experienced by caregivers of dementia patients receiving palliative care: Findings from the Palliative Excellence in Alzheimer Care Efforts (PEACE) Program. *Journal of Palliative Medicine*, 7, 797-807.

Docherty, S.L., Miles, M.S., Brandon, D. (2007). Searching for "the dying point": providers' experiences with palliative care in pediatric acute care. *Pediatric Nursing*, 33, 335-341.

Doka, K.A., & Martin, T. (2001). Take it like a man: Masculine response to loss. In D.A. Lund, (Ed.), *Men coping with grief* (pp. 37-47). Amityville, NY: Baywood Publishing.

Doka, K.J. (1981-82). Recent bereavement and registration for death studies courses. *Omega: Journal of Death and Dying*, 12, 51-59.

Doka, K.J. (Ed.). (1989). *Disenfranchised grief: Recognizing hidden sorrow*. Lexington, MA: Lexington Books.

Doka, K.J. (1993). *Living with life-threatening illness: A guide for parents, their families, and caregivers*. Lexington, MA: Lexington Books.

Doka, K.J. (1995). Coping with life threatening illness: A task based approach. *Omega: Journal of Death and Dying*, 32, 111-122.

Doka, K.J. (1996). The cruel paradox: Children who are living with life-threatening illnesses. In C.A. Corr, & D.M. Corr (Eds.), *Handbook of childhood death and bereavement*. New York, NY: Springer Publishing.

Doka, K.J. (1997). The effect of parental illness and loss on adult children. In I. Deitch & C.W. Howell (Eds.), *Counseling the aging and their families* (pp. 147-155). Alexandria, VA: American Counseling Association.

Doka, K.J. (Ed.). (1998). *Living with grief: Who we are, how we grieve*. New York, NY: Brunner/Mazel.

Doka, K.J. (Ed.). (2002). *Disenfranchised grief: New directions, strategies, and challenges for practice*. Champaign, IL: Research Press.

Doka, K.J. (2003). Death system. In R. Kastenbaum, (Ed.), *Macmillan encyclopedia of death and dying* (pp. 222-223). New York, NY: Macmillan.

Doka, K.J. (2003). The death awareness movement. Description, history, and analysis. In C.D. Bryant (Ed.), *Handbook of death & dying* (Vol. 1, pp. 50-56). Thousand Oaks, CA: Sage Publications.

Doka, K.J. (2005). Ethics, end-of-life decisions and grief. *Mortality, 10,* 83-90. doi:10.1080/13576270500031105.

Doka, K.J. (2009). *Counseling individuals with life-threatening illness.* New York, NY: Springer Publishing.

Doka, K.J. (2011). Introduction. In K.J. Doka & A.S. Tucci (Eds.), *Beyond Kübler-Ross: New perspectives on death, dying & grief* (pp. iii-xvii). Washington, DC: Hospice Foundation of America.

Doka, K.J., & Jendreski, M. (1985). *Clergy understanding of grief, bereavement and mourning.* Report prepared for the National Research and Information Center, Chicago, IL.

Doka, K.J., & Martin, T.L. (2010). *Grieving beyond gender: Understanding the ways men and women mourn* (rev. ed.). New York, NY: Routledge.

Doka, K.J., & Morgan, J.D. (1993). *Death and spirituality* Amityville, NY: Baywood Publishing.

Doka, K.J., & Tucci, A.S. (Eds.) (2008). *Living with grief: Children and adolescents.* Washington, DC: Hospice Foundation of America.

Doka, K.J., & Tucci, A.S. (Eds.). (2009). *Diversity and end-of-life care.* Washington, DC: Hospice Foundation of America.

Doll, G.A. (2006). Enhancing gerontological education. The role of older adults in a human development and aging course. *Journal of Intergenerational Relations, 4,* 63-71.

Donaldson, T. (1988). *24th century medicine.* Worcester, MA: Davis Publications.

Dooley, D., & McCarthy, J. (2012). *Nursing ethics: Irish cases and concerns* (2nd ed.), Dublin, Ireland: Gill & Macmillan.

Doss, E. (2012). *Memorial mania: Public feelings in America.* Chicago, IL: University of Chicago Press.

Douglas, C. (1992). For all the saints. *BMJ, 304,* 579.

Douglas, J.D. (1990). Patterns of change following parent death in midlife adults. *Omega: Journal of Death and Dying, 22,* 123-137.

Doukas, D.J., & McCullough, L.B. (1991). The values history: The evaluation of the patient's values and advance directives. *Journal of Family Practice, 32,* 145-153. Retrieved from http://www.jfponline.com.

Doyle, E. (2008). *A national conversation about death.* (Unpublished thesis). University of Edinburgh. Irish Health Service Executive (Accessed at www.hse.ie).

Drolet, J.L. (1990). Transcending death during early adulthood: Symbolic immortality, death anxiety, and purpose in life. *Journal of Clinical Psychology, 46,* 148-60.

Dubler, N., & Nimmons, D. (1993). *Ethics on call: Taking charge of life-and-death choices in today's health care system.* New York, NY: Vintage Books.

Duffy, S.A., Jackson, F.C., Schim, S.M., Ronis, D.L., Fowler, K.E. (2006). Racial/ethnic preferences, sex preferences, and perceived discrimination related to end-of-life care. *Journal of the American Geriatrics Society, 54,* 150-157. doi:10.1111/j.1532-5415.2005.00526.x.

Dula, A. (1994). African American suspicion of the healthcare system is justified: What do we do about it? *Cambridge Quarterly of Healthcare Ethics, 3,* 347-357. doi:http://dx.doi.org/10.1017/S0963180100005168.

Dunn, H. (2001). *Hard choices for loving people.* Herndon, VA: A & A Publishing.

Dunn, S.T.M. (2005). A place of transition: Directors' experiences of providing counseling and advising to distance students. *Journal of Distance Education, 20,* 40-57.

Durlak, J.A. (1978-79). Comparison between experiential and didactic methods of death education. *Omega: Journal of Death and Dying, 9,* 57-66.

Durlak, J.A. (1994). Changing death attitudes through death education. In R.A. Neimeyer (Ed.), *Death anxiety handbook. Research, instrumentation, and application* (pp. 243-260). Washington, DC: Taylor & Francis.

Durlak, J.A., & Reisenberg, L.A. (1991). The impact of death education. *Death Studies, 15,* 39-58.

Dyregrov, A., & Regel, S. (2012). Early interventions following exposure to traumatic events: Implications for practice from recent research. *Journal of Loss and Trauma: International Perspectives on Stress and Coping, 17,* 271-291.

Dyregrov, K. (2004). Strategies of professional assistance after traumatic deaths: Empowerment or disempowerment? *Scandinavian Journal of Psychology, 45,* 181-189.

Dyregrov, K., & Dyregrov, A. (2008). *Effective grief and bereavement support.* London, UK: Jessica Kingsley Publishers.

Eckersley, R. (1993). Failing a generation. *Journal of Paediatrics & Child Health, 29,* S16-S19.

Eckersley, R., & Dear, K. (2002). Cultural correlates of youth suicide. *Social Science & Medicine, 55,* 1891-1904.

Edwards, S., McCreanor, T., Ormsby, M., Tuwhangai, N., & Tipene-Leach, D. (2009). Maori men and the grief of SIDS. *Death Studies, 33,* 130-152.

Egan, R., MacLeod, R., Jaye, C., McGee, R., Baxter, J., & Herbison, P. (2011). What is spirituality? Evidence from a New Zealand hospice study. *Mortality, 16,* 307-324.

Eisenberg, N., & Silver, R.C. (2011). Growing up in the shadow of terrorism: Youth in America after 9/11. *American Psychologist, 66,* 468-481.

Eisenbruch, M. (1984). Cross-cultural aspects of bereavement: Ethnic and cultural variations in the development of bereavement practices. *Culture, medicine, and psychiatry, 8,* 315-347.

Eliot, T.S. (1936). *Selected writings.* New York, NY: Winggold Press.

Ellis, A. (1962). *Reason and emotion in psychotherapy.* New York, NY: Lyle Stuart.

Emanuel, E.J., Fairclough, D.L., & Emanuel, L.L. (2000). Attitudes and desires related to euthanasia and physician-assisted suicide among terminally ill patients and their caregivers. *Journal of the American Medical Association, 284,* 2460-2468.

Emanuel, L.L., Barry, M.J., Soteckle, J.D., Ettelson, L.M., & Emanuel, E.J. (2012). Advance directives for medical care – A case for greater use. *New England Journal of Medicine, 324* (13), 889-894.

Engel, G.L. (1980-1981). A group dynamic approach to teaching and learning about grief. *Omega: Journal of Death and Dying, 11,* 45-59.

Engel, S., Kiely, D.K., & Mitchell, S.L. (2006). Satisfaction with end-of-life care for nursing home residents with advanced dementia. *Journal of the American Geriatric Society, 54,* 1567-1572.

Enns, C.Z., & Williams, E.N. (Eds.). (2012). *The Oxford handbook of feminist multicultural counseling psychology.* New York, NY: Oxford University Press.

Epstein, D., Nisbet, E., & Gillespie, T. (2011) Who's responsible for the digital divide? Public perceptions and policy implications. *The Information Society, 27,* 92-104.

Epting, F.R., & Neimeyer, R.A. (1984). *Personal meanings of death: Applications of personal construct theory to clinical practice.* Washington, DC: Francis and Taylor.

Erickson, F. (2002). Culture and human development. *Human development, 45,* 299-306.

Erikson, E.H. (1963). *Childhood and society* (2nd ed.). New York, NY: W.W. Norton & Co.

Erikson, E.H. (1968). *Identity: Youth and crisis.* New York, NY: W.W. Norton & Co.

Erikson, E.H. (1982). *The life cycle completed: A review*. New York, NY: W.W. Norton & Co.

Erikson, E.H. (1982). *The life cycle completed: Extended version with new chapters on the ninth stage of development by Joan M. Erikson*. New York, NY: W.W. Norton & Co.

Erikson, K. (1976). *Everything in its path*. New York, NY: Simon & Schuster.

Espino, D.V., Macias, R.L., Wood, R.C., Becho, J., Talamantes, M., Finley, M.R., Hernandez, A.E., & Martinez, R. (2010). Physician-assisted suicide attitudes of older Mexican Americans and non-Hispanic White adults: Does ethnicity make a difference? *Journal of the American Geriatrics Society, 58*, 1370-1375. doi:10.1111/j.1532-5415.2010.02910.x.

Etzioni, A. (2000). Toward a theory of public ritual. *Sociological Theory, 18*, 44-59.

Eurotransplant International Foundation. (2011). Retrieved from www.eurotransplant.nl?id=statistics.

Evans, N., Meñaca, A., Andrew, E., Koffman, J., Harding, R., Higginson, R., Pool, R., Gysels, M., & for PRISMA (2012). Cultural competence in end-of-life care: Terms, definitions and conceptual models from the British literature. *Journal of Palliative Medicine, 15*, 812-820.

Everly, G.R., & Boyle, S.H. (1999). Critical Incident Stress Debriefing (CISD): A meta-analysis. *International Journal of Emergency Mental Health, 1*, 165-168.

Everly, G.R., Flannery, R.R., & Eyler, V.A. (2002). Critical Incident Stress Management (CISM): A statistical review of the literature. *Psychiatric Quarterly, 73*(3), 171-182. doi:10.1023/A:1016068003615.

Everly, G.S., & Mitchell, J.T. (1999). Critical Incident Stress Management (CISM): *A new era and standard of care in crisis intervention* (2nd ed.). Ellicott City, MD: Chevron.

Faber-Langendoen, K., & Lanken, P.N. (2000). Dying patients in the intensive care unit: Forgoing treatment, maintaining care. *Annals of Internal Medicine, 133*, 886-893.

Fadiman, A. (1997). *The spirit catches you and you fall down*. New York, NY: Farrar, Straus & Giroux.

Fagundes, C.P., Diamond, L.M., & Allen, K.P. (2012). Adolescent attachment insecurity and parasympathetic functioning predict future loss adjustment. *Personality & Social Psychology Bulletin, 38*, 821-832.

Fahrenwald, N.L., & Stabnow, W. (2005). Sociocultural perspective on organ and tissue donation among reservation-dwelling American Indian adults. *Ethnicity and Health, 10*, 341-354. doi:10.1080/13557850500168826.

Fairbank, J.A., Schlenger, W.E., Saigh, P.A., & Davidson, J.R.T. (1995). An epidemiologic profile of post-traumatic stress disorder: Prevalence, comorbidity, and risk factors. In M. Friedman, D. Charney, & A. Deutch (Eds.), *Neurobiological and clinical consequences of stress: From normal adaptation to post-traumatic stress disorder*. Philadelphia, PA: Lippincott-Raven.

Falicov, C. (2012). *Latino families in therapy: A guide to multicultural practice* (2nd ed.). New York, NY: Guilford Press.

Fan Z., Yang J., Kui Z., Zhuohong Z., Hao W., & Ning L. (2009). Post-trauma mobile service: A case study of psychological counseling service with mobile Internet technology. *Proceedings of the 2009 International Conference on New Trends in Information and Service Science* (pp. 1140-1144). Retrieved from http://ieeexplore.ieee.org/xpl/articleDetails.jsp?reload=true&arnumber5260427&content Type=Conference+Publications.

Farrell, K. (1998). *Post-traumatic culture: Injury and interpretation in the nineties*. Baltimore, MD: Johns Hopkins University Press.

Faschingbauer, T.R. (1981). *Texas Revised Inventory of Grief Manual*. Houston, TX: Honeycomb Publishing.

Faust, J., & Katchen, L.B. (2004). Treatment of children with complicated posttraumatic stress reactions. *Psychotherapy: Theory, Research, Practice, Training, 41*, 426-437.

Federal Trade Commission. (1994). *Funeral industry practices trade regulation rule: Final amended trade regulation rule*. Washington, DC: Bureau of Consumer Protection.

Feifel, H. (1959). *The meaning of death*. New York, NY: McGraw-Hill.

Feigelman, W., Gorman, B.S., Beal, K.C., & Jordan, J.R. (2008). Internet support groups for suicide survivors: A new mode for gaining bereavement assistance. *Omega: Journal of Death and Dying, 57*, 217-243.

Field, M. (2009). How people die in the United States. In J.L. Werth, Jr., & D. Blevins (Eds.), *Decision making near the end of life: Recent developments and future directions* (pp. 63-75). Philadelphia, PA: Routledge.

Field, M.J., & Cassel, C.K. (1997). *Approaching death: Improving care at the end of life.* Washington, DC: National Academy Press.

Field, N.P., & Friedrichs, M. (2004). Continuing bonds in coping with the death of a husband. *Death Studies, 28*, 597-620.

Field, N.P., Gao, B., & Paderna, L. (2005). Continuing bonds in bereavement: An attachment theory based perspective. *Death Studies, 29*, 277-299.

Figley, C.R. (Ed.) (1995). *Compassion fatigue: Coping with secondary traumatic stress disorder in those who treat the traumatized.* New York, NY: Brunner/Mazel.

Figley, C.R. (1995). Compassion fatigue as secondary traumatic stress disorder: An overview. In C.R. Figley, *Compassion fatigue: Coping with secondary traumatic stress disorder in those who treat the traumatized* (pp. 1-20). New York, NY: Brunner/Mazel.

Figley, C.R. (2002a). Compassion fatigue: Psychotherapists' chronic lack of self care. *Journal of Clinical Social Psychology, 58*, 1433-1441.

Fineberg, I.C. (2005). Preparing professionals for family conferences in palliative care: Evaluation result of an interdisciplinary approach. *Journal of Palliative Medicine, 8*, 857-865.

Fink, G.S. (2011). Legacy and spirituality at the end of life. In K.J. Doka & A.S. Tucci (Eds.), *Living with grief: Spirituality and end-of-life care.* Washington, DC: Hospice Foundation of America.

Finlay, I.G., Wheatley, V.J., & Izdebski, C. (2005). The House of Lords Select Committee on the Assisted Dying for the Terminally Ill Bill: Implications for specialist palliative care. *Palliative Medicine, 19*, 444-453.

Fins, J.J. (2006). *A palliative ethic of care: Clinical wisdom at life's end.* Sudbury, MA: Jones and Bartlett Publishers.

Fins, J.J., & Schiff N. (2005). In brief: The afterlife of Terri Schiavo. *Hastings Center Report.* 35(4):8. Retrieved August 2008 from Medscape.

Finucane, R.C. (1996). *Ghosts: Appearances of the dead and cultural transformation.* Amherst, NY: Prometheus Books.

Firth, P. (2011). Clinical supervision and reflective practice in palliative care: luxury or necessity? In I. Renzenbrink, (Ed.), *Caregiver stress and staff support in illness, dying and bereavement.* New York, NY: Oxford University Press.

Fish, S., & Shelly, J.A. (1978). *Spiritual care: The nurse's role.* Downers Grove, IL: InterVarsity Press.

Fitzgerald, H. (2003). *The grieving child* (2nd ed.). New York, NY: Simon & Schuster.

Flannery, R.R., & Everly, G.R. (2004). Critical Incident Stress Management (CISM): Updated review of findings, 1998-2002. *Aggression and Violent Behavior, 9*, 319-329. doi:10.1016/S1359-1789(03)00030-2.

Florian, V. (1985). Children's concept of death: An empirical study of a cognitive and environmental approach. *Death Studies, 9*, 133-141. doi:10.1080/07481188508252509.

Flynn, N., & Erickson, M. (2000). *Teen talk: A grief support group for teenagers (A curriculum in eight sessions for grief counselors, school counselors, and other professionals working with bereaved teens.)* Puyallup, WA: GriefWorks: A Bereavement Resource.

Foley, G.V., & Whittam, E.H. (1990). Care of the child dying of cancer: Part I. *CA: A Cancer Journal for Clinicians, 40*, 327-354.

Folkman, S. (1997). Positive psychological states and coping with severe stress. *Social Science & Medicine,* 45, 1207-1221.

Folkman, S. (1991). Coping across the life span: Theoretical issues. In E.M. Cummings, A.L.Greene, & K.H. Karraker (Eds.), *Life-span developmental psychology: Perspectives on stress and coping* (pp. 3-19). Hillsdale, NJ: Lawrence Erlbaum.

Folkman, S. (2001). Revised coping theory and the process of bereavement. In M.S. Stroebe, R.O. Hansson, W. Stroebe, & H. Schut (Eds.), *Handbook of bereavement research: Consequences, coping, and care* (pp. 563-584). Washington, DC: American Psychological Association.

Fook, J., & Kellehear, A. (2010). Using critical reflection to support health promotion goals in palliative care. *Journal of Palliative Care,* 26, 295-302.

Forbat, L., & Service, K. Pekala. (2005). Who cares? Contextual layers in end-of-life care for people with intellectual disability and dementia. *Dementia,* 4, 413-431.

Forbes, T.R. (1970). Life and death in Shakespeare's London. *American Scientist,* 58, 511-520.

Ford, S.G. (2006). *The role of imagined interactions and self-efficacy in psychosocial adjustment to spousal bereavement: A communication perspective.* (Unpublished doctoral dissertation). Louisiana State University.

Fortner, B.V., Neimeyer, R.A. (1999). Death anxiety in older adults: A quantitative review. *Death Studies,* 23, 387-411.

Foster, L.W., & McLellan, L.J. (2002). Translating psychosocial insight into ethical discussions supportive of families in end-of-life decision-making. *Social Work in Health Care,* 35(3), 37-51.

Foti, M.E., Bartels, S.J., Van Citters, A.D., Merriman, M.P., & Fletcher, K.E. (2005). End-of-life treatment preferences of persons with serious mental illness. *Psychiatric Services,* 56, 576-591.

Fowler, K. (2008). The wholeness of things: Infusing diversity and social justice into death education. *Omega: Journal of Death and Dying,* 57, 53-91.

Fox, M. (Ed.) (1981). *Western spirituality: Historical roots, ecumenical routes.* Santa Fe, NM: Bear & Company.

Frankl, V.E. (1959). *Man's search for meaning.* New York, NY: Pocket Books.

Freeman., H.P., & Payne, R. (2000). Racial injustice in health care. *New England Journal of Medicine,* 342, 1045-1047.

Freemont, W.P. (2004) Childhood reactions to terrorism-induced trauma: A review of the past 10 years. *Journal of the American Academy of Child and Adolescent Psychiatry,* 43, 381-392.

Freud, S. (1915). Thoughts for the times on war and death. In *Sigmund Freud: Collected Papers Volume 4.* New York, NY: Basic Books.

Freud, S. (1957). Mourning and melancholia. In J. Strachey (Ed.), *The Complete Psychological Works of Sigmund Freud* (pp. 152-170). London, UK: Hogarth Press.

Freud, S. (1961a). Totem and taboo. In J. Strachey (Ed., & Trans.), *The Standard Edition of the Complete Psychological Works of Sigmund Freud,* Vol. 13, pp. 1-162. London, UK: Hogarth Press. [Original work published 1912-13.].

Freud, S. (1961b). Mourning and melancholia. In J. Strachey (Ed., & Trans.), *The Standard Edition of the Complete Psychological Works of Sigmund Freud,* Vol. 14, pp. 243-258. London, UK: Hogarth Press. [Original work published 1917].

Freud, S. (1975). *The standard edition of the complete psychological works of Sigmund Freud.* J. Strachey, A. Freud, A. Strachey, & A. Tyson, (Trans.); originally published 1920. London, UK: Hogarth Press.

Freyer, D.R. (2004). Care of the dying adolescent: Special considerations. *Pediatrics,* 113, 381-388.

Friedman, M.J., & Marsella, A.J. (2001). Posttraumatic stress disorders: An overview. In A. Marsella, M. Friedman, E. Gerrity, & Scurfield (Eds.), *Ethnocultural aspects of posttraumatic stress disorder: Issues research and clinical application* (p. 11-32). Washington, DC: American Psychological Association.

Friedman, M.J., & Marsella, A.J. (2001). Posttraumatic stress disorders: An overview. In A. Marsella, M. Friedman, E. Gerrity, & Scurfield (Eds.), *Ethnocultural aspects of posttraumatic stress disorder: Issues research and clinical application* (p. 107). Washington, DC: American Psychological Association.

Fritzsche, P. (2004). *Stranded in the present: Modern times and the melancholy of history.* Cambridge, MA: Harvard University Press.

Fry, P. (2000). Religious involvement, spirituality, and personal meaning for life: Existential predictors of psychological wellbeing in community-residing and institutional care elders. *Aging Mental Health*, 4, 375–387.

Fryback, P., & Reinert, B.R. (1999). Spirituality and people with potentially fatal diagnoses. *Nursing Forum*, 34, 13–22.

Fullerton, C.S., Ursano, R.J., Reeves, J., Shigemura, J., & Grieger, T. (2006). Perceived safety in disaster workers following 9/11. *Journal of Nervous and Mental Disease,* 194, 61-63.

Fulton, R. (1987). Unanticipated grief. In C.A. Corr & R.A. Pacholski (Eds.), *Death: Completion and discovery* (pp. 49-60). Lakewood, OH: The Association for Death Education and Counseling.

Fulton, R. (2003). Anticipatory mourning: A critique of the concept. *Mortality*, 8, 342-351.

Fulton, R., & Fulton, J. (1971). A psychosocial aspect of terminal care: Anticipatory grief. *Omega: Journal of Death and Dying,* 2, 91-100.

Fulton, R., & Gottesman, D.J. (1980). Anticipatory grief: A psychosocial concept reconsidered. *British Journal of Psychiatry,* 137, 45-54.

Funeral Consumer Alliance. (2006). Common funeral myths and facts. *The FCA Newsletter,* 10(3), 8-9.

Furrow, B. (1991). Defining death. In B. Furrow, S. Johnson, S. Jost, & R. Schwartz (Eds.), *Health Law: Cases, Materials, and Problems* (pp. 1034-1055). St. Paul, MN: West Publishing.

Fuse, T. (1980). To be or not to be. *Stress*, 1(3), 18-25.

Gabbay, B.B., Matsumura, S., Etzioni, S., Asch, S.M., Rosenfeld, K.E., Shiojiri, T., et al. (2005). Negotiating end-of-life decision making: A comparison of Japanese and U.S. residents' approaches. *Academic Medicine: Journal of the Association of American Medical Colleges,* 80, 617-621. Retrieved from http://journals.lww.com/academicmedicine/pages/default.aspx.

Gaboury, J. (2001). *After the Sept. 11 attacks, industrial engineers pitched in to help where they could, but some found that they, too, had been hurt.* Retrieved from http://solutions.iienet.org.

Gallup International Institute. (1997). *Spiritual beliefs and the dying process: A report on a national survey.* Princeton, NJ: Nathan Cummings Foundation and Fetzer Institute, sponsors.

Galvin, K.M., Bylund, C.L., & Brommel, B.J. (2004). *Family communication, cohesion, and change* (6th ed.). Boston, MA: Allyn & Bacon.

Gamble, V.N., & Stone, D. (2006). U.S. policy on health inequities: The interplay of politics and research. *Journal of Health Politics, Policy and Law*, 31, 93-126.

Gambrill, E. (2012). *Critical thinking in clinical practice: Improving the quality of judgments and decisions* (3rd ed.). New York, NY: Wiley.

Gamino, L.A. (2003). Critical incident stress management and other crisis counseling approaches. In M. Lattanzi-Licht & K.J. Doka (Eds.), *Living with grief: Coping with public tragedy* (pp. 123-138). New York, NY: Brunner-Routledge.

Gamino, L.A. (April/May/June, 2005). Bereaved parents' reactions to media reporting: A case study. *The Forum,* 31(2), 9-10.

Gamino, L.A. (2011). Putting to rest the debate over grief counseling. In K.J. Doka & A.S. Tucci (Eds.), *Beyond Kübler-Ross: New perspectives on death, dying & grief* (pp. 113-130). Washington, DC: Hospice Foundation of America.

Gamino, L.A. (2012). Ethical considerations when conducting grief counseling online. In C.J. Sofka, I.N. Cupit, & K.R. Gilbert (Eds.), *Dying, death, and grief in an online universe: For counselors and educators* (pp. 217-234). New York, NY: Springer Publishing.

Gamino, L.A., Easterling, L.W., & Sewell, K.W. (2003). The role of spiritual experience in adapting to bereavement. In G.R. Cox, R.A. Bendiksen & R.G. Stevenson (Eds.), *Making sense of death: Spiritual, pastoral and personal aspects of dying, death and bereavement* (pp. 13-28). Amityville, NY: Baywood Publishing.

Garbarino, J., & Kostelny, K. (1996). The effects of political violence on Palestinian children's behavior problems. *Child Development*, 67, 33-45.

Garces-Foley, K, (2006). Hospice and the politics of spirituality. *Omega: Journal of Death and Dying*, 53, 117-136.

Gardner, J.E., Scherman, A., Efthimiadis, M.S., & Shultz, S.K. (2004). Panamanian grandmothers' family relationships and adjustment to having a grandchild with a disability. *International Journal of Aging & Human Development*, 59, 305-320.

Gary, J., & Remolino, L. (2010). *Coping with loss and grief through online support groups*. Retrieved from http://www.mental-health-matters.com/topics/grief-and-loss/932-coping-with-loss-and-grief-through-online-support-groups.

Gauthier, D.M. (2005). Decision making near the end of life. *Journal of Hospice & Palliative Nursing*, 2, 82-90.

Gazelle, G. (2007). Understanding hospice-An underutilized option for life's final chapter. *New England Journal of Medicine*, 357, 321-324.

Geiger, G. (2002). Racial and ethnic disparities in diagnosis and treatment: A review of the evidence and a consideration of causes. In B.D. Smedley, A.Y. Stith, & A.R. Nelson (Eds.), *Unequal treatment: Confronting racial and ethnic disparities in health care* (pp. 417-454). Washington, DC: National Academies Press.

Gelfand, D.E., Balcazar, H., Parzuchowski, J., & Lenox, S. (2001). Mexicans and care for the terminally ill: Family, hospice, and the church. *American Journal of Hospice and Palliative Care*, 18, 391-396.

Genevro, J.L., Marshall, T., & Miller, T. (2003). *Report on bereavement and grief research*. Washington, DC: Center for the Advancement of Health.

Gert, B., Culver, C., & Clouser, K.D. (1997). *Bioethics: A return to fundamentals*. Oxford, UK: Oxford University Press.

Gibbs, L. (2002). *Evidence-based practice for the helping professions: A practical guide*. Pacific Grove, CA: Brooks/Cole.

Gibson, A.B., Roberts, P.C., & Buttery, T.J. (1982). *Death education: A concern for the living*. Bloomington, IN: Phi Delta Kappa Educational Foundation.

Gibson, C.A., Breitbart, W., Tomarken, A., Kosinski, A., & Nelson, C.J. (2006). Mental health issues near the end of life. In J.L. Werth & D. Blevins (Eds.), *Psychosocial issues near the end of life: A resource for professional care providers* (pp. 137-162). Washington, DC: American Psychological Association.

Gil, E. (2003). Play Genograms. In C.F. Son & L.L. Hecker (Eds.), *The therapist's notebook for children and adolescents* (pp. 49-56). New York, NY: Haworth Press.

Gil, E. (2006). *Helping abused and traumatized children: Integrating directive and nondirective approaches*. New York, NY: Guilford Press.

Gilbert, K.R. (1989). Interactive grief and coping in the marital dyad. *Death Studies*, 13, 605-626.

Gilbert, K.R. (1996). "We've had the same loss, why don't we have the same grief?" Loss and differential grief in families, *Death Studies*, 20, 269-283.

Gilbert, K.R., & Horsley, G.C. (2011). Technology and grief support in the twenty-first century: A multimedia platform. In R.A. Neimeyer, D.L. Harris, H.R. Winokuer, & G.F. Thornton (Eds), *Grief and bereavement in contemporary society: Bridging research and practice* (pp. 365-374). New York, NY: Routledge.

Gilbert, K.R., & Smart, L.S. (1992). *Coping with infant or fetal loss: The couple's healing process.* New York, NY: Brunner/Mazel.

Gilbert, R. (1995) Protestant perspectives on grief and children. In E. Grollman, (Ed.), *Bereaved children and teens: A support guide for parents and professionals.* Boston, MA: Beacon Press.

Gilbert, R. (1999). *Finding your way after your parent dies.* Notre Dame, IN: Ave Maria Press.

Gilbert, R. (2002) A chaplain's perspective: The challenge for today. In R. Gilbert (Ed.), *Healthcare and spirituality: Listening, assessing, caring.* Amityville, NY: Baywood Publishing.

Gilbert, R. (2002a). *Healthcare and spirituality: Listening, assessing, caring.* Amityville, NY: Baywood Publishing.

Gilbert, R. (2002b). Spirituality and religion: Risks for complicated mourning. In G.R. Cox, R.A. Bendiksen and R.G. Stevenson (Eds.), *Complicated grieving and bereavement: Understanding and treating people experiencing loss* (pp. 179-192). Amityville, NY: Baywood Publishing.

Gilbert, R. (2006). A pastoral reflective on the spiritual dimensions of loss. *Illness, Crisis and Loss,* 14, 189-199.

Gijsberts, M.J., Echteld, M.A., van der Steen, J.T., Muller, M.T., Otten, R.H., Ribbe, M.W., & Deliens, L. (2011). Spirituality at the end of life: Conceptualization of measurable aspects—a systematic review. *Journal of Palliative Medicine,* 14, 852-863.

Gilliland, G & Fleming, S. (1998). A comparison of spousal anticipatory grief and conventional grief. *Death Studies*, 22, 541-569.

Giovanni, L.A. (2012). End-of-life care in the United States: Current reality and future promise: A policy review. *Nursing Economics,* 30(3), 127-134.

Girard, C. (1993). Age, gender, and suicide. *American Sociological Review*, 58, 553-574.

Gist, R., & Lubin, B. (1999) *Response to disaster: Psychosocial, community, and ecological approaches.* Philadelphia, PA: Brunner/Mazel.

Gladding, S.T. (2011). *The counseling dictionary: Concise definitions of frequently used terms* (3rd ed.). Upper Saddle River, NJ: Merrill Prentice Hall.

Glaser, B., & Strauss, A. (1965). *Awareness of dying.* Chicago, IL: Aldine.

Glaser, B., & Strauss, A. (1968). *Time for dying.* Chicago: IL: Aldine.

Glick, I.D., Weiss, R.S., & Parkes, C.M. (1974). *The first year of bereavement.* New York, NY: Wiley.

Goddard, A. (2011). Children's books for use in bibliotherapy. *Journal of Pediatric Health Care*, 25, 57-61. doi:10.1016/j.pedhc.2010.08.006.

Golden, T.R. (1996). *Swallowed by a snake: The gift of the masculine side of healing.* Kensington, MD: Golden Healing Publishing.

Goldman, L. (2000). *Life & loss: A guide to help grieving children* (2nd ed.). Washington, DC: Taylor & Francis.

Goldman, L. (2002). *Breaking the silence: A resource guide to help children with complicated grief: Suicide, homicide, AIDS, violence, and abuse* (2nd ed.). Washington, DC: Taylor & Francis.

Gone, J.P. (2011). Is psychological science a-cultural? *Cultural Diversity and Ethnic Minority Psychology,* 17, 234-242.

Goodkin, K.U., Baldewicz, T.T., & Blaney, N.T., Asthana, D., Kumar, M., Shapshak, P., Leeds, B., Burkhalter, J.E., Rigg, D., Tyll, M.D., Cohen, J., & Zheng, W.L. (2001). Physiological effects of bereavement and bereavement support group interventions. In M.S. Stroebe, R.O. Hansson, W. Stroebe, & H. Schut (Eds.), *Handbook of bereavement research: Consequences, coping, and care* (pp. 671-703). Washington, DC: American Psychological Association.

Goodman, N. (1992). *Introduction to sociology.* New York, NY: HarperCollins.

Gordon, A.K., & Klass, D. (1979). *They need to know: How to teach children about death.* Englewood Cliffs, NJ: Prentice-Hall.

Gorman, E. (2012). Death education in the cyberclassroom: Creating a safe space for student learning. In C.J. Sofka, I.N. Cupit, & K.R. Gilbert (Eds.), *Dying, death, and grief in an online universe: For counselors and educators* (pp. 183-197). New York, NY: Springer Publishing.

Goss, R., & Klass, D. (2005). *Dead but not lost: Grief narratives in religious traditions.* Walnut Creek, CA: AltaMira Press.

Goss, R., & Klass, D. (2006). Buddhism and death. In K. Garces-Foley (Ed.), *Death and religion in a changing world.* Armonk, NY: M.E. Sharpe.

Grad, O. (2011). The sequelae of suicide: Survivors. In R.C. O'Connor, S. Platt, & J. Gordon (Eds.), *International handbook of suicide prevention: Research, policy and practice* (pp. 561-575). New York, NY: John Wiley & Sons.

Graham, M. (2011). Time machines and virtual portals: The spatialities of the digital divide. *Progress in Development Studies II*, 3, 211-227.

Grassman, E.J., & Whitaker, A. (2006). With or without faith: Spiritual care in the Church of Sweden at a time of transition. *Omega: Journal of Death and Dying*, 54, 153-172.

Green, C.R., Anderson, K.O., Baker, T.A., Campbell, L.C. Decker, S., Fillingim, R.B., et al. (2003). The unequal burden of pain: Confronting racial and ethnic disparities in pain. *Pain Medicine*, 4, 277-294.

Green, C.R., Ndao-Brumblay, S.K., West, B., & Washington, T. (2005). Differences in prescription opioid analgesic availability: Comparing minority and White pharmacies across Michigan. *Journal of Pain*, 6, 689-699.

Greenberg, J., Solomon, S., & Pyszczynski, T. (1997). Terror management theory of self-esteem and cultural worldviews: Empirical assessments and conceptual refinements. In M.P. Zanna (Ed.), *Advances in experimental social psychology* (Vol. 29, pp. 61–139). Orlando, FL: Academic Press.

Grollman, E.A. (1967). *Explaining death to children.* Boston, MA: Beacon Press.

Grollman, E.A. (1977*). Living when a loved one has died.* Boston, MA: Beacon Press.

Grollman, E.A. (1990). *Talking about death: a dialogue between parent and child* (3rd ed.). Boston, MA: Beacon Press.

Grollman, E.A. (1993). Death in Jewish thought. In J.K. Doka & J.D. Morgan, (Eds.), *Death and Spirituality* (pp. 21-32). Amityville, NY: Baywood Publishing.

Grollman, E.A. (2000). *Living with loss, healing with hope: A Jewish perspective.* Boston, MA: Beacon Press.

Grunfeld, E., Coyle, D., Whelan, T., Clinch, J., Reyno, L., Earle, C.C., Willon, A., Viola, R.,

Coristine, M., Janz, T., & Glossup, R. (2004). Family caregiver burden: results of a longitudinal study of breast cancer patients and their principal caregivers. *Canadian Medical Association Journal*, 170, 1795-1801.

Gunaratnam, Y. (1997). Culture is not enough: A critique of multi-culturalism in palliative care. In D. Field, J. Hockey, & N. Small (Eds.), *Death, gender, and ethnicity* (p. 166-186). New York, NY: Routledge.

Gupta, L.M. (2008). *Traumatic losses among war-affected children in the developing world: Lessons learned for future post-conflict interventions.* Keynote address to the 30th Annual Conference of the Association for Death Education and Counseling, Montreal, Quebec, Canada.

Gutheil, T.G., & Gabbard, G.O. (1998). Misuses and misunderstandings of boundary theory in clinical and regulatory settings. *American Journal of Psychiatry*, 155, 409-414.

Gysels, M., Evans, N., Meñaca, A., Andrew, E., Toscani, F., Finetti, S., Pasman, H.R., Higginson, I., Harding, R., Pool, R. on behalf of Project PRISMA. (2012). Culture and End of Life Care: A Scoping Exercise in Seven European Countries. *PLoS ONE* 7(4): e34188. doi:10.1371/journal.pone.0034188.

Hagan, M.J., Tein, J., Sandler, I.N., Wolchik, S.A., Ayers, T.S., & Luecken, L.J. (2012). Strengthening effective parenting practices over the long term: Effects of a preventive intervention for parentally bereaved families. *Journal of Clinical Child and Adolescent Psychology*, 41, 177-188. doi:10.1080/15374416. 2012.651996.

Haine, R.A., Wolchik, S.A., Sandler, I.N., Millsap, R.E., & Ayers, T.S. (2006). Positive parenting as a protective resource for parentally bereaved children. *Death Studies, 30*, 1-28.

Halevi, M. (2012). *Meaning making and the Two-Track Model of Bereavement: Is it meaning in life or meaning with regards to the deceased we are talking about?* (Unpublished master's thesis). University of Haifa.

Haley, A., & Brody, B. (1996). A multi-institutional collaborative policy on medical futility. *Journal of the American Medical Association, 276,* 571-574.

Haley, W.E., Larson, D.G., Kasl-Godley, J., Neimeyer, R.A., & Kwilosz, D.M. (2003). Roles for psychologists in end-of-life care: Emerging models of practice. *Professional Psychology: Research and Practice, 34,* 626-633.

Hall, M., & Irwin, M. (2001). Physiological indices of functioning in bereavement. In M.S. Stroebe, R.O. Hansson, W. Stroebe, & H. Schut (Eds.), *Handbook of bereavement research: Consequences, coping, and care* (pp. 473-492). Washington, DC: American Psychological Association.

Hallenbeck, J., Goldstein, M.K., & Mebane, E. (1996). Cultural considerations of death and dying in the United States. *Clinics in Geriatric Medicine, 12,* 393-406. Retrieved from http://geriatric.theclinics. com/.

Hampton, K.N., Goulet, L.S., Rainie, L., & Purcell, K. (2011). Social networking sites and our lives: How people's trust, personal relationships, and civic and political involvement are connected to their use of social networking sites and other technologies. *Pew Internet & American Life Project, June 16, 2011.* Retrieved from http://www.pewinternet.org/~/media//Files/Reports/2011/PIP%20-%20Social%20 networking%20sites%20and%20our%20lives.pdf.

Hampton, L., & Emanuel E. (2005). The prognosis for changes in end-of-life care after the Schiavo case. *Health Affairs* 24, 972-975.

Hannay, M., & Newvine, T. (2006). Perceptions of distance learning: A comparison of online and traditional learning. *MERLOT Journal of Online Learning and Teaching*, 2(1), 1-11. Retrieved from http://jolt. merlot.org/Vol2_No1.htm.

Hannefield, G. (2009). Prader-Willi Syndrome needs early diagnosis. *Tulsa Kids*, July.

Hansson, R.O., Berry, J.O., & Berry, M.E. (1999). The bereavement experience: Continuing commitment after the loss of a loved one. In J.M. Adams & W.H. Warren (Eds.), *Handbook of interpersonal commitment and relationship stability* (pp. 281-291). Dordrecht, Netherlands: Kluwer Academic Publishers.

Hardt, D.V. (1979). *Death: The final frontier.* Englewood Cliffs, NJ: Prentice-Hall.

Hardwig, J. (1990). What about the family? *Hastings Center Report, 20*(2), 5-10.

Harrawood, L.K., Doughty, E.A., & Wilde, B. (2011). Death education and attitudes of counselors-in-training toward death: An exploratory study. *Counseling and Values*, 56, 83-95.

Harris, C.E., & Alcorn, S.P. (2001). To solve a deadly shortage: Economic incentives for human organ donation. *Issues in Law and Medicine*, 16, 215-225.

Harris, D.L. (Ed.). (2011). *Counting our losses: Reflecting on change, loss, and transition in everyday life.* New York, NY: Routledge.

Harrison, R.L., & Westwood, M.J. (2009). Preventing vicarious traumatization of mental health therapists: Identifying protective practices. *Psychotherapy Theory, Research, Practice, Training, 49,* 203-219.

Hawley, D.R. (2000). Clinical implications of family resilience. *The American Journal of Family Therapy, 28,* 101-116.

Hawley, D.R., & DeHaan, L. (1996). Toward a definition of family resilience: Integrating life-span and family perspectives. *Family Process, 35,* 283-298.

Hawton, K., Saunders, K.E.A., & O'Connor, R.C. (2012). Self-harm and suicide in adolescents. *The Lancet, 379,* 2373-2382.

Hayslip, B., Jr. (2003). Death denial: Hiding and camouflaging death. In C.D. Bryant (Ed.), *Handbook of death and dying* (pp. 34-42). Thousand Oaks, CA: Sage Publications.

Hayslip, B., & Hansson, R.O. (2003). Death awareness and adjustment across the life span. In C.D. Bryant (Ed.), *Handbook of death and dying* (Vol.1, pp. 437-447). Thousand Oaks, CA: Sage Publications.

Hayslip, B., Hansson, R.O., Starkweather, J.D., & Dolan, D.C. (2009). Culture, individual diversity, and end of life decisions. In J.L. Werth & D. Blevins (Eds.), *Decision making near the end of life: Issues, development, and future directions* (pp. 301-323). New York, NY: Routledge.

Hayslip, B., Patrick, J.H., & Panek, P.E. (2011). *Adult development and aging* (5th ed.). Malabar, FL: Krieger.

Hayslip, B., Jr., & Peveto, C.A. (2005). *Cultural changes in attitudes toward death, dying, and bereavement.* New York, NY: Springer Publishing.

Hayslip, B., Allen, S.E., & McCoy-Roberts, L. (2001). The role of gender in a three-year longitudinal study of bereavement: A test of the experienced competence model. In D.A. Lund (Ed.), *Men coping with grief* (pp. 121-146). Amityville, NY: Baywood Publishing.

Hayslip, B., & White, D.J. (2008). The grief of grandparents. In M.S. Stroebe, R.O. Hansson, H. Schut, & W. Stroebe (Eds.), *Handbook of bereavement research and practice: Advances in theory and intervention* (pp. 441-460). Washington, DC: American Psychological Association.

Hearsum, P. (2012). A musical matter of life and death: the morality of mortality and the coverage of Amy Winehouse's death in the UK press. *Mortality, 17,* 182-199.

Heckhausen, J., Wrosch, C., & Schultz, R. (2010). A motivation theory of life-span development. *Psychological Review, 117,* 32-60.

Hegedus, K., Zana, A., & Szabo, G. (2008). Effect of end of life education on medical students' and health care workers' death attitude. *Palliative Medicine, 22,* 264-269.

Heider, K.G. (2011). *The cultural context of emotion.* New York, NY: Palgrave Macmillan.

Heins, J.K., Heins, A., Grammas, M., Costello, M., Huang, K., & Mishra, S. (2006). Disparities in analgesia and opioid prescribing practices for patients with musculoskeletal pain in the emergency department. *Journal of Emergency Nursing, 32,* 219-224.

Helbok, C.M., Marinelli, R.P., & Walls, R.T. (2006). National survey of ethical practices across rural and urban communities. *Professional Psychology: Research and Practice, 37,* 36-44.

Hemmings, P. (2005). The family perspective in bereavement. In B. Monroe & F. Kraus (Eds.), *Brief interventions with bereaved children* (pp. 49-64). New York, NY: Oxford University Press.

Henig, N.R., Faul, J.L., & Raffin, T.A. (2001). Biomedical ethics and the withdrawal of advanced life support. *Annual Review of Medicine, 52,* 79-92. Retrieved from http://www.annualreviews.org/journal/med.

Hennings, J., Froggatt, K., & Keady, J. (2010). Approaching the end of life and dying with dementia in care homes: the accounts of family carers. *Reviews in Clinical Gerontology, 20,* 114-127.

Henry, A.F., & Short, J.F. (1954). *Suicide and homicide.* New York, NY: Free Press.

Henry, D.B., Tolan, P.H., & Gorman-Smith, D. (2004). Have there been lasting effects associated with the September 11, 2001 terrorist attack among inner-city parents and children? *Professional Psychology Research and Practice, 35,* 542-547.

Herman, J. (1992). *Trauma and recovery*. New York, NY: Basic Books.

Heron, M. (2012). Deaths: Leading causes for 2008. *National Vital Statistics Reports, 60*(6). Retrieved from http://www.cdc.gov/nchs/data/nvsr60/nvsr60_06.pdf.

Hickman, S.E., Hammes, B.J., Moss, A.H., & Tolle, S.W. (2005). Hope for the future: Achieving the original intent of advance directives. In *Improving end of life care: Why has it been so difficult? Hastings Center Report, 35*(6), S26-S30.

Hobfoll, S.E., Watson, P.E., Bell, C.C., Bryant, R.A., Brymer, M.J., Friedman, M.J., et al. (2007). Five essential elements of immediate and midterm mass trauma intervention: Empirical evidence. *Psychiatry: Interpersonal and Biological Processes, 70*, 283–315.

Hodge, D. (2005). Developing a spiritual assessment toolbox: A discussion of the strengths and limitations of five different assessment methods. *Health and Social Work, 30*, 314-323.

Hogan, N., & De Santis, L. (1992). Adolescent sibling bereavement: An ongoing attachment. *Qualitative Health Research, 2*, 159-177.

Hogan, N.S., Greenfield, D.B., & Schmidt, L.A. (2001). Development and validation of the Hogan Grief Reactions Checklist. *Death Studies, 25*, 1-32.

Hogan, N.S., Worden, J.W., & Schmidt, L.A. (2006). Considerations in conceptualizing complicated grief. *Omega: Journal of Death and Dying, 52*, 81-85.

Holinger, P.C. (1987). *Violent deaths in the United States*. New York, NY: Guilford Press.

Holland, J.M., Currier, J.M., Coleman, R.A., & Neimeyer, R.A. (2010). The Integration of Stressful Life Experiences Scale (ISLES): Development and initial validation of a new measure. *International Journal of Stress Management, 17*, 325-352.

Holland, J.M., Currier, J.M., & Neimeyer, R.A. (2006). Meaning reconstruction in the first two years of bereavement: The role of sense-making and benefit-finding. *Omega, Journal of Death and Dying, 53*, 175-191.

Holland, J.M., & Neimeyer, R.A. (2005). Reducing the risk of burnout in end-of-life settings: The role of daily spiritual experiences and training. *Palliative and Supportive Care, 3*, 173-181.

Holland, J.M., & Neimeyer, R.A. (2010). An examination of stage theory of grief among individuals bereaved by natural and violent causes: A meaning-oriented contribution. *Omega: Journal of Death and Dying, 61*, 105-122.

Hollander, J.A., & Gordon, H.R. (2006). The process of social construction in talk. *Symbolic Interaction, 29*, 183-212.

Homan, P. (2005). Responding to crisis: A bereavement perspective. *NHPCO Newsline Quarterly Insights Edition, 3*, 35-37.

Hooghe, A., Neimeyer, R.A., & Rober, P. (2011). The complexity of couple communication in bereavement: An illustrative case study. *Death Studies, 35*, 905-924.

Hooghe, A., Neimeyer, R.A., & Rober, P. (2012). "Cycling around an emotional core of sadness": Emotion regulation in a couple after the loss of a child. *Qualitative Health Research*, in press.

Hoover, J.H., Markell, M.A., & Wagner, P. (2004/2005). Death and grief as experienced by adults with developmental disabilities: Initial explorations. *Omega: Journal of Death and Dying, 50*, 181-196.

Hopkins, A.R. (2002). Children and grief. The role of the early childhood educator. *Young Children, 57*, 40-46.

Hopp, F.P., & Duffy, S.A. (2000). Racial variations in end of life care. *Journal of the American Geriatrics Society, 48*, 658-663. Retrieved from http://www.americangeriatrics.org/.

Horsley, G., & Horsley, H. (2012). Open to Hope: An online thanatology resource center. In C.J. Sofka, I. N. Cupit, & K.R. Gilbert (Eds.), *Dying, death, and grief in an online universe: For counselors and educators* (pp. 151-162). New York, NY: Springer Publishing.

Hosogoe, S. (Producer), & Itami J. (Director). (1984). The funeral. [Motion picture]. Japan: Fox Lorber.

Hospice and Palliative Care Training for Physicians (1997). *UNIPAC: The hospice/palliative care training for physicians.* Glenview, IL: American Academy of Hospice and Palliative Medicine.

Hostler, L. (1978). The development of the child's concept of death. In O.J. Sahler (Ed.), *The child and death* (p. 9). St. Louis, MO: C.V. Mosby.

Hoyert, D. (2001). The autopsy, medicine, and mortality statistics. *National Center for Health Statistics. Vital Health Statistics*, 3, 32.

Howarth, G. (2007). *Death and dying: A sociological introduction.* Malden, MA: Polity.

Huang, I., Guo, R., Xie, H., & Wu, Z. (2012). The convergence of information and communication technologies gains momentum. In S. Dutta & B. Bilbao-Osorio (Eds.), *The global information technology report 2012: Living in a hyperconnected world* (pp. 35-45). Retrieved from: http://www3.weforum.org/docs/Global_IT_Report_2012.pdf.

Humphrey, D. (2005). Farewell to hemlock: Killed by its name. Retrieved from http://www.assistedsuicide.org/farewell-to-hemlock.html.

Humphreys, K. (2011, September 14). Grief, Trauma, Exposure and the Internet. [Blog post]. Retrieved from http://www.washingtonmonthly.com/ten-miles-square/2011/09/grief_trauma_exposure_and_the032191.php.

Hunter, E.G. (2007-2008). Beyond death: Inheriting the past and giving to the future, transmitting the legacy of one's self. *Omega: Journal of Death and Dying*, 56, 313-329.

Hunter, S.B., & Smith, D.E. (2008). Predictors of children's understandings of death: Age, cognitive ability, death experience and maternal communicative competence. *Omega: Journal of Death and Dying*, 57, 143-162. doi:10.2190/OM.57.2.b.

Hutchinson, J., & Rupp, J. (1999). May I walk you home? Courage and comfort for caregivers of *the very ill.* Notre Dame, IN: Ave Maria Press.

Hutti, M.H. (1992). Parents' perceptions of the miscarriage experience. *Death Studies*, 16, 401-415.

Hwang, W. (2006). The psychotherapy adaptation and modification framework: Applications to Asian Americans. *American Psychologist*, 61, 702-715.

Hwang, W. (2012). Integrating Top-Down and Bottom-Up Approaches to Culturally Adapting Psychotherapy: Applications to Chinese Americans. In Bernal, G., and Domenech Rodriguez, M. (Eds.), *Cultural adaptations: Tools for evidence-based practice with diverse populations* (pp. 179-198). Washington, DC: American Psychological Association.

Imara, M. (1980). Director of the Center for Religion and Psychotherapy and the Psychological Counseling Center (Brandeis University), interview – Paramus, NJ.

Imber-Black, E. (2004). Rituals and the healing process. In F. Wash & M. McGoldrick (Eds.), *Living beyond loss: Death in the family* (2nd ed.) (pp. 341-343). New York, NY: W.W. Norton & Co.

Imber-Black, E. (2005). Creating meaningful rituals for new life cycle transitions. In B. Carter & M. McGoldrick (Eds.), *The expanded family life cycle: Individual, family, and social perspectives* (3rd ed.) (pp. 202-214). Boston, MA: Allyn & Bacon.

Imber-Black, E., & Roberts, J. (1992). *Rituals for our times: Celebrating, healing, and changing our lives and our relationships.* New York, NY: HarperCollins.

Impens, A. J. (2005). *Bereavement related mortality among older adults.* (Unpublished doctoral dissertation). University of Michigan.

Institute of Medicine. (2003). *Unequal treatment.* Washington, DC: National Academies Press.

International Work Group on Death, Dying, and Bereavement. (1992). A statement of assumptions and principles concerning education about death, dying, and bereavement. *Death Studies*, 16, 59-63.

International Work Group on Death, Dying and Bereavement. (1994) *Statements on dying death and bereavement.* London, Ontario, Canada: King's College.

International Work Group on Death, Dying and Bereavement. (1999). Assumptions and principles of spiritual care. In K.J. Doka & J.D. Morgan (Eds.). *Death and spirituality.* Amityville, NY: Baywood Publishing.

International Work Group on Death, Dying, and Bereavement. (2006). Caregivers in death, dying, and bereavement situations. *Death Studies, 30,* 649-663.

In re: Quinlan, 355 A.2d 647. (1976).

In re: Quinlan, 755A2A 647. (Cert. denied, 429 U.S. 922. 1976).

In re: the guardianship of Theresa Schiavo, an incapacitated person, Case No. 90-2908GD-003. (1998).

Irion P. (1999). Ritual responses to death. In J.D. Davidson & K.J. Doka, (Eds.), *Living with grief: At work, at school, at worship* (pp. 157-166.) Littleton, PA: Brunner/Mazel.

Irish Association of Palliative Care (IAPC). (2011a). *Artificial hydration in terminally ill patients: Position paper.* Dublin, Ireland: Author.

Irish Association of Palliative Care (IAPC). (2011b). *Palliative sedation: Discussion paper.* Dublin, Ireland: Author.

Irish Association of Palliative Care (IAPC). (2011c). *Voluntary euthanasia: Discussion paper.* Dublin, Ireland: Author.

Irish Council for Bioethics. (2005). *Bioethics research.* Dublin, Ireland: Author.

Irish Council for Bioethics. (2007). *Is it time for advance healthcare directives?* Dublin, Ireland: Author.

Irish, D., Lundquist, K.F., & Nelsen, V.J. (Eds.). (1993). *Ethnic variations in dying, death, and grief: Diversity in universality.* Washington, DC: Taylor & Francis.

Irish Hospice Foundation. (2010). *National audit of end of life care in hospitals in Ireland, 2008/9.* Retrieved from www.hospicefriendlyhospitals.net/national-audit-of-end-of-life-care-in-hospitals.

Irish Hospice Foundation. (2011). *Think ahead: Initiative of the forum on end of life in Ireland.* Retrieved from http://www.thinkahead.ie.

Irwin, W.H. (2006). Feeding patients with advanced dementia: The role of the speech-language pathologist in making end-of-life decisions. *Journal of Medical Speech - Language Pathology, 14.*

Iwashyna, T.J., & Christakis, N.A. (1998). Attitude and self-reported practice regarding hospice referral in a national sample of internists. *Journal of Palliative Medicine, 1,* 241-248.

Jackson, J.D. (2003). Justice for all: Putting victims at the heart of criminal justice? *Journal of Law and Society, 30,* 309-326.

Janet, P. (1978). *Mental state of hysteria.* New York, NY: University Publishers of America.

Jacobs, S. (1999). *Traumatic grief: Diagnosis, treatment, and prevention.* Philadelphia, PA: Brunner/Mazel.

Janoff-Bulman, R. (1992). *Shattered assumptions: Towards a new psychology of trauma.* New York, NY: Free Press.

Jezuit, D.L. (2000). Suffering of critical care nurses with end-of-life decisions. *MedSurg Nursing, 9,* 145-152.

Johnson, M. (2006). Terri Schiavo: a disability rights case. *Death Studies, 30,* 163-176.

Johnson, S.H. (2005). Making room for dying: End of life care in nursing homes. In *Improving end of life care: Why has it been so difficult? Hastings Center Report* 35(6), S37-S41.

Joinson, C. (1992). Coping with compassion fatigue: Taking care of one's self while taking care of others. *Nursing, 22,* 116-121.

Jones, J.H. (1992). *Bad blood: The Tuskegee syphilis experiment.* New York, NY: Simon & Schuster.

Jones, K. (2005). Diversities in approach to end-of-life: A view from Britain of the qualitative literature. *Journal of Research in Nursing,* 10, 431-454.

Jordan, J.R. (2008). Bereavement after suicide. *Psychiatric Annals*, 38(10), 679-685.

Jordan, J.R., Baker, J., Matteis, M., Rosenthal, S., & Ware, E.S. (2005). The Grief Evaluation Measure (GEM): An initial validation study. *Death Studies*, 29, 301-332.

Jordan, J., & McIntosh, J.L. (Eds.). (2011). *Grief after suicide: Understanding the consequences and caring for the survivors.* New York, NY: Routledge.

Jordan, J.R., & McIntosh, J.L. (2011a). Is suicide bereavement different? A framework for rethinking the question. In J.R. Jordan & J.L. McIntosh (Eds.), *Grief after suicide* (pp. 19-42). New York, NY: Routledge.

Jordan, J.R., & McIntosh, J.L. (2011b). The impact of suicide on adults. In J.R. Jordan & J.L. McIntosh (Eds.), *Grief after suicide* (pp. 43-79). New York, NY: Routledge.

Jordan, J.R., & Neimeyer, R.A. (2003). Does grief counseling work? *Death Studies,* 27, 765-786.

Juckett, G. (2005). Cross-cultural medicine. *American Family Physician,* 72, 2267-2274.

Jung, C.G. (1933/1971). The stages of life (Translated by R.F.C. Hull). In J. Campbell (Ed.), *The portable Jung* (pp. 3-21). New York, NY: Viking.

Jung, C.G. (1974). *The collected works of C. G. Jung.* Edited by H. Read, M. Fordham, & G. Adler. London, UK: Routledge & Kegan Paul.

Jupp, P.C. (2008). *Death our future: Christian theology and funeral practice.* London, UK: Epworth.

Kagawa-Singer, M., & Blackhall, L.J. (2010). Negotiating cross-cultural issues at the end of life: "You've got to go where he lives." In D.E. Meier, S.L. Isaacs, & R.G. Hughes (Eds.), *Palliative care: Transforming the care of serious illnesses* (pp. 329-347). San Francisco, CA: Josey-Bass.

Kagawa-Singer, M., Valdez-Dadia, A., Yu, M., & Surbone, A. (2010). Cancer, culture and health disparities: Time to chart a new course? *Cancer: A Journal for Clinicians,* 60, 12-39.

Kagle, J.D., & Giebelhausen, P.H. (1994). Dual relationships and professional boundaries. *Social Work*, 39, 213-220.

Kahana, B., Dan, A., Kahana, E., & Kercher, K. (2004). The personal and social context of planning for end-of-life care. *Journal of the American Geriatrics Society,* 52: 1163-1167.

Kalauokalani, D. (2006). Complementary and alternative therapies for pain management. In K. Doka (Ed.), *Pain management at the end-of-life: Bridging the gap between knowledge and practice* (pp. 183-196). Washington, DC: The Hospice Foundation of America.

Kalayjian, A.S. (1996). *Disaster and mass trauma: Global perspectives on post disaster mental health management.* Long Branch, NJ: Vista.

Kang, H.K., & Bullman, T.A. (2009). Is there an epidemic of suicides among current and former U.S. military personnel? *Annals of Epidemiology,* 19, 757-760.

Kaplan, E.A. (2008). Global trauma and public feelings: Viewing images of catastrophe. *Consumption Markets & Culture,* 11(1), 3-24.

Kaplow, J.P., Saunders, J., Angold, A., & Costello, E.J. (2010). Psychiatric symptoms in bereaved versus nonbereaved youth and young adults: A longitudinal epidemiological study. *Journal of the American Academy of Child and Adolescent Psychiatry,* 49, 1145-1154.

Kapust, L.R. (1982). Living with dementia: The ongoing funeral. *Social Work in Health Care,* 7, 79-91.

Karel, M.J., Gatz, M., & Smyer, M.A. (2012). Aging and mental health in the decade ahead: what psychologists need to know. *American Psychologist*, 67, 184-198.

Kastenbaum, R.J. (1977). We covered death today. *Death Education,* 1, 85-92.

Kastenbaum, R. (1989). Death system. In R. Kastenbaum & B. Kastenbaum (Eds.), *Encyclopedia of death* (pp. 90-93). Phoenix, AZ: Oryx Press.

Kastenbaum, R. (1993). Reconstructing death in postmodern society. *Omega: Journal of Death and Dying, 27*, 75-89.

Kastenbaum, R. (1996). A world without death? First and second thoughts. *Mortality, 1*, 111-121.

Kastenbaum, R.J. (2001). *Death, society, and human experience* (7th ed.). Needham Heights, MA: Allyn & Bacon.

Kastenbaum, R.J. (2004a). *On our way: The final passenger through life and death*. Berkeley, CA: University of California Press.

Kastenbaum, R.J. (2004b). Death writ large. *Death Studies, 28*, 375-392.

Kastenbaum, R. (2009). *Death, society, and human experience* (10th ed.). Boston: Allyn & Bacon.

Kastenbaum, R.J. (2012). *Death, society, and human experience* (11th ed.). Boston: Pearson Higher Education.

Kastenbaum, R., & Aisenberg, R. (1972). *The psychology of death*. New York, NY: Springer Publishing.

Kato, P.M., & Mann, T. (1999). A synthesis of psychological interventions for the bereaved. *Clinical Psychology Review, 19*, 275–296.

Kauffman, J. (2002). *Loss of the assumptive world: A theory of traumatic loss*. New York, NY: Brunner-Routledge.

Kauffman, J. (2002). Safety and the assumptive world. In J. Kauffman (Ed.), *Loss of the assumptive world* (pp. 205-211). New York, NY: Brunner-Routledge.

Kauffman, J. (2005). *Guidebook on helping persons with mental retardation mourn*. Amityville, NY: Baywood Publishing.

Kaufman, K.R., & Kaufman, N.D. (2006). And then the dog died. *Death Studies, 30*, 61-76.

Kavanaugh, K., Andreoni, V.A., Wilkie, D., Burgener, S. et al. (2009). Developing a blended course on dying, loss, and grief. *Nurse Educator, 34*, 126-131.

Kawamura, L. (2002). Facing life and death: A Buddhist's understanding of palliative care and bereavement. In J.D. Morgan & P. Laungani (Eds.), *Death and bereavement around the world, Volume I: Major religious traditions* (pp. 39-56). Amityville, NY: Baywood Publishing.

Kearney, M.K., Weininger, R.B., Vachon, M.L.S., Harrison, R.L., & Mount, B.M. (2009). Self-care of Physicians Caring for Patients at the End of Life. *The Journal of the American Medical Association, 301*, 1155-1164.

Keegan, O., McGee, H., Brady, T., et al. (1999). *Care for the dying-experiences and challenges: A study of quality of health service care during the last year of life of patients at St. James's Hospital, Dublin from their relatives' perspectives*. Dublin, Ireland: Health Services Research Centre, Irish Hospice Foundation and Palliative Care Service, St. James's Hospital.

Keeley, M., & Baldwin, P. (2012). Final conversations, phase 2: Children and everyday communication. *Journal of Loss and Trauma, 17*, 376-387.

Keesee, N.J., Currier, J.M., & Neimeyer, R.A. (2008). Predictors of grief following the death of one's child: The contribution of finding meaning. *Journal of Clinical Psychology, 64*, 1145-1163.

Khushf, G. (2010). A matter of respect: A defense of the dead donor rule and of "whole- brain" criterion for determination of death. *Journal of Medicine and Philosophy, 35*, 330-364.

Kieran, M. (1997). *Media ethics: A philosophical approach*. Westport, CT: Praeger Publishers.

Kilpatrick, D.G. (1986). Addressing the needs of traumatized victims. *The Practical Prosecutor* (pp. 15-18). Houston, TX: National College of District Attorneys, University of Houston Law Center.

Kilier, C.M., Geller, P.A., & Ritsher, J.B. (2002). Affective disorders in the aftermath of miscarriage: A comprehensive review. *Archives of Women's Mental Health, 5,* 129-149.

Kilpatrick, D.G., & Resnick, H.S. (1993). PTSD associated with exposure to criminal victimization in clinical and community populations. In J.R.T. Davidson and E.B. Foa, (Eds.), *Posttraumatic stress disorder: DSM-IV and beyond* (pp. 113-143). Washington, DC: American Psychiatric Press.

King, P.A., & Wolf, L.E. (1998). Empowering and protecting patients: Lessons for physician-assisted suicide from the African-American experience. *Minnesota Law Review, 82,* 1015-1043. Retrieved from http://www.minnesotalawreview.org/.

Kirkmayer, L.J. (2001). Confusion of the sense: Implications and ethnocultural variations in somatoform and dissociative disorders for PTSD. In A. Marsella, M. Friedman, E. Gerrity, & R. Scurfield (Eds.), *Ethnocultural aspects of posttraumatic stress disorder: Issues, research and clinical application.* Washington, DC: American Psychological Press.

Kirwin, K.M., & Harmin, V. (2005). Decreasing the risk of complicated bereavement and future psychiatric disorders in children. *Journal of Child and Adolescent Psychiatric Nursing, 18,* 62-78.

Kissane, D.W., & Bloch, S. (2002). *Family focused grief therapy.* Buckingham, UK: Open University Press.

Kissane, D.W., & Hooghe, A. (2011). Family therapy for the bereaved. In R.A. Neimeyer, D.L. Harris, H.R. Winokuer, & G.F. Thornton (Eds.), *Grief and bereavement in contemporary society: Bridging research and practice* (pp. 287-302). New York, NY: Routledge.

Kissane, D.W., & Lichtenthal, W.G. (2008). Family focused grief therapy: From palliative care into bereavement. In M.S. Stroebe, R.O. Hansson, H. Schut & W. Stroebe (Eds.), *Handbook of bereavement research and practice: Advances in theory and intervention* (pp. 485-510). Washington, DC: American Psychological Association.

Kissane, D.W., Lichtenthal, W.G., & Zaider, T. (2007). Family care before and after bereavement. *Omega: Journal of Death and Dying, 56,* 21-32.

Kissane, D.W., McKenzie, M., Block, S., Moskowitz, C., McKenzie, D.P., & O'Neill, I. (2006). Family Focused Grief Therapy: A randomized, controlled trial in palliative care and bereavement. *American Journal of Psychiatry, 163,* 1208-1218.

Klaiman, M.H. (2005). Whose brain is it anyway? The comparative law of post-mortem organ retention. *Journal of Legal Medicine, 26,* 475-490.

Klasen, F., Oettingen, G., Daniels, J., Post, M., Hoyer, C., & Adam, H. (2010). Posttraumatic Resilience in Former Ugandan Child Soldiers. *Child Development, 81,* 1096-1113.

Klass, D. (1986). Marriage and divorce among bereaved parents in a self-help group. *Omega: Journal of Death and Dying, 17,* 237-249.

Klass, D. (1988). *Parental grief: Solace and resolution.* New York, NY: Springer Publishing.

Klass, D. (1999). Developing a cross-cultural model of grief: The state of the field. *Omega: Journal of Death and Dying, 39,* 153-176.

Klass, D. (1999). *The spiritual lives of bereaved parents.* Philadelphia, PA: Brunner/Mazel.

Klass, D. (2001). The inner representation of the dead child in the psychic and social narratives of bereaved parents. In R.A. Neimeyer (Ed.), *Meaning reconstruction & the experience of loss* (pp. 77-94). Washington, DC: American Psychological Association.

Klass, D., & Hutton, R.A. (1985). Elisabeth Kübler-Ross as a religious leader. *Omega: Journal of Death and Dying, 16,* 89-109.

Klass, D., Silverman, P.R., & Nickman, S. (1996). *Continuing bonds: New understandings of grief.* Washington, DC: Taylor & Francis.

Kleespies, P. (2004). *Life and death decisions: Psychological and ethical considerations in end-of-life care.* Washington, DC: American Psychological Association.

Klein, A.C. (1998). Buddhism. In C.J. Johnson & M.G. McGee (Eds.), *How different religions view death and afterlife* (pp. 47-63). Philadelphia, PA: The Charles Press.

Klein, J. (June 11, 2012). End of life lessons. *Time, 179*(23), 18-25.

Klein, J., Stein, Z., & Susser, M. (1989). *Conception to birth: Epidemiology of prenatal development.* New York, NY: Oxford University Press.

Kleinman, A. (1990). *The illness narratives: Suffering, healing and the human condition.* New York, NY: Basic Books.

Kleinman, A. (2012). Culture, bereavement and psychiatry. *The Lancet, 379,* 608-609.

Klessig, J. (1992). The effects of values and culture on life-support decisions. *Western Journal of Medicine, 157,* 316-322. Retrieved from http://www.ncbi.nlm.nih.gov/pmc/journals/183/.

Klopfenstein, K.J. (1999). Adolescents, cancer, and hospice. *Adolescent Medicine, 10,* 436-43.

Knapp, S., & Slattery, J. (2004). Professional boundaries in nontraditional settings. *Professional Psychology: Research and Practice, 35,* 553-558.

Koch, T. (2005). The challenge of Terri Schiavo: Lessons for bioethics. *Journal of Medical Ethics, 31,* 376-378.

Kochanek, K.D., Xu, J., Murphy, S.L., Minino, A.M., & Kung, H-C. (2011). Deaths: Final data for 2009. *National Vital Statistics Reports, 60*(3). Retrieved from http://www.cdc.gov/nchs/data/nvsr/nvsr60/nvsr60_03.pdf.

Kock, W.J. (2001). *Diagnostic problems with PTSD.* Retrieved from http://www.drwilliamkoch.com/ptsd2.doc.

Koehler, K. (2010). Grief bibliotherapy and beyond for grieving children and teenagers. *Death Studies, 34,* 854-860. doi:10.1080/07481181003772721.

Koenig, B., & Davies, B. (2003). Cultural dimensions in end-of-life care for children and their families. In M. Field & R. Behrman (Eds.), *When Children Die* (pp. 553-579). Washington, DC: Institute of Medicine, National Academies Press. Retrieved from http://books.nap.edu/html/children_die/index.html.

Koenig, B.A., & Gates-Williams, J. (1995). Understanding cultural difference in caring for dying patients. *Western Journal of Medicine, 163,* 244-249.

Koenig, H.G. (1997). *Is religion good for your health?* Binghamton, NY: Haworth Press.

Koenig, H.G. (1998). Religious beliefs and practices of hospitalized medically ill older adults. *International Journal of Geriatric Psychiatry, 13,* 213-224.

Koenig, H.G. (2004). Religion, spirituality, and medicine: Research findings and implications for clinical practice. *Southern Medical Journal, 97,* 1194-1200.

Koenig, H.G., King, D., & Carson, V.B. (2012). *Handbook of religion and health* (2nd ed.). New York, NY: Oxford University Press.

Koenig, H., McCullough, M., & Larson, D. (2001). *Handbook of religion and health.* New York, NY: Oxford University Press.

Kogan, S.L., Blanchette, P.L., & Masaki, K. (2000). Talking to patients about death and dying: Improving communication across cultures. In K.L. Braun, J.H. Pietsch, & P.L. Blanchette (Eds.), *Cultural issues in end of life decision-making* (305-326). Thousand Oaks, CA: Sage Publications.

Konigsberg, R.D. (2011). *The truth about grief.* New York, NY: Simon & Schuster.

Koocher, G.P., & O'Malley, J.E. (1981). *The Damocles symdrome: Psychological consequences of surviving childhood cancer.* New York, NY: McGraw-Hill.

Korte, A.O. (1995-1996). *Despedidas* as reflections of death in Hispanic New Mexico. *Omega: Journal of Death and Dying, 32,* 245-267.

Kovacs, G. (1982). Death and the question of immortality. *Death Education, 1,* 5-24.

Kristensen, P., & Franco, M.H. (2011). Bereavement and disasters: Research and clinical intervention. In R.A. Neimeyer, D. Harris, H. Winokuer, & G. Thornton (Eds.), *Grief and bereavement in contemporary society: Bridging research and practice* (pp. 188-201). New York, NY: Routledge.

Kristjanson, L.J., & Aoun, S. (2004). Palliative care for families: Remembering the hidden patients. *Canadian Journal of Psychiatry, 49,* 359-365.

Krystal, H. (2002). What cannot be remembered or forgotten. In J. Kauffman (Ed.), *Loss of the assumptive world* (pp. 213-220). New York, NY: Brunner-Routledge.

Kübler-Ross, E. (1969). *On death and dying.* New York, NY: Macmillan.

Kübler-Ross, E. (1975). *Death: The final stage of growth.* Englewood Cliffs, NJ: Prentice Hall.

Kübler-Ross, E. (1991). The dying child. In D. Papadatou & C. Papadatos (Eds.), *Children and death* (pp. 147-160). New York, NY: Hemisphere Publishing.

Kübler-Ross, E., & Kessler, D. (2005). *On grief and grieving: Finding the meaning of grief through the five stages of loss.* New York, NY: Scribner.

Kübler-Ross, E., & Worden, J.W. (1977-78). Attitudes and experiences of death workshop attendees, *Omega: Journal of Death and Dying, 8,* 91-106.

Kuehn, B.M. (2009). Soldier suicide rates continue to rise. *Journal of the American Medical Association, 301,* 1111-1113.

Kuehn, B.M. (2010). Military probes epidemic of suicide. *Journal of the American Medical Association, 302,* 1427-1430.

Kushner, H. (2001). *When bad things happen to good people.* 20th Anniversary Edition. Schocken Books.

Kwak, J., & Haley, W.E. (2005). Current research findings on end-of-life decision making among racially or ethnically diverse groups. *The Gerontologist, 45,* 634-641. doi:10.1093/geront/45.5.634.

Kwon, S. (2006). Grief ministry as homecoming: Framing death from a Korean-American perspective. *Pastoral Psychology, 54,* 313-324. doi:10.1007/s11089-005-0002-1.

Lacey, D. (2006). End-of-life decision making for nursing home residents with dementia: A survey of nursing home social services staff. *Health & Social Work, 31,* 189-199.

Lester, D. (1996). Psychological issues in euthanasia, suicide, and assisted suicide. *Journal of Social Issues, 52,* 51-62.

Laituri, M., & Kodrich, K. (2008). On Line Disaster Response Community: People as Sensors of High Magnitude Disasters Using Internet GIS. *Sensors 8(5),* 3037-3055.

Lamb, V.L. (2003). Historical and epidemiological trends in mortality in the United States. In C.D. Bryant (Ed.), *Handbook of death and dying, Volume 1* (pp. 185-197). Thousand Oaks, CA: Sage Publications.

Lambrecht, M. (1991). The value of computer-assisted instruction in death education. *Loss, Grief, and Care, 4,* 67-69.

Lamers, E.P. (1995). Children, death, and fairy tales. *Omega: Journal of Death and Dying, 31,* 151-167.

Lamers, W. (2005). Autonomy, consent, and advance directives. In, K. Doka, B. Jennings, & C. Corr, *Ethical dilemmas at the end of life.* Washington, DC: Hospice Foundation of America.

Lancaster, J. (2011). Developmental stages, grief, and a child's response to death. *Pediatric Annals, 40(5),* 277-281.

Lancet, The (editorial). (2012). Living with grief. *The Lancet, 379,* 589.

Landsman, I.S. (2002). Crises of meaning in trauma and loss. In J. Kauffman (Ed.), *Loss of the assumptive world: A theory of traumatic loss* (pp. 13-30). New York, NY: Brunner-Routledge.

Lange, A., Schrieken, B., van de Ven, J.P., Bredeweg, B., Emmelkamp, P., van der Kolk, J., Lydsdottir, L., Massaro, M., & Reuvers, A. (2000). "Interapy": The effects of a short protocolled treatment of posttraumatic stress and pathological grief through the Internet. *Behavioural and Cognitive Psychotherapy, 28,*175-192.

Langs, R. (2004). Death anxiety and the emotion-processing mind. *Psychoanalytic Psychology, 21,* 31-53.

Larman, J.S. (2004). *Conjugal bereavement in younger and older* widows *and widowers: Influences of health and social support.* (Unpublished doctoral dissertation). Fielding Graduate Institute.

La Roche, M. (2012). *Cultural psychotherapy: Theory, methods and practice.* Thousand Oaks, CA: Sage Publications.

La Roche, M., and Christopher, M.S. (2009). Changing paradigms from empirically supported treatments to evidence-based psychotherapy practice: A cultural perspective. *Professional Psychology: Research & Practice, 40,* 396-402.

Larson, D.G., & Hoyt, W.T. (2007*)*. What has become of grief counseling? An evaluation of the empirical foundations of the new pessimism. *Professional Psychology: Research and Practice, 38,* 347–355.

Lattanzi-Licht, M., & Doka, K.J. (2003). Coping with public tragedy. In M. Lattanzi-Licht & K.J. Doka (Eds.), *Living with grief: Coping with public tragedy* (pp. 119-121). New York, NY: Brunner-Routledge.

Lattanzi-Licht, M., Mahoney, J.J., & Miller, G.W. (1998). *The hospice choice.* New York, NY: Simon & Schuster/Fireside.

Laungani, P. (1992). Cultural variations in the understanding and treatment of psychiatric disorders: India and England. *Counselling Psychology Quarterly, 5*(3), 231-244. doi:http://psycnet.apa.org/doi/10.1080/09515079208254468.

Laungani, P. (1996). Death and bereavement in India and England: A comparative analysis. *Mortality, 1,* 191-212.

Law Reform Commission. (2009). *Bioethics: advance care directives.* Dublin, Ireland: Law Reform Commission.

Leaman, O. (1995). *Death and loss: Compassionate approaches in the classroom.* London, UK: Cassell.

Ledger, S. (2005). The duty of nurses to meet patients' spiritual and/or religious needs. *British Journal of Nursing, 14,* 220-225.

Leenaars, A.A. (1989). Suicide across the adult life-span. *Crisis, 10,* 132-151.

Leenaars, A.A. (1996). Justin. In A. Leenaars & D. Lester (Eds.), *Suicide and the unconscious* (pp. 139-174). Northvale, NJ: Jason Aronson.

Lehman, D.R., Lang, E.L., Wortman, C.B., & Sorenson, S.B. (1989). Long-term effects of sudden bereavement: Marital and parent-child relationships and children's reactions. *Journal of Family Psychology, 2,* 344-367.

Leichtentritt, R.D. (2004). The meaning that young Israeli adults ascribe to the least undesirable death. *Death Studies, 28,* 733-759.

Leming, M.R., & Dickinson, G.E. (2007). *Understanding Dying, Death, & Bereavement* (6th ed.). Belmont, CA: Thomson/Wadsworth.

Leong, F.T., & Lopez, S. (2006). Guest editors' introduction. *Psychotherapy: Research, Practice and Training, 4,* 378-379.

Lester, D. (1982). The distribution of sex and age among completed suicides. *International Journal of Social Psychiatry, 28,* 256-260.

Lester, D. (1986). The distribution of sex and age among victims of homicide. *International Journal of Social Psychiatry, 32*(2), 47-50.

Lester, D. (1990). Suicide prevention in the schools. *High School Journal, 73,* 161-163.

Lester, D. (1994a). Are there unique features of suicide in adults of different ages and developmental stages? *Omega: Journal of Death and Dying*, 29, 337-348.

Lester, D. (1994b). A comparison of fifteen theories of suicide. *Suicide & Life-Threatening Behavior*, 24, 80-88.

Lester, D. (1996). Psychological issues in euthanasia, suicide, and assisted suicide. *Journal of Social Issues*, 52, 51-62.

Lester, D. (1998). *Suicide in African Americans*. Commack, NY: Nova Science.

Lester, D., & Frank, M.L. (1987). When are babies perceived as male or female? *Perceptual & Motor Skills*, 65, 698.

Lester, D., & Yang, B. (1998). *Suicide and Homicide in the 20th Century*. Commack, NY: Nova Science.

Leurquin-Hallett, L. (1999). Professional boundaries in nephrology nursing practice. *ANNA Journal*, 26, 80-82.

Levine, J.E. (1996). Oklahoma City: The storying of a disaster. *Smith College Studies in Social Work*, 67, 21-38.

Leviton, D. (1977). The scope of death education. *Death Education*, 1, 41-56.

Leviton, D., & Kastenbaum, R.J. (1975). Death education. *Death Studies*, 6, 179-181.

Lewis, S. (2008). *Beyond comprehension: The range of HIV/AIDS in Africa.* Keynote address to the 30th Annual Conference of the Association for Death Education and Counseling, Montreal, Quebec, Canada.

Lieberman, A.F., Compton, N.C., Horn, P.V., & Ippen, C.G. (2003). *Losing a parent to death in the early years: Guidelines for the treatment of traumatic bereavement in infancy and early childhood.* Washington, DC: Zero to Three Press.

Lichtenstein, R.L., Alcser, K.H., Corning, A.D., Bachman, J.G., & Doukas, D.J. (1997). African-Caucasian differences in attitudes toward physician-assisted suicide. *Journal of the National Medical Association*, 89, 125-133. Retrieved from http://www.nmanet.org/.

Lichtenthal, W.G., & Cruess, D.G. (2010). Effects of directed written disclosure on grief and distress symptoms among bereaved individuals. *Death Studies*, 34, 475-499.

Lichtenthal, W.G., Cruess, D.G., & Prigerson, H.G. (2004). A case for establishing complicated grief as a distinct mental disorder in DSM-V. *Clinical Psychology Review*, 24(6), 637-662.

Lichtenthal, W.G., Currier, J.M., Neimeyer, R.A., & Keesee, N.J. (2010). Sense and significance: A mixed methods examination of meaning-making following the loss of one's child. *Journal of Clinical Psychology*, 66, 791-812.

Lifton, R.J. (1979). *The broken connection.* New York, NY: Simon & Schuster.

Lifton, R., & Olsen, G. (1974). *Living and dying.* New York, NY: Bantam Books.

Lin, H., & Bauer-Wu, S. (2003). Psycho-spiritual well-being in patients with advanced cancer: an integrative review of the literature. *Journal of Advanced Nursing*, 44, 69-90.

Lin, K., Sandler, I. W., Ayers, T., Wolchik, S., & Laucken, L. (2004). Resilience in parentally bereaved children and adolescents seeking preventive services. *Journal of Clinical Child and Adolescent Psychology*, 33, 673-683.

Lindemann, E. (1944). Symptomatology and management of acute grief. *American Journal of Psychiatry*, 101, 141-148.

Little, M., Sandler, I.N., Wolchik, S.A., Tein, J-U., & Ayers, T. (2009). Comparing cognitive, relational, and stress mechanisms underlying gender differences in recovery from bereavement-related internalizing problems. *Journal of Clinical Child & Adolescent Psychology*, 38, 486–500.

Littlewood, J. (1993). The denial of death and rites of passage in contemporary societies. In D. Clark (Ed.), *The sociology of death: Theory, culture, practice* (pp. 69-84). Cambridge, MA: Blackwell.

Litz, B.T. (2004) *Early intervention for trauma and traumatic loss.* New York, NY: Guilford Press.

Litz, B.T., Gray, M., & Adler, A. (2002). Early intervention for trauma: Current status and future directions. *Clinical Psychology: Science and Practice, 9,* 112–134.

Lo, B. (2000). *Resolving ethical dilemmas: A guide for clinicians.* Philadelphia, PA: Lippincott, Williams, & Wilkins.

Lopez, S.A. (2011). Culture as an influencing factor in adolescent grief and bereavement. *The Prevention Researcher,* 18(3), 10-13.

Lowenstein, L., & Hertlein, K. (2012). Engaging children in family sessions: Three creative interventions. *Journal of Family Psychotherapy,* 23, 62-66. doi:10.1080/08975353.2012.654090.

Lohmann, R.I. (2005). The afterlife as Asabano corpses: Relationships with the deceased in Papua New Guinea. *Ethnology,* 44, 189-206.

Lomnitz, C. (2005). *Death and the idea of Mexico.* Cambridge, MA: MIT Press.

Lozano-Nieto, A., Guijarro, E., & Berjano, E.J. (2006). Critical assessment of the World Wide Web as an information resource in higher education: Benefits, threats, and recommendations. *MERLOT Journal of Online Learning and Teaching,* 2(1), 22-29. Retrieved from http://jolt. merlot.org/ Vol2_No1.htm.

Lubetkin, E.I., Jia, H., Franks, P., & Gold, M.R. (2005). Relationship among sociodemographic factors, clinical conditions, and health-related quality of life: Examining the EQ-5D in the U.S. general population. *Quality of Life Research,* 14, 2187-2196.

Luecken, L. (2008) Long-term consequences of parental death in childhood: Psychological and physiological manifestations. In M.S. Stroebe, R.O. Hansson. H. Schut & W. Stroebe (Eds.), *Handbook of bereavement research and practice* (pp. 397-416). Washington, DC: American Psychological Association.

Lund, D.A. (1989). Conclusions about bereavement in later life and implications for interventions and future research. In D.A. Lund (Ed.), *Older bereaved spouses* (pp. 217-231). New York, NY: Hemisphere.

Lund, D.A. Caserta, M.S., & Dimond, M.R. (1993). The course of spousal bereavement. In M.S. Stroebe, W. Stroebe, & R.O. Hansson (Eds.), *Handbook of bereavement: Theory, research, and intervention* (pp. 240-254). Cambridge, UK: Cambridge University Press.

Lunney, J.R., Lynn, J., Foley, D.J., Lipson, S., & Guralnik, J.M. (2003). Patterns of functional decline at the end of life. *Journal of the American Medical Association,* 289, 2387-2392.

Luthar, S. (2006). Resilience in development: A synthesis of research across five decades. In D. Cicchetti & D. Cohen (Eds.), *Developmental psychopathology: Risk, disorder and adaptation* (pp. 739-795). New York, NY: Wiley.

Lynn, C., & Rath, A. (2012). GriefNet: Creating and maintaining an Internet bereavement community. In C.J. Sofka, I.N. Cupit, & K.R. Gilbert (Eds.), *Dying, death, and grief in an online universe: For counselors and educators* (pp. 87-102). New York, NY: Springer Publishing.

Lynn, J. (2000). Rethinking fundamental assumptions: SUPPORT's implications for future reform. *Journal of the American Geriatric Society,* 48, S214-S221.

Lynn, J. (2005). Living long in fragile health: The new demographics shape end of life care. In *Improving end of life care: Why has it been so difficult? Hastings Center Report* 35(6), S14-S18.

Lynch, T., Connor, S.R., & Clarke, D. (2012). Mapping levels of palliative care development: A global update. *Journal of Pain & Symptom Management.* In press.

Lyon, M.E., Garvie, P.A., McCarter, R., Briggs, L., He, J., & D'Angelo, L.J. (2009). Who will speak for me? Improving end-of-life decision-making for adolescents with HIV and their families. *Pediatrics,* 123, 199-206.

Lyon, R., & Lyon, M.E. (2009). Adolescent end-of-life decision-making: family-centered advance care planning. In James L. Werth & Dean Blevins (Eds.), *Decision making near the end of life: Issues, development, and future directions* (pp. 11-26). New York, NY: Routledge.

Maasdorp, V. (2011). The challenge of staff support in hospice care in Zimbabwe. In I. Renzenbrink, (Ed.), *Caregiver stress and staff support in illness, dying and bereavement* (pp. 82-97). New York, NY: Oxford University Press.

MacConville, U. (2006). Mapping religion and spirituality in an Irish palliative care setting. *Omega: Journal of Death and Dying, 53*, 137-152.

Machado, N. (2005). Discretionary death: Conditions, dilemmas, and normative regulation. *Death Studies, 29*, 791-809.

Maciejewski, P.K., Zhang, B., Block, S.D., & Prigerson, H.G. (2007). An empirical examination of the stage theory of grief. *Journal of the American Medical Association, 297*, 716-723.

Maglio, C.J., & Robinson, S.E. (1994). The effects of death education on death anxiety: A meta-analysis. *Omega: Journal of Death and Dying, 29*, 319-335.

Maguire, T.V. (1997). A recovery bill of rights for trauma survivors. Retrieved from http://www._sidran.org_/recovery.htm.

Mahon, M.M., Goldberg, R.L., & Washington, S.K. (1999). Discussing death in the classroom: Beliefs and experiences of educators and education students. *Omega: Journal of Death and Dying, 39*, 9- 121.

Mahoney, M.J., & Graci, G.M. (2010). *The meanings and correlates of spirituality: Suggestions from an exploratory survey of experts* (pp. 521-528). Version of record first published: 11 Nov. 2010. doi:10.1080/074811899200867.

Malkinson, R.M. (2007*). Cognitive grief therapy*. New York, NY: W.W. Norton & Sons.

Malkinson, R., Rubin, S.S., & Witztum, E. (Eds.). (2000). *Traumatic and nontraumatic loss and bereavement: Clinical theory and practice.* Madison, CT: Psychosocial Press.

Mallory, J.L. (2003). The impact of a palliative care educational component on attitudes toward care of the dying in undergraduate nursing students. *Journal of Professional Nursing, 19*, 305-312.

Malone, P.A. The impact of peer-death on adolescent girls: An efficacy study of the adolescent grief and loss group. *Social Work with Groups, 35*(1), 35-49.

Mancini, A., & Bonnano, G. (2012). Loss and grief: the role of individual differences. In Southwick, S., Litz, B., Charney, D., and Friedman, M. (Eds.), *Resilience in mental health.* New York, NY: Cambridge University Press.

Manis, A.A., & Bodenhorn, N. (2006). Preparation for counseling adults with terminal illness: Personal and professional parallels. *Counseling and Values, 50*(3), 197-207.

Manning, M. (2009). Death, like sun cannot be looked at steadily. *Studies: An Irish Quarterly Review, 98*, 379-391.

Maris, R. (1985). The adolescent suicide problem. *Suicide & Life-Threatening Behavior, 15*, 91-109.

Markell, K.A. (2009). Educating children about death-related issues. In C.A. Corr and D.E. Balk (Eds.), *Children's encounters with death, bereavement, and coping* (pp. 294-310). New York, NY: Springer Publishing.

Markell, K.A., & Markell, M.A. (2008). *The children who lived: Using Harry Potter and other fictional characters to help grieving children and adolescents.* New York, NY: Routledge.

Marotta, S.A. (2000). Best practices for counselors who treat posttraumatic stress disorder. *Journal of Counseling and Development, 78*, 492-495.

Marrone, R. (1997). *Death, mourning, and caring.* Pacific Grove, CA: Brooks/Cole.

Marshall, G. (Ed.). (1994). *The concise Oxford dictionary of sociology.* New York, NY: Oxford University Press.

Martin, T.L., & Doka, K.J. (2000). *Men don't cry, women do: Transcending gender stereotypes of grief.* Philadelphia, PA: Brunner/Mazel.

Martin, T.L., & Doka, K.J. (2010). The influence of gender and socialization on grieving styles. In R.A. Neimeyer, D.L. Harris, H.R. Winokuer, & G.F. Thornton (Eds), *Grief and bereavement in contemporary society: Bridging research and practice* (pp. 69-77). New York, NY: Routledge.

Martsolf, D.S. (2002). Codependency, boundaries, and the professional nurse caring: Understanding similarities and differences. *Orthopedic Nursing*, 21, 61-67.

Marvin, C. (2000). On violence in media. *Journal of Communication*, 50, 142-149.

Maslach, C. (1982). *Burnout: The Cost of Caring.* Englewood Cliffs, NJ: Prentice-Hall, Inc.

Mason, J., & Haselau, C. (2000). Grief therapy: An experiential workshop. *Contemporary Family Therapy: An International Journal*, 22, 279-288. doi:10.1023/A:1007808523540.

Materstvedt, L.J., Clark, D., Ellershaw, J., Forde, R., Gravgaard, A.-M.B., Mueller-Busch, H.C., et al. (2003). Euthanasia and physician assisted suicide: A view from an EAPC Ethics Task Force. *Palliative Medicine*, 17, 97-101.

May, R., Angel, E., & Ellenberger, H. (Eds.). (1958). *Existence: A new dimension in psychiatry and psychology.* New York, NY: Basic Books.

May, R., & Yalom, I. (2005). Existential psychotherapy. In R. Corsini & D. Wedding (Eds.), *Current psychotherapies* (7th ed.). Belmont, CA: Thomson/Brooks/Cole.

Mayo Clinic Health Letter. (2005). *Meditation*, 23(3), 3-4.

Mayo, D. J., & Gunderson M. (2002). Vitalism revitalized: Vulnerable populations, prejudice, and physician-assisted death, *Hastings Center Report*, 32 (4), 14-21.

Mazzotti, E., Mazzuca, F., Sebastiani, C., Scoppola, A., & Marchetti, P. (2011). Predictors of existential and religious well-being among cancer patients. *Support Care Cancer*. Dec:19(12), 1931-1937. Epub 2010 Nov 25.

McAliley, L.G., Hudson-Barr, D.C., Gunning, R.S., et al. (2000). The use of advance directives with adolescents. *Pediatric Nursing*, 26, 471-480.

McCabe, M. (1994). Patient Self-Determination Act: A Native American (Navajo) perspective. *Cambridge Quarterly of Healthcare Ethics*, 3, 419-421. Retrieved from http://journals.cambridge.org/action/displayJournal?jid=CQH.

McCarron, M., & McCallion, P. (2007). End-of-life care challenges for persons with intellectual disability and dementia: making decisions about tube feeding. *Journal of Intellectual and Developmental Disability*. 45, 128-131.

McCarthy, J., Donnelly, M., Dooley, D., Campbell, L., & Smith, D. (2011). *End of life care: Ethics and law.* Cork, Ireland: Cork University Press.

McCarthy, J., Loughrey, M., Weafer, J., & Dooley, D. (2009). Conversations with the Irish public about death and dying. *Studies: An Irish Quarterly Review*, 98, 457-472.

McCarthy, J., Weafer, J., & Loughrey M., (2010). Irish views on death and dying: A national survey. *Journal of Medical Ethics*, 36, 454-458.

McClain, C.S., Rosenfeld, B., & Breitbart, W. (2003). Effect of spiritual well-being on end-of-life despair in terminally-ill cancer patients. *The Lancet*, 361, 1063-1067.

McConnell, Y., Frager, F., & Levetown, M. (2004). Decision making in pediatric palliative care. In B.S. Carter & M. Levetown, (Eds.), *Palliative care for infants, children, and adolescents.* Baltimore, MD: Johns Hopkins University Press.

McCracken, L.J., & Keogh, E. (2009). Acceptance, mindfulness and values-based action may counteract fear and avoidance of emotions in chronic pain: An analysis of anxiety sensitivity. *The Journal of Pain*, 10, 408-415.

McDaniel, S., Lusterman, D., & Philpot, C. (2001). *Casebook for integrating family therapy: An ecosystemic approach.* Washington, DC: American Psychological Association.

McDannell, C., & Lang, B. (1988). *Heaven, A history*. New Haven, CT: Yale University Press.

McDevitt-Murphy, M.E., Neimeyer, R.A., Burke, L.A., & Williams, J.L. (2011). Assessing the toll of traumatic loss: Psychological symptoms in African Americans bereaved by homicide. *Psychological Trauma*, in press.

McEnearney, B. (2010). *Messages: Signs, visits, and premonitions from loved ones lost on 9/11*. New York, NY: Harper Collins.

McGoldrick, M. (2011). *The genogram journey*. New York, NY: W.W. Norton & Co.

McGoldrick, M., & Walsh, F. (2005). Death and the family life cycle. In B. Carter & M. McGoldrick (Eds.), *The expanded family life cycle: Individual, family, and social perspectives* (3rd ed.) (pp. 185-201). Boston, MA: Allyn & Bacon.

McGovern, M., & Barry, M.M. (2000). Death education: Knowledge, attitudes, and perspectives of Irish parents and teachers. *Death Studies, 24*, 325-333.

McHugh, M. (1980). *Young people talk about death*. New York, NY: Franklin Watts.

McKeever, A. (1999). Psychobabble and edufads invade the church. *Education Reporter*, 167. Retrieved from http://www.eagleforum.org/educate/1999/dec99/focus_church.html.

McKinley, E.D., Garrett, J.M., Evans, A.T., & Danis, M. (1996). Differences in end-of-life decision making among black and white ambulatory cancer patients. *Journal of General Internal Medicine, 11*, 651-656. doi:10.1007/BF02600155.

McKissock, D. (1998). *The grief of our children*. Sydney, Australia: Australian Broadcasting Company.

McMaster, G., & Trafzer, C.E. (Eds.). (2004). *Native universe: Voices of Indian America*. Washington, DC: Smithsonian Institution.

McNally, M.D. (2000). *Ojibwe singers: Hymns, grief, and a native culture in motion*. New York, NY: Oxford University Press.

Meadors, P., & Lamson, A. (2008). Compassion fatigue and secondary traumatization: Provider self care on intensive care units for children. *Journal of Pediatric Health Care, 22*, 24-34.

Meads, C., & Nauwen, A. (2005). Does emotional disclosure have any effects? A systematic review of the literature with meta-analyses. *International Journal of Technology Assessment in Health Care, 21*, 153-164.

Medical Council of Ireland. (2009). *Guide to professional conduct and ethics for registered medical practitioners* (7th ed.). Retrieved from www.medicalcouncil.ie.

Mehrotra, C.M., & McGahey, L. (2012). Online teaching. In B.M. Schwartz & R.A.R. Gurung (Eds.), *Evidence-based teaching for higher education*. Washington, DC: American Psychological Association.

Meisel, A. (2005). The role of litigation in end of life care: A reappraisal. In *Improving end of life care: Why has it been so difficult? Hastings Center Report* 35(6), S47-S51.

Melhem, N.M., Day, N., Shear, M.K., Day, R., Reynolds, C.F., & Brent, D. (2004). Traumatic grief among adolescents exposed to a peer's suicide. *American Journal of Psychiatry, 161*, 1411-1416.

Mellor, P.A. (1993). Death in high modernity: The contemporary presence and absence of death. In D. Clark (Ed.), *The sociology of death: Theory, culture, practice* (pp. 11-30). Cambridge, MA: Blackwell.

Mellor, P.A., & Schilling, C. (1993). Modernity, self-identity and the sequestration of death. *Sociology, 27*, 411-431.

Merriam-Webster. (2011). Retrieved from http://www.merriam-webster.com/dictionary/death.

Merriam-Webster Online (2012). Definitions retrieved 7/26/12 from http://www.merriam-webster.com/dictionary.

Merrick, J.C. (2005). Death and dying: The American experience. In R.H. Blank & J.C. Merrick (Eds.), *End-of-life decision making: A cross national study* (pp. 219-241). Cambridge, MA: MIT Press.

Mesler, M.A. (1995). Negotiating life for the dying: Hospice and the strategy of tactical socialization. *Death Studies, 19,* 235-255.

Meyer, T.P. (2005). Media portrayals of death and dying. *The Forum,* 31(2), 3-4.

Middleton, W., Burnett, P., Raphael, B., & Martinek, N. (1996). The bereavement response: A cluster analysis. *British Journal of Psychiatry,* 169, 167-171.

Miller, E.J. (2002). A Roman Catholic view of death. In J.D. Morgan & P. Laungani (Eds.), *Death and bereavement around the world, Volume 1: Major religious traditions* (pp. 87-102). Amityville, NY: Baywood Publishing.

Miller, F.G., Truog, R.D., & Brock, D.W. (2010). The Dead Donor Rule: Can It Withstand Critical Scrutiny? *Journal of Medicine and Philosophy, 35,* 299-312.

Miller, G.R., & Steinberg, M. (1975). *Between people: A new analysis of interpersonal communication.* Chicago, IL: Science Research Associates.

Miller, J. (1994). *The transforming power of spirituality.* Paper presented at the conference on Transformative Grief, Burnsville, NC.

Miller, S., Gozalo, P., & Mor, V. Outcomes and utilization for hospice and non-hospice nursing facility decedents. Retrieved from http://aspe.hhs.gov/daltcp/reports/oututil.htm.

Miller, W., & Thoresen, C. (2003). Spirituality, religion, and health: An emerging research field. *American Psychologist, 58,* 1-19.

Mills, G., Reisler, R., Robinson, A.E., & Vermilye, G. (1976). *Discussing death: A guide to death education.* Palm Springs, CA: ETC Publications.

Mills, J.S. (1859). *On Liberty* (2002 ed.). New York, NY: Dover Publications.

Mills, T., & Wilmoth, J. (2002). Intergenerational differences and similarities in life-sustaining treatment attitudes and decision factors. *Family Relations,* 51, 46-54.

Mishell, D.W. (1993). Recurrent abortion. *Journal of Reproductive Medicine,* 38, 250-259.

Mitchell, B.L., & Mitchell, L.C. (2009). Review of literature on cultural competence and end of life treatment decisions: The role of the hospitalist. *Journal of the National Medical Association,* 101, 920-926. Retrieved from http://www.nmanet.org/.

Mitchell, J.T. (1983). When disaster strikes: The critical incident stress debriefing process. *Journal of Emergency Medical Service,* 8, 36-39.

Moberg, D. (2001). *Aging and spirituality: Spiritual dimensions of aging theory, research, practice and social policy.* Binghamton, NY: Haworth Press.

Modares, A. (2011). Beyond the digital divide. *National Civic Review,* 4-7.

Modi, S., Velde, B., & Gessert, C.E. (2010). Perspectives of community members regarding tube feeding in patients with end-stage dementia: Findings from African American and Caucasian focus groups. *Omega: Journal of Death and Dying,* 62, 77-91, doi:10.2190/OM.62.1.d.

Molaison, V., Bordere, T.C., & Fowler, K. (2011). "The remedy is not working": Seeking socially just and culturally conscientious practices in bereavement. In R.A. Neimeyer, D. Harris, H. Winokuer & G. Thornton (Eds.), *Grief and bereavement in contemporary society: Bridging research and practice* (pp. 375-387). New York, NY: Routledge.

Moore, C.M. (1989). Teaching about loss and death to junior high school students. *Family Relations,* 38, 3-7.

Moorman, S.M. (2011). Older adults' preferences for independent or delegated end-of-life medical decision making. *Journal of Aging Health,* 23, 135-157.

Moos, R.H., & Schaefer, J. (1986). Life transitions and crises: A conceptual overview. In R.H. Moos (Ed.), *Coping with life crises: An integrated approach* (pp. 3-28). New York, NY: Plenum.

Morel, E. (Ed.). (1970). *Fairy tales and fables.* New York, NY: Grosset & Dunlap.

Moreno, R.A., & Moore, M.K. (1994). Validity and reliability of the Multidimensional Fear of Death Scale. In R. Neimeyer (Ed.), *Death anxiety handbook: Research, instrumentation, and application* (pp. 3-28). Washington, DC: Taylor & Francis.

Morgan, J.D. (1993). The existential quest for meaning. In K.J. Doka & J.D. Morgan (Eds.), *Death and Spirituality* (pp. 3-10). Amityville, NY: Baywood Publishing.

Morgan, J.D., & Laungani, P. (2002*). Death and bereavement around the world: Major religious traditions (Death, value and meaning)*. Amityville, NY: Baywood Publishing.

Morgan, J.D., Laungani, P., & Palmer, S. (Eds.). (2002-2009). *Death and bereavement around the world* (5 vols.). Amityville, NY: Baywood Publishing.

Morgan, M.A. (1987). Learner-centered learning in an undergraduate interdisciplinary course about death. *Death Studies,* 11, 183-192.

Moro, T., Kavanaugh, K., Savage, T., Reyes, M., Kimura, R., & Bhat, R. (2011). Parent decision making for life support decisions for extremely premature infants: From the prenatal through end-of-life period. *Journal of Perinatal and Neonatal Nursing,* 25, 52-60.

Morrison, R.S. (2005). Health care system factors affecting end-of-life care. *Journal of Palliative Medicine,* 8(S1), S79-S87.

Morrison, R.S., Maroney-Galin, C., Kralovec, P.D., & Meier, D.E. (2005). The growth of palliative care programs in the United States Hospitals. *Journal of Palliative Medicine,* 8, 1127-1134.

Morrison, R.S., Wallenstein, S., Natale, D.K., Senzel, R.S., & Huang, L.-L. (2000). "We Don't Carry That" — Failure of Pharmacies in Predominantly Nonwhite Neighborhoods to Stock Opioid Analgesics. *New England Journal of Medicine,* 342, 1023-1026.

Mosk, J. (1972). *Ralph Cobbs v. Dudley F.P. Grant, Supreme Court of California, October 27, 1972. 8 Cal.* Retrieved from aw.gsu.edu/plombardo/Great%20Cases/Cobbs%20v%20Grant.doc.

Moss, M.S., Moss, S.Z., & Hansson, R.O. (2001). Bereavement and old age. In M.S. Stroebe, R.O. Hansson, W. Stroebe, & H. Schut (Eds.), *Handbook of bereavement research: Consequences, coping, and care* (pp. 241-260). Washington, DC: American Psychological Association.

Mouton, C.P., Espino, D.V., Esparza, Y., & Miles, T.P. (2000). Attitudes toward assisted suicide among community-dwelling Mexican Americans. *Clinical Gerontologist: The Journal of Aging and Mental Health,* 22, 81-92. doi:10.1300/J018v22n02_07.

Mowery, R.L. (2005). *Family decision-making about end-of-life care: A case study and commentary.* In B. Schragg (Ed.). Graduate Research Ethics Education Conference Proceedings. Indiana University, Bloomington, IN.

Muller, J., & Desmond, B. (1992). Ethical dilemmas in a cross-cultural context: A Chinese example. *Western Journal of Medicine,* 157, 323-327. Retrieved from http://www.ncbi.nlm.nih.gov/pmc/journals/183/.

Muller, W. (1997). *Touching the divine.* Boulder, CO: Sounds True.

Mulrine, A. (2012). Suicide 'epidemic' in Army: July was worst month, Pentagon says. In *Christian Science Monitor.* Retrieved from http://www.csmonitor.com/USA/Military/2012/0817/Suicide-epidemic-in Army-July-was-worst-month-Pentagon-says.

Murray, H., & E.S. Shneidman (1981). *Endeavors in psychology.* New York, NY: Harper & Row.

Murray, T., & Jennings, B. (2005). The quest to reform end of life care: Rethinking assumptions and setting new directions. *Hastings Center Report,* Nov-Dec. S52-57

Murphy, S.L., Xu, J., & Kochanek, K.D. (2012). Deaths: Preliminary data for 2010. *National Vital Statistics Reports, National Center for Health Statistics,* 60(4).

Mutran, E.J., Danis, M., Bratton, K.A., Sudha, S., & Hanson, L. (1997). Attitudes of the critically ill toward prolonging life: The role of social support. *Gerontologist,* 37, 192-199.

Myers, S.S., & Lynn, J. (2001). Patients with eventually fatal chronic illness: Their importance within a national research agenda on improving patient safety and reducing medical error. *Journal of Palliative Medicine*, 4, 325-332.

Nadeau, J.W. (1997). *Families making sense of death*. Newbury Park, CA: Sage Publications.

Nadeau, J.W. (2001). Meaning making in family bereavement: A family systems approach. In M.S. Stroebe, R.O. Hansson, W. Stroebe, & H. Schut (Eds.), *Handbook of bereavement research: Consequences, coping, and care*. Washington, DC: American Psychological Association.

Nadeau, J.W. (2008). Meaning-making in bereaved families: Assessment, intervention, and future research. In M.S. Stroebe, R.O. Hansson, H. Schut, & W. Stroebe (Eds.), *Handbook of bereavement and practice: Advances in theory and intervention* (pp. 511-530). Washington, DC: American Psychological Association.

Nagayama-Hall, G.C. (2001). Psychotherapy research with ethnic minorities: Empirical, ethical and conceptual issues. *Journal of Consulting and Clinical Psychology, 69*, 502-510.

Nagy, M.A. (1948). The child's theories concerning death, *Journal of Genetic Psychology*, 73, 3-27.

Nahm, E.S. & Resnick, B. (2001) End-of-life treatment preferences among older adults. *Nursing Ethics 8*, 533-543.

Nannis, E.D., Susman, E.J., Strope, B.E. (1978). *The adolescent with a life-threatening illness: Cultural myths and social realities*. Paper presented at *Human Needs and Political Realities: 13th Annual Conference of the Association for the Care of Children in Hospitals*, Washington, DC.

National Audit of End-of-Life Care in Hospitals in Ireland, 2008/9: *An assessment of the quality of care in the last week of life*. Dublin, Ireland: Irish Hospice Foundation. Retrieved from www.hospicefriendlyhospitals.net/national-audit-of-end-of-life-care-in-hospitals.ie.

National Center for Health Statistics (2000, July 24). Gun deaths among children and teens drop sharply. *HHS News*. Washington, DC: U.S. Department of Health and Human Services News Release.

National Consensus Project for Quality Palliative Care (2009). *Clinical practice guidelines for quality palliative care* (2nd ed.). Retrieved from http://www.nationalconsensusproject.org.

National Hospice and Palliative Care Organization. (2000). *Standards of practice for hospice programs*. Alexandria, VA: National Hospice and Palliative Care Organization.

National Hospice and Palliative Care Organization. (2012). *NHPCO facts and figures: Hospice care in America* (2011 ed.). Alexandria, VA: Author. Retrieved from http://www.nhpco.org/files/public/Statistics_Research/2011_Facts_Figures.pdf.

National Institutes of Health. (1997). *Symptoms in terminal illness: A research workshop*. Rockville, MD: Author.

National Institutes of Health Technology Assessment Conference Statement. (1995). *Integration of behavioral and relaxation approaches into the treatment of chronic pain and insomnia*. Rockville, MD: Author.

National Kidney Foundation. (2002). *Bill of rights for donor families: A revised document*. Retrieved from http://www.kidney.org/transplanation/donorFamilies/infoBooksDFBR.cfm.

National Vital Statistics System. (n.d.). *GMWK309: Deaths by place of death, age, race, and sex: United States, 1999-2005*. Atlanta, GA: Centers for Disease Control and Prevention. Retrieved from http://www.cdc.gov/nchs/nvss/mortality/gmwk309.htm.

Neimeyer, R.A. (Ed.). (1993). *Death anxiety handbook: Research, instrumentation, and application*. Washington, DC: Taylor & Francis.

Neimeyer, R.A. (1998). *Lessons of loss: A guide to coping*. New York, NY: McGraw-Hill.

Neimeyer, R.A. (2000). Searching for the meaning of meaning: Grief therapy and the process of reconstruction. *Death Studies*, 24, 541-558.

Neimeyer, R.A. (Ed.). (2001). *Meaning reconstruction and the experience of loss*. Washington, DC: American Psychological Association.

Neimeyer, R.A. (2002). *Lessons of loss: A guide to coping*. Memphis, TN: Center for the Study of Loss and Transition.

Neimeyer, R.A. (2002). Traumatic loss and the reconstruction of meaning. *Journal of Palliative Medicine, 5*, 935-942.

Neimeyer, R.A. (2006a). Complicated grief and the quest for meaning: A constructivist contribution. *Omega: Journal of Death and Dying, 52*, 37-52.

Neimeyer, R.A. (2006b). Widowhood, grief and the quest for meaning: A narrative perspective on resilience. In D. Carr, R.M. Nesse, & C.B. Wortman (Eds.), *Spousal bereavement in late life* (pp. 227-252). New York, NY: Springer Publishing.

Neimeyer, R.A. (2011). Reconstructing meaning in bereavement. In W. Watson & D. Kissane (Eds.), *Handbook of psychotherapies in cancer care* (pp. 247-257). New York, NY: Wiley.

Neimeyer, R.A. (2011). Reconstructing the self in the wake of loss: A dialogical contribution. In H. Hermans & T. Gieser (Eds.), *Handbook on the dialogical self*. Cambridge, UK: Cambridge University Press.

Neimeyer, R.A. (Ed.). (2012). *Techniques of grief therapy: Creative practices for counseling the bereaved*. New York, NY: Routledge.

Neimeyer, R.A., Baldwin, S.A., & Gillies, J. (2006). Continuing bonds and reconstructing meaning: Mitigating complications in bereavement. *Death Studies, 30*, 715-738.

Neimeyer, R.A., Botella, L., Herrero, O., Pacheco, M., Figueras, S., & Werner-Wildner, L.A. (2002). The meaning of your absence: Traumatic loss and narrative reconstruction. In J. Kauffman (Ed.), *Loss of the assumptive world* (pp. 31-47). New York, NY: Brunner-Routledge.

Neimeyer, R.A., Burke, L., Mackay, M., & Stringer, J. (2010). Grief therapy and the reconstruction of meaning: From principles to practice. *Journal of Contemporary Psychotherapy, 40*, 73-84.

Neimeyer, R.A., & Burke, L.A. (2011). Complicated grief in the aftermath of homicide: Spiritual crisis and distress in an African American sample. *Religions, 2*, 145-164.

Neimeyer, R.A., & Currier, J.M. (2009). Grief therapy: Evidence of efficacy and emerging directions. *Current Directions in Psychological Science, 18*, 252-256.

Neimeyer, R.A., & Harris, D.L. (2011). Building bridges in bereavement research and practice: Some concluding reflections. In R.A. Neimeyer, D.L. Harris, H.R., & Thornton, G.F. (Eds.), *Grief and bereavement in contemporary society: Building research and practice* (pp. 403-428). New York, NY: Routledge.

Neimeyer, R.A., Harris, D.L., Winokuer, H.R., & Thornton, G.F. (Eds.). (2011). *Grief and bereavement in contemporary society: Bridging research and practice*. New York, NY: Routledge.

Neimeyer, R.A., Hogan, N., & Laurie, A. (2008). The measurement of grief: Psychometric considerations in the assessment of reactions to bereavement. In M. Stroebe, R.O., Hansson, H. Schut & W. Stroebe (Eds.), *Handbook of bereavement research: 21st century perspectives* (pp. 133-186). Washington, DC: American Psychological Association.

Neimeyer, R., Keese, N.J., & Fortner, B.V. (2000). Loss and meaning reconstruction: Propositions and procedures. In R. Malkinson, S. Rubin, & E. Witztum (Eds.), *Traumatic and nontraumatic loss and bereavement: Clinical theory and practice* (pp. 197-230). Madison, CT: Psychosocial Press.

Neimeyer, R.A., & Jordan, J.R. (2002). Disenfranchisement as empathic failure. In K. Doka (Ed.), *Disenfranchised grief* (pp. 97-117). Champaign, IL: Research Press.

Neimeyer, R.A., Prigerson, H.G., & Davies, B. (2002). Mourning and meaning. *American Behavioral Scientist, 46*, 235-251.

Neimeyer, R.A., & Sands, D.C. (2011). Meaning reconstruction in bereavement: From principles to practice. In R. A. Neimeyer, H. Winokuer, D. Harris & G. Thornton (Eds.), *Grief and bereavement in contemporary society: Bridging research and practice* (pp. 9-22). New York, NY: Routledge.

Neimeyer, R.A., van Dyke, J.G., & Pennebaker, J.W. (2009). Narrative medicine: Writing through bereavement. In H. Chochinov & W. Breitbart (Eds.), *Handbook of psychiatry in palliative medicine* (pp. 454-469). New York, NY: Oxford University Press.

Neimeyer, R.A., Wittkowski, J., & Moser, R.P. (2004). Psychological research on death attitudes: An overview and evaluation. *Death Studies,* 309-340.

Nelson, H.L., & Nelson, J.L. (1995). *The Patient in the family: An ethics of medicine and families.* New York, NY: Routledge.

Neria, Y., & Litz, B.T. (2003). Bereavement by traumatic means: The complex synergy of trauma and grief. *Journal of Loss and Trauma*, 9, 73-87.

Neugarten, B.L., & Datan, N. (1973). Sociological perspectives on the life cycle. In D.A. Neugarten (Ed.), *The meanings of age: Selected papers [of Bernice L. Neugarten]* (pp. 96-113). Chicago, IL: University of Chicago Press.

Neugebauer, R., Kline, J., O'Connor, P., Shrout, P., Johnson, J., Skodol, A., Wicks, J., & Susser, M. (1992). Depressive symptoms in women in the six months after miscarriage. *American Journal of Obstetrics & Gynecology,* 166(1Pt1), 104-109.

Newman, B.M., & Newman, P.R. (1999). *Development through life: A psychosocial approach.* New York, NY: Brooks/Cole-Wadsworth.

Newman, E., Risch, E., & Kassam-Adams, N. (2006). Ethical decision-making about trauma-related studies. *Journal of Empirical Research on Human Ethics: An International Journal*, 1, 29-46.

Newson, R.S., Boelen, P.A., Hek, K., Hofman, A., & Tiemeier, H. (2011). The prevalence and characteristics of complicated grief in older adults. *Journal of Affective Disorders,* 132, 231-238.

New York State Department of Health. *Your rights as a hospital patient in New York State.* Pamphlet.

Ngo-Metzger, Q., Phillips, R.S., & McCarthy, E.P. (2008). Ethnic disparities in hospice use among Asian-American and Pacific Islander patients dying with cancer. *Journal of the American Geriatrics Society,* 56, 139-144. doi:10.1111/j.1532-5415.2007.01510.x.

Nichols, M.P., & Schwartz, R.C. (1998). *Family therapy: Concepts and methods* (4th ed.). Boston, MA: Allyn & Bacon.

Nolan, M.T., Sood, J.R., Kub, J., & Sulmasy, D.P. (2005). When patients lack capacity: The roles that patients with terminal diagnoses would choose for their physicians and loved ones in making medical decisions. *Journal of Pain and Symptom Management*, 30, 342-353.

Noonan, P. (1999, April 22). The culture of death. *The Wall Street Journal,* p. 1.

Noppe, I.C. (2004). Death education and the scholarship of teaching: A meta-educational experience. *The Forum*, 30(1), 4.

Noppe, I.C. (2007, April). *Bridging research and teaching: The role of SoTL and death education.* Presented at the 29th Annual Conference of the Association for Death Education and Counseling, Indianapolis, IN.

Noppe, I.C. (2008, May). *Teaching That Matters: Death Education and Interdisciplinarity.* Presented at the 30th Annual Conference of the Association for Death Education and Counseling, Montreal, Quebec, Canada.

Noppe, I.C. (2010, April). *Teaching That Matters: Death Education and Interdisciplinarity.* Presented at the 32nd Annual Conference of the Association for Death Education and Counseling, Kansas City, MO.

Noppe, I.C., Hames, C.C., & Schreiber, J.K. (April 2010). *Grief goes to camp: Models, outcomes and assessment.* Presented at the 32nd Annual Conference of the Association for Death Education and Counseling, Kansas City, MO.

Noppe, I.C., & Noppe, L.D. (1997). Evolving meanings of death during early, middle and later adolescence. *Death Studies, 21*, 253-275.

Noppe, I.C., & Noppe, L.D. (2004). Adolescent experiences with death: Letting go of immortality. *Journal of Mental Health Counseling, 26*, 146-67.

Noppe, I.C., & Noppe, L.D. (2009). Adolescent accidents and homicides. In Balk, D., & Corr, C. (Eds.), *Adolescents and death* (pp. 61-79). New York, NY: Springer Publishing.

Noppe, I.C., Noppe, L.D., & Bartell, D. (2006). Terrorism and resilience: Adolescents' and teachers' responses to September 11, 2001. *Death Studies, 30*, 41-60.

Noppe, L.D., & Noppe, I.C. (1996). Ambiguity in adolescent understandings of death. In C.A. Corr & D.E. Balk (Eds.), *Handbook of adolescent death and bereavement* (pp. 25-41). New York, NY: Springer Publishing.

Ober, A.M., Granello, D.H., & Wheaton, J.E. (2012). Grief counseling: An investigation of counselors' training, experience and competencies. *Journal of Counseling and Development, 90*, 150-159.

Ochberg, F. (1998). *When helping hurts*. Retrieved from http://www.giftfromwithin.org/html/helping.html.

O'Donahue, J. (2004). *Beauty: The invisible embrace*. New York, NY: HarperCollins.

Olive, K. (2004). Religion and spirituality: Important psychosocial variables frequently ignored in clinical research. *Southern Medical Journal, 97*, 1152-1153.

Oliviere, D., Monroe, B., & Payne, S. (Eds.) (2011). *Death, dying and social difference* (pp. 70-84). New York, NY: Oxford Press.

Olson, D.H. (2000). Circumplex model of marital and family systems. *Journal of Family Therapy, 22*, 144-167.

Olson, D.H., & DeFrain, J. (2006). *Marriages and families: Intimacy, diversity and strengths* (5th ed.). New York, NY: McGraw-Hill.

Orbach, I., & Iohan-Barak, M. (2009). Psychopathology and risk factors for suicide in the young. In D. Wasserman & C. Wasserman (Eds.), *Oxford textbook of suicidology and suicide prevention*, (pp. 633-641). Oxford, UK: Oxford University Press.

Orenstein, C. (2002). *Little Red Riding Hood uncloaked: Sex, morality, and the evolution of a fairy tale*. New York, NY: Basic Books.

Orona, C., Koenig, B., & Davis, A. (1994). Cultural aspects of nondisclosure. *Cambridge Quarterly of Healthcare Ethics, 3*, 338-346. doi:dx.doi.org/10.1017/S0963180100005156.

Osofsky, H.J., Osofsky, J.D., Arey, J., Kronenberg, M.E., Hansel, T., & Many, M. (2011). Hurricane Katrina's first responders: The struggle to protect and serve in the aftermath of the disaster. *Disaster Med Public Health Preparedness, 5*, S214-S219.

Osterweis, M., Solomon, & Green, M. (1984). *Bereavement: Reactions, consequences, and care*. Washington, DC. Institute of Medicine.

O'Toole, D. (1989). *Growing through grief: A K-12 curriculum to help young people though all kinds of loss*. Burnsville, NC: Mountain Rainbow Publications.

O'Toole, D. (1995). *Facing change: Falling apart and coming together again in the teen years*. Burnsville, NC: Compassion Books.

Ott, C.H. (2003). The impact of complicated grief on mental and physical health at various points in the bereavement process. *Death Studies, 27*, 249-272.

Oxford Dictionary. (2012). Oxford University Press. Retrieved from http://oxforddictionaries.com/ definition.

Palmer, L.I. (2000). *Endings and beginnings: Law, medicine, and society in assisted life and death*. Westport, CT: Praeger Publishers.

Panke, J.T., & Ferrell, B.R. (2005). Emotional problems in the family. In D. Doyle, G. Hanks, N.I. Cherry, & K. Claman (Eds.), *Oxford Textbook of Palliative Medicine* (3rd ed.), (pp. 985-992). Oxford, UK: Oxford University Press.

Papadatou, D. (1997). Training health professionals in caring for dying children and grieving families. *Death Studies*, 21, 575-600.

Papadatou, D. (2009). *In the face of death: Professionals who care for the dying and the bereaved.* New York, NY: Springer Publishing.

Pare, D., & Larner, G. (Eds.). (2004). *Collaborative practice in psychology and therapy*. New York, NY: Haworth Clinical Practice Press.

Pargament, K.I., Koenig, H.G., Tarakeshwar, N., & Hahn, J. (2004). Religious coping methods as predictors of outcomes of psychological, physical, and spiritual outcomes among medically ill elderly patients: A two-year longitudinal study. *Journal of Health Psychology*, 9, 713-730.

Paris, M.M., Carter, B.L., Day, S.X., & Armsworth, M.W. (2009). Grief and trauma in children after the death of a sibling. *Journal of Child and Adolescent Trauma*, 2, 71-80.

Paris, M.M., & Hoge, M.A. (2009). Burnout in the mental health workforce: A review. *Journal of Behavioral Health Services & Research*, 34, 519-528.

Park, H.L., O'Connell, J.E., & Thompson, R.G. (2003). A systematic review of cognitive decline in the general elderly population. *International Journal of Geriatric Psychiatry*, 18, 1121-1134.

Park, H.S., Shin, Y.S., & Yun, D. (2009). Differences between white Americans and Asian Americans for social responsibility, individual right and intentions regarding organ donation. *Journal of Health Psychology*, 14, 707-712. doi:10.1177/1359105309104917.

Parkes, C.M. (1972). *Bereavement: Studies of grief in adult life* (2nd ed., 1986; 3rd ed., 1996). London, UK: Tavistock.

Parkes, C.M. (1975). Determinants of outcome following bereavement. *Omega: Journal of Death and Dying*, 6, 303-323.

Parkes, C.M. (2001). Recent developments in loss theory and practice: Individual, family, national, and international implications. *Grief Matters: The Australian Journal of Grief and Bereavement*, 14, 36-40.

Parkes, C.M. (2011). Can individuals who are specialists in death, dying, and bereavement contribute to the prevention and/or mitigation of armed conflicts and cycles of violence? *Death Studies*, 5, pp. 455-466.

Parkes, C.M., & Brown, R.J. (1972). Health after bereavement: A controlled study of young Boston widows and widowers. *Psychosomatic Medicine*, 34, 449-461.

Parkes, C.M., Laungani, P., & Young, B. (Eds.). (1997). *Death and bereavement across cultures*. New York, NY: Routledge.

Parkes, C.M., & Prigerson, H.G. (2009). *Bereavement: Studies of grief in adult life* (4th ed.). New York, NY: Routledge.

Parkes, C.M., & Weiss, R.S. (1983). *Recovery from bereavement*. New York, NY: Basic Books.

Parkes, C.M., & Weiss, R.S. (1995). *Recovery following bereavement* (2nd ed.). New York, NY: Basic Books.

Parry, J.K., & Ryan, A.S. (Eds.). (2003). *A cross-cultural look at death, dying, and religion*. Belmont, CA: Wadsworth.

Pashler, H., McDaniel, M., Rohrer, D., & Bjork, R. (2008). Learning styles: Concepts and evidence. *Psychological Science in the Public Interest*, 9, 105-119.

Pattison, E.M. (1977). *The experience of dying*. New York, NY: Simon & Schuster.

Pattison, E.M. (1978). The living-dying interval. In C. Garfield, (Ed.), *Psychological care of the dying patient* (pp. 163-168). New York, NY: McGraw-Hill.

Pauley, M.D. (2008). *Medical futility: Dispute resolution and medical ethics in the hospital.* New York State Dispute Resolution Association, Inc. teleconference PowerPoint presentation.

Pearlman, L.A., & Saakvitne, K.W. (1995). *Trauma and the therapist: Countertransference and vicarious traumatization in psychotherapy with incest survivors.* New York, NY: W.W. Norton & Co.

Pearse, Jr., R.L. (1998). *Report of Guardian Ad Litem for In re: the guardianship of Theresa Schiavo, an incapacitated person.* Case No. 90-2908GD-003. Retrieved from http://www.hospicepatients.org/richard-pearse-jr-12-29-98-report-of-guardianadlitem-re-terri- schiavo.pdf.

Pence, G. (2008). *Medical ethics accounts of the cases that shaped and defined medical ethics* (5th ed.). New York, NY: McGraw Hill.

Penson, R.T., Rauch, P.K., McAfee, S.C., Cashavelly, B.J., ir-Hayes, K., Dahlin, C., et al. Between parent and child: Negotiating cancer treatment in adolescents. *Oncologist* 7, 154-162.

Perkins, H.S., Supik, J.D., & Hazuda, H.P. (1993). Autopsy decisions: The possibility of conflicting cultural attitudes. *Journal of Clinical Ethics,* 4, 145-154. Retrieved from http://www.clinicalethics.com.

Peteet, J.R., Ross, D.M., Medeiros, C., Walsh-Burke, K., & Rieker, P. (1992). Relationships with patients in oncology: Can a patient be a friend. *Psychiatry*, 55, 223-229.

Petersen, D. (2011). A decade of increased understanding. Retrieved from http://alumni.georgetown. edu/olc/pub/GTW/home/home.jsp.

Pfeffer, C. (1986). *The suicidal child.* New York, NY: Guilford Press.

Pfefferbaum, B., North, C.S., Doughty, D.E., Pfefferbaum, R.L., Dumont, C.E., Pynoos, R.S., Gurwitch, R.H., & Ndetei, D. (2006). Trauma, grief and depression in Nairobi children after the 1998 bombing of the American embassy. *Death Studies*, 30, 561-577.

Pfefferbaum, B., Tucker, P., North, C.S., Jeon-Slaughter, H., Kent, A.T., Schorr, J.K., Wilson, T.G., & Bunch, K. (2006). Persistent physiological reactivity in a pilot study of partners of firefighters after a terrorist attack. *Journal of Nervous and Mental Disease,* 194, 128-131.

Phelps, A.C., Maciejewski, P.K., Nilsson, M., Balboni, T.A., Wright, A.A., Paulk, E., Trice, E., Schrag, D., Peteet, J.R., Block, S.D., & Prigerson, H.G. (2009). Religious coping and use of intensive life- prolonging care near death in patients with advanced cancer. *Journal of the American Medical Association*, 301, 1140-1147.

Phillips, B.J. (2005). Determining brain death: A summary. *The Internet Journal of Law, Healthcare and Ethics*, 2. Retrieved from http://www.ispub.com/ostia/index.php?xmlFilePath=journals/ijlhe/vol1n1/ethics2.xml.

Picchi, T. (2011). Discovering the sacrament of the present moment: Catholic spiritual practices at the end of life. In K.J. Doka, A.S. Tucci, & K. Meador (Eds.), *Living with grief: Spirituality and end-of-life care.* Washington DC: Hospice Foundation of America.

Pine, V. (1977). A socio-historical portrait of death education. *Death Studies,* 1, 57-84.

Pine, V. (1986). The age of maturity for death education. A socio-historical portrait of the era 1976-1985. *Death Studies,* 10, 209-231.

Pines, A., & Aronson, E. (1988). *Career burnout: Causes and cures.* New York, NY: Free Press.

Pinquart, M. (2003). Loneliness in married, widowed, divorced, and never-married older adults. *Journal of Social and Personal Relationships*, 20, 31-53.

Pitman, A., Krysinska, K., Osborn, D., & King, M. (2012). Suicide in young men. *The Lancet*, 379, 2390-2399.

Pittman, R.K., & Sparr, L.F. (1998). PTSD and the law. *PTSD Research Quarterly,* 9 (2), 1-8.

Ponzetti, J.J. (1992). Bereaved families: A comparison of parents' and grandparents' reactions to the death of a child. *Omega: Journal of Death and Dying,* 25, 63-71.

Pousset, G., Bilsen, J., De Wilde, J., Benoit, Y., Verlooy, J., Bomans, A., Luc Deliens, L., & Mortier, F. (2009). Attitudes of adolescent cancer survivors toward end-of-life decisions for minors. *Pediatrics*, 124, 1142-1148.

Prensky, M. (2001). Digital Natives, Digital Immigrants. *On the Horizon*, 9(5), 1-6.

Prensky, M. (2009). H. Sapiens Digital: From Digital Immigrants and Digital Natives to Digital Wisdom. *Innovate*, 5 (3). Retrieved from http://www.innovateonline.info/index.php?view=article&id=705.

President's Commission for the Study of Ethical Problems in Medicine and Behavioral Research. (1981). *Defining death: A Report on the medical, legal and ethical issues in the determination of death.* Washington, DC: Government Printing Office.

Preston, T., & Kelly, M. (2006). A medical ethics assessment of the case of Terri Schiavo. *Death Studies,* 30, 121-133.

Prigerson, H. (2005). Complicated grief when the path of adjustment leads to a dead end. *Counseling and Psychotherapy Journal*, 5 (3), 10-14.

Prigerson, H., & Maciejewski, P. (2012). Dartmouth Atlas: putting end-of-life care on the map but missing psychosocial detail. *Journal of Supportive Oncology* 10, 25-28.

Prigerson, H.G., Frank, E., Kasl, S.V., Reynolds, C.F., Anderson, B., Zubenko, G.S., & Kupfer, D.J. (1995). Complicated grief and bereavement-related depression as distinct disorders—Preliminary empirical validation in elderly bereaved spouses. *American Journal of Psychiatry,* 152, 22-30.

Prigerson, H.G., Horowitz, M.J., Jacobs, S.C., Parkes, C.M., Aslan, M., Goodkin, K., Raphael, B., et al. (2009). Prolonged grief disorder: Psychometric validation of criteria proposed for DSM-5 and ICD-11. *PLoS Medicine*, 6(8), 1-12.

Prigerson, H.G., Horowitz, M.J., Pyszczynski, T., Solomon, S., & Greenberg, J. (2003). *In the wake of 9/11: The psychology of terror.* Washington, DC: American Psychological Association.

Prigerson, H.G., & Jacobs, S.C. (2001). Diagnostic criteria for traumatic grief. In M.S. Stroebe, R.O. Hansson, W. Stroebe & H. Schut (Eds.), *Handbook of bereavement research* (pp. 614-646). Washington, DC: American Psychological Association.

Prigerson, H.G., & Maciejewski, P.K. (2006). A call for sound empirical testing and evaluation of criteria for complicated grief proposed by the DSM V. *Omega: Journal of Death and Dying*, 52, 9-19.

Prigerson, H.G., Shear, M.K., Bierhals, A.J., Pilkonis, P.A., Wolfson, L., Hall. M., Zonarich, D.L., & Reynolds, C.F. (1997). Case histories of traumatic grief. *Omega: Journal of Death and Dying*, 35, 9-24.

Prigerson, H.G., Vanderwerker, L.C., & Maciejewski, P.K. (2008). A case for inclusion of prolonged grief disorder in DSM-V. In M.S. Stroebe, R.O. Hansson, H. Schut & W. Stroebe (Eds.), *Handbook of bereavement research and practice: Advances in theory and intervention* (pp. 165-186). Washington, DC: American Psychological Association.

Prilleltensky, I. (2012). Wellness as fairness. *American Journal of Community Psychology*, 49, 1-21.

Pritchard, D. (2000). The future of media accountability. In D. Pritchard (Ed.), *Holding the media accountable: Citizens, ethics, and the law* (pp. 186-193). Bloomington, IN: Indiana University Press.

Prochaska, J.O., & DiClemente, C.C. (2005). The transtheoretical approach. In J.C. Norcross & M.R. Goldfried (Eds.), *Handbook of psychotherapy integration* (2nd ed.), (pp. 147-171). New York, NY: Oxford University Press.

Prochaska, J.O., & Norcross, J. (2009). *Systems of psychotherapy: A transtheoretical analysis.* Pacific Grove, CA: Thomson/Brooks/Cole.

Propper, R.E., Stickgold, R., Keeley, R., & Christman, S.D. (2007). Is television traumatic? Dreams, stress, and media exposure in the aftermath of September 11, 2011. *Psychological Science*, 18, 334-340.

Psychological Work Group of the International Work Group on Death, Dying, and Bereavement. (1993). A statement of assumptions and principles concerning psychological care of dying persons and their families. *Journal of Palliative Care*, 9, 29-32.

Puchalski, C., Ferrell, B., Virani, R., Otis-Green, S., Baird, P., Bull, J., Chochinov, H., Handzo, G., Nelson-Becker, H., Prince-Paul, M., Pugilese, K., & Sulmasy, D. (2009). Improving the quality of care as a dimension of palliative care: The report of the Consensus Conference. *Journal of Palliative Medicine, 12,* 885-904.

Pynoos, R.S., & Nader, K. (1990). Children's exposure to violence and traumatic death. *Psychiatric Annals, 20,* 334-344.

Pyszczynski, T., Solomon, S., & Greenberg, J. (2003). *In the wake of 9/11: The psychology of terror.* Washington, DC: American Psychological Association.

Quinlan, C. (2009a). *Media messages on death and dying.* Dublin, Ireland: Irish Hospice Foundation.

Quinlan, C. (2009b). *Patient autonomy at end of life: literature review.* Dublin, Ireland: Irish Hospice Foundation.

Quinlan, C., & O'Neill, C. (2009). *Practitioners' perspectives on patient autonomy at end of life.* Dublin, Ireland: Irish Hospice Foundation.

Rabow, M.W., Hardie, G.E., Fair, J.M., & McPhee, S.J. (2000). End-of-life care content in 50 textbooks from multiple specialties. *Journal of the American Medical Association, 283,* 771-778.

Rai, R., Backos, M., Rushworth, F., & Regan, L. (2000). Polycystic ovaries and recurrent miscarriage – a reappraisal. *Human Reproduction, 15,* 612-615.

Rainer, J., & McMurry, P. (2002). Caregiving at the end of life. *Journal of Clinical Psychology: In Session, 58,* 1421-1431.

Randall, B. (2003). *Songman: The story of an Aboriginal elder.* Sydney, Australia: Australian Broadcasting Corporation.

Rando, T.A. (1984). *Grief, dying and death: Clinical interventions for caregivers.* Champaign, IL: Research Press.

Rando, T.A. (Ed.). (1986). *Loss and anticipatory grief.* Lexington, MA: Lexington Books.

Rando, T.A. (1988). Anticipatory grief: The term is a misnomer but the phenomenon exists. *Journal of Palliative Care, 4,* 70-73.

Rando, T.A. (1993). *Treatment of complicated mourning.* Champaign, IL: Research Press.

Rando, T.A. (Ed.). (2000). *Clinical dimensions of anticipatory mourning: Theory and practice in working with the dying, their loved ones, and their caregivers.* Champaign, IL: Research Press.

Rando, T.A. (2000a). Anticipatory mourning: A Review and critique of the literature. In T.A. Rando (Ed.), *Clinical dimensions of anticipatory mourning: Theory and practice in working with the dying, their loved ones, and their caregivers* (pp. 17-50). Champaign, IL: Research Press.

Rando, T.A. (2000b). The six dimensions of anticipatory mourning. In T.A. Rando (Ed.), *Clinical dimensions of anticipatory mourning: Theory and practice in working with the dying, their loved ones, and their caregivers* (pp. 51-101). Champaign, IL: Research Press.

Rank, O. (1958). *Beyond psychology.* New York, NY: Dover reprint.

Raphael, B. (1983). *The anatomy of bereavement.* New York, NY: Basic Books.

Redmond, L.M. (1989). *Surviving: When someone you love was murdered.* Clearwater, FL: Psychological Consultation and Educational Services, Inc.

Reed, P.G. (1987). Spirituality and well-being in terminally ill hospitalized adults. *Research in Nursing and Health, 10,* 335-344.

Regan, J.R.C., & Youn, E.J. (2008). Past, present, and future trends in teaching clinical skills through Web-based learning environments. *Journal of Social Work Education, 44,* 95-115.

Reiss, D. (1981). *The family's construction of reality.* Cambridge, MA: Harvard University Press.

Rendell, T.T. (2004). Medical and legal considerations of brain death. *Acta Anaesthesiologica Scandinavica*, 48, 139-144.

Report of the ad hoc committee of the Harvard Medical School to examine the definition of brain death. A definition of irreversible coma. (1968). *Journal of the American Medical Association, 205*, 337-340.

Ribbentrop, A.E., Altmaier, E.M., Chen, J.J., Found, E.M., & Keffala, V.J. (2005). The relationship between religion/spirituality and physical health, mental health and pain in a chronic pain population. *Pain*, 116, 311-321.

Rice, P.L. (2000). Death in birth: The cultural construction of stillbirth, neonatal death, and maternal death among Hmong women in Australia. *Omega: Journal of Death and Dying*, 41, 39-57.

Rich, D.E. (2000). The relationship between type and timing of post pregnancy loss services and grief outcome. *Dissertation Abstracts International, 60*(7-B), 3614.

Richards, T.S.A. (2001). Spiritual resources following a partner's death from AIDS. In R.A. Neimeyer (Ed.). *Meaning Reconstruction & the Experience of Loss* (pp. 173-190). Washington, DC: American Psychological Association.

Richardson, H., & Koffman, J. (2012). Embracing diversity at the end of life. In D. Oliviere, B. Monroe, & S. Payne (Eds.), *Death, dying and social difference* (pp. 70-84). New York, NY: Oxford University Press.

Richter, L., Somai, H., Zuma, T., & Ramsoomar, L. (2008). Children's perspectives on death and dying in Southern Africa in the context of the HIV/AIDS epidemic. *The Forum*, 34(1), 7-8.

River Dell Regional Schools Board of Education, 700 Series – Instruction, adopted September 8, 1970, p. 4.

Robinson, E.M, Phipps, M,, Purtilo, R.B., Tsoumas, A., & Hamel-Nardozzi M. (2006). Complexities in decision making for persons with disabilities nearing end of life. *Topics in Stroke Rehabilitation*, 13, 54-67.

Rodriguez, K.L., & Young, A.J. (2006). Patients' and healthcare providers' understandings of life-sustaining treatment: Are perceptions of goals shared or divergent? *Social Science & Medicine, 62*, 125-133.

Roediger, D.R. (1981). And die in Dixie: Funerals, death & heaven in the slave community, 1700-1865. *The Massachusetts Review*, 22, 163-183.

Rogers, C.R. (1980). *A way of being*. Boston, MA: Houghton Mifflin.

Rogers, L.S. (2004). Meaning of bereavement among older African American widows. *Geriatric Nursing*, 25, 10-16.

Romanoff, B.D., & Thompson, B.E. (2006). Meaning construction in palliative care: the use of narrative, ritual, and the expressive arts. *American Journal of Hospice and Palliative Care*, 23, 309-316.

Rosenberg, R.N. (2009). Consciousness, coma, and brain death. *Journal of the American Medical Association*, 301, 1172-1174.

Rosenblatt, P.C. (1993). Cross-cultural variation in the experience, expression, and understanding of grief. In D.P. Irish, K.F. Lundy, & V.J. Nelsen (Eds.), *Ethnic variations in dying, death, and grief: Diversity in universality* (pp. 13-19). Washington, DC: Taylor & Francis.

Rosenblatt, P.C. (1997). Grief in small scale societies. In C.M. Parkes, P. Laungani & B. Young (Eds.), *Death and bereavement across cultures* (pp. 27-51). London, UK: Routledge.

Rosenblatt, P.C. (2001). A social constructionist perspective on cultural differences in grief. In M.S. Stroebe, R.O. Hansson, W. Stroebe, & H. Schut (Eds.), *Handbook of bereavement research: Consequences, coping and care* (pp. 285-300). Washington, DC: American Psychological Association.

Rosenblatt, P.C. (2008). Grief across cultures: A review and research agenda. In M.S. Stroebe, R.O. Hansson, H. Schut, & W. Stroebe (Eds.), *Handbook of bereavement research and practice: Advances in theory and intervention* (pp. 207-222). Washington, DC: American Psychological Association.

Rosenblatt, P.C. (2012). The concept of complicated grief: Lessons from other cultures. In H. Schut, P. Boelen, J. van den Bout, & M. Stroebe (Eds.), *Complicated grief: Scientific foundations for health professionals* (pp. 27-39). New York, NY: Routledge.

Rosenblatt, P.C., & Elde, C. (1990). Shared reminiscence about a deceased parent: Implication for grief education and grief counseling. *Family Relations,* 39, 206-210.

Rosenblatt, P.C., & Nkosi, B.C. (2007). South African Zulu widows in a time of poverty and social change. *Death Studies*, 31, 67-85.

Rosenblatt, P.C., & Wallace, B.R. (2005a). *African American grief.* New York, NY: Routledge.

Rosenblatt, P.C., & Wallace, B.R. (2005b). Narratives of grieving African-Americans about racism in the lives of deceased family members. *Death Studies*, 29, 217-235.

Rosenblatt, P.C., Walsh, R.P., & Jackson, D.A. (1976). *Grief and mourning in cross-cultural perspective.* New Haven, CT: Human Relations Area Files Press.

Rosenblatt, P.C., & Yang, S. (2004). Love, debt, and filial piety: Hee Gyung Noh's view of Korean intergenerational relations when a mother is terminally ill. *Journal of Loss and Trauma*, 9, 167-180.

Rothera, I.C., Jones, R., Harwood, R., Avery, A.J., & Waite, J. (2002). Survival in a cohort of social services placements in nursing and residential homes: factors associated with life expectancy and mortality. *Public Health*, 116, 160-165.

Rothschild, B., & Rand, M. (2006). *Help for the helper: The psychophysiology of compassion fatigue and vicarious trauma.* New York, NY: W.W. Norton & Co.

Rourke, M.T. (2007). Compassion fatigue in pediatric palliative care providers. *Pediatric Clinics of North America*, 54, 631-644.

Rowling, L. (2005). Loss and grief in school communities. In B. Monroe & F. Kraus (Eds.), *Brief interventions with bereaved children* (pp. 159-173). New York, NY: Oxford University Press.

Rubin, S.S. (1981). A two-track model of bereavement: Theory and application in research. *American Journal of Orthopsychiatry,* 51, 101-109.

Rubin, S.S. (1999). The two-track model of bereavement: Overview, retrospect and prospect. *Death* Studies, 23, 681-714.

Rubin, S.S. (2012). Tracking through bereavement: A framework for intervention. In R. Neimeyer (Ed.), *Techniques of grief therapy: Creative practices for counseling the bereaved* (pp. 20-24). New York, NY: Routledge.

Rubin, S.S., Bar Nadav, O., Malkinson, R., Koren, D., Gofer-Shnarch, M., & Michaeli, E. (2009). The Two-Track Model of Bereavement Questionnaire (TTBQ): Development and findings of a relational measure. *Death Studies,* 33, 1- 29.

Rubin, S.S., Malkinson, R., Koren, D., & Michaeli, E. (2009). The Two-Track Model of Bereavement Questionnaire (TTBQ): Development and validation of a relational measure. *Death Studies*, 33, 305-333.

Rubin, S.S., Malkinson, R., & Witztum, E. (2003). Trauma and bereavement: Conceptual and clinical issues revolving around relationships. *Death Studies*, 27, 667-690.

Rubin, S.S., Malkinson, R., & Witztum, E. (2008). Clinical aspects of a DSM Complicated Grief Diagnosis: Challenges, dilemmas, and opportunities. In M.S. Stroebe, R.O. Hansson, H. Schut & W. Stroebe (Eds.), *Handbook of bereavement research and practice: Advances in theory and intervention* (pp. 187-206). Washington, DC: American Psychological Association.

Rubin, S.S., Malkinson, R., & Witztum, E. (2012). *Working with the bereaved: Multiple lenses on loss and mourning.* New York, NY: Routledge.

Rubin, S.S., & Schechter, N. (1997). Exploring the social construction of bereavement: Perceptions of adjustment and recovery for bereaved men. *American Journal of Orthopsychiatry*, 67, 279–289.

Ruffin, W.L. (2012). The importance of history: Teaching African-American perspectives in thanatology. *The Forum*, 36(4), 21.

Rurup, M.L., Onwuteaka-Philipsen, B.D., Pasman, H.R.W., Ribbe, M.W., et al. (2006). Attitudes of physicians, nurses and relatives towards end-of-life decisions concerning nursing home patients with dementia. Patient Education and Counseling, 61, 372-380.

Russac, R.J., Gatliff, C., Reece, M., & Spottswood, D. (2007). Death anxiety across the adult years: An examination of age and gender effects. Death Studies, 31, 549-561. doi:10.1080/07481180701356936.

Russell, E., Robinson, D.H.Z., Thompson, N.J., Perryman, J.P., & Arriola, K.R.J. (2012). Distrust in the healthcare system and organ donation intentions among African Americans. Journal of Community Health, 37, 40-47. doi:10.1007/s10900-011-9413-3.

Sakurai, M.L. (2006). Chaplains' view of role covers a wide range. Vision, April, 6-7.

Salmon, G. (2003). E-moderating: The key to online teaching and learning. London, UK: Taylor & Francis Books, Ltd.

Sanders, C.M., Mauger, P.A., & Strong, P.N. (1985). A manual for the Grief Experience Inventory. Blowing Rock, NC: Center for the Study of Separation and Loss.

Sanders, J.M. (2002). Ethnic boundaries and identity in plural societies. Annual Review of Sociology, 28, 327-357.

Sandler, I. (2001). Quality and ecology of adversity as common mechanisms of risk and resilience. American Journal of Community Psychology, 29, 19-61.

Sandler, I., & Ayers, T. (2001). Fostering resilience in families in which a parent has died. Innovations in End of Life Care, 3(6).

Sandler, I.N., Ayers, T.S., Wolchik, S.A., Tein, J.-Y., Kwok, O.M., Haines, R.A., Twohey-Jacobs, J., Suter, J., Kin, K., Padgett-Jones, S., Weyer, J.L., Cole, E., Kreige, G., & Griffin, W.A. (2003). The family bereavement program: Efficacy evaluation of a theory-based prevention program for parentally bereaved children and adolescents. Journal of Consulting and Clinical Psychology, 71, 587-600.

Sandler, I.N., Kennedy, C., Balk, D., Jordan, J.R., Nadeau, J., & Shapiro, E. (2005). Bridging the gap between research and practice in bereavement: Report from the Center for the Advancement of Health. Death Studies, 29(2), 93-122.

Sandler, I.N., Ma, Y., Tein, J.-Y., Ayers, T.S., Wolchik, S., Kennedy, C., & Millsap, R. (2010). Long- term effects of the family bereavement program on multiple indicators of grief in parentally bereaved children and adolescents. Journal of Consulting and Clinical Psychology, 78, 131-143.

Sandler, I.N., Wolchik, S.A., Ayers, T.S., Tein, J.-Y., Coxe, S., & Chow, W. (2008). Linking theory and intervention to promote resilience in parentally bereaved children. In M.S. Stroebe, R.O. Hansson, H. Schut & W. Stroebe (Eds.), Handbook of bereavement research and practice: Advances in theory and intervention (pp. 531-550). Washington, DC: American Psychological Association.

Satcher, D., & Pamies, R.J. (Eds.). (2006). Multicultural medicine and health disparities. New York, NY: McGraw-Hill.

Saunders, C.M. (1959). The problem of euthanasia: When a patient is dying (A series of articles). Nursing Times, October 9-November 13, 960-961, 994-995, 1031, 1091-1092, 1129-1130.

Saunders, C.M. (1967). The management of terminal illness. London, UK: Hospital Medicine Publications.

Saunders, C.M., & Kastenbaum, R. (1997). Hospice care on the international scene. Beverly Hills, CA: Sage Publications.

Sayeed, S., Padela, A., Naim, M.Y., & Lantos, J.D. (2012). A Saudi family making end of life decisions in the PICU. Pediatrics, 129, 764-768. doi:10.1542/peds.2011-1117.

Saylor, C.F., Cowart, B.L., Lipovsky, J.A., Jackson, C., & Finsh, Jr., A.J. (2003). Media exposure to September 11: Elementary school students' experiences and posttraumatic symptoms, American Behavioral Scientist, 12, 1622-1642.

Schaefer, D.J. (1988). Communication among children, parents, and funeral directors. In H.M. Dick, D.P. Roye, Jr., P.R. Buschman, A.H. Kutscher, B. Rubinstein, & F.K. Forstenzer (Eds.), Loss, grief and care (Vol. 2, Nos. 3/4, pp. 131-142). New York, NY: Haworth Press.

Scharlach, A.E. (1991). Factors associated with filial grief following the death of an elderly parent. *American Journal of Orthopsychiatry*, 6, 307-313.

Scharlach, A.E., & Fredriksen, K.I. (1993). Reactions to the death of a parent during midlife. *Omega: Journal of Death and Dying*, 27, 307-317.

Schiappa, E., Gregg, P.B., & Hewes, D.E. (2004). Can a television series change attitude about death? A study of college students and Six Feet Under. *Death Studies*, 28, 459-474.

Schiavo ex rel. Schindler v. Schiavo, 357 F. Supp. 2d 1378 (M.D. Fla.), *aff'd*, 403 F.3d 1223 (11th Cir.), *reh'g en banc denied*, 403 F.3d 1261 (11th Cir. en banc), *stay denied*, 125 S. Ct. 1692 (2005a).

Schiavo ex rel. Schindler v. Schiavo, 358 F. Supp. 2d 1161 (M.D. Fla.), *aff'd*, 403 F.3d 1289 (11th Cir.), *reh'g en banc denied*, 404 F.3d 1282 (11th Cir. en banc), *stay denied*, 125 S. Ct. 1722 (2005b).

Schiffman, D.D. (2004). *Coping with sudden infant death: An integrated approach to understanding family grief and recovery.* (Unpublished doctoral dissertation). Alliant International University.

Schindler v. Schiavo (In re Guardianship of Schiavo) 851 So. 2d 182 (Fla. DCA 2003); review denied, 855 So. 2d 621 (Fla. 2003) (table decision).

Schlafly, P. (1988). Death comes into the open. *Brooklyn Spectator*, April 13.

Schneider, K.R., Elhai, J.D., & Gray, M.J. (2007). Coping style use predicts posttraumatic stress and complicated grief symptom severity among college students reporting a traumatic loss. *Journal of Counseling Psychology*, 54, 344–350.

Schoeman, F. (1980). Rights of children, rights of parents, and the moral basis of the family. *Ethics*, 91, 6-19.

Schonfeld, D.J. (2011). Ten years after 9/11: What have we (not yet) learned? *Journal of Developmental & Behavioral Pediatrics*, 32, 542-545.

Schrag, D., Gelfand, S.E., Bach, P.B., Guillem, J., Minsky, B.D., & Begg, C.B. (2001). Who gets adjuvant treatment for Stage II and III rectal cancer? Insight from surveillance, epidemiology, and end results-Medicare. *Journal of Clinical Oncology*, 19, 3712-3718.

Schroeder-Sheker, T. (1994). Music for the dying: A personal account of the new field of Music-Thanatology: History, theory and clinical narratives. *Journal of Holistic Nursing*, 12, 83-99.

Schulz, R., & Aderman, D. (1974). Clinical research and the stages of dying. *Omega: Journal of Death and Dying*, 5, 137-143.

Schulz, R., Beach, S.R., Lind, B., Martire, L.M., Zdaniuk, B., Hirsch, C., Jackson, S., & Burton, L. (2001). Involvement in caregiving and adjustment to death of a spouse: findings from the caregiver health effects study. *Journal of the American Medical Association*, 285, 3123-3129.

Schut, H. (2010) Grief counseling efficacy. *Bereavement Care*, 29, 8-9.

Schuurman, D.L. (2003-2004). Literature for adults to assist them in helping bereaved children. *Omega: Journal of Death and Dying*, 48, 415-424.

Schwab, R. (1997). Parental mourning and children's behavior. *Journal of Counseling & Development*, 75, 258-265.

Seale, C. (1998). *Constructing death: The sociology of dying and bereavement.* New York, NY: Cambridge University Press.

Seale, C. (2010). The role of doctors' religious faith and ethnicity in taking ethically controversial decisions during end of life care. *Journal of Medical Ethics*, 36, 677-682. doi:10.1136/jme.2010.036194.

Searight, H., & Gafford, J. (2005). Cultural diversity at the end of life: Issues and guidelines for family physicians. *American Family Physician*, 71(3). Retrieved from http://www.aafp.org/afp/20050201/515.html.

Sehgal, A., Galbraith, A., Chesney, M., Schoefield, P., & Lo, B. (1992). How strictly do dialysis patients want their advance directives followed? *Journal of the American Medical Association*, 267, 59-63.

Sekaer, C., & Katz, S. (1986). On the concept of mourning in childhood. *The Psychiatric Study of the Child*, 41, 287-314.

Seligman, M. (1995). The effectiveness of psychotherapy: The *Consumer Reports* study. *American Psychologist, 50*, 965-974.

Sephton, S.E., Koopman, C., Schaal, M., Thoresen, C., & Spiegel, D. (2001). Spiritual expression and immune status in women with metastatic breast cancer: an exploratory study. *Breast Journal*, 7, 345-53.

Settersten, R.A. (2002). Socialization and the life course: New frontiers in theory and research. In RA. Settersten & T.J. Owens (Eds.), *New frontiers in socialization* (pp. 13-40). Amsterdam, Netherlands: JAI.

Shackford, S. (2003). School violence: A stimulus for death education—A critical analysis. *Journal of Loss and Trauma, 8*, 35-40.

Shah, S.K., & Miller, F.G. (2010). Can we handle the truth? Legal fictions in the determination of death. *American Journal of Law and Medicine*, 36, 540-585.

Shapiro, E. (2007). Whose recovery, of what? Relationships and environments promoting grief and growth. *Death Studies*, 32, 40-58.

Shapiro, E. (2012). Chronic illness and family resilience. In D. Becvar (Ed.), *Handbook of Family Resilience* (pp. 285-408). New York, NY: Springer Publishing.

Shapiro, E.R. (1994). *Grief as a family process: A developmental approach to clinical practice.* New York, NY: Guilford Press.

Shapiro, E.R. (1996). Family bereavement and cultural diversity: a social developmental perspective. *Family Process*, 35, 313-332.

Shapiro, F., & Forrest, M.S. (2004). *EMDR: The breakthrough therapy for overcoming anxiety, stress, and trauma.* New York, NY: Basic Books.

Shapiro, S. (1988). *Infertility and pregnancy loss.* San Francisco, CA: Jossey-Bass.

Shapiro, S.L., Astin, J.A., Bishop, S.R., & Cordova, M. (2005). Mindfulness-based stress reduction for health care professionals: Results from a randomized trial. *International Journal of Stress Management*, 12, 164-176.

Sharapan, H. (1977). "Mister Rogers' Neighborhood": Dealing with death on a children's television series. *Death Education*, 1, 131-136.

Sharma, R.K., Khosla, N., Tulsky, J.A., & Carrese, J.A. (2012). Traditional expectations versus realities: First and second generation Asian Indian perspectives on end-of-life care. *Journal of General Internal Medicine*, 27, 311-317. doi:10.1007/s11606-011-1890-7.

Shatz, M.A. (2002). Teaching thanatology in a foreign country: Implications for death educators. *Death Studies, 26*, 425-430.

Shavers, V.L., & Shavers, B.S. (2006). Racism and health inequity among Americans. *Journal of the National Medical Association, 98*, 386-396.

Shea, J. (2000). *Spirituality and health care: Reaching toward a holistic future.* Chicago, IL: The Park Ridge Center.

Shear, K., Frank, E., Houch, P.R., & Reynolds, C.F. (2005). Treatment of complicated grief: A randomized controlled trial. *Journal of the American Medical Association, 293*, 2601-2608.

Shear, M.K., Simon, N., Wall, M., Zisook, S., Neimeyer, R.A., Duan, N., Reynolds, C., et al. (2011). Complicated grief and related bereavement issues for DSM-5. *Depression and Anxiety, 28*, 103-117.

Shedler, J. (2010). The efficacy of psychodynamic psychotherapy. *American Psychologist, 65*, 98-109.

Sheets, V. (1999). Professional interpersonal boundaries: A commentary. *Pediatric Nursing*, 25, 657.

Sherell, K., Buckwalter, K.C., & Morhardt, D. (2001). Negotiating family relationships: Dementia care as a midlife developmental task. *Families in Society*, 82, 383-392.

Shimbun, Y. (1998). Teaching about death to learn about life. *The Daily Yomiuri*, 16. Retrieved online [LexisNexis Academic].

Shneidman, E. (1982, September). Reflections on contemporary death. Keynote presentation to the Forum for Death Education and Counseling, San Diego, CA.

Shneidman, E.S., & Farberow, N.L. (Eds.). (1968). *Clues to suicide*. New York, NY: McGraw-Hill.

Shrank, W.H., Kutner, J.S., Richardson, T., Mularski, R.A., Fischer, S., & Kagawa-Singer, M. (2005). Focus group findings about the influence of culture on communication preferences in end-of-life care. *Journal of General Internal Medicine, 20*, 703-709. doi:10.1111/j.1525-1497.2005.0151.x.

Siegel, D. (2012). *The developing mind : How relationships and the brain interact to shape who we are* (2nd ed.). New York, NY: Guilford Press.

Siegel, J.T., Alvaro, E.M., Hohman, Z.P., & Maurer, D. (2011). "Can you spare an organ?" Exploring Hispanic Americans' willingness to discuss living organ donation with loved ones. *Health Communication, 26*, 754-764. doi:10.1080/10410236.2011.566831.

Siegel, K., & Schrimshaw, E. (2002). The perceived benefits of religions and spiritual coping among older adults living with HIV/AIDS. *Journal for the Scientific Study of Religion, 41*, 91-102.

Siggins, L. (1966). Mourning: A critical survey of the literature. *The International Journal of Psycho-Analysis, 47*, 14-25.

Silveira, M.J., Kim, S.Y.H., & Langa, K.M. (2010). Advance directives and outcomes of surrogate decision making before death. *New England Journal of Medicine*, 362:1211-1218.

Silverman, P.R. (2000). *Never too young to know: Death in children's lives*. New York, NY: Oxford University Press.

Silverman, P.R. (2000). Children as part of a family drama: An integrated view of childhood bereavement. In R. Malkinson, S. Rubin, & E. Witztum, (Eds.), *Traumatic and non-traumatic loss and bereavement: Clinical theory and practice*. Madison, CT: Psychosocial Press.

Silverman, P.R. (2004). *Widow to widow: How the bereaved help one another* (2nd ed.). New York, NY: Brunner-Routledge.

Silverman, P.R. (2005). *Widow to widow* (2nd ed.). New York, NY: Routledge.

Silverman, P.R., & Kelly, M. (2009). *A parent's guide to raising grieving children*. New York, NY: Oxford University Press.

Silverman, P., & Worden, W. (1992). Children's reactions in the early months after the death of a parent. *American Journal of Orthopsychiatry, 62* (1), 93-104.

Silverman, P.R., & Worden, J.W. (1993). Children's reactions to the death of a parent. In. M.S. Stroebe, W. Stroebe, & R.O. Hansson (Eds.), *Handbook of bereavement: Theory, research, and intervention* (pp. 300-316). Cambridge, UK: Cambridge University Press.

Simon, R. (1995). The natural history of therapist sexual misconduct: Identification and prevention. *Psychiatric Annals, 25*, 90-94.

Simon, R.I. (1995). *Posttraumatic stress disorder in litigation: Guidelines for forensic assessment*. Washington, DC: American Psychiatric Association.

Simpson, E. (2011). Teaching empathy: Teacher mediation of a violent video game. In M. Koehler & P. Mishra (Eds.), *Proceedings of the Society for Information Technology and Teacher Education International Conference 2011* (pp. 1208-1210). Chesapeake, VA: Association for the Advancement of Computing in Education.

Slaughter, V., & Griffiths, M. (2007). Death understanding and fear of death in young children. *Clinical Child Psychology and Psychiatry, 12*, 525-535.

Smith, A., & Cherry, M.J. (2010). Death revisited: Rethinking death and the dead donor rule. *Journal of Medicine and Philosophy, 35*, 223-241.

Smith, H. (1994). *The illustrated world's religions: A guide to our wisdom traditions.* New York, NY: HarperOne.

Smith, L.H. (1981). Honk! If your school's got religion. *Today's Education,* Sept.-Oct., 64-71.

Smith, S.H. (2005). Anticipatory grief and psychological adjustment to grieving in middle-aged children. *American Journal of Hospice & Palliative Medicine,* 22, 283-286.

Smith, T.L., & Walz, B.J. (1998). The cadre of death education instructors in paramedic programs. *Prehospital and Disaster Medicine,* 13, 55-58.

Smith, W. (1997). *Forced exit.* New York, NY: Crown Publishers.

Smith-Torres, C. (1985). Lecture at Columbia-Presbyterian Medical Center, New York City March Conference of the Foundation of Thanatology.

Solomon, P., & Draine, J. (1995). Adaptive coping among family members of persons with serious illness. *Psychiatric Services,* 46, 1156-1160.

Sofka, C. (1997) Social support "internetworks," caskets for sale, and more: Thanatology and the information highway. *Death Studies,* 21, 553-574.

Sofka, C.J. (2009). Adolescents, technology, and the Internet: Coping with loss in the digital world. In Balk, D., & Corr, C. (Eds.), *Adolescents and death* (pp. 155-173). New York, NY: Springer Publishing.

Sofka, C.J. (2011). *Vamps, suicide, and grief – oh my! Death education in the public library.* Presented at the 33rd Annual Conference of the Association for Death Education and Counseling, Miami, FL.

Sofka, C.J. (2012). Appendix A: Informational support online: Evaluating resources. In C.J. Sofka, I.N. Cupit, & K.R. Gilbert (Eds.), *Dying, death, and grief in an online universe: For counselors and educators* (pp. 247-255). New York, NY: Springer Publishing.

Sofka, C.J. (2012). *Helping adolescents with dying and grief: Death education opportunities in the public library & online.* Presented at the 34th Annual Conference of the Association for Death Education and Counseling, Atlanta, GA.

Sofka, C.J., Cupit, I.N., & Gilbert, K.R. (Eds.). (2012). *Dying, death and grieving in an online universe. For counselors and educators.* New York, NY: Springer Publishing.

Sofka, C.J., Cupit, I.N., & Gilbert, K.R. (2012). Thanatechnology as a conduit for living, dying, and grieving in contemporary society. In C.J. Sofka, I. Noppe Cupit, & K.R. Gilbert (Eds.), *Dying, death, and grief in an online universe* (pp. 3-15). New York, NY: Springer Publishing.

Sofka, C.J., Dennison, J.R., & Gamino, L.A. (2012). Appendix B: Resources to assist with ethical issues in online service provision. In C.J. Sofka, I.N. Cupit, & K.R. Gilbert (Eds.) *Dying, death, and grief in an online universe: For counselors and educators* (pp. 256-264). New York, NY: Springer Publishing Company.

Soldini, M. (2005). The lessons for bioethics for the management of end-of-life conflict: The need for prudence and mercy. *Journal of Medical Ethics,* 31, 376-378.

Somerville, R.M. (1971). Death education as part of family life education: Using imaginative literature for insights into family crises. *Family Coordinator,* 20(3), 209-224.

Sourkes, B. (1996). *The psychological experience of the child with a life-threatening illness.* Pittsburgh, PA: University of Pittsburgh Press.

Speece, M.W., & Brent, S.B. (1992). The acquisition of a mature understanding of three components of a death concept. *Child Development,* 55, 1671-1686. doi:10.1080/07481189208252571.

Sperling, D. (2004). Maternal brain death. *American Journal of Law and Medicine,* 30, 453-501.

Spiro, J.D. (1967) *A time to mourn: Judaism and the psychology of bereavement.* New York, NY: Bloch Publishing.

Sprung, C.L., Cohen, S.L., Sjokvist, P., Baras, M., Bulow, H.H., Hovilehto, S. et al. (2003). End-of-life practices in European intensive care units: The Ethicus Study. *Journal of the American Medical Association, 290*, 790-797.

Sque, M., Long, T., & Payne, S. (2005). Organ donation: Key factors influencing families' decision making. *Transplant Procedures, 37*, 543-546.

Stanworth, R. (2004). *Recognizing spiritual needs of people who are dying.* New York, NY: Oxford University Press.

Starr, L. (2010). The educator's guide to copyright and fair use. Retrieved from http://www.educationworld.com/a_curr/curr280.shtml/.

Stately, J.E. (2002). Walking softly across the dialog of religion, spirituality, and the Native American experience of grieving. *New Direction for Philanthropic Fundraising, 35*, 79-96. doi:10.1002/pf.3506.

Stearns, P.N. (2010). Why death history? *The Forum, 36*(1), 3-4.

Steeves, R.H. (2002). The rhythms of bereavement. *Family Community Health, 25*, 1-10.

Stefanek, M., MacDonald, P., & Hess, S. (2005). Religion, spirituality and cancer: Current status and methodological challenges. *Psycho-Oncology, 14*, 450-463.

Stevens, M.M., & Dunsmore, J.C. (1996). Adolescents who are living with a life-threatening illness. In C.A. Corr & D.E. Balk (Eds.), *Handbook of adolescent death and bereavement* (pp. 107-135).

Stevenson, R.G. (1972). *Issues of life and death.* Oradell, NJ. (Unpublished school curriculum).

Stevenson, R.G. (1984). *A death education course for secondary schools: Curing death ignorance.* (Doctoral dissertation). Fairleigh Dickinson University, Teaneck, NJ.

Stevenson, R.G. (1990). The eye of the beholder: The media look at death education. *Death Studies, 14*, 161-170.

Stevenson, R.G. (1993). Religious values in death education. In K.J. Doka & J.D. Morgan (Eds.), *Death and spirituality* (pp. 281-290). Amityville, NY: Baywood Publishing.

Stevenson, R.G. (2010). Educating adolescents about death, bereavement, and coping. In C.A. Corr & D.E. Balk (Eds.), *Adolescent encounters with death, bereavement, and coping* (pp. 273-289). New York, NY: Springer Publishing.

Stillion, J.M. (2006). Understanding the end of life: An overview. In J.L. Werth, Jr., & D. Blevins (Eds.), *Psychosocial issues near the end of life: A resource for professional care providers* (pp. 11-26). Washington, DC: American Psychological Association.

Stimming, M., & Stimming, M. (Eds.). (1999). *Before their time: Adult children's experiences of parental suicide.* Philadelphia, PA: Temple University Press.

Stoddard, S. (1978, 1992). *The hospice movement: A better way of caring for the dying.* New York, NY: Vintage Books.

Stokes, J. (2005). Family assessment. In B. Monroe & F. Kraus (Eds.), *Brief interventions with bereaved children* (pp. 29-47). New York, NY: Oxford University Press.

Street, E., & Silbert, J. (1998). Post-traumatic stress reactions in children. *Clinical Child Psychology and Psychiatry, 3*, 553-560.

Stroebe, M., Gergen, M., Gergen, K., & Stroebe, W. (1992). Broken hearts or broken bonds: Love and death in historical perspective. *American Psychologist, 47*, 1205-1212.

Stroebe, M.S., Hansson, R.O., Stroebe, W., & Schut, H. (Eds.) (2001). *Handbook of bereavement research: Consequences, coping, and care.* Washington, DC: American Psychological Association.

Stroebe, M., & Schut, H. (1998). Culture and grief. *Bereavement Care, 17*(1), 7-11.

Stroebe, M., & Schut, H. (1999). The dual process model of coping with bereavement: Rationale and description. *Death Studies, 23*, 197-224.

Stroebe, M., & Schut, H. (2005). To continue or relinquish bonds: A review of consequences for the bereaved. *Death Studies*, 29, 477-494.

Stroebe, M., & Schut, H. (2010). The dual process model of coping with bereavement: A decade on. *Omega: Journal of Death and Dying*, 61, 273-289.

Stroebe, M., Schut, H., & Boerner, K. (2010). Continuing bonds in adaptation to bereavement: Toward theoretical integration. *Clinical Psychology Review*, 30(2), 259-268. doi:10.1016/j.cpr.2009.11.007.

Stroebe, M.S., & Stroebe, W. (1993). The mortality of bereavement: A review. In M.S. Stroebe, W. Stroebe, & R.O. Hansson (Eds.), *Handbook of bereavement: Theory, research, and intervention* (pp. 175-195). Cambridge, UK: Cambridge University Press.

Stroebe, W., & Stroebe, M. (1993). Is grief universal? Cultural variations in the emotional reaction to loss. In R. Fulton & R. Bendiksen (Eds.), *Death and identity* (3rd ed.) (pp. 177-209). Philadelphia, PA: Charles Press.

Stroebe, M.S., Van Der Houwen, K., & Schut, H. (2008). Bereavement support, intervention, and research on the Internet: A critical review. In M.S. Stroebe, R.O. Hansson, H. Schut, & W. Stroebe (Eds.), *Handbook of bereavement research and practice: Advances in theory and intervention.* (pp. 551-574). Washington, DC: American Psychological Association.

Stroebe, W., Schut, H., & Stroebe, M.S. (2005). Grief work, disclosure and counseling: Do they help the bereaved? *Clinical Psychology Review*, 25, 395-414.

Stroebe, W., Stroebe, M.S., & Abakoumkin, G. (1999). Does differential social support cause sex differences in bereavement outcome? *Journal of Community & Applied Social Psychology*, 9, 1-12.

Stroebe, W., Stroebe, M.S., Abakoumkin, G., & Schut, H. (1996). The role of loneliness and social support in adjustment to loss: A test of attachment versus stress theory. *Journal of Personality and Social Psychology*, 70, 1241-1249.

Stroebe, W., Zech, E., Stroebe, M.S., & Abakoumkin, G. (2005). Does social support help in bereavement? *Journal of Social & Clinical Psychology*, 24, 1030-1050.

Stubbs, D. (2005). Shrinking the space between people. In B. Monroe & F. Kraus (Eds.), *Brief interventions with bereaved children* (pp. 97-112). New York, NY: Oxford University Press.

Suárez-Orozco, M.M., & Robben, Antonius, C.M.G. (2000). The management of collective trauma. In C. Antonius & M. Suárez-Orozco (Eds.), *Culture under siege: Collective violence and trauma.* Cambridge, UK: Cambridge University Press.

Sudnow, D. (1967). *Passing on: The social organization of dying.* Englewood Cliffs, NJ: Prentice-Hall.

Sue, S., & Sue, D. (2003). *Counseling the culturally different: Theory and practice* (4th ed.). New York, NY: Wiley.

Suhail, K., & Akram, S. (2002). Correlates of death anxiety in Pakistan. *Death Studies*, 26, 39-50. doi:10.1080/07481180210146.

Sullivan, H.S. (1956). *The collected works of Harry Stack Sullivan*. New York, NY: W.W. Norton & Co.

Sulmasy, D.P. (2006). Spiritual issues in the care of dying patients : "…It's Okay between me and God." *Journal of the American Medical Association*, 296, 1385-1392.

Sunder, M. (2001). Cultural dissent. *Stanford Law Review*, 54, 495-567.

Surbone, A. (2008). Cultural aspects of communication in cancer care. *Supportive Care in Cancer*, 16, 235-240.

The SUPPORT Principal Investigators. (1995). A controlled trial to improve care for seriously ill hospitalized patients. The Study to Understand Prognoses and Preferences for Outcomes and Risks of Treatments (SUPPORT). *Journal of the American Medical Association*, 274, 1591-1598.

Sweasey, P. (1997). *From queer to eternity: Spirituality in the lives of lesbian, gay & bisexual people.* London, UK, and Washington, DC: Cassell.

Talwar, V. (2011). Talking to children about death in educational settings. In V. Talwar, P.L. Harris, & M. Schleifer (Eds.), *Children's understanding of death: From biological to religious conceptions.* (pp. 98-115). New York, NY: Cambridge University Press.

Tan, G.H., Totapally, B.R., Torbati, D., & Wolfsdorf, J. (2006). End-of-life decisions and palliative care in a children's hospital. *Journal of Palliative Medicine, 9,* 332-342.

Tanner, J.G. (1995). Death, dying, and grief in the Chinese-American culture. In J.K. Parry & A.S. Ryan (Eds.), *A cross-cultural look at death, dying, and religion* (pp. 183-192). Chicago, IL: Nelson-Hall.

Tatar, M. (Ed.). (2002). *The annotated classic fairy tales.* New York, NY: W.W. Norton & Co.

Traylor, E.S., Hayslip, B., Kaminski, P.L., & York, C. (2003). Relationship between grief and family system characteristics: A cross lagged longitudinal analysis. *Death Studies, 27,* 575-601.

Taylor, P.B. (1998). Setting your boundaries. *Nursing, 28,* 56-67.

Tedeschi, R.G., & Calhoun, L.G. (2004). *Helping bereaved parents: A clinician's guide.* New York, NY: Brunner-Routledge.

Tedeschi, R.G., & Calhoun, L.G. (2006). Time of change? The spiritual challenges of bereavement and loss. *Omega: Journal of Death and Dying, 53,*105-116.

Tein, J.-Y., Sandler, I.N., Ayers, T.S., & Wolchik, S.A. (2006). Mediation of the effects of the Family Bereavement Program on mental health problems of bereaved children and adolescents. *Prevention Science, 7,* 179-195.

Temel, J., Greer, J.A., Muzikansky, A., Gallagher, E.R., Admane, S., Jackson, V.A., Dahlin, C.M., Blinderman, C.D., Jacobsen, J., Pirl, W.F., Billings, J.A., & Lynch, T.J. (2010). Early Palliative Care for Patients with Metastatic Non-Small-Cell Lung Cancer. *New England Journal of Medicine, 363,* 733-742.

Templer, D.I. (1970). The construction and validation of a death anxiety scale. *Journal of General Psychology, 82,* 165-177.

Thirsk, L.M., & Moules, N.J. (2012). Considerations for grief interventions: Eras of witnessing with families. *Omega: Journal of Death and Dying, 65,* 107-124. doi:10.2190/OM.65.2.b.

Thomas, J. (2008). From people power to mass hysteria media and popular reactions to the death of Princess Diana. *International Journal of Cultural Studies, 11,* 362-376.

Thomas, N. (2001). The importance of culture throughout all of life and beyond. *Holistic Nursing Practice, 15,* 40-46.

Thomas, W.I., & Thomas, D.S. (1928). *The child in America.* New York, NY: Johnson Reprint.

Thomas, S., Quinn, S., Butler, J., Fryer, C., & Garza, M. (2011). Toward a fourth generation of disparities research to achieve health equity. *Annual Review of Public Health, 32,* 399-416.

Thompson, N. (2009). *Loss, grief, and trauma in the workplace.* Amityville, NY: Baywood Publishing.

Thompson, N. (2011). Workplace wellbeing: a psychosocial perspective. In I. Renzenbrink (Ed.), *Caregiver stress and staff support in illness, dying and bereavement* (pp. 25-31). New York, NY: Oxford University Press.

Tinker, G.E. (2004). *Spirit and resistance: Political theology and American Indian liberation.* Minneapolis, MN: Fortress Press.

Toedter, L.J., Lasker, J.N., & Alhadeff, J.M. (1988). The Perinatal Grief Scale: Development and initial validation. *American Journal of Orthopsychiatry, 58,* 435-449.

Tolle, S.W., Tilden, V.P., Drach, L.L., Fromme, E.K., Perrin, N.A., & Hedberg, K. (2004). Characteristics and proportion of dying Oregonians who personally consider physician-assisted suicide. *The Journal of Clinical Ethics, 15,* 111-118.

Tomer, A., & Eliason, G. (1996). Toward a comprehensive model of death anxiety. *Death Studies, 20,* 343-366.

Tong, K.L., & Spicer, B.J. (1994). The Chinese palliative patient and family in North America: A cultural perspective. *Journal of Palliative Care, 10*, 26-28.

Townsend,. M., Kladder, V., & Mulligan, T. (2002). Systematic review of clinical trials examining the effects of religion on health. *Southern Medical Journal, 95*, 1429-1434.

True, G., Phipps, E.J., Braitman, L.E., Harralson, T., Harris, D., & Tester, W. (2005). Treatment preferences and advance care planning at end of life: The role of ethnicity and spiritual coping in cancer patients. *Annals of Behavioral Medicine, 30*(2), 174-179. doi:10.1207/s15324796abm3002_10.

Tschann, J., Kaufmann, S., & Micco, G. (2003). Family involvement in end-of-life hospital care. *Journal of the American Geriatrics Society, 51*, 835-840.

Tucker, E. (2012). Social media and grief: How we experience loss is changing. *Global News*. Retrieved from http://www.globaltvedmonton.com/social+media+and+grief+how+we+experience+loss+is+chaging/6442685075/story.html.

Tulsky, J.A. (2005). Interventions to enhance communication among patients, providers, and families *Journal of Palliative Medicine, 8*(S1), S95-S102.

Turner, L. (2005). From the local to the global: Bioethics and the concept of culture. *Journal of Medicine and Philosophy, 30*, 305-320.

Umberson, D., Wortman, C.B., & Kessler, R.C. (1992). Widowhood and depression: Explaining long-term gender differences in vulnerability. *Journal of Health and Social Behavior, 33*, 10-24.

Ungar, M. (Ed.). (2012). *The social ecology of resilience: A handbook*. New York, NY: Springer Publishing.

United States Copyright Office. (November, 2009). Reproduction of copyrighted works for educators and librarians. Retrieved from http://www.copyright.gov/circs/circ21.pdf.

United States Department of Justice, Bureau of Justice Statistics. (2003). *Census of state and federal correctional facilities, 2000*. Washington, DC: Bulletin NCJ 198272.

Unruh, A.M., Versnel, J., & Kerr, N. (2002). Spirituality unplugged: A review of commonalities and contentions, and a resolution. *Canadian Journal of Occupational Therapy, 69*, 5-19.

Utz, R.L. (2006). Economic and practical adjustments to late life spousal loss. In D. Carr, R.M. Nesse, & C.B. Wortman (Eds.), *Spousal bereavement in late life* (pp. 167-192). New York, NY: Springer Publishing.

Vachon, M.L.S. (1987). *Occupational stress in the care of the critically ill, the dying, and the bereaved*. Washington, DC: Hemisphere Publishing.

Vachon, M.L.S. (2004). The stress of professional caregivers. In D. Doyle, G. Hanks, N. Cherny, & K. Calman (Eds.), *Oxford textbook of palliative medicine* (pp. 992-1004). New York, NY: Oxford University Press.

Vachon, M.L.S. (2007). Caring for the professional caregivers: Before and after the death. In K.J. Doka (Ed.), *Living with grief: Before and after the death* (pp. 311-330). Washington, DC: Hospice Foundation of America.

Vai, M., & Sosulski, K. (2011). *Essentials of online course design: A standards-based guide*. New York, NY: Routledge.

Vaillant, G. E. (1985). Loss as a metaphor for attachment. *American Journal of Psychoanalysis, 45*, 59- 67.

Valsiner, J. (2012). *Handbook of cultural psychology*. New York, NY: Oxford Press.

van Baarsen, B., & van Groenou, M.I. (2001). Partner loss in later life: Gender differences in coping shortly after bereavement. *Journal of Loss & Trauma, 6*, 243-262.

Vance, J.C., Najman, J.M., Thearle, M.J., Embelton, G., Foster, W.J., & Boyle, F.M. (1995). Psychological changes in parents eight months after the loss of an infant from stillbirth, neonatal death, or sudden infant death syndrome—a longitudinal study. *Pediatrics, 96*(5 Pt 1), 933-938.

Van der Kolk, B. (1987). *Psychological trauma*. Washington, DC: American Psychiatric Press.

Van Gennep, A. (1960). *Rites of passage Publications.* (M. Vizedom & G. Caffee, Trans.). Chicago, IL: University of Chicago Press.

Venhorst, C. (2012-2013). Islamic death rituals in a small town context in the Netherlands: Explorations of common praxis for professionals. *Omega: Journal of Death and Dying, 65,* 1-10.

Verheijde, J.L., Rady, M.Y., & McGregor, J. (2009). Presumed consent for organ preservation in uncontrolled donation after cardiac death in the United States: A public policy with serious consequences. *Philosophy, Ethics, and Humanities in Medicine, 22,* 15.

Vernon, G. M. (1970). *Sociology of death: An analysis of death-related behavior.* New York, NY: Ronald Press.

Vess, J.S., Moreland, J.R., & Schwebel, A.I. (1985). A follow-up study of role functioning and the psychological environment of families of cancer patients. *Journal of Psychosocial Oncology, 3*(2), 1-14.

Vicary, A.M., & Fraley, R.C. (2010). Student reactions to the shootings at Virginia Tech and Northern Illinois University: Does sharing grief and support over the Internet affect recovery? *Personality and Social Psychology Bulletin, 20*(10), 1-9.

Vig, E.K., Davenport, N.A., & Pearlman, R.A. (2003). Good deaths, bad deaths, and preferences for the end of life: A qualitative study of geriatric outpatients. *Journal of the American Geriatrics Society, 51,* 1541-1548.

Voices of September 11th: 9/11 Living Memorial. (2012). 9/11 living memorial: Commemorating the lives & preserving the stories of September 11, 2001. Retrieved from http://voicesofseptember11.org/dev/content.php?idtocitems=1,6.

Voigt, A., & Drury, N. (1998). *Wisdom from the earth: The living legacy of the Aboriginal dreamtime.* Boston, MA: Shambhala.

Volandes, A.E., Ferguson, L.A., Davis, A.D., Hull, N.C., Green, M.J., Chang, Y., Deep, K., & Paasche-Orlo, M.K. (2011). Assessing end-of-life preferences for advanced dementia in rural patients using an educational video: A randomized controlled trial. *Journal of Palliative Medicine, 15,* 169-177.

Volker, D.L., & Wu, H. (2011). Cancer patients' preferences for control at the end of life. *Qualitative Health Research, 21,* 1618-1631. doi:10.1177/1049732311415287.

Voo, T.C., Campbell, A.V., & deCastro , L.D. (2009). The ethics of organ transplantation: Shortages and strategies. *Annals of the Academy of Medicine, 38,* 159-164.

Wachter, R., & Lo, B. (1993). Advanced directives for patients with human immunodeficiency virus infection. *Critical Care Clinics, 9,* 125-136.

Waechter, E.H. (1971). Children's awareness of fatal illness. *American Journal of Nursing 71,* 1168-1172.

Waern, M. (2005). Suicides among family members of elderly suicide victims: An exploratory study. *Suicide & Life-Threatening Behavior, 35,* 356-364.

Wagner, B., Knaevelsrud, C., & Maercker, A. (2006). Internet-based cognitive-behavioral therapy for complicated grief: A randomized controlled trial. *Death Studies, 30,* 429-453.

Wakefield, J.C., & First, M. (2012). Validity of the bereavement exclusion to major depression: Does the empirical evidence support the proposal to eliminate the exclusion in DSM-5? *World Psychiatry, 11,* 3-10.

Wakefield, J.C., Schmitz, M.F., First, M.B., & Horwitz, A.V. (2007). Extending the bereavement exclusion for major depression to other losses: Evidence from the National Comorbidity Survey. *Archives of General Psychiatry, 64,* 433-440.

Waldman, D.A., & Davidshofer, D.A. (1983-84). Death anxiety reduction as the result of exposure to a death and dying symposium. *Omega: Journal of Death and Dying, 14,* 323-328.

Waldrop, D.P., Tamburlin, J.A., Thompson, S., & Simon, M. (2004). Life and death decisions: Using school-based health education to facilitate family discussion about organ and tissue donation. *Death Studies, 28,* 643-657

Walijarvi, C.M., Weiss, A.H., & Weinman, M.L. (2012). A traumatic death support group program: Applying an integrated conceptual framework. *Death Studies, 36,* 152–181.

Walker, A.C. (2008). Grieving in the Muscogee Creek tribe. *Death Studies, 32,* 123-141.

Walker, A.C. (2009). Building bridges in American Indian bereavement research. *Omega: Journal of Death and Dying, 59,* 351-367. doi:10.2190/OM.59.4.e.

Walker, A.C., & Balk, D.E. (2007). Bereavement rituals in the Muscogee Creek tribe. *Death Studies, 31,* 633-652. doi:10.1080/07481180701405188.

Walker, G., & Maiden, R. (1987). *Lifespan attitudes toward death.* Paper presented at the annual meeting of the Eastern Psychological Association, Arlington, VA.

Walker, P. (2001). A bioarchaeological perspective on the history of violence. *Annual Review of Anthropology, 30,* 573-596.

Walsh, F., & McGoldrick, M. (2004). *Living beyond loss: Death in the family* (2nd ed.). New York, NY: W.W. Norton & Co.

Walter. T. (1994). *The rebvival of death.* London, UK: Routledge.

Walter, T. (2008). Jade and the journalists: Media coverage of a young British celebrity dying of cancer. *Social Science and Medicine, 71,* 853-860.

Washington, H.A. (2006). *Medical apartheid: The dark history of medical experimentation on Black Americans from colonial times to the present.* New York, NY: Doubleday.

Wass, H. (1995). Visions in death education. In L.A. DeSpelder and A.L. Strickland (Eds.), *The path ahead. Readings in death and dying* (pp. 327-334). Mountain View, CA: Mayfield Publishing.

Wass, H. (2003). Death education for children. In I. Corless, B.B. Germino, & M.A. Pittman (Eds.), *Dying, death, and bereavement. A challenge for living* (pp. 25-41). New York, NY: Springer Publishing.

Wass, H. (2004). A perspective on the current state of death education. *Death Studies, 28,* 289-308.

Wasserman, J., Clair, J.M., & Ritchey, F.J. (2005-2006). Racial differences in attitudes toward euthanasia. *Omega: Journal of Death and Dying, 52,* 263-287. doi:10.2190/D3P0-2YY1-7E3A-0MQH.

Watchman, K. (2005). Practitioner raised issues and end of life care for adults with Down syndrome and dementia. *Journal of Policy and Practice in Intellectual Disabilities, 2,* 156-162.

Waters, C.M. (2001). Understanding and supporting African Americans' perspectives on end-of-life care planning and decision making. *Qualitative Health Research, 11,* 385-398.

Way, P., & Bremner, I. (2005). Therapeutic interventions. In B. Monroe & F. Kraus (Eds.), *Brief interventions with bereaved children* (pp. 65-80). New York, NY: Oxford University Press.

Weafer, J. (2004). *A nationwide survey of public attitudes and experiences regarding death and dying.* Dublin, Ireland: Irish Hospice Foundation supported by the Health Services National Partnership Forum.

Weafer, J. (2007). *Qualitative investigation of end-of-life issues.* Dublin, Ireland: Irish Hospice Foundation.

Weafer, J. (2009a). *Qualitative study of public perceptions of end-of-life issues.* Dublin, Ireland: Irish Hospice Foundation.

Weafer, J. (2009b). *The views of political representatives.* Dublin, Ireland: Irish Hospice Foundation.

Weafer, J., McCarthy, J., & Loughrey, M. (2009). *A nationwide survey of public attitudes and experiences regarding death and dying.* Dublin, Ireland: Irish Hospice Foundation.

Weaver, H.N. (2005). *Explorations in cultural competence: Journey to the four directions.* Belmont, CA: Brooks/Cole.

Webb, N.B. (Ed.). (2004). *Mass trauma and violence: Helping families and children cope.* New York, NY: Guilford Press.

Webb, N.B. (Ed). (2010). *Helping bereaved children: A handbook for practitioners* (3rd ed.). New York, NY: Guilford Press.

Webber, J.M., & Mascari, J.B. (2009). Critical issues in implementing the new CACREP standards for disaster, trauma, and crisis counseling. In G.R. Walz, J.C. Bleuer, & R./K. Yeps (Eds.), *Compelling counseling interventions: VISTAS 2009* (pp. 125-138). Alexander, VA: American Counseling Association.

Weber, J.A., & Fournier, D.G. (1985). Family support and a child's adjustment to death. *Family Relations, 34,* 43-49.

Weeks, O.D., & Johnson, C. (Eds.). (2001). *When all the friends have gone: A guide for aftercare providers.* Amityville, NY: Baywood Publishing.

Weiner-Kaufman, E. (2001). *Attitudes of physicians, clinical psychologists, and the public towards grief reactions and intervention methods in situations of loss and bereavement.* (Unpublished master's thesis). University of Haifa.

Weininger, R., & Kearney, M. (2011). Revisiting empathic engagement: countering compassion fatigue with 'exquisite empathy'. In I. Renzenbrink, (Ed.), *Caregiver stress and staff support in illness, dying and bereavement* (pp. 49-62). New York, NY: Oxford University Press.

Weir, D. (2012). *No place to die: The poetic of roadside sacred places in Mexico.* Retrieved from http://etd.lsu.edu/docs/available/etd-0403102-215300/unrestricted/Weir_dis.pdf.

Weisman, A.D. (1972). *On dying and denying: a psychiatric study of terminality.* New York, NY: Behavioral Publications.

Weisman, A. (1980). Thanatology. In O. Kaplan (Ed.), *Comprehensive textbook of psychiatry.* Baltimore, MD: Williams and Williams.

Weiss, B.L. (1988). *Many lives, many masters.* New York, NY: Fireside.

Wellman, R.J., & Sugarman, D.B. (1999). Elder and young adults' perceptions of the decision to withdraw from medical treatment: A replication and extension. *Journal of Social Behavior and Personality*, 14, 287-298.

Wenger, E., McDermott, R.A., Snyder, W. (2002). *Cultivating communities of practice.* Boston, MA: Harvard Business School Press.

Werth, J.L., & Blevins, D. (2002). Public policy and end-of-life care. *American Behavioral Scientist,* 46, 401-417.

Werth, J.L., Blevins, D., Toussaint, K.L., & Durham, M.R. (2002). The influence of cultural diversity on end-of-life care and decisions. *The American Behavioral Scientist*, 46, 204-223. doi:10.1177/000276402236673.

Westbrook, L.A. (2002). *The experience of mid-life women in the years after the deaths of their parents.* (Unpublished doctoral dissertation). Institute for Clinical Social Work.

Weston, D., Novotny, C.M., & Thompson-Brenner, H. (2004). The empirical status of empirically supported psychotherapies: assumptions, findings, and reporting in controlled clinical trials. *Psychological Bulletin,* 130, 631-663.

Whetstine, L. (2006). *Making decisions at the end of life.* Retrieved from Medscape.

Whetstine, I., Streat, S., Darwin, M., & Crippen, D. (2005). Pro/con ethics debate. When is dead really dead? *Critical Care Forum,* 9, 538-542.

White, J.M., & Klein, D.M. (2007). *Family theories* (3rd ed.). Thousand Oaks, CA: Sage Publications.

Wikan, U. (1980). *Life among the poor in Cairo.* London, UK: Tavistock.

Wikan, U. (1988). Bereavement and loss in two Muslim communities: Egypt and Bali compared. *Social Science and Medicine,* 27, 451-460.

Wikipedia (2006). Organ transplant. Retrieved from http://en.wikipedia.org/wiki/Death_education.

Wilcox, A.J., Weinberg, C.R., O'Connor, J.F., Baird, D.D., Schlatterer, J.P., Canfield, R.E., Armstrong, E.G., & Nisula, B.C. (1988). Incidence of early loss of pregnancy. *New England Journal of Medicine, 319*, 189-194.

Williams, A.L. (2006). Perspectives on spirituality at the end of life: a meta-summary. *Palliative & Supportive Care, 4*, 407-417.

Williams, A.L., & Merten, M.J. (2009) Adolescents' online social networking following the death of a peer. *Journal of Adolescent Research, 24*, 67-90.

Williams, C.M., Wilson, C.C., & Olsen, C.H. (2005). Dying, death, and medical education: Student voices. *Journal of Palliative Medicine, 8*, 372-381.

Williams, M.B., Zinner, E.S., & Ellis, R.R. (1999). The connection between grief and trauma: An overview. In E.S. Zinner & M.B. Williams (Eds.), *When a community weeps: Case studies in group survivorship* (pp. 3-17). Philadelphia, PA: Brunner/Mazel.

Wilson, G.T. (2005). Behavior therapy. In R.J. Corsini & D. Wedding (Eds.), *Current psychotherapies* (pp. 202-237). Belmont, CA: Brooks/Cole.

Windling, T. (2001). On Tolkien and fairy-tales. In K. Haber (Ed.), *Meditations on middle-earth* (pp. 215-229). New York, NY: St. Martin's Press.

Winkelman, W.D., Lauderdale, K., Balboni, M.J., Phelps, A.C., Peteet, J.R., Block, S.D., Kachnic, L.A., VanderWeele, T.J., & Balboni, T.A. (2011). The relationship of spiritual concerns to the quality of life of advanced cancer patients: preliminary findings. *Journal of Palliative Medicine, 14*, 1022-1028.

Winokuer, H.R., & Harris, D.L. (2012). *Principles and practice of grief counseling.* New York, NY: Springer Publishing.

Winston, C.A. (2006). African American grandmothers parenting AIDS orphans: Grieving and coping. *Qualitative Social Work: Research and Practice, 5*, 33-43.

Winter, L., & Parker, B., (2007). Current health and preferences for life-prolonging treatments: An application of Prospect Theory to end-of-life decisions. *Social Science & Medicine, 65*, 1695-1707. doi:10.1016/j.socscimed.2007.06.012.

Winzelberg, G.S., Hanson, L.C., & Tulsky, J.A. (2005). Beyond autonomy: Diversifying end-of-life decision-making approaches to serve patients and families. *Journal of the American Geriatrics Society, 53*, 1046-1050.

Wittkower, D.E. (2012). How can social media better support a community in mourning? *Future tense.* Retrieved from http://www.slate.com/articles/technology/future_tense/2012/07/aurora_shooting_how_social_media_can_support_a_community_in_mourning_.html.

Wizemann, T.M., & Pardue, M. (Eds.). (2001). *Exploring the biological contributions to human health: Does sex matter?* Washington, DC: National Academy Press.

Wolf, L. (Quoted by Lonnae O'Neal Parker, 2008, March 16). In Streets of the Dead; When Washington youths get killed, memorials pay testament to the victims—and to the grim realities of life in the District. *The Washington Post*, W.20.

Wong, P.T.P. (2003). Death education flourishes in Taiwan. *Science and Theology News.* Retrieved from http://www.stnews.org/rlr-1328.htm.

Worden, J.W. (1982, 1991, 2002, 2009). *Grief counseling and grief therapy: A handbook for the mental health practitioner* (ed. 1, 2, 3, 4). New York, NY: Springer Publishing.

Worden, J.W. (1996). *How children grieve: When a parent dies.* New York, NY: Guilford Press.

Worden, J.W., & Silverman, P. (1996). Parental death and the adjustment of school-age children. *Omega: Journal of Death and Dying, 33*, 91-102.

Worden, J.W., & Winokuer, H. (2011). A task-based approach for counseling the bereaved. In R.A. Neimeyer, D. Harris, H. Winokuer, & G. Thornton (Eds.), *Grief and bereavement in contemporary society: Bridging research and practice* (pp. 57-67). New York, NY: Routledge.

World Health Organization. (2006). Cancer Fact Sheet No. 297. Retrieved from http://www.who.int/mediacentre/factsheets/fs297/en/index.html.

World Health Organization. (2012). *World health statistics.* Geneva, Switzerland: Author. Retrieved from http://www.who.int/healthinfo/EN_WHS2012_Full.pdf.

World Health Organization. (2012). Definition of palliative care. Retrieved from http://www.who.int/cancer/palliative/definition/en/.

Wortman, C.B., & Silver, R.C. (1987). The myths of coping with loss. *Journal of Consulting and Clinical Psychology,* 57, 349-357.

Wu, A., Tang, C., & Kwok, T. (2002). Death anxiety among Chinese elderly people in Hong Kong. *Journal of Aging and Health,* 14, 42-56.

Wyatt, J. (2007). End-of-life decisions, quality of life and the newborn. *Acta Paediatrica,* 96, 790-791.

Xu, J., & Zhang, R. (2011). The theoretical basis and clinical practice of sandplay therapy applied to grief counseling. *Chinese Journal of Clinical Psychology,* 19(3), 419-421.

Yalom, I.D. (1980). *Existential psychotherapy.* New York, NY: Basic Books.

Yampolskaya, S., & Winston, N. (2003). Hospice care in prison: general principles and outcomes. *The American Journal of Hospice & Palliative Care,* 20, 290-296.

Yang, S.C., & Chen, S-F. (2009). The study of personal constructs of death and fear of death among Taiwanese adolescents. *Death Studies,* 33, 913-940. doi:10.1080/07481180903251687.

Yeo, G. (1995). Ethical considerations in Asian and Pacific Island elders. *Clinics in Geriatric Medicine,* 11, 139-151. Retrieved from http://geriatric.theclinics.com/.

Young, A. (1995). *The Harmony of illusions: Inventing post-traumatic stress disorder.* Princeton, NJ: Princeton University Press.

Young, E. (Trans.). (1989). *Lon Po Po: A Red-Riding Hood story from China.* New York, NY: Philomel.

Young, E.W.D., & Jex, S.A. (1992). The Patient Self-Determination Act: Potential ethical quandaries and benefits. *Cambridge Quarterly of Healthcare Ethics,* 2, 107-115. doi:dx.doi.org/10.1017/S0963180100000190.

Young, M., & Erickson, C. (1989). Cultural impediments to recovery: PTSD in contemporary America. *Journal of Traumatic Stress,* 14, 431-443.

Young, M. (1997). Victim rights and services: A modern saga. In R.C. Davis, W.G. Skogan, & A.J. Lurigio (Eds.), *Victims of crime* (2nd ed.) (pp. 194-210). Thousand Oaks, CA: Sage Publications.

Zalaznik, P. (1979). *Dimensions of loss and death education.* Minneapolis, MN: Ed-Pac Publishing.

Zech, E., & Rimé, B. (2005). Is talking about an upsetting experience helpful? Effects on emotional recovery and perceived benefits. *Clinical Psychology & Psychotherapy,* 12, 270-287.

Zerzan, J., Stearns, S., & Hanson, L. (2000). Access to palliative care and hospice in nursing homes. *JAMA,* 284, 2489-2494.

Zinner, E.S. (1992). Setting standards: Certification efforts and considerations in the field of death and dying. *Death Studies,* 16, 67-77.

Zisook, S., & Kendler, K.S. (2007). Is bereavement-related depression different than non-bereavement- related depression? *Psychological Medicine,* 37, 779-794.

Zisook, S., Schuchter, S.R., Sledge, P., & Mulvihill, M. (1993). Aging and bereavement. *Journal of Geriatric Psychiatry and Neurology,* 6, 137-143.

Index of Key Terms